CW00972440

About the Author

Julian Crowe was born in 1947. He was brought up in Greenwich but then left London and has lived mostly in Fife. He is married to the poet Anna Crowe, and they have three children and five grandchildren. The University of St Andrews awarded him an MA in Philosophy and a PhD for a thesis on Charles Dickens, and also employed him for many years as a computing adviser. The extraordinary story of Mary Ann Hunn was hidden in the Canning archive at Harewood House, and Julian came across it in the 1990s when he inherited the papers of the historian who first catalogued the Harewood documents. He has been working on this book ever since.

George Canning Is My Son

Julian Crowe

unbound

This edition first published in 2021

Unbound
6th Floor Mutual House, 70 Conduit Street, London W1S 2GF
www.unbound.com
All rights reserved

© Julian Crowe, 2021

The right of Julian Crowe to be identified as the author of this work has been asserted in accordance with Section 77 of the Copyright, Designs and Patents Act 1988. No part of this publication may be copied, reproduced, stored in a retrieval system, or transmitted, in any form or by any means without the prior permission of the publisher, nor be otherwise circulated in any form of binding or cover other than that in which it is published and without a similar condition being imposed on the subsequent purchaser.

ISBN (eBook): 978-1-78352-922-3
ISBN (Paperback): 978-1-78352-923-0

Cover design by Mecob

Printed and bound in Great Britain by Clays Ltd, Elcograf S.p.A.

MIX
Paper from responsible sources
FSC® C018072
FSC www.fsc.org

This book is dedicated with thanks to:

Chris Crowe & Daphne Jayasinghe
Swithun Crowe & Pomme Bour
Jessica Crowe & Jules Pipe

unbound

Unbound is the world's first crowdfunding publisher, established in 2011.

We believe that wonderful things can happen when you clear a path for people who share a passion. That's why we've built a platform that brings together readers and authors to crowdfund books they believe in – and give fresh ideas that don't fit the traditional mould the chance they deserve.

This book is in your hands because readers made it possible. Everyone who pledged their support is listed below. Join them by visiting unbound.com and supporting a book today.

Peter Adamson
Malcolm Bain
Bernard Barker
Cris Betts
Torben Betts
Marina Branscombe
Alan Bullard
Michael Callaghan
Dr Chris Carter
John Cassin
Elspeth and Antony Christie
Sanjit Chudha
Dot Clark
Martin Colley
Chris Collyer
John Collyer
Stewart Conn
Beverley Craw Eismont
Anna Crowe
Chris Crowe
Jessica Crowe
Rosalind Crowe
Swithun Crowe
Roz Currie
Alice Curteis
Ian Darling
Susan Davis
Christine De Luca
Nick Dibben
Claire Easingwood
Nick Eden-Green
Simon Eden-Green
Leisha Fullick
Bil Fulton
Carolyn George
Chris Gordon
Stephanie Green
Julie Grimble
Kiera Guest
John Henderson
Diana Hendry
John N.A. Hooper
Linley & George Hooper
Kate Hooper – Emma Smith

Kate Hooper – Peter Smith
Kate Hoskins
Sabine Hotho-Jackson
Maureen Jack
Angela Jarman
Peter Jarvis
Daphne Jayasinghe
Hasantha Jayasinghe
Lal & Priyanka Jayasinghe
Marine Joatton
Brian Johnstone
Peter and Stephanie Jupp
Susan Kakesako
Pete Kane
Dan Kieran
Jennifer King
Roger Knight
Eleanor Livingstone
Rebecca Lloyd
Samantha Lloyd
Valerie Lloyd
Chris Lockwood
Alice Lowe
Lindsay Macgregor
Robin MacKenzie
Phillip Mallett
Philippa Manasseh
Hugh Martin
Frances McKee
Jane McKie
Gill Merchant
Mike Merchant
James Mewis
John Mitchinson
Helen Moore
Joerg Mueller-Kindt
Graeme Munro
Charles Murray
Kylie Murray
Liz Murray
Ros Muspratt
Carlo Navato
Marion Newton
Penny & Oliver Ormerod
Terence Pepper
Katherine Perry
Birgit Plietzsch
Justin Pollard
Hilary Ranger
Peter Read and Chloé Gallien
Alan Reid
Toby Reid
Sioned-Mair Richards
Marie Robinson
Peter Robinson
Marc Schartz
Hamish Scott
Shamil Sharshek ULU
Josh Slocum
Daniel Smith
Karen Smith
Rachel Smith
Roger Squires
Cynthia Stephens
Bruce Stockley
Bridget Sudworth
Iain Suttie
Keith Sweetmore
Diana A Sykes
Maisie Taylor
Simon Taylor
Edward Thompson
Lucy Traves
Wendy Vacani
Paul Vysny
Tony Ward
Hannah Whelan
Hamish Whyte
David Williams
Elspeth Wills
Clevo Wilson
David Winkley
Kim Wright
Nathan Yeowell

Family Trees

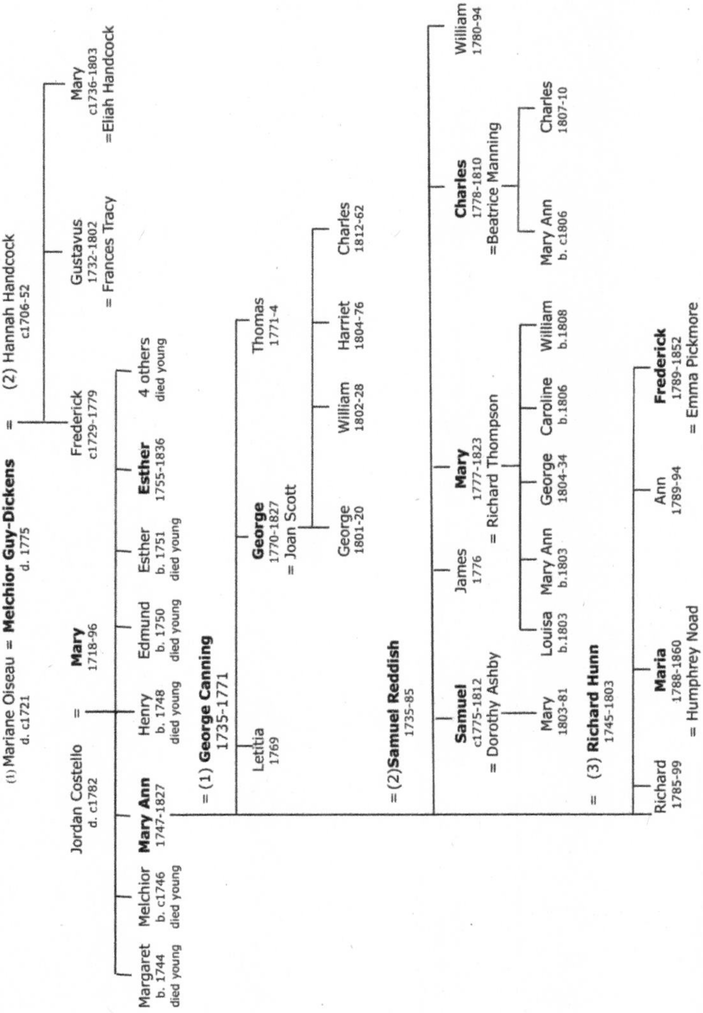

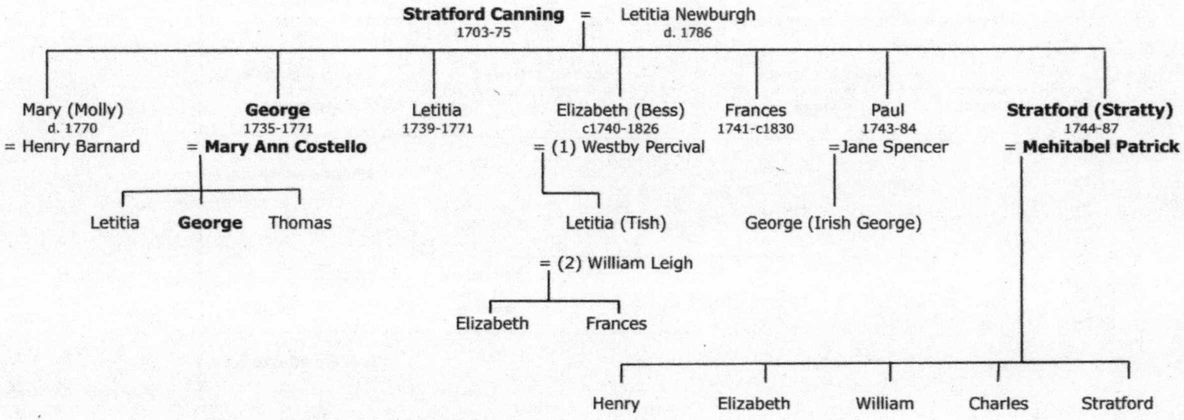

Stratford Canning = Letitia Newburgh
1703-75
d. 1786
Mary (Molly)
d. 1770
= Henry Barnard
George
1735-1771
= Mary Ann Costello
Letitia
1739-1771
Elizabeth (Bess)
c1740-1826
= (1) Westby Percival
Frances
1741-c1830
Paul
1743-84
=Jane Spencer
Stratford (Stratty)
1744-87
= Mehitabel Patrick
Letitia
George
Thomas
Letitia (Tish)
= (2) William Leigh
George (Irish George)
Elizabeth
Frances
Henry
Elizabeth
William
Charles
Stratford

Contents

Introduction

The story of George Canning and his actress mother Mary Ann Costello (married names Canning and Hunn, also known as Reddish) was known in outline to their contemporaries and to subsequent historians. Most biographies of Canning offer more or less accurate, but sketchy, accounts of his antecedents and early history, passing over Mary Ann with a few patronising words, but in the early part of the last century the genealogist Frederick Gale became interested in her for her own sake. His wife was a descendant of one of Mary Ann's other sons, and had inherited a clutch of family letters, a portrait of Mary Ann and other memorabilia, which gave him a starting point for his investigations. From contemporary newspapers and memoirs, as well as the baptismal and burial registers and wills that are the stuff of genealogical research, Gale sensed that Mary Ann was, as he put it, a 'remarkable woman', whose story deserved to be told. During the 1920s and 1930s he contributed a series of articles to *Notes and Queries* about her theatrical career and her family, and planned a book-length biography, but must have realised that, in the end, there were too many gaps in the record. The information he needed was hidden, along with much invaluable political material, in the Canning archive at Harewood House, and although Gale was in contact with the then Earl of Harewood he was not given access to the archive, which was at that point uncatalogued. Dorothy Marshall, whose book *The Rise of Canning* was published in 1938, made use of some of Canning's early letters, including the *Letter Journal* covering the first three years of his parliamentary career, but otherwise seems not to have dug deep into the Harewood papers.

The task of cataloguing the papers at Harewood fell to the historian Cedric Collyer, lecturer in history at the University of Leeds, and later at St Andrews. Apparently this came about as a result of a casual conversation between Cedric and the chancellor of the university, the dowager Countess of Harewood, Princess Mary, the Princess Royal. For several years in the late 1950s and early 60s Cedric and his assistant worked on the Canning papers, transcribing many of them and producing a catalogue. The archive was clearly important for a proper assessment of Canning's place in history, and Cedric planned to produce what would have been the first full-scale biography. He proposed to place more weight than other historians upon Canning's family and Irish background. Cedric continued his work after his retirement, but when he died in 1994 his book was incomplete. Meanwhile, in 1973 Wendy Hinde's fine biography had appeared, making full use of the Harewood papers. Cedric bequeathed his drafts and working papers to me, in the expectation that I would see his work through to some sort of completion. This placed me in a difficult position, since I am not a professional historian, and not equipped to write about Canning's political career. After much thought, and consultation with a former colleague of Cedric's, I concluded that it would be hard to find a scholar willing to take up Cedric's work. This is a great pity, because Cedric's narrative, so far as it went, was convincing and compelling, though perhaps somewhat old-fashioned in its approach, even for the 1970s.

When I came across Cedric's transcript of Mary Ann's own account of her life I realised that here was someone I could write about. Mary Ann's account, in a long letter to George, written in 1803 at a crucial point in their relationship, is precisely the document that Frederick Gale lacked. It fills in the gaps in his genealogical research, and confirms his intuition that Mary Ann was a remarkable woman. At the time I was working as an IT adviser at the University of St Andrews, and was also halfway through a part-time PhD on Charles Dickens, but I was determined to take on this new project.

The first thing was to obtain permission from the Harewood family to study and quote from the documents in their possession. This was quickly given, in an encouraging letter from the seventh earl. The papers were on loan to the West Yorkshire Archive Service, in their lovely 1930s art nouveau building at Sheepscar in Leeds, which I was to get to know well over the next fifteen years.

First of all I checked the transcript of Mary Ann's long letter against the original. The thrill of handling original documents never fades. Having read the transcript several times I knew the story, but nothing prepares you for the emotional impact of the real thing: the actual pen strokes, grains of the sand used to dry the ink still fixed to the paper or caught in the folds, and marks which you are easily persuaded were left by Mary Ann's tears as she remembered the events of her youth. I next made notes on the 2,000 or so letters that George wrote to his mother over almost half a century. Then there were the letters George wrote to his wife Joan, and his uncle and aunt, William and Bess Leigh. The West Yorkshire Archive Service also holds the Western Letters, a collection of letters handed down from the family of Mary Ann's brother- and sister-in-law, Stratty and Mehitabel Canning. There was, therefore, enough to occupy many visits, and I made steady but slow progress, travelling to Leeds whenever my other commitments allowed. I followed other lines of research in order to fill in the background to Mary Ann's narrative, including an exploration of contemporary newspapers held by the British Library in Colindale.

Some explanation is needed of the length of time I have taken over this project. Even allowing for the fact that until 2008 I was in a time-consuming job, I have allowed the work to drag on too long. The underlying reason is that researching and writing are more rewarding than the dismal task of finding a publisher, so I continued to explore new lines of research, some of them blatantly irrelevant, and went on rethinking and rewriting the story to the despair of my friends and family, who began to think it would never be finished. Another reason for delay was that I had to turn myself into an historian. In my job at the university I had dealings with many historians, and discussed my work with them and received much helpful advice, but I did not think to ask them for practical tips on how to conduct archival research. Had I taken a basic course on research methods, I would have saved myself a lot of trouble.

When I retired in 2008 there were new family commitments (grandchildren), but still I hoped my research would pick up speed, and so it did until, in 2010, I was told that the Harewood papers had been withdrawn from Sheepscar and were no longer available to the public. I was offered half a day of access to the papers in their new location at Harewood House, but that was all. This was disappointing, but not disastrous as I had almost completed my research on the letters, and I still had Cedric Collyer's transcripts which would fill in most of the gaps. What was more serious was that the Harewood family withdrew permission to publish extracts from their documents. There followed a period of fifteen months of frustration and anxiety, during which I started other writing projects. Eventually, to my great relief, the Harewood family's solicitors confirmed that I would be able to publish my work. In the meantime I had shown my manuscript to friends, and realised that more background research and rewriting were needed, particularly in order to get the balance right between Mary Ann and the glamorous George. This, and the tedious quest for a publisher, occupied the next six or seven years.

My extensive revisions were more or less complete when, in 2019, the book was accepted by Unbound and, thanks to the generosity of my family and friends, and friends of friends, fully funded.

A Note on the Sources

This book is largely based on letters from the collection of Canning papers which passed into the possession of the Harewood family through the marriage of George Canning's granddaughter to the fourth Earl of Harewood. The principal sources are Mary Ann Hunn's 65,000-word account of her life, written in 1803, which she and George referred to as the 'Packet', and the 2,000 or so letters that George wrote to his mother between 1780 and her death in 1827. For permission to study these papers while they were in the possession of the Harewood Estate I am grateful to the present Earl of Harewood, and more particularly to his late father, who responded most generously to my initial request.

As explained earlier, the Canning Papers at Harewood were withdrawn from public access around 2010, when my archival research was not quite complete. For certain aspects of the story I was therefore reliant on the notes and transcripts that I inherited from Cedric Collyer. Since then the papers have been transferred to the British Library, and are once more accessible. I have checked most of the details but a further visit to the library was required to finish the work. This projected visit has fallen victim to the restrictions to deal with the Covid-19 pandemic. For a few minor details, therefore, I remain dependent on Cedric's notes.

Among the Canning Papers is a series of diaries in which Canning recorded his engagements and expenditure, with occasional brief comments. Cedric left detailed notes on the diaries, but studying the originals was one of the tasks left undone when access to the papers was withdrawn in 2010. Quite apart from the present difficulties caused by Covid-19, it is impossible to consult the diaries because they are undergoing conservation at the British Library. All references to the diaries, therefore, are to Cedric's notes.

Personal letters give a direct view of the clash of wills and personalities, but they have their drawbacks. Most of the time the letter-writer is trying to make a case. This is especially true of Mary Ann's Packet, which like any memoir is something of a performance, crafted to play upon the feelings of an audience, in Mary Ann's case an audience of one. Furthermore, letters give an undue prominence to points of conflict, since it takes many more words to express disagreement than agreement, and George in particular seldom wrote at length except to enforce a point or reprimand his mother. It becomes only too easy to frame the narrative in purely adversarial form, which is sometimes a distortion.

At the age of six George was adopted by his aunt and uncle, and in the following half-century he and his mother can have spent in total not much more than a hundred hours in each other's company. Their relationship was conducted almost entirely by letter. But what happened when they did meet? Outside epistolary novels, people usually have no reason to give a blow-by-blow account of their meetings and confrontations. Mary Ann and George occasionally refer to their meetings, saying how they felt about them, but there is only one occasion when George enumerates the points they made face to face.

Apart from the Packet, only a handful of Mary Ann's letters have survived, because George destroyed most of them. More often than not, when I ascribe thoughts, requests and wishes to Mary Ann I am relying not on her own words, but on George's response. They wrote in very different styles, George sharply analytical and literal, Mary Ann more emotional and influenced by the extravagant language of the stage, which makes it likely that he did not always understand her letters, so that his answers may not always be a perfect guide to what she wrote.

The bibliography shows the range of published sources I have consulted. Some of them have been used just once or twice, to follow up odd details, while others have been constant companions. The literature on Canning the statesman is extensive; I have mainly relied on Wendy Hinde's biography and Dorothy Marshall's account of Canning's early career. P.J.V. Rolo's *Biographical*

Studies are particularly good on Canning's character, and Peter Dixon's biography was useful on political matters, particularly his account of Liverpool elections. For information on the Canning family I have used Giles Hunt's biography of Mary Ann's sister-in-law, *Mehitabel Canning, a Redoubtable Woman*, which is largely based on the collection of Canning family letters known as the Western Letters (because they were once owned by Hunt's aunt, Mrs Western). I have also been greatly assisted by the work of two genealogists, Frederick Gale, whose masterly articles in *Notes and Queries* have already been mentioned; and Linley Hooper, Fellow of the Genealogical Society of Victoria, who (like Fred Gale) is married to a descendant of Mary Ann. Linley has an extensive family history website, and has kindly shared her findings with me about the Reddish family.

I have relied heavily on a number of standard reference works, in particular the *Oxford Dictionary of National Biography*, the *Biographical Dictionary of Actors, Actresses, Musicians, Dancers, Managers and Other Stage Personnel in London, 1660–1800*, and parts four and five of *The London Stage 1660–1800*. In some cases these works are recycling a limited stock of anecdotes of dubious reliability, but at least for the peripheral figures in my story I have been happy to accept the judgement of specialist scholars whose grasp of the worlds of eighteenth century theatre and politics is greater than mine.

During the years I have been working on this project the research world has been transformed by the Internet. Thanks to the University of St Andrews I have enjoyed access to such online resources as the *ODNB* and Gale Historic Newspapers. Enormous numbers of eighteenth and nineteenth century books are online, enabling me to consult many more contemporary works than I could have found easily in libraries or bookshops. For comparatively trivial sums I have subscribed to the British Newspaper Archive (to fill gaps in the Gale collection) and Ancestry. Through Ancestry I have been able to examine baptismal and burial records, and wills, which otherwise would have necessitated long and costly journeys.

Fortunately the need for such expeditions has not been entirely done away with. It remains a pleasure to visit libraries and archives and handle actual documents and books. Even a microfilm reader seems closer to the original than a scanned image on one's screen at home.

The single most dramatic online moment was the discovery by my wife Anna of the text of Mary Ann's novel, *The Offspring of Fancy*. For several years the only known copy was in a library in Houston, Texas, and I despaired of ever seeing it. Suddenly a Google search found another, in the Library of Chawton House, Hampshire, and the text was available to download. But it was only by visiting the National Library of Ireland to check the microfilm of William Flyn's *Hibernian Chronicle* that I was able to establish that *The Offspring* is indeed Mary Ann's novel.

For many of the events described in the book the only evidence comes from the letters of Mary Ann and George. Where Mary Ann's account can be checked against outside sources she appears remarkably accurate, and so, within limits, I have tended to accept her word when there is no corroboration. I say 'within limits' because even when we accept a statement as correct as to the 'facts' we may want to dispute the 'interpretation' – and fact and interpretation are notoriously hard to disentangle. The external sources, whether they are in other people's letters or newspapers or the memoirs of her contemporaries, are liable to the same strictures. The reader should not be overimpressed by the thousand or so meticulous endnotes citing sources for what I allege in the book. Writing, or reading, a biography depends in the end on imagination. The endnotes serve as an anchor to prevent the imagination going into free flight, but like other anchors they should be kept below the surface. Sifting through the documentary evidence and weighing the different possible interpretations are activities deeply satisfying for the biographer, but at some point we have to look up, engage imaginatively with our subjects, and say that *this* is what we think was going on between them. There is no rule that says the reader has to agree.

1. Two Unhappy Families, 1760s

For almost fifty years Mary Ann Hunn kept up a regular correspondence with her son George Canning. Her letters were effusive, and full of incidents, plans, opinions and emotion; his replies were brief, dry, practical, often humorous, sometimes sarcastic, occasionally angry. The letter she started on her birthday in January 1803 was on a larger scale; she and George referred to it as her 'Packet'. 'At last I have acquired courage to sit down to the task which I have so long meditated,' she began. 'This day completes my fifty-third (or fifty-sixth – for I am not sure which) year…' She continued for twenty weeks and some 65,000 words to tell the story of her life, demanding passionately and forensically her natural rights as his mother and the grandmother of his children. George believed his mother's rights did not include the right to be received into his family home. She herself, he wrote in the only surviving document that gives his view of the relationship, had by her actions 'closed for ever' any 'intercourse' with his 'family and friends'.[1] The task she set herself was to expose her own conduct in its true light, to demonstrate that she did not merit this harsh judgement. She traced her story back to her origins, in Dublin.

In 1760, when she was thirteen,[i] Mary Ann's father's business

i Mary Ann was doubtful about her date of birth. When writing the Packet she was inclined to the view that she was born in 1750, but in 1813 she found evidence that she was born in 1747. She doesn't say what her evidence was, but it was probably correct; see the Appendix, 'When was Mary Ann born?'

collapsed for the second time. She was an intelligent girl, a centre of stability in a chaotic family. Her father Jordan Costello was a gambling man, and Mary Ann blamed his losses on 'a spirit of play [which] subdued his power of reflection'. He had been trained as a clothier, in the area of Dublin known as the Coombe, in the parish of St Luke, which in the first half of the eighteenth century was a centre of scientific and industrial enterprise, energised by an influx of Huguenot refugees.[2] Jordan was, Mary Ann recalled, 'one of the handsomest men of the Age', who boasted of his supposed descent from an Italian knight who married the daughter of Ulrick, king of Connaught. He deplored the fate that forced him to be a tradesman: 'Indeed,' Mary Ann wrote, 'his exterior woud have done better to personify a Prince.'[3]

In the early 1740s he had been employed in the cloth trade, with ambitions to branch out on his own. He had made the acquaintance of an inventive cloth merchant and dyer, Henry Smith, who also lived in the parish of St Luke.[4] A young woman, Mary Guy-Dickens, lived with Smith and his wife Esther as their ward. The Smiths had told Mary that both her parents were dead, and she had accepted the story without question and without any deep feeling, but Jordan knew better, having seen her father's name in the newspapers, and having heard what the neighbours remembered about him: he was Colonel Melchior Guy-Dickens, British Minister in Berlin until 1741, and then in Stockholm.[5] With such a father-in-law, Jordan thought as he listened to the gossip, he'd have plenty of money to finance his schemes and speculations. Marriage to Mary would have another advantage: Henry Smith had no children of his own, and would be sure to leave his business to his ward's husband, including the lucrative secret of a new process he had invented for dyeing mohair.

But Jordan was disappointed. First, although Mary was simple minded, she was obstinate, and had no wish to leave her home with the Smiths. He married her by trickery, and right from the outset she was resentful. She thought he was mad to talk of asking her father for money: didn't he know her father was dead? The Smiths were angry and for years refused to have anything to do with either of them. Bullied by her husband and rejected by her only friends, Mary was persuaded to make contact with her father. She and Jordan called their second child Melchior in honour of the Colonel, who gave Jordan £800 to establish his business. When the couple visited him in London before his Russian embassy, he was pleased with his princely son-in-law.[6] The £800 was probably less than Jordan had hoped for; the Colonel lived well on his salary and pension, but he was poorer than his style of life suggested. The funds proved inadequate and a few years later Jordan's business had collapsed, but by then there had been a partial reconciliation with Mr and Mrs Smith. Esther Smith was godmother to Mary Ann, and the affectionate couple took a fancy to the clever little girl. They made her their heir, and when they both died in 1756 she inherited six or seven hundred pounds. Henry Smith still didn't trust Jordan, and so the great mohair secret died with him. Jordan justified his distrust by appropriating Mary Ann's inheritance for his own purposes. By 1760 it had all gone and the business did not survive this second collapse.

Meanwhile, in eighteen years, Mary had borne eleven children, of whom two were still alive, Mary Ann and a sister, Esther, aged five. For four years the Costellos struggled on, husband and wife constantly quarrelling over money and religion. Only Mary Ann made the best of things, feeding the family with what she could earn from needlework. The name of the English colonel was long familiar to her from her parents' quarrels. His affluence made their poverty all the more galling. Ambassadors were naturally thought of as wealthy men, with the legendary diamond-encrusted snuffboxes that were their traditional perquisites. Jordan was all for tapping the Colonel for more funds. Mary protested that she didn't know where he was, and anyway they had already received, and squandered, her share of the Guy-Dickens money.

From what she overheard of her parents' quarrels, from her

mother's unreliable recollections and from information entrusted to her by Mrs Smith, Mary Ann had pieced together something of the family history. Her mother's mother, Mariane Oiseau, was the widow of a Huguenot pastor. When she married Melchior Guy-Dickens, then private secretary to the Lord Lieutenant of Ireland,[7] she was almost twice his age, with a son old enough to join the army. She had a vulnerable beauty which appealed to Melchior's romantic nature, but the marriage was brief: she died in childbirth. All this happened towards the end of the second decade of the century, Mary Ann calculated. Melchior, a young soldier with a career to make, left his infant daughter with his landlady Mrs Bevins, who soon passed her on to her daughter, Mrs Smith. In 1721/22, before leaving Ireland, he married a second time. This time his impressionable heart turned to a fifteen-year-old girl, Hannah Handcock, who climbed the orchard wall to run off with him.[8] Soon afterwards Melchior began the diplomatic career which would take him to Prussia, Sweden and Muscovy. For some years he sent money for his daughter's upkeep through his regiment's Dublin agent, Captain de Brisay, until the Smiths told him she had died. To explain why the money from her father had dried up, they likewise told Mary that he was dead.

Mary Ann does not say why the Smiths practised this deceit, nor is it clear when it originated. It may have been when Mary was twelve, or as late as 1741 when she was in her early twenties and her father about to set off for Sweden. The Smiths' motive was probably the obvious one: having brought the girl up they had grown fond of her and hated to lose her. They may also have felt that she would not take easily to life in a foreign court. And perhaps, having no family of their own, they hoped she might attract a husband worthy of inheriting the mohair secret.

One of the incidents that Mary related to her daughter was the moment when she learned that her father wasn't dead, which came about through a meeting, sometime after her marriage, with Captain de Brisay, who proved to her that the Colonel was alive and flourishing. De Brisay, Mary recalled, had greeted her as Miss Guy-Dickens, and then looked embarrassed when he saw she was pregnant. Although Mary remembered this *faux pas* as proof that the encounter was accidental, it's likely that Jordan had engineered it.

Resentment over such trickery, and bickering about money and religion, poisoned the Costellos' home life, but Mary Ann grew in beauty, intelligence and resourcefulness. Of her intelligence and resourcefulness her actions will provide ample evidence, and as for beauty, we shall see that in her youth she repeatedly drew men's eyes when she appeared in public. A portrait survives of her in middle age, but it gives little away.[9] With a long face, rouged cheeks, large hazel eyes, auburn hair almost hidden under an unbecoming cap, a long straight nose, small mouth and determined chin, she is not a conventional beauty. That she was beautiful is taken as given by all the Canning biographers, probably because, as we shall see, her first marriage was imprudent on both sides, and the most obvious explanation of such folly is that the girl must have been a great beauty. There is an impassivity, or severity, in the portrait. To find the loveliness in the face we must seek the things the artist hasn't shown. We must see Mary Ann alert, active, ardent, greedy for love. We can animate the face, and sense the feelings behind the mask, from her written record. The portrait shows her at her writing desk, a pen in one hand and a pair of glasses in the other. The mark of the glasses on the bridge of her nose is just visible.

In 1764 she was an uneducated, innocent girl, but energetic and practical, and whatever pretensions she might have to beauty later in life, she now had the liveliness of youth. She was the family's last hope. One day the unhappy mother had an idea. What if the Colonel could be persuaded to take Mary Ann under his protection? At least one child might be saved from the wreck. Given such a chance, a clever, pretty girl might find a way of retrieving the family fortunes. But how to do it? Impossible. She let the idea slip from her mind.

Not so Mary Ann. The suggestion galvanised her – it passed, she recalled, 'like electricity into my own breast'.[10] She was determined to make herself known to the Colonel. Sixteen years had passed since Jordan had traced the Colonel through his regiment's agent; Melchior had long been retired from the army, and the trail was cold. Another way was through the Irish relations of his second wife. Mary Ann tracked down a man called Eliah Handcock, Hannah's cousin, who wished her luck in her quest and told her that although the Colonel drew an Irish pension he lived in England,[11] in the village of Blockley in Gloucestershire.

Mary Ann dragged her mother across to Bristol and then to Blockley, only to find that her grandfather had moved to London, to Wigmore Street in the new development around Cavendish Square. When Mary and Mary Ann arrived on his fashionable doorstep, Melchior recalled (or was reminded by his other children) that his eldest daughter had already had, years before, her share of his fortune. He firmly refused to give her anything more than the cost of her journey home, but he took an immediate fancy to Mary Ann, and agreed to take her in and help her find a husband.

The household she now entered was not a happy one. The girl Melchior had romantically eloped with never effaced the memory of his real love, the Huguenot widow Mariane. Hannah too was now dead, and their three grown-up children gave him little satisfaction, quarrelling with him and amongst themselves, although there had as yet been no final breach. The family lived comfortably on their income, but there was little capital to be shared among the three children, who watched each other jealously. The eldest, Frederick, who was a lawyer and occasional man of letters when Mary Ann lived with the family, was ordained in 1775, at the age of forty-six, and died four years later as curate of Wootton-under-Edge. Gustavus was a soldier and courtier who had done well in the Seven Years War, had made a good marriage, and was rising in the Queen's household. Mary, the youngest, lived at home. Her brothers, who had reason to distrust her influence over their father, described her as 'incapable of loving anything but herself'.[12] Bilious was how Mary Ann remembered her. Mary and Gustavus may not have been the wicked aunt and uncle of novels, deliberately engineering Mary Ann's downfall, but they were selfish and worldly, and had an interest in getting her out of the house before the old man was charmed into leaving her all his money. Into this tense atmosphere came Mary Ann, innocent, lovely and nobody's fool. She soon learned how to dress Melchior's nightcap, read to him, write his letters, make his tea and soothe his servants.

Back in Dublin, Jordan, Mary and little Esther waited to see what would come of the London venture. Jordan had cousins called French who owned land in County Mayo. They gave him board and lodgings in return for working as an unpaid steward.[13] For a man who claimed descent from the ancient kings of Connaught it was a sad decline, and he blamed it on his Protestant wife, on her father and his English family living comfortably in London, and on her old guardian who had jealously taken his valuable secret to the grave. Where Mary and Esther lived while Jordan was in Mayo, and how they survived, is not known. All they could do was hope that clever, pretty Mary Ann would put things right.

**

While these changes were happening among the Costellos another unhappy family was living more affluently in another part of Dublin. Stratford Canning, lawyer, antiquarian and landowner, had a house in respectable Abbey Street, and a country estate at Garvagh in County Londonderry. The rents from the Garvagh property and other smaller farms amounted to some £3,000 a year. He and his wife Letitia had four daughters and three sons. Molly, the eldest, was married in 1763 to a clergyman, Henry Barnard, son of the Bishop of Derry. Stratford had approved of the marriage, but after the ceremony inexplicably quarrelled with all the Barnards.[14] Molly's brothers and sisters were constantly anxious about her delicate health and frequent pregnancies, but their father forbade them to visit her. In 1766 she and her husband were at last permitted to visit Garvagh, but three years later normal intercourse between the Garvagh household and the Barnards was still forbidden. In 1769, when Molly was recovering from her latest lying-in, her brother was prevented from riding across to see her. 'I am used to such mortifications,' she wrote.[15]

Although his tyrannical behaviour lies at the heart of this whole wretched story, Stratford Canning was in some ways an attractive character. In politics he was a libertarian Whig, an enthusiastic reader of 'Junius';[i] he was equally progressive on matters of religion, a freethinker who admired Voltaire. From his long, pedantic letters, written in the legal hand he'd learned in his youth, you'd picture an eccentric, scholarly old chap, with interesting bees in his bonnet about matters such as the history of the Druids. Writing to his youngest son, his namesake known as Stratty, he appears genial enough, careful over money but not unreasonably so, perhaps over-ready with detailed advice, but showing an affectionate interest in the young man's travels and business affairs. Stratty replied carefully, knowing how easy it would be to fall from favour, how irrevocable such a fall would be.[16]

The eldest son, George, had been in London since 1757, sent there to study law and get over an unsuitable love affair. All love affairs were unsuitable in Stratford Canning's eye; he hated anything that loosened his grip on his children. He may have been simply a supremely selfish and parsimonious man, or an obstinate stoic, or a father whose jealous love for his children could only express itself in a compulsion to control them. Whatever the reason, his family suffered from his unaccountable ways, which they called the Abbey Street Logic. His wife and sister seem to have treated him more indulgently, referring to him as 'Him', as in 'Him had more business to do in the country'.[17] His daughter Bess stood up to him, and the middle son Paul learned to dissemble. The

i The letters of 'Junius' were anonymous attacks on the government, published between 1769 and 1772.

two other daughters, Letitia, who died young, and Fanny who lived a long life and remained unmarried, may have mixed some genuine affection with their fear of him. All the girls watched and trembled for 'sweet little Stratty', uncertain whether he would be corrupted like Paul by the Abbey Street Logic, or expelled and lost to them like George.[18]

George was enrolled at the Middle Temple, but neglected his legal studies in favour of poetry, politics and women. Stories reached home of the splash he was making, or was expected to make, in literary and political circles. His talents – 'the Mind of a Prince and the Abilities of a Pitt', in Mary Ann's words[19] – were bound to take him far, to earn him powerful patrons, leading to a seat in Parliament. He published a long poem on the Whig hero Lord William Russell, executed in the purges following the Rye House Plot of 1683. In the confused politics of the 1760s George was (like his father) a strong Whig; he belonged to the circle around John Wilkes and the poet Charles Churchill,[i] and produced pamphlets, newspaper paragraphs and political poems, in support of the opposition to the new King's favourite, Lord Bute. In George's poem 'Humanity', in praise of William Augustus, Duke of Cumberland ('Butcher Cumberland', the Whigs' favourite royal duke), Cumberland's 'mild, humane, undaunted, generous Mind' is contrasted with a succession of different types of inhumanity – murderers, seducers and torturers, with the longest passage dwelling on Siraj ud-Daula, Nawab of Bengal who was responsible, the poem claims, for the Black Hole of Calcutta. Cumberland's butchering of the Jacobites in 1745/46 gets a passing mention: 'Behold the *Hero* – who, supremely great, / From curst Rebellion sav'd a sinking State.'[ii] Charles Churchill

i John Wilkes (1725–1797): politician, founder in 1762 of the *North Briton*, an anti-government weekly. Charles Churchill (1732–1764): satirical poet, collaborator on the *North Briton*.

ii 'Humanity' appeared in 1766, the year following Cumberland's death. To a modern mind it seems bizarre to describe Cumberland as mild and humane, and although at the time it was widely accepted that the extirpation of the rebels in 1746 was necessary for the security and liberty of the nation, the thought must cross one's mind that the poem is ironical in intention. But this is unlikely, if only because George senior (unlike his son) died in 1764, and in a draft of an unpublished poem George refers to him – 'Churchill the free! Alas! was Passion's slave!' – before going on to attack a whole clutch of anti-Wilkesite politicians.[i] It sounds as though he was bidding to take Churchill's place as the poetic mouthpiece of the extreme anti-government faction, but he may have overestimated his own importance to the cause, because in the extensive published correspondence between Wilkes and Churchill there is no mention of him.[20]

George's most significant poetic achievement was nothing to do with politics, but a translation into rhyming couplets of the *Anti-Lucretius* by a French diplomat of the early eighteenth century, Cardinal Melchior de Polignac.[ii] Widely distributed during the Cardinal's lifetime, and first published soon after his death, the *Anti-Lucretius* is an attack on materialism, in nine books of Latin hexameters, placing scientists and philosophers such as Newton, Gassendi, Bayle and Hobbes in the atomist tradition that dates back to Democritus and Lucretius. To start with George planned to test the market with a limited publication of the first three books, deciding in the end to publish the first five. The title page gives the date as 1766, but it was still in the press in February 1767, delayed by the printers, he said, although he had not completed Book Four until the end of 1766. In December 1767 he reported that the subscribers were slow to pay, and sales were sluggish, perhaps, he admitted, because he had translated only half of the work.[21]

The rectitude that George professed in politics and literature

seems not to have gone in for irony: 'I never stoop to ironie, not I, / For I'm no joker, and I hate a Lye,' he wrote in the draft poem referred to below.

i The draft was written in a manuscript book among George's letters to Stratty. Among the enemies of Wilkes attacked in the poem are: Fletcher Norton (1716–1789) who, as solicitor-general, conducted the prosecution of Wilkes; Lord Sandwich (1718–1792) who betrayed Wilkes's trust by using his private writings to discredit him; Lord Halifax (1716–1771) who issued the warrant for the arrest of Wilkes; Philip Webb (1702–1770), the barrister who enforced the warrant and seized Wilkes's papers; Tory writers such as Tobias Smollett (1721–1771) and the virulent polemicist John Shebbeare (1709–1788); and culminating with Lord Bute himself.

ii Cardinal Melchior de Polignac (1661–1742): diplomat under Louis XIV and one of the chief negotiators at the Treaty of Utrecht (1712). In leisure hours in the course of his long career he composed the nine books of his *Anti-Lucretius*. The first book was translated into English by William Dobson in 1756.

did not extend to his dealings with 'the sex'. He made no secret of his 'vehement desire for sensual gratification', and admitted that keeping chaste for three months was an unusual experience, giving rise to 'constitutional turbulences'.[22] His letters contain scattered references to pretty girls, but apart from a flirtatious affair with a well-to-do Irish woman called Peggy Arbuckle, and a narrow escape from marriage to an Islington tavern-keeper's widow, there's no record of any particular attachments.

Gossip travelled easily between London and Dublin, so Stratford knew what was going on. The most easy-going father might have felt George was wasting his time and his talents; the most generous father would have been anxious about the rising debts. Stratford, who was neither easy-going nor generous, kept George short of funds, expecting him to live the life of a stoic, and imposing his will by keeping him poor. George eluded him by raising 'imaginary funds' from money-lenders. They were willing enough to oblige the heir to a substantial estate, but when the family quarrel became known, they demanded payment. Stratford had never paid his meagre allowance with any regularity; now it dried up altogether. George went into hiding, deserting his usual place at the Grecian Coffee House, changing his name and burying himself in semi-rural Islington. Stories reached home of his poverty, of how he was reduced to selling the buckles off his shoes to buy three-halfpence-worth of breakfast, and was tempted to marry that tavern-keeper's friendly widow. He had supporters in Ireland who besieged Stratford with petitions on his behalf. Even members of the family dared to protest: 'every Engine [was] set to work to force open the long closed Heart of his Father.'[23]

Eventually Stratford gave in, but in a typically grudging and ungracious way. He wrote a letter, witnessed by a family friend, saying he would unconditionally pay off George's debts and resume the allowance. George used this to gain respite from his creditors, until, in a nice example of Abbey Street Logic, Stratford let it be known that he would make this unconditional payment only if George emigrated to America.[24] Fearing that their victim would escape, the money-lenders again closed in. George narrowly escaped arrest when the owner of the Grecian Coffee House demanded his arrears. Stratford altered his terms. He would pay on condition that George surrendered to his brother Paul his rights and expectations as heir and consented to receive his allowance from Paul's hands. This would make it harder to borrow in the future. George submitted to the humiliation, but remained convinced that his brother was playing a double game, friendly to him in London, obsequious to Stratford when back in Ireland. Paul was likened to the treacherous Blifil in *Tom Jones*.[25]

The debts continued to accumulate, but George was able to resume his old life and his own name without fear of immediate arrest. He continued to play the national lottery in partnership with Peggy Arbuckle or Stratty, devising a 'manoeuvre' involving insurance to double his chances of a prize. He began to prepare the first five books of the *Anti-Lucretius* for the press, and set about the urgent task of finding subscribers, persuading them, if he could, to pay in advance, and using the proceeds to cover his most pressing needs. His haphazard approach to canvassing left him unable to publish a list of subscribers, for which he apologised in the preface to his collected poems.[26]

Meanwhile Stratford remained on friendly terms with Stratty. He procured him a place to learn business in the counting-house of a Dublin merchant called Robert Patrick, and things went well until Stratty fell in love with Patrick's daughter Mehitabel. Stratford dealt with Stratty as he had with George, sending him away to get over his infatuation. His sisters and his aunt begged Stratty to avoid offending their father, who, they assured him, loved him dearly – 'his heart is along with you wherever you go,' his aunt told him, while his sister Letitia wrote, '… indeed Stratty I did not know the tenderness of his affection for you till you were gone… Never neglect to contribute all in your power to his happiness…'. With surprisingly generous funds at his disposal, for which he had to account minutely, Stratty went on an extended tour of the great business centres of Europe, Bordeaux, Paris, Amsterdam, Rotterdam, Hamburg, Riga, St Petersburg. Friendly letters passed between father and son throughout this journey, the only tension emerging when Stratty tried to gloss over his occasional extravagances. He sent his father antiquarian notes, and wrote of those he met along the way. He asked for samples of basalt from the Giant's Causeway to be sent to the Prince of Orange, and made a detour to visit Voltaire at Ferney near Geneva, obtaining a set of the great man's works for his father. Old Stratford was visibly moved when he read of his son's conversation with Voltaire.[27]

What we know of old Stratford Canning comes mainly from George, Stratty and Mary Ann. Seen through their eyes the old man seems a monster, using his economic power, and exploiting his children's strong family loyalty, to impose his arbitrary will. Without exculpating old Stratford, we should note that things in Abbey Street and at Garvagh might not have appeared in the same light to everyone. Those who should have known him best, his wife and his sister, undoubtedly feared the violence of his reactions and the obstinacy with which he clung to his decisions, but they could laugh at Him and also seem to have understood the powerful and baffled love that he felt for his disobedient children. As well as being biased against Stratford by what they suffered at his hands, Mary Ann and Stratty were to some extent anglicised by their long residence in London, sharing the metropolitan incomprehension of Irish social attitudes and customs. Three decades later we'll see Mary Ann's son fully reconciled with surviving members of old Stratford's family, and puzzled by the events that had led to his father's disinheritance and his mother's life of struggle.

**

While George Canning was battling against poverty, and hoping that his translation would help him retrieve his fortune, Mary Ann was firmly settled in the household in Wigmore Street. Mary Guy-

Dickens found her useful. When her doctor prescribed a trip to Bath for her biliousness, she took her niece with her. Mary Ann was eighteen years old when she was 'taken from the most extreme degree of retirement and thrown upon the surface of the world.'[28] Contemporary representations of the Pump Room at Bath full of the old and sick do not make a pleasant picture. Twelve years later, when Mary Ann came to write a novel of fashionable life, she recorded her impressions of Pump Room society:

> The pump-room is all in a bustle; every body here knows every body's affairs; and, from the antiquated virgin, who endeavours to make chastity atone for the want of every other virtue—to the pert coxcomb, with pink-sattin heels to his shoes, who does not pretend to any virtue at all—every individual is a self-erected judge of every other person's conduct.[29]

It was an oppressive place, particularly for a lively young person dependent upon an antiquated, or at least middle-aged, virgin like Aunt Mary. Nonetheless, for Mary Ann, as for countless other young women, it offered a first glimpse of fashion, made all the more thrilling by comparison with the long dreary Dublin years. Mary Ann learned that she was a beauty. Heads turned. There was a Captain Lawley, for example, who noticed her.

She was a serious young woman, and was more interested in a middle-aged doctor called Zephaniah Holwell. She was to have a lifelong interest in medical matters, and an admiration for 'the faculty', but there was more than just medical knowledge to recommend Holwell as a companion. He'd led an exciting life as a surgeon with the East India Company, and events had made him, briefly, a significant player in Company politics.[i] In 1756 he had been left in charge of the garrison at Calcutta to face the attack of the Nawab of Bengal. After the fall of the fortress the European prisoners were confined overnight in the notorious Black Hole, which resulted in many deaths – although perhaps

i John Zephaniah Holwell (1711–1798): Holwell's account of his actions in India is now widely regarded as unreliable.

not as many as Holwell was to allege in the tendentious and self-glorifying account that he published as soon as he got back to England. The 'old sinner', as Mary Ann called him, hatched a plot to abduct her, which was thwarted not by her aunt, who should have been looking after her, but by the watchful Captain Lawley. 'Black-hole' Holwell recovered from his disappointment, and soon afterwards married a milliner who was, the story went, strikingly like Mary Ann.[30]

Holwell was one of a succession of notable men who were to show an interest in Mary Ann, and capture her interest in return. Her grandfather was another; in his time he had played a prominent part in several diplomatic coups. He had been expelled from Sweden, and earlier in Prussia had taken the part of the Crown Prince Frederick (later 'the Great') against his father King Frederick William I. When the comfortable but dull Wigmore Street routine was resumed – carriage exercise with Aunt Mary, dinners with uncle Gustavus, little domestic dramas such as the coachman's wife giving birth to twins – things were enlivened by her conversations with the old man. Melchior enjoyed her company, and she was happy to listen to his stories as she dressed his nightcap or made his tea. He told her about his youth in the army in Ireland, as the Duke of Bolton's aide-de-camp, and about the friends he had made among the Huguenot refugees in Dublin. He remembered Mariane Oiseau, and fancied he saw a likeness between Mary Ann and his lost love.[31]

Next summer, when Aunt Mary was again ordered to Bath, Melchior insisted on accompanying them, perhaps mindful of Zephaniah Holwell and unwilling to entrust Mary Ann to her aunt's care.

Once again Mary Ann attracted attention. A young clergyman fell in love with her and she with him. She remembered his name as Henry Harley, and that he was a younger brother of the then Earl of Oxford.[i] They met regularly at the house of a pious lady,

i The then Earl of Oxford, had two brothers who were clergymen, and who were unmarried in 1766, but neither was called Henry, and neither was particularly young. John Harley, an acquaintance of both Aunt Mary and the young man's mother, the Dowager Countess of Oxford. Aunt Mary and her pious friend must have seen what was going on, but at first they did nothing to interfere. At the same time a Mr Stone, who had made a fortune in the West Indies and was on the lookout for a wife, decided after 'long and attentive observation' that Mary Ann was artless and pure enough for his purpose, but withdrew when he heard about young Harley. Mary Ann knew nothing of this at the time, but Stone's interest is unlikely to have escaped Aunt Mary, and fear of losing this lucrative connection may have been what prompted her to look more closely at the Harley romance. She found that while the young man was willing to be married privately, in defiance of his family, Mary Ann, believing that the discord of her parents' marriage had stemmed from the disapproval of their respective families, refused to countenance such a move – or at least that is how she recalled it in the Packet. Aunt Mary, realising that nothing would come of it, torpedoed the affair by getting her friend to reveal all to the Dowager Countess. A message was sent to young Harley pretending his mother was seriously ill; he hurried home and Mary Ann never saw him again. It was, she recalled, the first time her heart was touched.[32]

The field was now open for Mr Stone and when the party was back in London he came forward with a very generous offer, including a large sum in pin-money, enough to provide comfortably for Mary Ann's parents. This is the first of several occasions on which West Indian money, slave money, will make an appearance in this story; we can hardly avoid noticing the connection with slavery, but at the time it was so ubiquitous and commonplace that it passed without remark: it was just money. Money was what the Costellos needed, and Mr Stone had a great

---

later bishop of Hereford, was 38 in 1766; William Harley, Rector of Everleigh, Vicar of Uffington and Prebendary of York and Canon of Worcester, was 33, and died unmarried three years later. Assuming Mary Ann is correct in recalling her clerical wooer as a brother of the Earl of Oxford, the likeliest candidate would be William. She is unlikely to have invented the story, because she knew that one of the things the Cannings held against her was that 'I had refused a nobleman to throw myself away on a Player' (Packet, 66).

deal of it. He was alive to the dangers of taking a young wife (he was fifty-two; Mary Ann was twenty, and thought she was seventeen) but was satisfied that he'd found a girl who would neither deceive him nor hanker for his death. Mary Ann could see it was a good offer, but her heart was not touched. Sensing perhaps that her aunt had reasons of her own for wanting to see her married, she turned to her grandfather for disinterested advice. Melchior was still a romantic, still after almost half a century thinking of his beautiful Mariane; he understood the human heart and warned Mary Ann against a loveless marriage. Mary Ann turned Mr Stone down, and like Zephaniah Holwell he soon found consolation, marrying a woman closer to his own age. He lived on for many years, Mary Ann noted, congratulating herself on having avoided a long and tedious marriage.[33]

Another year went by, and Melchior grew fonder of Mary Ann, while Aunt Mary was torn between a wish to get her away from the Colonel and a growing dependence on her for the little comforts of life. That summer the doctor suggested Islington Spa for Aunt Mary's biliousness; she could go daily in the coach from Wigmore Street, and the doctor said to Mary Ann that the main benefit was that it would force her aunt to get up and about early in the morning.[34] Back and forth they went in the grand Guy-Dickens carriage, from Wigmore Street north to Islington, sometimes stopping on the way to pick up one of Aunt Mary's friends. Once again Mary Ann attracted attention, and soon she was all but betrothed to a pompous clergyman called Rash, curate of Stanfield in Norfolk.[i] She thought him a fool, and told him so, which he bore meekly, but he was from a good Norfolk family and had recently inherited a property from his mother. Aunt Mary encouraged him. In July Mr Rash entrusted his future happiness to the care of his dear Miss Guy-Dickens while he went down into

i It is not clear from the Packet whether the name is Rush or Rash, and Mary Ann says only that he was from Norfolk. The best fit to be found in the *Clergy of the Church of England Database* is John Rash, who was appointed curate of Stanfield, Norfolk, in 1758, and so may well have been in his early thirties in 1767. The vicar of Stanfield at the time was Rev Rash Bird, possibly a relative.

the country to prepare his family for the news that he proposed to marry a penniless Irish girl he had picked up at Islington Spa.

It was only when Mr Rash was about to leave town that Mary Ann realised what was going on. His manner of bidding farewell made his intentions, and Aunt Mary's, only too clear. Mary Ann did not openly protest. It was a year since her grandfather had discoursed upon the human heart and warned her against a loveless marriage, a year of tedium – the old Colonel's nightcap and tea, Aunt Mary's peevishness, the grumbling of the servants – which may have made an escape into marriage, even marriage to Mr Rash, look less unattractive. She was innocent enough to imagine that he would be as meek after marriage as he had shown himself as a suitor. She knew (and Aunt Mary was there to remind her if ever she forgot) that it was her duty to retrieve her family's fortunes by a good marriage. But despite her docile, fatalistic acceptance, she knew it wasn't right. Zephaniah Holwell, the chivalrous Captain Lawley, young Henry Harley and the fabulously rich Mr Stone all had tempted her, and she had resisted. After these escapes she was now drifting into marriage with a dull, silly man, because her family wished it and because she could see no other way of ending her dreary existence as a poor relation in Wigmore Street. She looked on as though it were happening to someone else – it was a mighty odd proceeding, she thought, which gave her neither pleasure not pain.[35] Her will to resist was worn down, she gave in, she would marry Mr Rash down in Norfolk – unless something happened over the summer.

2.
Courtship and Marriage, 1767–1771

Islington in the 1760s was a suburban village, not yet submerged by the spread of London. There were several medicinal springs in the neighbourhood whose waters and tree-lined walks had enjoyed a brief vogue when patronised by royalty, but which were now past their best. Socially, the Islington resorts were less strictly stratified than Bath. They courted the public with a variety of entertainments, and were places of relaxation, of dishabille, which attracted all sorts of people, from respectable hypochondriacs like Aunt Mary to prostitutes and pickpockets. Somewhere in between were the fortune-hunters and excitement-seekers, adventurous girls and young men on the prowl, who hoped to evade some of the strict rules of class distinction and decorum which governed life in fashionable London: 'Wits, captains, politicians, trulls, / Sots, devotees, pimps, poets, gulls'.[36]

In the summer of 1767 George Canning drifted back to his old refuge in Islington. He was in a melancholy mood. His small winnings on the lottery were never enough to keep him ahead of his creditors. His life seemed to have come to a halt, his ambitions, both literary and political, were leading him nowhere. Peggy Arbuckle had gone back to Ireland and turned sentimentalist.[37] Although he had overcome his dislike of royalty enough to dedicate his translation to the Queen, he doubted if any good would come of it. He was sniped at by the critics, and deterred potential patrons by setting himself up as the one righteous man in a world of liars and time-servers.

> O! Should I ever prostitute the Muse
> To mean, corrupt, or arbitrary views,
> Aught but the dictates of my heart disclose,
> Or say in Verse what I would not in Prose,
> By Dulness blotted from the roll of Fame
> May cold Oblivion shroud my blasted Name![38]

This obstinate and self-centred man had something about him that inspired affection and loyalty. His friends were not without influence. One of them was a rising Irish politician and member of a large landowning family, John Beresford, who repeatedly urged him to swallow his pride and place himself and his talents at the service of some powerful political figure.[i] Another crony was Isaac Heard, Lancaster Herald at Arms, who would later rise to become Garter King of Arms,[ii] while yet another, Sir William Duncan, was physician to George III and a principal investor in the ill-fated New Smyrna settlement in Florida. Duncan's court position and Scottish nationality made him a surprising friend for George; the connection may have originated when George was considering emigration to America. Heard and Duncan wanted to do their best for their friend, and schemed to find him a rich wife, although what part Duncan played in these events is not clear.[39]

Isaac Heard and another young man followed George to Islington, where the three of them went lounging under the trees of the Spa. Isaac had spotted a pretty girl in the crowd, and he wanted to point her out to George. The first time they went to spy on her it was sunny, and her hat was pulled down over her eyes, so they came back next day. There she was, her face uncovered for

---

i John Beresford (1738–1805): MP for Co. Waterford, holder of numerous government posts and sinecures, and brother of the second Earl of Tyrone. A contemporary of George Canning at Trinity College, Dublin, Beresford had come to study law in London at about the same time.

ii Isaac Heard (1730–1822): a sailor and merchant turned antiquarian. He was knighted in 1786.

all to see, Mary Ann with her aunt and her aunt's fat friend Miss Gwyn. Mary Ann noticed them noticing her. 'She's a trimmer, I assure you. Nothing escapes her,' said Isaac, loud enough to be overheard by Miss Gwyn.[40] Isaac was presumably using the word *trimmer* not in the sense of a political trimmer or time-server, but to represent Mary Ann as one who could hand out a severe thrashing or reprimand.[i] It's not clear how he had reached this assessment of her character – perhaps from his acquaintance Mr Rash, who had felt the sharp edge of her tongue – but he had got her measure pretty accurately.

Why did Isaac single out Mary Ann for George? He may (like Jordan Costello) have had an exaggerated idea of Melchior's wealth and thought he was putting George in the way of a rich marriage. Or perhaps he thought the Guy-Dickens connection could be useful in other ways: Uncle Gustavus might use his court position to encourage the Queen to take notice of the dedication. But the simplest explanation is probably the best: whatever might come of it all, Mary Ann's lovely face, high spirits and mocking tongue would surely rouse George from his lethargy.

Isaac used heraldry as an excuse to get into conversation with the Guy-Dickens party, asking about the foreign coat of arms on the side of the Colonel's coach. This led to general introductions and further encounters. When asked to give an account of himself, George told the ladies that he was a lawyer. Isaac and the other young man soon withdrew, leaving George to charm Aunt Mary and win the heart of Mary Ann. Miss Gwyn helped by carrying letters between the young couple. When poor Mr Rash returned, having gained his family's approval for the match, he was told by the waiters at the Spa that the thin lady's niece was going to marry Counsellor Canning.[41]

Meetings at the spa and in Wigmore Street were chaperoned

i Both senses of *trimmer* (a time-server or an outspoken critic) are to be found in the newspapers of the time. For the application of the word to one who inflicts severe punishment or sharp rebuke see the *OED* and Eric Partridge, *Dictionary of Historical Slang*. It's possible, however, that to young men on the prowl in 1767 it meant something different, something like our *smasher* or *stunner*.

by Aunt Mary. George teased her and called her Mamma, which she may have preferred to Mr Rash's *My dear Miss Guy-Dickens*. Melchior sanctioned their meetings on condition that there should be no touching, but Aunt Mary enforced the ban only fitfully. They found opportunities to exchange kisses, and in September George committed an indiscretion sufficiently grave to make him seek forgiveness, both from Mary Ann and Aunt Mary. Her lips, he said, had now confessed 'in more ways than one' that she loved him entirely. The lightheartedness of his apology shows how confident he felt that what he called his 'foibles and irregularities' were not deplored too seriously by either of them.[i] Aunt Mary read some, but not all, of their letters, probably more out of prurience than in order to protect Mary Ann's innocence. When Mary Ann managed to smuggle out unseen a particularly passionate letter to her lover, Aunt Mary saw the reply in which George paraphrased Mary Ann's effusion.[42] The laxness of her supervision was due in part, perhaps, to a willingness to indulge the young, in part to a selfish indifference, but most of all to impatience to get Mary Ann away from her too doting grandfather.

The same mixture of motives was at work in Gustavus, who was deputed by Melchior to investigate George's circumstances. He asked some friends of friends what they knew, but when George protested furiously against having his character enquired after like a servant's Gustavus did not pursue the matter. George was particularly anxious that nobody in Ireland should be approached, because he did not want his father to get to hear of the proposed marriage. Mary Ann hastened to assure George that neither she nor her aunt were involved in this enquiry.[43]

George himself offered a spectacularly unconvincing account of his situation and prospects. Yes, he had been disinherited, he told Mary Ann in a letter to be shown to Gustavus,[44] but he was sure his mother and brother would make good provision for him

i George's easy assumption that he would be forgiven might not have struck us as particularly out of place until recent events (2017-2019) heightened our sensitivity to the sound of male entitlement.

after his father's death. No, he had not yet earned a penny from his profession, but many famous lawyers had started at the bottom of the ladder, married early and risen to eminence and riches. He gave examples, neither of them particularly apt, since the men in question did not marry until well established in their careers. One, he says, whose beloved 'leaped out of a window into his arms' nonetheless rose to be attorney-general of Ireland; George omitted to mention that the lady was a substantial heiress and niece of a senior member of the judiciary. As for his own current financial situation, certainly he was burdened with many debts, but only, he explained, because of his youthful extravagance, 'boyish ebullitions', and his need for sensual gratification. No responsible parent or guardian could have regarded such a man as an eligible husband for an innocent girl with no fortune of her own. Gustavus did nothing to interfere, and probably concealed the truth from Melchior.

Since Mary Ann believed she was only eighteen the question arose of her father's consent to her marriage. Explicit parental consent was not required if the banns were called, but George may have feared that calling the banns in a fashionable London church would tempt officious friends to communicate the news to Jordan and to Abbey Street. This might lead Jordan to forbid the banns and would also sabotage George's plan of presenting his parents with a *fait accompli*. Marriage by licence involved less publicity, but for that written parental consent was needed.[45] It is likely that Jordan would have withheld consent, since Mary Ann had been sent to London to restore the family's fortunes, and marrying the penniless George Canning was no way to achieve this. There was also a risk that, if notified of the intended marriage, he would make contact with Abbey Street. To avoid these difficulties the lovers considered eloping to 'the banks of the Tweed', but then Aunt Mary produced a simpler remedy. Mary Ann, she announced, was three years older than had hitherto been thought, and would come of age on 27 January 1768. If they married on the twenty-eighth George could obtain a licence by swearing that Mary Ann was of age, and so save the cost of a journey to Scotland. Despite his infatuation, he was happy to delay the marriage.[46]

Mary Ann wrote in the Packet that Aunt Mary 'pretended to have gained her intelligence by writing to my Mother for your Fathers information'.[47] For the rest of her life Mary Ann remained uncertain as to her true age. Mrs Costello maintained that Mary Ann was her third child, born in 1750, but with eleven births and nine children dying in infancy she may have forgotten when she was herself married, and the order in which her children were born. Aunt Mary was probably right, but her discovery was also convenient not only for the lovers but for herself, since it removed a potential obstacle to her plan for getting Mary Ann out of the house. Apart from the purely legal matter of written consent, Aunt Mary must have known that she and her brother and father were gambling unwarrantably with their niece's future. The new calculation relieved them of responsibility: if Mary Ann was of age, they were powerless.

In the meantime no obstacle, apart from Aunt Mary's indulgent supervision, was placed to their corresponding, meeting and touching, as often and as intimately as they wished. On the twenty-eighth of each month George wrote suggestively of the pleasures to be enjoyed on 28 January. 'Be sure when you go to bed not to think of this night three months,' he wrote on 28 October. On 28 December they entered what he called the 'honeymoon of expectation' and his expectations were clearly centred on the sexual demands they would make of each other. Commenting on the extravagance of her Christmas purchases, he wondered whether she would be as eager to spend his strength in the Elysium of bed, sheets, blankets and pillows. She protested that his love was bodily and transient, to which he replied that bodily and mental love enhance each other, adding that he appreciated the joys and comforts of a shared bed, even if she as yet didn't.[48]

At the beginning of October, when he was living in lodgings in Kensington and planning to return to his chambers in the Middle

Temple – either place being within easy reach of Wigmore Street – he abruptly announced that they could not meet for six weeks. He gave no reason, and in language that would not have disgraced the Abbey Street Logic he wrote: 'It is scarcely possible to imagine an occasion wherein I would not chuse to be explicit; yet such an occasion has occurred.'[49] And that was that. He was annoyed when, in her anxiety over his health, Mary Ann attacked his 'garrison' by sending the Guy-Dickens coachman with a message to his lodgings. She must use only the penny post, and even if they met in the street she was not to approach him, he said. In moments of doubt Mary Ann suspected that he was living a double life. Such suspicions, he said, made him fear she had died and been replaced by a different Mary Ann. A woman who loves should trust her lover; even if he has done what is alleged against him she should trust that it was done for the best. He begged her not to seek out 'naughty meanings' in everything, and lectured her on the evils of sentimentalism.

> A sentimentalist may write with any meaning or with no meaning, and pretend she had this meaning or that meaning or t'other meaning, she may joke and say she was serious, or be serious and say she was joking, while she holds her Slave of a Correspondent bound in fetters of Cold Iron.[50]

Sentimentalism was a sort of irresponsibility which allowed a woman to take refuge in a fog of words and evade the reality of physical love.

George's motives for the separation are hard to establish. He hinted that meeting her was a distraction from his legal studies,[51] which would be more convincing if there was evidence that he devoted his time to study. Creditors may have been forcing him to go incognito, or he may have been still in the process of freeing himself from an earlier entanglement. It may be that he had contracted a venereal disease. Although he prided himself on having remained celibate since meeting Mary Ann in the summer, he had not lived chastely before that, and may have wanted to ensure that he was clear of infection before his marriage. Since cures for venereal diseases required intensive and prolonged treatment, typically involving mercury or silver nitrate which had visible and disgusting side effects, such as drooling at the mouth or discolouration of the skin, men often preferred to hide from everyone except their doctor for the duration.[52] Another possible explanation is that the separation was intended to give added piquancy to their love letters. A few years later George made preparations to publish their correspondence, and there is a literary quality to his letters, as though he were writing for a wider readership than Mary Ann alone. He may have contrived the situation in order to impart narrative tension to the projected book. When Mary Ann looked back on these events she found it incredible that her aunt and uncle did not find George's behaviour alarming enough to cast further doubt on his eligibility: 'it seems as if we were all under the influence of some illusion that Obscured our Judgments & fetter'd our actions, for some purpose which Heaven had preordain'd.'[53]

Only George's side of the correspondence has survived. He made much of his experience in love, taunting Mary Ann for her simplicity, criticising her naïve morality, and teasing her with the promise of delights to come. He congratulated her on her frank response to his advances, evidence that her desires were as strong as his, but since she lacked the language to express her feelings he lectured her on the nature of Love. Love, he declared, like Mind in the *Anti-Lucretius*, must be one, indivisible, indestructible, and not, as she seemed to think, 'a most salutary composition made up by Reason of the choicest ingredients, as friendship, esteem &c &c most accurately and judiciously blended together, to be gulped down at once after shaking the bottle.'[54]

> I mean by that [he continued], that when the ceremony is once over the happy Pair are to lead very rational lives in concert, till Death comes to separate them, and then the survivor wears black for so many months, and so the Tragi-Comedy is concluded with very great decorum and prodigious applause. Depend upon it, that Love which is not it's own pure principle, but is made up of a combination of any other principles, will immediately after marriage be resolved into those principles, that is, in other words, it will not be love at all … fifty thousand [other principles] … can no more make true Love than fifty thousand Rubies can make a Diamond.

When she told him primly that she would love him as well as he deserved, he replied angrily that love is not to be reasoned over and measured out according to deserts. What mattered in love was the spontaneous emotion generated between 'those sources of inexpressible delight: our sympathetick Hearts'. If she persisted in her heresy she would be disciplined, he said, promising to punish her body for the errors of her mind, and adding that 'a little wholesome discipline applied smartly now and then will add a prodigious zest to our love.'[55]

In the event their marriage did not take place on 28 January. George repeatedly put it off – another suspicious circumstance that Mary Ann's friends remarked upon, without taking any action. The reason may have been lack of funds or poor health. Every winter he was ill, and throughout January he was receiving the attentions of a 'periwig-pated doctor', but it's not clear what was wrong.[56] He was also labouring under political difficulties, having been persuaded to enter negotiations with members of the government and write a pamphlet attacking the American Colonists' demand for no taxation without representation.[57] His usual allies, the Wilkesites, were pro-Liberty and pro-American, and he had hitherto agreed with them. In order to prove that he was not prostituting his muse by denying his principles he offered a convoluted argument about the nature of 'representation' and obligations that passed from one generation to another to reconcile the exactions of the government with the constitutionalism of the Glorious Revolution. This may have unsettled him enough to take his mind off marriage, and although he did not tell Mary Ann about it she suspected that while he was in seclusion he was making a 'desperate effort' over some literary task. To make up for postponing the marriage, he composed a 'Birthday Offering': 'Ere this short Winter's day be gone,/ My Mary Anne is twenty-one.'[58]

George's sister Molly Barnard and her husband Henry were in London, staying with Henry's uncle Andrew Stone in Privy Gardens, Whitehall. The Barnards visited other acquaintances in and around London, including Andrew Stone's niece who was married to a John Arbuthnot in Mitcham, Surrey, but Molly spent much of the time with Mary Ann in Wigmore Street.[59] Andrew Stone was a government and court insider, now in retirement, but still holding his position as treasurer to the queen. His name probably impressed Melchior and Gustavus, and together with George's connection with Lord Hillsborough, and friendship with coming men like John Beresford and George Macartney, may have helped persuade them it was safe to entrust Mary Ann to a disinherited poet.[i] Macartney had been a fellow student in Dublin, but had outdistanced his brilliant but feckless friend and may have begun to find the connection irksome. He complied with a request from George to provide Stratty with letters of introduction to his successor in St Petersburg, Lord Cathcart, but regarded a later request on behalf of Henry Barnard as unreasonable. George felt this refusal as a snub. Macartney's recommendation of Stratty came to nothing, which may have led Stratty to think his efforts had been half-hearted.[60]

Mary Ann and Molly grew increasingly fond of each other. Since it was important to have someone from the Canning family present at the wedding, and Molly was impatient to get home to her sickly children in Ireland, George eventually fixed the date for

i George Macartney, first Earl Macartney (1737–1806): Envoy to Russia in 1764, he rose steadily in the diplomatic and colonial service.

21 May. But for the pressure from his sister he might have put off the day indefinitely, because he had no home to take a wife to. His situation was desperate, as he wrote later in the summer to Stratty: 'The poor precarious half-yearly fifty pounds, which I have got in the most ungracious manner for these two years, is near half swallowed up in the payment of interest for money necessarily borrowed within those memorable years of total dereliction.' Mary Ann knew nothing of this: 'I knew not his resources. Reserve was a characteristic of his mind, — and I never sought to violate a feeling which tho its Effects were painfull to me, I held sacred to the last hour of his life.' He arranged temporary lodgings in Islington and a day or so before the wedding he summoned Mary Ann to his chambers in the Middle Temple to pack up his belongings ready for the move.[61]

They were married by licence in the parish church of Marylebone, with Molly and Henry Barnard in attendance, and with Gustavus giving Mary Ann away on behalf of her grandfather. The witnesses were Albinia Gwynn and Gustavus. The wedding breakfast was held in Melchior's house. Molly presented Mary Ann with a set of silver table-spoons and a lock of her hair. She also informed Abbey Street of the marriage. In their eagerness to reconcile Stratford to the event, she and Paul emphasised Mary Ann's gentle birth and perhaps exaggerated her grandfather's fortune. After the ceremony the Barnards hurried back to Ireland and their children.[62]

Mary Ann had made herself popular with the servants in Wigmore Street, and one of them accompanied her when she and George set up house in Islington. George told Stratty that his domestic happiness made him see things in a new light, making him all the angrier at his treatment by the world and disgusted at being forced to 'scramble amongst expedients for a miserable subsistence.'[63] It was not long, however, before Mary Ann received another hint that her husband had inherited some of the Abbey Street Logic. At first he made a point of being at home to dine with her, but soon his bachelor habits reasserted themselves. She received a note written from the King's Head, Holborn. As it was the first time that he had 'baulked your expectation of seeing me at home', he was letting her know that he was detained. 'On future occasions,' he added, 'I shall not probably be so ceremonious.'[64]

Paul carried out the task of paying George his allowance so high-handedly that George quarrelled with him, though not so violently as to sever the relationship. Stratty, on the other hand, though he wrote home dutifully of the 'misconduct of my brother in London', and promised to obey his father 'strictly in every possible command', nonetheless remained on good terms with George. Like his mother and sisters, George understood the need to placate 'Him', and would have forgiven the abject tone of some of Stratty's letters home, but Paul had gone too far, having decided that his future lay in swallowing whole the Abbey Street view. George confided in Stratty about the 'astonishingly extraordinary' behaviour of Paul.[65] Mary Ann looked on with interest and apprehension. She had had her own family problems, but being afraid of her father had never been one of them.

On the expiry of their six months in Islington George and Mary Ann went into new lodgings in Featherstone Buildings, Gray's Inn Passage.[66] Over the next twenty years Mary Ann was to spend various periods in London, mostly in the Bloomsbury, Gray's Inn Road, Somerstown and Battlebridge areas, on either side of the New Road (nowadays, the Euston Road). When they moved into the new lodgings she was pregnant, and in March 1769 her first child was born there. They called her Letitia, in honour of George's mother. For George this was a matter of principle, to assert the indissoluble family bond.[67] Mary Ann may also have hoped that the birth of a grandchild would soften her mother-in-law's heart, but if she expected the women in Abbey Street, George's mother, his aunts and sisters, to circumvent Him's intransigence, she was disappointed.[68]

A few months later the family transferred to a third set of

lodgings, close to where George had his chambers in the Temple. This was a temporary measure while a much grander house was being prepared for them in Queen Anne Street. The arrangements were slowed down by having to do everything on credit. In the lodging house Mary Ann's nerves were constantly irritated by quarrels that erupted whenever her loyal servant suspected that the landlady was taking advantage of their inexperience to cheat them. They decided to move to Queen Anne Street immediately, whether the house was ready or not. Within a week or so of their quitting it the lodging house near the Temple was burned to the ground.[69]

Queen Anne Street is parallel to Wigmore Street and Marylebone Road. Now it runs from Welbeck Street to Chandos Street, but in 1769 it continued east of what is now Portland Place at least as far as Great Portland Street. It was into a house at this end of the street that George and Mary Ann and baby Letitia moved in the summer of 1769. Their neighbours included artists, physicians, writers and the occasional MP. As the street names reveal, the land round about belonged to aristocratic families such as the Oxfords and Portlands, who were cashing in on the demand for fashionable addresses from members of the upper middle class keen to place a distance between themselves and the money-grubbing City.[70] George insisted that a liveried manservant was essential to maintain one's standing in this aspiring neighbourhood. It seems strange that George, after his bohemian life, attached such importance to prestige, but he never lost his sense of who he was, the heir to a substantial landed estate. It was not just a matter of prestige for its own sake. A man in livery would impress creditors, and so had a cash value. At this point Mary Ann thought it an extravagance, but as time went on, in different circumstances, she came to see its importance. The young couple had started married life with just one servant, the faithful cook from Wigmore Street; in the course of events they had acquired a nursemaid, and now there was also an ex-waiter from the Grecian Coffee House.[71]

In the autumn Letitia was almost ready to be weaned. Installed in her new home with its new furniture and fittings Mary Ann thought that after a few false starts her married life proper was at last beginning, and her husband was starting to make his way in the world. He went out every morning to do business. What his business was, she didn't know. It is said that George was engaged in the wine trade, which may explain references to a certain Mr Cromie in his correspondence. Several wine merchants in Dublin were called Cromie, and one may have been the William Cromie who was a neighbour of the Cannings in Abbey Street, so it is possible that through this connection George was employed to sell wine on commission, which was a genteel kind of commercial activity, though probably not very lucrative.[72] This was an occupation even less congenial than the law, but he was forced to accept it. Mary Ann didn't know how much of his time he devoted to selling wine, how much he spent writing, and chasing possible patrons and subscribers – and how much just sitting in coffee houses grumbling about his unaccountable father and proclaiming himself to be out of tune with the times, a lone honest voice.

> Ah London! London! Bane of rising youth,
> Nurse of deceit, eternal foe to truth!…
> By thy fell poison blasted soon depart
> The rustick blush, and honesty of heart;
> Falsehood succeeds, with all her motley train,
> Of wiles collusive, and deceptions vain …[73]

Twice a week they dined with Melchior, who enjoyed discussing politics with George. They disagreed, of course, the old Colonel's instincts being those of a courtier and diplomat, while George was a defender of liberty and intransigent opponent of the king. Melchior could see that George's talents should take him far, if only he would attach himself to some faction. Lords Temple and Lyttelton as well as Hillsborough showed an interest in him, commissioned pamphlets from him or offered to procure a seat in

Parliament, but he refused to be bound by party loyalty to either government or opposition. His friends begged him to come to terms with one or other of these powerful men, but he always failed to strike while the iron was hot, as John Beresford put it.[74] Melchior couldn't understand how any man of talent and spirit could turn down a seat in Parliament.

After one of their dinners in Wigmore Street Mary Ann and George returned to find their house in uproar. Letitia was in the kitchen with the servants, suffering convulsions. The experienced nursemaid, claiming to know better than the young mother, had tried to hurry on the weaning process by giving the baby solid food, probably a sort of bread and water paste. Mary Ann, who subscribed to the views of a popular doctor, Hugh Smith, on the importance of a milk diet,[i] had overruled the nurse, believing that the unsuitable food was making Letitia constipated. She was probably right. But while the parents were out of the house the baby was taken down to the kitchen and given more of the forbidden pap. This, Mary Ann was convinced, was the cause of the convulsions. Three days later the child was dead.[75]

Among the letters of condolence was one from Stratty, now home in Dublin. He could imagine her grief, he said, having long thought that her maternal feelings were too intense, that her emotional investment in the fragile life of her infant had been too great, too risky. He ventured to suggest that such extreme feeling was 'a sort of self-gratification', but admitted that it was easy to philosophise when he had not himself been in the position of a bereaved parent. Many years later, in very different circumstances, he would repeat the charge of self-gratification, and condemn her for it. Now he ended his letter with an assurance that he felt 'an esteem and affection for you which I am sure will remain till my latest breath'. This inaugurated a series of affectionate letters from Stratty over the next four years; Mary Ann clearly felt its importance, because she endorsed it 'the first'.[76]

i There were two doctors called Hugh Smith at this time, one known for his benevolence, the other for his entrepreneurial flair. Mary Ann's Dr Smith was the second.

Molly Barnard too had invested heavily in short infant lives. She knew all too well the pain of loss: she '[twines] herself round my heart,' she wrote, as she watched over one of her own dying babies.[77] She sent a conventional letter of condolence immediately after Letitia's death, but when she heard that Mary Ann's second baby was almost due she wrote again. Calculating that Mary Ann's new pregnancy had begun before Letitia was weaned, Molly sent her this terrible warning, urging her dear Mary Ann not to breastfeed her next baby unless she was resolved to do it justice:

> … the milk of the healthiest woman upon Earth [she wrote] is in a state of corruption from the moment she is with child, and therefore Deem'd by every Body the most pernicious thing a child can take, for tho it may not be the immediate cause of their Death, it may lay up store of misery for them, and no one can tell when or in what shape it may break out.[78]

Mary Ann had evidently not picked up this warning from her reading of Hugh Smith. Writing on the danger of employing a wet nurse, Smith mentioned that when a woman was pregnant her milk was less nutritious, and her charge would either pine away and die or grow up weakly, but his warning was less stark and explicit than Molly's.[79] But she believed her sister-in-law. The letter, as she recalled thirty years later, 'harrowed up my soul', but she was grateful for the warning – testimony to the strength of the two women's friendship. She took it in better part than George, who almost quarrelled with his sister over it. He was annoyed at the interference, because it upset Mary Ann, and meant that until the baby was weaned he and Mary Ann would have to sleep apart.[80]

Having dismissed the disobedient servant, Mary Ann made up her mind to provide better care for her next baby. She suggested that she should summon her mother and sister from Dublin. Old Mrs Costello had lost nine of her eleven children, which may have raised doubts about her child-rearing skills, but Mary Ann could at least rely on her to do as she was told. Esther was about fifteen, with a lifetime of looking after other people's children ahead of her. Perhaps surprisingly, George agreed. No doubt the thought of saving the wages of a nursemaid weighed with him, and having grown up in a household full of obedient aunts and sisters he may have had thoughts of recreating the same environment in his own home, with himself in the patriarchal role. Mrs Costello and Esther duly came across, and with Jordan Costello installed on his cousin's estate in Mayo it seemed that Mary Ann's family was at last taken care of. George took a fancy to Esther, who may have treated him with more uncritical respect than his sharper-tongued wife.[81]

Money worries deepened. Faced with the prospect of gaol for a debt of £111 13s 0d, George used John Beresford's name to raise the money, only telling his friend of the 'complex transaction' after the event. Now that it was too late, Aunt Mary remarked on the young couple's struggles, but George resented her enquiries, which he suspected would not lead to any substantial help. He instructed Mary Ann to go direct to her grandfather and ask for immediate payment of the legacy that she had been led to expect. Melchior, she recalled, had once shown her a will in which she was left £270 – she remembered it because it was an odd sum. The old man was beginning to lose his wits and could do nothing without consulting his daughter. Aunt Mary called on her brothers to put pressure on the old man to refuse. The excuses they used were first that George had brought his difficulties on himself by refusing the offer of a seat in Parliament, and then that Mary Ann would need the money still more desperately if George were to die leaving her unprovided for. This eventuality, which they had not considered seriously at the time of Mary Ann's marriage, now struck them as likely. Mary Ann, mindful of what had happened when her mother had asked Melchior a second time for assistance, admitted that their argument was sound enough. She saw no need to quarrel over it, but the incident led to a breach between George and the Guy-Dickens family. The quarrel was mainly on George's side: he had his father's gift for severing links and writing people off, whereas Melchior's children, less violent in their affections and animosities, might have kept in contact, provided there was no danger of Mary Ann getting her hands on the old Colonel's money.[82]

George was now actively thinking of publishing his and Mary Ann's love letters, despite objections from Mary Ann herself, and from Molly. He planned to include an appendix giving full details of his family's conduct towards him, hoping that fear of exposure would make his father come round. The previous summer old Stratford had sent Stratty a message for George concerning some letters, and although the contents of the message are not known it may mean that news of the publishing plan had already reached Abbey Street. George's publication of the 'Birthday Offering' may have been a signal that he was serious about pushing his private affairs into public view. John Beresford subscribed, with a handsome cheque, but begged George to satisfy his subscribers by publishing something else. Shortly before her death, when she was ill and heavily pregnant, Molly set about raising money from friends to send to George, in the hope of preventing publication. George saw no contradiction between this indifference to the wishes of his entire family and his often stated view that the demands of family were sacred. It's impossible to say how serious he was over this, but he went on seeking subscribers both in London and, through Beresford, in Dublin. He sent Beresford fifty blank subscription forms, reminding him to indicate which subscribers wanted the deluxe version on royal paper.[83] However much he tightened the pressure, he should have known that his father was the last person to give in to blackmail.

The baby was born on 11 April 1770, a son, christened George, 'the delight, the blessing of my fond heart,' Mary Ann wrote. A new routine was established. In the mornings her husband would go out about his mysterious affairs until dinner time, while she attended to the baby. Between dinner and tea they both played with the baby before handing him over to Mrs Costello in the nursery, which left Mary Ann free to attend to her husband. In the course of those summer evenings he described his years of poverty and struggle, and his conflict with his father. Even the moments of relaxation with baby George were clouded by bitter memories. He could not look on his heir without remembering how he had wronged him by signing away his inheritance. Interrupted only by the baby's last feed at ten o'clock, these melancholy conversations went on until they separated for the night, Mary Ann to sleep in the nursery, George to his solitary bed, his anxieties and the 'constitutional turbulences' arising from enforced celibacy.[84]

The one time George consulted Mary Ann on his affairs was when Lord Hillsborough offered to appoint him governor of Grenada. If they went there, George told Mary Ann, the climate would kill him within a year, and she and the baby would be isolated far from home; whereas if they stayed in Britain and he were to die, his father and mother would not, he believed, withhold their protection. With these arguments against the proposal, Mary Ann could hardly have urged him to accept it, and she wondered why he bothered to ask her opinion. She disliked his casual allusions to his own death, 'sallies of fixed despair', as she called them.[85]

George's thoughts returned obsessively to the rupture with his family. He was fierce in his denunciations of the Abbey Street Logic, especially when he heard from Stratty that their father had forbidden any mourning on the death of Molly in October 1770, ordering the household to carry on as usual. 'Never can they lose a Fellow to what they have lost,' George wrote, 'and bearing this affliction so stoically… what Infraction of Mortality upon any remaining connection can possibly stagger their stoicism henceforth.' George's gesture of making his mother godmother of his first child had elicited no response, but he insisted that nothing his parents did or failed to do could cancel his obligations towards them.[86]

Even political discussions came back to this bitter personal wound. He described the conflict with the American colonists in terms of a painful relationship between an indulgent parent and undutiful son, and his whole argument on the topic turned upon the idea of inherited obligations.[87] In the course of one of his fireside conversations with Mary Ann and Stratty, he expressed his dislike of the Scots (a common political topic at the time) in particularly extreme language, and when challenged explained that they were a cold people – look at King James the Sixth, who was content to shake the hand of Elizabeth while it was still red with his mother's blood. It was irrelevant to point out Mary Stuart's guilt: 'Mary was his Mother — and by Every law of God & Nature he was her Defender — not her Judge!'[88] Mary Ann would remember this many years later when her own son, she felt, was setting himself up as her judge.

Things in Queen Anne Street would have been gloomier still but for Stratty's presence in London. He remained on reasonable terms with his father – just. By the time he got home from his travels his passion for Mehitabel Patrick had abated, or so he told his father, but Mehitabel had no intention of giving him up. He set off again, this time on a walking tour of Ireland, gathering information on ancient sites to assist his father's study of Ireland's Druidical past. By this time things had gone still more sour between Stratford and George; the old man may have seen the danger of pushing Stratty too far. When Robert Patrick died leaving his business in disarray, Stratford was all the more determined to prevent the match, while Stratty felt it would be ungenerous to desert the Patrick family in their time of trouble. Neither would he desert George and Mary Ann, although when his father complained that he was being unduly influenced by his rebellious older brother he pretended that Queen Anne Street was too far from his usual haunts for him to have 'frequent intercourse' with them.[89] Paul was also in London from time to time, and professed friendship for George and Mary Ann, but they and Stratty remained wary of him.

Having recently returned from his travels Stratty had much to talk about apart from these family vexations. He took life more easily than George, of whom he was much in awe. Born in 1744, he was only three (or six) years older than Mary Ann, and having been the baby of the family he remained guileless and immature. While in receipt of a generous allowance from his father he had tried to save enough to pay off some of George's debts, but his money ran through his fingers: 'he had an Heart capable of the strongest and most Active Affection,' Mary Ann recalled, 'and Had his Head been equal to it He woud have acted more worthy of himself — but he was the slave of his Affections.'[90] He'd been just thirteen when George left Ireland, and for ten years or more his sisters had fed him stories of their brother's genius and unmerited suffering. As winter came on Stratty and Mary Ann's shared anxiety about George's declining health developed into friendship. Over the years to come Mary Ann would have occasion to think deeply about the many ways in which a woman can be made wretched in marriage, and her reason would tell her that a man like Stratty, reasonable, practical and respectful, might have made an easier partner than the gloomy and autocratic George, who, she recognised, had his share of his 'Fathers Illness'.[91] But, as George had impressed upon her, reason was not what counted in love, and she remained till the end passionately attached to her husband.

One evening in January 1771, when Stratty had gone back to his lodgings and Mary Ann and George were about to separate for the night, George stopped on the stairs. Mary Ann recalled the incident:

> he looked piteously in my face, & said Am I still to be deserted?— My Heart was smote severely, and I ask'd him what was to become of George?— he replied that I had Two Georges, but it seemed [that] One was to be sacrificed to the other — His Bed was lonely, he said, and his thoughts unfit for Solitude — horror froze my blood — [92]

What froze her blood was Molly's warning – a warning made all the more poignant by Molly's recent death. Rushing to the nursery she asked her mother to look after the baby for the night. She didn't reveal that she was going to sleep in her husband's bed, saying just that he was too ill to be left alone. Immediately she set about weaning the baby earlier than planned, but not quickly enough. Convinced that she had conceived that first night, she was terrified of the effect on baby George. He was teething and would wake and cry in the cold January nights,[93] and as she left the conjugal bed and made her way back to the nursery to quieten him by giving him the breast, she feared she was poisoning him. All seemed well, but what of the secret damage done by her corrupted milk? 'No-one can tell when or in what shape it may break out,' Molly had written.

In the last months of his life, as his physical health fluctuated, and creditors began again to press for payment, George's behaviour became erratic. He wrote bitterly to Beresford of Lord Hillsborough, who had tempted him to seek office, but had proved to be 'in all lights, and in all moods and tenses, a most hollow-hearted, double-tongued, cajoling scoundrel'. Desperately he knocked on friends' doors to beg them to pay in advance for one of several projected books, including the book of love-letters, breaking into tears of gratitude when an old family friend from Dublin, Robert Crowe, immediately produced five guineas.[i] Thomas Newburgh, a relative of old Mrs Canning, sent a christening present – too late for little George, too early for the unborn child. George told Mary Ann to keep it safe and to remember, because he would not be around to remember for her, that the new child was to be called Thomas. She used the money to pay some of her most pressing bills. At the same time, George could not suppress the instincts of a gentleman and man of property: when a circular appeal came to him from Catherine Jemmat, an author crippled with rheumatism and even more unfortunate than himself, he promised a subscription.[94]

Knowing that his death was near, he bitterly surveyed the

---

i Crowe heightened the drama by saying he met George on the very day Mary Ann gave birth to her son. His account is inaccurate in detail, and reads like a well-turned anecdote, but there is no need to doubt that the encounter happened.

ruins of his life, and saw that his son's hope of prosperity lay in recovering the lost Garvagh inheritance. He left the following injunction: 'You are born, my dear George, with all my Rights and all my wrongs upon your head: Assert my Rights, avenge not my wrongs.' The words are written on the back of a sheet containing notes for a projected book. In a letter to John Beresford, Mary Ann suggests there was something more elaborate, a 'sacred scroll' left by George for his son, detailing his rights and his wrongs, but I've not found it.[95] In the event, young George would take no more than a passing interest in his father's wrongs, never questioning the right of Paul's son to inherit the Garvagh property.

In his 'fixed despair', George became reckless, as though to prove that the tyrant Cromie would be the death of him. The weather, Mary Ann recalled, was dismal on 20 March, and George had 'an Alarming degree of sore throat', but he insisted on going out on foot in the rain and sleet to transact some necessary business on behalf of friends in Ireland. He met Stratty in the City and they came back together. George was confined to bed for several days, but as soon as he could he went out again, until on 4 April he took to his bed for the last time. Mary Ann sat with him night after night until he seemed to show a slight improvement, upon which she felt she could relinquish her post to Esther. But in the night Esther became anxious, sent a servant for the doctor and summoned Mary Ann. Mary Ann rushed to the bedside, sending Esther to bring the baby to be blessed by his father. George could not speak. As he struggled to lift himself to kiss her he fell back and died.[96]

Mary Ann sat alone with the body, rousing herself only when the baby was brought to her. All around, the house was in uproar, her mother and Stratty both weeping uncontrollably, while she maintained a tragic calm. She refused food, and sat speechless in George's room, not allowing the coffin to be closed until forced by the onset of putrefaction. She insisted on accompanying Stratty to the funeral. When they returned the baby George was placed in her arms, and then she broke into a 'gush of tears'. After drinking a cup of tea laced with opium, she slept.[97]

She composed a simple and touching epitaph:

> Thy virtue and my love no words can tell
> Therefore a little while, my George, farewell.
> For faith and love like ours Heaven has in store
> Its last best gift—to meet and part no more.[98]

The sentiments are conventional, and against them we have to place Mary Ann's unblinking recognition, implicit in her account of her marriage, that her husband was obstinate, autocratic and irresponsible. But there's no reason to question the reality of her passion and her grief. The 'little while' that she had to wait before re-joining him turned out to be fifty-six years of extraordinary life.

3.
Widowhood, 1771–1773

Mary Ann knew something of her husband's money troubles, but he had disguised their true extent. Stratty had to tell her there was nothing; none of the furniture, not even her bed, was paid for. As they went through George's papers together, searching fruitlessly for a will, they came across an unopened letter from John Beresford, containing £30. Arguing that this gift had never been received by George and that therefore it could not be reckoned as part of his widow's inheritance, Stratty sent it back. This seems a perversely scrupulous act, the sort of thing George himself would have done. It may also have been due to timidity towards Beresford. He must have been a distant and imposing figure, and Mary Ann seems to have hesitated before communicating with him, beginning a letter on 25 May, finishing it four weeks later and not sending it for another three weeks. Beresford returned the money, which settled some of the debts. Soon afterwards, Mary Ann lighted upon another banknote hidden amongst the scattered papers, but she suspected that Stratty had planted it from his own meagre funds, and begged him to take it back.[99] As they shared the task of bringing order to George's affairs, dealing with his creditors and reviewing the remains of an unfulfilled life, the easy friendship between Stratty and Mary Ann deepened into a strong bond of sympathy and affection.

Aunt Mary visited with offers of help. The family's quarrel had been with George, and now he was gone they were prepared to help his widow. Although there was no more talk of the £270, their intervention suggests that they felt some residue of affection for the girl who had brightened their household for three years, and perhaps accepted some responsibility for her plight. Aunt Mary also, no doubt, wanted to set a limit to the demands that Mary Ann and her mother might make upon the Colonel. Mary Ann was pregnant, believing that her baby was due in October. Nothing could be decided until then. In the meantime it was arranged for Mary Ann to stay over the summer on a farm close to a house that Melchior had taken in Hornsey.[100]

Paul Canning told his father that George had died, leaving a son, another George. Old Stratford immediately sent Mary Ann £20, telling her he would send the same amount every six months for the child's support, so long as she remained in England. Mary Ann immediately saw she would need somehow to supplement this allowance, which, however, she acknowledged fulsomely, addressing her parents-in-law as the 'Honoured Father and Mother of the Lost Partner of my Soul'. Thereafter her letters became angrier, while Stratford remained blandly dismissive, refusing to provide anything for her own maintenance, and no more than £40 a year for little George, rising to £50 if the second child was born alive. Beresford, to whom she confided the details of the correspondence, begged her to be more conciliatory, but it would have made no difference. Stratford recalled that George had boasted of her good family, a claim that Mary Ann repudiated – George had boasted of her personal virtue, not her birth – although it was true that Molly and Paul had made the most of the Guy-Dickens connection. The old man remained intransigent. So far as he was concerned, Mary Ann had a grandfather who enjoyed a handsome pension from the Irish government – let him take care of her. For himself, he 'begged to be excused'. Mary Ann endorsed the letter: 'What my Dear George used to call Abbey Street Logic'.[101]

Stratty visited her at Hornsey, and wrote when he couldn't visit. He was preoccupied with business worries as he tried to establish himself in the City. His relationship with Mehitabel Patrick, on which his future standing with his father depended, was still unresolved. He wrote bitterly of his parents. He was anxious for news of his ailing sister Letitia, and feared that no one would trouble to tell him if, as he expected, she died. When he wrote to his father after George's death he received no reply. Someone, probably his aunt or one of his sisters, explained why. 'My letter is still unopened,' he told Mary Ann, '– the silent and despised Tenant of the corner of some pocket – perhaps they wait to ransack the Library for a second Quotation, or they must suppose Time to be absolutely in their own power, when months are employed to do the work of moments.' He writes 'they' – he found his mother as infuriating as his father. And yet, like his brother George, he still proclaimed his affection for them, and when he eventually heard, apparently from someone outside the family, that Letitia had died, he did not believe that his father's stubborn stoicism would shield him from feeling the loss: 'Nature may be kept down,' he wrote to Mary Ann, 'but cannot be stifled.' He had a friend, another young man starting out in business in the City, Thomas Raikes. When Raikes took him to his home in Gloucester he saw a house filled with 'filial love and a mother's love for her children', which made him reflect sadly on the 'perversity' of his own situation.[102]

Another visitor to the farm was a friend of George's called Major Molesworth. It was he who first raised the idea that Mary Ann should go on the stage. This was an unthinkable proposition, and yet at the same time the obvious solution. Unthinkable, because a modest woman, used to a private life, could not suddenly parade herself on a stage, submitting her figure and her face to the scrutiny of the public; no lady could contemplate lowering herself to the social level of a paid play-actor. But if you looked at the hard facts, as presumably the major did, Mary Ann's one indisputable asset was her beauty, and where better to exploit it than the stage?

Major Molesworth's suggestion did not stop there. He proposed that she should make her debut as Isabella in *The Fatal Marriage* because there was a tyrannical father in the play, and it would be a way of shaming the Canning family.[i] Such conflation of the actress with the character she plays was common in the theatre of the time, and is not unheard of nowadays. When the north-country actress Charlotte Johnston[ii] played Isabella in her home town of Wigton, people recalled that she had quarrelled with her family and accused her of composing some of her speeches herself to denounce her dead father.[103]

Mary Ann was not ready for such a drastic step so soon after her bereavement. Nothing in her life to date, she said, had prepared her for appearing in public and defying the 'general and indiscriminate censure which it had been usual to bestow upon [actors]'. As for playing the heroine of *The Fatal Marriage*, she could not even bring herself to read the play in private, such was her intense sympathy for Isabella's predicament. Stratty was vehemently opposed.[104] The major's suggestion came to nothing, and he disappeared from Mary Ann's life, like George's other friends.

One of the gaps in Mary Ann's narrative covers the circumstances in which she lost contact with the Guy-Dickens family. As the summer drew to a close she seems to have been less at ease with them. The only real supporter she had ever had in Hornsey and Wigmore Street was her grandfather, and he was now increasingly under the control of his daughter. There was a suggestion – it's not clear how serious it was – that the family should take her in. Fearing that this meant that they would take care of her but leave George to the mercy of the Cannings in Ireland, she said she would starve rather than be deprived of her son. She asked her aunt and grandfather what help she might expect from them, and they told her they could give her nothing immediately, but held out vague hopes for the future.[105]

---

i *The Fatal Marriage* was an adaptation of Thomas Southerne's play usually attributed to David Garrick, but described by Mary Ann as '[John] Hawkesworth's Isabella'.

ii Charlotte Johnston or Deans (1768–1859), actress and writer. See below, chapters 5 and 13.

Stratty did not encourage her contacts with the 'great house' and around the beginning of September, before her planned six months on the farm at Hornsey were up, he found lodgings for her above a carpet warehouse in Holborn. It was close to his chambers at Carpenter's Hall, and within reach of medical assistance for her confinement, which they assumed was imminent. His eagerness to get her away from the Guy-Dickens orbit made her worry that he wanted her to remain dependent on him.[106] It was probably at this time that a small sum of money reached her from Ireland, the money raised by Molly shortly before her death. Molly's husband entrusted it to a cousin, who half a century later remembered the day when she visited Mary Ann's wretched garret and saw the future statesman in his cradle.[107]

Any fears Aunt Mary had that Mary Ann and her children would become a charge on the Guy-Dickens family, not to mention the mother and sister who now formed part of Mary Ann's household, can only have been intensified by the arrival of another impecunious Irish relation, Eliah Handcock, the cousin of Melchior's second wife who had helped Mary Ann to locate her grandfather. Having now fallen on hard times himself he had come to London, and was currently living in rat-infested lodgings. He looked on Mary Ann as a channel offering access to the Guy-Dickens family.[108]

Mary Ann awaited her confinement with great anxiety. If the baby didn't arrive soon the Cannings would question whether George was the father. She had two fears: first that her son would be taken away from her, transported to Ireland and lost from view, and secondly that the Cannings' insistence that she should remain in England was part of a plan to dismiss her son as an impostor. She begged Beresford to come and see little George, so that he would know him and could vouch for him if his identity was ever questioned. Such long term fears were intensified by a more immediate concern: if she died in childbirth, as she expected, who would take care of George and ensure that he was given no improper food? But she was a practical woman, and more provident than her husband. She made a will appointing four of his friends to act as guardians. In addition to Beresford and Macartney there were two Dublin lawyers, William Dunkin and Arthur Wolfe. The appointment of men with power and influence in Ireland shows clearly where she believed the threat would come from. Of the four, Beresford seems to have been the most helpful in the short term. He had shown himself generous towards poor George Canning while he was alive, and had written warmly to him, congratulating him on marrying for love in defiance of family and material interests.[109] Now he tried to be helpful to his friend's widow. The letter returning the £30 was followed by others containing advice on how to deal with the Canning family. We know little of Mary Ann's dealings with Dunkin and Wolfe, although she was still in touch with Wolfe some fifteen years later.

She was particularly disappointed in George Macartney, who made no reply when she asked him to act as guardian. Probably echoing what she had heard her husband say of him, she wrote in the Packet:

> George Canning was the Eldest son of a Man of near Three Thousand a year — with superior talents, & superior expectations — George Macartney was the Son of a man whose Property was small — and who was of such incapacity of talent that at the death of His Father he was passed over as an Idiot, and the property, about Twelve Hundred a year, came immediately to George… Poor George Canning died the victim of a broken heart after struggling for years with poverty & all its consequences! — George Macartney still lives a Peer of the Realm — wise but mysterious are the decrees of Heaven![110]

Macartney was married to Lady Jane Stuart, the daughter of George Canning's enemy, Lord Bute, a woman, Mary Ann wrote, 'of an uncommon plain person – tall, meagre, and some years older than himself – but she secured him great and useful connections …' Lady Jane, however, did more than any of the others to help, using her useful connections to inform the Queen of Mary Ann's plight and the cruelty of old Stratford Canning. Stratty distrusted the 'Quality', saying they were 'all alike', and was certain nothing would come of this intervention.[111]

Shortly after Mary Ann moved to Holborn, Eliah Handcock's fortunes changed and he received the invitation he'd been angling for. On the day appointed for his visit to Hornsey his landlady and laundress feared he was absconding without paying his bills. They presented demands for half a guinea and eight shillings respectively, locking him in his room and withholding his clean linen until he paid. His hopes of making a good impression on his grand relations were all threatened for the lack of just 18s. 6d. He wrote to Mary Ann, ending with the words 'A splendid guinea is a Treasure to a person in distress.' When the letter arrived she was sitting with the baby and her mother. She had a guinea in her purse, and a handful of loose change. What should she do? Her mother told her to do as God directed. She looked at George and asked herself how it would be when he was a man if he found himself in the same predicament as the unfortunate Eliah. Perhaps she recalled her husband's response to Catherine Jemmat's appeal. She sent her splendid guinea and invited Eliah to call for dinner in Holborn on his way out to Hornsey. They dined cheerfully, and were still at table playing with the baby when a carriage drew up outside the carpet warehouse, and a gentleman asked for Mrs Canning. He presented her with a packet bearing a duke's coronet on the seal. It was from the Duchess of Ancaster, one of the Queen's ladies-in-waiting, who was currently at her house in Lincolnshire but hoped soon to call in person. The packet contained fifty pounds in banknotes from the Queen, which Mary Ann prudently kept to herself until Eliah had left.[112]

Mary Ann now had two noble supporters. The Duchess was always amiable, whereas Lady Jane made Mary Ann feel her dependent position. The Duchess was not a born aristocrat. Her father, Thomas Panton,[i] was Master of the King's Running

i Mary Panton (died 1793) married the third Duke of Ancaster in 1750. Her father Thomas (1697–1782) was was described by Horace Walpole as a 'disreputable horse jockey', but

Horses at Newmarket, which may have been what brought his daughter into contact with the Duke of Ancaster, the Master of the Horse. The Duke had political ambitions, but was described as an 'egregious blockhead... mulish and intractable',[113] so his Duchess may have welcomed the diversion provided by Mary Ann and her troubles. She called regularly at the Holborn lodgings while Mary Ann was awaiting her confinement.[114]

October came and went. Mary Ann still believed that she had become pregnant in January. November and December were terrible months of anxiety about this epic pregnancy and fear of the hidden effects of her corrupted milk on George. The dark days were lightened by visits from the Duchess and by Stratty's constant attentions. These two had little sympathy for each other, the one serious and domestic, the other rich and irresponsible. They each had their own ideas about Mary Ann's future, but for now all thought was suspended.

Thomas 'broke from the confines of his melancholy prison' on 23 December, a big, healthy baby. Mary Ann, who recovered quickly from the ordeal, contrasted her own case with that of the widowed Lady Tavistock, who suffered a similarly protracted pregnancy from which she never recovered.[i] Mary Ann approved of Dr Johnson's saying that if Lady Tavistock had been obliged to provide for her family, if she had been a washer-woman or had kept a chandler's shop, she would not have died.[115] But although she was never as idle as Lady Tavistock, Mary Ann was not yet in a position to take active steps to secure her future livelihood. Her days and her energy were spent in placating young Thomas's voracious demands. Fearing for her health, in the spring Stratty, 'our dear Friend and guardian Angel', took lodgings for her in Dulwich.[116]

Mehitabel, who was now in London, along with her mother and younger sister Betsy, had no time for Mary Ann's determination

---

his daughter brought the Duke a fortune of £60,000.

i Lady Elizabeth Russell, wife of Lord Francis Russell, Marquess of Tavistock, was left a widow in March 1767; her third son was born five months later, and she herself died in November 1768. I have not found authority for the story that Lady Elizabeth's pregnancy was unduly prolonged.

to go on nursing as a final duty to her dead husband. Her view, expressed strongly to Stratty, was that it was affecting Mary Ann's health. She may also have felt that it was preventing the young widow from moving on to the next phase in her life. Mary Ann's pretty face had brought her one husband; it was time to show herself in public and catch another. Mehitabel was not thinking only of Mary Ann's interests: so long as this beautiful and unfortunate sister was unprovided for Stratty would not settle down. It was not that Stratty could think of marrying his brother's widow, but Mary Ann had a powerful hold upon him. Mehitabel was prepared to put up with a lot for Stratty's sake, but his dithering irritated her. When asked her opinion on anything, she said she would ask Stratty, and he would ask his sister. When friends asked her why she was not yet married she said Stratty was waiting for his sister to give her consent. Meanwhile Mary Ann saw her warm-hearted, weak-willed brother-in-law slipping away from her, falling more and more under Mehitabel's influence. She felt Stratty would be better off with Betsy, who was, she thought, more ladylike. Marriage to Mehitabel was bound to lead to Mary Ann's eventual exclusion from Stratty's life, whereas Betsy, being younger, might have been more susceptible to Mary Ann's influence.[117]

Despite these tensions, Stratty and Mehitabel paid regular visits to Dulwich during the summer, glad perhaps to get away from Mehitabel's mother, who had come to London to sort out her late husband's affairs. There was a room in the Dulwich house where Stratty could sleep, while Mehitabel shared Mary Ann's bed. This was a deplorable Irish custom, Mary Ann thought,[i] but Mehitabel's presence may have saved her life one morning when she collapsed on the floor, exhausted after satisfying Thomas's prodigious appetite. Now Mehitabel could enlist Stratty on her side of the argument: strong measures were needed. With Mrs

i Sharing a bed with a female relative, abhorrent though it was to Mary Ann's refined feelings, remained an acceptable practice in Mehitabel's view. Twenty years later she reported that she was sharing a bed for several nights with her sister-in-law Bess Leigh. She was happy to do so, despite Bess's liking for brandy and water (Hunt, 114).

Costello's collusion they whisked Mary Ann up to town, leaving both children in their grandmother's care. Mary Ann felt she was abandoning her last duty to the departed George. She was right: it marked the end of an era in her life.[118] The struggle to make a future for herself and her children could no longer be postponed.

That Mary Ann only had to show her face in public in order to attract a husband was confirmed almost as soon as she moved to Dulwich. She was returning from a walk with George when she was greeted by two young gentlemen, Charles and Henry Phipps, younger sons of Lord Mulgrave. Charles was a lieutenant in the navy, Henry had just left Eton.[i] Charles made a few attempts at polite conversation, gallantly expressing surprise at learning that George was Mary Ann's son rather than her brother. How alike they were, she and George, he said, to which she replied that it was hardly surprising since she was his mother. Undeterred by her sharp tongue, Charles came next day to see her. George was at the window and spotted him: 'Mamma,' he cried, 'The man, the man!' Mary Ann overheard the man enquiring of a neighbour whether it was true that she was a widow. For days Charles Phipps besieged her, sending young Henry with messages and begging for an interview. He sought out Stratty and obtained his permission to pay his addresses. Lady Mulgrave seconded his suit, saying that Mary Ann and her children could come to live with her while Charles was away with his ship, and the marriage could take place on his return. But Mary Ann remained obdurate, whether because of a dislike of second marriages, or because she had not been impressed by Charles Phipps's conversation, or because she did not fancy being patronised by his mother. By September the affair, such as it was, had fizzled out. Over the years to come Mary Ann kept an eye on the progress of Charles Phipps's promising career as naval officer and politician, until he died in his thirties.

---

i Charles Phipps is the only one of the three sons of the first Lord Mulgrave not to have an entry in the *ODNB*. He and his elder brother had brief but distinguished careers. The youngest brother inherited the title and was a political colleague and rival of George Canning. See below, chapter 31.

Her refusal to take advantage of the opportunity he offered (like her husband's refusal to sacrifice his principles to become an MP) was remembered and held against her.[119]

Back in Holborn after the Dulwich interlude the search for an income began in earnest. Mehitabel suggested that Mary Ann, with her experience and medical skill, could easily find a place in a family, supervising the children as a sort of upper nursemaid. She might get away without having to take her meals with the servants, Mehitabel said hopefully, but even so Mary Ann rejected the idea. The wife of one George Canning and the mother of another could not, she said, descend to servitude – the line she would stick to through all her years of struggle. Very well, said Mehitabel, what about a genteel sort of shop in a country town? Despite her approval of the widow who kept a chandler's shop, Mary Ann rejected this too. When the Patricks went back to Ireland at the end of the summer her future was undecided, and Mehitabel's marriage was in doubt.[120]

It may be that Mehitabel exaggerated Mary Ann's part in Stratty's hesitancy. He was equally, or even more, concerned about his father's attitude. Family ties were strong among the Cannings; there was affection as well as wariness in the letters exchanged during Stratty's travels. Stratty was unwilling to displease old Stratford, who had treated him handsomely so far. Furthermore, he had started his business with his father's support; it was not yet well established and he could ill afford a final rift.[121] He would be disinherited for sure if he married Mehitabel.

The Duchess, when she first visited Mary Ann, had held out the prospect of various royal appointments. One was as wet nurse to the Queen's next child, but nothing came of the suggestion, probably for no more sinister reason than that there was at that point no royal baby in view. Nor was there necessarily anything sinister in the failure of the Duchess's second idea, the housekeeper's job at Dublin Castle, but Mary Ann suspected there were powerful forces working against her: although his daughter, Lady Jane, was well disposed towards her, Lord Bute would remind the King that Mary Ann's husband had been hostile to the Court.[122] Mary Ann persisted all her life in the belief that she and her son suffered from the hostility of the king because of the political writings of her husband.

What could be done without royal patronage? She could start a school. The Duchess would dragoon all her friends' daughters into Mary Ann's establishment. No matter that Mary Ann had herself received no education; she could employ masters to do the teaching, and all that was asked of her was to inculcate ladylike manners. The scheme fell through for lack of capital. So why not write a book? She could expose her father-in-law's conduct. All the Duchess's friends would subscribe. Authorship needed no capital. But Mary Ann felt that here her lack of education would be fatally exposed. She would willingly have resorted to needlework, as she had years before in Dublin, were it not that such work was, like being a servant or keeping a shop, unbecoming for the widow of one George Canning and the mother of another: 'every body thought their plan better than that'.[123]

A different idea was floated by Mary Ann's doctor, Hugh Smith. He had shown himself a good friend, attending the children and inoculating them against smallpox without charge. An enterprising man whose family medicine chests and accompanying book of advice had been on the market since the early 1760s,[124] Smith had spotted an opening for a female dentist. He reckoned Mary Ann had all the relevant qualifications – presumably physical strength, common sense, a lack of squeamishness, and that all important gift of a ladylike manner. He undertook to train her and provide the equipment. Since no fine lady could be expected to employ a dentist who arrived at her house on foot he would provide a carriage, but this carried alarming implications. To provide professional equipment was a straightforward matter of business, but to set her up with a carriage was the sort of thing a man might do for his kept mistress. Stratty agreed that the arrangement could prove embarrassing, but he could not afford to provide her with a carriage himself, so the scheme fell through.[125] Later events suggest that their suspicions of Smith's motives were justified.

The Duchess was disappointed by the rejection of her schemes, particularly the plan for a school, but admired Mary Ann's determination to save Stratty expense and to avoid interfering with his marriage plans – he had at last made up his mind to marry Mehitabel, despite his father, although as yet no date was fixed. By the end of 1772 Mary Ann's friends had nothing left to propose except to revive Major Molesworth's suggestion of the stage. Mary Ann still shrank from it, but the Duchess had recognised that 'fortitude' was a 'decided part' of Mary Ann's character, and believed that she could carry it off.[126] By *fortitude* the Duchess probably meant a capacity to outface critics and naysayers – something she may have known about, if, as the daughter of a horse-trainer, she had had to deal with hostility from her husband's friends and relations.

Stratty was roused to one last effort. Frances and Hannah Gore were the natural daughters of an army officer who had established them as milliners in Jermyn Street. Finding that business was not as brisk as they'd hoped, they were on the look out for a partner who could invest further capital, and at the same time draw in more fashionable customers. Stratty, having audited the books and found everything in order, offered to put up some £700 himself and undertook the negotiations on Mary Ann's behalf. The Duchess advised against it, saying that while she would support Mary Ann in anything, it would be hard to drum up custom among her friends because the Gore sisters were not well thought of. They wished, Mary Ann recalled, 'to increase, & to raise their Style of connections — in me they calculated upon a certain mode of achieving that point.' Mary Ann herself was impressed less by the Gores than by Stratty's exertions; she was touched, and acceded to his desperate wish to keep her off the stage.[127]

A date in January was fixed for concluding the articles of

partnership. In the morning, however, there came a letter from Mehitabel that made Mary Ann change her mind. Mehitabel expatiated on the disadvantages of going on the stage and repeated her suggestion of taking a position in a family. She offered to take care of the two boys when she and Stratty were married; Mary Ann should not be so reluctant to be parted from them. Mehitabel added that if Mary Ann could raise £200 or so with no risk to anyone but herself it would be worth investing it in some enterprise in order to avoid the stage, but then she came, obliquely, to the point of the letter: that she could understand Mary Ann's 'fear of involving a dear Brother, who could ill afford to lose £4 or 500' – it seems that Stratty had been afraid to tell Mehitabel that he was planning to invest as much as £700.[128]

When Stratty called to take Mary Ann to Jermyn Street, bringing his close friend Dick Weld, a fellow Irishman who shared his business and political interests, to act as witness, she shocked them by going back on the whole deal. In a long and painful discussion she refused to give any reason, but Stratty guessed that it was the result of the letter he had forwarded from Mehitabel, and his suspicion was confirmed when Mary Ann declined to show it to him. Stratty wrote to Mehitabel commanding her to authorise Mary Ann to show him the letter. When he read it he turned pale and tried to make out that Mehitabel didn't really mean to prevent the deal going through. Mary Ann agreed to submit the letter to the judgement of Dick Weld. He said the meaning was unequivocal, and that on receipt of such a message from Stratty's future wife Mary Ann had no option but to back out. Stratty wrote a thunderous letter to Mehitabel who sent a bemused apology, denying any intention of throwing out 'a low dirty Hint to prevent your accepting from your Brother the Means he offers for establishing you comfortably in Business'. She feared that her intervention would leave Mary Ann no option but to 'embrace the stage plan' and foresaw that this would lead to 'future Distresses'.[129]

Given the part which Mehitabel was to play in her life, Mary

Ann's animosity towards her is understandable. As she looked back Mary Ann sometimes accused her of malice, but more often of nothing worse than insensitivity, tactlessness and vulgarity. In the Packet her verdict on the decisive letter was this:

> I did not blame Miss Patrick for the apprehension she implied — far otherwise — I thought her Justified — A mind of more Candour woud have spoken its opinion more openly & unequivocally — a mind of more delicacy woud have convey'd it more tenderly — A mind of extremely fine feeling — woud not perhaps, (under the circumstances & situations of all the parties — woud not perhaps) have express'd it all — but neither Candour, delicacy, nor extreme fine feelings mark'd her Character — She was a good Sort of young woman, with a showy figure and a prettrish face — but her Mind was evidently, "The Ordinary of Nature's sale work" — No shining beauties — nor great defects [130]

Mehitabel's intervention was for the best. Within weeks the Misses Gore went bankrupt, which doesn't say much for Stratty's auditing of their books. Dick Weld called on Mary Ann to show her the announcement and congratulate her on her escape. Now Stratty began to look more tolerantly on the 'stage plan'. There was no alternative.[131]

The Duchess introduced Mary Ann to David Garrick, manager of Drury Lane Theatre.[i] Garrick was the greatest actor, and one of the greatest men, of the age, who in the course of his career had done much to improve standards of acting and production and enhance the general reputation of the profession. One of his foibles was, as he told Lord Lyttelton, his pride in winning 'the kind thoughts of the great and good', so the Duchess's recommendation may have influenced him in Mary Ann's favour.[132] During the summer he told her to prepare one of Monimia's scenes in Otway's *The Orphan*,[ii] which he would hear her rehearse in a few days

---

i David Garrick (1717–1779): manager of Drury Lane from 1747 to 1776. When Mary Ann knew him his health was already failing.

ii Thomas Otway (1652–1685), author of *Venice Preserv'd* (1682). *The Orphan* (1680) was time. She did more than he had asked and learned the whole part. He was happy with her rehearsal and told her to spend the rest of the summer preparing for her debut. He flattered her by comparing her with the great Mrs Cibber, and made it clear where he thought her strengths might lie by the other parts he advised her to study, Fanny in *The Clandestine Marriage* and Indiana in *The Conscious Lovers*, both of them examples of genteel and sentimental comedy.[133] John Home, author of *Douglas*, one of the most popular plays of the time, undertook to coach her and help her find a suitable character for her first appearance.[i]

At the same time Mary Ann considered the implications for her moral reputation and her standing as a lady in the informal and socially promiscuous life of the theatre. She was anxious for approval. She wrote to John Beresford, not for advice – her mind was made up – but seeking his endorsement and begging him to judge her by her conduct in her new life:

> For that conduct I have many securities, the Memory of a beloved Husband, the Love and Duty I owe to Our darling Orphans, my own peace of mind, and let me add what I owe to that amiable and exalted character who stands forth to countenance, as she avows she has advised, me to it.[134]

The Duchess of Ancaster did not envisage her friend grubbing along in the lower ranks of the profession. The gamble of going on the stage, Mary Ann told Beresford, was only worthwhile if she could start in 'first rate style'. This meant above all starting at the top under the protection of Garrick, but she also expected to assert her status in the theatre by living in style. She took and furnished a house in Great Queen Street. Since the beginning of the century,

---

a domestic tragedy set on a country estate. The heroine, Monimia, was to prove one of Mary Ann's favourite roles.

i John Home (1722–1808): a minister of the Scottish church and a playwright. His *Douglas* had been rejected by Garrick at Drury Lane, but when produced in Edinburgh and at Covent Garden it met with great success. In the early 1760s Home was private secretary to Lord Bute, and one of the London Scots whose presence in the capital had so enraged George Canning.

when Sir Godfrey Kneller established his Painting Academy there, Great Queen Street had been home to painters and engravers, as well as writers and leading actors.[135] There she established herself, her children and her mother and sister, with servants, including a man in livery, which she believed was necessary to respectability. All this was done on credit. Mr Yateman the upholsterer was so impressed by Garrick's name that he agreed to take his payment in two instalments, after her first and second benefit nights.[136]

The faithful Stratty, despite his misgivings, supported her in all these steps. He had worries of his own. Having made up his mind to defy his father and marry Mehitabel, he had taken a house in the City, 10 Clements Lane, Lombard Street, but it was still unfurnished when he set off to Dublin for the wedding. He left it to Mary Ann to choose the tables and chairs. He thought it a reasonable thing to ask, since she was fitting up her own house at the same time and would employ the same upholsterer. Mehitabel seemed happy with this arrangement, writing from Dublin that Mary Ann should buy the counterpane and 'anything else which you think necessary and not extravagant', but when she reached Clements Lane she found fault with everything: 'it was neither the Tables being high, not the chairs being low — but it was a fixed prejudice against the person who chose them,' Mary Ann recalled.[137]

Mehitabel considered that Mary Ann had been drawn to the stage in order to avoid more humdrum and less prestigious work. Mary Ann was merely consulting her own pleasure, regardless of morality, regardless of her family. Stratty found such plain-speaking distressing – Mary Ann saw his lip quiver and turn pale – but in time he adopted Mehitabel's view. As we shall see, the formula became axiomatic in the Clements Lane logic.[138] Their view had something to be said for it. Had she not clung to social pretensions she could not afford, Mary Ann might have done well enough elsewhere for herself and her family, so it was easy to accuse her of being influenced by the glamour of the stage. If nothing else, she must have been flattered and excited by the contact with the great Garrick. But Mehitabel's attitude was coloured by jealousy and perhaps by her sense of insecurity as a wife whose husband's family looked down on her. Furthermore, with her outsider's view of the acting profession she was too quick to assume that its allure was all to do with passion, glamour and excitement.

The breach with Stratty and Mehitabel did not happen all at once. During her summer of preparation Mary Ann continued to visit them, and as late as three or four months after her debut, Mehitabel wrote a jokey letter from Bath about the beaus and beauties and the problems of Stratty's 'corpus'. The visits were not always easy. On one occasion Stratty's friend Dick Weld was at dinner. Serving the cod's head Mehitabel found something lacking in the household equipment: 'What, have you no trowel, Stratty?' she asked, using what Mary Ann regarded as either a provincialism or shopman's slang for a fish slice. She then turned on Dick Weld and told him that as a regular dinner guest he should bring her a trowel for a house-warming. Mary Ann looked at Stratty as he almost fell off his chair with mortification, but Dick took it in good part, bringing the trowel when he next visited. It was Mehitabel's way. She enjoyed boisterous fun, including games of physical contact, like blind-man's buff, the sort of thing Mary Ann disapprovingly called 'hot-cockle sport'. Mehitabel once flared up at this prudishness and told her she needn't come if she didn't like their ways. Stratty tearfully begged his wife to apologise, which she did readily enough.[139]

Mehitabel was quick to take offence. She would complain that Mary Ann was too taken up with fashionable company to have any thought for mere City people like her and Stratty. Mehitabel seems to have particularly objected to a certain Mrs Hankey, to which Mary Ann 'always replied that with Mrs. Hankey I was always sure of finding pleasure, & never disgust or incivility'. Once Mary Ann stayed away for ten days while George and Thomas were unwell, until a message came saying Stratty was very ill.

She rushed round to Clements Lane and found him in tears at the thought that he might have died without seeing her again. Mary Ann also wept copiously, whereupon Mehitabel burst into a fury, telling her not to make such a hypocritical fuss, and saying Stratty had been far worse earlier on, as she might have seen for herself if she had not been 'racketing about' with Mrs Hankey. 'Oh how my soul despised her!' recalled Mary Ann. Mehitabel's invective was deflated when Dr Smith arrived (recommended to Stratty and Mehitabel by Mary Ann) and confirmed that Mary Ann had indeed been confined to her house by the illness of her children. For the rest of the day Mehitabel made a conspicuous effort to be civil to her.[140]

**

By the autumn of 1773 Mary Ann and her household were well established in Great Queen Street. She attended the theatre and spent days reading plays with Lord Lindsey, the Duchess of Ancaster's son. The search went on for a suitable role for her first appearance. The Duke, like Major Molesworth, thought Isabella in *The Fatal Marriage* would be a good choice. Lord Lindsey, recommended Andromache in *The Distress'd Mother*, which was the somewhat understated title of Ambrose Philips's version of Racine's *Andromaque*.[i] 'Linds[e]y,' his mother replied, 'do find something less dolefull.' While her friends argued, Mary Ann was already leaving them behind, beginning, with the help of John Home, to see things not as a connoisseur of the theatre, but as an insider, a professional. Garrick suggested she might like to try Juliet, and when she said she thought she was too old for the part he laughed at her naïveté and said she would think differently in a dozen years' time.[141]

In the end they hit upon the title part in *Jane Shore*, Nicholas

---

i Ambrose Philips (1674–1749): poet and playwright, and member of the Irish House of Commons. His work in general was not greatly admired in his day (he features in a comic verse of the time as 'Namby-Pamby') but his *Distress'd Mother* (1712) remained popular throughout the eighteenth century.

Rowe's play first produced in 1714.[i] The choice of Jane Shore, Edward IV's mistress, as her first part was in one sense a safe one, since Rowe's tragedy was well known and popular, being the tenth most frequently performed tragedy during Garrick's time as manager.[142] But it was also a daring decision. *Jane Shore* belongs to a tradition of so-called 'she-tragedies' which typically showed women as victims of both a cruel society and their own merciless passions. By 1714 women rather than boys had been playing female roles on the English stage for half a century, and writers were beginning to present female emotions in a less stylised and idealised manner. Later in the century, as attitudes changed, the representation of female sexuality in she-tragedies was sentimentalised to meet more fastidious tastes; it was a development fostered by Garrick as he raised the moral reputation of the theatre. Nonetheless, the continued popularity of the she-tragedies was still due in part to their frank treatment of sexual feelings, temptations and misconduct. The public's willingness to identify the actress with the character, which Mary Ann's friends had acknowledged when they proposed Isabella as a suitable part for her, led to an assumption that the actress herself must be possessed by the emotions and sensations that she represented on stage. These ideas contributed to the widespread opinion that the theatre was a morally dangerous place.

Within this widespread opinion there were different strands. There were those who believed, like Mary Ann herself, that a stage career was disadvantageous because it was widely regarded as immoral; and then there were those who believed it really was immoral. The prevalence of the latter view is well documented, but its adherents varied greatly. They included 'serious' Christians like the mother of the actor manager John Bernard,[ii] who believed that playhouses led to workhouses, and the minister at Hull Low Church

i Nicholas Rowe (1674–1718): poet laureate from 1715, mainly known for his tragedies.

ii John Bernard (1756-1828): appeared at Covent Garden during many winter seasons in the 1780s and 1790s, but spent his summers building a base for himself in the provinces. As we shall see, he managed the theatre in Plymouth. He spent the latter half of his career in America. His *Retrospections of the Stage* was published posthumously in 1830.

who was mocked by Tate Wilkinson[i] for preaching that 'Every one who entered a playhouse was, with the players, equally certain of *eternal* damnation', but also others who cheerfully patronised the theatre, even while deploring the immodesty and moral danger inherent in what Mary Ann called the actress's public character.[143]

According to a complacent article published in 1772, English actors received large salaries and 'far from being stigmatized with the mark of reprobation, as in other countries, they are esteemed by the public, and caressed by the best company, provided they preserve their morals untainted.' In this, as in many other pronouncements about the theatre, moral judgments are entangled with other considerations, such as social standing and profitability. In John Bernard's mother's favourite dictum it's hard to say whether moral condemnation predominated, or fear of the economic precariousness of the career. The hypocrisy is closer to the surface in a story told by the actress Mary Robinson[ii] of her sister-in-law, whose righteous indignation against the stage was mollified when it proved profitable. There were sharp social distinctions within the theatre, so that what might sound like moral condemnation of the profession as a whole, sometimes turns out to be directed only at the more degraded parts of it. The controversial actress Charlotte Charke,[iii] for example, wrote of her time as a strolling player that it would have been 'more reputable to earn a groat a day cinder-sifting at Tottenham Court', but her point was not that all actors were disreputable, but that those she encountered at the bottom end of the profession were vulgar, ignorant and inept.[144]

Moral disapproval, economic anxieties and social distinctions make a powerful and disturbing combination, as we shall see in the second half of Mary Ann's life, dominated as it was by her

---

i Tate Wilkinson (1739-1803): one of the leading actor managers, who tried to spread Garrick's reforms to the more anarchic world of provincial players..

ii Mary Robinson (née Darby, 1756/8–1800): actress, poet and novelist, who started her Drury Lane career just as Mary Ann's came to an end.

iii Charlotte Charke (1713-1760), actress, playwright and novelist, was the daughter of the playwright Colley Cibber. Disowned by her family and barred from the London theatres, she worked with small troupes of strolling players.

son's sometimes hysterical reaction to her theatrical past. In an area where there was, and still is, much hyperbole and thoughtless moralising we should consider the measured verdict of the Quaker and social reformer Priscilla Wakefield.[i] When surveying the professions open to women she named the stage as one of the few where the number of celebrated women proved that there was 'no inequality of genius, in the sexes, for the imitative arts'. She admitted that the stage was nonetheless unsuitable for women, because of the courage needed to face an audience, and the 'variety of situations incident to it, which expose moral virtue to the most severe trials,' making it 'a line of life, in which it is scarcely possible to preserve that purity of sentiment or conduct, which characterizes female excellence.' Nonetheless, Wakefield recognised that under pressure from 'unpropitious circumstances' even the most virtuous woman might take the decision to become an actress.[145]

Cultural historians are sometimes blunt in their pronouncements on eighteenth century attitudes to the stage. We are told, for example, that the professions of courtesan and actress were 'wilfully confused and conflated' by a male audience, and that Charlotte Charke was understood by her contemporaries 'as a whore: a public woman defined primarily by her sexuality'.[146] These statements are less startling than might seem at first glance, because 'courtesans' were quite distinct from common prostitutes, while Charke, though called a whore, was not generally accused of trading sex for money. What Mary Ann expected, what made her apprehensive, was that an actress was a 'public character'; it was this move from a private to a public character that 'all the propensities of [her] mind' made her wish to avoid. Her face, figure, voice and manners would be public property, to be discussed and joked about in the newspapers, and even her private virtue would be made matter for speculation:

---

i Priscilla Wakefield (1750–1832) was writing a quarter of a century after Mary Ann first went on the stage. During that time attitudes hardened, with the spread of serious Christianity, and increasing idealisation of women.

How well the modest woman plays the whore,
How well fair Canning plays the part of Shore.

An early biographer of George Canning said that this couplet eulogised 'at once [Mary Ann's] beauty, her talents, and her virtue'.[147] Others might find it less bland, a suggestion that even the honest woman has about her something of the whore. Some actresses encouraged this prurience 'as a way of increasing their popularity or notoriety'.[148]

A striking example was provided by the case of another new actress, Elizabeth Hartley,[i] whose London debut as Jane Shore provoked a newspaper storm the previous winter. Arising originally from a complaint that the Covent Garden managers had replaced an established actress with the newcomer, the controversy quickly moved on to a cold appraisal of Mrs Hartley's personal charms, with innuendoes about her morals. She would be, a correspondent suggested, entertaining company for a man anywhere but in the theatre, and was better suited to play the adulteress Jane Shore than the virtuous Queen Catherine in *Henry VIII*.[149] Joshua Reynolds painted Mrs Hartley three times, to represent different elements of female sexuality, as a nymph, as a Madonna, and as Jane Shore.[150]

The attitude of Stratty and Mehitabel to the theatre was as ambivalent and confused as anyone's. They numbered the playwright and theatre-owner Richard Brinsley Sheridan and his wife Elizabeth amongst their closest friends,[ii][151] and almost certainly applauded the line taken by Sheridan in forbidding Elizabeth to continue her professional singing career after their marriage. However much they regretted Mary Ann's decision, with Stratty doing all he could to find an alternative, they did not quarrel with her over it, and continued to visit her after her first appearances, and

---

i Elizabeth Hartley (c.1748–1824): she has attracted the notice of cultural historians. Martin Postle discusses Joshua Reynolds's portrait of her in the role of Jane Shore. Reynolds knew Elizabeth in 1771, when she was living in lodgings with a bawd called Mrs Kelly (Cruickshank, *The Secret History of Georgian London*, 348)

ii Richard Brinsley Sheridan (1751–1816): playwright, theatre manager and politician. Born in Dublin; his mother was a playwright, his father an actor. Elizabeth Linley (1754–92), one of a family of singers, appeared on the stage from an early age, and was much painted.

still received her in their home. Despite his distrust of aristocrats, Stratty may have been impressed by the Duchess of Ancaster's backing. The Duchess, once the decision was taken, was happy to be involved in the excitement of launching her protégée's career, thinking it more respectable than doing business with the questionable Gore sisters. Lady Jane Macartney supported Mary Ann's preparations by organising reading parties.[152]

Hastings in Rowe's play was one of Garrick's most famous characters, and to the surprise of some he agreed to revive it and play opposite Mary Ann. Her sessions with John Home now concentrated on preparing the part of Jane. Then came her introduction to the theatre as a member of the company. The mere size of the backstage area was enough to surprise her, with its maze of corridors and rooms. The players she had seen and admired on stage were now revealed as ordinary men and women, and for the first time she also saw the many backstage specialists without whom the great machine of the theatre would never spring to life – scene-painters, mechanics, rope-men, costume-makers and laundresses, lamp-lighters, musicians, copyists, money-takers and the rest. Among them was the prompter William Hopkins,[i] a powerful figure who supervised the performances on the night and kept a detailed record, passing judgement on the actors and noting audience reactions. Having a wife and two daughters in the company, all trying to make their way in the profession, Hopkins took a jaundiced view of Garrick's habit of giving big roles to ladies who had never acted before. After meeting her future colleagues Mary Ann was taken onto the stage to look out over the vast, empty and very cold auditorium. Drury Lane at that time accommodated an audience of some 1,800 or 2,000 (some put it even higher) in the pit, boxes and lower and upper galleries.[153] Perhaps she tested the acoustics – would her voice carry to all

i William Hopkins (died 1780) held the post of prompter at Drury Lane from 1760 until his death. His notes on performances, in the manuscript diaries of the theatre held in the Folger Library, Washington, are quoted extensively in *The London Stage*, and will be frequently referred to in the following chapters.

parts? – but the only real trial would come in the presence of an audience whose clothing would muffle the sound.

A powerful enough voice, a retentive memory and stamina to support long hours of tiring work[i] were fundamental requirements without which nothing else mattered, so Garrick, however willing he was to please Mary Ann's aristocratic sponsors, must have been satisfied on these counts before allowing the experiment to proceed. Of course much more was needed to make an actor. Tate Wilkinson wrote that until the actual performance it was impossible to be certain whether a new actor, however promising he or she might seem, would be convincing.[154] Managers had to trust their instinct. Years earlier Garrick had gone to hear a country actor with a view to bringing him to Drury Lane, but when he attended the performance his attention was immediately arrested by another member of the cast, Samuel Reddish. 'That man's an actor,' Garrick exclaimed as soon as Reddish spoke.[155] It was Reddish, not the other actor, who got the job, and he was now, after Garrick himself, one of the leading men at Drury Lane. But for all his instinct and experience, Garrick was fallible, and in Mary Ann's case may have been influenced by her aristocratic backers and, perhaps, by her sad story and lovely face.

Because too often actors would declaim their own lines without taking notice of anyone else on the stage, one of Garrick's reforms had been his insistence on rehearsals of the whole cast together. Even the most experienced performers were required to attend, since while they might manage with only one or two rehearsals, the rest of the dramatis personae needed more and would be 'perplex'd and disjointed' if the whole cast were not present.[156] Nonetheless, once a production was established newcomers might be expected to slot themselves into the action without a full rehearsal. This was a lot to ask of a novice like Mary Ann, and both Garrick and

i The evening's entertainment might last five hours or more, although where there was a large company, as at Drury Lane, it was not usual for leading actors to perform in both the main piece and the supporting programme. In smaller provincial theatres actors might be taking part all through the evening.

Reddish, who had the part of Dumont (who turns out to be Jane Shore's husband in disguise), went through their scenes with her. Elizabeth Younge,[i] who was cast as the second female lead, Alicia, was an established actress who had played Jane in her time, but was new to the part of Alicia; she and Mary Ann rehearsed together, devising some new pieces of stage business.[157]

Well before her first night, therefore, Mary Ann had entered her new world. Many things had come to separate her from her beloved Stratty – his marriage, Mehitabel's jealousy, her own disdain for the vulgarity of Clements Lane – but the most impenetrable barrier was that between the audience and the professional actress, enveloped in mystery and dedicated to the discipline of body and mind needed to perfect her skill. Even frequent theatregoers could barely imagine what went into producing the performance that delighted them on stage. In the inexhaustible mine of theatrical anecdotes one of the richest veins is the initiation story, in which a novice's naïve assumptions about the actor's craft are brutally overturned. Once, a young actor, criticised by Garrick for reading a part with too little feeling, replied that he would do better when he was dressed for the part and on stage in earnest. Garrick reprimanded him: 'Then, you are no actor! If you cannot make a speech, or make love to a table, chair or marble slab, as well as to the finest woman in the world, you are not, nor ever will be a great actor.' As Tate Wilkinson drily remarked, 'even an indifferent performance on the stage is not so easy a task as is generally imagined.'[158]

Even now Mary Ann made a last appeal to Stratford Canning to increase her allowance to something more reasonable, so that she could avoid going on the public stage. Stratty, who knew his father better, told her it was hopeless.[159]

---

i Elizabeth Younge (1740?–1797) had been at Drury Lane since 1768, her first two roles having been Imogen in *Cymbeline* and Jane Shore. Garrick admired her and by the end of his time as manager she was his fifth highest paid actress.

4.
Jane Shore, November 1773

In Rowe's tragedy, Jane Shore, left unprotected by the death of her royal lover, is helpless against the intrigue of the Duke of Gloster. As a woman, she is also helpless against her own passions, as Hastings puts it in a speech that sums up the she-tragedies' understanding of female psychology:

> How fierce a Fiend is Passion! With what Wildness,
> What Tyranny untam'd, it Reigns in Woman!
> Unhappy Sex! Whose easie yielding Temper
> Gives way to every Appetite alike;
> Each gust of Inclination, uncontroul'd,
> Sweeps through their Souls, and sets 'em in an uproar;
> Each Motion of their Hearts rises to Fury,
> And Love in their weak Bosoms is a Rage
> As terrible as Hate, and as destructive…[160]

Although Jane protests against the 'partial justice' by which women are so severely judged, compared with the 'lawless libertine' who roves 'free and unquestion'd through the wilds of love', she acknowledges that Woman is 'Sense and Nature's easy Fool'.[161] She is, however, more than the slave of her senses. In the course of his complicated conspiracies Gloster offers to spare her on condition that she use her charms to persuade Hastings to desert the young princes; she refuses to come between the boys and their only protector. Mary Ann, with her two unprotected sons, must have warmed to this side of her character. Similarly, with her belief in the indissolubility of the true love bond, she will have approved of the play's ending, in which, before the death that releases her from shame, the now penitent Jane is reunited with her faithful husband. Mary Ann can hardly have foreseen when she made her choice of play how sadly appropriate it was, since, like poor Jane Shore, she was to learn that when a woman allows herself to be fooled by sense and nature:

> Ruin ensues, Reproach and endless Shame,
> And one false step entirely damns her Fame;
> In vain, with tears the loss she may deplore,
> In vain, look back on what she was before;
> She sets, like Stars that fall, to rise no more.[162]

The play's run was due to begin on 22 October 1773, but was postponed because Elizabeth Younge was ill. The postponement was opportune, because Elizabeth Hartley's Jane Shore had been revived that month at Covent Garden. After this nerve-racking delay, at last the first night arrived, Saturday 6 November.[163] Nothing in her months of practice had prepared Mary Ann for the moment of stepping out onto the stage in front of those eighteen hundred spectators. The auditorium was not darkened; their faces were clearly visible – and their fidgeting. Theatre audiences were generous to newcomers, but quick to spot weakness, and merciless if they thought they were being fobbed off with something less than the real thing.

Jane's first entrance is in the second scene, where Dumont's friend Belmour gives her the cue: 'The blessings of the cheerful morn be on you / And greet your beauty with its opening sweets.' The audience applauded. Garrick's eyes were upon her from the wings, encouraging her, challenging her to rise to the occasion.[164] There was more applause throughout the performance as she won her way through to the play's tumultuous final scene, in which Dumont, revealed as her wronged husband, just has time to forgive her before she dies. The play then ends with an icily correct speech from Belmour, enjoining the audience to teach their children that repentance cannot save the adulteress 'From want, from shame and an untimely grave'. A less stark verdict was to be found in the epilogue:

> Well, peace be with her, she did wrong most surely;
> But so do many more who look demurely.
> Nor should our mourning madam weep alone,
> There are more ways of wickedness than one.
> . . .
> And since sh' has dearly paid the sinful score,
> Be kind at last and pity poor Jane Shore.[165]

'There are more ways of wickedness than one' was a sentiment that Mary Ann was to cherish over the coming years, when she attacked the notion that female virtue began and ended with chastity.

Stratty had been too much affected by first night nerves to attend but he and Mehitabel were waiting in Great Queen Street to hear how the performance had gone. When they heard that the play was to be repeated on Monday, and that the announcement had been greeted with 'torrents of applause', they each embraced Mary Ann – with apparent pleasure, she recalled, and also, no doubt, with relief. They attended the Monday performance.[166] The first step had, to that extent, been successful.

The reviews were mixed. The longest and most detailed, by *Candidus* in the *General Evening Post*, described her performance in three different scenes:

> It is not to be wondered at that she was animated in the scene with Hastings; but in that trying one also with Gloster, she displayed her own feelings, and supported the character with amazing sensibility; *she was really great.* In the dying scene,

> which is altogether playing, her looks, her attitudes, her feelings, did what language could not do, they reached the hearts of the audience, and, like Garrick in Lear, commanded such a still silence, that every sigh was heard throughout the house, which was only now and then interrupted by a well timed applause.[167]

This analysis provides a gloss on the tendency to conflate the actress with the role. In the scene in which Jane refuses to betray the young princes Mary Ann showed her own feelings; it was a situation requiring the actress to place herself in the dilemma faced by the character, and respond as she herself would respond. In the dying scene, on the other hand, she was 'altogether playing' – because the events were so far out of her own experience that she had to *imagine* how her character would respond. The scene with Hastings is different again, and *Candidus* says little about it, except that she was 'animated', which probably means that she gave herself up to the passions that are at work in the scene. This, he says, is not to be wondered at, which suggests that he regards success in this scene as the first essential for any representation of the part. Overall, the review is highly favourable, praising Mary Ann's grace and elegance, her accents and articulation, describing her as showing 'all the dignity of a woman of fashion' and concluding that she 'promises to be an elegant refinement upon Mrs Cibber'. There could hardly be higher praise than comparisons with Garrick's Lear and Mrs Cibber.[i]

Other reviewers were less fulsome. Mention was made of Mary Ann's powerful backers and high expectations which had not been justified by the event. Some found fault with her voice, some with her figure; some found her too unexpressive, others suggested that she overacted. The *Morning Chronicle* was pleased with her figure and countenance, but otherwise critical: 'she has a bad voice, an unfortunate sameness of tone, and wants a power to

---

i Susannah Cibber (1714–1766): wife of Charlotte Charke's brother, Theophilus Cibber. Seven or eight years after her death, she still provided the standard against whom every new actress was measured. Mary Ann would recall that Garrick himself likened her to Mrs Cibber – a claim also made by Mary Robinson (*Memoirs*, 29).

vary her features, as well as spirit in her delivery.'[168] Unlike some other reviews this one gave prominence to other performances, discussing Elizabeth Younge's Alicea at some length, and suggesting that she went too far in the frantic scene: 'the stage requires a decency of conduct even in the extremity of the most violent passion'. The *London Chronicle*'s reviewer, who waited until the third performance, reported that Mary Ann 'surprized the audience by all the feelings of a great actress.'[169] This paragraph was reprinted in *Morning Chronicle*, which had been much severer after the first night.[170] One writer noted Mary Ann's timidity, but hoped that with experience she might become 'a considerable ornament to the stage'. Another felt that Jane Shore was the wrong part, and hoped she might be more successful in a different one, whereas another foretold that though she would never be a great actress, she might, with practice, arrive at 'middling merit'.[171]

Something which several reviewers noticed, including those most favourable, was that Mary Ann's voice lacked power, although some added that it was sweet or harmonious. *Candidus* explained the problem away by hinting, rather oddly, that it would have been unbecoming for a newcomer to burst too boldly on the scene with a powerful voice, while the *London Chronicle* blamed first night nerves and said that by the third night she was displaying 'great power of voice'. Although it was known that Mary Ann was Irish, no one suggested that she betrayed a provincial accent. In December, *The General Evening Post* published a discussion of Mary Ann's performance in the form of a dialogue between an Englishman and an Irishman. The two debaters agree that her voice was too weak to reach the whole auditorium, but the Englishman asserts that her feelings were so well conveyed that they touched the hearts of the audience even when her words could not be made out. The conclusion reached by the discussion is that Mary Ann needed to 'module her voice', and then try other characters in which she might satisfy even her 'testy countrymen'.[172]

We also have three professional comments on Mary Ann's acting.

The first is her own admission that her voice lacked power; she may have meant only that she had difficulty making herself heard, but she was probably also confessing to an inability to declaim in the full tragic fashion. Secondly, among the audience on that first night was John Bernard, a stage-struck youth rebelling against his mother's strictures on playhouses, who went on to become a distinguished actor-manager in the West Country, where he knew Mary Ann, and in America. He remembered her performance and at the time thought it promising, although he later had reservations about her abilities. He remembered also the buzz of publicity that surrounded her debut, and the strong support she received from a distinguished cast, including Garrick. Most ominously, Hopkins the prompter was unimpressed. He admitted that she was well applauded, but his own opinion was briefly given: 'a small mean figure very little power (very So, So)'. *Very So, So* was one of his favourite expressions of disapproval.

Jane Shore was played six times over the course of a month, but then the run ended because Garrick was ill. Mary Ann was offered the option of continuing with a different actor playing Hastings, but followed the advice of friends to wait for Garrick, thus losing the momentum of her successful debut.[173]

Mehitabel offered her opinion one evening when she and Stratty were taking tea in Great Queen Street. Mary Ann, she said, had shown 'too much affection for her husband in the dying scene'. Many emotions are on display in the eventful final scene, and Mehitabel may have felt that Mary Ann did not get the balance right, that guilt and horror should have predominated, rather than renewed love for her wronged husband. Mary Ann detected a more personal and damaging accusation: that she had allowed a liking for Samuel Reddish, who played the part of Dumont/Shore, to show through. That this was indeed Mehitabel's meaning is suggested by an exchange earlier that same evening. Before attempting another role, Mary Ann had been advised to take advice from an experienced member of the company, and

Samuel Reddish had offered his services. He and Mary Ann had just finished a practice session as Stratty and Mehitabel arrived in Great Queen Street. When Reddish had left Stratty said he was a genteel-looking man, to which Mehitabel added 'and very handsome', asking what had brought him to the house. 'Not his beauty but his Business,' Mary Ann replied, with the professional actor's impatience with a gossip-hungry outsider. But Mehitabel went on probing. She quizzed little George when Esther brought him round to Clements Lane. Which of the actors did he like best? When he replied that he never met any of them, she said she supposed that was the story his mother had told him to tell.[174]

So it wasn't true, as Mary Ann later insinuated, that alienation from Stratty forced her to take to the stage, nor that Stratty and Mehitabel dropped her as soon as she went on the stage. Nonetheless the two things were connected. As she became more and more absorbed in her new life, relations with Stratty and Mehitabel grew more strained; as she found less and less of a welcome in Clements Lane she looked for friendship and support in the theatre.

Whether or not Mary Ann had succeeded in launching herself in 'first rate style', her theatrical adventure secured its first goal: she was paid. She says the treasurer brought her £50 on account after her third night; the treasurer's book says it was ten guineas, which was later deducted from what was due to her at the end of the season. However these divergent figures might be reconciled, the essential point remained that she was at last able to 'spread my own Table with the Produce of my own Exertions', experiencing a satisfaction 'which those who love the Exercise of their duties, & prize the independance which every good mind feels — will know how to appreciate.'[175]

Independence meant more than putting food on the table. She feared that her two sons would be swallowed up by the Canning family. She still looked forward to the day when George would assert his rights as heir to the Garvagh estate. If he or little Thomas fell into the hands of the family in Ireland it would be all too easy for two defenceless boys, like the Princes in the Tower, to be lost in what most Londoners regarded as a wild and lawless country. She hinted at these fears in a letter to another of her aristocratic friends, Lady Nuneham: 'I have made the great sacrifice of a private to a public life, that I might keep my children in the face of the world in opposition to every effort that has been made to plunge them into an obscurity where friendship itself might forget and leave them.'[176]

What exactly did she fear? From our perspective, Stratford Canning appears as an irascible, eccentric, stubborn old man, while Paul is a prudent and cautious son dealing carefully with a difficult father. Mary Ann can be forgiven for seeing them more luridly, as malevolent and devious, plotting against her friendless children. While she probably did not picture her sons rotting away in a dungeon beneath the great house at Garvagh, some such Gothic nightmare may have lurked not far below the surface of her imagination, but if Paul was, as she thought, like the treacherous Blifil, she had more to fear from deceit than from outright violence. She suspected that a determination to keep her sons out of their inheritance lay behind Stratford's requirement that they should remain in England. The previous summer she had begged John Beresford to help her bring her sons to public attention to prevent their 'annihilation'.[177]

Eventually Mary Ann would feel the disadvantages of being a public figure as she fell under intense scrutiny from both the theatre audience and the newspapers, but at the outset, encouraged by her friends, she hoped to invoke the power of the press on her side against the Canning family. It was not an unreasonable hope, given the unflagging attention paid by the newspapers to the private lives of actors and, especially, actresses in the London theatres. Such assistance would not have been available to her if she had lapsed into obscurity by following Mehitabel's advice to take a position in a great man's family, or hide herself away in a shop in some little town.

5.
London and Bristol, 1774–1776

Samuel Reddish was a useful actor, always able to command a good salary. His most famous role may have been Posthumus in *Cymbeline*, but there were those who said his real talent was for playing villains. When Garrick brought him to London he was immediately popular with audiences but found it hard to settle in the company. He was mocked for his provincial accent and lack of education, and right to the end of his career faced taunts over the mispronunciation of obscure words such as *orisons*. He suffered from fits of some sort, but whether these had a physical cause or were mental breakdowns is unclear. He was insecure and quarrelsome, and acquired a reputation, perpetuated by historians but perhaps not altogether deserved, for drunkenness, womanising, extravagance, untruthfulness and unreliability.[178] In the theatre, where everyone depends on everyone else, it was this last vice that was hardest to forgive.

Mary Ann testifies in his favour: 'I never saw him drunk, never knew him spend an Evening at a Tavern, nor ever heard of a wish to Gamble or to associate in any Societies, but of Family parties.' If he had a history of womanising before 1773 she might well not have known about it, so her testimony on this point is not worth much. Had he been a drunkard or gambler, however, she could hardly have failed to notice. The story of his drinking may well have been invented or exaggerated as a plausible explanation for his chronic unreliability. He was a spendthrift; he had a taste for fine clothes, and books, and when his household effects were auctioned off they included luxury goods such as a fortepiano, a telescope and a globe. There's a story that he owned a racehorse. Mary Ann says of his prodigality, '<u>folly</u> was the worst colouring that coud be given to this propensity — he wasted his money upon Articles of dress & Furniture, many of them useless — On Paintings which he did not understand, and Horses which he seldom wish'd to ride.' She refers to debts of some £800.[179]

Whether he was more untruthful than others is hard to say, but he was undoubtedly quarrelsome. He was involved in a long-running dispute with the actor Charles Macklin of Covent Garden, in the course of which he is said to have conspired to hiss Macklin off the stage. This occurred in October and November 1773, and it led two years later to a well-publicised court case, which was still remembered after twenty years. From the evidence presented it is hard not to conclude that Reddish behaved badly.[180] In Bristol, as we'll see, he was challenged to a duel. In all such disputes truth was an early victim on all sides.

Reddish was a flashy dresser and a handsome man. As a youth he had married his landlady's daughter, but they quarrelled and separated, and she became the mistress of a furrier in the Strand. In addition, according to his enemies, he produced a succession of Mrs Reddishes – a whole bundle of Reddishes, people said, one of whom, particularly masculine in appearance, was nicknamed Horse-Reddish. The woman most often associated with Reddish was the actress Polly Hart, who was said to have been the kept mistress of a succession of baronets, one of whom left her an income of £200 a year; one story was that Reddish had married her in order to get his hands on the money.[181] Traces of a Mrs Reddish, presumably Polly, can be found on playbills and in newspapers in the 1770s.[182] Following Polly Hart and the wife in the Strand, Mary Ann was at least the third Mrs Reddish. Whether the bundle of Reddishes was larger than this is unclear.

In the green room at Drury Lane these scandals were, no doubt, common knowledge, but Mary Ann kept aloof, and nobody thought it their business to warn her, so she knew Reddish only as a well-regarded actor. She was, she said, 'born with an Admiration for Talent – and Mr R had infinite Genius', just the man to help her make her way in this new world. Her goal now was to prepare the part of Fanny in the comedy *The Clandestine Marriage*.[i] If she could learn it in time she hoped to be given the part in the Christmas charity performance, but Hopkins the prompter intervened and it went to one of his daughters. This was Mary Ann's first introduction to what she called the 'intricacies' of backstage life.[183] Her first instinct was to seek Stratty's support, but since he was no longer 'master of his own judgement', anything she told him would be passed on to Mehitabel.[184] She fell back on Reddish for practical advice and protection. His capacity for making enemies was to cause Mary Ann much trouble in the future, but his quarrelsomeness may have seemed a point in his favour so long as it took the form of championing her against the Hopkins faction.

She may also have been dazzled by his extravagance, excited by a visit to the races, impressed by the telescope and globe. Reddish seems to have been equally impressed by Mary Ann. The seduction may have started as the automatic reflex of a philanderer, but he soon fell under her spell. She was young and beautiful, and a lady. She was clever and strong minded, would take him in hand, sort out his everlasting money problems. In the early months of 1774, as no more parts came her way and the excitement of *Jane Shore* wore off, Mary Ann realised that in this new world effort and talent might not be enough. She began to feel her isolation. At the same time Reddish became more and more assiduous in his attentions, until towards the end of March she capitulated, and went away with him, intending to go to Scotland for a clandestine

i A comedy by George Colman the Elder and David Garrick, first performed in 1766, and thereafter a regular favourite.

marriage. Rumours that something was in the air had already reached Mehitabel, prompting her to warn Mary Ann to take care to preserve 'that Blessing… which if once lost, however you may at present slight it, you would certainly deplore.' Since both Mary Ann and Reddish were of age to marry in England, there was no need to go to Scotland. Reddish may have hoped that by going far away he could get away with the bigamous marriage, but Mary Ann must have queried the necessity, and it was presumably then that he told her of the wife in the Strand. By then she was, she found, irretrievably compromised. We don't know how far she had gone – how far they'd got on the road north, and how far their relationship had developed – but before long it was known at the theatre that she had become Reddish's latest conquest. How and why she allowed this to happen is unclear. Apart from admiration for his talent, Mary Ann admits to no positive feelings for Sam Reddish. In the absence of further explanation from Mary Ann herself, there are several possibilities. Although later on Sam came to be dominated by Mary Ann, at the outset he may have been the predator; he may have forced her into bed, either by physical violence or deceit, or by claiming he could influence her career. Alternatively she may have set out to manipulate and use him to protect her in the theatre – or perhaps she was simply overwhelmed by the feelings of her 'sympathetic heart', as at the time of her first marriage. There was probably something of all these forces working together to place Mary Ann in what she recalled thirty years later as 'a snare which my cooler Judgment had deprecated, and which my own recollection scarce can yet give credit to'.[185]

Mary Ann's horror when she realised her predicament was intensified when Reddish told her that Garrick did not intend to engage her for the following year. She fell seriously ill, with a burning fever. Her mother and sister nursed her and, not knowing what had happened, were surprised at Reddish's constant attention. He accepted his responsibility and was abjectly contrite, swearing to dedicate the rest of his life to caring for her and her family.[186]

It seems that she took his protestations at face value, and there's no reason to assume that he was insincere. Whatever may have been true of his past behaviour towards women, in Mary Ann he acknowledged a stronger and more determined personality.

She was sufficiently recovered by 12 April to appear as Perdita in *Florizel and Perdita*, the afterpiece adapted from *The Winter's Tale*.[i] This was the first of several substantial parts that she played that month. The next was Hero in *Much Ado about Nothing*, which she had been promised back in November. It might seem surprising that these parts came her way just as Garrick had made up his mind not to re-engage her, but she was entitled to a benefit, and it was only fair to keep her before the public in the run-up to her night. For her benefit on 26 April she played Mrs Beverley, the wronged and virtuous wife of a compulsive gambler in Edward Moore's domestic tragedy *The Gamester*.[ii][187] The pathetic Beverley, victim of his own weakness, was one of Reddish's stock parts, and here it is hard to avoid the fallacy of identifying the actor with his character. The man to whom Mary Ann had yoked herself was, like Beverley, too weak to protect her from the dangers of a treacherous world but, despite his inadequacies, and despite the informality of their relationship, she never deserted him. In an aside Mrs Beverley declares that it is not the marriage contract that binds a woman to a man, but love: 'She who can love, and is beloved like me, will do as much. Men have done more for mistresses, and women for a base deluder.'[188]

Although Mary Ann, unlike the helpless Mrs Beverley, would soon become capable of thinking and acting for Reddish as well as herself, for now she still had much to learn about the 'intricacies' of her new life. The arrangements for her benefit were mismanaged due to her inexperience and unclear advice from Reddish, but

i There were adaptations of *The Winter's Tale* by Garrick and by MacNamara Morgan (c.1720–1762). Morgan's version omits Leontes and Hermione, and appears to be the one used on this occasion (Stone, iii. 1801).

ii *The Gamester* by Edward Moore (1712–1757) was a popular part of the repertoire from its first performance in 1753, when Garrick played Beverley. It was based on a play of 1721, *The Fatal Extravagance* by Aaron Hill.

nonetheless raised a respectable £114, including twenty guineas from the Duchess, who was out of town and could not attend in person, and seventy-six guineas from Lady Jane, who managed to dispose of seventy-five box tickets among her friends. Two days later Mary Ann played Octavia in *All for Love*, with Reddish as Antony.[189]

This was her last role of the season. When *Florizel and Perdita* was next performed, on 7 May, her role of Perdita was taken by another actress. She hoped that the success of her benefit and the run of appearances in April meant that Garrick intended to relent, and this hope was strengthened when he told her that over the summer she should extend her experience by playing in the provinces, where the playhouses were smaller and the audiences less demanding.[190]

Reddish owned a part share in the theatre in Bristol, and he offered to employ her there. Bristol was not an ideal place for an actress to build up her confidence, since its theatre was almost as large as Drury Lane, so if part of Mary Ann's trouble was the weakness of her voice, she would experience the same difficulties.[191] Mary Ann agreed to go with Reddish, but not as his mistress; they must live apart, she insisted. She was pregnant, however, and by the end of the summer it would be hard to hide. It is not known exactly when her child was born, but her condition was known to Stratty before she left London for the summer, and little Samuel was baptised the following April.[192]

Mary Ann had not achieved the instant success she had depended on – nothing like the éclat achieved a year or so later by Mary Robinson. She was not to be a grand actress in a fine house, with servants and a carriage. But there was no going back, not now she was carrying Reddish's child. She had no alternative but to 'make the most of my talents'. 'There is an Elasticity in the Human Mind,' she wrote, 'that rises under oppression — Mine has a large portion of it, and in this instance, as well as others, it served me nobly.' While Stratty was in Bath it occurred to him that she must be in want, and so he sent her £50. She added up her bills, paid what she could, and prepared to dismiss the expensive manservant.[193] She had retrenched before, when her husband died, and she could do it again. But in the meantime her elasticity was severely tested by three further blows.

The first came from an unexpected source. Dr Hugh Smith had never sent a bill. Mary Ann regarded him as a friend; he used to stay on after doctoring the children to talk about medical matters or poetry, but her refusal of his offer to provide her with a carriage shows her determination to place a clear limit on their intimacy. He heard of her vulnerability at the theatre, and hoping that after her affair with Reddish she would be less scrupulous, he called one evening at Great Queen Street, ostensibly to discuss Milton, and offered to set her up as his paid mistress. She assumed he was drunk and called her manservant to throw him out. Next day, to show her the cost of her scruples, Smith sent in his accumulated bill. Thirty years later she bitterly remembered the amount: £61 19s 10d. She paid it in full, apart from ten guineas for her sons' inoculations which Smith had explicitly undertaken to administer for nothing. She was further humiliated to learn that he had been discussing her affairs with Mehitabel.[194]

When Stratty heard of the Bristol plans he intervened to prevent her taking George and Thomas out of London. He was not impressed by the promise that she and Reddish would be living apart. If she attempted to take the boys with her, he would remove them from her care. Unable to say this to her face, he sent his partner, a kindly man called Hugh Johnson. Mary Ann couldn't believe that Stratty would be so cruel, but Johnson assured her, as gently as he could, that the threat would certainly be carried out unless she left the boys behind with her mother. Looking on Johnson as a friend, she asked if she should seek the protection of the law. He said nothing, but wept sympathetic tears. Courts at that time were willing to grant custody of children to their mothers, but either Mary Ann didn't know the law, or was unwilling to bring on the final break which would undoubtedly follow on legal proceedings, whatever the result. Or perhaps she simply couldn't afford a court case. Anyway, the result would have been uncertain; prejudice against the theatre might have told against her. She had to submit, having extracted a promise that no attempt would be made to take the boys away from Mrs Costello and Esther.[195]

Before long Yateman the upholsterer heard that she was 'done for' at the playhouse. He immediately demanded full payment, rather than waiting until her second benefit night for the second instalment. It now looked as though she would not have a second benefit, in which case he could 'go whistle' for the rest of his money. In accordance with their agreement, Mary Ann offered exactly half the total, once more calling on her manservant to escort Yateman from the house. Yateman then had her arrested for the whole debt. The bailiff was scandalised at the upholsterer's behaviour. The writ being made out in the name of Mrs Canning, he winked at her to suggest that she should deny that she was Mrs Canning, since she was now beginning to be known as Mrs Reddish. Her manservant seconded this suggestion, but she scorned to sink to a deception which would have risked transferring her debts onto Reddish. Leaving the children in the care of Mrs Costello and Esther, and taking her book and her weeping maid with her, she followed the bailiff to a sponging-house (a private house where debtors were temporarily held) in Fetter Lane. All the windows were barred, but the bailiff promised she would be treated like a queen. There she read until she felt tired and then settled down to sleep.[196]

In a panic, Mrs Costello sent for Stratty, who paid Yateman in full, and then hurried to Fetter Lane to secure Mary Ann's release. They had a tearful meeting. 'Go back to your children, Mary Ann,' Stratty said. At the mention of her children she begged him to relent and allow her to take them with her to Bristol, assuring him she would not be living there as Reddish's wife. Alarmed at the turn she was giving to the conversation, he offered what he thought was the best way out of her difficulties: she should go to

France until the scandal had passed – in other words she should have her baby and, if it survived, find a nurse over there, in the expectation that it would conveniently die – and then come back to George and Thomas. She said she would go to France provided she could take George and Thomas with her. That, he said, was impossible. He abruptly tore himself away, afraid of her old magic, afraid he would not be able to maintain the firm line that he and Mehitabel had agreed. Of all the men Mary Ann had to do with, Stratty was probably the one she loved most dearly. So far as we can tell this heartbreaking encounter in the sponging-house was the last time they met. 'He left me free,' Mary Ann wrote, meaning that he had freed her from the bailiff, and also that she was free of the Cannings. She did not feel equal to eating the veal cutlets that the bailiff's good-natured wife had prepared for her, but she had a cup of tea, and then went home.[197]

Before going to Bristol, Reddish too had debts to settle. A notice appeared in the *Public Advertiser* instructing his creditors to present their bills to the stage door keeper at the theatre, 'that they may be immediately inspected and discharged'. By taking over the administration of Reddish's affairs the theatre could use its credit to persuade his creditors to accept a partial settlement. Reddish had, possibly at Mary Ann's suggestion, agreed to this arrangement, although he was not satisfied with the way the theatre management carried it out. It benefited the theatre, because if the creditors remained unsatisfied they might grow impatient and threaten arrest, in which case Reddish would not be able to perform. A letter from an actor seeking work at Drury Lane suggests that during the summer Garrick was preparing for just such a contingency. Furthermore, by owning Reddish's debt the management had a hold over him, to prevent him leaving – a hold they attempted to exploit a few years later.[198]

Mary Ann left her mother, sister and the two boys in the Great Queen Street lodgings, but with just one servant. In Bristol she kept the name Canning and, as she had promised Stratty, lived a 'life of solitude and singleness'. Although some may have known of her relationship with Reddish, it doesn't seem to have been common knowledge. Since they lived separately Mary Ann possibly wasn't with Reddish when highwaymen robbed him of nine guineas – an example of the bad luck that seems to have dogged him. It's surprising that Mary Ann doesn't allude to such a dramatic occurrence; perhaps Reddish invented the story to cover up some foolish extravagance.[199]

Two years later Reddish's promotion of Mary Ann met intense opposition, but this year no such resentment was apparent. At the beginning of the season he staged *Jane Shore*, playing Hastings himself, with Mary Ann as Jane. Her London experience justified her choice for this exacting role, but otherwise he did not try to promote her as the leading lady – that place was taken by their Drury Lane colleague, Elizabeth Younge. Nonetheless, Mary Ann repeated several of her London roles, Octavia in *All for Love*, Perdita in *Florizel and Perdita* and Mrs Beverley in *The Gamester*. In her first month she extended her repertoire with genteel parts in comedies such as Samuel Foote's *The Lyar*, and *The Way to Keep Him* by Arthur Murphy,[i] as well as the second female lead in tragedies, such as Lavinia in Rowe's *The Fair Penitent*, and Statira in Nathaniel Lee's *The Rival Queens or the Death of Alexander the Great*, the most lurid of all she-tragedies.[200]

Lee's play, described by a critic as a 'mad play wrote by a mad poet',[201] was popular throughout the eighteenth century.[ii] As its double title suggests, it deals with the conspiracy against Alexander as well as the rivalry between his two wives, Roxana and Statira. Both women are consumed by love for Alexander, and both are betrayed by him. The rival queens represent two versions of womanhood, both prey to violent passion, but one having her feelings under control, accepting her betrayal passively,

i Samuel Foote (1721–1777): comic playwright and actor, and an enterprising and innovative theatre manager. Arthur Murphy (1727–1805): playwright and actor.

ii Nathaniel Lee (1653?–1692) was a friend and protégé of Dryden, with whom he collaborated on the tragedy *Oedipus*. *The Rival Queens* (1677) is discussed at length by Nussbaum (chapter 2).

and the other not. Roxana is malevolent and violent, while Statira, 'Diana's Soul, cast in the flesh of Venus', is restrained and dignified. She plans to retire from the world, but when Alexander begs forgiveness she gives in, and goes to prepare their marriage bed. Before he can join her he is poisoned by the conspirators, and she is stabbed by Roxana. Although she is going to die, while Roxana will live to bear Alexander's child, Statira declares herself the moral victor: 'This death will crown me with immortal glory, / To dye so fair, so innocent, so young, / Will make me Company for Queens above.'[202] Although the two roles are more or less equal in length and in importance for the plot, Roxana is more spirited, more assertive, at times driven mad with jealousy and injured pride; she has all the tragic fury. Statira is undoubtedly the secondary role, which no doubt was why Mary Ann took it, but in view of the willingness of audiences to identify the actress with her character it was also safer for her to play injured innocence rather than the more active, interesting and wicked Roxana. The same is true of Octavia, and of her part in Thomas Francklin's *The Earl of Warwick*[i] in which she played the colourless and virtuous Lady Elizabeth Grey, rather than the malevolent and powerful Queen Margaret.[203]

After an exhausting run in June and July her appearances were less frequent as the season wore on. This may have been because of her pregnancy, although it didn't prevent her appearing now and then. She calculated that she appeared some thirty times altogether over the summer, which, to judge by the press announcements was no more than a slight exaggeration.[204] On the last night of the season she was Celia in *As You Like It* to Miss Younge's Rosalind.[205] All in all, the summer was encouraging, and she earned enough to pay off her debts.[206] Although she had no regular engagement at Drury Lane to look forward to, Reddish might be able to secure her the occasional part. She set off back to London in good heart.

---

i Thomas Francklin (1721–1784) was a clergyman, who (without acknowledgement) based his *Earl of Warwick* on a French play by Jean-François de la Harpe. He also collaborated on a translation of the works of Voltaire.

During the summer she had written to Stratty begging to have her sons with her, but when there was no response she decided that 'I now owed something to myself, and I no longer sought what I no longer hoped to Obtain'. All summer there were encouraging reports from her mother about the boys, and just as she left Bristol she heard again that they were well – 'my Heart beat high at the Thought of meeting my little darlings,' – but when she reached her mother's lodgings she found Thomas dangerously ill. Within days he was dead.[207] The loss of her children was always the greatest challenge to her elasticity of mind. She spent weeks in a state of nervous collapse, during which time she heard nothing from Clements Lane, whereas Reddish came daily to express his condolences. Struck by this contrast, and feeling more than ever alone in the world, she made up her mind to throw in her lot with him. Paul Canning heard of the death of Thomas and that Mary Ann was taking Reddish's name, and told his father, who wrote to Mary Ann asking what she proposed to do about her surviving child. She replied that nothing had changed, she would always be his mother, and Stratford left it at that. 'He neglected but did <u>not</u> persecute me,' was her final word on this strange, unaccountable man.[208]

Mary Ann kept her options open; everything was uncertain, including whether Reddish's child would survive. Despite what Paul had told his father, she seems not to have made up her mind to call herself Mrs Reddish until late in 1775, after the baby's christening, and after her second summer in Bristol, during which she was billed as Mrs Canning. Mrs Costello opposed the change. Her violent dislike for Reddish[209] may have been for domestic reasons, such as the clutter of belongings, which it presumably fell to her to look after, or perhaps she distrusted his seductive charm. When she heard how Mary Ann had been compromised by the trip to Scotland it may have reminded her of how she herself had been tricked by Jordan. All we know about Mrs Costello's character is that she quarrelled with her own husband, and with

Reddish. The two men may have been alike, vain, plausible and irresponsible.

Another change came with the death of old Stratford Canning in 1775. His will,[210] which cut Stratty off with a shilling on account of his marriage, left a small provision for George's maintenance, with a prospect of more when Mrs Canning died. Stratty once more suggested taking George into his family to ensure he had a good education – a proposal that had first been made as a threat, and then hinted at gingerly during the encounter at the sponging-house, and was now offered through Hugh Johnson as an amicable arrangement. Reddish was devoted to young George, and feared that the proposal was making Mary Ann ill. He begged Johnson to go away and never raise the matter again. Mary Ann would die if she lost her child, he said.[211]

Reddish's hopes of reviving Mary Ann's London career were disappointed. Towards the end of March 1775 she appeared, anonymously, in Garrick's *The Guardian*, the afterpiece on Reddish's benefit night. Apparently successful in this, she allowed herself to be pushed forward by Reddish into an altogether more testing role, Andromache in *The Distress'd Mother*. Other actresses had pulled out and in the emergency Mary Ann was given the part, which she had learned at the time of her debut. It was not a success. She was repeatedly hissed, and Hopkins noted that her performance was very bad, worse than anything he had seen at Drury Lane. The shock of this humiliation had a greater impact on Reddish than on Mary Ann. Next day he came to the theatre in despair, 'as mad as a March Hare,' as Hopkins put it. He had been kept awake all night with 'all the Terrors of the Damn'd upon him' and 'call'd the Great Gods and the dear woman (Mrs Canning) that lay by his side to witness the Truth of this Assertion'.[212]

Reddish was out of action throughout April, and only appeared once or twice more before the theatre closed for the summer. He and Mary Ann again travelled down to Bristol, leaving George behind with his grandmother and aunt in new lodgings near the New Road, the district in which Mrs Costello was to spend the remaining twenty years of her life.[213] The Bristol theatre had been re-fitted, and now boasted of its improved lighting with spermaceti candles. Garrick's friend William Parsons, a well respected comic actor and co-proprietor of the theatre, sent bulletins on Reddish's state of health and state of mind. These were of concern to Garrick, partly, no doubt, from human sympathy, but also for business reasons. If Reddish decided not to return to Drury Lane the following season, or if he was too ill to act, the theatre would lose a useful actor, not to mention the substantial sums of money advanced to him. Parsons' first letter reassured Garrick that Reddish had no intention of deserting Drury Lane, but otherwise his prognosis was gloomy. Early on, Reddish was out of action for more than a week, showing alarming symptoms, sudden contortions of the face and failure of memory. He was, Parsons believed, 'hastening to insanity'. John Henderson, the leading man in Bath, opened the 1775 Bristol season with his Shylock. He seems to have faded out as Reddish recovered, but was back in August in Robert Jephson's tragedy *Braganza* for both Reddish's and Mary Ann's benefits.[214]

From mid-June until September Reddish and Mary Ann were both appearing regularly, with Mary Ann taking the lead, mainly in comedies, but also in such major tragic roles as Aspasia in Rowe's *Tamerlaine*, Jane Shore to Reddish's Hastings, and Desdemona to his Othello. Reddish's promotion of Mary Ann still did not provoke the protests that would erupt the following summer, and when the benefits came round in the latter half of the season, many of the company were happy to secure her services on their nights, in roles such as Viola in *Twelfth Night* and Hero in *Much Ado about Nothing*. Audiences may have been well disposed towards Reddish because of the extravagance of some of his productions, which included a revival of Garrick's Shakespeare Jubilee pageant, a fête champêtre with a thousand lamps, a Chinese Festival and a lavish production of Dryden's *King Arthur*, which, Reddish claimed, had always been considered too expensive to be properly staged outside London, but which he now attempted – 'it being his chief study and greatest Pleasure to procure the public of Bristol as many rational and Novelle Entertainments as the short space of three Months will permit.'[215] Among these rational entertainments were some of the successful new plays of the 1775 London season, such as *Braganza* and Thomas Francklin's *Matilda*.

It was a punishing schedule. On their benefit nights Mary Ann and Reddish both had leading roles in the afterpiece as well as the mainpiece. It was, it seems, too much for some of the audience, who complained that the performances included too many 'interludes', for which Mary Ann apologised, declaring she was 'ever studious to show her respect to the Public, with whose displeasure she would not trifle, nor whose Understanding insult.' Reddish and Mary Ann stayed in Bristol until mid-September, by which time some of the other actors had dispersed, leaving Reddish unable to stage *Richard III* as he wished. Instead they played Otway's *The Orphan* for their final night, with Mary Ann as Monimia.[216] While we don't know what tensions there may have been beneath the surface, Reddish seems to have worked well with his colleagues, and Mary Ann was accepted as one of the leading players. At the end of the season Reddish paid off more of the money he owed the Drury Lane management, at the same time apologising, in a letter endorsed 'Mr Reddish's penitent letter', for his unreliability the previous winter.[217] In both of these steps we can see Mary Ann's influence.

The season of 1775/76 saw Garrick's farewell to Drury Lane with a series of last performances – the last Hamlet, the last Richard III, the last Lear, and then the final performance of all, as Felix in Susanna Centlivre's *The Wonder*. Reddish played throughout the season without the ructions of the previous year. Garrick may have been grateful to Mary Ann for her management of his difficult colleague, but it did her no good. He told her he had sworn not to employ her, such was the pressure upon him, but we don't know where the pressure came from, nor exactly why he swore his oath: it may have been extracted from him by her enemies, or he may have sworn voluntarily, to place the matter beyond his control and so put an end to demands from friends and enemies alike. At the end of the season Reddish's engagement with the theatre had just one more year to run, and he asked to be released so that he and Mary Ann could look for employment together, but Garrick said it was impossible; presumably he had undertaken to hand over the company intact to his successors.[218]

Mary Ann's only appearance this season was on Reddish's benefit night in March, playing Monimia in *The Orphan.* Otway's tragedy portrays a family idyll destroyed by selfishness, secrecy and obstinacy – not unlike the Cannings of Abbey Street. Mary Ann was now convinced that she was best suited to comedy, but she knew the part, and Monimia's tragedy was on a domestic scale which was within her range. The audience received her well enough. She was advertised as 'a Lady, being her first appearance this season'. The critic in *The Morning Chronicle* identified her as the lady who had appeared three seasons earlier as Jane Shore, and, while praising her 'great sensibility', detected the inexperience which made her 'extravagant in her action and deportment'. Hopkins recorded that she was 'very so, so'.[219]

Mary Ann and Reddish spent the season in a house in Great Russell Street, Bloomsbury. It wasn't a harmonious household, with George, the new baby Sam, Mrs Costello and Esther, and Sam's wet nurse. Mrs Costello's quarrel with Reddish was as violent as ever, and the nurse added to the uproar with complaints that Sam was cruelly neglected. When advertising his benefit night, Reddish announced that tickets could be had not from Great Russell Street, but from an address in Great Queen Street, either because it was closer to the theatre, and so more convenient for the public, or because he had been driven out by Mrs Costello. Everyone, Reddish included, thought only of George, except perhaps the unassuming

Esther, about whose opinions we never hear anything.[i] One of her jobs was to take George to visit Clements Lane, where she had to put up with Mehitabel's outspoken jibes. George was fastidious, and when Mehitabel's baby Harry did something to annoy him he said he never allowed his brother Sam to do that. Irritated, perhaps, by the boy's primness, and reminded of Mary Ann's disdain for hot-cockle sport, Mehitabel snapped that he should not refer to that player's brat as his brother. Legally Mehitabel was correct, illegitimate children had no family. When he got home George asked Mary Ann why poor Sam was a brat.[220]

The centre of everyone's attention, with a doting mother and an unstable and indulgent stepfather, thoroughly spoiled but at the same time neglected, undisciplined and untaught – what would become of George? An old Irish actor, John Moody,[ii] a kindly man who took an interest in the welfare of his colleagues, was sufficiently concerned to speak to Stratty. The story was told in later years that Moody warned Stratty that if young George went on as he was going, he would end on the gallows. It's the sort of thing that's said about literary anti-heroes like Tom Jones. Moody may have used the phrase, but more probably it was put into his mouth in later years by admirers or opponents of George Canning who wished to portray him as an adventurer or picaresque hero. However Moody expressed himself, he only confirmed what Stratty and Mehitabel had already concluded, that George should not be left in his mother's care. In the spring of 1776, therefore, they sent Hugh Johnson again to press Mary Ann to sign away her rights as George's guardian to Stratty and Paul. They would send him to school, paid for by old Mrs Canning, and Mary Ann could have him to stay with her for part of the school holidays. [221]

Johnson found George seriously ill, with a fever so severe that the doctor had insisted that his long ringlets should be cut off. In

---

i Mary Ann never so much as mentions her sister's name. We only learn for certain what it was from the record of her marriage in 1796.

ii John Moody (1727–1812) had a reputation for benevolence and was a leading figure in the foundation of the Theatrical Benevolent Fund.

place of the treacherous Hugh Smith, Mary Ann had called in the famously benevolent and conscientious Richard Jebb.[i] Seeing how reluctant she was to destroy the boy's beauty, Jebb brusquely told her that she must cut off his hair or have 'Issues' in his arms. As she watched over the bed Mary Ann must have asked herself what was to happen in the summer while she was working in Bristol. Could she entrust this shorn lamb to the clumsy care of Mrs Costello? It was perhaps this immediate anxiety as much as George's long-term advantage that finally made her agree to Stratty's terms. Mehitabel had her faults, but she was a sensible woman and, as a modern mother, more likely to understand the latest techniques of child-rearing than Mary Costello. Mary Ann gave in, and an order of adoption was obtained from the Master of the Rolls in May 1776. Different dates are given for the transfer of custody to Stratty, and it may be that George spent time at Clements Lane before the adoption was made official. Looking back, George believed the separation came when he was four. 'Almost the first recollection that I have of any passage in my life,' he wrote, 'is that of being taken away from her.'[222]

Mary Ann's memory of this painful period remained confused. She had her suspicions of Mehitabel, but at this point she was, as she recalled in the Packet, 'not sure your Mind would be poison'd – your Affection, your pious fondness for me – taught to tread the mere cold path of duty'. When she came to write the Packet she could not remember when exactly she had surrendered George, except that she was sure it was around the time of his illness and the loss of his precious curls. 'Indeed from 73 to 77,' she wrote, 'my Mind was often in a State so near to annihilation that long pauses seem to have been made in my Existence.'[223] She wrote nothing in the Packet about what was to be a disastrous summer in Bristol, not even mentioning the birth of her baby James. Another fragile life that twined around her heart.

This summer Mary Ann was known in Bristol as Mrs Reddish.

i Richard Jebb (1729–1787): physician at St George's Hospital. He attended the royal family and was made a baronet in 1778.

After her comparative success in the previous two seasons she was not prepared for the hostility of her reception. Early on she was cast as Queen Elizabeth in *Richard III*, but the writer and teacher Hannah More, who regularly reported to her friend Garrick on theatrical events in Bristol, wrote that in the end Reddish 'had the prudence not to suffer the woman to appear'. According to a version put about by the actor Samuel Cautherley,[i] she did appear, but was 'expelled from the Stage on her first appearance by the united Voice of the audience'.[224] She was not cast again until later in the season.

Mary Ann's benefit night, on which she was counting for the upkeep of her mother and sister in the coming year, was fixed for Monday 29 July, when the mainpiece was to be Isaac Bickerstaff's *The Maid of the Mill*.[ii] Her pregnancy was well advanced, and whether or not she could appear was in the balance. Actresses would typically work right up to the start of their labour, but could hardly return to work immediately after giving birth. A prosperous actress like Dora Jordan, with her royal protector the Duke of Clarence, might take a few weeks' rest, and even the hard-pressed Charlotte Deans, who tells of one child, her seventeenth, born as the doors of the theatre were opening and another delivered during a performance of *The Battle of Hexham*, gave herself a few nights to recover.[225]

In this crisis Mary Ann claimed to have been the victim of 'Malevolence, Artifice and ill Design'. What happened can only be guessed from partisan and elliptical accounts by Hannah More, Samuel Cautherley, Reddish and Mary Ann herself. Perhaps because her enemies in the theatre controlled the publicity, the newspaper announcements for *The Maid of the Mill* made no mention of her benefit. Two days before the performance it was reported that the part of the Maid would be taken by Mrs

i Samuel Cautherley (1747-1805): an undistinguished actor, the ward and, according to some, the illegitimate son, of David Garrick. He was employed at Drury Lane for some years, but quarrelled with Garrick and resigned in 1775.

ii Isaac Bickerstaff (1733–after 1808), librettist: *The Maid of the Mill* (first produced in 1765; music by Samuel Arnold) is based on Samuel Richardson's novel *Pamela*.

Wrighten, 'to strengthen the performance'.[i] Whether Mary Ann was consulted on the substitution we don't know; it's possible that the first she knew was when she saw the newspaper. She then went into labour, and her son James was born on Sunday 28 July.[226] It was suggested that because she had not appeared she should forfeit her benefit, but Reddish, and possibly the audience on the night, protested, and she received a satisfactory £112.[227]

After her confinement Reddish cast her as Constance in Cautherley's benefit production of *King John*, and Eltruda in James Wrighten's benefit, *King Alfred*. Actors had a say on who played in their benefits, and first Cautherley and then Wrighten ignored Reddish's arrangements and chose Mrs Jackson instead. Reddish was to play in both productions, but he now refused to appear in either. He conceded that Mary Ann had been in no condition to learn the new and demanding role of Constance, but Eltruda was a part she knew well and could have played, so his real quarrel was with Wrighten. He extended his retaliation to include Cautherley because, he said, Wrighten had pointed at Cautherley's action as a precedent. Reddish claimed that he was chivalrously punishing Cautherley for a slight that would be damaging to Mary Ann's career. There arose a furious public quarrel between the two actors, whose exchange of letters in the Bristol newspaper was picked up by the London press.[228]

In the course of another quarrel, unrelated to Mary Ann, an actor called Robinson, who had come from Dublin to play in the opening production but seems not to have been employed since, claimed that his articles had been breached and challenged Reddish to a duel. Reddish was said to have replied that he could not afford to die until after his benefit night.[229] If he meant that he had to wait until he had paid off his debts, he would never be ready to die.

It's not clear why the uproar in Bristol was greater this summer

i Mary Ann Wrighten (1751–1796). A leading singer at Drury Lane, she later went to America, where she died. She is reported to be the first woman composer to have music published in the USA. James Wrighten, her first husband, was a less talented performer who became prompter at Covent Garden and Drury Lane.

than during the previous two. It may have been that Mary Ann's baby and change of name made it harder to ignore the scandal – it was this year that Hannah More described her as the latest of the 'bundle of Reddishes' – or perhaps ill health affected her performance in the opening production of *Richard III.* Perhaps Reddish's behaviour was becoming more erratic, and people were tired of him, audiences and fellow actors alike. There may too have been larger forces at work. The following summer season would see a number of Reddish's Drury Lane antagonists, including the whole Hopkins family, in Bristol. In 1778 the Bristol theatre would be granted a royal patent, and in 1779 the enterprising John Palmer[i] would inaugurate a joint venture between the Theatres Royal in Bath and Bristol. These changes may already have been in the air, giving rise to a feeling that they would work better without the unpredictable Reddish. For whatever reason, the situation had become untenable, and Reddish decided to retreat. He sold his interest in the theatre, and after his benefit night, which attracted a large though hostile audience, he and Mary Ann went to Plymouth for the last few weeks of the summer season.[230]

However relieved the new managers may have been to see him go, Reddish's defection left them pleading for the indulgence of the audience as they sought 'to extricate themselves from the Difficulties they are under by the absence of their Colleague'. Unlike Reddish at the end of the previous summer, they persevered with their planned performance of *Richard III*, but the comedian John Quick playing Richard was unable to persuade the audience to treat him seriously.[231]

The past three years had shown that it was not as easy as Mary Ann had hoped to achieve a 'first rate style'. At times she had almost succumbed under the pressure of her new life, but she had survived, thanks to Reddish's support and her own resilience and

i John Palmer (1742–1818): theatre manager and postal reformer, who inherited his family stake in the Theatre Royal, Bath. His experience running rapid communications between Bath and Bristol to enable his actors to work in both locations contributed to his plans for speeding up the postal service.

intelligence. She had learned from the experience, and if these three years had not made her a first-rate actress, they had given her a certain professional pride and understanding of the workings of the theatre.

6.
Semiramis, 1776

After Plymouth, Mary Ann and Reddish returned to London for the winter season. Drury Lane was entering the post-Garrick era in the hands of Richard Brinsley Sheridan, although Garrick's partner, Willoughby Lacy, held on to his share for another two years.[i] Mary Ann had made a good impression in Plymouth and when she reached Drury Lane she hoped that Garrick's fatal promise would be a thing of the past. Lacy agreed, or so she thought, that she should be given a trial in a play of her choosing, and her salary should depend on how she was received, but he seems to have promised more than he could fulfil. The decision lay with Sheridan, who was eager to employ Reddish, but refused to offer Mary Ann a regular engagement. Her few weeks in Plymouth had not effaced the stories of the disastrous season in Bristol. Sheridan said there was a 'violent sensation' to be overcome, but whether this was among the public or the other players is not clear. He conceded that if an author stipulated that she was to act in his play the management would not oppose the request – and there was, as it happened, just such an author, George Ayscough, a captain in the Guards and the translator of Voltaire's tragedy *Semiramis*.[ii]

i Willoughby Lacy (1749–1831) inherited his share in Drury Lane from his father James Lacy (1696–1774), Garrick's partner since 1747. Willoughby sold up to Sheridan in 1778.

ii Captain George Ayscough (died 1779) was the son of Anne Lyttelton, sister of the first Baron Lyttelton. In addition to his translation he also published a collection of his uncle's works and a book of travel writing.

The leading actress Mrs Yates was to play Queen Semiramis, and Ayscough wanted Mary Ann to play Princess Azema. As a man of fashion, Ayscough had enough friends, Sheridan hoped, to counterbalance Mary Ann's enemies.[232]

Meanwhile there were a few days left before George was due to start school, and he spent them with Mary Ann. Despite her agreement with Stratty, this was to be the last time she had George to stay with her. He was six, and apart from one brief meeting in 1779 he would not see her again until he was almost sixteen. The image of his mother that he carried in his head during the long separation was based on how she was now, in her late twenties, a young mother nursing her new baby, not yet scarred by years of hardship. During the next ten years he thought much about her, but with only occasional letters, and odd scraps of information gleaned from the conversation of his aunt and uncle, he knew almost nothing of her life, just enough to be sure that it was difficult and that he couldn't be with her.[233]

While the Packet is eloquent about Mary Ann's own sadness at the separation, and her continuing concern for George's physical well-being, there is nothing about his feelings. The only psychological impact that Mary Ann envisaged was that he might be induced to transfer his loyalties from her to the Cannings. In later years, when she criticised George for behaving unnaturally towards her, it's not clear how far, if at all, she recognised that the unnaturalness might be the natural result of the pain attached to his early memory of their separation. We marvel at the things, self-evident to us, that people in the past were unaware of – the evil of slavery, for example, and the hypocritical double standard in sexual morality – and to these blind spots we should add widespread lack of insight into the minds of children. It was not unusual for children to be farmed out to more prosperous relatives. The practice could generate confusion and uncertainty in the future, making it a common plot device in plays and novels, with both comic and tragic outcomes. In Voltaire's tragedy, for example, after Queen Semiramis has murdered her husband, her son is sent away; when he returns incognito fifteen years later she falls in love with him and is accidentally killed by him.

The 1776–77 season did not start well for Reddish. He was cast as Vainlove in Congreve's *The Old Batchelor*[i] but objected that it was a minor character, a complaint which, he believed, Garrick would have treated sympathetically. Expecting, therefore, to be relieved of the part, he didn't bother to study it. The new management, less accommodating than Garrick, insisted that he should play Vainlove, so at the last minute he set about learning the lines. At the first performance on 19 November he was hissed for repeatedly stumbling over the words, until eventually he came forward and apologised, accusing the management of not giving him long enough to prepare. The audience, which had been shouting 'Off, Reddish, off!', now applauded him. Sheridan agreed that another actor should take over the part, but demanded that Reddish withdraw his accusation. Reddish himself published several detailed accounts, giving his own side of the story, but Sheridan insisted on a complete public retraction, which he made before his next appearance, in yet another revival of *Jane Shore.* He claimed that he had not intended to mislead the public, but had been thrown off balance by the hissing, which may well have been true, because all through his career he was sensitive to hostile audiences. The audience applauded him generously. At the end of the month he appeared in the leading role in another Congreve comedy, *Love for Love.*[234]

Reddish was not the only member of the company finding it hard to get on with the new management. The quarrel over Vainlove followed hard on a similar incident affecting Mary Ann Yates, one of the highest paid performers at Drury Lane.[ii] Illness necessitated a change of programme, and at short notice the

---

i William Congreve (1670–1729) was a leading exponent of Restoration comedy. Sheridan revived three of his plays in the 1776/77 season.

ii Mary Ann Yates (1728–1787) was well known for her willingness and capacity to stand up to her employers.

management announced the Colley Cibber version of Vanbrugh's *The Provok'd Husband*, with Mrs Yates as Lady Townly. This was a stock play and Mrs Yates was familiar with the part, but she insisted it was against her articles of employment to appear at less than twenty-four hours' notice. The management did not justify her absence by the usual pretence that she was ill, and the quarrel erupted into an exchange of letters in the newspapers. Mrs Yates defended herself vigorously. Hopkins the prompter joined in on behalf of the management. Mrs Yates claimed that he had helped to stoke the flames by reporting matters to Sheridan in a way that was prejudicial to her. Meanwhile another correspondent congratulated Sheridan on having stood up to Mrs Yates, which suggests a deliberate policy on the part of the new management to curb the power acquired by leading actors under Garrick's regime. The matter was concluded, as in Reddish's case, with a climbdown by Mrs Yates, a dignified address to the audience at the start of an evening performance and liberal applause.[235]

Once Mrs Yates was reconciled with the management, preparation for *Semiramis* could go ahead. It was a risky proposition, a new play by an inexperienced author, with an unfamiliar story.[i] It's not clear why Ayscough had asked Mary Ann to play Azema. It may be that Reddish, or Mrs Yates, made it a condition of their own appearance, or Ayscough, whose uncle, Lord Lyttelton, had once tried to help George Canning senior, may have known and been moved by Mary Ann's story. She herself was in two minds, keen for another chance at Drury Lane, but afraid that this was a bad vehicle. It may be that she was offered the part only after more knowing members of the company had declined. She reminded Sheridan that her style and especially her voice were better suited to comedy than tragedy, but her request for a part in comedy was turned down, probably because it didn't fit into Sheridan's wider plans. In his own plays he was breaking with the

i An Italian opera, *Semiramide Riconusciuta* by Gioacchino Cocchi, was produced three times at the King's Opera House, Haymarket, in February 1771 (Stone, iii. 1527–1528). The opera does not tell the same story as Voltaire's play.

tradition of sentimental comedy that had dominated Garrick's time at Drury Lane, and to prepare audiences for the new style he was planning a revival of the more hard-hitting and satirical comedies of Congreve. This project was dear to Sheridan's heart, but it was not without risk, and an inexperienced and controversial actress would make extra difficulties. He told Mary Ann it was *Semiramis* or nothing.[236]

Paragraphs announcing that the play was being 'got up' were inserted in the press, and plot summaries were given, along with background information on the legends about Semiramis. This suggests a conscious effort to familiarise audiences with the outlandish name and to counter attempts to 'depreciate' the play in advance. Both Voltaire's original and Ayscough's translation were criticised. It was reported that Thomas Francklin, author of a rival translation, had declared the play unsuitable for presentation on the English stage. The controversy may have stimulated interest among the public, but also tended to justify Mary Ann's reservations. One newspaper concluded grudgingly that the play 'may crawl its nine nights by the assistance of Mrs Yates as an actress and Mr de Loutherbourg as a Painter and the men who roll the wretched Thunder Machine, and Fire Rosin behind the Scenes.'[i][237]

Preparations did not go smoothly. It was found during rehearsals that, owing either to Ayscough's lack of theatrical experience or to the elaborate technical requirements of de Loutherbourg's designs, a scene needed to be lengthened to allow time for the set to be changed. Ayscough couldn't think of anything, so Mary Ann, who three years before had proclaimed her complete lack of education, composed an extra speech for Azema.[238] She also complained that at one point the scene design was flatly inconsistent with her lines, and since it was easier to change the script than the scenery,

i Philippe Jacques de Loutherbourg (1740–1812) was a French landscape painter who became chief scene designer at Drury Lane in 1771. Under both Garrick and Sheridan he introduced new techniques, 'creating new and astounding scenic effects' (Stone iii. 1741). The sets for *Semiramis* were elsewhere criticised as 'old, and in general very indifferent', the best being the tomb scene (*London Evening Post*, 14–16 Dec. 1776).

the lines were deleted.[239] These problems further confirmed her suspicion that *Semiramis* was not a good play.

Another unfavourable circumstance noticed by the press was that *Semiramis* was interrupting, after only two nights, a popular run of *Romeo and Juliet*. Mary Ann, preoccupied though she was with her preparations, can hardly have been indifferent to the huge success of the new Juliet, Mary Robinson, making her first appearance on any stage, another of Garrick's protégées who, like Mary Ann, reminded him of Mrs Cibber. The critics granted that Mrs Robinson had much to learn, but enthused about her figure and face, her graceful arms and 'fine marking eyes', her voice and her 'wild, untutored genius'. Even Hopkins conceded that she made 'a very tolerable first Appearance, and may do in time'. It may be significant that the least enthusiastic review of Mrs Robinson was in the *St James's Chronicle*, which as we shall see was on the whole the most favourable to Mary Ann. When the *Morning Chronicle* wrote that Mrs Robinson had made a 'better impression… than we remember… from any new actress for some time past', the new actress they must have had most in mind was Mary Ann, whose debut three years before had not been forgotten.[240]

The first night of *Semiramis* was Saturday 14 December. The problems and controversies may have increased the first night tension, but cannot have prepared Mary Ann for the violence of what happened. Hostility towards the play was suddenly all concentrated upon her. As she made her entry in the second act there was some applause, but it did not reassure her. At once there arose a determined hissing. Accounts differ as to whether the hissing was a reaction to her opening speech or, as it seemed to her, began even before she opened her mouth. It may have begun in one place before she spoke, and spread to other sections of the audience as they blamed her for not making herself heard above the noise. The disorder continued throughout her performance; someone threw an apple. With encouragement from Mrs Yates she persevered to the end, but not one word that she uttered was heard. Her enemies 'knew their business – and they did it effectually'. Hardened play-goers were shocked at this brutality, praising Mary Ann's 'modest firmness', and blaming the management for exposing her in a part for which she was ill qualified. Unlike Reddish in *The Old Batchelor*, she did not break out of character to plead with the audience, but it is surprising that neither Reddish nor Mrs Yates had the courage to plead on her behalf. Hopkins noted that Mary Ann 'was hissed all through and must never perform again. Indeed she was very bad.' Her friends in the theatre and the newspapers claimed that the hissing was clearly premeditated. Mrs Yates called on the management to investigate the matter. Even hostile critics deplored the behaviour of the audience as a shameful reflection on the English play-going public.[241]

The second performance had been announced for the Monday. On Sunday morning Ayscough and Sheridan agreed that Mary Ann should persevere, but in the course of the day they both came under pressure, either from among the actors or from whoever was responsible for the organised hissing, and withdrew their support, feeling perhaps, as some of the newspaper commentators did, that it would be cruel to expose Mary Ann any further. Sheridan, realising that Mary Ann had the only copy of Azema's extra speech, told Reddish to get it from her. It's a measure of the discipline of the theatre that neither Reddish nor Mary Ann disputed Sheridan's right to reassign the part. Though shaken by her ordeal Mary Ann maintained her professionalism, acknowledging that the authority of the theatre manager is like that of 'every other master of a family'. Hopkins's elder daughter took over as Azema.[242]

The *St James's Chronicle*, which had been a supporter of Mary Ann ever since *Jane Shore*, recalled that she had in the past given complete satisfaction, and insisted that the hissing had begun before she had a chance to prove herself. Other reviewers agreed with Hopkins's verdict. The correspondent in the *Morning Chronicle*, writing that Mrs Reddish 'speaks sensibly and has feeling, but the thinness of her tone rather excites laughter than serious attention', was clear about the sequence of events: she was heard patiently for some time, and was hissed only when she had 'totally failed'. Part of the newspapers' anger was directed at the theatre management for casting Mary Ann as Azema, underlining Mary Ann's point that it was an unsuitable play in which to launch an untried actress. The *Morning Post* asked why they did not choose Miss Younge. As the controversy raged, the hostile *Morning Chronicle* raked up the Bristol disaster, and also threw in the insult about Mary Ann being the latest in the 'bunch of Reddishes'.[243]

Mary Ann bravely attended the Monday performance. She suspected that the Hopkins faction had had a hand in her humiliation and was on the lookout for evidence. She and her adherents thought they had found it when her replacement was word perfect throughout, apart from the two changes introduced during rehearsals, which suggested she had learned the part in advance. Mary Ann went on to argue that if it had not been known that she would be deprived of the part, there would have been no need to supply a replacement, and if it was known in advance there must have been a deliberate plot. The case is not conclusive. If Hopkins did tell his daughter to prepare the part, he may have been acting merely on his long-held low opinion of Mary Ann's talent. As a newspaper pointed out, it was reasonable enough to provide an understudy. But a hint of suspicion remains, partly because the same pattern of events had occurred shortly before, when another actress, Miss Essex, made her first Drury Lane appearance in the troubled production of *The Old Batchelor*; Hopkins described her as 'a mean figure and a shocking actress', and the next night she was replaced by his younger daughter.[244]

Miss Hopkins' reviews were mixed, the newspapers dividing along the same lines as they had over Mary Ann. The *Morning Chronicle* said Miss Hopkins, having taken the part at short notice, handled it with great spirit and propriety, but the *St James's Chronicle* complained that she was a 'mere apology for a Tragic Heroine, in which the Mother's want of politeness, and the

Mechanism of her Father (who, it seems, is the Prompter at the Theatre) is so unhappily blended. The poor Girl this night spoke nonsense without seeming the least conscious of it.' This last point presumably refers to the lines which were incompatible with the scenery. In her own account Mary Ann describes Miss Hopkins in the same terms: 'the poor girl had studied [this passage] *so long*, and *so thoroughly*, that she could not on Monday evening leave it out'. The *Morning Chronicle* noticed the similarity and described the *St James's Chronicle*'s comment as a paraphrase of Mary Ann's. Since the *St James's* review was probably written before Mary Ann's comments were published there is a suspicion that she collaborated with its author, or indeed wrote it herself.[245]

The experience demoralised Mary Ann entirely and she fell ill, but this did not prevent her from writing a series of letters to the *Morning Chronicle* during the second half of December, giving her side of the story. In these letters, which have already been referred to, Mary Ann signed herself 'an Injured Woman'. The first is dated just three days after the disaster. The *Morning Chronicle* was firmly in the Hopkins camp, but agreed to publish Mary Ann's side of the story in the interests of fairness, they said, but also no doubt in order to keep the scandal alive. They prided themselves on being a 'Theatrical paper'.[246] Mary Ann's letters are written in the same detailed, forensic style as Reddish's about *The Old Batchelor* the previous month. They contain some intemperate personal attacks on the unrefined Miss Hopkins, but for the most part they are an obsessive raking over of the details of what happened, going back to the start of her career.

Once, she reminded readers, she had been deemed worthy to play opposite Garrick in *Jane Shore*, and the great man had likened her to Mrs Cibber. Some of her readers remembered the story differently, believing that Garrick had employed Mary Ann in order to ingratiate himself with the Duchess of Ancaster; to them Mary Ann's boasts now seemed absurd. When the *St James's Chronicle*, usually supportive of Mary Ann but presumably keen, like the *Morning Chronicle*, to seem impartial, published a hostile letter bringing up her recent failure in Bristol, she replied that she had been well received for two summers in Bristol, ignoring the disastrous summer of 1776. She also pointed out that in the previous two seasons at Drury Lane she had twice appeared and twice been well received, referring to the afterpiece, *The Guardian*, and to her Monimia on Reddish's benefit night, but passing over her less successful Andromache. She recalled the prompter's duplicity (as she saw it) over *The Clandestine Marriage* in the early months of her career, when she was 'unpractis'd in the Intricacies of a Theatre', and alleged the same sharp practice now. Recalling the preparations for *Semiramis* she emphasised her unwillingness to take the part of Azema, and admitted that it was not suited to her particular talents. Her voice, she said, was known to lack the power expected of a tragic heroine. By being forced to play Azema, she implied, she had been set up to fail.[247]

Her self-justification stretched to some five thousand words before 2 January, when the editor of the *Morning Chronicle* called a halt, perhaps afraid of giving offence to Sheridan, or alarmed at the undignified exchange of insults, and possibly also feeling that Mary Ann was doing herself a disservice by the shrill tone of the letters. Her critics also became more shrill as the controversy raged on. The *Morning Chronicle* wrote on 27 December: '… from her miserable figure, and still more miserable voice, she made the Princess [Azema], from scene the first to scene the last, an object of laughter and contempt.' Readers were, no doubt, losing interest. There was a flurry of disagreement over the prologue and epilogue to *Semiramis*, but then there were other plays and other actors to think about, not least Mary Robinson, who appeared twice more as Juliet, and was then established in the company, becoming celebrated in the role of Perdita, and as the mistress of the young Prince of Wales.

Much of what Mary Ann wrote seems well argued, even if she labours over small details in a way that can hardly have appealed to readers, but sometimes her anger gets the better of her and she's stung to make an ill-considered response. Picking up a phrase in the *Morning Chronicle*'s paragraph on Miss Hopkins, Mary Ann wrote:

> Your correspondent adds, that the part became a "new one in [Miss Hopkins's] hand," ha! ha! ha! – this puts me in mind of a *bon mot* of an honest Hibernian, who having been in London, in the late reign, at his return, was asked what sort of *person* his late Majesty was,—ashamed to confess that he had not had the honour of an opportunity of judging, he replied, "By my soul, he's every inch a *king*, for he's not a bit like a *gentleman!*" – the application is obvious.

This is hardly the 'language of Billingsgate', as a correspondent in the *Morning Chronicle* later claimed, but such an ill-judged attempt at satire shows that Mary Ann was too narrowly focused on her grievance to imagine the likely reactions of her readers. The same correspondent commented on Mary Ann's wild appearance since the incident: 'a wandering, unmeaning look and manner, a certain odd arrangement of the ornaments of her head, which generally accompanies a *derangement* within'.[248]

Mary Ann defended herself against this and other insinuations that she was in need of the attentions of a mad-doctor:

> Lest Dr. Monro,[i] with his usual humanity, should… think me worthy of a visit, I shall endeavour to support my own cause against the united efforts of false wit, false reasoning, false promisers, and those who are of too much consequence to startle at falsehood of any kind, in such a manner, as to convince the world that I have a sufficient degree of common sense, thanks to the bounteous giver! "to *stay the babbling of these vain gainsayers*"—and to blunt the arrows of the most pointed wit,

---

i Dr John Monro (1715–1791) was physician in charge of Bethlem and Bridewell, and also licensee of a private madhouse, Brooke House, in Hackney. He was a patron of the arts with a particular interest in Shakespeare.

> unsupported by the sacred pillar on which I lean,—unalterable truth—"*let that speak for me, and make up my deserving!*"[249]

The tone of the 'Injured Woman' letters is hardly more hyperbolic than that of Mary Ann's detractors. The letters are certainly not proof of insanity, but they suggest that she had been thrown off balance by an affair that was still remembered in theatrical circles twenty years later as 'a regular attack, uniform in its sound and direction where she filled her part tolerably, as well as where she failed'.[250]

After the stimulus of writing the letters, Mary Ann fell into a state of apathy which lasted through January and February. Reddish continued at the theatre, and things went on as usual in the disunited house in Bloomsbury, but without George her delight and purpose in life were gone. On 1 March 1777 she suffered a fresh blow when her baby, James, died. She believed it was because of the effect of the *Semiramis* disaster on her milk. Her elasticity deserted her and for several weeks she seemed to lose all interest in life. Then, realising that 'Either an Effort of Activity or a decided despondency was inevitable', she decided to try something new.[251]

7.
The Offspring of Fancy

Back in 1772, the Duchess of Ancaster had urged Mary Ann to write a novel, using the story of her own troubles and including a stinging portrait of old Stratford Canning as a wicked father-in-law, but she had rejected the idea. She felt her lack of education too acutely. Since then she had been learning by heart great chunks of the best authors, and mixing with writers and artists as well as actors. Her years in the theatre had given her the self-reliance that goes with learning a trade and earning your own keep. She had the confidence to appear before 1,800 people and hold their attention, and the resilience to stand her ground against their hostility. Perhaps authorship was not so impossible after all. The 'Injured Woman' letters showed, if nothing else, that she could organise an argument and write fluently. But what to write about? She had no wish now to antagonise unnecessarily the family who had the care of her son. Nor did she choose to go back over her experiences in the theatre. The intensity of her efforts at self-justification had threatened her mental equilibrium; she couldn't go on for ever being an injured woman. It would have to be a work of imagination, her fancy setting her free from the difficult realities of her life.

When she was strong enough, Mary Ann would go with a friend to church. One Sunday she was too unwell and stayed at home, but rebuked herself for her listlessness, picked up her pen and started writing as her fancy directed. By the end of church time she had written a couple of letters, for her fancy had settled on the epistolary form. She showed them to her friend, who encouraged her to go on. Within a few weeks she produced 83 letters, enough for two small volumes. Her friend recommended a publisher called Nicolls, who had published *The Anti-Lucretius* ten years earlier. He thought the novel might sell, but as it was not in his line he passed it to John Bew of Paternoster Row, who offered her good terms: he would print 750 copies, of which she would have 100 to sell for herself, and if the proceeds from the remainder covered the costs and bookseller's margin she would receive the balance.[252]

The Offspring of Fancy is a rare book, with just two out of Bew's 750 copies known to have survived the vicissitudes of two and a half centuries, one in America and the other in England.[i] It is not a great work of fiction demanding to be recognised, but it is entertaining, and certainly good enough to make us regret that Mary Ann didn't write more. Its weakness is in the plot; there are a number of good subplots composed from the commonplaces of eighteenth century novels – long-lost relatives, duels, forced marriages, elopements, seductions, disappearances and reappearances – but there's no main plot driving the whole narrative. Its strengths lie in the variety of clearly delineated characters, and the lively, engaging style of many of the letters. There is perceptive social commentary on such matters as female education, child-rearing, gender inequality and the double standard in judging sexual misconduct. Such observations were not original – protests against the poverty of female education, for example, had been raised many times before – but they are effectively dramatised by the events of the novel and were directly informed by Mary Ann's own experience.

Recognisable autobiographical allusions can be found in

i One copy is in the Harry Ransom Center at the University of Texas, Austin; another is at the Chawton House Library, Hampshire (formerly part of the University of Southampton). The Chawton copy is accessible online. Nowadays, when finding things on the Internet is so commonplace, it is hard to recall how miraculous it seemed in the early 2000s when, after many unsuccessful trawls, the search engine suddenly lighted on this copy.

almost every episode, while many of the characters contain strong elements of people in her own life – her mercurial father and slow-witted, docile mother; her arbitrary and unaccountable father-in-law; strait-laced and unsympathetic Mehitabel; gloomy, secretive George Canning. The central figure of Marianne Clement is plainly an idealised self-portrait. She describes her letter-writing style in terms that recall Mary Ann's own letters, rushing ahead with little regard for any punctuation but the dash. Marianne defends this rattling spontaneity as preferable to a style concocted according to conventional recipes.[253] Her husband, who respects and trusts her and speaks freely with her, is a cultured London merchant. Amidst all the unhappy marriages described in the novel, the Clements alone are happy and equal, presenting Mary Ann's vision of what life might have offered her as Stratty's wife in Clements Lane.

Marianne has friends from the fashionable West End, including a young wife and mother called Mrs Belmour. The fashionable lady, idle, selfish and superficial, was a stock figure in plays and novels, and Mary Ann may have taken much of Mrs Belmour's character (as she took her name[i]) from the genteel comedies of the day, but there are some elements in the characterisation which reflect her own preoccupations. Mrs Belmour is shockingly indifferent to her children, for example, and is a thoughtless and lazy letter-writer. Marianne points to her friend's unhappy marriage to a dull husband as an extenuation of her defects.[254] Mary Ann's own experience of this milieu derived from her three years in her grandfather's house in Wigmore Street and her contacts with the Duchess and other West End friends, of whom Mrs Hankey is the only one whose name is known. The Duchess's house was in Berkeley Square, Mrs Hankey's in Arlington Street, so by locating Mrs Belmour in Dover Street, which is the continuation of Arlington Street north of Piccadilly in the direction of Berkeley Square, Mary Ann may be hinting that she

i There is a Mrs Belmour in Arthur Murphy's *The Way to Keep Him*. Belmour is also the name of the character in *Jane Shore* who first praises Jane's beauty but at the end icily condemns her.

is based on a conflation of these two friends.[255] Marianne's uneasiness about some aspects of the *bon ton* circles that Mrs Belmour inhabits reflects the tension between the City and the West End. Mary Ann herself experienced this tension when Mehitabel resented her friendship with Mrs Hankey. In the novel the criticism of the *bon ton* comes both from Marianne's City businessman husband and from her pious country-loving sister Charlotte.[256]

Amongst all the details of Marianne's family and social life, one would expect to find trips to the theatre, but apart from two passing allusions there is no mention of the stage. When the requirements of the plot lead her protagonists into morally compromising situations, Mary Ann locates them not in the theatre but at a masquerade party and at the Ranelagh pleasure garden. Prompted by Mrs Belmour but criticised by Charlotte, Marianne attends a masquerade. During the preparations she hears of the death of an old acquaintance, but cannot bring herself to excuse herself from the party, saying that not one in a hundred of her London friends would understand how she could forego the pleasures of the masquerade because of the death of an old man who was 'no way connected but by the general tie of humanity'.[257] The night of the masquerade coincides with the first dramatic episode in the novel, when Mr Clement brings home his niece to protect her from her lover and her husband. Shocked by this juxtaposition, Marianne reflects more deeply on what she has witnessed:

> I could not help wondering at Mrs. Belmour and Mrs. Colville, who are both women of sense, being so entertained with the flimsy stuff of every masquerader's brain.—Lady Bridget T—— and her two sisters were in the characters of nuns: they did not seem to have any ideas to support the appearance; but they looked handsome, and that was a sufficient reason for the choice.[258]

This may reflect Mary Ann's disenchantment with the masquerade she was taken to by Mrs Hankey,[259] and with the *flimsy stuff* of the theatre as well, but what we sense above all is the scorn of a professional actress for amateurs who have given no thought to the character they are trying to represent.

It's at Ranelagh that Amelia, Mr Clement's niece, makes an assignation with her lover Charles Mason. At first Marianne describes this in terms of the popular play, *The London Merchant*, likening Charles to the naïve George Barnwell, and Amelia to the scheming prostitute Sarah Millwood, but things are not as they seem.[260] Amelia and Charles have entered the morally dubious space of the pleasure garden, but contrary to expectations created by popular prejudice and melodrama, remain virtuous. The explanation emerges in the course of Amelia's narrative, the strongest plot line in the book, which occupies much of the second volume.

Amelia traces the origins of her predicament back to her mother's unsatisfactory upbringing and disastrous marriage. Her mother's mother is 'a very amiable woman but not possessed of any great understanding', married to a 'man of quick and transitory feelings'– clear echoes there of Mary and Jordan Costello. Cast adrift by these ill-suited parents for refusing to accept the elderly husband they had chosen for her, Amelia's mother, Miss Clement, is determined to marry Thompson, the former drawing master at her school, who now, by a lucky inheritance, has become a country gentleman. Thompson tricks and bullies her into becoming his mistress rather than his wife, as he now has his eye on a more advantageous match. A clergyman, however, forces him to fulfil his promise to marry Miss Clement.[261] Thompson turns out to be a selfish, niggardly and unscrupulous man, who tyrannises over his wife, grudges the money needed to educate his son and neglects his daughter, Amelia, until such time as she becomes a marriageable commodity, useful as a way of pursuing his own devious ends.

The bright point in Amelia's life has always been her brother William and his university friend Charles Mason. She and Charles have fallen in love. Charles wants to ask for her hand in marriage, but both Amelia and William, cautious and fearful, like the Cannings in their dealings with the arbitrary and unpredictable Stratford, persuade him that it would be madness to approach their father. Afraid that Thompson will find another suitor for Amelia, Charles insists on an informal marriage ceremony, which takes place without a parson or any witnesses except her brother and the stars above. The couple consummate the marriage, perhaps beneath the stars, an act which at the time seems natural and innocent. Immediately after the ceremony the brother is killed in a freak riding accident, and with Charles back in Cambridge Amelia is left at the mercy of her father and his plans for her marriage.[262]

The first husband he proposes is a penniless gambler, and Amelia is saved by the intervention of the family lawyer. The next is Anthony Wolfe, a young Irishman who has made a fortune in India, a man of substance, generous and sensitive – quite unlike the stereotype that the reader might have expected of a suitor who introduces himself as the third of seven children whose father was the ninth child of a gentleman of Southern Ireland.[263] Thompson hopes to sell off part of his estate to Wolfe and doesn't see why he shouldn't make a similar bargain out of his daughter. Wolfe sees the matter in the same light, exclaiming to Thompson's agent, 'She's the handsomest creature I ever saw! Why did you not tell me this? and you might have asked what you pleased for the purchase.' Amelia confesses that although her heart was already bestowed elsewhere she was pleased to know that she could excite such admiration. Attracted to Wolfe, she is almost ready to abandon Charles, but before she can make up her mind Wolfe dies of 'a nervous complaint' aggravated by the strain of suspense. Shortly before his death Wolfe makes over a substantial sum of money to Amelia, but her father spitefully throws the deed of gift in the fire, declaring, in an outburst worthy of the Abbey Street Logic, that she should not profit from the death of a man she had 'murdered'. Thompson drives Amelia from the house to take refuge with her old nurse, but his feelings suffer a reversal and he is reconciled with her after the death of his wife.[264]

Thompson now produces a third suitor, Merisford, a vulgar and uneducated beast. Amelia declares herself already married to Charles and appeals passionately to be spared a forced marriage, declaring it unnatural, and calling on her brother's 'sacred shade' to save her from it. Merisford asks what it all means, and Thompson dismisses her words contemptuously, blaming the strolling players who were recently at York.[265] Amelia's speech is undeniably 'theatrical' in style – her invocation of her brother's shade recalls the repeated prayer to the shade of Ninus in *Semiramis* – but, theatrical or not, her words do better justice to the realities of her situation than the coarse terms used by Merisford and Thompson.

As Amelia unfolds her story in letters to Marianne, episodes which seemed enigmatic or shameful in the first volume are shown to have been driven by her determination to escape from a degrading marriage, transforming the initial impression of Amelia as a fallen woman. The forced marriage is described in great detail, starting with a period of imprisonment and isolation in which she is reduced to 'violent hysterics' and loss of consciousness. When she recovers she learns that her tormentors had 'taken advantage of some of those moments when speech just anticipates sense, and joined me to Merisford and misery'. The clergyman, Mr Parfect, complacently satisfied by the form of words, declares the marriage valid. Amelia acknowledges that she is bound to Merisford by the vows extracted from her; she never 'wronged his bed'. Her eventual withdrawal from the marriage is sanctioned when Merisford finds a woman prepared to treat him more kindly, and takes her as his mistress. Having married Amelia on the basis that her marriage to Charles was invalid, Merisford now finds it convenient to take the opposite view, setting himself free to marry his mistress.[266]

These dubious transactions show the married state to be not a natural or divine dispensation, but an imperfect human institution, artificial and provisional. Both Marianne and Amelia refer to marriage without love as legalised prostitution, a point that is vividly illustrated by Merisford's offer to increase Amelia's pin-money by £100 if she can 'bring yourself to fancy me', and his willingness to share her with another man, provided she manages it discreetly.[267] Merisford is a brutal man, who beats his wife, but he's also weak and stupid, whining and wheedling, and genuinely baffled by Amelia's refusal to see things as he sees them. But however weak and pathetic, he is a man, invested by society with the power to imprison Amelia in his own narrow vision of life. As he is about to drag her back to his home she protests:

> Mr. Merisford... I never deceived you—I never will—it is out of nature for you and I to be happy—I cannot love you—I cannot obey you—the woman who can long continue a good wife to one man, whilst her wishes are all another's, must have the possession of a virtue for which I know no name—it is not patience—it is not fortitude—it is not self-denial—it is not chastity: but it is a combination of all those virtues in one. I do not possess it.—My duty is yours, if an involuntary vow can bind the free-born soul:—but my heart, my soul, my virgin-vows, were all bestowed before I saw you.[268]

Forced marriages were a common theme in eighteenth century novels and plays, and even Amelia's repudiation of the vows in the marriage service finds an echo in a highly successful new comedy, Hannah Cowley's *The Runaway*, which was performed at Drury Lane seventeen times between February and May 1776. Right at the end of the play, with three happy weddings in prospect, the subversive Bella considers the words of the marriage service: '*Love*, one might manage that perhaps – but *honour, obey* – 'tis strange the Ladies had never interest enough to get this ungallant form mended.'[269] Hannah Cowley's play shows two silly old men attempting to force their offspring into unsuitable marriages, dealing in comic mode with issues that are grittily realistic in Mary Ann's novel. The play takes for granted that the two old men are driven by a desire for family aggrandisement, a conventional and recognisable motive, suitable to drive the comic plot. In the novel, by contrast, Amelia's mean-spirited father mires himself in a series of shabby bargains in which his determination to impose his will on his daughter plays a larger part than any hope of actual profit. His treatment of his children, exercising mastery for its own sake, is as futile and baffling as old Stratford Canning's.

The novel comments bitterly upon the conventional morality which makes chastity the beginning and end of female virtue. Like Mary Ann herself, Amelia has 'fallen', has succumbed to her passion for Charles Mason. Charles blames himself for seducing her, but Amelia does not base her own claim for compassion on a plea of having been forced or deceived by him; she accepts her own fault, but nonetheless claims pure and virtuous intentions: 'we loved each other; and, conscious as we were of having no intentions but such as were prompted by nature, and warranted by innocence and virtue, we indulged them without restraint,' she writes.[270] We can detect here the influence of Mary Ann's husband George and his lectures on 'those sources of inexpressible delight: our sympathetick Hearts'.

Amelia knows all about the cruelty of virtuous women:

> Had you treated me with that conscious superiority which unblemished virtue entitled you to, [she writes to Marianne] and which will always appear where the virtues of generosity and social sympathy are not as powerful as that of chastity; I should, perhaps, have revered you for the possession of the latter, but the want of the former would have made reverence alone all the tribute I should pay.[271]

A generous woman, a woman of 'true and unaffected virtue' might be wise enough to keep her virtue unblemished, but she will be slow to condemn others. In years to come Mary Ann would read this argument in Mary Wollstonecraft's *Vindication of the Rights of Woman* and, later again, she would make the same plea most eloquently on her own behalf in her Packet.

The theme of the novel is the theme of Mary Ann's own life: the vulnerability of women in a man's world. Mary Ann accepts that it is a man's world. She doesn't dispute the right of fathers, husbands or even brothers to determine women's lives. That is the way things are – more grandiosely, it's the natural order – but she demonstrates vividly the consequences that follow when this power is placed in the hands of men who are too weak, stupid, selfish or narrow-minded to use it with wisdom, moderation and generosity.

She shows too that when women are let down by the men they have trusted, their inadequate education leaves them unable to take charge of their own affairs. Even those who have skills and talents are prevented from using them by principles of perverted sentiment. Amelia refers to a married man who 'in circumstances where common honesty called for every exertion of their talents for the support of their family, refused to suffer [his wife] to obtain, by a laudable use of hers, a very considerable sum, lest other men should impertinently fall in love with her.'[272] This comment, which is not altogether in character for the diffident Amelia, is in the voice of Mary Ann defending the rights of female performers, and is almost certainly an allusion to Sheridan's refusal to allow Elizabeth to sing in public after their marriage.

The Offspring of Fancy was published in the first half of 1778, anonymously, the author described as 'a Lady'. It was noticed by the literary reviews. Tobias Smollett's *Critical Review* noted superciliously that it was a passable novel for anyone looking merely to be entertained who preferred variety to excellence, but criticised it for having 'neither regularity of design, nor attention to embellishment, as is necessary to give the stamp of genius to a literary production'. The *Monthly Review* made the same points, complaining of 'too much confusion in the plan and negligence in the execution'. The least unfavourable notice appeared in the *London Review of English and Foreign Literature*: 'Fancy is so very prolific in this fantastical age, that very few of its offspring are worth notice. We have met, however, with worse *effusions* of *fancy*, than this novel teems with.'[273] This is faint praise, but words like *effusions* and *teems* do suggest something of the quality of Mary Ann's writing. Mary Ann escaped the still harsher treatment given to *The History of Melinda Harper*, which *The Critical Review* described as good only for inducing sleep. Reviews of novels in these magazines were more often scathing than complimentary, and were particularly patronising towards women writers – the sleep-inducing author was advised by the *Monthly Review* to stick to her needle. The criticisms of the design and structure of the *Offspring* are justifiable, but there is skill in the way the mystery surrounding Amelia is built up in the first volume and gradually resolved in the second. The reviews say nothing about the novel's positive virtues, the intelligence and vitality of the writing and the variety and sharpness of the characterisation.

All this time Mary Ann was still living in the house in Bloomsbury, with Mrs Costello still at war with Reddish. There was just the one child now, little Samuel. Esther was over twenty and able to take on much of the running of the household, and perhaps earn something to contribute to her own and her mother's upkeep. Mary Ann therefore had the leisure to consider a new career as a writer. It was a time when publishers were willing to experiment with new authors, knowing that there was an expanding demand, particularly, as *The Monthly Review* put it, among female readers with many tedious hours to beguile. Even so, it's surprising how easily Mary Ann found a publisher for her first effort; she may have had contacts and supporters in the bookselling world, which would be a measure of how far, despite her failures at Drury Lane, she had managed to acquire what she described to Lady Nuneham as a 'publick character'.

We don't know how straightforward Mary Ann found the task of writing. In the four years since she assured the Duchess of Ancaster that writing a novel would be entirely beyond her, she had learned much about language and dialogue, and how to create an effect and construct a plot. From what little she says about the experience, it sounds as though ideas came to her easily enough. She composed the first letter in an hour or so, and the whole thing was completed in barely two months. Writing in her own informal manner, as her heroine Marianne wrote, may have been relatively effortless, but the formal prose of the other characters' letters was more demanding, although the rapidly composed 'Injured Woman' letters show that grammatically correct writing came to her readily enough. It might seem surprising, therefore, that *The Offspring of Fancy* was to be her only novel. Its plot is probably its weakest element, so perhaps she just found it too difficult to construct another one.

She may also have been discouraged by the dismissive tone of the reviews. Perhaps her experience in *Semiramis* made her less resilient than usual, less able to brush off the hostility of critics and learn from her mistakes. But the most likely reason for not following up with another work of fiction is that *The Offspring of Fancy* had fulfilled its main purpose. The original motive for taking up her pen had been therapeutic, to help her get over the accumulated shock of losing George, the *Semiramis* disaster and the death of little James. The therapy worked. By the middle of May she was ready to contemplate a return to the stage.

8.
Ireland, 1777–78

Reddish performed regularly through that winter and spring, but by May 1777 he was so disgusted with the behaviour of the Drury Lane management towards both himself and Mary Ann that he insisted on terminating his contract. For Mary Ann it was too early to judge whether novel-writing would yield enough to live on, and her needs were urgent. Reddish was willing and able to provide for her and their child, and he left his financial affairs entirely in Mary Ann's hands, but given the animosity between him and her mother she was unwilling to divert any of his money to support her own family. During the hopeful time when she thought she was established at Drury Lane, Mary Ann had promised to send a guinea a month to her father, who was fretting away on his cousin's estate in County Mayo. By now the flow of guineas had long run dry, and Jordan had come across to join Mrs Costello and Esther in London. Mary Ann made up her mind to return to the only paid work she knew, but not wanting to influence Reddish she said nothing until he had committed himself to leaving Drury Lane. When he signed up with Thomas Ryder, whose company was based at the Theatre Royal, Crow Street in Dublin and also made summer tours to Cork and Limerick, she decided to go with him. She had no regular contract, but it was understood that she would take any suitable part that came along.[274]Ryder was a good manager to work for in every respect except one: he was notoriously unreliable about money.[i]

Sheridan was annoyed to be losing Reddish who, for all his faults, was popular with the public and a versatile member of the company. Mary Ann, shrewdly looking after his affairs, thwarted what sounds like a plot on the part of the management to stop him leaving London. Despite her efforts over the last three years, he still owed the theatre £176. Most of it was liquidated by giving up his benefit night to Sheridan, who was keen to buy up nights in order to maximise his own profits from his new play, *The School for Scandal.* The treasurer suggested Reddish should let the rest run on until he got back from Ireland. Mary Ann insisted on paying off the whole debt, and felt vindicated when it emerged that arrest had been imminent. She, or his creditors, also persuaded him that as they were going away for an indefinite period he should sell his household goods, including his books and wines, his reflecting telescope, fortepiano and spring clock.[275]

Before setting off for Ireland Mary Ann found a home for her parents, Esther and young Samuel. For a while Esther kept up relations with the family in Clements Lane, and although by the time George went to Eton he had lost her address, these early contacts laid the foundation for his lifelong affection for his aunt.[276]

Mary Ann and Reddish left for Ireland in late May 1777, so only caught the tail end of the season at Dublin's Crow Street theatre. Reddish opened with *Venice Preserved* on 17 June, the advertisements declaring it his first appearance in Dublin for ten years. During June and early July Mary Ann appeared in several of her regular roles, starting with Monimia in *The Orphan*, when she was billed as 'from the Theatre Royal in Drury Lane, being her first appearance in this Kingdom', and continuing with Lady Townly in *The Provok'd Husband* and Harriet in *The Guardian.* She

i Thomas Ryder (1735–1791): actor and manager of the Crow Street Theatre, Dublin, 1772–1782. His *ODNB* entry makes no mention of his controlling the theatre in Cork, but Mary Ann in the Packet says that Reddish 'closed with Rider for Dublin, Corke and Limerick'. For anecdotes about Ryder see W.C. Oulton, *History of the Theatres of London*, ii. 94-99 and Bernard, i. 299.

also played what was for her the new part of Charlotte Rusport in Richard Cumberland's *The West Indian.*[277]

Towards the end of *The Orphan*, Reddish, playing Castalio, accidentally stabbed Polydore, played by a Mr Smith, in the side. The story was reported in a 'Letter from Dublin' in a Bristol newspaper, feeding an appetite there for discreditable stories about Reddish, but there's no reason to suppose the accident was his fault rather than Smith's.[i] Presumably it happened at the moment when Polydore runs onto Castalio's sword. They were both experienced actors, familiar with the play, so the mishap was probably due to their not having rehearsed together. Smith's injury was not grave; he was back on the stage by the following week. The incident did not damage Reddish's relations with the other actors and seems to have had no effect on his own delicate mental balance. He continued with a punishing schedule; in addition to his appearances with Mary Ann, in the last week of June he played Osman in Aaron Hill's *Zara,* and Romeo.[278]

There is a story that the Abbey Street Cannings tried to organise a boycott of Mary Ann's performances, but this sounds unlikely. Perhaps they spread malicious gossip, or tried to fan the professional antagonism that Reddish incurred wherever he went, but there's no sign that it had any material effect on the theatregoers of Dublin – the Lord Lieutenant evidently saw no reason not to attend the *The West Indian.* The only problem was getting Ryder to pay the actors' salaries on time. In this respect Mary Ann herself was better off; being employed on a casual basis she received payment for each appearance out of the night's takings.[279]

In July they moved south to Cork, opening their campaign early in August with two performances of *The Provok'd Husband*, the second being for the benefit of the House of Industry, the charitably funded precursor to the workhouse.[280] Theatres everywhere tended to support charities with benefit performances, and the Irish theatres seem to have been particularly generous in this respect. Other causes supported while Mary Ann was in Ireland were relief for

i This Mr Smith was not William 'Gentleman' Smith who had been a colleague at Drury Lane.

imprisoned debtors, and help for an officer's widow with a large family to support. Then as now charity was good publicity, and it was also a way for the stage to assert its respectability, but there's no need to be too cynical about it. Theatrical people were sometimes seen as outcasts, and they kept themselves apart because of the exacting discipline of their profession, but they remained by and large functioning members of the community.

The Reddishes would remain in Cork for more than two months, with an excursion in September to Limerick during which Thomas Arne and his wife arranged charitable concerts in the cathedral in Cork.[281] On reaching a new town there were people to see and arrangements to make. The leaders of opinion had to be squared – the landlords of the major inns, the magistrates, the doctors, the auctioneers, the booksellers, and above all the printer of the local newspaper. Ryder and his associate Tottenham Heaphy had ambitious plans for the Cork season, and ensured extensive publicity in the form of playbills and carefully planted stories about the magnificence of the productions to come – so many hundred coloured lights, a storm scene showing all the workings of a ship of war in distress, or a new musical entertainment called *The Coopers* with a view of a dry cooper's workshop in operation.[282] They encouraged interest in their production of Sheridan's new work *The Duenna* by letting it be known that the author had issued an injunction forbidding unauthorised performances, but adding that since the 'disagreeable order of injunction' had not yet reached Cork the play would go on. The story of the injunction may have been exaggerated to stimulate interest in the production and divert attention from the inferiority of the pirated version.[283]

For his benefit night on 6 October Reddish appeared as Richard III with Mary Ann as Queen Elizabeth. She may have played the part in her unhappy 1776 season in Bristol, but the advertisement improved on this by claiming she had played it in London. The night's entertainment was to open with an address to the ladies and gentlemen of Cork, spoken by Mr Reddish, and also include a 'humorous Satirical Dissertation on Hobby Horses to be spoken by Mr Moss' and Arthur Murphy's comedy *The Way to Keep Him*, with Mary Ann as the Widow Belmour. A few days after the first announcement a further paragraph appeared in which Reddish admitted that he could have presented a 'much longer Bill', but could not have selected 'any pieces for the reputable performance of which he could so confidently answer'. On the night he may have been disappointed by the 'thinness of the Boxes', which a paragraph next day attributed to an 'engagement in which a great part of the citizens were concerned'.[284]

The newspaper where these theatrical announcements appeared almost daily, *The Hibernian Chronicle*, was in the hands of an important local figure, William Flyn, bookseller 'at the sign of Shakespeare'.[i] He had a range of business interests: he was local agent for the National Lottery, and, like many printers and booksellers, sold patent medicines; he was also prominent in local affairs and charities, such as the relief of debtors. Actors handled their own publicity, particularly in the days leading up to their benefit night, and when there was a problem over paying for printing the playbills, whether because of Reddish's extravagance or Ryder's irregularity, it fell to Mary Ann to sort out the problem. She went down to the newspaper office to negotiate with Flyn, who proved accommodating.[285] It was thirteen years since Mary Ann had left Ireland, almost half her lifetime, but she made sure he was aware of her Irish origin. She got on well with him, as she usually did with intelligent, forceful men.

For her own benefit night Mary Ann chose to play the self-sacrificing Eleonora in James Thomson's sentimental *Edward and Eleonora*. The play was written in 1739 but banned under the Licensing Act and not given a licence until it was adapted and produced at Covent Garden in March 1775.[ii] Without the

i William Flyn (1740–1811) is a good example of the Catholic businessmen who, though excluded from the civic government, were the dominant element in the commercial life of eighteenth century Cork (R.F. Foster, *Modern Ireland* 211).

ii James Thomson (1700–1748) is best known for his poems *The Seasons*. *Edward and Eleonora* (1739) was the second play to fall foul of the 1737 Licensing Act. The text edge of contemporary polemic which led to the ban in 1739, it is lacking in incident and provides, as one of the 1775 reviewers pointed out, only scanty materials for a five-act tragedy. Prince Edward, leader of the crusader army, is stabbed with a poisoned dagger by an Assassin, acting under the orders of the Old Man of the Mountains, and is saved by his wife Eleonora, who sucks out the poison, believing that she must die in the attempt. After a protracted dying scene, and an equally long scene in which Edward refuses to be comforted for his loss, Eleonora is cured by the Saracen chief Selim (played by Reddish), who comes to the English camp in disguise, bringing the antidote. Eleonora's great act of devotion, the sucking out of the poison, takes place while Edward is asleep at the end of the second act. Thomson supplies no accompanying words, so it either happens offstage or, more probably in dumb-show. The advertisement promised that a 'very favourite song' would be performed at this point in the drama. The tragedy was followed by an occasional address by Reddish, and Garrick's afterpiece *The Guardian*, in which Mary Ann played her usual role of Harriet which, as the advertisement stated correctly this time, she had taken two years before at Drury Lane.[286]

Despite the thinness of the drama in *Edward and Eleonora*, Thomson draws from the story a powerful lesson about reason and tolerance, invoking the 'ruling Wisdom' that has made men different from each other, with different opinions. Edward, reminded by his and Eleonora's narrow escape of the bloodshed caused over the centuries by the bigotry of the crusades, repents of his 'mistaken Zeal', and Selim draws the play to a close:

> Let Holy Rage, let Persecution cease;
> Let the Head argue, but the Heart be Peace;
> Let all Mankind in Love of what is right,
> In Virtue and Humanity unite.

---

was adapted for the 1775 performance by Thomas Hull, who heightened the pathos by introducing Eleonora's children into the dying scene.

Whether or not Mary Ann chose the play for political reasons, the application of this message to Ireland in 1777 was clear. From childhood experience of her parents' quarrels Mary Ann was aware of the religious strife that divided Irish society;[287] now it may have seemed that reconciliation was in the air. The following year Parliament would repeal some of the most flagrant of the penal laws against the Catholic majority, and so begin the cruelly protracted process of unpicking the system of oppression imposed by the Protestant Ascendancy. Mary Ann's acquaintance William Flyn embodied the hopeful possibilities of reconciliation. A Catholic, he was excluded from the official organs of power in Cork, but he had nonetheless established himself as a substantial and influential figure in the city through charitable activity and his publishing and bookselling business.[288] We can't know how far, if at all, Mary Ann discussed the politics of tolerance with Flyn, but it would have been in character for her to do so. One thing we know she talked to him about was *The Offspring of Fancy*. He asked for fifty copies to sell on her behalf.

After several 'last nights' in Cork the company returned to the Crow Street theatre in Dublin. Later in her life, as she travelled by coach between the West of England and London, Mary Ann was to take close notice of the state of agriculture and the plight of the farm workers, recording her observations in letters to her son. Perhaps she used her time on the road between Dublin and Cork, and between Cork and Limerick, to observe the wretched state of the Irish countryside. But she left no record of her time in Ireland beyond her brief account of her theatrical activities and her dealings with William Flyn. One of the unanswered questions about Mary Ann is what she felt about her Irish origins. Her years with her grandfather in Wigmore Street, and her intimacy with the Duchess of Ancaster, had given her a taste for metropolitan refinement and a fastidious dislike of such Irish practices as sharing a bed with another woman. Her Dublin childhood had been clouded by poverty and religious wrangling. Since her marriage,

Ireland had been associated above all with the sinister hostility of the Canning family in Abbey Street. Perhaps she had little reason to think kindly of her native land, but it's impossible to be sure.

Reddish played a succession of tragic roles at Crow Street during the winter and spring, including Osman in *Zara*, Achmet in *Barbarossa* by John Browne, Hastings in *Jane Shore* (with Jane played by yet another young lady making her first appearance on any stage) and several appearances as Richard III and Macbeth. He also played some of the comic parts from his Drury Lane repertory, such as Townly in *The Provok'd Husband* and Sir Charles Easy in *The Careless Husband*, both perennially popular pieces by Colley Cibber. When he had last played Sir Charles at Drury Lane six years earlier, the part of Lady Graveairs had been taken by Polly Hart, the then Mrs Reddish. His appearances were largely confined to mainpieces, but he took his regular Drury Lane character of Heartley in *The Guardian* when it was presented as the afterpiece following *The Governess*, the title by which Ryder's version of *The Duenna* was advertised.[289]

In December, Mary Ann's daughter Mary was born. As a young woman Mary would take the name of her stepfather, Richard Hunn, leading to confusion over her date of birth, but the evidence in the Packet is clear, and unlike Mrs Costello Mary Ann was not likely to make a mistake. Following her confinement Mary Ann's first appearance was on 10 March, as Queen Eltruda in Reddish's benefit performance of Thomson's masque *King Alfred*. She employed a local woman as wet nurse, who then accompanied the family when they left Ireland in the early summer.[290] Mary Ann makes only fleeting references to her servants, so we can't be certain, but this Irishwoman may be the servant known only as Dennis who was still with Mary Ann fifty years later.

Mary Ann played Monimia in *The Orphan* at the end of March; this time Reddish and Smith managed to fight without mishap. Although she had only appeared twice in the season she was granted a benefit on 21 April. Her first plan was to revive Rowe's

Tamerlane, but soon changed her mind in favour of something less ambitious, Arthur Murphy's comedy *All in the Wrong*. Her night included an interlude of music from *Alfred*, and a new farce, *The Man of Quality*, based on an old play, Vanbrugh's *The Relapse*. The advertisements emphasised that the local favourite Thomas Ryder would have a prominent part in both plays.[291] Taking advantage of her public character, Mary Ann inserted the following beneath each of the newspaper announcements of her benefit night:

> Mrs Reddish takes the opportunity of informing her friends and the public of this her native city, that in consequence of their many obliging demands, she has ordered from London a new importation of *The Offspring of Fancy*…

She had made the same arrangement with James Potts, printer of *Saunders's News-Letter*, that she had with William Flyn in Cork.

The tour of Ireland had been a success, and the Reddishes crossed the sea to Scotland feeling unusually prosperous. Mary Ann would have liked to remain in Ireland, but Reddish said he had already opened negotiations with Covent Garden. London was still where he could command the best price for his talents, and if they based themselves there he would try to secure an engagement for her and she would have access to provincial centres, where she had proved herself successful. He also reminded her of the difficulties he had experienced with Ryder over payment of his salary. True to his promise to put Mary Ann's interests first, he said he would go back to Ireland with her if she insisted, but she would not accept such a sacrifice.[292]

After a brief and lucrative Scottish tour, they returned to London to ratify arrangements with Covent Garden, and settle the affairs of the family. The Irish earnings more than covered the debts incurred by her parents and sister during her absence. Reddish had arranged engagements in Plymouth for the rest of the summer. The new baby and her nurse stayed in London with Mrs Costello, while Esther and Samuel, now three or four years old, accompanied Mary Ann to Plymouth.[293] In five weeks Mary

Ann confirmed the good impression she had made there two years before.

They were back in London in time for the winter season. One of the first things Mary Ann did on her return was to take delivery of her hundred copies of her novel and send supplies to Flyn in Cork and Potts in Dublin. For three months at the end of 1778 notices appeared prominently in Flyn's *Hibernian Chronicle* announcing *The Offspring of Fancy*, by 'an Irish Lady'.

9.
Hamlet and Posthumus, 1778–79

Despite his year's absence Reddish remained a popular name in London, and Thomas Hull at Covent Garden was happy to sign him up at a salary of twelve guineas a week, more than he had been getting from Garrick and Sheridan. Mary Ann budgeted to live on six guineas, putting the other six towards slowly paying off Reddish's remaining debts. They could afford to take a good house in Bow Street, close to the theatre.[294] Having no wish to make another attempt on the London stage, she now permitted Reddish to contribute to the upkeep of her parents and sister. As the consort of one of the leading actors of the age, and with a good chance of summer employment for herself in Plymouth, her prospects were better than at any time since the death of her husband. With two small children, Sam aged four and baby Mary, she was once more pregnant.

Hull didn't make use of Reddish for the first few weeks of the season, allowing anticipation to build up before his appearance as Hamlet, a role he had not previously played in London. Much is made of the professional jealousy of actors and the cruelty of audiences, but the reality is that a play is a collaborative enterprise for the actors, while the audiences are eager to be pleased, so when Reddish stepped onto the stage old differences were forgotten and everyone in the vast auditorium was willing him to succeed. A sympathetic reviewer recalled that an actor's first attempt at Hamlet was a formidable challenge, worse than making one's debut. Mary Ann was ill and could not be present, but a friend told her that the audience welcomed him as a 'restored favorite' with 'torrents of applause'.[295]

But when it came to the climax of the duel scene, disaster struck, something far more serious than the mishap in Dublin. John Whitfield,[i] the actor playing Laertes, injured Reddish not in his body but where it hurt him worse, in his pride and dignity: with a careless thrust of his rapier he whipped off Hamlet's wig. The audience now dissolved in laughter as high tragedy collapsed into low farce. It would be humiliating at any time to lose one's wig in this way, but in the 1770s fashions in headgear had gone to absurd extremes and wigs were a particular target for low farce – the comedian Samuel Foote having recently caused the king and queen themselves to 'laugh immoderately' when in one of his cross-dressing roles he had lost his extravagant headdress.[296] Habit and professionalism enabled Reddish to carry on to the end, but not to banish the farcical mood or restore the dignity of the action.

Always hypersensitive to audience reactions – 'professional vanity was his weakest place'[297] – Reddish nonetheless set about preparing for his next performance, in his favourite role of Posthumus, but on the morning of the performance the servant noticed that something was wrong. When Mary Ann went to him she found 'He was lost – he knew not anything we said to him – denied the fact of his being to play that night'. All day he continued in a state 'of almost inanity'. Remembering that after the death of her husband it had been her baby George who had restored her to life, Mary Ann called on the nurse to bring Mary to her father. Reddish smiled; they were hopeful; but then he asked weakly, 'Whose little angel are you?' They took him out in a carriage for fresh air, but to no avail. Thomas Hull, who had

---

i John Whitfield (1752–1814) was a long-serving actor who regularly played subordinate characters like Laertes, and was known for his ability to prepare a part at short notice. Mary Ann was to come across him later on in Exeter (*BDA*, xvi. 39-43).

been an apothecary before becoming an actor and was regarded as an oracle on medical matters, was called in, took one look at the patient, diagnosed poisoning and recommended an emetic.[298] He then hurried off to find another actor to take Reddish's place, and to reconcile an angry audience to the loss of a favourite player in his most popular role. William Brereton[i] of Drury Lane, having played the part twice the previous season, agreed to take it on.[299]

Dr Jebb, now Sir Richard, considered the case all but hopeless, but so long as the barest possibility of a cure remained he continued daily attendance at the patient's bedside. Mary Ann remembered with gratitude his devotion, particularly, perhaps, because it encouraged the management to anticipate a rapid cure. For a month they paid Reddish's salary, but then regretfully informed Mary Ann that the payments would have to cease until Jebb could hold out definite hope of recovery.[300]

At this point Mary Ann went into labour and after thirty hours gave birth to a sickly boy, little Charles Reddish. She was too ill to suckle and he was too weak to drink even from Hugh Smith's patent infant-feeding bottle. Mary's affectionate Irish nurse saved his life by taking him to her bounteous bosom, as Mary Ann gratefully recalled – comparing this generous Irishwoman with her other servant, a Scotswoman, who chose to desert the family at the height of their troubles. Mary Ann herself was seriously ill, but her surgeon Dr Bromfield pulled her through.[301]

She immediately set about another retrenchment. She now had the invalid Reddish, three children, a servant and her parents and sister to maintain, and her total resources were five guineas and a few odd shillings. It was the third time since her marriage that she had sold up her household furnishings and moved to cheaper accommodation. She took lodgings on Tottenham Court Road, close to where Esther and Mrs Costello had lived with George a few years earlier. As she was making these arrangements she was warmed by three incidents which proved that her world was not

i William Brereton (c.1751–1787) was married to Priscilla Hopkins. In the 1780s he became infatuated with Sarah Siddons, and died in the Hoxton lunatic asylum.

entirely hostile. The first was Dr Bromfield's generous waiving of his fee for his assiduous attendance during her confinement and illness. Next William Flyn sent a first payment of £7 10s from sales of her novel in Cork. Finally, she was visited by one of the actors from Drury Lane with an offer from the theatre's benevolent fund to pay Reddish a pension of £70 a year.[i] The immediate crisis was solved, therefore, but £70 would not maintain her and all her dependants. She would have to work.[302]

She and Reddish had arranged to return to Plymouth for the summer; now she wrote to the management to explain that Reddish could no longer fulfil his engagement, and was surprised to be told she would be welcome in her own right. But still, there were new and old debts to be paid before she could leave London, and she would have to find the costs of the journey into the West Country, as well as provision for her family during her absence. Without this, she couldn't take up the Plymouth offer. Miraculously, as winter turned to spring, Reddish's condition seemed to improve. Friends began to think he might return to the stage, even if for just one last benefit night. Mary Ann approached Thomas Harris, Hull's partner at Covent Garden, and eventually he agreed to give her a night in the first week of May. He was less confident than Mary Ann about Reddish's capacity. Reddish himself was reluctant, but Mary Ann coaxed him to make this final effort. She rehearsed three of his Shakespearean roles, Romeo, Richard III and Posthumus, and found he was most proficient as Posthumus. Mary Ann was assured by the Fund committee that Reddish's annuity would be unaffected by a single performance.[303]

Harris asked Mary Ann to name her play, and she chose *Cymbeline*. He offered her the part of Imogen, but she didn't want to jeopardise things by raising the spectre of the past. In any case she had enough to do to manage Reddish – in a reversal of roles, she was now coaching him. A cast was gathered which included

---

i A Theatrical Fund for the benefit of impoverished old and infirm actors was established at Covent Garden in 1765, and at Drury Lane the following year. Both funds were secured by Act of Parliament in 1776 (Hogan, vol. i p. cxxxiv).

William Smith from Drury Lane as Iachimo, old animosities forgotten in the crisis. Reddish's demeanour on the day led to much apprehension, but the performance went as well as ever.

> Smith declared that in one Scene with him, Posthumus never play'd so well!— yet it is a certain Fact, that during the whole of the Night — the poor unhappy Being who was perhaps for my Sake upheld & supported by Superior power — was quite unconscious of the cause which brought him there — did not know it was his own Benefit — nay at several different times during the representation was unconscious the part he was playing and, even supposed he was Acting Romeo! — perhaps a Circumstance so wonderfull in the History of Insanity never was heard of, nor may again?[304]

Like Mary Ann's *Semiramis* disaster, the story of Reddish's final appearance found a place in theatrical legend. It was described in 1786 by one of Reddish's friends, John Ireland,[i] to illustrate his contention that when an actor's understanding fails nature can take over.[305] To make his point Ireland may have exaggerated the extent and depth of Reddish's delusion, and Mary Ann, always ready to dramatise a situation, may possibly have allowed her memory to be influenced by his account, but what has a clearly authentic ring is her real anxiety, her sense that a 'Superior power' was sustaining Reddish for her sake. Reddish's share of the takings was £180, which was just enough for Mary Ann's purposes. As soon as she had settled her family she and Reddish set out for the West. Jebb recommended sea bathing for Reddish's condition.[306]

Mary Ann's departure represented capitulation and recognition that she was never going to succeed on the London stage, not in 'first rate style' as she had hoped, nor in any style at all. Her great gamble had not come off. After almost six years, her future was as uncertain as when she had discussed it with the Duchess – it was worse, because she was on her own, her patroness having

i John Ireland (1742–1808): poet and writer about the theatre, known for his store of literary anecdotes.

moved on to new hobbies, new protégées. Mary Ann faced at best the drudgery and obscurity of the provincial theatre; at worst the squalid and dangerous life of a strolling player.

But she described herself as having in her nature a 'predisponent cause to happiness',[307] a resilience in the face of misfortune. As she rattled along in the Winchester coach with Reddish at her side and five-year-old Sam between them, she could look back on the last six years and find some consolation. In 1773, when she played opposite the great Garrick, innocently hoping for a glorious career, she had known nothing; now, even if she was to be neither a second Mrs Cibber nor, like Mary Robinson, a Prince's mistress, she was an experienced actress, with a solid grounding in the craft, able to play the leading women in many of the standard works in the repertory. She had fallen under the spell of Reddish, a man whose talent, looks, charm and vulnerability prompted a passionate response from her sympathetic heart. Her love for him may not have survived the realisation that he was weak and boastful and, like all the men she ever depended on, utterly undependable, but she had held fast to him, nursed him through a succession of crises, and sorted out his chaotic finances. In return he had helped her to acquire whatever skill she possessed. Now the father of her three children (and she was already pregnant with a fourth), he was completely dependent on her, pensioned off, half-crazy. She was no longer an impressionable girl, but a determined and mature woman.

She was to break her westward journey in Winchester in order to visit George at his school.[308] The loss of George was one failure that even her predisposition to happiness could not disguise. The original agreement that she could have him with her during part of his holidays had been quietly dropped, and she had not seen him since before the *Semiramis* debacle.

10.
Such a Portion of Romance, 1776–1782

So far as is known, George made the transition from Bloomsbury to Clements Lane easily enough, but who can tell what went through a six-year-old's mind? We have only two glimpses into his life before 1776. One is a fictional account that he wrote towards the end of his time at Eton, describing a chaotic early education, and the other is a passing reference, in a letter of 1800, to a Mrs Agnes Thompson, one of his father's creditors: 'we were great friends when I was four years old'. Before the adoption became official he had been used to his mother's absences, and to spending time in Clements Lane. Since he was almost immediately sent off to Hyde Abbey School in Winchester he may not have realised how completely and irrevocably he had been removed from his mother's care. Stratty and Mehitabel neither helped nor hindered his attempts to keep in touch by letter, but they told him nothing, except that his mother was a stage actress, travelling the country, and couldn't afford to look after him. As the years passed and the separation stretched on, nothing was said about the reasons for it. He was afraid to probe the mystery.[309]

Stratty and Mehitabel's second child, Bessy, who was born around the time George arrived in Clements Lane, would always be his favourite cousin. There was an elder brother, Harry, born in 1774, and a younger, William, born in 1778. Two further brothers, Charles and Stratford, would come later, in 1783 and 1786. George was fond of them, but felt at a remove from them, if only because he was older. He had brothers and a sister of his own, but he wasn't allowed to see them, or even speak of them. He longed to kiss them, he told his mother,[310] which suggests that he watched Bessy kissing her little brother and envied his cousins. Did he join in the kissing and, if not, did he himself shrink from such intimacy, or was a barrier placed in his way?

The Cannings of Clements Lane were sociable. Dick Weld was still a regular visitor; George liked him, and remembered him fondly.[311] From the sparse testimony concerning his childhood George seems to have been studious and old for his years, so he may sometimes have found Mehitabel's household uncongenial, with young children and a good deal of hot-cockle sport. Mehitabel must have been irritated by a superciliousness in her nephew that recalled her old brushes with Mary Ann. She also noted his inclination to argue, to defend and justify himself in the face of criticism,[312] a character trait that time would only accentuate. Although he was never less than grateful towards Mehitabel, he found Stratty's sister Bess Percival more sympathetic. She was a widow with a daughter, Letitia, and was soon to marry an easy-going and well-to-do clergyman called William Leigh. Mr Leigh had contacts with university men and members of Parliament; he kept a curate and lived the life of a country gentleman. From mid-teens onward George chose to spend his holidays with the Leighs.

The Packet gives an unsympathetic and one-sided view of Mehitabel, portraying her as provincial and vulgar, and alleging that she had tried to alienate George from his mother while promoting a match between him and her daughter Bess. Mary Ann admitted to being prejudiced, conceding, 'in justice to a Woman whom I have no reason to love', that at least Mehitabel had done nothing to justify her father-in-law in disinheriting Stratty for marrying her.[313] A more balanced and attractive picture emerges from Giles Hunt's biography of Mehitabel. Mary Ann, for example, complained bitterly that Mehitabel, while condemning her affair with Reddish, was indulgent towards her friend Elizabeth Sheridan's affair with Lord Edward Fitzgerald, but Hunt shows that Mehitabel was indeed troubled by Elizabeth's adultery. Their friendship was broken off, and only resumed when Sheridan himself begged Mehitabel to give comfort to his wife, who was now dying of consumption.[314] Hunt describes Mehitabel as strong, practical and down to earth, a staunch Whig and a convinced Christian, a 'redoubtable woman'; the family letters in his book show her to have been intelligent, humorous and tolerant. It's hard to say how well she played the part of mother substitute in young George's life. Was her tactless reference to Sam Reddish as a player's brat an aberration, caused by some momentary irritation, or part of a recurrent pattern throughout George's childhood? George retained his affection for the family he grew up in, even if he never treated Mehitabel with the easy confidence that marked his dealings with the Leighs.

In Clements Lane George picked up his politics from the conversation of Stratty and Whig friends, such as Richard Weld – big ideas like constitutional reform or the abolition of slavery, and more specific controversies to do with commercial law and Irish trade.[i] Stratty had no time for royalty, and this, combined with a study of Roman history, led George towards the mild republicanism for which he would be known at Eton and Oxford.[315] Politics apart, there were other words that the young George will have heard as he listened to the talk in Clements Lane – Nature, Feeling, Duty, Reason – words which were used in those days by thinking people to make sense of their lives. How was he to apply them to his own predicament? Did he feel the natural affection of a son

i Stratty joined the Society for Constitutional Information, was treasurer of a fund to support the Whigs in legal actions following the 1784 election, and acted as steward for a dinner of the Benevolent Society of St Patrick (*Parker's General Advertiser*, 11 July 1783; *Morning Chronicle*, 22 Feb., 15 Mar. 1785). He was London agent for the Irish State Lottery, and a director of the Royal Exchange Assurance (*Morning Chronicle*, 29 May 1783; *Public Advertiser*, 5 July 1783). His friend Richard Weld was a public opponent of the American war and supported American prisoners (*London Evening Post*, 14 Oct., 27 Dec. 1777). See Hunt, 51–2.

for his mother, and if not could reason and duty create a feeling where none arose naturally? Was it unnatural to feel more for his Aunt Bess Leigh than for his mother? Was it his duty to follow the rational injunctions of his uncle and benefactor, or should nature be his guide? Should he not consult, if he could, the beliefs of his dead father and the feelings of his absent mother?

He seldom mentioned Mehitabel to his mother, but he told her about his aunt Bess Percival, later Bess Leigh, and in return asked repeatedly the names and ages of those he still called his brothers and sister. He sent his love to them and to his Aunt Esther, and asked for his grandmother's address.[316] He had one family in Clements Lane; he could talk to them, laugh with them, learn to make their ways his own. And there were the others, his mother's family, whom he could neither see nor talk to, nor touch and kiss.

In a letter of 1782, shortly before George left Hyde Abbey for Eton, Mary Ann made her feelings clear enough, although one wonders how far the twelve-year-old was able to understand and sympathise.

> How shall I find words to convey to thee, [she wrote] my precious child, the gratification of a mother's best expectations? How tell thee what raptures even thy anxious *wish* to see me can bestow? Doubt not, my Life, we shall meet; that Power whose gift alone such filial virtues are; that God, who gave thee at first to my fond maternal bosom, will one day restore thee to its throbbing wishes, its often repeated prayers! When it will please His divine mercy and wisdom to permit me to be so blest, He only knows; but I feel a full and perfect confidence in the fact, and wait His time with resignation![317]

In later life George would be quick to repulse with humour and irony any excessive show of emotion. He learned, if not at once, then certainly by the time his childhood was over, that such an outpouring of love contained a demand for something in return, a demand he was unwilling or unable to meet.

Looking back in 1799 he recalled the confusion in his mind:

> I maintained a constant correspondence with her, yet, as She of course, was silent upon the subject, and as I dreaded to enquire of any body else into the causes of our separation, I had no other idea concerning her, than that she was in misery, and I unable to relieve her. And as our correspondence (though I have not the least doubt it was in fact known and permitted all along) had to me an air of mystery and clandestineness, I had mixed up in my feelings towards her such a portion of romance, as if it had not been corrected and subdued by subsequent reflection, would have led me to fly to her as to my natural home, at any moment when my Uncle's authority over me was removed.[318]

As he grew up, he swung from one extreme to another, at one time sorry for himself, unsure who he was and where he fitted in, at another overwhelmed with pity for his mother as she struggled amidst unimaginable hardships, at another intrigued by the mystery and romance of her life – and all the while capable of putting this baggage to one side as he flexed his intellectual muscles and tasted the pleasures of scholarship, literature and controversy.

At Hyde Abbey School he appeared old for his age, he didn't join in games,[319] and seems to have missed out on other boyish activities. When he was a young man his friends were amazed to find that he didn't know that frogs came from tadpoles.[320] Not knowing what every schoolboy knows is a mark of an isolated childhood. He was bookish, and proud of his literary father. When the boys were required to recite a poem in class he chose his father's long account of the last days of Lord William Russell. He was keen to get hold of a copy of the *Anti-Lucretius*.[321]

The visit from Mary Ann at Hyde Abbey in 1779 did nothing to dispel the romantic mystery that surrounded her, and nothing to lessen his sense of being different from his schoolfellows. Some of the older boys may have had a good idea who she was and what she did for a living – Mr Richards, the headmaster, almost certainly knew – and George picked up the sense that there was something in his mother's story that it was better not to talk about. Uncle Stratty kept the secret from him, and he had to keep it from others. He understood that the visit would not be repeated until his uncle gave permission.

Schoolboys are used to the idea that home and parents are embarrassing. Before long he was happy enough. He was clever, with a good memory and lively imagination, and despite his dislike of physical games he commanded loyalty and affection as he rose through the school. After his death contemporaries sent their schoolboy reminiscences to the press. He learned by heart the poems of Thomas Gray, and showed a precocious talent for versification. Taking the main part in a school production of the *Orestes* of Euripides he showed 'surprising judgement and sensibility' in portraying the 'madness of the matricide in all the horrors of conscious guilt'.[322] Whether this experience, at the age of eleven or twelve, helped him understand his feelings about his own mother is impossible to say.

George was close enough to one of his schoolfellows, a delicate boy called Thomas Garnier, to spend part of one of his holidays with the Garniers at Rooksbury, in Hampshire. There he met a friend of the family, Henry John Richman, a scholarly and eccentric young clergyman, who was drawn to the precocious and lonely boy.[i] This friendship led to a correspondence that lasted throughout George's schooldays and beyond. Richman's letters were written with great affection, informality and a touch of naïveté. He followed George's political rise with interest, and sent him copies of his poems for advice and criticism. Unfortunately no letters survive from the earliest period of their friendship, but later on Richman knew about Mary Ann. Most of their discussions were on scholarly topics or on academic prospects, but if George ever revealed to anyone the complicated feelings he was grappling with, it was probably to Richman, whose kindness left a lasting

---

i Henry Richman (1754?–1824) later became master of the grammar school at Dorchester, and rector of Holy Trinity, Dorchester.

impression. Though he was not in a formal sense George's tutor, that was how George thought of him, and when he rose to power he made an effort to procure a living for him.[323] But his feelings of gratitude did not stop there: we shall see that in later life George would follow Richman's example and show himself attentive to the needs of friendless young men.

In 1782 George had measles, and was sent home to convalesce under Mehitabel's care. In September, having got over his illness and recovered from a riding accident, he started at Eton. It took him a few months to settle down to the new life. Several letters to his mother have survived from this time, and their tone is plaintive, hesitant, uncertain. 'Allow me my dear Mother the pleasure of knowing the state of yr Circumstances,' he wrote, expressing both anxiety on her behalf and curiosity. Having no reply he begged for a letter, confessing that he was 'excessively uneasy' about her. He worried that being so straitened in her circumstances she would be unable to pay the postage on his letters.[324]

Before long he had gathered around himself a group of devoted friends, some of them friends for life. More than ever he was conscious of his secret. It was not yet, in his mind, positively shameful, but something that always prevented openness and intimacy. Over the years he gradually brought to perfection the protective devices that were to last him all his life: wit, sarcasm, fun and an unstoppable fluency. He made his cousins laugh, he made his schoolfellows laugh, and while they were laughing they were not probing. He mastered the skills that won prizes and applause: rhetorical writing and versification, in Latin and English. With words he imposed his own terms and kept all his relationships under control. As a last line of defence he had his Canning legacy, an obstinate determination to bend people to his will. His Eton friends recognised that he was already 'quite a man'.[325] Quite a man, yes, but also a confused boy.

11.
Plymouth and Exeter, 1779–1785

Mary Ann, Reddish and little Sam travelled on from Winchester, arriving in Plymouth in time for the summer season. Plymouth, with the wilds of Cornwall just across the river, was something of a frontier town, known to the rest of the country mainly through the shipping columns of the newspapers: the comings and goings of ships of war and trade, their cargoes, their adventures – storms, privateers, mutinies – and the messages they brought from ships they had passed, with news and rumours of events in the West Indies and America. Activity had been intense for a year or so as the war with the American colonists and their French allies took hold. Plymouth felt close to the war, on the front line. In December 1778 there had been a mass breakout from the Millbay prison in the town by more than a hundred American prisoners – the most dramatic of a series of escapes. In May, about the time Mary Ann arrived, a fleet was gathering to sail for New York.[326]

For some twenty years there had been a theatre at Frankfort Gate on the western edge of Plymouth, near what later became the Globe Tavern, and beside a little thoroughfare called Love Lane by some and by others Burying Place Lane. The stage and auditorium were tiny by comparison with Drury Lane or the theatre in Bristol.[327] The company at Frankfort Gate also supplied those in Dock (what is now Devonport) and Exeter. The manager in Exeter was Richard Hughes, and in Plymouth a Mr Wolfe.[i] There was some sort of business relationship between the two of them – they employed the same group of actors and both depended on the gentry of their part of Devon for a significant part of their audiences – but how closely they were connected is not clear. Things were fluid in the world of provincial theatre, with improvisation off stage as well as on. These were the men who, for the next six years, would hold power over Mary Ann, the men she had to satisfy. Hughes was an established actor with a reputation for kindliness, but Wolfe, it was said, was aptly named; both were businessmen, who had to make the theatre pay. Also involved in the management of the three theatres was Thomas Jefferson, a leading Drury Lane actor who had played Gloster when Mary Ann appeared as Jane Shore.[328] Another figure who would be important for Mary Ann was Robert Trewman, the owner of the *Flying Post*, which was printed in Exeter but catered for all three communities. Like Flyn's in Cork, Trewman's newspaper office and bookshop provided a meeting place for local writers and their readers. Trewman was a lottery agent and was involved in the trade in patent medicines. He was also a part proprietor of the theatre in Exeter.

Reddish had been an apothecary's apprentice in Plymouth until an itinerant group of players inspired him to take to the stage.[329] It's doubtful whether many now remembered the apprentice turned actor of a quarter of a century before, but he had been back since and had contacts in the town. Plymouth had offered him and Mary Ann a friendly retreat when they made themselves unwelcome in Bristol, and now they found lodgings with old associates. Reddish's illness meant that Mary Ann quickly got to know the local members of the 'faculty'.[330]

After several weeks of sea bathing Reddish's symptoms showed signs of improvement, and Hughes and Wolfe suggested that his

i Richard Hughes also managed the theatre in Weymouth and his provincial success eventually enabled him to take over the management of Sadlers Wells (*Thespian Dictionary* s.n. Richard Hughes). Very little is known of Wolfe.

name on the bills would be good for business. For a little while things went well, but then the pressure began to tell. Reddish's old instability resurfaced, with a new ingredient of violence directed particularly at Mary Ann and her unborn child. Friends hurried Mary Ann away from Plymouth to Dock, while Reddish was kept under restraint. The stage fraternity was compassionate when it came to looking after one of its own, and since Reddish was already being supported by the Theatrical Fund in London its directors were informed. When Mary Ann returned to Frankfort Gate things seemed calmer, but one night there was a disturbance behind the scenes, loud enough to alert a group of her friends in the audience. Two of them, Richard Hunn, a well-to-do draper, and a surgeon called Gashing, rushed backstage and were in time to rescue her from a sudden murderous assault. Concluding that Reddish now needed constant supervision, the directors of the Theatrical Fund agree to take responsibility for him, provided he could be got up to London. Jordan Costello travelled down to Plymouth to act as escort.[331]

On arrival in London Reddish placed paragraphs in the newspapers asserting his sanity and denying that his family was in need of support from the Theatrical Fund. Fecklessness, unreliability and occasional 'fits', which had long been a feature of his life, had now become a settled inability to manage his affairs and pursue his profession, but despite the new element of violence, his protest may well have been justified. His manner of expressing himself, however, was typical of the effrontery and self-delusion that had made him so many enemies, and may have reinforced the belief that he was mad. He was incarcerated briefly in Bedlam, and then after living for a while at Newington Green on the edge of London, was transferred to the Asylum in York. In choosing the recently established York Asylum, the Fund directors were trying to do their best for their unfortunate colleague; they couldn't know that the institution's fine new buildings and impressive ideals concealed a regime of incompetence and cruelty. Reddish died there in 1785.[332] He was not forgotten; the trade in theatrical prints and actors' memoirs kept his face and his name in the memory of the play-going public. The Fund, continuing its support for Reddish's family, paid for young Sam's education.

When Mary Ann watched the coach leave for London it was the last she saw of the man who had been a husband to her for some six or seven years. Later in her life, she claimed to regard her years as Mrs Reddish with disgust, and the name as a badge of infamy. There must have been something of this in her mind as she watched him go, but there were also other feelings at work. She could reflect with pride that she had stood by the father of her children through his suffering.[333] There may have been more tender feelings too, but if so the Packet is silent about them. She was now in her early thirties, about to give birth for the eighth time. If her child was born alive she would have four to provide for. She must work. And however shameful the name of Reddish was, she would have to keep it until she won the right to another. It was the name by which she was known at the theatre, it was part of her 'publick character', and to abandon it now would be to admit before the world what much of the world knew, that she was not Reddish's lawful wife.

It was also the last known appearance of her father in her life. He was apparently still alive in the autumn of 1782, when George wrote that something in one of Mary Ann's letters had left him anxious about his 'poor grandfather'.[334] Neither father nor lover had served Mary Ann well. Instead of protecting her and providing for her, they had let her down at every turn. She saw all this clearly. Hadn't her novel been a catalogue of the ways in which weak and selfish men let women down? From what little is known of Jordan Costello, he seems to have been unreliable and ineffectual, so much so that it is almost a surprise that he was entrusted with, and discharged satisfactorily, the responsible task of conveying Reddish to London. He had been, back in Dublin days, a man of talent and enterprise but, as Mary Ann knew from her own experience, talent and enterprise were not enough. The hostile world, and human failings, could defeat the bravest efforts.

Jordan brought the babies, Charles and Mary, down to Plymouth for Mary Ann to look after, and took young Sam back with him to London.[335] Presumably Mary Ann wanted her younger children with her, rather than entrusting them to her mother. Charles was now the age that Thomas had been when he died in her mother's care. The whole family, whether in London or Plymouth, depended on Mary Ann's earnings, so after the birth of William she continued going the rounds of Frankfort Gate and Dock in the summer, and Exeter for the winter season.

Mary Ann described the ten years following her Drury Lane debut as 'years of such suffering as to retrace in all the minutia of colouring, woud be to suffer over again'. These words belong to a narrative designed to demonstrate that she had not chosen to become an actress for her own pleasure, but we should not dismiss them on that account. It was a hard life. George's letters from Eton, presumably reflecting what he heard from his aunt and uncle, repeatedly refer to Mary Ann's straitened circumstances. But although she had to scrape around for money and had many burdens to bear, her exertions in the theatre were by now providing her and her dependants with 'the necessaries and some of the Comforts of Life'.[336]

The provincial stage had benefited from the improvement in the profession that had come about during the reign of Garrick in London. There were a number of influential actor-managers with strings of theatres under their control. Some, like Tate Wilkinson, were intelligent and impressive men who kept in touch with the latest professional developments. New theatres were being built, some with royal patents, and some designed according to the latest practice in stagecraft. While London theatres were closed in the summer, metropolitan actors would descend on the major provincial towns. The playhouses in Plymouth and Exeter were not in the first rank of provincial theatres, but neither were they on the lowest rung. Hughes, the manager in Exeter, had high standards, demanding from his actors strict attention to business in return for punctuality in payment of salaries.[337]

Mary Ann could still assume the air of a lady of fashion, securing patrons amongst the leading people in and around Exeter and Plymouth. Her social circle included a leading Plymouth doctor, William Farr, Lord Courtenay of Powderham Castle, Sir Frederick Rogers, Plymouth's current MP, and his successor Captain John MacBride, a devotee of cock-fighting as well as the theatre.[338] How well she knew them is unclear, but they were at least friends of friends. She also made loyal and lasting friends, such as Dr Gashing in Plymouth, and Dr and Mrs Downman and Bridget Moore[i] in Exeter. Hugh Downman was a poet and dramatist as well as physician, and his wife was related to the Courtenay family. Conscious that in the eyes of the Cannings her past liaison with Reddish amounted to a disqualification from polite or decent society, Mary Ann was gratified that her friends' wives were happy to call on her and receive her in their homes.[339] This roll call of respectable connections is a reminder that, although the letters from which her story emerges are sharply focused on George and the Cannings, she had a broad social life apart from them, about which we know hardly anything.

Sometime in 1781 or 1782 a young actress called Elizabeth Kemble came to work at Frankfort Gate. Her father was a successful actor-manager in the Midlands, while her sister, Sarah Siddons, and her brother, John Philip Kemble, were to become the most famous tragedians of their day.[ii] Her parents had apprenticed Elizabeth to a mantua-maker, but she was determined to follow her sister to Drury Lane. She was a wilful girl, 'wild as a colt untamed,' according to Tate Wilkinson, who knew her in York in 1783. Her parents granted her wish and sent her to Plymouth to

i Mrs Bridget Moore: mentioned several times in the Packet and in George's letters to Mary Ann. She is probably the Mrs Moore who appeared in *The Maid of the Mill* and *The Provok'd Husband* in 1778 (*Exeter Flying Post*, 11 Dec. 1778).

ii Elizabeth Kemble (1761–1836) was the fifth of twelve children of Roger Kemble and his actress wife Sarah Ward.

learn the craft. She soon rebelled – she was a Kemble, and wasn't going to let a bunch of provincials tell her how to act – and when she made enemies and found herself isolated within the company, Mary Ann sympathised, only too well aware what it was to suffer the hostility of the green room. She used her influence to protect Elizabeth, at the same time advising her, if she wanted to survive in the profession, to work harder and be more conciliatory. Early in 1783 Mrs Siddons procured Elizabeth an opening at Drury Lane, and not long after that she joined a touring company in the North of England, and married the manager Charles Whitlock.[340]

When Mary Ann first established herself in Devonshire in 1779, she coincided briefly with the young John Bernard, who remembered having seen her as Jane Shore six years before. While Mary Ann was descending in the theatrical world, Bernard was on the way up. Before joining Hughes he had been in the north of England with Tate Wilkinson, and then in Norwich. He was ambitious and did not stay long in Exeter. After another spell with Wilkinson, an extensive tour of Ireland and several seasons in Bath, he was engaged by Harris at Covent Garden.[341] By the late 1780s he was joined with Wolfe in the management of the summer theatre in Plymouth, and we shall see him having a part to play at the end of Mary Ann's acting career.

In the six years since he had seen Mary Ann as Jane Shore, Bernard had learned more of the art of acting, and his assessment of her talents is revealing. Her efforts, he wrote, 'were more characterised by judgement than genius; but Nature had gifted her in several respects to sustain the matrons.' By judgement Bernard meant those elements of the actor's craft that can be acquired through intelligent application; by genius he meant the inventive ability, analogous to the poet's inspiration, that enables actors to create a character whose emotions and actions lie beyond their own, and the audience's, everyday experience. Mary Ann was an intelligent woman who used her own experience of life, in particular her experience as a mother, to portray recognisable figures. He added that she owed some of her local popularity and patronage to her 'domestic' character rather than her acting skill, surrounding her talents 'with the halo of her becoming principles', which suggests that in her choice of parts she tried to avoid if she could those which might reflect badly on her private character.[342]

She played in a wide range of productions, many of them melodramas and light comedies now long forgotten, but also Shakespeare, Dryden, and Sheridan, even returning to *Jane Shore*.[343] Most of the productions were 'from stock' – plays that could be got up with minimal rehearsal because the experienced actors knew them well, and the theatre possessed a ready supply of suitable scenery and props. There were new plays, including recent London successes, such as *The School for Scandal* in which Mary Ann played Lady Sneerwell. This was a revival, in December 1781, of a production that Hughes had originally mounted three years earlier, before Mary Ann's arrival. Then, unable to procure a copy of the text, he had employed the youthful Bernard, in return for an extra ten shillings a week, to compile a version from his own knowledge of three of the parts combined with the recollections of his wife and friends who had seen the play performed at Drury Lane.[344]

Early in 1782 Exeter saw the first performance of Hugh Downman's play *Editha*, set in the city at the time of the Viking invasions. Mary Ann played the title role.[345] Against a background of the siege of Exeter, the play tells a melodramatic story of courage, treachery, mistaken identity and virtue triumphant. Editha's 'air above the vulgar' persuades her Danish captor, Rodolph, to woo her rather than ravish her,[346] but when she resists his entreaties, he reverts to savage type. Uncontrolled jealousy drives him to make an attempt on her life, but in the darkness he stabs the treacherous Gunhilda instead. Editha survives, refuses to betray her country and is reunited with her brother, mother and long-lost father. In the midst of violence and deceit she stands firm, subject to none of the stormy and illicit passions that ruin heroines such as Jane Shore.

She inspires unlawful lusts in the barbarous Rodolph, but not, as Jane does, through the contagion of her own sensuality. Editha declares her virtue, in contrast to the deceitful Gunhilda, in a manner that recalls Mary Ann's first husband's conscious rectitude:

> O pure Sincerity! O holy Truth,
> When I shall cease thy mandates to adore
> May ignominy be my portion here,
> And Heaven refuse me happiness hereafter![347]

Although *Editha* was never widely performed it had local appeal. Mary Ann returned to the part in 1784, and it was revived again after she had left Exeter, with Mrs Kemble, Elizabeth's mother, as Editha.[348] Editha's transcendent virtue places her at the centre of the drama while raising her above the violence and duplicity with which she is surrounded. It was an excellent part for an actress trying to efface a stain upon her reputation by wrapping herself in a halo of becoming principles. Downman composed the play to honour his city; he may also have hoped it would do some good for his friend Mrs Reddish.

By 1783 Mary Ann was the leading actress in the three theatres. Refinement was an important part of the actor's craft, particularly valued by Hughes, who according to the *Thespian Dictionary* would 'suffer no actor, nor actress to appear on his boards in an improper dress, nor allow those liberties which country performers are too apt to take'. Tragic heroes and heroines were almost invariably of royal or noble birth, like Editha with her 'air above the vulgar', and an actor had to display the instincts of a gentleman or lady in order to sustain them convincingly in the eyes of a class-conscious audience. Or so it was frequently said in the theatrical criticism of the day. It was what Mary Ann herself had argued when criticising Miss Hopkins. Her London life had left her with a fashionable gloss which could not be matched by provincial colleagues. Not that it was entirely gloss and manner, since Mary Ann had a strength of character that made her stand out, the fortitude remarked on by the Duchess of Ancaster. Fine manners and fortitude, unsupported by influence, spotless reputation and superlative talent, had not been enough to secure success at Drury Lane, but in the provinces they made her the 'ruling favourite'.[349] It was not what she had hoped for ten years before, and it could not last for ever, but for now it was enough. Her regular salary met her day-to-day needs, and her benefit nights paid for nurses and schools for her children.

In these years, she made no further attempt to see George, either because she knew it was futile or because she was too busy, and too poor, to make the journey to Winchester. When she heard in the summer of 1782 that he had left Hyde Abbey for Eton, he was that much further beyond her reach, physically and socially.

By 1783 Mary Ann was thirty-six years old (or thirty-three) and ten years of work and childbearing had left their mark. Escape from the laborious and not particularly lucrative life of a provincial actress must have been an appealing prospect, but she was no nearer finding an alternative than when she first became a widow. Mary Ann's Exeter friend, Bridget Moore, actress turned schoolteacher, may have prompted dreams of leaving the profession, and revived the idea of opening a school, first suggested ten years earlier by the Duchess of Ancaster. There was another possibility, which she had refused to contemplate back in 1772: marriage. Marriage – to the right man – would guarantee support for her dependants, and enable her to leave the theatre and change her name; it would confer the sort of respectability which must weigh with Stratty and make him grant her access to George.

Of the two men who had rescued her from Reddish's violence, one, Dr Gashing, was a married man, but the other, Richard Hunn, was single. His father was a master cooper in the naval dockyard and an alderman,[350] and he himself had a business as a draper and silk mercer. A devotee of the theatre, Hunn wrote occasional reviews in the newspapers, his sharp pen making him unpopular among the actors, but his criticisms had not been directed at Mary Ann. He had saved her life, and appeared devoted to her, and although 'he was undoubtedly a tradesman, yet by a sort of general consent, I think, it appear'd, he moved in the superior circle'.[351] Nowhere in the Packet does Mary Ann admit to a romantic attachment to Richard Hunn, any more than to Samuel Reddish, but in neither case can we draw any conclusion from this silence. She was older now, and the long-term prudential reasons for an alliance with Hunn seemed stronger than in the case of Reddish, so it looks more like a marriage of convenience than a meeting of 'sympathetick hearts' – but it is impossible to be certain. They were married in Exeter in February 1783, Mary Ann signing her name as Canning.[352]

She wrote at once to George, enclosing a letter to Stratty. In her new position, with her new name, she could no longer be denied access to her son. She invited Stratty to make enquiries, to satisfy himself of the respectability of her husband. Her first husband had been angry when Gustavus Guy-Dickens dared to enquire after his character, as though he were a servant applying for a place. It's a measure of how far Mary Ann had slipped in social standing that she was prepared to submit to this humiliation. Her letter arrived at Clements Lane during the school holidays, but Stratty waited until the evening before George went back to Eton before making known his decision.

The answer was No. No, he wouldn't enquire into Mr Hunn's character, and No, she and George could not meet. George had eagerly seconded his mother's request, and Stratty must have been reluctant to inflict pain by refusing. He didn't reply to Mary Ann himself, but told George what to say. 'He expatiated on your bad conduct,' George wrote, 'and he said he thought you had on all occasions rather consulted yr own immediate pleasure and satisfaction, than the interest of your family, and me in particular.' Stratty was a kind man, and almost certainly delivered his verdict as gently as possible, but there is no gentle way of expatiating to a thirteen-year-old boy on his mother's bad conduct. Mary Ann recalled it with bitterness: '... in the barbarous policy which he had inveteratly adopted, dictated to you an answer, unworthy of him to conceive & unnatural for you to be made the channell of — God forgive him!' George's letter is smudged, and he needed several attempts at spelling the unfamiliar word *expatiated*. 'Judge my dr Mother, how cruel, how afflicting a sentence this was to me,' he went on, 'but all is over now, he seem'd quite determin'd... Write to me as soon as you can; come if possible...' He ended with the formula that was to serve him in rough times and smooth for the next forty-four years: 'believe me yr ever dutiful and affectionate Son, G. Canning.'[353] In years to come it may have become a mere formula, a flourish, but for now he was surely pledging himself in earnest. So one of the hopes she had pinned on her marriage was disappointed.

Within a few weeks of the wedding she was back on stage in a programme consisting of *Cymbeline*, a musical interlude by Isaac Bickerstaff based on Farquhar's *The Recruiting Sergeant*, an address 'by Mrs Hunn', and a farce, *The Register Office* by Joseph Reed, with five-year-old Mary Reddish giving an epilogue in the character of the muse Clio.[354] How the child reacted to this exposure we can only guess; it was the prelude to a life in which her wishes were subordinated to the stronger will of her mother and, later, her half-brother. This was Mary Ann's benefit night, and now she was married to a man of substance she may have expected it to be her last, but this hope crumbled too when Richard Hunn revealed his secret longing to go on the stage himself.

He was, we can assume, the unnamed gentleman who appeared as Posthumus on her benefit night. He can hardly have impressed her, since she was used to seeing Reddish in the part, but the night went better than she feared, and Hughes was willing to persevere, giving him next the less demanding character of Lubin in Charles Dibdin's comic opera *The Quaker*. After these two attempts it seemed that the experiment had ended, so Mary Ann was horrified to learn soon afterwards that Hunn intended to sell his drapery business and invest the money in the theatre. He 'languished for

Heroics', as she put it, and fantasised that together they would found another great theatrical family to rival the Kembles. She told him he had no aptitude for acting, a piece of straight talking that he took badly from his new wife.[355] He could point out that it was not unusual for amateurs to try their luck, particularly if they had a little pot of capital to back them, and that some went on to make a career. She had done it herself, and had maintained herself for ten years. You couldn't always calculate the results in advance. Gentility, refinement, that was what marked her out amongst her provincial colleagues, and he too would command attention with his gentleman-like manner. She admitted that he might pass in small supporting roles in polite comedy, which required no more than a good manner, but for tragedy, for Heroics, much more was needed – physical presence and theatrical understanding, neither of which he could command.

There was to be no relief for Mary Ann. In May she was in Dryden's tragicomedy *The Spanish Friar or the Double Discovery*, taking the comic role of Elvira rather than the more substantial and tragic Leonora. Whether she preferred Elvira because she was happier in comedy, or because the character's wit and repartee make it the more exciting part to play, is not certain. With Hughes himself cast in the role of the fat friar Dominic it is likely that the comic element was allowed to dominate. Elvira's frank lasciviousness cannot have done much for Mary Ann's halo of good principles. Soon afterwards the company left for the summer in Plymouth and Dock, returning to Exeter for the winter season, with the advertisements promising that the theatre had been well heated after lying unused for so many months.[356]

Hunn had sold his business, which may have been failing anyway, and bought shares in the Exeter and Plymouth theatres.[357] The actors could have warned him not to trust Wolfe, who still controlled the Frankfort Gate theatre, but his stinging paragraphs over the years had made him unpopular, so they may not have been sorry to see him fleeced. Now he could have all the heroic parts he longed for, exposing his spindly legs in tights to the ribaldry of the farmers of Exeter and sailors of Plymouth.

When Mary Ann appeared, probably as Cleopatra rather than in the role she had taken in London and Bristol, Octavia, in Dryden's *All for Love*, Hunn insisted on playing Mark Antony. The strength and beauty of Dryden's verse and the pathos of the tragedy may not have been fully appreciated by some sections of the Exeter audience, but they knew that Antony is supposed to be a great general, and that he is passionately loved by the Egyptian queen. When Richard Hunn, the draper, came forward in the part they knew they were being short changed. Whether he was booed and hissed from the outset, like Mary Ann in *Semiramis*, or whether it was only gradually that his incapacity became apparent, he soon could not make himself heard above the uproar. Mary Ann had to plead with the audience to give him a hearing. 'I'll tell 'ee what, marm,' called out a witty farmer, 'if Mr. Mark Antony doan't go whoam directly, I'll throw my hat at 'un and break both his legs.' The incident was reported to John Bernard by Whitfield of Covent Garden, the same actor whose unlucky sword thrust had caused the downfall of Reddish. Bernard believed that some of the actors had fomented the trouble in revenge for Hunn's scathing reviews.[358]

Hunn hung on, blaming everyone but himself. In March 1785 a paragraph appeared in the *Flying Post* attacking unruly elements in the audience, accusing them of throwing stones and bricks onto the stage.[359] Unpopular though he was, Hunn's financial stake in the theatre and Mary Ann's value to the company meant that Wolfe and Hughes couldn't easily get rid of him. Mary Ann understood the business well enough to see his efforts were hopeless, but whenever she suggested he should give up, he bullied her into silence. The marriage already seemed a bad bargain, having brought professional embarrassment, while failing to resolve the unhappiness at the heart of her personal life, the separation from George.

George's letters were affectionate, but stiff and constrained, as though he didn't know what to write. Mary Ann's responses were, we can assume, longer, overflowing with emotion. In later years, when George wrote to her every week, and when she was living less hectically, their correspondence was the centre of her life. How far the same was true at this period is hard to say. 'Meantime,' she had written in 1782, thinking of the long years they would have to wait before they could meet, 'be assured of my daily remembrance, my daily prayers; and fail not to feed my anxious hopes in thee with frequent repetitions of those sweet feelings, which blunt the sharpest arrows of adversity, and rob hard, hard fate of its power to render entirely wretched.'[360] With all allowance made for Mary Ann's hyperbole, it's likely that he was indeed seldom far from her thoughts, however much her current worries pressed upon her.

Prevented as she was from participating in George's life, she could supplement his letters with occasional glimpses of events at Eton. They didn't yet feature George himself (though that would come later as he rose up through the school) but almost daily there was some testimony in the newspapers to the importance and glamour of Eton. Such and such an Etonian was made a bishop, or entered the government – or died, full of honour, with his obituary recording precocious genius and schoolboy glory. Towards the end of 1783 the school featured in news reports of a different nature, when the assistant masters refused to work, in protest at some grievance, and the boys, left unsupervised, broke out in a riot against the Master, Dr Davies. 'No Davies! Down with him!' the boys shouted, like a theatre audience abusing an unpopular actor. Tables and windows were broken, an egg was thrown. The situation was saved, it was said, by the intervention of a 'Great Personage' (possibly the King). When Mary Ann read of the violence she immediately thought the worst and wrote to George asking if he had been hurt. The anxiety made her all the more eager to see him, and her mind raced on to imagine a meeting. Would he recognise her? she wondered, to which he made a characteristically practical response, asking if there was any hope of a trial – as though she was the one who could bring it about.[361]

In time to come, when he was making his career amongst the country's great men, George would be quick to squash any attempt by his mother to open up a link, however tenuous, between her life and his. Sometimes, as we'll see, his reaction came close to panic. For now, however, he seems not to have resented it when she enquired about a schoolfellow who happened to be the son of one of her Exeter acquaintances. The circumstances were strange and sad. At the end of 1784 two boys had a savage fight in which one, the older boy, received fatal injuries. She asked George what he knew of it. The newspapers had disagreed on most of the circumstances, including the names of the combatants, but George could confirm that the dead boy was indeed Kitson, the son of her Exeter friend. He did not enlarge on the affair, so Mary Ann was none the wiser about the origins of the quarrel.[362]

George included a further piece of news in this letter, the death of his uncle Paul Canning. Mary Ann had no reason to think kindly of Paul, but as the brother of her first husband, his passing raised memories of different, if not happier, days. This was the juncture at which George, had he been older, might have asserted his rights, but the moment passed; the Garvagh inheritance went without dispute to Paul's son, another George Canning, known in the family as Irish George. Paul's death would have an impact on George and Mary Ann a few years later, because it left his widow in control of the Canning estate in Ireland, and she was to prove uncooperative.

Early in 1785 the first of Mary Ann's children by Richard Hunn was born, another Richard, who was afflicted with some never specified congenital disability. He is hardly ever mentioned in the surviving letters, and always in tones of pity. 'The poor little infant you mention as labouring under that dreadful affliction may heaven preserve,' wrote George in April. Esther came down from London to help. While she was in Plymouth she took to the boards, a brief experiment which she didn't repeat.[363] But she would have to do something. With the family's future threatened by Hunn's irresponsible gamble, some provision was needed for Mrs Costello's declining years. When Esther's brief attempt on the stage came to nothing, Mary Ann wrote to a friend, asking for assistance.[364] Esther, she said, often helped her to dress, so might be well suited to be a lady's maid. George Canning's mother could not sink to being a servant, but evidently his aunt could. The friend replied that there was all the difference in the world between assisting a sister out of affection and being bound to carry out every whim of a demanding mistress: the life of a servant was intolerable to anyone not born to it. Nothing came of the proposal.

The Hunns appeared regularly in Plymouth and Exeter throughout 1784 and 1785, with their benefit nights sponsored by local dignitaries such as Lord Courtenay and Captain MacBride. For his Plymouth benefit in October 1784 Hunn played one of the principal men in Hannah Cowley's *A Bold Stroke for a Husband*.[365] It's a play in which the men, young and libidinous or old and tyrannical, are much less engaging than the women, who manage to maintain their integrity by their resourcefulness and deception. Mary Ann took the part of the injured wife, Donna Victoria, who dares to disguise herself as a man in order to recover her husband's property from the hands of his mistress. Of the principal women in the play, Victoria and her cousin Olivia, Mary Ann had this time taken the more virtuous and, despite the cross-dressing, duller part. Victoria's situation offered a parallel to Mary Ann's own, as she struggled to save the family's livelihood, which her husband's infatuation had so recklessly jeopardised.

As time went on, the resentment of his fellow actors and hostility of the audiences made life increasingly difficult for Hunn, until Mr Wolfe eventually took advantage of his unpopularity to push him out.[366] There was nowhere in the South-West for the Hunns to go, so at the beginning of 1786 they jumped at the opportunity to make a fresh start at the theatre in Worcester. Mary Ann prepared a farewell speech to the people of Exeter, to be delivered at her last benefit night, but then came news that the manager in Worcester was bankrupt and in gaol. The theatre was closed. Her friends the Downmans, who were with her when she heard, begged her to stay, offering to use their influence with Hughes in Exeter, and promising that Lord Courtenay would intercede on her behalf. But she knew it would be hopeless. Wolfe was implacable, while Hunn himself had been so often humiliated that he was determined to move on.[367]

Even before the news of the Worcester failure Mary Ann's thoughts had been turning to Ireland,[368] to the genial, if unreliable, Thomas Ryder, and the accommodating William Flyn. Although she never allows herself to say anything positive about her time in the theatre, the year in Ireland with Reddish seems to have been a happy time.

12.
The Meeting, 1785–1786

When Mary Ann's marriage did not result in her leaving the stage, Stratty and Mehitabel must have felt that their doubts and mistrust were justified. Here she was, following her own inclination, indifferent to the effect on George. In the midst of all her troubles in Plymouth, and not long after the birth of poor Richard early in 1785, she once more begged to be allowed to meet George, and he seconded her.[369] Stratty again kept them in suspense for a more than a month, reluctant as before to send an answer that would cause disappointment, and increasingly uncertain what to do for the best. As before, he made George the bearer of the bad news.

Two years earlier Stratty had justified his prohibition by expatiating on Mary Ann's bad conduct. Now he focused rather on a fear that George might be inveigled into following his mother onto the stage. With hindsight this seems an unrealistic fear, but at the time Stratty, remembering Orestes at Hyde Abbey and recognising an histrionic streak in his nephew, had grounds for apprehension. How could George not be interested in the theatre, given his romantic curiosity about his mother? In his schoolboy letters he asked about her troubles and wondered where she might find a more appreciative audience. Even if he was not lured onto the stage, there was a risk that he would decide that his proper place was at his mother's side, and give up all the advantages of

Eton in order to throw in his lot with her. It was, he admitted later, only respect for his uncle that kept him from doing so.[370] Stratty knew how spellbinding Mary Ann could be; it would be irresponsible to expose the boy to this dangerous influence until he had built up other interests and acquired a wider understanding of the world. He wrote to George, without mentioning the stage, but making his meaning clear:

> I am far from wishing to counteract or diminish those filial feelings of regard, which you naturally possess for your Mother, but I wish to have interwoven with those feelings such sentiments as may prevent all possibility, or at least probability of your Mind receiving any Biass from your Visit to her, which might be Prejudicial to you during the rest of your Life. Time only can give you a sufficient Stock of such Sentiments, and therefore the longer you delay the Visit, the less Danger there will be from it.

George passed the message on to Mary Ann.[371] They both took comfort that the ban was evidently not to be permanent, and from a hope that Stratty had only refused because he was planning to take George to Ireland.

Meanwhile George continued to shine at Eton. Quite apart from the secret of his mother, as the nephew and ward of a not particularly successful City merchant he naturally felt at a disadvantage amongst the sons of the country's elite, but brains and wit trumped everything. Some of his aristocratic friends may have had reservations about the Clements Lane connection, and some may even have picked up rumours from older brothers and uncles about pretty Mrs Canning who had played Jane Shore, but they succumbed nonetheless to his charm, applauded his literary and academic successes, laughed at his jokes, and enjoyed the frisson of his extreme Whig and republican opinions.

An arcane question arose about how his education should proceed. Stratty was cautious, wanting him to take the safe route through school and university: a scholarship to enable him to stay at Eton as a Colleger until he was nineteen, then on to Kings College, Cambridge, with a fellowship to follow. George observed the comparative discomfort of the Collegers' living quarters, and the mild contempt in which they were held by the more aristocratic boys, and was also apprehensive that Stratty's plan might lead inexorably to taking holy orders. He chose the more prestigious status of Oppidan, risky though it was for a boy without fortune or connections. Two family friends, Sheridan and Charles James Fox,[i] both of them risk-takers, persuaded Stratty to let George have his way.[372]

While Stratty may have deplored the recklessness of his choice, he could take comfort from George's determination to align himself with Eton's aristocrats. This was the sort of sentiment that would make a young man hesitate to throw up everything to become an actor. Quite apart from the higher ambitions implied by his choice, George was learning from his friends the advantages of a good income. Luxury never attracted him, but he was fastidious in his habits and impatient over the practical matters of domestic life; the idea of good servants and a well-run house was appealing. Mehitabel's homes (she and Stratty now had a small house in Putney as well as Clements Lane) were bustling and friendly, but full of children.[373]

George's stock of suitable sentiments was augmented further in the summer of 1785 when Stratty and Mehitabel took him to Ireland to meet more of his Canning relations. Mrs Canning, who was now in her late sixties, had been subsidising George's education and wanted to see him.[374] Now that the Garvagh estate had passed to Irish George, it was important that English George should understand the situation and not be tempted in later life to raise wasteful legal disputes about the succession. The message got through; George never showed any inclination to right the wrongs done to his father.

---

i Charles James Fox (1749–1806) was leader of the radical wing of the Whig party. He had three brief periods in office, but like his ally Sheridan spent most of his career in opposition. Fox was godfather to Stratty and Mehitabel's third son (Hunt, 48).

While staying in Abbey Street, George did not forget his mother and her growing family. He speculated on where her latest 'theatrical campaign' was to take her. The last address he had for her was the theatre at Plymouth Dock. Had she moved on? he wondered. What were her plans?[375] Mary Ann asked what had prompted these speculations. Had Stratty been talking about her? She clutched at the idea that Stratty was once more taking an interest in her career, and even wrote to him directly.[376] Now that Plymouth and Exeter, because of her husband's behaviour, were closed to her she was contacting theatres in Bath and London. Although Stratty had no influence in theatrical circles, he knew people who might be able to help, such as John Palmer, the proprietor of the theatre in Bath, or Sheridan's parents-in-law, Mary and Thomas Linley, who were managing Drury Lane. Mary Ann would never lose the outsider's conviction that friends, and friends of friends, on the inside could provide a helping hand if only they would exert themselves. Stratty refused to speak to Palmer. 'Interest on such occasions,' he told George dismissively, 'is of very little Use, everything depending on the merit of the Persons, as Actors.' And as for Drury Lane, he said, Mary Ann must realise there was 'not much chance there'.[377]

All through the autumn and winter of 1785–86 George's letters from Eton were taken up with the prospects for Mary Ann's campaign. He wanted her to join the company that the Leighs had taken him to see at Norwich, and hoped that the 'removal' of the leading actress there, Mrs Belfille, would offer her an opening, because Mrs Belfille had previously 'engag'd all the characters in the Comick line', a comment which suggests he was aware of Mary Ann's preference for comedy. She told him of possibilities in the north, in Richmond or Beverley, and he pressed her for details, but he suspected that audiences in Beverley would be 'mere country people', and repeated his hopes for an engagement in Norwich.[378] In a few years the thought of his mother appearing where she might encounter the Leighs would horrify him, but now he welcomed it as offering the promise of security. Meanwhile her plans for an Irish tour were well advanced, and Stratty, aware that the sea voyage involved some risk, agreed that before she set off George would come down to Exeter to see her.[379]

By January Mary Ann's plans had changed. Instead of Ireland, when the Worcester plan finally fell through, she made one last bid for work in London. First she tried George Colman at the summer theatre in the Haymarket. When Colman refused, there was another, less attractive, option. An actor-manager called John Palmer (known as Plausible Jack, not the John Palmer of Bath, nor yet the Drury Lane actor of an earlier generation, Gentleman John Palmer) was trying to launch a new theatre in the East End of London, which he hoped was beyond the range of the monopoly held by the three licensed West End houses, Drury Lane, Covent Garden and the Haymarket.[380] The legal position was contested, and so among the many obstacles encountered by Palmer was the difficulty of recruiting actors, who feared prosecution or blacklisting by the established theatres. If this scheme failed Mary Ann and her husband would try their luck in the North of England. They took lodgings in Great Wild Street, close to Drury Lane and not far from her old house in Great Queen Street. Esther and Mrs Costello, meanwhile, had lodgings in Tottenham Court Road, and later in Battlebridge, beside the New Road. It was shortly afterwards that Esther first lived with the family of the organ-builder John Byfield, though in what capacity, whether as lodger, servant, nurse or companion to Mrs Byfield, is not clear.[381]

The news that Mary Ann was in London came as a surprise to George. Although she was no longer planning to cross the sea, the promise of a meeting was not withdrawn, but George begged her not to come out to Eton, assuring her that he could easily come to Great Wild Street. The meeting was fixed for Monday 20 February. He had a fine, though overcast, day for his trip to London; spring had come early. As he approached the neighbourhood of Drury Lane he may have noticed bills announcing that Mrs Siddons was to appear as Jane Shore in a Royal Command performance that night.[382] He was eager and excited as the years of waiting came to an end. Apart from the Winchester visit and a few weeks during his first school holidays, his last memories of Mary Ann were of her nursing him through his illness ten years before, when he was six and she twenty-nine, still, no doubt, retaining much of her Wigmore Street refinement. His mental picture of the pretty young mother who had tenderly watched over his sickbed had been idealised through the lonely years of mystery, and supplemented perhaps by theatrical prints of actresses in character, either statuesque and dramatic or simpering and sentimental.

What he found when he entered her room was a middle-aged woman, marked by her years of hardship and her nine pregnancies. While his tastes and habits had become increasingly refined, she had been living amongst provincial actors, struggling to maintain her fragile gentility. To the audiences of Plymouth and Exeter she might still seem a fine lady, but not to the fastidious Etonian. 'Never shall I forget the ardent and tumultuous feelings with which I went to this interview,' he would write thirteen years later, '— and my heart even now sickens at the recollection of the sudden revulsion which all those feelings experienced.'[383] Nowhere does he say what it was that caused this revulsion. Perhaps she was not as clean and neat as he expected a lady to be. Her clothes were perhaps gaudy, but threadbare and patched – fine for a lady on the stage, but not at close quarters. Her voice and theatrical diction may have overwhelmed him. In the years of separation he had dreamt of being reunited with an idealised mother, of living with her and supporting her by his labours. Now, in a single moment of disillusionment, he saw distinctly that such a future was impossible. Supporting her by his labours, yes, that would always be his first duty, but living with her, seeing her day after day, listening as she invoked the claims of Motherhood and Nature in her stage voice, submitting to her passionate maternal embraces – never. What had been a vague and awkward secret now became an urgent and insoluble dilemma. At the end of that February day, as the coach took him back to Eton, he wrestled with the problem.

Dutiful and Affectionate Son – other sons,[i] more secure in their family and more confident in their sense of who they were, might find that the words fitted their feelings and expressed their duty quite comfortably, but for George the formula he had learned to use when writing to his distant mother now collided with his sudden feeling of revulsion. Duty required him to love his mother, and he would do his duty, but how much love was required, and how much had he to give? A son who is forced to ask such questions has already lost his way. Feeling and duty, nature and reason – could these abstractions help him cut through the thicket? Literature and society gossip alike abounded with undutiful sons and unnatural parents. His reading will have furnished striking examples of unnatural parents such as the Countess of Macclesfield who disowned her son, the poet Richard Savage, and notoriously undutiful sons like the Prince of Wales or Edward Wortley Montagu. Could such spectacular cases of family breakdown throw light on his own situation? He had not been told much of his own father's story, but he must have picked up enough to work out that something had broken down. He had met his Grandmother Canning, a kind old lady. Had his father failed in his duty to her? Had she unnaturally cast him out?

He reached no conclusions about how all that he had seen and felt that day would affect his own future, whether it meant abandoning his nascent ambition for a public career, and contenting himself with the obscurity of the legal profession, but one thing was certain: the secret must be buried still deeper beneath a brilliant surface. He confided in no one. What he feared was the sympathy of friends. Some of them, he suspected, would willingly open their purses to help him, but this would undermine his position; he would no longer be their brilliant leader, but their sordid dependant. Outside

i William Pitt, for instance, regularly ended his letters to his mother, 'Your ever dutiful and affectionate W. Pitt' (Hague, *William Pitt the Younger*, 52, 118).

school, who was there he could confide in? Stratty and Mehitabel were biased against his mother and would not give disinterested advice. The Leighs would at least have listened sympathetically, but as yet he didn't know them as intimately as he would later on. He was still in touch with his mentor Henry Richman, to whom he would later mention practical matters to do with Mary Ann, but no letters survive from the period immediately following the meeting in Great Wild Street.

Mary Ann's own response to this longed-for meeting was surprisingly muted. She had found him, she recalled, 'full of the tender duty which … still proved a solace to my distant sorrow', the melancholy tone hinting perhaps at a vague disappointment, as though she had sensed George's horrified reaction.[384]

In the summer of 1786 George accompanied Stratty and Mehitabel to Bath where old Mrs Canning was taking the waters. She was dying, her condition being, as Mary Ann surmised in one of her few surviving letters to George, 'one of those undescribable cases, which Physical sagacity rather seeks to alleviate, than pretends to understand'.[385] The old lady died in October, and was buried in Bath Abbey. George's sympathy at this sad time can only have intensified his sense of connection with his aunt and uncle, drawing him further from his mother and consolidating the feelings left behind by the meeting in Great Wild Street. He told Mary Ann that his dying grandmother had received him with great affection, which she must have read with mixed feelings – pleasure on his behalf, jealousy on her own.

Back in London in September George tried several times to find Esther and Mrs Costello's lodgings in Battlebridge, not knowing, perhaps, which side of the New Road to look. By then Mary Ann had left London. He received long letters from her, to which he sent brief replies. All his life this would be the pattern – pages and pages from Mary Ann, and hurried notes from George, interrupted by the demands of his busy life. In September he brought his letter to an abrupt end when the man came to cut his hair. But however brief his letters, he could not dismiss his mother's plight from his mind. 'Good God!' he wrote in October, 'That a Mother should labour under such disadvantages and such mortifications, and I not have the power to alleviate them.'[386]

13.
Northern Campaign, 1786–1787

Plausible Jack Palmer hoped to open his East End theatre in May 1786, but it soon became clear that this date could not be met. The Hunns' needs were pressing, so in March they launched themselves into the unknown territory of the North of England. They made the right choice; in the end, as actors who committed themselves to join him, such as Mrs Belfille from Norwich, would find to their cost, Plausible Jack's venture fizzled out.[387]

There were several theatrical circuits covering the northern counties, some more prestigious and lucrative than others. Companies of actors would travel from town to town, aiming to coincide with race meetings, fairs and assizes, sometimes in the larger towns staying for a season of several weeks or months, but in others playing for no more than a few nights before moving on. The actor-manager Tate Wilkinson, one of the great figures of eighteenth century theatre, controlled the licensed playhouses in York and Hull, with other bases in Wakefield, Doncaster, Pontefract, Sheffield and Leeds. He also visited theatres as far afield as Edinburgh and Norwich. Beverley had once been part of his circuit, but ownership of theatres was always fluid, as is clear from Wilkinson's characteristic comment on a rival manager, Samuel Butler: 'Like the French troops he seized upon my neighbouring territories of Beverley.' Wilkinson bore no grudge; he went on to describe Butler as 'a very honest man, indefatigable in his endeavours, and deserves the esteem and good will with which he is generally supported.'[388] He could afford to be generous; his own audiences were large enough to tempt major London players such as Mrs Siddons and her brother John Philip Kemble, and Mrs Jordan.

Another circuit, controlled by Joseph Austin and Charles Whitlock, husband of Mary Ann's old acquaintance Elizabeth Kemble, took in Lancaster and Chester,[i] and they were chosen by the proprietors of the new theatre in Newcastle upon Tyne to inaugurate their first season in 1788.[389] The company managed by Thomas Bates and his nephew James Cawdell had in the past played in a temporary theatre in the Moot Hall in Newcastle,[390] and now served the theatres in North Shields, Durham, Darlington, Stockton and Whitby.[ii] At a humbler level was an itinerant troupe who went the rounds of small towns in Lancashire under their manager Thomas Bibby.[iii] All these companies were, strictly speaking, itinerant, but the term was commonly used contemptuously for players without access to regular theatres, as in a pompous and graceless claim made a few years earlier by Whitlock, that his own productions had 'a more elegant and theatrical stile than can possibly be in the power of any little itinerant company who arrogate to themselves a species of theatrical merit which they are entirely unacquainted with.'[391]

As Wilkinson found, Samuel Butler was ambitious. In the early 1770s he had left his job as a stay-maker to join a company of

---

i Charles Whitlock (died 1822): According to Mary Ann, Charles Whitlock had started out in the theatre alongside William Siddons, and that they had each got on by marrying one of the talented and lucky Kemble women. (Mary Ann to George, 24 Aug. 1788).

ii James Cawdell (1749–1800) was an actor and poet who shared in the management of the theatre company founded by his uncle Thomas Bates, and took over sole control in 1788. The theatre at Whitby was included in Butler's circuit from 1793 (Rosenfeld, *Georgian Theatre of Richmond, Yorkshire*, 20).

iii Thomas Bibby is a shadowy figure. According to the *BDA*, a certain Mr Bibby who appeared in London in 1746 'may have been (or been related to) Thomas Bibby, the provincial manager active in the 1780s' (*BDA* ii. 108). He could possibly be the Mr Beeby encountered by Charlotte Deans in the 1790s in Carlisle (Marshall, ed., *A Travelling Actress in the North and Scotland*, 29).

players managed by a widow, Mrs Tryphosa Wright. Her first and second husbands had both been managers of the company, and on the death of Mr Wright she had taken over. She was in her mid-forties when Samuel joined and, although he was half her age, and indeed younger than her two daughters, she married him and handed the management to him. The company had a reputation for respectability, possibly enhanced by the fact that Tryphosa was a child of the clergy, as were both her sons-in-law. Butler himself had no pretensions about his acting abilities; what he contributed was energy and discipline. He planned new theatres at Richmond and Harrogate.[392]

The Hunns joined Butler's company in March 1786 at Beverley. One of Tryphosa's daughters had died the year before, depriving the company of one of its leading actresses, and it may have been this that gave Mary Ann her opportunity. Beverley was Butler's base until the summer, with a brief excursion to the small town of Howden, perhaps to catch the crowds attending a race meeting. The company then moved on to Harrogate for the summer, and then to Bedale and Northallerton, and perhaps to Ripon or even as far away as Kendal.[393] Samuel Reddish had died the year before in York asylum, but his name was not entirely forgotten, it seems, since Mary Ann found it worthwhile to let it be known that she was the former Mrs Reddish; it reminded northern playgoers that she had appeared on the London stage.[394]

Where the theatres were unlicensed the actors were still theoretically liable to be prosecuted under ancient laws against vagabonds, so along with all the other leaders of opinion who had to be conciliated, such as the local newspaper editor and the landlords of the larger inns, it was important to sound out the attitudes of the magistrates. It was not until 1788 that the Theatrical Representations Act gave magistrates the power to license players to perform in non-patented theatres, a move that coincided with the foundation of several new provincial theatres, such as Butler's in Harrogate and Richmond in 1788, and Kendal in 1789. Before then, although a blind eye seems to have been turned to illegal performances, the threat of prosecution always remained.

For the sake of negotiating with the local powers, and to look after the baggage and provide an escort on the dangerous roads, Mary Ann must have found it useful to have her husband with her, but as an actor he was a liability. Mary Ann had come across several couples who were employed as a package, and often there was a disparity in talent between them. She and Reddish had been such a couple, and the Wrightens, whom Mary Ann had known in Bristol, were another. But Richard Hunn was less talented than most. Any part that required him to do more than lounge in a gentlemanly manner on stage was beyond him. Worse still, he was ridiculously vain, and thought that Butler, who would stand no nonsense from his actors, treated him unfairly. He dragged Mary Ann into his dispute.[395]

One of Mary Ann's letters from Harrogate has survived.[396] Since the new theatre would not open for another two years, the company still used a converted barn. This was a common enough practice, and in some cases the barn was turned into a reasonable substitute for a theatre, with a proper stage and decent seating, but sometimes it was a very patched-up job. Harrogate's barn behind the Granby Hotel was probably better than most, but Mary Ann told George that it was 'not very well calculated for its guests'. Compared with Bath (where George was just then staying with the Cannings) the number of wealthy visitors was small. Mary Ann put the number at about 300, spread across the eight principal inns. Audiences at the theatre were always elegant, she said, but sometimes very thin. She had seen the plans for the new theatre and doubted whether it would be a success, but Butler knew his business. In the theatre's second season, for example, he was able to raise a subscription from the wealthier visitors to tempt Dorothea Jordan to break her journey to Edinburgh and play four nights in Harrogate.[397]

The cost of maintaining her children at school was a growing anxiety, and Mary Ann was counting on a good benefit night.

Members of the audience the previous week had been heard praising her performance as Violante in Susanna Centlivre's *The Wonder*, so she was hopeful. The company at one of the inns, The Dragon, ordered forty-two box seats. On the day of her benefit there was a tremendous thunderstorm with torrential rain, and it looked as though the performance might be cancelled, but the weather cleared by six o'clock and, although the pit and gallery were emptier than usual, the boxes, whose occupants presumably came by carriage, were unaffected.

While Mary Ann was making the most of slim pickings in Harrogate, Sarah Siddons was enjoying her lucrative visits to York and Hull, and back again to York for the race week. Tate Wilkinson recorded that Mrs Siddons played to unprecedentedly large audiences across Yorkshire, making 1786 a 'Sidonian year', but the expense he incurred in transporting the star actress from place to place meant it was not also a 'Wilkinsonian' year.[398] News of the this triumph travelled across Yorkshire, leading Mary Ann to comment sourly that Mrs Siddons 'was born in One of Fortune's favorite Moments – and yet her natural Parsimony makes her as miserable as if she had never emerged from the Obscurity in which she was born.'

In the hope of returning closer to her familiar haunts Mary Ann took advantage of George's visit to Bath to ask again about the state of the theatre there. Could he confirm that John Palmer, whom she had hoped Stratty would speak to on her behalf the year before, had handed day-to-day management of the theatre to his partner William Keasberry?[i] If decisions were up to Keasberry she was hopeful of securing a recommendation from Keasberry's son-in-law, Nathaniel Peach, who was in the clothing trade and was, Hunn claimed, a former business associate.[399] It was a flimsy hope, but she grasped it, telling George (in answer to Stratty's assertion to the contrary) that in the theatre 'interest is the best recommendation to get engagements', even if merit is the only way to keep them. In contrast to his eagerness to help the previous year, before the Great

i William Keasberry (1726–1797) was a joint-patentee of the Bath theatre with John Palmer. Palmer's many other interests may have left Keasberry in control.

Wild Street meeting, George replied coolly to her questions. He kept her letter, which may indicate a willingness to make enquiries on her behalf, but all he came up with was the truism that a 'constant situation [would be] more eligible, both as being more creditable, and indeed from considerations of travelling expenses.'[400]

Two years later, when Mary Ann was, briefly, in markedly better circumstances, she wrote of this phase of her career in disparaging terms: she had mortified her feelings, she said, in several small companies, ending in a 'disgracefull Company of Itinerants'.[401] There was no reason for Mary Ann to be ashamed of Butler's company. But when Hunn quarrelled once too often with the Butlers, he and Mary Ann had to move on. In December 1786 Mary Ann was in South Shields, appearing in *The Gamester* at the request of the Freemasons.[402] The part of Beverley was taken by James Cawdell from North Shields. Cawdell was sufficiently impressed by her performance to take her on, along with her husband. They travelled with their new companions down the coast, and in February were appearing at Whitby. Since Bates and Cawdell's theatres were mainly in coastal towns, the company usually travelled by sea. Cawdell's poem 'The Royal Cargo, or the Company's Voyage from Scarborough', describes how they were wind-bound for nearly a fortnight.[403] By the summer Hunn had quarrelled with Cawdell, and so he and Mary Ann crossed the Pennines to join Mr Bibby's strolling company in Lancashire.

While Mary Ann says little about her life on this lowest rung of the theatrical profession, actresses of a later and of an earlier generation have left vivid accounts. Around the turn of the century Charlotte Deans of Wigton tramped on foot through Cumberland and the Scottish Borders, leading her children and wading across rivers in spate.

> We must have perished at one place, [she wrote] but for the kindness of a traveller from Galashiels, the water taking his horse to the shoulders as he carried us across. It was dark long before we reached our place of destination; we had only one guide which

> was the volcanic-like blazing of Carron Iron Works. A little boy hearing our youngest child but one crying from fatigue, as she walked, (Mr Deans carrying the infant,) took her on his back and bore her, like a little hero, to the door of our lodgings, and left us without waiting for thanks.[404]

At the end of these epic journeys there was, if they were lucky, a friendly innkeeper who would feed them on credit while they set up a makeshift theatre and hoped for an audience. At Jedburgh, for instance, Charlotte and her husband had a barn to perform in, the cobwebs and holes in the roof covered up with miscellaneous pieces of scenery, and they were lucky to find a blind musician to play their music and French prisoners-of-war to swell their audience.[405] This passage, from towards the end of her long career, gives a sense of her journeyings:

> We went to Kirkoswald and did very well, we next went to Cumrew and Brampton, then the Mauldsmeaburn, where… we continued here a few nights, and then went to Appleby a month, to Brough a fortnight, and then over Stainmoor to Barnard Castle, where we did well until the death of King George the Fourth put an end to our performances, when we returned across Stainmoor to Kirkby Stephen without success, passing through Sedburgh to Kirkby Lonsdale, where we were also unsuccessful: proceeded to Bampton for two nights and Mauldsmeaburn two nights, to Greystoke, Hesket-newmarket, Caldbeck, Wigton, Aspatria, and Maryport, … we then went to Allonby and Skinburness, crossed the Solway to Annan, and then to Gretna.[406]

Charlotte Charke, the estranged daughter of Colley Cibber, experienced the whole gamut of theatrical life in the mid-century. She knew the regular playhouses of fashionable London, but her memoirs deal mainly with her life on lower levels of the profession. She writes contemptuously of her time amongst ragged groups of actors – ‘a complete tragical emetic for a person of the smallest degree of judgement’ – and country audiences made up of snoring butchers and their chattering wives. She complains of the tedious routine of dragging bundles of costumes and props from town to town, and describes a night that she and her companions spent in a Gloucestershire gaol.[407] Mrs Charke's memoirs are highly satirical and entertaining, but her respect for her craft was genuine enough. She hated to see it debased. Mary Ann likewise was a dedicated professional who had performed with the likes of Garrick, Reddish and Mrs Yates. She was appalled at the depths to which her husband's vanity and folly had reduced her.

As they moved on from one town to another Mary Ann left instructions for her letters to be forwarded, and kept in precarious touch with George until February 1787, when she was with Cawdell in Whitby. Then there seems to have been silence between them for three months or more. George was ending his Eton career on a high note of excitement. Then in June, needing to contact her urgently following the sudden death of his Uncle Stratty, he found he had lost track of her movements altogether, and so sent his letter to Esther in the hope that she could forward it.[408]

By then the Hunns were in the town of Bury in Lancashire with Bibby. As there was no regular playhouse in Bury, Bibby and his troupe set up their stage in a large barn in Moss Lane. With audiences large enough to require a gallery to be erected, the makeshift arrangement acquired an air of permanence, and people referred to the barn as the 'theatre'. Like the converted barn in Harrogate, it was more elaborately furnished than that described by Charlotte Deans, and clearly, for a town with neither a theatre nor assembly rooms, made a good substitute. Nonetheless, acting in a barn was associated with the lowest rank of the profession, suggesting scenes like Hogarth's *Strolling Actresses Dressing in a Barn*, with all its squalor, moral laxity and vitality.[409]

On 4 July 1787 the company was offering a long programme at the request of the local Freemasons. What happened is passed over in a brief sentence in the Packet, and the account given here is taken from press reports and the work of a local historian, Benjamin

Barton, who wrote some ninety years after the event.[410] The main piece was *King Henry IV with the Humours of Sir John Falstaff*, Thomas Betterton's adaptation from Shakespeare, supported by John O'Keefe's pantomime *The Lord Mayor's Day*. There were incidental songs, including one with words by Emmanuel Swedenborg, likely to be of interest to Freemasons, and a tableau showing a masonic dinner and featuring local members of the brotherhood. Late in the proceedings (past midnight in Barton's account, about half past ten according to the *Whitehall Evening Post*) the external brick wall gave way under the pressure of the crowd in the gallery, bringing down the gallery itself and much of the roof. As many as 300 members of the audience were buried beneath the debris; many were crushed under the weight of the slate roof, with broken limbs, fractured skulls and seven or eight killed outright.

The correspondent in the *Times*, who was present and lost a brother and sister in the disaster, referred to 'riotous' behaviour in the gallery, which could mean anything from boisterousness to actual fighting. The *Manchester Mercury* points to the weakness of the external wall, and although it blames the 'rude behaviour of the lower class of people pressing into the gallery' the root cause seems to be that the barn was not constructed for the use to which it was now being put. Barton claims that 'evidence of this night's troubles might be seen in limps, and distorted limbs, down until half a century afterwards', which suggests that the story lingered in local legend. He gives colourful touches – people climbing on rafters, the stillness of the midsummer night, and the cracks and booms of the falling timbers – which are plausible enough, but may be the product of Barton's dramatic imagination.

Mary Ann and her husband were badly shaken but unhurt. They moved on to Wigan, more determined than ever to leave Bibby and his company.[411]

14.
George's Progress, 1786–1788

In London, George read about the Bury disaster, but his mind was full of other things, and since his mother's engagements had hitherto been to the east of the Pennines, it did not occur to him that she was involved. The fifteen months that had passed since the Great Wild Street meeting had brought dramatic changes in his own life. His Eton career had come to a glorious end, with the prize composition of 700 Latin verses in commemoration of the restoration of Charles II. His wit, wide reading and gift of language are all evident in a project which brought still greater acclaim. This was the *Microcosm*, which started as a school magazine but was taken up by an enterprising publisher, and sold to the public. It was a joint effort with his friends John Frere, Robert (Bobus) Smith and John (Easley) Smith. They invented an editor called Gregory Griffin, and the magazine was made up of papers supposedly written by him or submitted to him, which was a literary device adopted in publications such as the *Gentleman's Magazine*. It allowed the boys to display their own fine writing while poking fun at the periodical literature of the day. The fame of the *Microcosm* reached the King, who congratulated George personally on the Terrace at Windsor, and remembered it years later when George was a rising politician. Urging his mother to buy a copy, George told her proudly that his articles were those signed *B.*[412]

His contribution to the final number included a fragment of Gregory Griffin's 'Life':

> Of my birth and parentage I shall say nothing; for, from an account of either no instruction could be gathered. Of my education—the first circumstances, which I have any recollection of, are, that I was, at the age of six years, employed in learning the rudiments of my mother tongue, spinning cock-chafers on corking-pins, and longing for bread and butter, at a day school, near—— My proficiency here was so great, that I actually got through within a month, by far the greater part of a gingerbread alphabet, and might be literally said to devour my learning with an astonishing avidity. In my hours of relaxation from study, the utmost stretch of my intellects was the acquisition of the aforesaid bread and butter; the highest notion I could conceive of rational amusement, was enjoyment of that delight, which arose from the contemplation of the above mentioned cock-chafer, writhing, or, as I then, in compliance with the custom of my schoolfellows, termed it, *preaching*, in the agonies of impalement.[413]

Biographers of Canning refer to this mock-reminiscence as justification for John Moody's fears about George's misspent childhood. '[A]n illuminating scrap of autobiography,' one calls it,[414] but it betrays less about George's childhood than about the seventeen-year-old boy who wrote it. With all the secrets he was determined to keep safe, he still dared, albeit under the cloak of a fictional persona, to draw the attention of his schoolfellows to his own unmentionable birth and parentage, and to the poverty of his early years. Always reserved and secretive, and alert to any threat to his reputation, he possessed also a streak of recklessness, particularly when he had a pen in his hand and an idea in his mind.

He now had a small income of his own under Mrs Canning's will, some £220 of Irish rents, out of which, with Stratty's permission, he made an allowance of £20 a year to Mary Ann. He told her that Mr Hunn should 'draw on my uncle' for the sum.[415] This locution would become familiar, but this was the first time it appears in George's letters and we can imagine that he wrote it with a certain mental flourish, with the amusement that he would always feel when confronted with a new piece of jargon, and with some emotion as he made the first step towards fulfilling his duty towards his mother. Mary Ann also, as she read and re-read his letter, must have felt, along with gratitude for the much needed subsidy, a glow of pride at this sign that George was becoming a man.

Stratty's death in May 1787 gave George a further opportunity to demonstrate his maturity and capacity for business. He came away from school to help his bereaved aunt, accompanying the coffin from Brighton to London, and discussing affairs with Stratty's partner Walter Borrowes.[416] The news reached Mary Ann while she was in Bury. It was almost twenty years since sweet little Stratty had enlivened evenings with her gloomy husband in Queen Anne Street, and more than ten since their last tense meeting in the sponging-house. He had judged her severely and had stood between her and her son, but he was also the one out of all the men in her life who had, for a time at least, served her most disinterestedly. She had not forgotten his ingenuous attempt to help her by hiding banknotes around her house.

George asked William Leigh to act as his guardian, but it's not clear how formal the arrangement was. In August he told Mary Ann that Walter Borrowes was now his guardian. Over the years George came to trust Borrowes on money matters, but even at this early stage he saw that his uncle's business partner was incapable of advising him more widely. He did not break with Mehitabel or the cousins he had grown up with, but without Stratty in Clements Lane he was all the more inclined to spend time with the Leighs. William Leigh lived the life of a country gentleman, and Bess was a woman who took life easily, assisted by the occasional strong drink, whereas Mehitabel was a harassed widow, bringing up five children and struggling with the financial tangle that Stratty had left behind. George's first independent act, which neither Borrowes nor William Leigh could oppose, was to raise Mary Ann's allowance from twenty to fifty pounds. He told her of this intention in August, although it was three months before the money was ready for her to draw on Borrowes' bank for the extra £30.[417]

For part of the summer of 1787 George lived with Richard Brinsley Sheridan, who took an interest in him, both for the sake of old friendship with the Cannings and because he saw a promising recruit to the Whig cause. Agitation for the emancipation of Catholics from the remaining disabilities and for radical political reform made these interesting times. The French Revolution had not yet brought about the change in the political mood in England which was to shut down hopes of progressive reform and keep the Whigs out of power for a generation. Sheridan's friendship with the young Canning was so close that the story got about that he was George's guardian. Sheridan was the one person who could have provided George with an insight into his mother's past, but if he did so there is no record of it. Perhaps reticence ruled. Sheridan himself was ambivalent towards the theatre – apart from money-lenders it remained his only source of income, but he had vetoed his wife's singing career and quarrelled with his father over the old man's refusal to stop performing. George remained all his life grateful to Sheridan for his kindness at this critical period, but of all the advice he picked up from their conversations the one thing he referred back to was the warning that a theatrical connection was a drawback for an aspiring politician.[418]

This same summer a trivial incident occurred which was to have a lasting effect on George. He sought the advice of his father's friend Sir George Macartney. Macartney, through his wife, knew about Mary Ann. Mary Ann had not warmed towards Lady Jane, even while benefiting from her assistance, and the relations between the two women must have become frostier still with the scandal over Reddish. Macartney was an ambitious social climber, not the man to risk anything on behalf of the son of one of his wife's cast-off protégées. In any case, George approached him at a bad time, when he had recently come home from India, was facing severe criticism for his conduct of affairs there and had narrowly survived a duel. Macartney seemed well disposed towards George, and wrote platitudinous letters recommending diligence in his studies (underlining diligence), but later received him coldly.[419] Mary Ann, had she heard of this rebuff, would have seen in it the malign influence of Macartney's father-in-law, Lord Bute. George made up his mind to have nothing more to do with Macartney, and the incident left him with a lifelong horror of being snubbed by great men.

Macartney, Sheridan and William Leigh all offered George advice on the next step in his education. Without much difficulty they fixed upon Oxford and Christ Church, but then there was disagreement about whether he should go as a Commoner or a Gentleman Commoner, another arcane issue, like the Colleger/Oppidan question at Eton. Macartney advised becoming a Gentleman Commoner, and George agreed, but William Leigh argued that this was a needless extravagance, persuading George to take the safer, less glamorous option.[420] It may be this change of plan that caused Macartney's coolness. These matters were speedily resolved. It was more difficult for him to fix upon his ultimate choice of career – law, politics or literature? – the conundrum that his father had never solved. There was no need to decide immediately, since the same course of studies would prepare for all three.

During his first year at Christ Church George was seduced into joining an aristocratic debating society whose members included Robert Jenkinson, the son of Lord Hawkesbury. Jenkinson's career and George's would run in parallel for the next forty years. George was the more brilliant, but it was his friend who was destined to succeed more quickly – his father bought him a seat in Parliament before he was twenty-one. Although the debates (and indeed the society's very existence) were supposed to be secret, it was common knowledge that George espoused the radical reformist side. The King is said to have remarked that 'Mr Canning's republican principles had done great harm at Christ Church'.[421] In his second year George gave up the debates and acquired a more useful reputation for hard work. He won the university prize for Latin verse, and in his third year he was awarded a studentship. But giving up the debates and concentrating on academic success did not mean giving up his friendships. He did not go back on the choice he had made at Eton to side with the wealthy and aristocratic Oppidans, rather than the Collegers, the scholarship boys who swotted away in the hope of a fellowship and a comfortable college living.

At Christmas 1787 Mary Ann sent him a 'GC' seal that had belonged to his father, part of his pitifully meagre inheritance. When he wrote to thank her for it on Boxing Day he used it to seal his letter. She took care when opening it to preserve the wax intact. She believed that one of the holds she had over George was that she was the keeper of his father's memory. Unfortunately, although George was always respectful, he was only fitfully interested in the father who for all his talent had achieved so little.

No letters from George have survived from the eight months following the letter with the GC seal. Mary Ann began a letter from Lancaster in August 1788 by remarking on his silence, but adding: 'But my sweet Boy I woud have every Act towards me, spring from the heart; nor coud I accept, a duty I enforced. – Write then, my love, when you can, when you will; let not thy Mother be a tax upon your liberty and happiness.' Having heard of his 'Zeal in politics', his debating club and the notoriety of his republican views, she warned him not to offend the King as his father had. 'I hope that time has deaden'd the Royal resentment,' she added, 'and that you will never feel those consequences from it which have so severely sunk me.' William Reddish, now eight years old, was with her in Lancaster, and he caught her enthusiasm, declaring that George was destined to be the Glory of his Country and the Blessing of his Mother. She repeated William's words to George, not suspecting that for many years these two destinies would be in conflict, as his pursuit of public glory meant their lives would run along separate paths.[422]

15.
The Whitlock Circuit 1787–1788

In Wigan, shortly after the Bury disaster, Mary Ann met Charles and Elizabeth Whitlock. As managers of the playhouses at Lancaster and Chester, the Whitlocks were aristocrats of the theatre in the region. When news of what had happened at Bury reached them they were about to inaugurate a new theatre in Preston, and either stopped in Wigan on their way or hurried there specially to help the survivors. Elizabeth Whitlock showed herself friendly towards Mary Ann, grateful for past help, suggesting that the Hunns should join the company. Mary Ann would take a share of the 'first business', while Hunn could pick up any small parts that might come his way. This was a big step up after Bibby's troupe, and the Hunns accepted gratefully.[423]

For Mary Ann, who had patronised and protected Elizabeth in Plymouth, it was a sad reversal. No doubt she compensated for her humiliating circumstances, as she would so often in later years, by talking about her son's achievements – his prize poem, his success with the *Microcosm*, and his summer in London with Sheridan. Charles Whitlock saw an opportunity to boost the coming season at Chester by securing the endorsement of the locally influential Frances Crewe, the celebrated political hostess and toast of the Whigs, whose husband was MP for the county and a parliamentary supporter of Charles James Fox. It was well known that Sheridan was a regular visitor at Crewe Hall. Whitlock suggested that perhaps Mary Ann might ask her son to ask his friend Sheridan to ask Mrs Crewe to lend her name to support the theatre.

Mary Ann duly asked George. He may not have known that Sheridan had been Frances Crewe's lover, and that now, despite their political alliance, they were personally estranged, but even without this extra twist it was clearly an embarrassing request. He tactfully evaded the problem, saying it was a bad time to raise the matter because Sheridan was preoccupied with the death of his wife's sister ten days earlier. In a single letter which encapsulated the contrasts and tensions of their lives he announced that he was increasing her allowance to £50, commiserated over the Bury disaster, lamented that he did not know where she now was, described his conversation with the King, and apologised for not being able to pass on her request to Sheridan. Later in the autumn when Mary Ann raised the matter again, George went to Battlebridge to discuss it with Aunt Esther, who wrote to assure Mary Ann that there was nothing to be done. This is one of only two letters from Esther that have survived. On the other half of the sheet George told Mary Ann to draw her extra £30 allowance.[424] Since he had decided on this three months earlier it had nothing to do with the disappointment over Mrs Crewe, but it made a convenient way of softening the blow. It was to be a pattern that he followed repeatedly in the years to come: disagreement and disappointment followed by gifts of money.

Even without Mrs Crewe's endorsement Mary Ann's first season at Chester went well enough, although the statement in the Packet that she was to 'divide the first business' with Mrs Whitlock gives a misleading impression. Mrs Whitlock took a large share of the first business, and there was more competition for the remainder than Mary Ann implies. A puff in the *Cumberland Pacquet* declared Austin and Whitlock's to be 'the best Company out of London' and included Mary Ann among its six 'Capital Actresses', describing her, inaccurately, as 'from the Theatre Royal, Bath'. The list also included Mrs Belfille, who had come north following the failure of Plausible Jack Palmer's venture in London's East End.[425]

An account of the season in Chester can be constructed from Frederick Gale's study of surviving playbills together with the theatrical announcements in the *Chester Courant.* Neither source is comprehensive, and the picture is incomplete. Gale notes on some of the bills the handwritten comment that Mrs Hunn was Mr Canning's mother.

Mary Ann began on 7 November with the leading part of Mrs Sullen in Farquhar's *The Beaux' Stratagem*, and a few days later played Gertrude in *Hamlet*, but thereafter she had less prominent roles. Mrs Belfille now took the first business in comedies, such as Hannah Cowley's *A School for Greybeards* and Arthur Murphy's *All in the Wrong*, and made what was billed as her first appearance in tragedy as Adelaide in Robert Jephson's *Count of Narbonne.* Mrs Whitlock retained the other major tragic roles, leaving Mary Ann to play subsidiary characters in plays such as *The Gamester* and *Edward and Eleonora* in which she had been used to taking the lead. For her benefit on 14 December Mary Ann chose *The Rivals* (Sheridan contributing something to her benefit after all) in which she took the second lead, Julia, with Mrs Belfille as Lydia. Mr Hunn played Fagg, the servant. Mary Ann did not take part in the afterpiece, Thomas Betterton's *Barnaby Brittle*, in which Mrs Belfille again played the leading lady. Richard Hunn played servants and other minor roles throughout the season, including Osric in *Hamlet*, perhaps the ideal character for him, since Mary Ann thought his only assets as an actor were his gentlemanlike manners.[426]

On 7 December Mary Ann played Elmira in the afterpiece, Isaac Bickerstaff's *The Sultan*, and her husband took part in the night's mainpiece, Hannah Cowley's *A Bold Stroke for a Husband.* This was probably the night that Mrs Crewe's house guests visited the theatre, among them Elizabeth Sheridan. When someone remarked that one of the actresses had been one of the many

Mrs Reddishes, Elizabeth realised who she was and remembered meeting her, as Mrs Canning, years before. With a shock, Mary Ann recognised her in the audience and, according to Elizabeth, 'never took her eyes from my face, which quite distressed me.' In a letter to Mehitabel, Elizabeth described Mary Ann as 'thinner, older and more ugly than you can imagine'. She was more disgusted still by the illiterate and vulgar Hunn: 'With her understanding and talents (for she certainly had both) to make such a choice!' She also noted that Mary Ann was very big with child, which may have been an exaggeration because at this point Mary Ann was less than six months pregnant. Elizabeth attributed Mary Ann's wretchedness not to poverty, misfortune and injustice but to her 'vices'.[427]

Between Christmas and New Year Mary Ann repeated her performance as Gertrude in *Hamlet*, and played Queen Elinor in *King John* and Irene in *Barbarossa*, in both of which the leading female part was taken by Mrs Whitlock. In January Mr Hunn played Stukely in *The West Indian*, with Mary Ann not listed and the female lead taken by Mrs Belfille. Again, on the last night of the season Mary Ann was not listed, but her husband had a part in the afterpiece, a brand new farce by Edward Topham, *Bonds without Judgement or the Loves of Bengal*.[428]

After Chester the Whitlocks moved to Newcastle, to inaugurate the new Theatre Royal. In the first two weeks Mary Ann, billed as a newcomer to Newcastle, appeared in the afterpieces, but not in the mainpieces. Elizabeth Whitlock and Mrs Belfille shared the first business. [429] From mid-February onwards Mary Ann was in no condition to perform, being confined for a full seven weeks before the birth of her daughter Maria in the first week of April. She told George of the event in a letter on his eighteenth birthday, writing warmly of her husband's attentiveness during her long and difficult confinement.[430] Whatever her own feelings about Richard Hunn, she wanted George to think well of him.

Mary Ann, who had zealously suckled Letitia, George and

Thomas, over-zealously according to her friends, entrusted her Reddish and Hunn children to wet nurses. 'Poor Richard' was being cared for in the West Country, and now Maria was left with a nurse outside Newcastle while the company moved back to Chester for the race week in May, and then on to Lancaster. This distressing separation probably saved Maria's life, because at Lancaster the European influenza pandemic caught up with the company. The newspapers told of high-placed individuals such as the Austrian Emperor and the King of Poland who suffered during that summer. The disease reached London in June, and Scotland by August. Mary Ann described it as 'an Epidemic sore throat and scarlet fever which raged all round me, and swept many to the grave' and her treatment as 'an enormous blister and the nauseous regimen of Bark and Port'. The disease was said to be seldom fatal if treated carefully, as is confirmed by the fact that while the poor died in large numbers the prominent sufferers seem to have survived. Mary Ann mused on the uncertainties of life: she had written to Esther, she said, reporting herself well enough to appear on consecutive nights as Mrs Beverley in *The Gamester* and Lady Randolph in *Douglas*, but 'while she [Esther] was reading my own attestation of being in perfect health, I was in the high road (apparently) to the grave.'[431] From this it appears that she now had a share of the first business, possibly because other actresses were already sick.

We don't know what prompted George to preserve this letter and the earlier one from Newcastle, but it may be because they reported Mary Ann's safe delivery from the perils of childbirth and disease. The Lancaster letter went on to describe deteriorating relations with the Whitlocks. Charles Whitlock was autocratic and boorish, but his conduct was not 'wrong by the rules of the Theatre'. As Mary Ann had acknowledged at the time of *Semiramis*, the manager of a company had to command obedience like any other head of a family. She herself was well enough rewarded for her patience, she said, but her husband's feelings 'which are exquisite, are sometimes severely, and often unnecessarily sported with'. Disenchanted with the theatre, Hunn was now looking out for some other occupation to tide him over until he might come into his inheritance – his father, Mary Ann noted, was over seventy and 'at his Death we ought to be independant'.

Mary Ann's complaints prompted George to write that he hoped to rescue her 'from a line of life, in which you have endured so much'. This letter, addressed to her in Chester, was long and painful, marking the end of his lingering romantic feelings for the theatre. Mary Ann recalled that it was during this second Chester season, that 'in several of your letters a sort of regret appeared at my precise situation in the world'. He moved from mere commiseration to active hostility to her profession. His calm hope to rescue her from her line of life was followed by a more emotional outburst: suspecting that Mary Ann planned to put Mary (then aged eleven and at Mrs Moore's school in Exeter) on the stage, 'For God's sake,' he exclaimed, 'for her sake and your own – do not permit a thought of theatrical attachments to take root in her breast.'[432]

The main purpose of his letter was to respond to her renewed request for Sheridan's help in applying to Mrs Crewe. The previous year's excuse no longer applied, and George had approached Sheridan and discussed the matter with Aunt Esther, who told him it was customary for actresses to call on their patronesses in person. He begged his mother not to do this, assuring her that Sheridan was confident he could prevail upon Mrs Crewe. The situation was particularly embarrassing because his university reputation had reached Crewe Hall, and he had been invited to stay there in the autumn. His mother's presence made this unthinkable. He wrote to Mrs Crewe, not making a bland excuse but explaining exactly why he couldn't come, and asking her to support Mary Ann's benefit. Just as Mary Ann was reading of Sheridan's assurance that the application would succeed, Mrs Crewe herself was changing her mind, writing regretfully that she had to consider the effect of a theatrical connection on her husband's electors. George was sure Mrs Crewe's regrets were sincere, but if Mary Ann suspected otherwise she was probably right: John Crewe was invariably returned for the county unopposed.[433] George had hesitated before making his request, and Mrs Crewe's friendly snub told him he had been right to hesitate. The lesson he had learned from George Macartney's cold reception was confirmed: great people were to be treated with caution.

The autumn season at Chester was preceded by three performances at Eaton, home of Lord Grosvenor, before opening at the Theatre Royal on 22 September 'by Desire of Lord Viscount Belgrave', Lord Grosvenor's son. Mary Ann played Lady Capulet in *Romeo and Juliet* on 24 September, with her husband having a part in the afterpiece, Hannah Cowley's *Who's the Dupe?* Then neither of the Hunns is listed until the end of October, when Mr Hunn had small parts in both *The Merchant of Venice* and the afterpiece, *The Farmer* by John O'Keefe. When *Jane Shore* was performed on 5 November Mr Hunn played the minor character of Ratcliffe, but Mary Ann did not appear, the part of Jane being taken by a Miss Henry, making her first appearance at Chester.[434]

For Mrs Whitlock's benefit on 12 November the mainpiece was a new tragedy, *The Regent* by Bertie Greatheed, which had had a controversial first performance at Drury Lane in the spring.[i] Richard Hunn had a small part, but Mary Ann is not listed that night, and indeed, so far as we know she appeared only twice more in the season, on her benefit night, 14 November, and five days later as Lady Loveall in the afterpiece, Elizabeth Inchbald's *Appearance is Against Them.* For her benefit she played Pulcheria in Nathaniel Lee's *Theodosius,* a strange play with little of the energy of Lee's *Rival Queens.*[435] At the end the feeble emperor Theodosius, thwarted in love, retires from the world, handing over his power and responsibilities to his strong-minded and intelligent sister

i Bertie Greatheed (1759–1826) was the nephew of the Duke of Ancaster. When his play was first produced in London it was generally well received, but the audience protested against a scene in which a child was mistreated onstage.

Pulcheria – another apt character for Mary Ann, who in her own life so often found herself tidying up after weak and ineffectual men.

There were performances at the Theatre Royal on three nights each week, but the *Chester Courant* seldom had space to advertise them all, and even when a play was advertised not all the *dramatis personae* were listed.[i] The evidence is therefore incomplete, but it seems that in 1788 Mary Ann was less prominent than she had been the year before. This may have been because her health had not recovered following her illness in Lancaster, or it may indicate a loss of status within the company, in which case her reliance on Mrs Crewe's backing was more desperate than George realised. Unlike Mary Ann's, Mrs Whitlock's benefit was sponsored by a local magnate, Sir Watkin Williams Wynn, MP for Denbighshire and a keen theatre-goer. This, together with the enthusiastic support given to the company by Viscount Belgrave, who already at twenty-one was an MP, casts doubt on the sincerity of Mrs Crewe's excuse for withholding her name. It may reflect a difference in the political circumstances of John Crewe compared with the others, since as a Whig, Crewe depended in part on the non-conformist interest which would generally be more hostile to the theatre than the Tory squires who supported Belgrave and Williams Wynn. Neither the Whitlocks nor Mary Ann, however, are likely to have understood this, so Mrs Crewe's refusal must have left a bitter taste, and may have precipitated the next setback in Mary Ann's career.

**

Running a provincial theatre was a precarious business, and the Whitlocks appreciated the value of endorsement by the local gentry. For some time Mary Ann had been contributing less to the work of the company, and when it became clear that she had no influence with Sheridan and the Crewes Charles Whitlock

i On 23 Sept. 1788, for example, a third of the space in the four-page newspaper was taken up with lists of holders of game licences.

decided to part with her at the end of the season. Getting rid of her troublesome husband would be a further advantage. Relations worsened steadily, but Mary Ann was used to the storms of theatrical life, and was not prepared for the announcement at the beginning of December that she would not be required in Newcastle.[436]

She found herself stranded in Chester, 180 miles from Maria in Newcastle and from George in London, but she had not lost her old elasticity. By selling some of her more valuable costumes and props she raised just enough to pay her fare to Newcastle and her husband's to London. Hunn's infatuation with the theatre had completely evaporated, and he promised to look for other employment in the West Country. Mary Ann gave him a letter to present to George asking for an advance on the next half-year's allowance. Once she had collected Maria she would follow him down to Plymouth by sea. She was pregnant again, and would be with him before her confinement, she said.[437]

George had now had repeated intimations of how precarious the theatrical life could be – the Bury accident, the epidemic at Lancaster, the treachery of the Whitlocks, the humiliating dependence on capricious patrons. In three years his romantic view of the theatre had been replaced by precisely the sentiments Stratty had hoped for. At the time of his embarrassment over Mrs Crewe he told Bess and William Leigh of his determination to rescue Mary Ann from the theatre:

> I hope to God the time will come when it will be in my power to effect something more permanent for her ease and comfort, and to snatch her, at least in her decline of life, from a profession, which even in its most brilliant situations the prejudice and perhaps illiberality of mankind has stamped as disreputable, but which in her line of it has much, much more than even that consideration to make it the least eligible of all the stations in which a woman can be placed.[438]

The words run smoothly on the page, but he did not write them without hesitation. The phrase 'and perhaps illiberality' was an afterthought, an attempt to distance himself from the prejudice of mankind. But the final exaggerated denunciation is his own, not that of illiberal mankind. As will often be the case with George's pronouncements, apparent precision obscured an underlying confusion of feeling. What exactly was it that made Mary Ann's 'line' the 'least eligible' station for a woman? It was indisputably precarious, and her liaison with Reddish seemed to substantiate the belief that it was immoral. Mixed with these reasons was something more personal, more deeply felt: the revulsion experienced at the Great Wild Street meeting.

But he could not persuade Mary Ann to give up the stage unless he had something better to offer. She had to live and support her family. The uncertainty of his own position was brought forcibly to his attention by the bankruptcy of his late uncle's firm in the autumn of 1788. It is not clear whether Stratty had left the firm in a bad way, or whether Borrowes, without Stratty's guidance, had bungled things. George didn't lose anything himself in the crash, because he had nothing in his account, but it meant delay in receiving his income from Ireland. Matters were arranged by Borrowes and Mehitabel's brother Paul Patrick, so that when Richard Hunn turned up in London at the beginning of 1789 and presented Mary Ann's letter, the money was there to give him ten guineas and send him on his way.[439]

16.
Newcastle and Bristol, 1789–1791

When George thought of his mother's 'line of life' his imagination dwelt on its hardships and disappointments, taking no account of any pleasure or satisfaction she might have derived from her work. After fifteen years, he thought, she must welcome release should a reasonable alternative offer itself. He may well have been right. When her husband left for the South to make a new life outside the theatre, she hoped to follow his example after a few years. Her struggles had left her destitute and exhausted. Nonetheless, when she came to look back on her life she reckoned that the two or three years following her abandonment by the Whitlocks were as wretched as any she'd known – no more eligible than her time on the stage.[440]

When she reached Newcastle from Chester at the beginning of January 1789, she was reunited with her baby daughter. Her plan was to travel by sea to Plymouth in the expectation of an engagement at the theatre, but the winter weather prevented her sailing. By the time the storms abated she had fallen ill and would have to stay where she was, cared for by friends, until after her lying-in. For the seven months she was in Newcastle all she had to support herself was her allowance from George, plus twelve guineas raised by selling the remainder of her theatrical trinkets. She remembered later with pleasure that when the half-year's instalment fell due George sent her twenty pounds, deducting only half of the money he had advanced to her husband. Her pregnancy was difficult and her anxious friends contacted George. He sent five guineas, all he could scrape together; 'trifling assistance', he called it. The twins, Frederick and Ann, were born at the end of May, after which she was again ill. In June, George, not having heard from her for a month, wrote anxiously from Oxford to inquire after her and, incidentally, to tell her of his Latin verse prize.[441]

When she recovered she was impatient to leave Newcastle, but was detained because her husband had not sent the £20 she was expecting to pay her debts and her fare. He was working by now for a draper, William Stephens, in Wine Street, Bristol. She believed he had the money and could have sent it, but Stephens may have been slow to pay his salary. Relations between Hunn and his employer were bad from the outset. At last, in July, the twenty pounds arrived, enabling her to settle with her creditors and board the boat for London, along with her three babies and a servant. Years later she remembered the kindness shown her by the 'social and hospitable Northumbrians' at this all but fatal crisis in her life.[442]

The fatigue of her nine days' sea voyage, on top of her confinement and illness, gave Mary Ann a reason for staying in London, close to her sister and mother. It was the vacation and George came to town, affording her the delight, she said, that only happy mothers know. It was three years since the meeting in Great Wild Street, when George had been 'almost a man'; now he was quite a man, more assured, more assertive. Mary Ann's idea of proceeding to the theatre in Plymouth had been dropped, either because she was still in poor health, or because she expected her husband to support her. George hoped she would settle down 'with some degree of comfort' in Bristol, but his optimism would prove misplaced: it would be eighteen years before she could settle anywhere with any comfort, material or mental. As he would put it in 1794, she was forever 'jigging about up and down, from place to place, when God knows how she contrives to be able to live at any place'.[443]

As she made her way to Bristol, Mary Ann too hoped that the worst of her troubles were over. Her husband would be less well off as a travelling salesman than if he had stuck to his own drapery business, but there would be something to live on, and there were still expectations from Alderman Hunn. Whether she intended to give up her career for good is not clear. She needed to pay for schooling for her Reddish children, and Hunn's income would hardly stretch that far. Nonetheless, with the twins and Maria going out to nurse, and their disabled eldest child, Richard, who was now four years old, probably in the care of Hunn's sisters in Devonshire, Mary Ann could look forward to a period of stability and recovery. This did not take account of Hunn's irresponsibility, which was evident as soon as she reached Bristol. He had found lodgings for her in a confined street, damp and unhealthy, possibly above Stephens's shop or warehouse in Wine Street. Perhaps fearing her reaction, he was not there to welcome her. When he eventually came home it was to tell her that there was no money for nurses or a second servant, so she would have to nurse the twins and look after the one-year-old Maria by herself. 'You all look very well here,' he observed, before setting off again on his own thankless work of drumming up customers for Mr Stephens.[444]

Before the end of August, with Mary Ann in Bristol, George felt free to visit Crewe Hall. He twice went to the theatre, in Chester and at the Grosvenor family seat at Eaton Hall. At the Theatre Royal 'your friends' the Whitlocks appeared in Arthur Murphy's *Know Your Own Mind*, with Mrs Whitlock yielding the leading role to the visiting star Dorothy Jordan. At Eaton, Viscount Belgrave was 'surprisingly good' as Othello, although the company as a whole, including other members of the Grosvenor family and their friends, was bad, and the performance dragged on for six hours in a cold theatre. Whitlock was 'a sad stupid stick', George wrote, and he couldn't see Mrs Whitlock's affected performance 'without great anger'.[445] His companions at Crewe Hall must have been puzzled by such vehemence. However gratified Mary Ann may have been by his criticism of the Whitlocks, he touched a sensitive spot when he praised Lord Belgrave. As a man and an aristocrat, Belgrave risked nothing by indulging his appetite for the theatre, whereas Mary Ann, a woman, and sordidly dependent on her wages as an actress, was too dangerous to support. Mary Ann, who gave more attention to reading George's letters than he to writing them, undoubtedly saw the double standard implicit in his casual reference to Belgrave's Othello.

When Mary Ann recalled her time in Bristol what she remembered was that she had been ill, exhausted, neglected by her husband, and harassed by a hostile landlady. Her natural resilience was overcome and there were moments when she longed for death. She developed 'symptoms of a rapid dropsey', and her doctor warned that she must move to a healthier location, stop nursing the twins and get help in the house. In March or April 1790 she moved to lodgings in the newly developed Bath Street, owned by a woman who had a tea warehouse, one of the more genteel forms of retail trade. The twins were sent to wet nurses, but there was no money for domestic help. Mary Ann thought, perhaps, of calling on her sister, but Esther was caring for Mrs Costello in London. The solution was to summon Mary from Exeter. Twelve years old, Mary had been doing well at Mrs Moore's school, and may already have seen herself as a schoolteacher, but now she was installed as housemaid and nursemaid in the lodgings above the tea warehouse. She was less well suited for the work than Esther, less robust and more highly strung, sweet-natured and perhaps afraid of her mother. Her stepfather resented her presence and mistreated her, possibly taunting her with her illegitimacy. George's fondness for her, although they would not meet for another ten years, dated from this time when she was caring for their sick mother in Bristol. He sent his love 'especially to Mary'.[446]

Mary Ann kept the three Reddish boys out of her husband's

way. Samuel, Charles and William were all by now at a school in the village of Scorton, near Catterick in Yorkshire, run by an enterprising clergyman called James Milner, author of several textbooks and occasional contributor to scientific journals.[i] At his establishment (in the words of his advertisement in the *Times*) boys were 'boarded, clothed and expeditiously qualified for any commercial or genteel department' for £16 a year. As at the most famous of all Yorkshire schools, Dotheboys Hall, there appear to have been no holidays. It sounds bleak, but even Charles, who would later turn out to be nervous and unsettled, seems to have got on well enough with Milner to want to keep in touch with him after leaving the school. Sam, whose fees were paid by the Drury Lane Theatrical Fund, was nearing the end of his time at the school, where he was, by his own account, the leading classical scholar. Never afraid (as George would find in years to come) to ask for favours, in September 1789 fifteen-year-old Sam sent a cheeky letter to the Theatrical Fund asking for an extra grant to cover Italian lessons, cricket bats, new breeches and dancing lessons. He was particularly keen to have the dancing lessons, to give him confidence to enter polite society. The directors of the Fund agreed to everything except the dancing.[447] Charles and William seem not to have qualified for the Theatrical Fund's bounty. Years before, in her early relations with Reddish, Mary Ann had scrupulously avoided making her parents and Esther a drain on Reddish's purse, and she may have felt the same reluctance to pay for the Reddish boys out of her husband's earnings. But the question hardly arose, because the money Hunn gave her was inadequate even for her immediate needs. The school bills mounted up.

Hunn blamed his employer for their poverty, but he was himself carrying on an affair with the landlady of their old lodgings, whose addiction to drink must have been a drain on his salary.

---

i James Milner (c.1747–1834): his published works include *A Collection of English Exercises: for the use of schools and academies* (York: 1792); and *The New Penman's Delight* (of which I have found no trace); and an article 'On Hay-Making in general, and particularly in Wet Weather' (1812).

Although she may have suspected him of infidelity, Mary Ann still hoped all would be well. They kept up appearances. At the end of 1789 Hunn sent George a present of a basket of oysters, and the following autumn Mary Ann received an apparently friendly visit from his sisters and father. She put the best gloss she could on her husband's failures, telling George he was held back by timidity and despondency. George did not yet know of Hunn's bad relations with his employer; all he knew was that Stephens was a respectable man, and that Hunn's position in the business was the very lowest, a 'rider', or commercial traveller.[448]

In March 1790 Mary Ann annoyed George by giving a Mr Hutton of Exeter College a letter to deliver to him. Resenting the attempt to make him acquainted with someone from a less fashionable college, and perhaps afraid that she was trying to install herself by proxy in his Oxford life, George did not reply for some time. She asked why he had not responded, displaying an anxiety that he thought unreasonable. 'Look after the health of your mind as well as your body,' he wrote, while apologising stiffly for having been unable to 'return Mr H's civility'. He was learning to be more guarded in his dealings with his mother, but at the same time, to make up for the snub, he promised to visit her soon.[449]

This was George's first visit to her in Bristol, arranged to fit in with a stay in Bath with the Leighs. He was in time to witness the squalor of her original lodgings, but how he reacted to it, and whether he was instrumental in her move to the tea warehouse, is not clear. The Leighs had been in Bath for some months while Bess Leigh's daughter Tish took the cure, and at Christmas had been joined by Bess's sister, Fanny Canning.[450] It may have been now that Bess and Fanny put up a memorial plaque in Bath Abbey to their mother. At some point during her unhappy time in Bristol Mary Ann visited Bath and read the inscription. When she considered how her husband George had been treated by his family, including his mother, the lines of conventional praise made her angry, as she recalled in the Packet:

> her Husband had enjoin'd her to withhold all succour from her child — and she obey'd — yet her Life was respected and her Death lamented — her Memory made sacred by a testimonial of her virtues placed in the sacred repository where her ashes moulder — These Eyes have seen it — God of Nature! Can it be! [451]

George visited again in January or February 1791, catching a bad cold on the journey, which he said he cured when he was back in Oxford by good hours, moderate exercise and 'much Bark'. On one of the visits Mary Ann showed him a collection of his father's letters and manuscripts.[452] In almost two decades of traipsing round the country she had somehow kept these relics safe. There wasn't much – a few dozen letters from friends and family, a notebook containing drafts of poems, and the eighty or so love letters that she received before her marriage – and they would not have taken up much space, tucked in amongst her costumes and theatrical props. We can picture the two of them sitting together in the Bristol lodgings, turning the dusty papers over and over in their hands, Mary Ann with her memories, George with his questions. Who was this father whose misfortunes and untimely death had created such a tangled problem for his wife and son? 'Assert my rights,' his father had written, 'avenge not my wrongs.' What was he to do about asserting his father's rights? He could hardly go to law with the Irish Cannings who had, on the whole, treated him kindly.

George and Mary Ann were by now in frequent contact, although it would be some years before their routine of regular weekly exchanges was established. Between his first visit to Bristol at the end of March 1790 and his next in February 1791 there are only two letters from George, one from Oxford and one from Crewe Hall. It is possible that he wrote others which have been lost, but if there really was a long blank on his side it suggests that Mary Ann did not write to him during those ten months. She says she was in Bristol from August 1789 to March 1791,[453] but a summer excursion to Devonshire might not have seemed worth mentioning in the Packet, and if she was renewing contacts with her friend John Bernard, now managing the summer theatre in Plymouth, she would not have wanted to draw attention to it, which would explain the gap in her letters. As she recovered from her dangerous dropsy, and as memories faded of her humiliation at the hands of the Whitlocks, she may well have allowed her thoughts to wander back to her career. Money was one motive; another was frustration and a longing to escape the confines of her dreary home and unhappy marriage.

If she did spend time in Devonshire, she was back in Bristol by the winter. Although her accommodation in Bath Street was clean and airy, she was not happy. She needed a change, and circumstances brought it about. There were many tea dealers in Bristol at the time, and the warehouse in Bath Street succumbed to the opposition. Mary Ann learned that her landlady was selling up and she would have to vacate her lodgings at Lady Day (the end of March) 1791. Hunn, keen to save money and at the same time perhaps hoping to keep the sharp-tongued Mary Ann out of the way while he carried on his adulterous affair, proposed that they should give up their joint home for a while. She should go down into Devonshire taking Mary and Maria, while he set off for his summer on the road. In the autumn he would bring the twins to Exeter, which would require him to pay off their nurses. Mary Ann willingly fell in with this suggestion.[454] She didn't realise it when they went their different ways after Lady Day but, although it would be seven or eight years before there was a formal separation, she and her husband would not live together again.

17.
Burying Place Lane and London's New Road 1791–1793

George stayed for a fourth year in Oxford. His college was as much his home as anywhere. It provided him with books and intelligent conversation, as well as board and lodging, and in Dr Cyril Jackson, the Dean, a shrewd clergyman keen to see his talented protégé launched on the world, he had a trustworthy adviser.[i] At the end of his first year, when he had given up the debating society and foregone his visit to Crewe Hall, George felt gloomy about his future and disenchanted with Christ Church, a 'dungeon' which only the Dean's kindness made tolerable. How much the Dean knew about Mary Ann one can't tell. When he criticised George for a habit of turning conversations into negotiations and an 'appearance of reserve' that inhibited friendship, George blamed this manner on his 'situation', but Jackson thought it was 'at bottom nothing but pride', which suggests that he did not appreciate the complexity of George's difficulties. What the Dean knew was that George was alone in the world, with a small income and no family to support him. As Stratty had once feared the lure of the theatre, Jackson feared George would be intoxicated by the greater stage of politics. Concentrate on the law, he advised, avoid a dangerous reputation for political ambitions, and keep clear of

i Cyril Jackson (1746–1819), used his position as Dean of Christ Church, 1783–1809, to gather gossip and exert influence in government circles. After George entered Parliament Dr Jackson continued to favour him with long letters of advice.

'unprofessional' companions who would encourage late hours and a penchant for superficial arguments and easy applause.[455]

In April 1791 George came into his inheritance from his grandparents, a cash sum of £3,000, and a slight addition to his Irish rents. He calculated his prospective income to be £326, a misleadingly precise figure, but he soon discovered that getting money from Ireland was not to be straightforward. His uncle Paul's widow, acting on behalf of her son, was in no hurry. She wanted to pay the £3,000 in two instalments, but the Dean advised him to insist on having it all at once. Always vague about money matters, and finding the details distasteful, George had no clear idea how much his Oxford debts amounted to. William Leigh and Walter Borrowes were sorting them out – Leigh bridging the gap until the Irish money was available, and Borrowes providing the financial expertise. In the event it was November 1792 before the £3,000 arrived. After satisfying all his creditors and his own immediate needs, only £600 remained, which he lodged with William Leigh.[456] Leigh, despite having children of his own to support, and a stepdaughter from Bess's first marriage, would be a regular source of subsidies for some years to come. In return George gave the Leighs all the affection that found no outlet elsewhere, and kept them entertained with his letters.

When Mary Ann left Bristol at the end of March 1791 she went to stay with her friend Bridget Moore in Exeter. They discussed Mary's future. Mrs Moore offered to take Mary as an apprentice teacher, but required a premium of a hundred guineas, which George undertook to pay as soon as he received his £3,000. Mary Ann innocently supposed that his inheritance would be immediately available on his birthday, 11 April 1791, but he explained, optimistically, that he couldn't expect to be paid until June. Mary Ann would have to find Mrs Moore's hundred guineas in some other way. In this emergency she made up her mind to resume her career. John Bernard was currently appearing at Covent Garden, but as part owner of the Frankfort Gate theatre was making arrangements for the coming summer season. She wrote to him and he willingly agreed to employ her. When Hunn heard, he disapproved, but she discounted his views. The season at Frankfort Gate was due to begin on 20 June.[457] Mary Ann made her preparations, but how enthusiastically we don't know.

George was in despair. With no immediate prospect of receiving his Irish money he reluctantly offered Mrs Moore a promissory note, on condition that she undertook not to negotiate it. Such 'paper' had a life of its own. Bonds could be sold on by the immediate creditors, or bequeathed to their widows and heirs, to be presented for payment many years later. George knew enough of his father's history to have a horror of finding his own signature circulating in this way. The failure of his Uncle Stratty's business can only have intensified his distrust. Reluctantly he sent Mrs Moore two notes of hand, one for ten guineas to be cashed immediately, and the other for ninety at two months' date. When the ninety guineas fell due and the money was not there to meet it, Borrowes renewed the note without consulting George, who was away. George was angry, fearing there was something underhand about the procedure, but Borrowes satisfied his scruples and explained that it was all in the way of business.[458] Scrupulous gentlemen like George often find it useful to have a Walter Borrowes at their side.

Just days before the start of the Plymouth season George's notes reached Exeter. His financial affairs, he confessed in the covering letter, were more complicated than he had thought. He went on to discuss Mary Ann's proposed return to the stage, choosing his words carefully. 'Any line of life' was preferable, he said, which is obviously an exaggeration, but he didn't enlarge on his objection, finding it a matter of too much delicacy. He admitted he had no right to advise her while he lacked the means to assist her, which seems on the surface to be a confession of weakness, but because it accompanied the gift of a hundred guineas, very material assistance, it amounted to an assertion of his right to intervene.[459]

If Mary Ann was tempted by the prospect of returning as John Bernard's leading lady, she may also have felt a certain reluctance. She was now in her forties; she had undergone eleven pregnancies, travelled the length of both England and Ireland, recovered from at least two severe physical illnesses and suffered from the vagaries of three difficult men. Three of her children had died in infancy, while the rest were scattered with nurses, foster parents and schoolmasters. She may have felt it was time to do something less demanding. She may have had no intention of joining Bernard's company, only raising the possibility as a way of proving to George and her husband how desperate she was, but it's more likely that her feelings were mixed, that she would have returned to the stage with her old gusto, had it become necessary.

George assumed, and wanted to believe, that Mary Ann would be happier if she retired, and he looked on his hundred guineas as enabling her to do so. But this wasn't the same as the ten pounds he gave to Hunn two years before, or the five pounds for comforts and medicine in Newcastle, or even the £50 allowance. The hundred guineas were not explicitly a bribe, but neither were they any longer the spontaneous gift of an emotional boy, desperate to do something – anything – to relieve his mother. By laying down that assistance implied a right to guide her actions, he was marking a change in their relationship. Neither his advice nor the hundred guineas prevented Mary Ann from going to Plymouth.

When his letter did not elicit an immediate recantation, he wrote another in which he overcame his feelings of delicacy, and poured out his arguments against the theatre. He based his case on public opinion, carefully not saying outright that he agreed with the general prejudice against the theatre. He said it would harm Mary's chances in her chosen profession if it were known that her mother was on the stage; parents, he said, would not want their daughters' manners and morals 'form'd on the model of the green-room'. If, as seems likely, Mrs Moore was herself a retired actress, it may be that George overestimated the squeamishness of West Country parents. His final argument was that his own prospects would be harmed, as Sheridan's had been, by theatrical associations. And, he added, he was determined to make rapid progress for her sake so that he could provide for her. What he said about Sheridan may have been true, although there were many other things in Sheridan's rackety life to explain why he did not advance in politics as far as his talents deserved. What is more significant is that by comparing his prospects with Sheridan's experience he was revealing an intention to follow Sheridan into public life, even though six months later he would still be telling Mehitabel that he was concentrating on Law, Law, Law.[460]

George's letter was forwarded to Mary Ann in Plymouth. A fortnight later, he was congratulating her on having given up her theatrical plan in favour of another which was, he said, more eligible and practicable.[461] It's not clear why Mary Ann capitulated, whether she was persuaded by his money or his arguments, or whether she was already inclined to abandon her demanding career, and the hundred guineas left her free to do so.

Her break with the theatre was not quite as clean and complete as her assurances to George would suggest. Her Plymouth lodgings, found for her by John Bernard, were in Burying Place Lane, next to the theatre, above the workshop of the theatre's carpenter, a man called Symonds. When Bernard came to write his memoirs almost forty years later, he remembered working with Mary Ann in the summer of 1791. He wrote that she was his leading lady that year, which, if true, would mean that she told George a direct lie at the time, and tacitly repeated it in the Packet by passing over her summer in Plymouth without any mention of what she did there.[462] This is unlikely, although there is no independent evidence that she did not appear.[463] But even if she did not become the leading lady at Frankfort Gate for one final season, Bernard's recollection may not have been entirely groundless. When she told George she had given up acting she may have felt that the odd appearance, to help out, didn't count. There were also many other things, apart from appearing on stage, that an intelligent and experienced woman of the theatre could do to make herself useful, from stitching costumes to supervising rehearsals or copying and adapting texts. But whatever happened that summer, when Bernard's 1791 season at Frankfort Gate was over Mary Ann's professional career was at an end.

Bernard records a curious incident. The rent for her lodgings above Symonds' workshop was unusually low because it was believed in the neighbourhood that the building was haunted by a 'perturbed and perambulating spirit'. Strange noises were heard at night, and no one wanted to live there. Mary Ann either didn't believe in ghosts or didn't think this one would do her any harm. On the first night she sat up in bed with her book waiting to see what would happen. Soon from downstairs came noises of hammering, sawing, planing – all the sounds of a carpenter's shop. Mary Ann laid aside her book and her spectacles and went down in her stockinged feet, as quietly as she could, to avoid frightening off whoever was making the noises. When she looked into the workshop all was still – there was no one there; she examined everything, nothing had been disturbed. She went back to bed. The noises started again and then, eventually, fell silent. It happened night after night. She persuaded Symonds and Bernard to sit with her to witness the phenomenon. When the noises started up and Mary Ann went downstairs, Symonds fled, while Bernard stayed to admire her coolness. From then on Mary Ann lived rent free. She got used to the commotion, joking that if she didn't hear the carpenters at work she'd begin to think they were coming upstairs.[464]

Such, at least, is Bernard's story. Assuming it is true, it's surprising that Mary Ann makes no mention of it. Her role in the episode would have fitted in with the picture of herself presented in the Packet as the strong, calm influence when all around are confused and in panic. It was how she responded to her husband's death, to her arrest for debt and to each successive blow that life dealt her. She may have kept quiet because she didn't want to remind George of her theatrical contacts in Plymouth, or perhaps the episode was less sensational than Bernard makes it seem, but it's a pity we don't have her observations. In the Packet she now and then invokes the 'God of Nature' and 'the Hand that guides this vast Machine',[465] terminology which suggests that she took a thoughtful approach to religion, and is unlikely to have had much sympathy with superstition. Her version of the haunted carpenter's shop would have been intriguing. She felt secure enough to stay on in Symonds' lodgings until the beginning of 1792.

Though relieved to have got his way, George was struck by a new thought. Hitherto he had accepted the obligation to support his mother as any son might feel it; now that he had intervened decisively and cut off her means of supporting herself his general obligation had been replaced by a strict contract making it his first duty to provide for her.[466] His sense of obligation would become more intense over the years, but at the same time he became more convinced that his assistance and subsidies gave him the right to impose conditions, such as where she should live. He was a young man now, and he asserted himself with some hesitation, but he would become more peremptory and arbitrary as he grew in assurance and the Canning instinct for autocracy became stronger.

Mary Ann's alternative source of income, though George described it as more eligible and practicable, was as yet untried and uncertain. It involved manufacturing and selling an eye salve. She does not say what drew her to the patent medicine trade, but the name she gave to her product, Costello's Collyrium, suggests that it was developed by her father. She was optimistic about an occupation that appealed to her scientific interests while involving nothing that could be stigmatised by a prejudiced world as unfeminine. Priscilla Wakefield, for example, considered the compounding of medicines a suitable profession for middle-class women. There is something ludicrous about patent medicines, and in later years the satirist 'Peter Pindar' would make fun of Canning's association with the ointment, while Canning's biographers tend to mock Mary Ann's endeavour, adopting the ironical tone that will be evident in George's later references to it.[467] But it was a serious undertaking, and Mary Ann was to devote much of the next fifteen years to prosecuting it.

At the end of the summer of 1791 Mary Ann remained in Plymouth waiting for her husband to recover the twins from their nurses and make a home for them all back in Bristol, as promised. She wrote to remind him, but there was no reply. Now convinced of Hunn's infidelity, she no longer hid the truth from George. She told him that she was getting no financial support from Hunn himself, although his sisters were probably caring for the disabled Richard, and also took an interest in Maria, who was named after one of them. In the new year Mary Ann left Plymouth for Exeter, where at least she could be with Mary. She planned a visit to London. George advised against it, mainly on grounds of cost, but she persuaded him that she was needed to care for her mother, and could use her time in town to find positions for Samuel and Charles. Aged sixteen and thirteen respectively, the boys needed to earn their keep.[468]

Mary Ann did not leave Exeter immediately, but she was restless and short of money. The twins were approaching their third birthday, and she wanted them with her, while the ointment project needed capital. For the present she hardly had enough for day-to-day expenses. She did not despair of her marriage, keeping on good terms with her sisters-in-law, and writing regularly to her husband, leaving him in no doubt about her circumstances and her view of his behaviour: 'I saw that he was too conscious of his own breach of faith & duty, & knew too well my Sentiments on those points to expect forgiveness: I saw too, that there was on his part no apparent intention of either altering his conduct, or attoning for it.' She kept copies of her letters and of his replies to show to George.[469]

George might refer lightly to his mother jigging about up and down, but the journey between Devonshire and London was not one to be undertaken lightly. It meant a day and a half at the very least in an uncomfortable coach, which cost £1.11s.6d for an outside seat, or £2.12s.6d inside[470] – this at a time when Mary Ann's main or only income was her £50 annual allowance, or as she thought of it, 'nineteen shillings a week… far from independance'. George could do nothing about the discomfort of the journey, but in March when he left £2.12s.6d with Esther in Battlebridge, it was probably to cover the cost of an inside seat. Mary Ann was well used to travelling; she was sociable, and probably enjoyed talking to her fellow travellers, discussing the state of the harvest and events in France, telling them about her eye salve, her theatrical past and her brilliant son. She arrived in London in the summer and went to stay with her mother in Tottenham Court Road. George called on her before leaving for a holiday in Norfolk with the Leighs, who lent him a horse to take him on a round of visits including Crewe Hall and Oxford.[471]

By now George had reached a conclusion about his future. When he told his Aunt Mehitabel that he had spent his Christmas reading Law Law Law, it may have been true, but he had also been thinking through the options open to him. Despite the Dean's warnings, it's unlikely that he seriously considered anything but politics. There remained the question of how to enter Parliament, and how to support himself and his mother while making his way. He would be dependent on what he could earn from political office. The Cannings had always been Whigs, and Sheridan and Charles James Fox assumed that George's talents would be placed at the service of the Whigs. But it was the governing party, under William Pitt, that offered the best chance of office. This mercenary motive was backed up by what seems to have been a genuine change of mind. For some time George had been mixing with radical politicians in London, taking part in debates and gaining a reputation as an effective speaker. There was a story, which may well have been true, that William Godwin[i] discussed the political situation with him and predicted a great future for him as a revolutionary leader. At

i William Godwin (1756–1836) was a leading intellectual among the radical reformers in the 1790s. He was married to Mary Wollstonecraft in 1797.

the same time, George had been working for government lawyers, getting up cases against radical reformists, which led him to adopt the Pitt administration's assessment of the strength of organised sedition in the country. When he saw that serious people like Godwin were preparing for revolution, he came to believe there was a real threat to established order. Another event that propelled George towards supporting the government was the formation of the Friends of the People[i] by leading Whigs such as Charles Grey and Sheridan. This move, George believed, not only threatened the security of the country but had split the Whig party and made them lose all credibility. He acted cautiously, but by the summer was making overtures to the governing party. In July, while staying with Fox and his mistress Mrs Armistead in Chertsey, he wrote to Pitt asking for a meeting.[472]

When they met in August, the two men came to a good understanding, and the prime minister promised to secure George a seat in Parliament. This was the beginning of an intense personal and political friendship which was to last until Pitt's death in 1806. Observers would note how close they were to each other; the childless Pitt, they said, had adopted Canning, while Canning's feelings for Pitt were those of a son. The two had much in common; they were both highly intelligent, literate, sensitive, hard-working and far-seeing men, in a political class where such qualities were rare. George accepted that the unsettled times and the contagion from revolutionary France made it necessary to curtail political liberty, but he held out for the right to vote according to his conscience on issues such as Catholic emancipation. Pitt allowed that on such 'speculative' subjects a member was, so far as the government was concerned, free to vote as he wished. George would have to follow the views of the proprietor of his seat,[ii] however, and this could prove an embarrassment because

i The Society or Association of the Friends of the People consisted largely of aristocratic and middle class supporters of parliamentary reform who were opposed to the unconstitutional extremism associated with Thomas Paine. Charles Grey, later Earl Grey, never forgave George's abandonment of the Whigs and remained a bitter political enemy.

ii In the unreformed House of Commons most seats were in the gift of a local landowner his firm commitment to the Catholic side separated him from the bulk of his party. The slave trade was another issue on which George differed from many Tories and which Pitt regarded as speculative, because there was no prospect of getting a bill for abolition through the current parliament.[473] But agitation for constitutional reform was not speculative, and there George would have to follow the government's increasingly repressive line. The charge of 'tergiversation' was to follow him throughout his career, making him unusually sensitive to accusations of inconsistency, both in politics and in his dealings with his mother.

None of these developments are mentioned in George's letters to Mary Ann and it's unlikely that he was any more forthcoming when they met face to face, which they did several times over the summer, at her mother's lodgings in Tottenham Court Road. Mary Costello was now well into her seventies and could no longer manage on her own. How the old lady supported herself is hard to say. There may have been some money from Jordan's family in Ireland, and perhaps she remained in contact with her Guy-Dickens half-siblings, Mary and Gustavus. More probably, Esther contrived to give her something, although what Esther did for money is not known. At the end of August Mary Ann and her mother moved from Tottenham Court Road to 23 Wilsted Street, Somers Town, north of the New Road. Esther was not far away, with the Byfields in Constitution Row, Gray's Inn Lane, the other side of the New Road.[i] This was a significant boundary: north of the road, Esther informed George, was 'off the stones' so far as the Post Office was concerned, which meant that letters would take an extra day to be delivered. George therefore sent most of his letters to the Byfields' address, and Esther took them over to Wilsted Street.[474]

Samuel and Charles, whose future provision was Mary Ann's

---

who controlled the choice of the small number of men entitled to vote in elections.

i Wilsted Street was the southern end of what is now Ossulston Street; Gray's Inn Lane, including Constitution Row, is now Gray's Inn Road. (Horwood, *Plan of the Cities of London and Westminster*).

other reason for coming to London, seem to have done well at James Milner's school. Sam had come to London early in 1791, staying close to Drury Lane with his mother's old colleagues the Wrightens and acting as agent for Milner's school,[475] but how long this arrangement continued is not clear. He had thought of joining the Navy, but been deterred when the prospect of war with France seemed to be receding. Now that war was more likely he had hopes that a brother-in-law of Mr Hunn, Captain Featherstone, might use influence on his behalf. Charles was still at school, but the unpaid bills were mounting and Mary Ann hoped she had a job lined up for him in London. An old acquaintance called Morton, a coach-maker, had stood godfather to Charles when he had seemed unlikely to live. But Charles had lived, and Morton now offered to take him into his business, either for old times' and friendship's sake, or in deference to one of his titled customers, Lord Courtenay, whose father had been among Mary Ann's supporters in the theatre in Plymouth. Charles wasn't keen. Perhaps aware of this, Morton was slow to honour his promise. Mary Ann tried to see him at his place of business, but he told her to come to dinner at his house instead. She duly went, but he still prevaricated, and told her to come again. Perhaps he enjoyed her company, but these evenings in central London were inconvenient, particularly after the move to Somers Town, because she could not afford the expense of a hackney carriage (they charged double after sunset), and had to walk the length of Gray's Inn Lane to get home.[476]

One day at dinner another of Morton's guests, a clergyman called Colman, was intrigued by Mary Ann. She was evidently a lady, so how was it that she was hoping to make her son a coach-maker? Morton told him that she was living apart from a husband who was incapable of valuing her at her true worth. Whatever else he revealed about Mary Ann's past, nothing he said affected the favourable impression Colman had formed. He had a friend called Mercier, a widower who had made a fortune in the West Indies and was now looking for a respectable companion for his three daughters. The terms that Mercier was offering were generous, including a pension for life after her time in the family came to an end. She considered the proposal seriously, enquiring about the characters of her prospective charges, but in the end she refused. It seemed hard, as she trudged back home in the rain, to turn down this opportunity, but George's mother could not 'descend to servitude, however splendid'.[477] This makes the second time that Mary Ann chose not to solve her troubles by taking a share of the profits of slave labour, the first being when she rejected Mr Stone twenty-five years earlier. The tainted origin of the money seems to have had nothing to do with her refusal, unless it was that she feared that a man accustomed to owning slaves might prove an uncongenial employer for an English gentlewoman.

At about the same time a Covent Garden actress called Harriet Esten offered Mary Ann an engagement in the company she was forming in Edinburgh, where she was licensee of the Theatre Royal. Although it's unlikely that Mary Ann really wanted to resume her career, at such a distance from her family and with all its uncertainties, she went as far with the Edinburgh negotiations as fixing her salary at the good rate of £6 a week. She turned it down, out of deference to George. Whereas she kept him informed about the progress of her dealings with Morton, she said nothing about the offers from Mercier and Harriet Esten, but nonetheless hoped her compliance with his wishes would entitle her to a mother's place in his affection.[478]

She might refuse these offers, but she needed something. The ointment business was not yet profitable and she could not rely on her husband for money. Hunn's 'extraordinary' behaviour and endless complaints were making 'a comfortless situation worse', George wrote. Instead of sending the money she asked for, Hunn promised a supply of linen for the Wilsted Street house, but didn't keep his promise, and when he eventually sent her five guineas, it was swallowed up by more pressing needs. George, although already overdrawn on his account with Borrowes, scraped together enough for her coals and her rent. He discussed the problems with Bess Leigh, who packed up a box of linen for him to give to Mary Ann.[479]

In the autumn of 1792 Hunn's sister Martha died, and he reported that under her will £1000 was destined for their four children, most of it for the two girls, but there was no immediate relief, apart from the interest on £500 for Hunn himself. George wrote hopefully that this 'must have called forth his recollection of his family', but there is no sign that any of this extra income reached Mary Ann. Nonetheless she could still feel indignation on her husband's account, complaining that his employer, 'that despicable wretch Stephens', had deliberately sent him to South Wales to prevent him going down to Devonshire to see his dying sister.[480]

While Mary Ann was in London trying to launch her two Reddish sons on the world, she was equally uneasy about Maria and the twins, who were down in the West Country. Maria may have been with her Aunt Maria Hunn, but the twins were still with nurses. She had not seen them since she left Bristol in 1791, and could not recover them until her husband paid the nurses. As she struggled through a gloomy London winter, she longed to be reunited with her little ones.[481]

Mary Costello had never been much company for her clever daughter, so Mary Ann spent her time reading. She read Mary Wollstonecraft's *Vindication of the Rights of Woman*, in which she found a vindication not only of her rights, but of her whole life. In the dedication of her work, Wollstonecraft protests against 'tyrants of every denomination, from the weak king to the weak father of a family'. It was the recurrent theme of Mary Ann's novel, the tyranny of incompetent and inadequate men. She had suffered from them all her life, most notably her father-in-law Stratford Canning, author of all her troubles, but also her own father who appropriated her inheritance, and the secretive husband who expected her to obey him without question. Wollstonecraft writes admiringly of the widow who exerts her strength and talents to maintain her family, despite the obstacles placed in her way by society; understandingly of the young woman carried away by natural passion; respectfully of the unmarried woman who remains loyal to the father of her children. In all these portraits Mary Ann could see reflections of her own experience. This passage must have leapt out at her:

> A woman who has lost her honour, imagines that she cannot fall lower, and as for recovering her former station, it is impossible; no exertion can wash this stain away. Losing thus every spur and having no other means of support, prostitution becomes her only refuge, and the character is quickly depraved by circumstances over which the poor wretch has little power, unless she possesses an uncommon portion of sense and loftiness of spirit.

In this protest against the *Jane Shore* doctrine, that for a woman 'one false step forever damns her fame', Mary Ann appreciated Wollstonecraft's general argument that female education and the prejudices of society leave women with 'no other means of support'. She will also have noted the particular application to her own life: she had not taken refuge in prostitution, and could take comfort in the reflection that this was due to her 'uncommon portion of sense and loftiness of spirit'.[482]

Evening had come on as Mary Ann read, and she was now writing enthusiastically to George in the dark: 'She has raised my sex (and in consequence myself) to a state of dignity,... asserting the native nobility of our minds.'[483] Mary Wollstonecraft might not have chosen Mary Ann's rackety life as an ideal illustration of the native nobility of women's minds, but her philosophy was compelling precisely because it was embodied in the unsatisfactory lives of countless women of her time.

What George thought of his mother's enthusiasm is hard to guess. He did not approve of women who interfered in politics.[484] He had just extricated himself from involvement with other advanced thinkers and radical politicians, including

Wollstonecraft's future husband William Godwin. Throughout their long correspondence Mary Ann's opinions would be consistently more radical than George's. She would draw his attention to the sufferings of the poor and he would respond with the government line, sympathising impotently with genuine hardship while accusing agitators of stirring up grievances.

George could ignore Mary Ann's political ideas, but in other respects he remained on his guard. When she passed on the locket that Molly Barnard had given her on her marriage, he wondered ungraciously what she expected him to do with it. She replied that if he didn't want it himself he could give it to either Bess Leigh or his other Canning Aunt, Fanny Canning. In the end he gave it to Mehitabel, which did not please Mary Ann. She told him she had a still more precious locket, containing the hair of his 'sainted father' and of Letitia, 'a little angel sister, whose happy spirit was snatch'd to Paradise before you were born'. She had hesitated to give this to him because she could tell he had no taste for such 'baubles', and it may be that she used Molly's locket as a test to see how he would respond. While he had little taste for lockets of hair, he was becoming interested in his past and in his father. This coincided with his break with the Canning family's Whig sympathies, about which his aunt Mehitabel had been very angry. He had arrogantly dismissed her rebuke, but was nonetheless curious to learn more of what his father had thought. He asked Mary Ann for the family papers she had shown him in Bristol.[485]

18.
Bitter Words, 1793

By the beginning of 1793 Richard Hunn had freed himself from the objectionable Stephens, and was working for another firm, based in Manchester, which enabled him to offer reasonable provision for Mary Ann's future. He told her to meet him in Guildford, saying that his business commitments wouldn't let him come into London, but his real reason may have been fear of having to face George. At the Guildford meeting he repeated his offer, and they reached what Mary Ann took to be a clear understanding. He would join her in Bristol and liberate the twins from their nurses, and she would then make a home for all four of their children in Exeter. His salary would be £130 per annum, out of which he promised to send her £80 in the first year and £100 in each of the next two years, after which time his contract would expire and they would have to think again. He also assured her that the bulk of the Hunn family's money would come to their children on the death of his sister Maria. Finally, they agreed to collaborate in manufacturing and marketing the eye salve. They discussed details such as the size of the packaging, and he told her to follow advice she'd been given by Dr Downman to open negotiations with Francis Newbery of St Paul's Churchyard,[i]

i Francis Newbery (1743–1818) belonged to a family of printers and booksellers, a trade often combined with the marketing of patent medicines. His wife belonged to the Raikes family of Gloucester, friends of Stratty.

one of the leading sellers of patent medicines.[486]

They fixed 1 February for their rendezvous in Bristol. It was inconvenient to interrupt her protracted negotiations with Morton and leave Esther to look after their mother, but she was determined to recover her babies and establish herself in her new career. She reported to George on the Guildford meeting. Delighted at the prospect of a resolution of her affairs, he called on her in Wilsted Street to say goodbye and to deliver Bess Leigh's box of linen. When she got to Bristol she found that her husband was already tampering with their agreement. He said now that he would take care of Frederick along with his elder brother Richard, leaving her with Ann and Maria. She was happy with this, but puzzled and annoyed when he warned her that now wasn't the time to put the ointment on the market. It was too late, she told him, she had already bought the boxes and written to contacts in Exeter and Plymouth.[487]

From Bristol she went down to Exeter, staying a few weeks with Mrs Moore before finding lodgings close by. Maria already showed a preference for living with her aunt, and Mary Ann did not prevent her, but Ann stayed in Exeter and began her schooling under her sister Mary. She was, Mary Ann told George, 'so good that every body delights in her'.[488]

Mary Ann sent the family papers George had asked for to Somers Town in a box, telling him that it contained 'every line of your Father's writing which the wreck of time has left me possess'd of… His letters to me are precious testimonials of his real, and my imputed worth. – Cherish them my love, and when you reflect that you are the Offspring of the two people concerned, do not value yourself, nor love the Survivor less.' If his father's pitifully slender literary remains told him anything it was that his political inheritance was as meagre as his fortune. Mary Ann also enclosed Molly Barnard's letters, which were full of sisterly affection. Having been hurt by George's thoughtless reaction to the gift of Molly's locket she used the occasion to administer a subtle rebuke. Passing the relic on to Mehitabel was evidently the last thing she had wanted. It should have gone to one of Molly's surviving sisters, she said, adding stiffly: 'You have, however, had my permission to use it, as I am convinced you delight to use every thing you possess, for the happiness of others – particularly, of those you love.' Finally she enclosed a copy of the 'Birthday Offering', pointing out the error concerning her age, since at this point in her life she believed she had been born in 1750. Esther, she said, would forward the 'treasure' to his chambers, and she asked him to let her know when it arrived: 'I shall be more anxious for their safety, than if every page was a Bank Note.' She asked him to use the box to send her the works of Mary Wollstonecraft. George took delivery of the papers when he visited his grandmother and aunt. He reported to Mary Ann that Mrs Costello was unchanged, but that Aunt Esther was worn and harassed from looking after Mrs Byfield.[489]

George was now waiting impatiently for a suitable seat in Parliament. In June 1793, almost a year after his meeting with Pitt, he was returned for the borough of Newtown in the Isle of Wight.[i] He mocked the absurd procedure by which he was returned without a contest by the handful of docile electors in the borough,[490] but he was a young man and no amount of irony could disguise his delight at being in Parliament. He relished such trappings as the privilege of franking letters, a substantial perquisite which would over the years play a crucial part in his dealings with his mother and her family. The cost of postage was high, and usually borne by the recipient. MPs did not have to pay, and if they signed their name on outgoing letters they were delivered free of charge. Members could use (or misuse) the privilege on behalf of other people, and Mary Ann would regularly send George her mail to be franked, and sometimes her

i The owner of the Newtown seat was Sir Richard Worsley, who used it over the years as a lever for extracting favours from the government. He put it at Pitt's disposal in return for being appointed Minister to Venice. In view of Worsley's unreliability Pitt later arranged for George to be returned for Wendover, which he represented from 1796 to 1802 (*HoP 1790–1820*, s.n. Sir Richard Worsley).

friends' mail as well.[i] This was to be an irritant over the years, but for George there was the advantage that with much of the family's correspondence passing through his hands he was able to monitor it and occasionally insist on changes.

George sat out his election in Oxford, and it was from there that he first sent a letter bearing his own frank to Mary Ann, who was in London for business to do with the ointment. She was overjoyed, although she grumbled that he had not told her straight away, leaving her to hear the news casually in the course of discussions with Francis Newbery. George explained that he had waited until his election had been officially announced, to make sure that his frank was honoured. He came to town to see her and, as he told the Leighs, to try to persuade her that 'a seat in Parliament is not exactly the same thing in point of dignity with the Sultanship of all the Indies, nor precisely equal in profit to £500,000 three per cent Consols'. To persuade her to go back to Exeter, he undertook to contact Newbery and negotiate with Morton the coach-maker on her behalf.[491]

Mary Ann got on well with Francis Newbery, a shrewd businessman, but also a cultured man who had studied chemistry and medicine, and was a keen musician and devotee of amateur dramatics. During their discussions Mary Ann said, or hinted, that in due course George would publicly acknowledge her. One day, she was convinced, he would have a home where she would share his family life, 'lay[ing] up my nearly shatter'd bark in the sweet harbour of domestic affection and tranquillity'.[492]

> … I was counting upon all that I look'd forward to, by all that I had known of your affection and your dutiful tenderness – when your future wife, your prattling Infants floated in my delighted anticipation – when I reckon'd amongst the blessings in store for me, the tracing in one Boy his Father's Infancy, in another a

i Successive acts of Parliament attempted to control MPs' franking privilege, which adversely affected the revenue of the Post Office; in a Parliamentary debate in 1784 Pitt claimed that the annual loss amounted to £40,000, and that his proposed changes would reduce this by half. Further attempts to curb abuse were made in 1795.

> likeness to the happy Mother at whose Bosom I contemplated in fond fancy, a George as dear and lovely as I once fed at mine.[493]

In this idyll Newbery spied a useful commercial opportunity. An endorsement from the young member for Newtown would look well in the advertisements. Knowing that this suggestion would annoy George, Mary Ann hesitated to tell him, only letting it slip in a letter once she was back in Exeter. She was entirely unprepared for the ferocity of his response. Never, he said, never would he publicly acknowledge her. He was determined to make this plain, so that she would understand it once and for all. Their future relationship, he told her, would involve no 'Publicity of visiting in promiscuous intercourse with the World'. We don't know all that he said, because she destroyed part of his letter, but those words were still fixed in her mind when she came to compose the Packet ten years later. They were, she said, the first bitter words she had received from him; it was the first time her tears had blotted a letter of his.[494]

George believed his letter had set out unequivocally the terms on which they were to live; he would refer back to it repeatedly in their future disputes. Unfortunately his words were less unequivocal than he imagined. She accepted that public acknowledgement of the sort envisaged by Newbery was out of the question – she claimed, perhaps disingenuously, that she had never thought otherwise – but it did not occur to her that George could mean anything so unnatural as barring her from private intercourse with his family. Such an interpretation would have 'blasphem'd your Virtue, your Piety, your Humanity'.[495] He saw things differently. He was a young man in bachelor chambers, just severing ties with his childhood home, and with no immediate prospect of settling down in a house of his own. For him there was no middle ground between the lonely and secret place where he acknowledged his duty and affection for his mother, and the great stage of fashionable dinners and comfortable country houses where he lived in promiscuous intercourse with the world. It didn't occur to him that his ponderous and careful phrases had left any doubt as to his meaning, any room for Mary Ann to hope that she would one day live in tranquillity with him in the privacy of his family home.

He was staying with the Leighs at Ashbourne in Derbyshire when he wrote this terrible letter. They realised something was wrong and tried to help in the only way they could by giving him money to send to his mother – she had asked for £10 and he sent her £20, telling her to pass some on to Samuel. It may have been at this point that Bess Leigh suggested that she and William might ease matters by meeting Mary Ann themselves, something he always forbade.[496] In subsequent letters he went out of his way to soften the violence of his response – he asked after Samuel, hoped that Hunn was sticking to his agreement, and wished her well in her negotiations with Morton and Newbery. He thought up the name under which she should market the ointment: Costello's Collyrium.[497] His attempts to mollify her worked too well; in the end he had all but effaced the clear impression that he had intended to make. She remembered the bitterness, but was left with the feeling that perhaps he didn't really mean it.

When Newbery learned that the Canning connection could not be used to promote the ointment, he lost interest. It's hard to believe that the chance of exploiting the name of the newest member of the Commons would have been so crucial, but then as now great store was set by celebrity endorsement – as we saw with the Gores' millinery business, and the Whitlocks at the theatre in Chester. Anything that prised open the door into the closed world of wealth and fashion was all important. But perhaps Newbery was glad to find an excuse to back out. He lectured George on the economics of the medicine trade, and seems to have sensed that the Collyrium would not make money.[498] He may also have found that Mary Ann wasn't an easy person to do business with.

George had been suspicious of Newbery from the start, or so he claimed, and was angry when he heard of his defection. He took two lessons from the incident. The first was that by interfering in her dealings with Newbery he had once more undermined her attempts to earn a living, which strengthened his obligation to provide for her himself: 'How I regret the want of wealth,' he wrote at the beginning of December, 'and pant for the attainment of some portion of it, that I may be enabled to relieve your distresses.' Secondly, he began to fear that Mary Ann would always be a chink in his armour through which he could be attacked by the unscrupulous, which made him all the more determined to keep her hidden away. Mary Ann remembered 1793 as the year of the 'first bitter words'. For George it was the moment when he clarified in his own mind the need to keep her at a distance. It would be some years before Mary Ann realised with horror the 'precise boundary which was to be marked out between us'.[499]

19.
Brothers, 1794–1798

Like Mary Ann in the theatre, George needed to launch his parliamentary career in first-rate style. He couldn't afford to lounge on the back benches. He made his maiden speech on 31 January 1794, a month into his first session – perhaps the most important day of his life, he told the Leighs. The speech was well received for its wit and erudition, but he was warned that he gesticulated too wildly; members on the government bench in front of him edged out of the way of his flailing arms. He gave the Leighs a circumstantial account of the day, but Mary Ann had to be satisfied with the 'sketches' in the newspapers. He sent the *Sun* and the *Star* to her and the *Herald* to Aunt Esther.[500]

Shortly afterwards he fell ill – like his father he was usually ill in the winter, but this time it was worse. Mehitabel came to nurse him, for which he was not at all grateful at the time, because he disliked being told what to do and was embarrassed to think of her witnessing the 'indelicacies and uncomfortablenesses' of the sick room. He wrote to the Leighs about his ambivalent feelings towards the aunt who had brought him up, and who now seemed to be invading his bachelor home. Not offended by his rudeness, Mehitabel invited him to convalesce at her house in the suburban village of Wanstead, which he accepted, although he feared a house full of children would not be restful. In the event, he told the Leighs, he had enjoyed 'great comfort and tranquillity' while benefiting from a regimen of 'asses' milk and bark'. He assured Mary Ann that he was recovering and told her on no account to come up to see him. As soon as he left Wanstead, before going back to his chambers, he went to Somers Town to show himself to Aunt Esther, to prove he was alive.[501]

In the weeks following his illness an incident took place which reminds us that George was still very young. His friend Robert Jenkinson responded to the threat from Revolutionary France by forming a regiment of Volunteers, much to the amusement of friends who couldn't see him as a gallant colonel. George wrote a set of satirical verses, a mock call to arms, in Jenkinson's name. Others in the plot pretended to have had them printed, and told Jenkinson that bill-stickers would be out first thing in the morning to distribute them far and wide. Jenkinson fell for the story and was upset, but when he found out the truth he was angrier still, considering George's part in the affair a betrayal of friendship. George apologised, but although nothing had been printed or distributed Jenkinson refused to accept the incident as a harmless joke. George claimed that Jenkinson's refusal to accept the apology was in its turn a failure of friendship. The quarrel reduced both young men to tears, and it took the combined efforts of their friends to bring about a reconciliation. 'Why, child,' Dr Jackson exclaimed when he visited George at the end of May 1794, 'this is more nonsensical than you used to be at Christ Church… pretty people to govern a nation truly.'[502] The incident revealed two sides of George's character that were to bedevil his career: the carelessness with which he gave offence to others, and his readiness to take offence himself.

Pitt invited George to second the address on the King's speech at the beginning of his second session,[503] but in the weeks and months that followed there was no further sign of progress. In frustration, George called on Pitt, and without asking outright made it plain that he needed a salary. Pitt promised to do what he could, but although George heard in August that one of the under-secretaryships at the Foreign Office was likely to come his way, he had to fret anxiously through the autumn waiting for confirmation. The newspapers were reporting his appointment from the middle of December onwards, but he didn't get his official paper and pen until 5 January 1796. As George stepped into the world of government he expressed his awe in a metaphor which for others would have been trite enough, but for him had a certain poignancy: it was pleasant, he wrote, to get behind the scenes and see 'the mechanism and machinery by which the actions of the great Pantomime are guided.' He was young and fresh enough to relish the extension of his privileges: 'I might frank you down forty feather beds,' he told the Leighs.[504]

Although he had discharged his substantial debt to William Leigh when he received his £3,000 from Ireland, he continued to borrow smaller sums from him, and from his aunt Fanny Canning. In March 1794, when Mary Ann wanted to raise finance for the ointment business, she asked him to underwrite a £100 loan with a promise to repay in August 1795. He refused to put his signature to any paper, but offered a verbal promise, which seems to have been accepted. When August 1795 came round it was only through the generosity of a friend that he was able to discharge his obligation. His salary of £1,500 per annum enabled him straightaway to insure his life for £4,000, for his mother's benefit. In March 1796, however, before he had received the first instalment of his salary, he was shocked to learn that medicines Mary Ann had taken when she was ill in Bristol five years earlier had never been paid for, the sort of shock that her precarious existence would deliver again and again. Unable to raise the full amount, he sent her £15 against her next quarter's allowance. In December Mary Ann reminded him that the debt was still outstanding, and he offered to send a further £20.[505]

Hitherto he had feared to tell his friends about his mother, in case they thought he was angling for financial assistance. That at least was the reason he acknowledged, but it may be that he was inhibited by a deeper sense of shame – it was not easy to admit that his mother had once been Samuel Reddish's mistress, and had produced a string of player's brats. The burden of secrecy had been a barrier between him and even his closest associates. Now he felt sufficiently secure to break his silence. The friend he singled out for this confidence was Charles Ellis, a fellow MP, a gentle, generous, modest man, whose large fortune was derived from slave labour on his family's plantations in the West Indies. On every topic but slavery, Ellis followed George's lead. He was unambitious, saying that he valued his seat in Parliament only because it enabled him to support those he loved. He had recently given £5,000 to his old tutor, making it impossible for the tutor to refuse by settling the money on his wife and children. On hearing about Mary Ann, Ellis proposed to buy her an annuity, warning George that an under-secretary's salary was subject to the uncertainties of political fortune. George wondered whether he had any right to refuse, and when he did refuse he reflected that this made the third time that he had deprived Mary Ann of an income, which underlined yet again his obligation to provide for her himself. Six months later Ellis prevailed on him to accept the gift of a horse.[506]

Ellis persuaded George to approach Pitt about Mary Ann. Pitt took the revelation calmly. In earlier discussions there had been no mention of her, but it's unlikely that he was unaware of his protégé's family circumstances. Now he pointed out that he had several sinecures at his disposal and, furthermore, when the time came for George to leave the Foreign Office, the government could award a pension, to be paid to his mother.[507]

**

Meanwhile, Mary Ann's other sons still needed to be launched in life, even if not in first-rate style. When he committed himself to providing for Mary Ann's future comfort George was also undertaking (though he may not have realised it at first) to provide for her children. The first instalment was the hundred guineas for Mary. The boys presented more complex problems. He no longer referred to the Reddishes, Sam, Charles and William, as his brothers. In his letters to the Leighs, and even in his diary, they were always 'my mother's sons'.

When Captain Featherstone failed to get him into the Navy, Samuel enlisted as a soldier – and soon regretted it when he found he was to be sent to Botany Bay, as sergeant of marines on a convict ship, the *Surprize*. He complained to Mary Ann, and she complained to George. 'What can I do? I cannot prevent it,' George wrote in his diary. Most entries in the diary are drily factual, so this exclamation stands out, suggesting unusual depth of feeling. Over the next few months he enquired after posts that might be more agreeable to a young man of education, but he had no influence to exert and no wish to stick his neck out or to advertise the connection. He contented himself by meeting Samuel as he prepared to leave, and giving him a bag of books.[508] If Samuel found no sympathetic company among the soldiers, he may have hoped for it among the convicts, who included the Scottish political martyrs, the agronomist William Skirving, the lawyer Thomas Muir and the unitarian minister Thomas Fysshe Palmer, all three prosecuted for sedition by a nervous government.

The *Surprize* sailed in May 1794. Some eight months later news reached the London papers of an enquiry at Rio de Janeiro into an alleged mutiny on the ship. The allegations involved elements of both crew and prisoners, including two of the political prisoners, Thomas Fysshe Palmer and William Skirving. Sam was a prominent witness at the enquiry. What happened is far from clear, except that the biggest villain appears to have been Captain Campbell, who was described by Samuel's commanding officer, Ensign Pattullo, as a 'savage'. Mary Ann undoubtedly read the reports, and George may well have been in a position to find out more of the background, but they didn't discuss it in their letters. When the *Surprize* reached Botany Bay, Palmer and Skirving were released and honourably acquitted on the mutiny charges.[509]

George thought Samuel a good fellow, but bold and wild, and as such probably safer on the other side of the world. In July 1795 a stranger arrived bringing letters and, as George complained to the Leighs, a bill for £10 'drawn upon me by Saml Reddish at Botany Bay'. He forwarded the letters to Mary Ann, but didn't mention the bill. Despite criticising Samuel for making unreasonable demands, George occasionally made tentative moves to improve his position, but in the end all he could do was keep Mary Ann informed of sailings to Australia so she could have her letters ready. Samuel remained in the colony for several years, and with a grant of land and two convicts to help him cultivate it he considered settling for good.[510]

In 1794 two of Mary Ann's children died. Ann's death in August, barely eighteen months since she had been recovered from her nurse, left behind bitter memories. It is probable that the little girl died in Taunton,[511] which suggests that Mary Ann, with calls upon her attention in both Exeter and London, had once more handed her over to someone else's care, giving Hunn's sisters, who presumably took their brother's side in the increasingly open quarrel, an excuse to reproach her as a bad wife and mother. No such bitterness clouded her memory of William Reddish who died in Scorton later that same year, aged thirteen or fourteen. She believed that the Milners did what they could for his comfort. George sent them five pounds for medicines and comforts, and on hearing of William's death fitted Charles with a suit of mourning. He did not go into mourning himself, and acknowledged no personal involvement in the tragedy of 'the poor little object of your regrets' except on Mary Ann's behalf.[512]

In the Packet Mary Ann remembered William as a 'sweet boy', but the only glimpse she gives of him is the moment in Lancaster when he made his prophecy about George being the glory of his country. As for Samuel and Charles, she wrote about their prospects in life, and cared in a practical way about their well-being, but we are left to imagine her feelings. She and George were both exercised over what to do about Charles in particular, but she made no mention of his feelings, his hopes or ambitions – or if she did, George ignored it. The one exception is chilling: Charles was with her as she wrote to George from Somers Town in 1793 and 'He beg'd leave to write to you in this letter, but I told him I coud not spare a corner.'[513]

Although she now had no children at school with Mr Milner, her dealings with him were not at an end. She still owed him money. It might seem a modest enough sum, £28 3s 2d, but for Mary Ann it was over half her annual income, while for Milner it represented almost twice the annual fee for a boy at his school. He eventually appealed to George, who sent him £10. Annoyed and distressed at not being able to do more, George wrote an amusing account of the matter to the Leighs, telling them that Mary Ann, instead of paying Milner, had sent 'cart-loads' of Costello's Collyrium. Taking this literally, Canning's biographers use the incident to illustrate how unreasonable Mary Ann had become, but it's likely first of all that 'cart-loads' is a rhetorical flourish, and secondly that the ointment was not sent entirely out of the blue.[514] James Milner was an enterprising man with an interest in scientific matters. While she was arranging her sons' education Mary Ann may well have discussed her ointment with him and he may well have expressed an interest in acting as her agent in the North of England. He wasn't far from Harrogate, with its constant supply of wealthy invalids. While she may have overestimated his willingness to be involved, her behaviour was not necessarily as absurd as it can be made to appear.

It would be some time before George shook off the ambitious Mr Milner, who applied to him for testimonials as a teacher and for support in his pursuit of clerical preferment. Although George said repeatedly that he couldn't help – he had no knowledge of Milner's abilities as a teacher, and church appointments were not in his gift – he sympathised, and recognised that the poor man had grounds for complaint.[515]

Charles Reddish was to pose an intractable problem. Eventually, before the end of 1793, Morton the coach-maker fulfilled his promise, but he did it ungraciously, and made Charles's life difficult. At first George told Charles to put up with things, giving him a guinea as encouragement, but when he realised that the boy's complaints were justified he asked Mehitabel's brother Paul Patrick to find him alternative work. This resulted eventually in a post in the counting house of the tea importing firm of Popplewell and Styan, where Charles got off to a bad start by not coming prepared with money to tip the servant who made tea for the clerks. Slight of stature, he liked smart clothes but spoiled the effect by being slovenly and dirty. The other clerks made him their butt. There were quarrels, Charles would lose his temper and he once took a knife to a colleague. He was eventually dismissed either because of incompetence – there were complaints about his handwriting from the beginning – or, as Paul Patrick believed, because of his 'ungovernable temper'. George listened to Charles's explanation and decided he was not greatly at fault.[516]

George took a close, but intermittent, interest in Charles's activities. Shortly after Charles started at Popplewell's, something occurred for which George lectured him and forced him to write a 'penitentiary letter', but whether this was the knifing incident, or indeed whether it had any connection with the counting house at all, is impossible to say. It may have been to do with a letter Charles sent to Mr Milner. When Mary Ann wrote from Exeter exhorting Charles to behave better, George, monitoring the correspondence, sent back one of her letters, pointing out an inaccuracy which weakened the force of her exhortation. In the hope that Aunt Esther could be a good influence, he used his position as postmaster to direct Charles's letters to Somers Town to force him to visit every Sunday. When George visited his aunt he was amused to find her mending Charles's stockings; she complained that they wore out very fast, and asked his advice 'about *double-heeling* them – an expedient that in a great measure counteracts the rubbing of the shoe. I highly approved of it.'[517]

One explanation of the boy's erratic behaviour emerged when he confessed to Aunt Esther his wish to be an actor. Esther kept his secret for a while, but then felt obliged to reveal it to George and Mary Ann. George was furious, although he tried to make light of it, saying Charles was just a silly boy. He made him swear to abandon forever any thought of the stage. Mary Ann seems to have done nothing to defend Charles. There's no reason to assume that Charles's ambition was unreasonable. Like his father he was subject to fits, and he had also inherited his father's extravagance and habit of falling back on lies and prevarication, so why not his genius as well? He was never given a chance to try. 'I represented the matter to him in such a light as I flatter myself has shewn him the folly of his notions about it,' George told the Leighs. When his eyes were bad Charles would read to him, very well and for hours on end, but it did not strike him that this might indicate some histrionic talent.[518]

At the outset George had been well disposed towards 'little Charles Reddish', telling the Leighs hopefully, possibly quoting a school report from Milner, that he 'writes admirably and is an excellent accountant'. It had seemed easy, slipping him the occasional guinea, passing on old clothes, sending him on errands, but soon he was drawn into supervising many aspects of Charles's life – finding him to a good tailor; hectoring him about his behaviour and his handwriting; checking up on his correspondence. For Charles's increasingly alarming fits he at first relied on his own apothecary, but later consulted a leading society doctor, Richard Warren,[i] who prescribed cold baths, as Dr Jebb had recommended for Charles's father. In February 1796 George introduced Charles to a new landlady, perhaps because the previous one was encouraging his theatrical aspirations, but after less than three weeks, having discovered something wrong with the new landlady, he insisted that Charles should move out and stay with Mary Ann, who was

i Richard Warren (1731–97), physician to the Prince of Wales, was said to be the highest earning physician in the country.

visiting London and had lodgings in Devonshire Street, not far from Gray's Inn Lane and Somers Town.[519]

Although irritated by Charles's habit of writing too many pointless and often illegible letters, either as an excuse for not doing other things or so that he could be seen addressing 'George Canning MP', George tried to be fair, reflecting that perhaps the habit arose from affection. He didn't want to suppress 'anything that indicates feeling'. What he found harder to forgive were the lies that Charles told, which he first learned about at the same time as he heard about the fits. Teach him truthfulness, George urged Mary Ann, or there's no hope 'of success, of happiness, or of respectability for him in this life'.[520] George's deepest worry, however, was a suspicion that Mary Ann was encouraging her sons to look on him as their brother, partly for their own sakes, but also because it was another way of laying claim to her own place in his life. He understood now why Mehitabel had rebuked him for calling the player's brat his brother.

There remained the problem of Mary Ann's marriage. In the spring of 1795, when she was in Devonshire and Hunn was back in his home town of Plymouth, their paths occasionally crossed, but he would take no notice of her. 'He is a scoundrel,' George wrote. 'Good God, that she could ever link herself to such a fellow.' He was so fearful of being drawn into their quarrels that he refused to visit his friend Lord Boringdon at Saltram near Plymouth.[521] George made up his mind that separation was the only solution, but for Mary Ann it was hard to sever all ties with the father of her children. Whether she still had any sympathy for him is doubtful. He presents a dismal figure, a seedy middle-aged man who had made a hopeless mess of his life, looking to George to rescue him.

**

Mary Ann had an eye for what was going on in the world; she read the newspapers and formed her own opinions. She had felt at home in a Duchess's drawing room, but equally she could walk into a tavern or squeeze into the corner of a coach without embarrassment. As she jigged up and down to London she took note of what she saw, and listened to what people were saying – all sorts of people. She noted the suffering and unrest in the towns and countryside, and became convinced that the scarcity of grain was artificially maintained to keep prices high. People were hungry, and the government was responding to their protests with harsh measures. Believing that her glorious son, if he knew the truth, would relieve the suffering of the people, Mary Ann sent him her observations, as we can tell from his occasional, brief responses. Many years later she still recalled the impression made on her by what she saw on her travels in 1795.[522]

She may well have been disappointed by his answers. His response to her accusation about hoarding was a counter-accusation that the discontent was instigated by agitators. The Seditious Meetings Act, he said, was 'necessary and salutary' in order to suppress 'profligate associations of sedition'. She was despondent about the war and the new taxes, to which he replied that the war was 'just and unavoidable' and that the taxes would not bear heavily on the poor. He reminded her complacently that opposition is easier than government. Later he seems to have enlarged upon the conduct of the war, but half a sheet is missing: perhaps she disapproved so strongly of what he said that she destroyed it, or sent it back. He had no intention of going into greater detail. A woman, he wrote in his *Letter Journal*, 'has no business at all with politics, or if she thinks at all about them, it should be at least in a *feminine* manner, as wishing for the peace and prosperity of her country – and for the success and credit of those of her family (if she has any) who are engaged in the practical part of politicks.' Mary Ann certainly wished for his success and credit, scouring the newspapers for information and wondering why he was not more often on his feet in Parliament.[523]

**

While Mary Ann was living in Devonshire Street, George was engaged in the final negotiations about his under-secretaryship, and getting to know his principal, the Foreign Secretary, Lord Grenville.[i] She had come to town to be close to her mother, arriving in early December 1795, and taking George by surprise. Although it was Esther who had borne the main burden of looking after Mrs Costello over the years, the old woman wanted Mary Ann to be with her at the end – Mary Ann and George. She lingered several weeks, 'in a dying way' as George told the Leighs. He visited, and when she eventually remembered who he was she acknowledged his importance by declaring that she could now die contented. The old lady died on 20 January 1796, on the day of George's first royal levée as a member of the government, a coincidence that Mary Ann recalled with obscure satisfaction. George supported Mary Ann throughout this period, agreeing reluctantly to dine with her on New Year's Eve, but determined to resist any further invitations by pleading business. While he was grumbling at being dragged into these sad events in his mother's life, he was entering wholeheartedly into the Leighs' anxiety about Bess's sister Fanny Canning, whose proposed marriage to Colonel Spencer, brother of Paul Canning's widow, was off and then on and finally off.[524]

The new under-secretary's life was dominated by official labours; he was at the mercy of the winds and tides that brought the mails. His letters to Mary Ann were full of apologies for not visiting (when she was in town), or for not writing more than a note, scribbled hastily to catch the evening post. He was now writing almost every week, more frequently if he had particular business or a complaint to make, but it is plain enough where she came in his priorities. He told her how long and late he laboured, and during the recesses she could follow his progress from one country house to another, but he told her nothing about affairs of state or his relationships with political colleagues. He was freer, even to

i William Grenville, first Baron Grenville (1759–1834) was leader of the powerful Grenville family interest in Parliament. A cousin and early political ally of Pitt, he was hard working, but not always easy to get on with. He was Foreign Secretary for ten years from 1791.

the point of indiscretion, in his letters to the Leighs. In February 1797 he told them of the '1200 sheep-stealing Frenchmen' who had landed near Fishguard in Pembrokeshire, while to Mary Ann he wrote like a government spokesman that he was confident in the security of the country. More indiscreetly still, in September 1797 he kept the Leighs informed of the delicate and ultimately unsuccessful negotiations with France, marking his letter 'Secret'.[i] He reminded his mother that he would never discuss politics with her, reassuring her with generalities: 'the spirit and unanimity of the Country will convey it safe thro all difficulties and trials'.[525]

Esther was set free by her mother's death, and less than two months later, at the age of 41, married Joseph Murch.[526] Not long afterwards Mary Ann left for Exeter, travelling by way of Bristol, where she had to explain to the druggist that she could not yet pay her five-year-old medicine bill in full. Esther soon followed. Mr Murch had interests in Devonshire, including the Globe Tavern, near the theatre in Plymouth.[527] Aunt Esther's removal from London deprived George of a link with his childhood. He had never been barred from meeting her, because Stratty had not feared her influence, and he could still see her without apprehension. She made no demands on him, either for money or for demonstrations of affection.

Since his dismissal from Popplewell & Styan in the autumn, Charles had been at a loose end, staying with his mother in Devonshire Street, calling on his aunt and grandmother and running errands for George, who even contemplated taking him on as his private secretary. Then in March 1796 Walter Borrowes offered to employ him. For a week or so things went well, but Charles didn't settle down any better than at Popplewell's. Borrowes made allowances, reporting mildly that Charles 'could be more diligent and steady', but by May the fits were getting worse and Charles had to leave. Mary Ann, in Exeter, was not

i Lord Malmesbury's peace mission was sabotaged by the more extreme elements on the French side, and by disagreements among the British. The episode provided Canning with an early insight into the intricacies of high politics (Hinde, 49–51).

aware of the seriousness of his condition. George hoped to avoid alarming her and was annoyed when Charles himself told her how bad his latest fits had been. Believing that Charles had brought them on himself by not taking his medicine and cold baths, he sent him down to the West Country, where Mary Ann could supervise him. Since sea bathing had been recommended she transferred her base from Exeter to Plymouth. At the beginning of July, George saw Charles off on the coach, with five guineas and the doctor's prescription in his pocket. He told Mary Ann to smarten him up, make him improve his handwriting, make him more self-reliant, teach him French and, above all, persuade him to tell the truth.[528]

By October 1796 George had taken advice and reached his decision: Charles should go as a 'guinea pig' on an East India Company ship to Madras or Bombay. A guinea pig was a probationary midshipman, and the initial voyage could lead to a career with the Company on either land or sea. Charles was to be in Portsmouth, he told Mary Ann, ready to sail by the middle of November, although it turned out to be at least two months before his ship left port. Mary Ann, at George's suggestion, came to London at the end of the year to help Charles with his preparations and to see him off. She stayed on after Charles left, first in Devonshire Street, and then in lodgings near Red Lyon Square, before going back to Plymouth in June. The post of guinea pig seems unsuitable for a boy with Charles's problems, but although he remained subject to fits the voyage appeared to improve his general health: 'If he is as much improved in mind as he is increased in person,' George wrote on Charles's return in August 1798, 'he must be a prodigy.'[529] Unsurprisingly the East India Company declared him unfit for service.

20.
Plagues, 1798–1799

At the end of 1798 George counted his five plagues. One was Charles, home from his guinea pig trip. Another was Sam, who planned to leave the army and come home from Botany Bay in search of employment. Then there was an Irish cousin called Hugh Doherty, a lieutenant of marines, who likewise hoped for a civilian post.[i] It's not known exactly what Doherty wanted, nor what George could do for him, beyond a gift of £20 in March 1799. The slippery Mr Hunn was a more time-consuming plague, while the most distressing of all was Mary Ann's refusal to leave London.[530]

While she was in Devonshire Street preparing Charles for his expedition, George asked Mary Ann where she wanted to settle, hinting at the possibility of a house near, but not in, the capital. He gave Wanstead, where Mehitabel lived, as an example of the sort of suburban village he had in mind; he would be able to visit her as easily as he visited his aunt. Mary Ann recalled, no doubt, that he had stayed more than a week in Wanstead after his illness in 1794, and interpreted his suggestion as confirmation that his bitter words at the time of the Newbery affair did not mean that she could have no place in his domestic arrangements. He had got

---

i Hugh Doherty had not yet achieved the notoriety that would attend his publication of his matrimonial troubles in *The Discovery, or The Mysterious Separation of Hugh Doherty Esq, and Ann his Wife* (1808).

as far as discussing with Borrowes the possibility of raising a loan of £2,000 for this purpose, but Mary Ann objected that he could not afford it and the matter was dropped.[531]

The plan was revived in the autumn of 1797, when Pitt made good on his offer to find George an extra income, appointing him to a sinecure as receiver-general of the Alienation Office, worth £500 or £600 a year. George described it to Mary Ann as a small office and a proof of Pitt's esteem.[532] He told Borrowes to go ahead and look for a house. Borrowes was a competent man of business, well able to raise a loan and negotiate a lease, but not the best man to choose a house for a lady. George would have done better to entrust his servant Fleming with the task. Fleming was occasionally called on to advise the Leighs on practical matters such as recruiting a butler, but George was afraid of letting his servants know too much about Mary Ann. He feared the knowing wink, the look of complicity, amongst those around him. Borrowes was discreet and, in any case, as Stratty's close associate he had always known the story, as Mary Ann couldn't help reflecting apprehensively when she first met him.[533]

By the beginning of 1798 Borrowes had taken a lease on a small house in the village of Totteridge near Barnet, about ten miles from Westminster. It was not much further from Mehitabel in Wanstead, but in the absence of good cross-country roads there was little danger that she and Mary Ann would come across each other. The rent, and an allowance of £200, took up all that George could spare from his Alienation Office salary.[534] He took into his confidence a fellow MP, William Manning of Copped Hall, one of the largest houses in Totteridge. Manning was a banker and supporter of the government, whose London home was close to George's new chambers in Spring Gardens.

Mary Ann at first embraced the scheme enthusiastically, but as soon as she saw the house (or so she would claim with hindsight) she realised that living there would cost more than she could afford. Her account of her time in Totteridge gives a vivid insight into the genteel pressures of life in a suburban village. There were no shops nearer than Barnet, and having no transport she was dependent on expensive tradesmen who came to the village with their carts. Mehitabel had complained of the same problem when she first moved to Wanstead. Fleming would have foreseen this. When Mary Ann began to explore village society she found more painful problems than tradesmen's carts. Those in the village she naturally expected to mix with, such as the Mannings, kept liveried servants, who would humiliate her if she visited without a carriage. She didn't have a manservant, not even an 'urchin' in livery, except for a part share in an old man who kept the garden tidy, so when she held a party, who would carry her invitations round the village? Obviously not the gardener! – something else that Fleming would have grasped at once.[535] Considering the hardships and humiliations she'd overcome in her life it may seem surprising that Mary Ann was so unresilient in the face of such irritants, but readers of Jane Austen and Fanny Burney don't need to be reminded of the ferocity with which small social distinctions were enforced.

As Mary Ann was preparing for the move, George told the Leighs that Totteridge afforded 'plenty of good neighbourhood', but this was wishful thinking. Mr Manning warned that Totteridge, though one of the prettiest of the suburban villages, was also the 'most unsocial'. His family found all the society they wanted in London and hardly mixed with their neighbours.[536] Even today Totteridge is a pretty place, full of fine houses, with little outward sign of community life. But Manning may have been telling only half the story, unwilling to add that the ladies of Totteridge, with their sensitive social and moral antennae, had detected something not quite right about their new neighbour, the same ambiguity that had puzzled Mr Colman when he met Mary Ann at Morton's dinner table. She found no welcome, and the experience left her bitter.

The main disappointment, however, was George himself. Up until now neither she nor he had had a home they could share.

When he came to her in Bristol, for instance, they were flying visits, and when she was in London he could not be expected to share her lodgings, and she could hardly stay at his bachelor establishment, even in the comparative magnificence of Spring Gardens. All this she had accepted. But now she had a roof and a bed for him, close to London, where he could easily spend a night or two. Surely he would come to relax in his mother's company after his week's labours. To the Leighs he made no secret of how much he disliked visiting her. His reluctance was partly due to the cramped accommodation and the economies that she had to make in her housekeeping; his squeamishness in this respect is evident in his description of a dinner at Walter Borrowes' villa in Banstead, near Epsom: 'a little, little room in a little, little house, the sun full upon it – smoking victuals – the company fresh, or rather foul from the Race Course…'. He did stay once or twice at Totteridge: she kept the pillow he slept on, she recalled, and always fancied that it gave her sweeter rest, and she hoped to die upon it.[537] If she spoke like this at the time it will have been a stronger deterrent than the physical discomfort.

To add to his reluctance, Charles Reddish, back from India, was often to be found there. Mary Reddish too had left her post with Mrs Moore to live with her mother, partly to save the expense of an extra servant, but also because her compliant and sympathetic presence was a comfort. It was now that George met Mary for the first time. He was already well disposed; her letters showed her to be very different from her brothers. After their meeting, his feelings were warmer still. She was young, just twenty when they met, and very shy. She hardly managed a word. He found he couldn't quite regard her as his sister, but he was moved by the encounter. In years to come his letters to Mary Ann would frequently include good wishes to Mary, or anxious enquiries after her health. When he had occasion to write to Mary herself his letters were warm; he was never sarcastic as he was sometimes with Mary Ann, and now and then he signed himself her affectionate brother.[538]

Charles moved back and forth between Totteridge and London, threatening to make himself at home in Spring Gardens. George was complaining of this overfamiliarity to his friend John Frere when Charles barged into the room. Charles told Mary Ann what he had overheard, and when she chided George he replied that he had done it deliberately, intending to impress upon Charles the impropriety of entering a room without knocking. The boy was a constant anxiety to Mary Ann, and she passed on her worries to George: one day he had a fit or wanted to be married, the next he bought too many waistcoats, or slept out all night. Having now lost all sympathy with Charles, George was helping him, he said, out of dry duty – he might have added that it was also because it had become vital for his peace of mind to get rid of Charles once and for all.[539]

George never forgot how coldly he had been received by Sir George Macartney in 1787. Never again would he willingly risk such humiliation by asking a great man for a favour. Nonetheless, for his mother, for Sam Reddish, and now for Charles, he did ask. Within three weeks of Charles's return he approached Pitt's lieutenant, Henry Dundas, who among his other offices was president of the Board of Control.[i] George was beginning to understand the game of patronage, and to realise that he played it with a very weak hand. He had no money, no powerful relations, no boroughs in his pocket, no favours to barter with his political colleagues. His position was further weakened by an unwillingness to admit the closeness of his relationship with Charles. Although it was accepted that one might seek favours for family members, petitioning on behalf of a stranger could be resented almost as an insult. Nonetheless Dundas procured a cadetship in the East India Company's army. Over the next few months George waited impatiently for a ship to take Charles away for ever. Neither Charles himself nor Mary Ann was consulted. Mary Ann knew

i Also known as the India Board. Henry Dundas (1742–1811), later Viscount Melville, was concurrently president of the Board, treasurer of the Navy, and secretary of state for War, while also supervising the affairs of Scotland.

that if he went to India she was unlikely to see him again. She must also have known how ill suited he was to the rigours and temptations of military life, but she accepted George's decision. She told Charles that if he went George would do what he could to advance his career, or at least Charles had that impression, and the hope stayed with him through the slow years of his exile. Whether George authorised this undertaking is not known – perhaps he was so desperate to persuade Charles to go that he was prepared to make vague promises for the indefinite future. Arrangements were almost upset because a letter was missed when Mary Ann unexpectedly went on a visit to London, but eventually, after more mistakes and misunderstandings, the poor young man left for India at the end of 1798. Mary Ann sent him one last packet, which George assured her arrived in time.[540] With the departure of Charles the first of the five plagues was over.

The purpose of Mary Ann's London visit was to meet Captain Philip King who had recently been appointed Governor of Botany Bay, and to talk to him about Samuel's future. George promised to write to Captain King but told her firmly that she was not to mention his name.[541] Her trip may also indicate a feeling that she too, like the Mannings, could find a more congenial social life in London.

Realising that Mary Ann was disillusioned with Totteridge, and hearing that Mrs Manning's brother was interested in the house, George told Borrowes to look into transferring the lease. He urged Mary Ann to reach an arrangement before the winter set in, but warned her firmly not to settle in London. Thus what George liked to describe as the Totteridge 'experiment' came to an acrimonious end within a year. He blamed the failure on Mary Ann's unreasonable expectations. He had the impression (common to many children of exigent parents) that nothing he could do would satisfy her, that the more of his time he gave her, the more she would demand.[542] Mary Ann always resented the term *experiment*, believing quite plausibly that George had set the whole thing up to fail, to prove that it was impossible for her to live anywhere near London.

It was a hard winter with horses and people freezing to death, and roads and canals blocked by ice and snow. The mails were delayed, disrupting George's work at the Foreign Office, while his private affairs were impeded by the illness of his groom. Mary Ann too was ill, and her departure, planned for November, was delayed until February. Whatever she had felt about Totteridge over the past few months, when she came to leave its advantages were uppermost in her mind. It would have been the ideal place if only she had enjoyed a better income, but the sort of establishment needed to live there comfortably would have been ruinous to George, and so she felt it was for his sake that she was leaving, which may have lowered her sense of obligation. She felt free to choose for herself where to settle next. Borrowes arranged her move and stored her furniture. She found lodgings in Hart Street in Bloomsbury, not far from where she had lived with Reddish at the time of the *Semiramis* episode.[543]

By the middle of February the thaw had set in, leaving the streets awash. George said he would 'swim' to Hart Street to see her at the start of what he optimistically called her 'short stay' before she continued her journey into the West. A clear hint, which she ignored. She asked him to arrange for her newspaper to be delivered in Hart Street, making him suspect she was digging in. March came and went, and she stayed on. She gave no reason, but her determination to have her own way was clear enough. For George, having her in London would be '10,000 times worse' than Totteridge, and her obstinacy in this regard, he told the Leighs, 'vexes and almost angers me'.[544]

Mary Ann's presence in London was connected in George's mind with the problem of what to do about her husband. Her relations with Richard Hunn had deteriorated since the supposed settlement of their affairs in Guildford in 1793, and George had long decided that the only solution was a complete separation.

Hunn appears from the exchanges between Mary Ann and George to have been a thoroughly untrustworthy man, but allowance must be made for the bias of an estranged wife and her son. He claimed (in a letter that George described as 'impudent') to be supporting the three surviving children, and although Maria joined Mary Ann in the autumn of 1795 he continued to support the two boys, Richard and Frederick.[545] How much he, or his sisters, did for the children, the disabled Richard in particular, is unclear, but he did not abandon them, and that should be said in his favour.

George was considering a deal, offering Hunn a lucrative position on condition that he signed articles of separation. He used the ten-year-old Maria as a channel of communication with her elusive father. The first plan was to place Hunn in the Customs, but he was too old. He could have the comptrollership of St Vincent, 'a healthy island', George said confidently. Disposing of him far away was George's favourite option, but when Hunn objected, he procured the post of paymaster of the Gentlemen Pensioners,[i] which at £300 per annum was half the value of the St Vincent post, but Hunn doubtless preferred not to travel to the West Indies, however healthy the island.[546]

In return, Hunn signed articles of separation. George met him briefly to discuss the terms, but left the details to Borrowes. Things seemed to be going well, and George introduced a lighter tone into their correspondence by responding to Mary Ann's concern about his bad cold with a joke: it was right that he was taking James's Powders because he had caught the cold at a royal levée at St James's. But the mood soon soured. She noticed on one of his visits to Hart Street that he looked 'thoughtful', and he explained it by saying he was concerned about the effect that living in London would have on Mary, but this was almost certainly cover for his anger at Mary Ann's obstinacy. He became ever more explicit in his hints that she

i The Honourable Band of Gentlemen Pensioners were bodyguards to the King, later referred to as Gentlemen at Arms. It's not clear exactly what, if anything, their paymaster was required to do, but as there were only forty of them it was unlikely to have been onerous.

should leave London, until in the end she complied with the letter of his demand by moving to Penton Street, Pentonville, which was a newly developed area north of the New Road, with fields beyond – 'off the stones' – and so technically out of town.[547]

Whether by unlucky coincidence or by design, Hunn also was living in Pentonville. If it was by design, it's not clear what the design was nor whose it was, Mary Ann's or her husband's. However it had come about, George thought the situation improper. It introduced renewed uncertainty. The deed of separation was something George had insisted upon, with a view to putting an end to the Hunn plague once and for all. Mary Ann's feelings in the matter had not been considered. She probably approved, but George could not be sure. Would she change her mind and decide after all to stand by the father of her children? Would Hunn exercise a hold over her, coming upon her when she was without the support of George or Borrowes and persuading her to vary the terms of the separation in his favour? George's demands for Mary Ann to leave became strident.

We can only speculate on the precise reasons for this stridency. He was frustrated at not getting his own way, but there was also, perhaps, some deeper anxiety. He didn't trust her. She was a woman, and there was no telling what further entanglements her emotions might lead her into. Her anger at the failure of the Totteridge experiment could only contribute to her volatility. He presumably knew by now of Hunn's open adultery down in Bristol, and by an illogical but inevitable association of ideas this would recall uncomfortable facts in Mary Ann's own history. In Pentonville Hunn might look in at her lodgings windows, encounter her in the street, meet her at the houses of friends; the two of them might get together, collude, allow the thoroughly unsatisfactory situation to drag on and on. Were they so lacking in self-control that they would resume their conjugal life? So long as he permitted her to remain in Pentonville he would feel he was himself colluding in the disgraceful affair.

When he wrote to her in Penton Street (under the 'impulse of the most strong duty and affection, and after the most deliberate reflection') he was so embarrassed at the thought of his servant seeing her address that he took his letter to the post himself. He could hardly bear to visit her. On one occasion he got halfway to Pentonville but couldn't go on, and turned back. A few days later they met and quarrelled and he said he would not visit her there again. His words left a bitter memory. 'I cannot forget the anxiety you shew'd to send me away again,' she wrote, '— What coud have influenced you then — and what has been ever since increasing that desire to get rid of me — God knows! and I suppose you know — but I cannot guess!'[548]

He admitted to the Leighs that he had been forced to speak to her in a 'manner extremely unpleasant'. We cannot know how this extremely unpleasant scene played out. As his political associates would learn over the years, George had a varied armoury with which to impose his will: volcanic temper, icy criticism, sarcasm, self-righteousness, mulish obstinacy, eel-like sophistry. By some combination of tactics he overcame Mary Ann's resistance. When her own sharp tongue failed her and she was forced to acquiesce, we can only guess what she said to avoid the worst thing of all, a complete breakdown of their relationship. What he thought he heard from her was a firm resolution to fix her residence permanently in the West Country.[549]

At the beginning of June she took the coach for Exeter. George wrote a cheerful letter to greet her arrival. As for Hunn, George inserted a new clause in the agreement, making it a condition of his appointment with the Gentlemen Pensioners that he should have no contact whatsoever with Mary Ann. Since Hunn had already agreed the terms, this variation was irregular, and George felt himself to be uncomfortably in the wrong. But Hunn went quietly. He took up his post later in June, and held it until his death four years later. Mary Ann was staying in Plymouth, at Esther's husband's hotel, the Globe, near the old theatre, when she finally signed the deed of separation.[550]

With Charles on the high seas, Hunn disposed of and Mary Ann tucked away in Devonshire, George felt his three greatest plagues were safely dealt with. Meanwhile his career had got off to a good start. At the Foreign Office he had proved that he was hard working, quick to learn and skilled in argument. In addition to winning the good opinion of his colleagues, and above all of Pitt, he was recognised in the country as a coming man. This had been signalled soon after he took office by his appearance in a Gillray cartoon, *Promis'd Horrors of the French Invasion*, where he is shown in the background hanging from a lamp-post. This macabre debut was not achieved by chance. Disappointed not to have featured as one of Pitt's supporters in Gillray's earlier cartoon, *The Death of the Great Wolf*, George used the good offices of his friend John Sneyd to ensure that the artist had an opportunity to find out what he looked like. *Promis'd Horrors* proved that he had at last caught up with Jenkinson; they are shown together, hanging from the same lamp-post.[551]

In addition to his solid work at the Foreign Office, he was also a leading propagandist for the government, in particular through his contributions to the pro-government review *The Anti-Jacobin*,[i] where he used his sharp satirical wit and facility as a versifier in the bad cause of suppressing dissent. The title of the magazine recalls Canning senior and *The Anti-Lucretius*; when we think of the partisan use to which George was now putting his poetic gifts, it's hard not to think also of what his father had written about prostituting his muse.

Early in 1799 George was moved from the Foreign Office to a place on the Board of Control. Departure from the Foreign Office provided the occasion for the award of the promised pension. In February he discussed it in some detail with Pitt, who initially suggested £200. It was eventually fixed at £500, to be granted to Mary and Maria for their lifetimes, on the understanding that the bulk of it, £300, was for Mary Ann, with a small share also for Aunt

i Not to be confused with its successor, *The Anti-Jacobin Review*, which George described as 'detestably bad and stupid' (Diary, 3 Sept. 1798).

Esther – the precise division varying over the years. Borrowes and Paul Patrick were trustees. The Royal Warrant was granted in May, and by July the arrangements were almost complete. In case the girls died before Mary Ann, their lives were to be insured. There was a slight hitch over Mary's name, since she was usually known as Mary Hunn, which confused the lawyer drawing up the documents.[552]

Later George would claim that it was understood between them that the pension was in some way dependent on her keeping out of London, but Mary Ann's recollection of events was different, and since we don't know what was said face to face, we can't know who was right. Perhaps George meant to make the stipulation, but lost his nerve and fell back on impressive sounding periphrases. Mary Ann was not mollified: why had he not told her sooner that she was to have an income that would have enabled her to live respectably in Totteridge?[553] It confirmed her suspicion that he had intended the Totteridge experiment to fail, although he had other reasons for not mentioning the pension. He was always careful not to hint at future benefits until they were certain, and in this case it was prudent to say nothing until the separation from Hunn was irreversible.

Late in the summer, while Mary Ann was in Plymouth, Sam Reddish arrived home, taking her by surprise, since his recent letters had not mentioned an imminent return, and it was not many months since she had been petitioning Governor King on his behalf. In September 1799, when Samuel turned up in London, George was staying at Walmer with Pitt and Dundas. Although there were important matters, both public and private, to detain George at Walmer, the thought of Sam at large enquiring after him was sufficiently alarming to make him hurry back to town. He met Sam, probably genially enough, and instructed him to go down to Mary Ann in Plymouth and stay there.[554]

George offered to help Samuel make the transition to civilian life. Although it would be possible to obtain an army commission for him, it was not a secure prospect, not because a soldier was all the time risking his life, but because one could never be sure how long hostilities would last. He was, however, adamant that Sam would have to go far away from London, and hoped to find him a West Indian post. His immediate worry was that Samuel would intervene violently in his mother's quarrel with her husband. He told Mary Ann to keep an eye on her fiery son, who, he said, should occupy his leisure by writing a book about his adventures in Australia. Above all she must detain him in Devonshire.[555]

Letters had already begun to arrive from Charles, dispatched from ports of call on the way to India, including packets containing batches of letters to frank and send on. Some were overweight, and some were not from Charles but from friends to whom he had offered the convenience of Mr Canning's frank. One of Charles's own letters infringed the rules George had laid down, perhaps because it was addressed to a young woman, or to a public figure. George refused to frank it, lest he should seem to endorse its contents. He sent it to Mary Ann to do with as she wished. Now and then alarming reports would filter back. As early as February 1800, George learned that Charles had fallen foul of the governor-general, Lord Mornington, possibly by using George's name to claim special treatment.[i] Mary Ann wanted George to do something, and he vaguely promised to write to Mornington about it.[556] All this was troublesome, but less so than Charles's actual presence.

George's plagues had posed difficult problems which he thought he had approached coolly and reasonably, whereas sometimes he had made things worse by oversensitivity and exaggerated fears – the old fears about Charles and the theatre, for example, or the new fear about Mary Ann in Pentonville. It was perhaps too much to expect him to be entirely cool and rational: he was still a young man, unsure of his future, moving in circles that he had not been

i Richard Wellesley, second earl of Mornington, later Marquess Wellesley (1760–1842) was Governor-General 1798-1805. On his return he became a political ally of Canning. He was the elder brother of the Duke of Wellington. George also mentions contacts on the subject of Charles with Henry Wellesley, Mornington's brother and private secretary in India.

born to, and with his hands as yet unused to the 'machinery and mechanism' of power. There had not yet been time to heal the wounds of his adolescence; he had forgotten neither the horror of his meeting with Mary Ann in 1786 nor his humiliation at the hands of Sir George Macartney in 1787.

Meanwhile, Mary Ann in Devonshire brooded over the unpleasant words that had forced her out of London. George tried to change the subject by opening a protracted discussion about the eye salve, but although she answered his questions, and was grateful for the help he promised Samuel, she was convinced that he had grown proud, was ashamed of her and wanted her out of the way.

21.
Two Outsiders

The story of the actor John Moody warning Stratty that the six-year-old George was on the road to the gallows reads like the opening of a picaresque novel, with George as another Tom Jones. When Mary Ann refers to her sinister brother-in-law Paul Canning as another Blifil, she underlines the analogy. George's own fantasy in the *Microcosm* about cockchafers and bread and butter belongs to the same genre. For some, Canning remained until the end of his life a picaresque figure, a rogue, an adventurer, a boy from nowhere.

By 1799 he had made a good start. With the support of his network of friends from Eton and Oxford, and now from Parliament, he was welcomed into the best houses, but he went there not from hereditary right but because he was entertaining company, because men like Charles Ellis loved him and because he was thought to be a coming man. His job at the Foreign Office had brought him into contact with the inner councils of state, where affairs of the highest importance and secrecy were conducted, but an under-secretary, if he did his work properly, was still a clerk, inky fingered, tied to his desk, wearing out pen after pen, straining his eyes in the candlelight. In 1799 George's climb to the summit was far from complete, and the path could lead down as well as up. It was by no means certain that he would, as he hoped and planned, make it into the Privy Council by the time he was thirty.[557] The classic reward for the successful picaro, and his ladder to further success, was a good marriage. George knew, his sponsors Pitt and Dundas knew, all the world knew that if he was to make his way in politics he needed a wealthy wife.

Conversely, the classic picaresque pitfall was sexual transgression, which might take many forms. George's father, for example, after a decade of promiscuity, had completed his ruin by marrying a penniless girl for love. For George himself, the first temptation of this sort may have been his cousin Bess, whom he knew from a baby. A gentler character than her mother, she must have helped to make his time in Clements Lane less lonely than it might have been, and as she grew up and George left home she was a diligent and sympathetic letter-writer. In the Packet Mary Ann accused Mehitabel of scheming to promote the match. For her it would have been the final defeat, with George lost forever, swallowed up by the Cannings.[558] It's easy to see why, in her loneliness and frustration, Mary Ann came to believe her accusation, but although the cousins were fond of each other, there is no reason to think George seriously contemplated marrying Bess.

As a young woman, Bess Canning used to stay regularly with the Leighs, which enabled her to observe an affair that could have proved a more dangerous temptation. Early in 1798 George was with the Leighs in Bath when he met a Miss Newenham, possibly one of the eighteen children of a controversial and somewhat disreputable Irish politician, Sir Edward Newenham. Attracted by her looks and intelligence, he almost allowed himself to fall in love with her, but her family was a drawback: 'the devil of a connection,' he wrote in his diary. 'Two brothers that deserve to be hanged for murder in Ireland – ruined fortunes! numerous family, and this added to my own embarrassments.'[i] He pulled up

i What George says about 'Miss New's' family would fit with some of what is known of Sir Edward Newenham's large family, but it's not certain that any of his surviving daughters were still unmarried in 1798, nor what his sons might have done to deserve hanging. So perhaps George's Miss Newenham belonged to another branch of the family.

short, and by the end of the year was carefully retreating from the entanglement. He told Bess Leigh that he was 'free' but warned her not to break with Miss Newenham too abruptly, in case it should be apparent that she had been cultivating the Irish girl's acquaintance for his sake.[559] His cousin Bess observed that he had lost 'a piece of his heart' in the affair.[560]

Mary Ann's uncle, General Gustavus Guy-Dickens, had taken a different route to disaster. He was indicted in 1793 for an assault on a soldier with intent to commit an 'unnatural crime'. Influential friends went bail for him and interfered with the witnesses, mounting an unsuccessful prosecution of one and shipping another off to the front line. Although these tactics seem to have prevented the case coming to trial, Gustavus resigned from his regiment and the Queen's household. He died nine years later in the Fleet debtor's prison. Mary Ann, recalling her uncle's presence at her wedding, described him as 'the unfortunate Col Guy-Dickens, who has since that so fatally forfeited the worlds Esteem'.[561] George was not tempted by good-looking soldiers any more than by childhood fancy or romantic love, but there were other possibilities.

The courtesan Harriette Wilson claimed in her memoirs that Canning was among the many leading statesmen who shared her body, and the accusation has been repeated in a recent book, even though there seems to be no evidence to support it apart from the scattergun testimony of Harriette herself.[i] More socially secure targets of Harriette's memoirs, such as the Duke of Wellington, could afford a certain insouciance in the face of her allegations, whether true or false, but Canning knew that he was vulnerable, and this would probably have saved him from the temptation – even if he wasn't saved by his primness, his sense of decency and his horror of appearing ridiculous. Prim, decent, cautious men are capable of

i Harriette Wilson (1786–1845): The story of her life and her accusations against many members of the political elite, including Canning, is wittily told by Frances Wilson in *The Courtesan's Revenge*. While endorsing the allegations against Canning, Frances Wilson provides no additional evidence.

making themselves ridiculous for sex, however, and George, for all his caution, had a risk-taking streak. Harriette's story might be true, but there's no compelling reason to suppose that is, and it probably referred, in any case, to a later period in his life.

But even if he did none of the things that Harriette accused him of, we can't conclude that as an unattached man about London in the 1790s he was always prudent and chaste. Our knowledge of his goings on derives chiefly from family letters, and although he was happy enough to tell the Leighs about the foolish trick he played on poor Jenkinson, or a drunken escapade with his friend Osborne Markham, or his 'cheary' celebrations after his maiden speech,[562] he is unlikely to have regaled his uncle and aunt with accounts of visits to a brothel. He kept a diary, but its entries tend to be terse and businesslike rather than confessional. Lack of evidence does not imply that he never indulged what his father coyly referred to as 'constitutional turbulences', either with prostitutes or with discreet women from his own circle. If he did, he got away with it, since predatory sexual behaviour was liable to pass without censure and even without notice. A greater danger would be posed by involvement in a scandalous affair with a married woman, leading to an action for criminal conversation or a duel. Those with a more assured place in the world could, and did, play this game with a degree of impunity; an outsider, who might easily be written off as an adventurer, had to think twice.

There would be no reason to speculate on George's behaviour if it were not that his relationship with his mother was largely determined by his condemnation of her sexual transgression. He applied the double standard which judged women more severely than men, a piece of hypocrisy which was so pervasive that it hardly needs to be mentioned. George's attitude to his mother's conduct, however, would be much more distasteful if he were personally implicated in an illicit sexual relationship.

He had a number of warm friendships with women. One was Lady Malmesbury, whose husband was an important influence on him during his time as under-secretary, and who herself advised the young man on social graces, during the Volunteers incident, for instance. Another was Lady Susan Leveson-Gower, sister of his Oxford friend Granville Leveson-Gower, younger son of the Marquess of Stafford. On visits to Leveson-Gower's extensive family George found himself more than once the only person, in a large company, who was not related to everyone else. But, he told the Leighs, 'they soon forget that one is a stranger'. As a young man without a comfortable family life of his own he was touched by this welcome, but his comment shows he knew his place, as a stranger, on probation. He had the good sense not to jeopardise his position by making love to any of the daughters, but he was interested enough in the lively Lady Susan to be dismayed when she married the politician Dudley Ryder, who was ten years her senior, and rather dull.[563]

Leveson-Gower's brother, Lord Gower, was married to Elizabeth, Countess of Sutherland. All her life, the countess was a controversial figure: as a baby she had been the subject of a famous law suit, as wife of the British ambassador in Paris in 1792 she sent clothes and comforts to the imprisoned Marie Antoinette, and as an 'improving' landowner in the early nineteenth century she would bear much of the odium for the north Highland clearances. Some found her overbearing, but George declared, 'I like Lady Sutherland mightily. She is very handsome – and very pleasant – and clever – and ATTENTIVE.' Her attentiveness extended to taking an interest in his Oxford verses and the *Microcosm*.[564] She was, at the time he came to know her, in her late twenties, just about the age his beautiful and intelligent mother had been when he was taken from her in 1776.

Apart from Lady Susan, most of George's women friends were older than him; Mrs Crewe was much older, of his aunt and uncle's generation. They were also intelligent and independent – though not too independent, for he hated a female politician – and appreciative of his wit and ambition. They responded to his need for intimacy and affection without expecting him to make love to them. To some he seemed cold and intimidating; Leveson-Gower's mistress thought him too serious and disapproving.[565] He had no small talk and no time for sentimentality; he was reserved and self-contained, slow to show emotion, having learned since boyhood to keep everything on a tight rein.

One relationship, however, showed signs of running out of control: his growing intimacy with Caroline, Princess of Wales. He must have known the risk, although he can hardly have foreseen the political embarrassment this friendship would cause him later on. He seems to have been motivated by a genuine liking for the princess, and by chivalrous feelings for a badly used woman; he also enjoyed the bohemian ethos of Montague House in Blackheath, where she was virtually imprisoned. Even republicans can feel the allure of royalty, while Caroline's predicament appealed to George's inherited dislike of the reigning family. So when she made a pass at him he was, he wrote to Leveson-Gower, 'bewildered', but perhaps also flattered and excited. It appealed to his reckless streak. We don't know how far they went in the strange atmosphere of Montague House, but in the end caution prevailed and he was glad to make an amicable retreat. It would have been ruinous to both of them, he admitted.[566] The rumour that they were lovers soon died down, only to surface a quarter of a century later to add fuel to George IV's animosity.

The outsider seeking to establish himself among those born to privilege might fly high, astonish all who remember where he came from, spend comfortable evenings with beautiful and intelligent women, make love to a princess, but in the end, if he is to succeed, he needs money. He needs that rich wife.

Mary Ann too was a girl from nowhere when she arrived on her grandfather's doorstep, an Irish poor relation determined to force her way into the tight little world of Wigmore Street, threatening to disrupt the comfortable expectations of her aunt and uncle. Had things gone smoothly a fortunate marriage might have made her a great lady, but instead she followed her heart and married George's father, an obstinate outsider. After his death she remained an outsider. We use the word of Canning the politician because, however far he penetrated the ruling elite, he remained an outsider among insiders, uncertain of himself, secretive, sardonic, intent on his own goals, not a team player as we would say nowadays, and always suspect. Mary Ann was an outsider in a starker sense; she belonged forever to the crowd on the outside, looking in.

Now aged about fifty she could look back on more than thirty years of battle and compromise. She had lived on her wits, grabbed what she could for herself and her dependants, enjoyed life when things went well, bounced back when things went wrong, faced temptations, made mistakes, bestowed her trust and been let down, and through it all she had maintained her self-respect. But for a woman these picaresque peaks and troughs were hard to sustain. Hampered by rigid social limitations and moral inhibitions, by pitifully inadequate education and by legal and economic disabilities, the female adventurer faced a more daunting challenge than her male counterpart.

The facets of her nature that Mary Ann identified as helping her in her struggle were resilience, initiative and a predisposition to be happy. We might add strength of will and sheer force of character and intelligence. We are bound to admire her as she struggled onwards, and admire her all the more because she three times turned her back on the traditional resource of her kind, a rich husband. But these virtues appeared to George in a different, less favourable light. Her resilience meant she would never take no for an answer, her initiative meant he could never guess what she might do next. Always thin-skinned, he winced under her trimming tongue. A schemer himself, he feared her indirect ways and felt her intelligence working against him.

Down in Plymouth after her expulsion from London, Mary Ann pressed on with the ointment business, with the support of her old associate Robert Trewman, proprietor of the *Flying Post.*

By 1800 she had established a network of agents selling Costello's Collyrium across the West Country, from Bristol to Penzance. Its curative powers were not limited to sore eyes, but included chapped hands and 'excoriated nipples'. She also developed new products based on the original collyrium, a cerate or wax-based ointment for the treatment of burns, wounds and piles, and a 'most beautiful preparation, called Costello's Coral Lip Salve'.[567]

In the summer of 1799 George was a customer. Following three years' close attention to the correspondence of the Foreign Office, his eyes were in a bad state. He was treated by the celebrated eye doctor Jonathan Wathen Phipps, but also followed Mary Ann's prescription of nightly applications of Collyrium. Mary Ann evidently thought that Phipps's 'operation' did more harm than good. George's letters over the summer were full of descriptions of his symptoms and requests for advice. It provided a safe topic, and kept them well away from the controversies of the winter, but neither the doctor nor Mary Ann managed to cure his eye problem. Things went well at first and George declared that he had faith, but soon he was reporting that the treatment caused a redness and rawness that was worse than the original symptoms. Mary Ann blamed Gowland's Lotion, which he was using as an aftershave, but the trouble persisted after he had left off the Gowland's. He used a blob of Collyrium about the size of a large pea, rubbed in with a finger. Mary Ann said he should apply it with a camel-hair brush, but he said he couldn't manage that. One inconvenience was that on waking in the morning after using the ointment at night he couldn't see to read without first washing his eyes with warm water. Since the hours between waking and getting washed and dressed provided him with much of his reading time, when he would prepare himself for the business and controversies of the day, he was naturally afraid of having to use the ointment every night for the rest of his life. When he asked if he would become dependent on it she interpreted his question as a hint that he was about to go to Ireland where he might not find fresh supplies.

He explained the reason for his question, assuring her that he was not about to visit 'savage Climes where Collyrium does not abound'. He left off the ointment for a few days in September, but the symptoms got worse, so he carried on with it until the middle of October, when he gave up, saying it caused too great an irritation.[568]

'Must I always be red and raw?' George asked Mary Ann in July after a few weeks of using the Collyrium. 'Without being a great coxcomb, I had full as lief not do.' In September he was bathing his eyes each morning in brandy and water, because he suddenly had an added inducement to make himself look agreeable.

22.
Marriages, 1799–1801

Having overcome whatever feelings he had for Miss Newenham, and extricated himself from his entanglement with the princess, George felt free to look elsewhere for a wife. The pension likewise set him free. Mary Ann's future was now secure, he believed, and his obligation to provide for her discharged. The pension was derived from West Indian sugar revenues which meant not only that Mary Ann, who evidently shared George's abolitionist views,[569] would live the rest of her life on the proceeds of slavery, but also that her income would be affected by fluctuations in the sugar trade. In years to come, as well as providing subsidies when she overspent her income, George would advance instalments of the pension from his own pocket whenever the sugar revenues were delayed. But for now he believed that the provision he had made was both secure and sufficient, that she would no longer be troubled by her husband, and that her children were provided for – Mary having her share of the pension, the Reddish boys with posts abroad, and the Hunn children supported by their father's family. He was over-optimistic; with the possible exception of Maria, Mary Ann's children were never satisfied; they would all expect him to do more.

In August 1799 Pitt and Dundas were at Walmer Castle, Pitt's official residence as warden of the Cinque Ports, anxiously waiting for bad weather in the Channel to lift and for the Anglo-Russian invasion of the Netherlands to get under way. The party at the castle included Dundas's wife Lady Jane and his great-niece Joan Scott (Joan being pronounced with two syllables). Joan was twenty-three, and an heiress. George may not have known previously of her existence, but he knew something of her family, having attended a ball at her mother's house in Piccadilly five years previously. Mrs Scott, with her three marriageable daughters, had been a notable member of fashionable London society, a regular attender at court functions, and her wealth had been widely advertised when jewels to the value of £4,000 were stolen from her.[570] Since Mrs Scott's death in 1797 Joan had divided her time between her aunt, Lady Jane Dundas, and her sister Henrietta, now a marchioness, married to the heir of the Duke of Portland.

George was invited to stay at Walmer. The idea was in the air that he was coming down expressly to meet Joan, but despite this hint of manipulation, despite his rawness and redness, and despite his sarcastic manner, they seem to have been favourably impressed with each other. George denied that he was an impetuous, romantic or enthusiastic lover, and his careful response to the charms of Miss Newenham seems to confirm this, but he left Walmer in a state of high excitement, and broke his journey halfway to dash off a letter to Lady Susan Ryder confessing his passion for 'a girl with God know how many thousand pounds, the sister of one who had recently blended her name with a Dukedom'. He asked for advice, which, when it came, he didn't follow. Within days he was back at Walmer for a further interview with Joan, at which they reached a good understanding. He was impressed by the frank and almost manly way in which she had discussed things.[571] If she didn't grasp at the outset what was involved in being married to a politician, she soon had a demonstration, as George approached their courtship as a political problem. Joan's wealth, while it made the marriage possible, and from George's point of view desirable, was also a stumbling block, because it made him look like a fortune-hunter.

Although Joan herself was satisfied, he had to convince her family of his sincerity.

Their liking for each other increased during the autumn, but although Joan's mother's family, the Dundases, favoured him, George feared opposition from her closest relatives, her sister and brother-in-law, the Marchioness and Marquess of Titchfield. George begged his friend John Sneyd, a regular visitor at Welbeck, the home of the Portlands, to encourage Lord Titchfield to approve of the match. But the courtship stalled. George was determined to do nothing underhand. While Joan and her aunt publicly behaved as though the engagement was a *fait accompli*, he still held back until the Titchfields could be brought round fairly. Joan's recovery from a near-fatal illness in the spring gave her a powerful emotional weapon to bludgeon the Marchioness into relenting, but George said it would be wrong to take advantage of it. Despite a mild outburst against the Titchfields in a letter to the Leighs, he refused to quarrel, admitting frankly that from many points of view he was not an eligible husband.[572]

But already before Joan's illness, and more particularly after her recovery, he was very keen to succeed: 'I cannot bear the idea of giving her up,' he told Lady Susan.[573] He was undoubtedly in love. He could also see, as Pitt and Dundas had seen, that Joan was the ideal match. She had a large fortune (although it turned out to be less than the £100,000 that the gossips gave her)[574] and was well connected, but she was not too highly born. She might have done much better from a mercenary point of view, but she was not demeaning herself by marrying George. In terms of social standing their antecedents were much the same. The men in her family had been lawyers, soldiers and landowners, as in his.

Her father, General John Scott of Balcomie in Fife, came from an old family, and had a career in the Army and Parliament.[575] His vast fortune was said to have come from gambling. Stories abounded of his skill at whist and billiards. He played carefully and soberly, and invested his winnings in land. Still, it's hard not to suspect that he may have supplemented those winnings from other sources – possibly from bribes and commissions from the time when his associate Lawrence Dundas was a highly successful contractor supplying the army.[i] Whether or not he gained his wealth corruptly, it is well documented that a good bit of it was expended in bribes in the course of his 1761 election for the notoriously venal Tain Boroughs. General Scott was married briefly to a very young noblewoman, Lady Mary Hay, but when she eloped with an officer in his regiment he divorced her and married instead the mature and respectable Margaret Dundas.[576] After three years of marriage he died, leaving two infant daughters and the third, Joan, on the way.

The Marchioness, realising that her younger sister knew her own mind, capitulated not long after Joan's recovery, and soon even the cautious Lord Titchfield was brought round by Joan's determination, and also by further proof that George had a promising future: in a complicated re-shuffle Pitt appointed him paymaster-general and a member of the Privy Council. He missed by a few weeks his aim of being Right Honourable before he was thirty.[577]

There was one other point in George's favour, arising from an eccentric provision in General Scott's will. Scott left his substantial landed property in Fife and elsewhere to his eldest daughter, with the proviso that if she married a peer or the eldest son of a peer the land should pass to her younger sister. On his marriage Lord Titchfield had obtained legal opinions to the effect that the stipulation was probably unenforceable, but that it would have to be tested in court. The middle daughter, who had likewise disobeyed her father's will by marrying a peer, had since died. When Joan married, her husband might be tempted to launch an expensive lawsuit, a possibility which had held up administration of the General's will. As part of the marriage negotiations George

i One of the stories told about Scott's gambling (Wood, *The East Neuk of Fife,* 219) is that he won Dundas House in the New Town of Edinburgh from its owner Sir Lawrence Dundas, and that to avoid losing it Dundas undertook to build an equivalently grand house for Scott nearby. This story may have been true, but equally it would make a good cover story to disguise a bribe.

and Joan signed an undertaking not to dispute the Marchioness's inheritance.[578] A suitor who was more mercenary, or less sensible, or who felt himself to be in a stronger position than George, might have been less willing to waive his claim.

Early in 1800 Mary Ann down in Devonshire picked up hints from the newspapers that something was in the air, hints which George told her to disbelieve. The winter and spring proved difficult for her. George lightly assumed that once out of London she and her daughters would settle down in Devonshire, but it was not easy. They could stay with her friend Mrs Moore in Exeter or with Esther at her husband's Globe Tavern in Plymouth, but neither could provide them with a permanent home. The year 1799 ended sadly with the death of her afflicted son Richard, aged fourteen.[579] We don't know anything about the poor boy's disability, nor how great a part Mary Ann had played in caring for him, but as George himself would find during the short life of his own eldest son, a disabled child will, in the words of his father's sister Molly, twine itself around the heart. Mary Ann had now lost six of her twelve children.

Of those that remained one, Charles, was beyond her reach, unlikely to return. Now Samuel was about to be dispatched to a new life overseas. In the new year, after protracted negotiations, George obtained a post in the West Indian Revenue service for him. As soon as he heard it was in the air Samuel impetuously rushed up to London, much to the annoyance of George, who foresaw endless delays during which Sam would be inconveniently hanging around. In the event, a place was found on a convoy leaving Portsmouth around the end of January. Mary Ann went to see Samuel off. Walter Borrowes assisted by raising a loan to pay Samuel's travelling expenses and keep him going until he could draw his salary. It was only when Sam was on the point of leaving (or perhaps after he had set sail) that George revealed that there would be a 'noviciate' during which he would not be paid, and that the appointment was conditional on completing the noviciate satisfactorily.[580] Sam had something of his mother's resilience, embracing his fate more cheerfully than Charles, and thinking right from the outset of ways of making good and getting ahead. He was intelligent and good company; his departure left Mary Ann feeling flat and deserted. Although his posting allowed for home leave every three years, she couldn't fail to recall what her husband had said about life expectancy in the West Indies.

She had another son to look after. Under the separation agreement Frederick had been left in his father's care, but now Hunn persuaded Mary Ann to take charge of him. She may have been pleased to do so, although she did not keep him with her for long. He was eleven and she sent him to a school at Kingsbridge, some twenty miles from Plymouth and forty from Exeter.[581] How often she visited him in the course of her travels between the two towns is not clear. From what one can gather of Frederick's personality later in life he seems to have grown up with a sense of being an unwanted child.

On 8 May 1800 Mary Ann was in Exeter. Rumours about George and Joan could no longer be ignored, and she had a premonition that the evening mail would bring important news. She waited up for the postman, and just before midnight George's letter arrived with its first mention of a 'person who has engrossed my attention'. She wrote at once. Her first paragraph was all exultation and joy, but her second noted how sparing he had been with his information. She thanked him for this 'portion of your confidence', and promised to wait patiently until his 'unabated love – (for I love that word better than duty)' prompted him to tell more. She then referred to Joan as 'the dear object whom my heart admits to its maternal kindness'. The periphrasis, which was necessary because George had not yet told her the name of her future daughter-in-law, contained an assertion of her right to be connected with the event, and with Joan herself. It never occurred to Mary Ann that she was to have no such connection. Let him keep her out of his public life if he must – that much she had accepted since the Newbery incident of 1793 – but surely he would not deny her right to embrace her daughter-in-law.

Friends who were travelling north from Exeter offered to take her as far as Bristol, and she took the opportunity to go to London to repeat in person the prayers contained in her letter. She was not permitted to see Joan, who went to Brighton with her sister; it's not clear whether this was a pre-existing arrangement or improvised to prevent a meeting with Mary Ann. George himself had little or no time to spare, and when he went to join Joan, Mary Ann 'having no other attraction in London, return'd to the Country'. It was a shocking indication of how things really stood, a revelation of how much had been kept from her during the past eight months, while George was writing to her about his eyes and the ointment or Samuel's future. She rebelled inwardly against this treatment, and her personal discontents opened her eyes all the more to the greater discontents of the people. As she travelled back down to Devonshire she listened to stories of hunger in the countryside, and took note of what she saw in the fields and the towns along the way.[582]

George was not much more open with the family at Wanstead. He had his differences with Mehitabel, he told the Leighs, which he wanted to hide from Joan, lest they raise 'untimely questions'. It may be that Bess Canning was upset by her cousin's marriage. George wrote to her that he expected her and Joan to love each other. The Leighs were kept informed of all the ups and downs of the courtship and the arrangements for the wedding, at which William Leigh was to officiate. They knew early on the identity of George's intended, although even with the Leighs it was not until her illness that he first referred to her simply as Joan. George showed them the letters of advice and encouragement he had received from Lady Susan Ryder, and they knew all about a long letter that George wrote to his ally Lady Jane Dundas in which he gave a detailed account of his situation and prospects.[583]

The letter, which has been referred to several times already as evidence for George's feelings towards his mother, was written at the suggestion of Lady Jane herself, while Lady Susan may have given hints on what to say. Lady Jane was to hand it to Joan and the Titchfields when she thought the time was right. George showed himself more realistic about his prospects than his father had been when he wrote a comparable letter to Gustavus Guy-Dickens. He admitted that apart from the rents from a tiny Irish estate his only income was his official salary, and although he was well advanced in his career, politics was an uncertain business. He explained why he had deserted the Whigs, and admitted that he could not have contemplated marriage to a poor woman. That he had changed sides in politics, and that he was a poor Irishman who needed a wealthy wife, were facts too well known to be denied. It was hard to admit them frankly, but they were not grounds for personal shame. It was harder to write about his mother.

He describes how his mother, a widow without friends or money, made the mistake of going on the stage. He expresses his horror of the stage as a career for a woman, and implies that it led directly to the greater mistake of her liaison with Reddish. He tells how he was adopted by his uncle, and for many years speculated about his absent mother, constructing a dreamy, romantic image of her, which was cruelly shattered by the meeting in Great Wild Street when he was fifteen. He describes his revulsion, the pain of carrying his secret for so long, and the relief of confiding at last in Charles Ellis. He also told of his immediate resolution to make his mother's needs the first call upon his resources. This determination became still firmer, he says, when he persuaded her to give up the stage, and again when he refused Ellis's offer to help her.

The words he uses to describe Mary Ann's conduct – imprudence, shame, guilt, degrading, misfortune, misconduct, suffering, atonement, unfortunate – testify to the tension he felt between pity and condemnation. He also strikes a balance between explicitness and delicacy towards the feelings of his readers, Joan and her sister. Joan's almost masculine mind may have been strong enough to hear the facts without embarrassment, but he could be less sure of the Marchioness. She was timid and seemed to be afraid of him. He lets fall that Mary Ann had children by both her present husband and her other 'connection', but the whole thing is wrapped up in conventional terms, without details – without saying, for instance, that the connection with Reddish (who is not named) lasted six or seven years and that she bore him five children, three of whom were still living. There is an awkwardness in his expressions, a sign of the care with which he was treading a difficult middle way: while assuring his future wife that she would not have to meet the former mistress of Samuel Reddish, he had to avoid seeming so harsh and unfilial that Joan would think twice before placing her own future in his hands. It was just the sort of balancing act that would mark many of his political speeches, but just because it's cleverly done we should not assume that it was insincere. There is no ambiguity about his conclusion: his mother's liaison with Reddish, though now almost twenty years in the past, is a blot that cannot be effaced, rendering her unfit to mix with his wife.

> At no point have I omitted to impress upon her mind (especially at the moments when I was most labouring for her essential comfort and welfare) that her lot in life had no connection with mine; that, befall me what might, it should be the first object of my exertions to secure to her a competency beyond the reach of any accident that might affect my fortunes; but that on the other hand, be my political advancement, or private situation what they might, – that competency once secured to her, I should conceive my duty done; – that my relation was to her, and her alone... that her relation was to me alone, and that with my connections or friends she had nothing to do.... Do you require any further explanation to satisfy you, that, whatever my feelings of affection and duty towards my Mother may be, I have them at least under such regulation and controul, that they can never be productive of inconvenience, or even awkwardness, to any Connexion that I may form?

When Joan read the letter, before her illness, she expressed herself satisfied.[584] Her sister and brother-in-law took longer to make up their minds, but whether it was Mary Ann's past or George's uncertain future that gave them pause is not clear.

Once the Titchfields had consented, arrangements went ahead quickly, with Charles Ellis helping George to choose and buy a curricle, Pitt giving advice on choice of a country residence, the lawyers tackling the obscurities of old Stratford Canning's will, and the Herald's office coming to an agreement on the Canning coat of arms. The wedding took place on 8 July 1800, William Leigh officiating. Pitt gave the bride away, and George's friend John Frere was best man. Frere recalled that Pitt could not have been more moved by the occasion if George had been his own son, although Pitt's latest biographer suggests that his emotional reaction may have been due to other things, such as illness, anxiety about the war, or alcohol.[585]

Joan's understanding of the guarantee contained in the letter to Lady Jane was clear from the chilling letter she wrote to Mary Ann after the wedding:

> I am aware indeed, (as he has disguised nothing from me) of the circumstances which preclude a personal intercourse between us but from your experience how little distance of place and length of separation have had the effect of abating anything of his filial regard and tenderness, I hope, you will be disposed to give me credit, when I assure you, that they cannot impair in me that share of those sentiments which I derive from him…

Mary Ann was shocked: 'I read this anticipated letter, and I read in it my future Fate!' She was to be cut out of George's life. Although she read her fate in Joan's letter, she did not accept it. Had she known of his unequivocal undertaking to Lady Jane she might have realised her protests were futile. Like Garrick swearing not to re-engage her, George had given his word, although he was always too tactful, or too ashamed, to tell her so. Every bit as distressing was the revelation that George had told his wife the story of her past – and not her own version of it, but the version he had received from Stratty and Mehitabel. He had, like Stratty all those years before, expatiated on her misconduct. 'I think I never was less equal to the business of an Epithalamium,' she wrote immediately. 'I think I feel as I shou'd do if you were gone upon a long Embassy—and I was—an Old woman.'[586] In 1793 George had decreed that there could be no public contact between them; now he had gone further, there could be no personal intercourse between her and his family. It confirmed everything she had suspected since their struggle after the Totteridge episode. He had been changed by success, made proud by his newly acquired wealth, and persuaded by his grand associates to cast off his mother.

The future now filled her with horror. Her reaction was extreme. Rather than settling for an existence on the outer fringes of George's world, she contemplated a complete withdrawal, seeking out an impoverished clergyman's wife in the depths of the country who would take her as a paying guest. She made the threat, but the shock had thrown her into such a fit of lethargy that she did nothing about it. It's hard to believe she would ever have withdrawn completely, since even in a rural backwater she would have been within reach of the postman, but the idea took hold of her imagination and made her eager to get her girls settled in life: Mary should find a respectable husband, and then provide a home for Maria.[587]

**

George was to find that it was not only in London that embarrassments could arise. It was in Devonshire that the most painful of all the disagreements between mother and son had its origins. It was there that Mary made the acquaintance of a naval officer called Parker. There were a number of Parkers in the Navy just then; circumstances suggest that Mary's captain was Edward Thornborough Parker, Nelson's youthful aide-de-camp.[588] Edward

Parker had been sent by Nelson to England with dispatches in October 1799, earning praise from his captain on the way for his conduct under fire during a skirmish on shore near Gibraltar. He was promoted to the rank of commander that month, which entitled him to be known as Captain Parker, but since he seems not to have had a ship it is not clear what he had to occupy him while waiting for Nelson to leave Palermo and complete his slow journey home. Where and how he met Mary is unclear, but there are some possible avenues: Edward had relations in Devonshire, and was connected through his mother with Stratty's friends the Raikes family in Gloucester.[589]

The affair gave rise to a dispute between George and Mary Ann which raged through the second half of 1800 and on into the new year. George's preoccupation with his wife's difficult pregnancy, together with a crisis that threatened to bring his political career to a premature end, might partly explain why he was blind to the devastating effect the Parker affair had on his mother's already troubled mind.

Mary now was twenty-two years old. Already, while she was with her mother in Totteridge, she had attracted the attention of a businessman called Richard Thompson. Thompson was a lawyer who worked as London agent for country gentlemen,[590] and was always on the lookout for other things, including government posts. Born in 1765, he was thirteen years older than Mary. It's a measure of how little is known about Mary Ann's life apart from George that we do not know how Richard Thompson came to know Mary; perhaps he was related to the Agnes Thompson who had been one of George Canning senior's creditors. When he proposed marriage, Mary took fright. She had, she said, no wish to be married, and was perhaps relieved when George expressed his disapproval. At that point he was still trying to find places for the Reddishes and for Hunn, and didn't want another job-hungry man in the family. 'It will not do,' he wrote in his diary, and he must have been equally forthright when he discussed the matter with Mary Ann. He approved of Mary's 'pretty and sensible' letter putting an end to the affair.[591] Mary went on living quietly with Mary Ann.

Captain Parker appeared on the scene while Mary Ann was in Plymouth coming to terms with her disappointment over George's wedding. The affair with Mary may have started, on Parker's side, as a summer flirtation, a way of filling up his time while he waited for Nelson. We don't know how seriously Mary was smitten, but Mary Ann encouraged her, possibly, as George suspected, pushing the timid Mary into the affair. Parker may have found himself drawn in deeper than he intended. His family were alarmed and registered their disapproval. George also disapproved, as he disapproved of anything that might bring his mother's children to public attention, but he refused to express an opinion. He was annoyed that Mary Ann had asked for his views without telling him about the opposition of the Captain's parents. Mary Ann wrote several times to the Captain, and was excited, both on Mary's account and on her own, at the prospect of an alliance with a respectable, even glamorous, naval officer. George's position as the family's postmaster became an embarrassment, since by franking the letters he might appear to be endorsing their contents. He read what Mary Ann had written and found a hint that Parker might look to him for help in gaining promotion. When he told her to remove this impression, she merely added that she was not, of course, promising anything, which he said made things worse, because it implied that she could promise something if she chose. How far Mary Ann eventually went in her letters is unclear, but she seems to have entered into an 'engagement' with the Captain in George's name, or at least that is how George saw it. Parker was probably confused; he certainly felt that promises had been made, and wrote to Borrowes seeking clarification. This made George suspect that for Parker the whole thing was just a 'speculation', but if he was indeed the Parker who was Nelson's favourite, the nephew of another senior naval figure, and already a commander at the age of twenty-one, he is unlikely to have needed any help from a junior member of the government.[592]

As the affair continued George's anger grew until it affected his concentration. He suspected that Mary Ann had given the Captain a false idea of their relationship by failing to mention that she was herself excluded from George's home, and that George did not recognise Mary as his sister and would never recognise her husband as his brother-in-law. This suspicion was so painful that he did not put it into words until more than a year later, when fresh disputes drove him to renew his recriminations.[593] His worst fear was that if Mary Ann had deceived Parker, he himself would be seen as aiding the deception. When pleading his own cause to Joan and her family he had been scrupulous in telling them the truth about his 'connections'; now he was being drawn into a conspiracy to foist a player's brat onto a respectable naval family.

By the winter the affair had fizzled out. The Captain returned to his duties, Mary acknowledged that stronger wills than hers had prevailed, and George told Joan that it was 'finally' settled. He used a bad cold as an excuse for missing a dinner in honour of Nelson, and so avoided a meeting with Captain Parker, who was bound to be in attendance. George expressed approval of Mary's conduct, both to Mary herself and in a letter to Joan. Mary Ann told him how pleased Mary was to have won his approbation; he replied that 'never was any approbation more completely deserved.'[594] In this ponderous exchange of compliments we might see an attempt to bring things to a close, but if that was George's hope, he had failed to understand the devastating effect of his anger.

Under his onslaught Mary Ann's resilience failed. Her letter telling of her collapse reached him while he and Joan were at Welbeck Abbey in November, and his distress was aggravated by the need to keep everything hidden from his hosts. Unusually, he did not reply at once, but waited until the next morning to read her letter again. His response veered between concern for her health and frantic self-justification:

> I cannot be at ease or be reconciled to myself (though still my conscience nor my judgment do not reproach me) – I cannot rest till I hear from you again – and hear that you no longer tax me with unkindness.... Good God! how I should reproach myself if I thought I had given just ground for complaint and remonstrance for my Mother !... that I have inflicted a wound where I entended only to suggest the correction of an error, and that in shewing how I had been misled – But I will not say a word that shall look like arguing this point at this moment. No, my dearest Mother, I have at this moment but one wish, but one object, to entreat you to let me hear that you are well, and that you rely as confidently as ever on the unvarying tenderness and respect of your most dutiful and affectionate son G.C[595]

He prepared a lengthy memorandum on the affair, which he asked her to read and then return, so he could keep it as a record – although he said a few days later that he would destroy it. He apologised in advance for the difficulty he had in expressing himself clearly. Well aware that it would sound harsh, and be interpreted as a sign of pride, he tried to assure her that he had not changed, but had been 'animated by the same sentiments, which have animated all my feelings, and guided all my actions towards my mother from my childhood up to the present hour.' Mary Ann knew what to expect and it was several days before she summoned courage to open his packet. He told her he had not shown the memorandum to Joan, to allay any suspicion that Joan had influenced him, but she replied that he ought not to keep anything from his wife. Having suffered in her first marriage from her husband's secrecy, she was always a believer in openness. Although it was true that Joan had not seen the packet, he had kept her informed of all the developments, so she knew what it contained.[596]

He hoped that Mary Ann's characteristic piece of advice about marital frankness was a sign that she was recovering, but after the unpleasant words that had driven her from London the year before, and the disappointment caused by Joan's icy letter, the bitterness of the Parker correspondence left her sunk in 'absolute, and inevitable despondence', with her mind 'shook from its Characteristic Centre'.[597] She brooded on his words, twisting their meaning. Recalling that at the outset he had declined to give a view on the affair, she accused him of abandoning her and her problems altogether.

Things were quieter over the new year. George told Borrowes to arrange a £40 allowance for Frederick, who was still at school in Kingsbridge. George was probably anxious to ensure that there was no accumulation of arrears of fees as had happened with Mr Milner. Mary Ann sent a present to Joan, who then made a small contribution to a charitable collection that Mary Ann was interested in. There were uncontroversial matters to occupy them, such as the death of Paul Patrick, Mehitabel's brother, whom George described as 'liberal in his conduct – though perhaps, from education, not so much so in his ideas'.[598]

But then, in February 1801, Mary Ann wrote telling George that she thought they would meet no more, reviving the idea of withdrawing to a country vicarage. He was shocked; with political upheavals and his wife's difficult pregnancy on his mind he had put the autumn's quarrels behind him. He replied indignantly, asking for clarification of her hints. Fearing that she would interpret his words according to her own wishes and ideas, he asked Joan to copy his letter for the record. Mary Ann was probably not serious about her threat, but it was a possibility that hung in the air for some time, an extreme solution that might appeal to one who declared herself 'not born for Mediocrity'.[599]

In the spring Mary Ann roused herself to take an interest in public affairs, the distresses of the poor and unrest in the countryside. The price of bread was high. There was famine in Ireland, while in England there was great scarcity and persistent rumours of hoarding. Some called for legal fixing of the price of grain as under the ill-fated *Loi du Maximum* during the worst years of the French Revolution. A committee of the House of Commons recommended offering premiums totalling thousands of pounds to encourage the cultivation of potatoes, the diet of the poor. The distress was widely reported, but Mary Ann felt, as she had in 1795, that she needed to present George with the testimony of her own eyes. George told her to wait for the harvest, when things would get better. A day or two later he returned to the subject, giving the government line that the distresses of the poor only turned to riot under the 'instigations of the wicked'. The government, he said, could not relieve the poor entirely, but could, and should, suppress the wicked.[600] More than ten years later she would recall these events, and the controversies over hoarding and the *Loi du Maximum*.

Even at the height of the Parker crisis, when Mary Ann heard that Joan was pregnant her practical interest was aroused. She offered copious advice. Joan's reply was as cool as her wedding letter: 'I shall not fail to profit by your kind instructions as well those which you have already sent me, as those which you have the goodness to promise me in future.' During a difficult pregnancy Joan found some of Mary Ann's comments brisk and unsympathetic: 'I do not believe that I suffer more than other persons,' she wrote, 'and yet I confess I think my sufferings rather greater than you seem to make allowance for.' [601] She signed herself 'your dutiful and affectionate daughter', which must have seemed an empty formula, reinforcing a suspicion that it was equally empty when employed by George.

Joan's baby was born at the end of April. Afraid that Mary Ann would use the event as another excuse for rushing up to London, George emphasised Joan's indisposition after her long forty-eight-hour confinement. There was, he told Mary Ann, no question of her being the baby's godmother. He made a mystery of this matter for a week or so, before revealing that the Princess of Wales had offered herself. He hoped this would put an end to Mary Ann's disappointment – who, after all, could resent being superseded by a princess? – but the bitterness of exclusion remained. When he was a boy at Eton chatting to the King about the *Microcosm*, and she a poor actress who had narrowly escaped from the accident at

Bury, she could make light of the gulf between them, confident that he would in due course raise her to his level. Now here he was again, hobnobbing with royalty, and all she could think of was how completely his grand connections had taken him from her. But, according to the pattern that was already established in their correspondence, he looked for an olive branch, for common ground. Knowing her views on breastfeeding he assured her that he and Joan shared her disappointment over Joan's inability to nurse the child. And of course there was no disagreement about the name: the boy was to be George. This could have caused a difficulty, since the baby should have been named Charles after his royal godparent, Caroline – but the good-natured princess was satisfied with Charles as the second name.[602] George facetiously referred to the baby by his initials in lower case, *gcc*.[603]

The excitement of the birth of her grandson passed. Mary became more and more anxious about her mother's 'State of unnatural Torpor', and, perhaps blaming herself for it, would do anything to help. Mary Ann was still in contact with the Thompsons, Richard's brother William being a doctor with an interest in the eye ointment.[604] Hearing that Captain Parker had withdrawn, Richard returned to renew his offer of marriage. Mary still had no wish to be married, felt no love for the estimable Mr Thompson and could see no material advantage to be gained from the marriage. But instead of saying no outright, she turned to her mother for guidance.

Mary Ann trod a fine line, unwilling to force the marriage on her chastened and compliant daughter, but equally unwilling to lose the advantages such a marriage offered. Thirty-five years earlier she had found herself in much the same situation as Mary, asking her grandfather how she should reply to the handsome offer from Mr Stone, the rich West Indian. Melchior advised her to follow her heart. Mary Ann, like her grandfather, understood the human heart; she also understood the lottery of marriage, the vulnerability of women, the unreliability of men. She told Mary to follow her heart, influenced by no 'foreign considerations, however laudable', but at the same time she made clear what these laudable foreign considerations were. Thompson was not as rich as Mr Stone, but he was an 'honest, worthy man', and as Mrs Thompson, Mary would be able to provide a home for her sister Maria and help her find a husband.[605] Mary Ann may also have thought that Thompson was a solid and enterprising businessman with experience of finance and commerce and the labyrinth of public offices; someone she could trust to look after her interests, and those of her sons. Faced with such arguments Mary felt she could not refuse. She bowed to her mother's stronger will, desperate to make amends for the anguish caused by her entanglement with Captain Parker, and perhaps also anxious about her own uncertain future if Mary Ann were to die. Without her mother's masterful personality to protect her, what inducement would the all-powerful George have to afford Samuel Reddish's bastard daughter his precious advice and support?

George had opposed Thompson when he first appeared at Totteridge, but now his objections were withdrawn. At the time of his own marriage George had claimed that his duty towards his mother and her children had been discharged; he was already coming to realise that he had been over-optimistic. Hitherto he had looked to Paul Patrick and Walter Borrowes for help in managing the affairs of Mary Ann and her family, but Patrick was dead and Borrowes was getting old, and may already have been showing signs of unreliability. He saw a potential ally in Richard Thompson.

Mary and Richard were married in Plymouth on 19 November 1801. Thompson proved a conscientious husband, and the marriage turned out happier than seemed likely at the outset. Maria, who already at the age of thirteen was sharper than Mary, noted her sister's reluctance to be married. Four years later, staying with the Thompsons in Kennington, she observed that Mary's esteem for her husband had deepened into genuine affection, and that Thompson had grown to appreciate his wife's uncommon amiability.[606]

George wrote to congratulate Mary, signing himself her 'affectionate brother',[607] and he called on her once or twice at her new home in Millbank Row, Westminster. But, as he had said of Mary Ann, the connection was with him alone, not extending to any of his family. So when he and the Leighs passed the Thompsons in the street he made some acknowledgement of Mary, but there were no introductions. The Leighs probably guessed who she was, but she had no idea who they were.[608] And although over the years George had many dealings with Richard Thompson, and although he sometimes condescended to refer to Mary as his sister, he never acknowledged her husband as his brother-in-law.

By the time Mary was married Edward Parker had died a hero's death, mortally wounded on the ill-planned Boulogne expedition, deeply and publicly mourned by Nelson. Mary Ann, thinking of her own experience as a young widow facing the hostility of her husband's family, commented on Mary's merciful escape.[609]

**

While the angry letters about Captain Parker were going to and fro, George was dealing with the first setback in his political career.[610] Early in 1801 Pitt was forced to resign over Catholic emancipation, and George insisted on following him out of office. The new government was still Tory, under the leadership of Henry Addington, a man for whom George had long felt, and expressed, unbounded contempt: 'Pitt is to Addington as London is to Paddington.'[i] With his own strong position on the Catholic question, George felt he couldn't honestly stay in government without his leader, even though Pitt instructed his followers to support the new administration, to keep out the Whigs. The tensions arising from this prolonged crisis, in particular the personal distress of disagreeing with Pitt, probably contributed

i Henry Addington (1757–1844), the son of a fashionable doctor, was a personal friend of Pitt. He had been Speaker of the Commons (1789–1801) and was prime minister from 1801 to 1804. In 1805 he was elevated to the peerage as Viscount Sidmouth, and was home secretary for the first ten years (1812–1822) of Lord Liverpool's administration. The Paddington gibe is frequently quoted, but I've not found where it originated.

to George's failure to manage effectively and tactfully his tricky dealings with Mary Ann.

On leaving office he had to give up his official residence. It happened just as Joan's confinement was due. His successor as paymaster, Lord Glenbervie, allowed them to stay on until the baby was born, a chivalrous offer which was only extracted after a battle, since George had not endeared himself to Glenbervie by his attacks on the new administration. Nor did George feel particularly grateful, making fun of Glenbervie behind his back, calling him Glenbubby. For his retirement, George took a small estate, South Hill, near Bracknell. It was here that the Cannings entertained the Princess of Wales after little George's christening. Writing facetiously to the Leighs and to Mary Ann, George described his new life as a country gentleman, slaughtering his own mutton and worrying about the hay; Mary Ann, ever interested in all that concerned him, was looking out for a harvest moon. But it was a charade: all his attention was on the parliamentary battle. It galled him to see Robert Jenkinson, now Lord Hawkesbury (or Hawkinson, as George put it), the friend he had always regarded patronisingly as a dull plodder, occupying the post of foreign secretary in the new cabinet.[611]

Resentment over Captain Parker remained never far from the surface – on both sides. Mary Ann wrote in the Packet:

> What I suffer'd in that dreadfull period God only knows! May you never guess at it!— Several of your letters — I never dared to give a second reading, but sealed them up with a superscription in my own hand — "Never to be open'd". One I burned — My Brain woud have burst else — It has always been understood by the rest of my family that all your letters are to be buried with me — they are to form a pillow for a head that will Ache no longer! but that woud have disturbed the Slumbers even of death — so I destroy'd it.

– while George would refer back to the affair whenever what he called 'painful discussions' arose between them.[612]

23.
Millbank and Tufton Street, 1802–1803

It may have been a relief for both Mary Ann and George to turn from the Parker affair to the safer ground of her sons' misbehaviour. George complained about each of them in turn. Charles in Calcutta was showing signs of his ungovernable temper, and seems to have made dishonest use of George's name in an attempt to raise money. Worse still, at one point he threatened to return to England, to which George replied that he hoped Charles was not coming back to seek his fortune, because 'I have no other to help him to'. The news that Charles had been promoted elicited from George only the grudging hope that it would 'produce the merit that would justify it'. Even twelve-year-old Frederick was misbehaving, sending George an obscene anonymous letter. But George tried to pass over such irritations lightly, admitting, for instance, that Frederick's prank was 'no proof of a hardened ill disposition'.[613]

Right at the end of 1801 a dispute blew up between Samuel and Walter Borrowes, for which George blamed Mary Ann. Samuel had recently married Dorothy Ashby, the seventeen-year-old daughter of a Barbados planter. Mary Ann made much of Dorothy's fortune, without mentioning that it would be some years before she could touch her inheritance. The omission of this detail prompted Borrowes to ask for repayment of the money advanced to Samuel when he first went to the West Indies. Samuel replied indignantly to what he regarded as an 'unlooked for, unwelcome and unanswerable' demand. He had been led to believe the loan could be carried over until he had saved enough to repay it. Mary Ann, Borrowes and Samuel came to an understanding on the issue, but not before Samuel had antagonised Borrowes, and written things about George 'which I heartily forgive, but shall not readily forget'. As always when driven to defend himself, George did it in stiff and sanctimonious terms, writing of Samuel's 'ebullitions of spirit which an irregular mind mistakes for grandeur of sentiment and just pride of temper', adding that now he was out of office his income was less than Samuel's £600 salary. This was not strictly true, but he may have forgotten his Irish rents and was thinking only of the salary from the Alienation Office, and it also ignored the fact that Joan's substantial income was also at his disposal. He added that his income had been earned (a debatable claim to make about the Alienation Office), unfairly implying that Samuel's had not.[614]

One disadvantage of Mary's marriage from George's point of view was that Richard Thompson's various business interests were centred in the capital. Mary would have to live there, providing a standing excuse and opportunity for Mary Ann to spend time in London. She was not really settled down in Devonshire. She was some months in Exeter, then in Cullompton where Esther and Joseph now lived, and then in Plymouth. At the beginning of 1802, meditating a visit to the Thompsons, she decided to give up her Plymouth house on Lady Day, 25 March. George's refusal to give an opinion on the Parker proposal, she told him, made her think he no longer wished to be consulted about her affairs, leaving her free to make up her own mind.

George wrote a long and angry response, lamenting the unexpected resumption of 'painful discussions' of the Parker affair. He claimed that he had merely refused to interfere in that one affair, and it was absurd to conclude he had relinquished his duties of 'comfort and counsel' towards her. But in any case, she didn't need to ask, she knew quite well his opposition to her living in London. Such a move would force into focus those facts which it was better for them both to keep vague and unspoken. He raised now, as he would raise repeatedly over the next few years, his suspicion that she had misrepresented his own relationship with her and her children. She had, he believed, told Captain Parker, by implication if not by positive statement, that if he married Mary he would be accepted as George's brother-in-law; and she had insinuated that she was herself received by George's wife, enjoying the privileges of grandmother to George's child. Now George suspected that she had said the same to Richard Thompson, even allowing him to believe that Mary was Hunn's daughter and legally entitled to use his surname. If she had deceived Thompson in this way, then… For now he wrote only, 'I truly lament the error', not yet uttering the threat to defend himself by telling Thompson the truth, or his side of the truth, about Mary Ann's illicit liaison with Reddish and Mary's illegitimate birth. Instead he invoked the opinion of 'the world' – of his intimate friends, of the Canning family, of everyone who knew her story – in support of his refusal to introduce her into his family. She might think him wrong, might think he was actuated by false pride, but the world thought otherwise, and he would not brave the opinion of the world, he said, and if he did, it would be in vain. What he thought was a harmless appeal to public opinion merely confirmed Mary Ann's view that it was because of his grand connections that he was driving her away.[615]

This letter included another, less veiled, threat. He said he would have made the payment of the pension conditional on her residing outside London if he had not assumed that, in the light of the Totteridge experiment, her move to the West Country was permanent. Perhaps in their highly charged quarrel while she was living in Pentonville she had given an undertaking to that effect. If so, she had either forgotten what was said in the heat of their quarrel, or regarded a promise extorted by his bullying tactics as meaningless. It's unlikely that he ever could have brought himself to leave her destitute, both because he recognised an unconditional obligation towards her and also because by giving her money he could to some extent influence her decisions. Money could be used, and would be used in years to come, to soften the effect of his harshness, deflect her anger and keep her at an emotional distance. Nonetheless, by linking the pension with her place of residence he was reminding her that he had a powerful sanction in his hands. It was the closest he ever came to threatening to cut off her means of support – a measure of how exasperated he had become.

Grieved by the 'perplexity and vexation' of it all, George sought the Leighs' sympathy,[616] but there's no doubt that he was the stronger party in the quarrel. As the weaker party, Mary Ann wasn't always scrupulous and frank, she didn't hold back and was not afraid to employ special pleading or emotional blackmail, as in her declaration the year before that they would meet no more. George was becoming more wary in his handling of her. Although he held all the power she was proving a formidable opponent. She was exasperated by what she felt was his repeated misrepresentation of events. He complained that she kept repeating the same arguments, but he too returned again and again to his versions of the Newbery and Parker affairs, and the Totteridge experiment.

George now added a further reason against Mary Ann's move to London: his aunts, Mehitabel, Bess Leigh and Fanny Canning were in town, and it would be awkward if they ran into each other. This was for Mary Ann the last straw. She thought he would be less willing to sacrifice her happiness to the Cannings' convenience if he knew more of her history. The idea came to her of writing a full account of events to give her side of the story. She told him to expect a 'packet' in March. Meanwhile she suggested that they should call a truce and keep off these painful topics. But as March approached she had not begun her 'packet'. Instead she broke her own truce, flinging out 'insinuations and accusations' which stung him to another furious response. Her accusation was that it was social pride that was making him ashamed of her; he had changed towards her since his rise in the world and his grand marriage. He refused to defend himself; if she brought it up again he would be 'compelled to absolute silence'.[617] This threat to stop writing to her was perhaps even more terrible, because more credible, than the threat to cut off the pension. It made her think twice about producing her proposed packet; it would be almost a year before she embarked upon it.

When Lady Day came, Mary Ann left Plymouth, but only for Exeter. For a few months she and George exchanged letters on uncontroversial family matters: Joan's miscarriage and subsequent difficulties when she became pregnant again; the progress of little Georgey, and his disability; communications from and about Samuel and Charles; a call George paid on Mary. There was also politics, such as the great Pitt celebratory dinner which George organised, and for which he wrote the song 'The Pilot who Weathered the Storm'. Then, in July 1802, she arrived in London to stay in Millbank Row.[618]

At first all was well: George accepted that she had adequate reasons for her visit. One was the business of the ointment, which had now become 'formidable'. She was still actively engaged in promoting it and, although she worked through a network of agents across the country, and also, during the brief halt in the war, on the Continent, she could argue that London made the best base for her growing enterprise, particularly as her two main collaborators were Richard and William Thompson. Her pension was only secure so long as the government revenues were secure, and she looked on the Collyrium as an insurance against the possibility of revolution. She had come across French aristocrats in exile who were incapable of maintaining themselves. If revolution came to Britain and her pension was lost she hoped to avoid the fate of an émigrée marchioness reduced to begging because she 'unhappily had <u>no</u> <u>executive</u> talent of any kind'.[619]

This independent resource was all the more necessary because after their recent arguments she could not bear to receive further help from George. She had gratefully taken his bounty in the past because she believed it was given from filial affection, but now 'The veil had unhappily been torn from my Eyes — and now it must come thro the cold road of mere duty — or of Charity. I coud not take it on either terms.' She may have overstated in retrospect her determination to take nothing more from him. Perhaps at the time she was less single minded, still holding on to a hope that things would somehow be made right between them. She recalled that he had himself recoiled in horror at the idea of their meeting no more – and yet he did not want her to come to London: where else were they to meet, she asked, if not in London? 'Inconsistency is surely the characteristick of all mankind,' she wrote, criticising him, but perhaps also thinking of her own confused state of mind.[620]

The Thompsons were not poor, but they lived modestly, and Mary Ann may well have felt cramped and unwelcome in their house beside the river. Millbank was an unfamiliar neighbourhood, her previous homes in London having all been some way to the north, in Bloomsbury, Gray's Inn Lane, Tottenham Court Road, Somers Town and Battlebridge; those friends she had in town were far away.[621] George visited her, but less frequently than she wished. Being so close to where he spent his days only emphasised her exclusion from his grand life, which kept her resentment alive. Towards the end of the summer it came once more to the surface.

George and Joan were staying at Walmer Castle, which Pitt had lent them to give Joan the benefit of sea air, when she repeated her accusation that his refusal to receive her in his home was a new development brought on by his grand marriage. He replied at length. It was she, he said, who was responsible for the awkwardness between them, and it was she who had changed her mind. He referred back to the Newbery affair of 1793, when he had laid down, in terms that she had not forgotten, that there was to be no 'Publicity of visiting in promiscuous intercourse with the World'. He was saying now no more than he had said then, he insisted. She knew the reason for it, he said, and knew that it was nothing to do with social pride or his marriage. He was acting on 'the same grounds that from my childhood had formed the barrier between us, God knows not of my choice'. If she went on spreading her accusations of social pride, it would be 'almost more than human forbearance can suffer, to put up with misconstructions so injurious, and so undeserved, without an effort to set myself in right'. Earlier in the year he had stopped short of threatening to reveal his side of the story. He was still unwilling to make the threat quite explicit, but it was clearer than ever. Mary Ann endorsed this letter 'Never to be opened'.[622]

Mary's first confinement was expected in March 1803, and George could see that there was little chance that Mary Ann would leave before then; he told the Leighs that he thought she proposed staying for ever. After their holiday at Walmer, he and Joan settled for the autumn at South Hill, their Berkshire estate. Their second child was expected in December, and Joan was undecided whether to stay in the country or come to town to be closer to medical attention. When George come to London it was usually on political business, and he could not always find time for Mary Ann. Most of his letters are short notes arranging and then rearranging visits, and apologising for not keeping appointments. A difference of opinion occurred when he high-handedly destroyed a 'heterogeneous mixture' of Charles's letters to people he had not heard of or did not approve of. Mary Ann disagreed with George over at least one of these correspondents, but they managed to avoid an escalation of ill-feeling. George tried to take the edge off his anger by kind words. He asked after Mary, discussed the prospects for Samuel, and described his styes and sore eyes, which he was once more treating, not very effectively, with Costello's Collyrium.[623] Even his angry letter of 25 September began with a discussion of the ointment, and a hope that sea water would not counteract 'the operation of the panacea'.

Joan opted for London for her lying-in, and it was therefore at lodgings in Conduit Street, near Hanover Square, that William Pitt Canning was born on 16 December. George knew that Mary Ann would have two questions: whether Joan would be able to nurse the baby herself, and who would be godmother. On the first point he assured her that Joan wanted to nurse but had been forbidden by the doctor.[624] The other matter he carefully avoided mentioning. It would be more than a month before Joan was well enough to travel, but although George was constantly in town he didn't find time to visit Mary Ann more than once or twice. The new year began uncomfortably.

The business partnership with the Thompsons was successful, the ointment now being produced and marketed as a liniment as well as an eye salve and cerate. Mary Ann took a house round the corner in Tufton Street, large enough to serve as a manufactory for the ointment. She hoped that Esther and her husband would come up from the country to help with the work, but Mr Murch was understandably reluctant to abandon his various interests in the West Country. At home things were not going smoothly. Mary Ann, who cannot have been an easy house guest, felt she had outstayed her welcome. Richard Thompson may have thought his delicate wife would get on better without the presence of an outspoken mother with robust views on childbearing. He told Mary Ann that her room would be needed for a nursery, although perhaps to soften the blow Mary hinted that in a few years, when money was less tight, they might have a larger house where she would once more be welcome. Mary Ann therefore moved into the Tufton Street house. This was all arranged tactfully, Mary Ann declaring that it was a bad idea for a mother to live with a married daughter.[625]

To furnish the new house she sent for her things from Devonshire, and also the furniture from Totteridge, which Walter Borrowes had been looking after since the end of the ill-fated episode. But there were other things to buy, and she applied to Borrowes for an advance on the next instalment of the pension.

In the past Borrowes had raised no objection to similar requests, but this time he said no. Mary Ann wrote him a number of furious letters. Borrowes defended himself by saying he was acting in accordance with a promise that George had exacted from him. Stunned by her outburst and not knowing how to respond, Borrowes sent for George, who, when he saw what Mary Ann had written, immediately sat down at Borrowes' desk in Austin Friars to tell her of his 'alarm and regret'. He warned her against reopening the 'uncomfortable' matters that had made them both so unhappy over the past year or so. Too angry to trust himself, he put off answering her accusations further.[626]

What Mary Ann minded most was that George had deliberately prevented Borrowes from showing kindness. If George had simply refused the money in a fit of anger, or because he was suddenly short of funds, it would have been inconvenient, but to have acted in so premeditated a manner was far worse. It was all of a piece with the coldness he had shown her since the quarrels of the Totteridge episode and his grand marriage. It produced 'sensations I hope never to experience again'.[627]

Now Mary Ann reached the heart-rending conviction expressed in the opening paragraph of the Packet: 'My boasted Son … is ashamed of his Mother – thinks it contamination to suffer his Wife to visit her.' She may have come to this conclusion as a result of turning over and over in her mind all the things he had said and written since he became a great man in Parliament – the Newbery affair, the Totteridge experiment, the expulsion from London, Joan's icy marriage letter, the Parker affair – but perhaps when they met, in a moment of exasperation, he had uttered the word *contamination* out loud. Now she was convinced that there was to be no home for her, no shelter at George's fireside, no chance to hold her grandchildren in what she called 'the embrace of Nature'. She asked George to visit her in her new house on her birthday, which fell in a few days' time. With the press of political commitments and anxiety over Joan's projected journey to Welbeck, he told her he couldn't be sure of coming. This evasive answer angered her as much as the fact that in the end he did not come, the more so because she had promised Mary and her husband that he would include them in his visit.[628]

George, the glorious son whom she had always favoured above all her other children, had spurned her. When her birthday came and there was no visit she could not face her other children. She shut herself in her room and settled down to the long deferred task of writing the story of her life, a justification of her past decisions, and a plea to George to return to the natural affection that had warmed her heart when he was a boy. She planned to spend a month or so on the writing, and to hand him the completed packet around the middle of March.[629]

24.
The Packet, 1803

'My Beloved George,' she began. 'At last I have acquired courage to sit down to the task which I have so long meditated.' Courage was needed to face uncomfortable truths, particularly because so much hung upon the verdict of her one powerful reader. The 'Injured Woman' letters had demonstrated Mary Ann's capacity for special pleading and her skill at marshalling facts. Back then she had concentrated on the events of just a few days. Now she had a whole lifetime to work with, to present in such a light that George would have to withdraw the charge that it would be 'contamination to suffer his wife to visit her'. All the injustices she had suffered would be cancelled if she could only enjoy 'the Embrace of Nature'. Like many of the phrases she and George used, this is more impressive than precise. It sounds as though she were asking just a limited thing – a meeting, a sight of her grandchildren, an embrace, nothing more substantial – but the phrase stood for a future in which she enjoyed her natural place in the life of his family.

The Packet was conceived and composed as a private letter and (unlike the love letters written by George Canning senior) was not written with even half an eye to the public, or posterity. There was a readership of one. Nonetheless Mary Ann's account bears comparison with published theatrical memoirs, such as those of Charlotte Charke, Mary Robinson and Charlotte Deans. Charke and Robinson were professional writers, hoping to make money, but they no less than Mary Ann and Mrs Deans were also determined to put the record straight, to show that their suffering was not their fault – 'to rescue my name from an unmerited odium that has been heaped upon it' as Deans puts it in her preface. Robinson declares at the outset that her life has been passed in a world of 'duplicity and sorrow'. Charke, like Mary Ann, states that her purpose in writing is to regain the affection of a man – in her case the father who has repudiated her, under the influence of enemies who 'have not always too strictly adhered to truth, but meanly had recourse to falsehood to perpetrate the ruin of a hapless wretch, whose real errors were sufficient without the addition of malicious slanders'. All four writers, however, do much more than show themselves to have been victims of malice, duplicity and other people's folly. Their writing takes on a life of its own. It has been said of Charke that she was 'a performer, both on- and off-stage, who takes up her pen as one in a series of costumes'.[630] She continued in her memoirs the exploration and assertion of her own personality and agency, in defiance of both family and society, that had been the business of her life as a public woman. Mary Ann seldom strays far from her central purpose of persuading George she had been at all times a victim, but the picture she conveys of what she achieved in her life is no less vivid and compelling than her complaints of what was done to her.

Her opening paragraph refers to the mystery surrounding her age: 'This day completes my Fifty third (or Fifty Sixth— for I am not sure which) year…' And the letter goes rattling on for another 65,000 words of anecdote, revelation and rhetorical appeal, until some twenty weeks later she brought her 'long and heartbreaking manuscript' to a close, writing the final paragraphs to the accompaniment of a summer thunderstorm. The events were often painful, rousing her to indignation or wringing tears from her eyes, but still there was pleasure to be had in recalling incidents, turns of phrase and snatches of conversation. She could take pride in her professional skill, her ability to face facts, her self-reliance and resilience under the buffeting of events; she was vain enough, perhaps, to enjoy placing herself at the centre of things, persecuted by the mighty, suffering the enmity even of the King himself, calm and strong in a crisis. There was artistic satisfaction too. The letter was written with almost no revisions or corrections – a few words changed or added above the line, a single sheet inserted with a newly recalled incident, a final section added after a break of two months – but for all its spontaneity it is a well-crafted production. She knew how to tell a story, hold an audience, and play upon her reader's feelings.

She wrote long into the night. On that first day she poured out some 4,600 words, describing her mother's origins and marriage, and the difficulties of the Costellos' life in Dublin, and bringing the story down to the point where she was herself installed in the Guy-Dickens household. She quickly became engrossed as she recalled her childhood and pieced together scraps of family history picked up from her parents. Her own part in events naturally dominated the narrative: *she* brought about the reconciliation with her mother's foster-parents, the Smiths; *she* worked with her needle to earn comforts for the family; *she* took the initiative in tracing her grandfather and throwing herself on his protection. Picturing herself as she was when she left Dublin, an innocent girl, she felt a sudden surge of indignation: she was still innocent, her heart was still pure. 'I have been, I repeat it, the Victim of too much feeling,' she wrote, picking up the idea from the she-tragedies she knew so well, 'but guilt I never knew — yet — had I been the vilest — the most depraved of all human beings, what punishment coud have been prepared for me keener than what is implied in your Conduct?'[631] She apologised for the digression, admitted she was tired after writing so long, and promised to go to bed when she reached the end of her current sheet.

She went on to describe her life in Wigmore Street, her trips to

Bath, the attempted seduction by Zephaniah Holwell, the offers of marriage. She reached the summer of 1767 and her daily journey with her aunt to Islington. She laughed again at the self-satisfied and dull-witted Mr Rash – 'He sometimes attempted to mark his attention to me — but I laugh'd, & he was dumb' – and then there came the momentous moment for which she took a new sheet and a new pen: 'Two new Comers attracted our Notice – One look'd like a man of science – or of the better order of Traders – the other – God of Heaven! – the other was your Father!'[632]

She kept her project secret from her daughters, although they suspected she was up to something, and that it had to do with George. Mary begged her to visit, insisting on a family meal on Sundays. Maria, now fifteen and less docile than her sister, was installed in Tufton Street and Mary Ann found she could only work on the letter at night or when she had persuaded Maria to go round to Millbank Row. At the same time she kept up her regular weekly correspondence with George, and also attended to the ointment business and saw to furnishing her new house. George paid occasional visits, and was aware that she was writing something out of the ordinary. He referred ruefully to the expected 'packet' that he would have to read and reply to.[633]

Now and then she inserts the current date, enabling us to trace the progress of her work. By the end of the first week in February, after some 12,000 words, she had covered her courtship and marriage, the birth and death of Letitia, and the birth of George, 'the Delight, the Blessing of my fond Heart'. One evening she was deep in the story of her husband's early struggles, his ill-treatment by his father and the reckless idealism of his anti-government pamphlets, when she broke off. It was late at night, and her recollections had taken an unpleasant turn. Her romantic picture of her husband as the high-principled victim of his father's malice and the King's resentment was suddenly clouded as she recalled another side of his character, his secretiveness, his insistence on unquestioning obedience. 'He had some of his father's Illness,' she concluded, 'although the deference I paid to his will generally averted its influence from me.'[634]

Next day she was suffering from pains in her face and head, the result, no doubt, of writing long into the night. The trouble persisted for the rest of the month. At times she lay in her room, unable to read or write. When her condition improved the exceptionally cold and stormy weather kept her indoors. On some days it was too wet to send Maria round to Millbank Row, but her illness gave her the excuse to shut herself away and carry on without being observed. It was also a spur: she was afraid of dying before completing the task.[635] She had reached the most difficult point in her narrative.

After describing her widowhood, and her efforts to find an income, she had to account for the events which had separated her from George: her decision to go on the stage and her liaison with Reddish. Special care was needed over the presentation of these two fatal steps, to avoid any suggestion that she had hankered after the excitement and satisfaction of an actor's life, or that she had slept with Reddish because she fell in love with him. There must be nothing to lend credence to Stratty's dreadful verdict, that she had all the time consulted her own immediate pleasure and satisfaction. Her argument was that she had been driven by circumstances. With no friends or family to support or advise her, she had to grasp anything that came her way, and when every other opening proved illusory the opportunity offered by Garrick was too good to refuse. Since she took it for granted that George would agree that the alternative occupations suggested by Mehitabel, keeping a shop or employment as a higher nursemaid, were impossible for the wife of one George Canning and the mother of another, she must have felt she had made her first point effectively enough.

She was on shakier ground when she went on to suggest that she couldn't help taking Reddish as a lover and protector, tracing this decision also back to the loss of Stratty's support. As the 'dear and sacred prop of Fraternal Affection' was withdrawn, 'what was

I to do? My Heart wanted a resting place'. This admission that Reddish had taken Stratty's place in her heart was the closest she came to admitting that she had followed her affections. It was safer to imply that on entering the new and sometimes treacherous world of the theatre she needed guidance and protection. Reddish helped her, praised her, advised her, when everyone else deserted her. It was not through any 'foul or unworthy' motive or 'coarse passion' that she yielded to his 'assiduities'.[636] After a digression describing her brief acquaintance with Charles Phipps in Dulwich, she returned to the origin of her liaison with Reddish, summing it up without any tinge of passion:

> I saw that my point in life was fixed — and as I had no doubt of an Engagement, tho I coud not guess how productive it might be — I was not irrational in concluding that my Interest woud be secured by having the protection of a person who knew what every portion of merit deserved, & woud probably be able to make the best bargain when a permanent Engagement was to be made[637]

She blurred the issue by her vagueness about the sequence of events, implying first of all that she accepted Garrick's offer of work only when entirely deserted, whereas in fact she remained on reasonable terms with Clements Lane even after *Jane Shore*; and then claiming both that she eloped to Scotland with Reddish because she was isolated in the theatre, and that her isolation was caused by the malicious gossip arising from her elopement. This imprecision was not necessarily a deliberate tactic. Her motives at the time must have been confused, and the passage of thirty years is unlikely to have made them any less so. Although her memory for incidents was clear, it was another thing to place them in a neat sequence of cause and effect. Her early association with Reddish following her first appearance as Jane Shore gave rise to gossip, which had reached Mehitabel's ears before the journey to Scotland. This pushed her more and more towards Reddish, until the salacious speculations of the rumour-mongers became a reality.

Mary Ann recalled her sense of achievement in providing for her family by her own labours, and she mentioned her admiration of Reddish's professional talent, but for the most part she was content to describe her actions of thirty years before in neutral, practical terms, with little indication of what she thought or felt. She wrote nothing of the thrill and glamour of the theatre, the excitement of working with David Garrick, or the intellectual challenge of learning her lines, understanding her roles and becoming initiated in the mysteries of her profession. She wrote of Reddish's attention to her during her illness, of his 'assiduities', and his care and attention to George, but nothing of his good looks, his lavish generosity, the flattery of his attentions. Beyond her brief reference to her heart seeking a resting place she gave no hint of the passions and desires of a young woman whose sexual nature had been first aroused in her brief marriage to an experienced and demanding sensualist.

She was similarly evasive concerning her relationship with Stratty. She recalled how he had lightened the gloom of life with her sick and moody husband, supported her during the first years of her widowhood and attempted ineffectually to combat Mehitabel's animosity towards her, but in all these recollections he was always her brother, his affection for her always fraternal. There was no question of their marrying – marriage to a dead husband's brother was against both the law and the teaching of the church – but the story of Marianne Clement in *The Offspring of Fancy* makes it clear that Mary Ann had contemplated, even if only fleetingly, what might have been if she had become Stratty's wife. The relationship of Mehitabel, Stratty and Mary Ann was troubled from the start by money problems and differences of class and education, and later on by the trauma of Mary Ann's sacrifice of her child, but at root it was a love triangle. When Mehitabel expressed frustration at her delayed marriage she was not merely exasperated at Stratty's indecisiveness or anxious about the expense of supporting Mary Ann, but jealous of the sexual hold exercised by a more sophisticated rival.

The passions had faded, making it hard to take seriously her sentimental yearning for Stratty or her infatuation with Reddish, easier to think of it all as a matter of putting food on the table, of sustaining her position in the theatre, of keeping going. At fifty-three, weary and depressed, these were the things she found most real – these, and the suffering of an injured mother. In the second week of March, after 164 pages, when she thought she was near the end of her 'heartrending task', suddenly new recollections flooded her mind. The antagonisms of her youth sprang to life. Recalling that one of George's reasons for wanting her to leave London was to prevent her coming into contact with his aunts, she launched into a ferocious attack on Mehitabel, accusing her of having from the outset done everything in her power to alienate George from his mother and even of having plotted to capture him as a husband for her daughter Bess. To Mehitabel, she wrote, she owed 'every Misery of my Life since the year 1772'.[638]

Exhausted, and perhaps shocked at this sudden vehemence, she brought her account to an end. There were still many things she might have written, new episodes from her long and troubled history which might have made George see things her way, but it was too late; she lacked the patience and energy to recast her letter; it must stand as it was. She moved to her final appeal. Having told her story as best she could she begged George to consider the sufferings that drove her to act as she did, and to judge her mercifully. She went further: he should not be judging her at all. She recalled the conversation between Stratty and her husband on the subject of the Scots, whom George Canning senior regarded as a hateful, selfish people. Perhaps Mary Ann recalled as she wrote this that George's wife was from Scotland, but the point of the anecdote was to repeat her husband's saying about James VI: 'Mary was his Mother… and by every Law of God and Nature he was her Defender – not her Judge.'[639]

Then she went further still, risking an allusion to the passions that had swept her into Reddish's arms. Like Amelia in *The Offspring of Fancy* she admitted that she had erred, but it was error without guilt: 'I was neither impel'd nor guided by Guilt – my Heart was Pure.'[640] Women like Amelia are, in the formula of *Jane Shore*, 'Sense and Nature's easy fool', or in Mary Wollstonecraft's more sympathetic words, 'dupes of a sincere, affectionate heart'.[641] Mary Ann claimed that she too had been natural, sincere, affectionate. As she recalled her husband's denunciation of cold-hearted King James, she must also have remembered his lectures on love. Hard though it was, after thirty years, to recall the feelings that had animated her in her twenties, when she insisted that her heart was pure she was doing more than claiming to have been driven by practical necessity. She couldn't say it to George – it would sound too much like seeking her own pleasure – and most of the time she hardly admitted it to herself, but now, as she summed up her arguments, she seems to have stolen a glimpse at her younger self and recognised that she and Reddish had been moved (to borrow the words from her husband's letters) by 'those sources of inexpressible delight: our sympathetick Hearts'.

The justification of her decisions forms the main argument of the Packet. Another part of her case was to assert the importance of family ties, both by rhetorical appeals to the God of Nature, and by carefully chosen examples of filial duty. She criticised her own parents, but continued to love them and work for them. Her husband was appallingly treated by the old people of Abbey Street, but, she said, never lost his love and reverence for them. In particular, it had gone without question that his mother should be godmother of their first child, Letitia. 'Nature was his guide.'[642]

Mary Ann writes of the joy she took in George from the moment of his birth, of the love and care she had bestowed on him – all of which, so long as Nature was his guide, he had amply repaid. In her letters over the preceding year she had accused him of changing towards her out of false pride. Now she suspected something more, something for which 'Nature knows no name'; she suspected that 'some imperious and irresistible influence must have counteracted Nature's Laws'.[643] It's as though she understood the compact he had made with Joan's family in his letter to Lady Jane Dundas.

In a sense, she hardly needed to insist upon the sacred duty of a son to his mother; George accepted it, and repeatedly asserted that his obligations to her were the first concern of his life. From childhood he had been taught to sign his letters to her as 'ever my dear Mother's affectionate and dutiful son'. To Mary Ann this conventional formula seemed increasingly hollow. He did his duty so far as her material needs were concerned, but his affection went no further than the occasional grudging visit and his hurried weekly scrawl. All he did, as she said at the beginning of the Packet, was done out of cold charity and duty. But as she nears her conclusion she admits, in one of the Packet's most powerful passages, that she cannot be angry with him:

> For you my beloved George, I have preserved an Affection that even the unexpected harshnesses of the last three years cannot weaken — and if I am Sensible of any thing like injustice in myself, it is a good consciousness that had any other of my Children acted exactly in the same way — what I now feel of regret — woud have been anger & resentment — I cannot be angry with you; my brain woud not sustain a conflict so dreadfull — as the process of rooting out all the fondness, all the pride, all the enthusiasm of Thirty Three years, and placing anger in the desolate region of a bankrupt heart[644]

The peroration of her letter was written in March against the background of new quarrels. George was busy, his time divided between political manoeuvring in London, supervising building work at South Hill and visiting his family at Welbeck. He shrank from calling on Mary Ann. On the last day of February, following an acrimonious letter from her, he actually turned back on his way to Tufton Street. She interrupted work on the Packet to complain of a letter which was 'of a Complexion, which for your sake I hope will not meet again the Eye of a Mother — For the present Adieu to Narrative'.[645] A few days later he was passing through London again and made a brief visit, in the course of which he said things that led to another furious exchange.

It seemed trivial. For some years now Mary Ann had been receiving a pro-government newspaper, *The True Briton*, from George's newsman. George kept the newsman informed of Mary Ann's changes of address. He didn't want her to contact the man herself, and had been annoyed once before when she had done so. Now Richard Thompson, possibly with George's assistance, had acquired an interest in a rival, *The Oracle*, and Mary Ann wanted to support her son-in-law by changing to his paper.[i] She mentioned her intention in the course of George's visit. He was put out and told her crossly that on no account was she to write to his newsman, in his name, to make the change. She was so hurt by his peremptory tone that when he had gone she once more left off the task of winding up her Packet in order to compose a bitter remonstrance. How could he have spoken to her so roughly and angrily? Why did he suppose she was about to write to his newsman? Couldn't he trust her not to make use of his name? If it mattered so much, why hadn't he mentioned it before, and why didn't he explain clearly? She wrote at such length that when he received her letter he thought it was the long-promised packet. Surprised by her unexpected fury, he composed a careful response consisting of three numbered points, concluding that if she didn't understand why she was not to contact his newsman he couldn't explain further and she would have to take his word for it. 'I should have believed – (had not the event disappointed me) that my mother would take my word without explanation,' he wrote,

---

i The following year Thompson gave up his association with the paper, apparently encouraged to do so by George, who arranged an extra payment for Mary to make up for the loss of income. Then a little later he found a post for Thompson in the Revenue service (Diary, 27 May, 14 Nov. 1804).

in a manner that recalled his father, and his father's father – the Canning 'Illness'.[646]

What he did not tell her was that the *True Briton* was financed by the government, and the copy she received was one of the many hundreds bought by the government in order to keep the paper afloat. Since the beginning of the Addington administration the paper had followed Pitt's line of supporting the new government, but in the course of 1803 it moved towards demanding the return of Pitt, a change that George approved of and may have been instrumental in bringing about.[647] The goings-on at the *True Briton* were closely watched by opponents such as William Cobbett,[i] and it would have been embarrassing if it got about that a subscription to the paper in Canning's name had been cancelled. Without this explanation, the incident confirmed everything Mary Ann suspected about his changed feelings towards her.

The weather was bitter in the middle of March. George, staying at Lothian's Hotel during the parliamentary session, was confined to his room by 'la grippe'. Mary Ann, after a sociable evening with William Thompson and his wife, was hurrying out to a waiting coach when she slipped on newly fallen snow, knocking her head against the stone steps. Dr Thompson established that her skull was not broken, but for a day she found herself unable to put the finishing touches to the Packet. Once she had recovered enough to read and write she was impatient to get it off her hands, becoming increasingly irritated by the demands made on her time by Maria and the Thompsons. Having read the whole letter she did not want to make any changes, but still she feared to draw her story to a close. Ending it, she said, would be 'like drawing an important bolt — that may either open wider the door of our intercourse, or close it for Ever'. The result depended on George, and she begged him to consider carefully before he responded.[648]

She referred to the two incidents that had precipitated her

i William Cobbett (1763–1835) was a prolific political writer who campaigned for constitutional reform as the way to end corruption and (his main preoccupation) improve the lot of agricultural workers.

writing of the Packet (his failure to visit on her birthday, and the dispatch of his children to Welbeck) and then added some inconclusive remarks about her plans, emphasising that she saw her future lying in London, close to Mary, though not living with her. Alluding indirectly to the recent quarrel, she told George how well the *Oracle* was doing. None of this was relevant to the grand theme of her letter, and when she could postpone the end no longer she wrote a conclusion of great dignity and grace.

> I know not that I have any thing more to say — but my heart lingers on the momentous subject, and clings to it, as a sort of link of the chain that binds us to each other — and I fear to snap it rudely, lest it never shoud close again — but I must release you — This consideration decides — and I will say farewell!— May all the fondness my Heart treasures for you, support me under the consequences whatever they may be! And my prayers be heard with mercy proportioned to the Zeal that offers them for every Blessing on your beloved head — and on those you love!— Accept that blessing my Darling George, & believe that Never Mother loved a Son — as you are loved by your Ever Aff: Mother!—[649]

When George was fully recovered from his cold he called on her and took delivery of the Packet, promising to read it as soon as he found time to be alone with it. He expected to have an opportunity on the journey to Welbeck, but it turned out that he had to travel by night, so the chore was postponed. Six weeks went by and he still hadn't found the right moment. In May, as she thought of the Packet lying unread in George's writing box, Mary Ann wondered anxiously whether she could add or change anything to make her story more persuasive. Having asked him to return the Packet, she now looked at it apprehensively, hesitating to open it, until she heard that he was planning to go out of town, so that if she was to make any changes it would have to be done soon.[650]

Re-reading the story was, she said, a dreadful task, but on the whole she was satisfied with it. She added a few words here and there, inserted a sheet about *The Offspring of Fancy* and her dealings with William Flyn, and appended twelve pages at the end. She began this new section by begging to be allowed to stay in her house, even though the Thompsons, whose proximity in Milbank Row was her original reason for choosing Tufton Street, were planning to move to the southern suburb of Kennington. All her life, she said, she had been driven from place to place, never able to settle; now she had a house and garden that pleased her, and she hoped to stay in peace. Whatever one might think of her larger claims, this plea for peace after her turbulent life seems unanswerable. But she knew what George's answer would be, and she feared to hear it. 'Oh my George! When at this period of the year 1770 you hung at my fond Bosom – drew the Supply of your precious life from mine and clasp'd in my supporting Arms – look'd in my delighted face conscious of the sweet gratification which as Natures delegate I administered to you – who coud have foreseen that at this day I shoud fear to meet you!' [651] But in the middle of this outburst she was interrupted, and a further fortnight passed before she took up her pen again.

In the interim she had come across some old letters, including the one written by Mehitabel which put an end to the negotiation with the Jermyn Street milliners, and which now provided a further cue to reflect on the coarseness of Mehitabel's mind. She had also seen George, and he had been kind to her. He had even seemed to take pleasure in her company, staying with her for an hour, well beyond the time he had stipulated. Ever alert to slights, she was no less eager to recognise kindness. He told her that if she wanted him to take the Packet with him into the country it would have to be ready by 10 June. On the eighth, therefore, she resumed her task. His unexpected kindness precipitated a cascade of disjointed sentences encapsulating her whole argument:

> In the middle of the last sentence I was interrupted, and forced to lay aside my pen — since that I have seen you – and I think with kinder looks than I have lately met with – my heart expanded

> with delight when I found you had pass'd more than an hour with me – how often it shoud seem, I might have such indulgence, and neither God nor Man offended! – but I will not ask, what is so much sweeter when volunteer'd – I am sure, my Hearts own transcript, your natural course coud not have been easily turn'd aside – form'd with every gentle, every affectionate propensity – I saw you – all my breaking heart coud pray for, and with reluctance that was too prophetic, I yielded your Infancy to the forming hands of – but what coud I do? – It was not for their sakes – but for yours – your Education – the cultivation of those talents in which my proud heart delighted, and all my future glory was anticipated – that was the price of my fatal acquiescence – Well, well, to you it has been as profitable as to me it has been fatal – I was not sure your Mind would be poison'd – your Affection, your pious fondness for me – taught to tread the mere cold path of duty – that to give me bread – a Nurses claim, would be the prescribed conduct of a darling Child to a Mother whose bitterest Enemies coud not charge with a want of a Mothers love for you – I am going over ground which I have already trodden bare – I did not intend to return to it again – but the discovery of those letters which I have not seen for years, has brought back recollections, which I had either lost, or which time had weaken'd & obscured – in some of your Uncles, I find references to facts that will act as a sort of interpretation of some parts of my History – but I had quite forgotten Miss Patricks kind advice respecting my seeking for a place in some family, as a sort of Upper nurse maid – she thought it would be very eligible – and I now remember she mention'd as an inducement, that there were many families, such as the Duchess of Ancaster or Lady Jane coud recommend me to, where it woud not be necessary perhaps for me to dine with the servants – this was whilst she was in London – I saw poor Strattys lip quiver and then pale; so I let it pass[652]

The most material addition was a circumstantial account of the offer made in 1793 by the West Indian merchant, Mr Mercier.[653]

This incident showed how axiomatic it had always been in her mind that it was unthinkable to enter any form of domestic service, however dignified, and so reinforced her argument that there really had been, back in 1773, no alternative to the stage. She also pointed out that when she turned down both this offer and the proposal from the theatre in Edinburgh, she was still in the happy state of not realising the 'precise boundary' that George was to place between his life and hers:

> ... then I held present poverty at Nothing, for there in that sweet perspective I looked for my compensation – had I known (God of nature! how shoud I ever guess at such an unnatural calamity being in store for me) had I know[n] that no such blessing was in reserve – what might not the frenzy of my brain have led to – Mr Mercier's servant coud have been laid no lower![654]

On 9 June it was raining too hard for Maria to leave the house, so Mary Ann made an excuse to retire to her room, to round off her letter. She summarised again the current state of the ointment business, in order, she said, to assure him that she would be able in the future to maintain herself and discharge her debts without his help.[655] She was almost dismissive:

> You have been the best of Sons – and tho I had rather have held your affection and Esteem for my advocates within your pious breast – than mere duty and the portion of Natural affection inseparable from it – and if I may so express myself – have felt it more an equal communication than a dependant good – yet under whatever colour – I bless you for your conduct to me and mine – and when I sometimes regret the burdens I have been, and have brought upon you, I feel a counter argument in the opportunity it has afforded to the heightening of your Character, and the exercise of your Virtues – Heaven has rewarded your pious works, with every Species of Earthly blessing; and even shoud some of those blessings take a temporary flight – the hand that guides this vast Machine will point your way to such

> comforts and consolations as only the good & virtuous can taste here, and hope for hereafter.[656]

The rain continued to pour down and there was thunder as the summer day came to an end. She summed up her blessings, her joy in her new grandchildren, Mary's twin daughters, and her own resilient nature with its predisposition to be happy, but then the thought of her separation from George came back to her, undermining her peace of mind and threatening to embitter the love and duty she owed to her other children. But no, she would not reopen the great question. She drew her letter abruptly to a close, reminding him that she was about to leave London for a few weeks in Devonshire, asking him visit Mary and Maria, and finally calling on him to 'pity the hard Fate of your Ever affectionate Mother!!!' – echoing that plaintive epilogue: 'Be kind at last and pity poor Jane Shore.'

25.
Shatter'd Bark, 1803–1806

George called at Tufton Street on 10 June 1803 and once more took possession of the Packet, noting glumly that it was thicker than ever. He carried it away with him, promising to read it at the earliest opportunity. They were both leaving London. He was to join Joan and the two boys at Welbeck; she was going to collect Frederick from his school in Kingsbridge, pay the arrears of his fees and Maria's, and take him on a tour of her old Devonshire haunts. She took him to the theatre in Plymouth.[657]

Frederick was fourteen. He had run up bills with Kingsbridge shopkeepers, which irritated George, who knew he'd have to find the money. In any case, he wasn't well disposed towards Frederick. The obscene anonymous letter of a year or so ago may have been just a schoolboy prank, a dare suggested by his classmates, but it showed that Frederick had been boasting of his connection with the famous Mr Canning. It was high time for him to leave school and find a career. His own fancy was for the sea, but George warned that the fate of a midshipman 'unless of transcendent merit' was uncertain.[658] As he had warned Samuel, the Army and Navy were good careers in time of war, but war could not last for ever. His real objection may have been that he foresaw decades of lobbying the Admiralty on behalf of Frederick, in whom he did not detect transcendent merit.

The case of Samuel showed that no settlement was ever final. Samuel was the least troublesome of Mary Ann's sons, but even he kept coming back for more, or so it seemed to George. That summer of 1803, he was on leave from the West Indies, on the lookout for a better position. His wife, Dorothy, had given birth to a daughter, christened just before he left for England. George had consented to be godfather, *in absentia*, which generated ill-feeling with Mary, who said he had gone back on an undertaking to be godfather to her firstborn. He reminded her, through Mary Ann, that his promise had referred to her first son, and so far she had only produced twin girls. Dorothy's young brother, Nathan Ashby, was also in London, hoping for employment in England.[659]

These matters occupied George's letters while Mary Ann was in Devonshire over the first half of the summer, together with advice on her tax return, and a long discussion of little Georgey's health. The boy's lameness seemed for the moment to be less pronounced, but he suffered from roughness of the skin, all over his body and on his face. Mary Ann offered detailed medical advice, which included using Costello's Cerate. Whether or not Joan was willing to use it, George ordered supplies, and Maria sent him two boxes from the Tufton Street store.[660]

Nothing was said about the Packet, although it was weighing on both their minds – George reluctant to open it, Mary Ann anxious to know his reaction. It was the beginning of August before he read it (on another coach journey to Welbeck) and even then he didn't immediately say what he thought. Mary Ann was back in London by then; he could not avoid meeting her, and so could not postpone his response indefinitely. Even so, she had to wait until the end of September before hearing that after reading her story he could assure her that he remained unchanged in his 'constant, anxious, unalterable affection and duty' towards her. It was small reward for her heart-rending task, to be told that he thought no worse of her than he had before. He disliked being put in the position of having to form an opinion on his mother and judge the facts of her life that she had put before him. Recalling James VI, he apologised for using the words *opinion* and *judge*, but could think of no less offensive way of describing the task she had presented him with.[661]

What he had learned from the Packet may have dented the assurance with which he faced the world. This stay at Welbeck was his last until 1817, a gap he would explain by saying that when in office he was too busy, and when out of office too proud to visit his wife's ducal connections, which suggests that the 1803 visit may have left a lasting impression of awkwardness and even humiliation. How much this was due simply to his political setbacks, which meant he was no longer the coming man he had been at the time of his marriage, and how much to the long and sometimes shocking history he had just read, is impossible to say. While political disappointment left him less buoyant, less able to separate himself from his mother's story, the humiliating thought of where he had come from must have made the prospect of a political comeback seem more remote. He recorded a long response in a packet of his own. It was now her turn to fear what she would read. She was ill when he called at Tufton Street in September, so he didn't leave it with her, and since it was too large for his frank he left it at Walter Borrowes' office for her to collect when she felt ready for it. We don't know what he wrote because he insisted on her returning it to be destroyed, but there was no concession: she was to have no contact with his family.[662]

Their arguments grew, with a life of their own, one disputed point leading to another; she was, he felt, always shifting her ground, now seeming to acquiesce in his ruling, now protesting against it. It all, he wrote, afflicted him and wore him out. There remained some safer topics, such as the weather and income tax, and, above all, medical matters. When Georgey's skin condition improved George said he thought it was the ointment's doing, even though the nurses were more doubtful. Mary Ann's 'medical dissertation' extended to advice on antimonial wine for Georgey, and the use of the ointment as an aftershave lotion for George himself. In return George expressed concern for Mary Ann's health. It's not clear what her symptoms were, but she eventually saw a doctor and George was reassured. He sent money for the doctor, and a consignment of port wine.[663]

Even discussion of Frederick's future was preferable to reopening the old argument. Frederick still hankered after the sea, but George had talked it over with Samuel, who offered to take Frederick with him when he went back to Jamaica. George remarked sarcastically that the boy could do less harm on an island than on a ship. Mary Ann didn't want another of her children dismissed to an insalubrious corner of the world. Frederick's father distrusted Samuel and shortly before his death registered a strong protest. George, who had not placed much weight on Hunn's views when he was alive, took no account of them once he was dead. He tried to reassure Mary Ann by reminding her that Samuel's brother-in-law was now living in London and beholden to her, so they had, as it were, a hostage to ensure that Samuel, and his wife's family, treated Frederick well. But Frederick got his way and with help from Mary's husband (possibly making use of George's name) he sailed as a midshipman on the sloop *Dolphin* in January 1804. George did not come to Tufton Street to see him off. 'Tell him,' he wrote, 'I shall be more pleased to see him on return from a cruise where he has done his duty, than to take leave of him.'[664]

Joan was at South Hill awaiting her third confinement while George was jigging about on political business between there and London. He was in London when Harriet was born, and Joan's sister wrote to inform him. Her note reached him just as he set out for Tufton Street, but he didn't pass on the news to Mary Ann, preferring to tell her later, in writing. This seems strange, but he may have hoped to escape her effusive congratulations. Later he assured her that Harriet 'sucks like a pig'. Mary also was pregnant that spring, and in poor health.[665]

George called at Tufton Street every few weeks. His diary entries are fuller for 1804 than for most years, but he says nothing of these meetings beyond the bare fact that they occurred. He probably came prepared with a stock of safe topics – Joan's health, Mary's health, the children's progress, the benefit he was deriving from the ointment. At one meeting Mary Ann confessed the extent of her debts, and at another they discussed the changing political situation. His business in town was to promote the changes in every way he could. He was forever apologising for missing appointments. By the middle of May 1804 Pitt was once more prime minister and George was back in office, as treasurer of the Navy, with a salary of £4,000 per annum, and an official residence in Somerset House. But Pitt had been obliged to balance his appointments in order to keep the Addington group happy; there was no place for George in his cabinet. It was only his loyalty to and dependence upon Pitt that made George swallow the bitterness of being left out.[666]

Nonetheless the resolution of the long political crisis, together with relief over Joan's safe delivery from her confinement, brought about a relaxation. He immediately sent Mary Ann £200 in anticipation of his new salary, telling her to pay off the debts that had been troubling her since she moved into Tufton Street, and share the rest with Aunt Esther. He warned her, gently enough, that she needed to keep within her income, as he had debts of his own which he reckoned he might pay off in four years if he remained in office, which, he reminded her in confidence, could not be guaranteed. He also surprised and delighted her with talk of the possibility of a meeting with Joan and the children. The first mention of this in his letters is a brief assurance that Little George would pay her a visit.[667] This may have been the first intimation Mary Ann had of his change of heart, but it is likely that they had spoken of it face to face. We don't know whether it was a concession wrung from him by her passionate appeals, or by her anger, or whether he came round to it slowly in his own time, calculating that, properly handled, the concession could do no harm and would persuade her to leave London.

Properly handled, that was the great thing. No foreign embassy could have been planned with greater care. The meetings were fixed for the middle of September, and in the preceding week George wrote four times making and clarifying arrangements, when and where the meetings should take place and who should be present. Joan lost patience. Why make so much fuss about the choreography of the visits? He reminded her how necessary it was to impress upon his mother that the visits were a concession granted entirely on his terms: 'Dearest dear will think I have been harsh perhaps,' he wrote, 'But I found a little curb absolutely necessary.' Bess Leigh also offered advice on how to conduct the meetings.[668]

At one level it was probably fear of 'awkwardness' – of too many people in a cramped room, of embarrassed silences and attempts at small talk – that drove him to be so strict, but underneath there was a deeper anxiety. Anything to do with Mary Ann was a potential plague. He had been reminded of this a few weeks previously when a complete stranger attempted to open a negotiation on behalf of Samuel, who had evidently made unauthorised use of his, George's, name. It was, George wrote, with the inelegance that he always fell into when struggling to control his fury, 'an instance of rapaciousness and indelicacy... beyond what I had suffered myself to think possible'.[669] Now he suspected that, without his little curb, Mary Ann would exploit his concession, feeling herself entitled to a permanent place at his fireside, opening him to further attack from the rapaciousness and indelicacy of her sons.

He was also afraid that gossip linking him with Mary Ann would be used by the opponents of the government to wound him and damage Pitt. This wasn't entirely groundless. Mary Ann's pension was already a grievance well publicised by opposition writers, and would remain so for the rest of her life. The satirist 'Peter Pindar'[i] wrote of George's host of poor relations as 'a beautiful nest of

i 'Peter Pindar' was the pseudonym of John Wolcot (1738–1819). He was involved in a very public quarrel with the pro-government journalist William Giffard of the *Anti-Jacobin*.

cater*pillars*, ordained by the Heaven-born *oeconomical* minister to devour the few remaining leaves of the old oak.' The *oeconomical* minister was Pitt, whose government was imposing retrenchment on the country to pay for the war. Peter Pindar's list of George's relations was extensive: 'Madame Hun; the Miss Huns, alias Cannings, alias Reddishes; a pension for her Husband, Mr Hun; a place in the West Indies for *one* Master Reddish, and military promotion in the East for the *other*; and to crown the whole, a pension for poor Uncle Tommy, the tinker of Somers Town.' At the same time Peter Pindar also used the connection with Joan's dead father to discredit George, noting that General Scott made a great fortune 'by his profession and a *lucky* throw of the dice' and that such a fortune is not honestly made in a hurry.[670]

To aggravate his fear of publicity, as soon as he had taken up his job as treasurer of the Navy George discovered that the office was embroiled in two major scandals. One involved malpractice in the payment of sailors' wages to their wives, legitimate and otherwise, and was comparatively easy to contain, because the 'prostitutes' of Wapping who were victims of this official rapacity and indelicacy were of no account.[671]

The second scandal had emerged from parliamentary enquiries into long-standing practices at the Pay Office and, being taken up by the opposition, eventually brought about the downfall of Henry Dundas (now Lord Melville), who had been an early supporter of George's career, and was also Joan's great-uncle, husband of Lady Jane. Dundas had managed the affairs of Scotland on behalf of the government (and for the benefit of his own extended family) throughout Pitt's first administration, and had been Pitt's loyal lieutenant in Parliament. For many years he had held the office of treasurer of the Navy as a sinecure, leaving the business in the hands of his deputy, the paymaster, Alexander Trotter. Trotter was part of another large Edinburgh family whose interests were intertwined with those of the Dundases. His function at the Pay Office was to pay the salaries and pensions of sailors, and he was therefore responsible for handling large sums of public money, which he found it convenient to hold in his private bank account until the salaries fell due. Opponents pointed out that while this procedure might, as Trotter claimed, expedite payments to the sailors, it also meant that interest on the funds was paid to him rather than the government. For George this was an uninteresting technical matter and so long as the sailors got their wages, he was inclined to accept Trotter's view of the case. He was forced to say something to Mary Ann about the affair because Richard Thompson was asking questions, hinting that he was interested in a post in the Pay Office, where Trotter's misconduct was likely to lead to a reorganisation of the personnel.[672]

Throughout the summer the new administration faced more serious problems than Trotter's peculation. London was in the grip of repeated invasion scares, which may, by putting his personal worries in perspective, have contributed to George's decision to allow a meeting. To intensify the atmosphere of crisis and foreboding, the weather was exceptionally hot, with meat rotting in the butchers' shops and cheese melting on the market stalls.[673] George and Joan were detained in town well into September by the international situation and the trouble at the Pay Office, but planned to go down to South Hill on the fourteenth.

On the thirteenth, according to George's carefully worked out protocol, they took little Georgey, in a new pair of trousers and without his nursemaid, across the park from Somerset House to Tufton Street. George had stipulated that Mary Ann was to be quite alone, meaning that Mary and Maria were to keep out of sight. One imagines them watching excitedly from the upstairs landing as George hurried Joan and little Georgey into the best parlour. Mary Ann gave her grandson an extravagant present, which he was not allowed to open on the spot, and sixpence to give to 'poor starved people'.[674] There's no account of how the meeting passed off, but to judge by the known character of those involved we can picture George standing somewhat stiffly in the background, perhaps recalling his own painful encounter with Mary Ann in 1786, and trying so far as he could in the cramped drawing room, to keep out of the women's way, while Georgey submitted to his grandmother's enthusiastic embrace and Joan looked on protectively.

When George and Joan got back to Somerset House they sent all the servants, except the cook, on ahead to South Hill, to get the house ready for a visit from Georgey's godmother, the Princess of Wales. There was therefore no one to witness Mary Ann's return visit next day. She came escorted by Mary and her husband – but not Mary's children, George had insisted – and saw her two younger grandchildren, William and baby Harriet. Everything passed smoothly. As soon as the Thompsons' carriage had moved away, George, Joan and the children, with Fatty Bowers the cook, set off for the country. In recognition of Richard Thompson's part in managing the affair George sent him a gift of port and sherry. He also took an interest in Thompson's pursuit of public office.[675]

The visits had gone better than expected, apparently unobserved by prying servants and hostile newspapermen, and Mary Ann did not exploit her advantage by raising new demands. She expressed her satisfaction in a letter, which George forwarded to the Leighs to give them 'some notion of how the thing passed'.[676] His deviation from his usual custom of destroying his mother's letters once he had answered them suggests that the Leighs had shown particular interest in the meetings, and may even have been instrumental in persuading him to grant the favour. The occasion was, perhaps, sufficiently important in his eyes to make him reluctant to destroy Mary Ann's expression of thanks out of hand, and yet he may not have wanted to keep her letter with him, in which case sending it to the Leighs solved his dilemma.

Thankful that the ordeal was over, George hoped that Mary Ann would now capitulate, settle in the West Country and live quietly on the pension. From their discussions he believed this was her intention. To make certain, he pressed her to make it plain to

Mary that she didn't propose to return, but she refused. It would be better to say nothing until she had left, to avoid 'inquiries and remonstrances'. Once she was down in Devonshire it would, she said 'repeatedly', be easy to invent excuses for staying there. To George this could only mean that she had made up her mind to give up her London home.[677]

Mary Ann had achieved the thing she said she wanted above all else, but she could see how reluctantly George had granted it. She didn't complain, she said she was delighted with the visits, but when she went a week without writing he feared she was dissatisfied.[678] He was probably right. His little curb, restricting who could be present, had put a constraint on everything. Furthermore, in practical terms she was no better off. She still had two children, Maria and Frederick, to establish in life, while Mary, Sam and Charles continued to make demands. Life remained a struggle. In this struggle she had, in addition to the power of her own personality, three principal assets: the pension, the income from the ointment and what she could get from George's growing influence in the world. While she could receive the pension wherever she lived, her other two assets could best be exploited from a London base. She left at the beginning of October to visit Esther in Cullompton and old friends in Exeter and Plymouth, but she intended to return.

**

During the princess's stay at South Hill George injured his leg in an accident, which possibly explains the bad-tempered tone of some of his letters. It was also an excuse for not attending the christening of Mary's son George in November, although he kept his promise to be godfather. He felt unwelcome pressure from Mary Ann to attend. It was as though her whole object was to place him in embarrassing and awkward situations: why will she do so? he asked in his diary. He wrote to her about his convalescence, arranged supplies of wine, and acknowledged a gift of Devonshire cream from Aunt Esther in Cullompton,[679] but all the time in the background lurked the unresolved matter of where Mary Ann should live.

The Thompsons planned to move to Kennington, which would remove one of the attractions of Tufton Street. Unwilling to go back to living permanently with them, Mary Ann was uncertain what to do when her round of visits in Devonshire came to an end. George refused to offer advice on the subject, saying that she knew what he thought and it was futile to go over the ground yet again. He offered to find employment for Mary Ann's Plymouth friend Dr Gashing and for relations of Hunn's sister, hoping, no doubt, that this would strengthen her ties in the West Country.[680]

She would not let the argument die down. There were practical reasons for wanting to come back to London, but her tenacity suggests that something more than mere convenience was at stake: she wanted to win the argument, wanted George to *want* her living close to him. She wrote from Plymouth asking him again for advice and when he replied that she would never live in London with his *concurrence* she pounced upon the word and angrily sent his letter back.[681] She had asked him to advise her, as her son, and he had replied by presuming to dictate to her. His pride was reaching new heights, she said, repeating her old grievance. It was too much for George's patience.

His response, dated 8 November 1804, was the harshest letter he ever wrote to her, a cleverly woven mixture of charm, self-justification and menace. He complained that when he had accused her of going back on what they had agreed in their face-to-face discussions her reply was that at their meetings 'we talked under the influence of feelings that naturally made us liable to mutual misunderstanding'. He flatly denied this: ' I never talked,' he wrote, 'nor ever to the best of my recollection heard you talk with more clearness and collectedness …' This affords a glimpse of their confrontations: Mary Ann overwhelmed by her feelings, terrified of losing her son altogether, willing to say anything to appease him;

and George, angry, proud, obstinate, unhappy, baffled, repressing his feelings, allowing the storm to rage around him, and when it was over drawing the conclusion he wanted from what she had said. If she refused to abide by their verbal agreements, however, he would have to express himself clearly in writing, but when he did so she sent back his letter. What was he to do?

Her accusation that he had changed towards her out of pride was not true, he wrote, and was not generous; had anyone but his mother accused him he would have called it a lie. He had laid it down as long ago as the Newbery affair of 1793 that she had no connection with his family. She would never be admitted to his house or introduced to his friends and associates. If she consented to stay out of London this unhappy situation could be covered up, but if she insisted on living close to him her exclusion would be obvious to all. She can have been in no doubt that *obvious to all* meant obvious to Richard Thompson and his family, who would be bound to demand an explanation. What was new in this letter was an explicit threat that if she went about telling people that her exclusion was due to his pride, he would not take the injustice silently but would defend himself by revealing the real reason, and, he said, she knew what that real reason was. In other words, her continued presence in London would lead inevitably to Thompson, and Thompson's family, learning the truth about her past and Mary's illegitimate birth. This threat had always been in the air – had been signalled in the course of the angry exchanges of two years before – but it was in this letter that he spelled it out with the starkest clarity.

We don't know what Richard Thompson thought about Mary Ann and her past. His will stipulates that on no account were his daughters to be domiciled with their grandmother, and Mary's will repeats the ban, but neither gives a reason.[682] On the whole, it's unlikely that he would have been shocked and disgusted, or even surprised, to learn that Mary was illegitimate. He had probably made it his business to unearth all he could about her family. Although Mary had taken Hunn's name, and although it was as Mary Hunn that she had been awarded her share of the pension, he must have realised she was Reddish's child, if only because she was older than Charles Reddish. The one thing he may not have known (although he could have found out, since the dates of Reddish's death and Mary Ann's marriage to Richard Hunn were both matters of record) was that Mary Ann had never been legally married to Reddish. The threat to tell him the scandalous truth may well have been less terrible than George supposed. But perhaps Mary was the real target. If she naïvely believed that Thompson had accepted her as Mary Hunn, it would be disturbing for her to learn that he was to be told the truth about her birth. George was fond of Mary, so if this was the burden of his threat it is a measure of how desperate he was to carry his point. Three months later, in February 1805, George and Thompson had a long discussion about Mary Ann, after which George noted that Thompson 'understands her', but without enlarging on what exactly Thompson understood.[683]

The letter of 8 November was as full of emotional and moral blackmail as Mary Ann's Packet. George was pained that his grand gesture of September had met with no answering concession from her. He was hurt too that she was unwilling to comply with his wishes when he was so tireless in working for her benefit and that of her connections, and to underline the point he dropped a broad hint that he was on the point of securing a substantial position for Richard Thompson as Supervisor of the Receiver General's Receipts and Payments in the Port of London.[684] With its skilful combination of pathos and reasoning, the letter exhibits vividly the rhetorical qualities which, in public life, charmed and disarmed some, and made many others regard George Canning with deep suspicion.

It is not clear how Mary Ann responded to this letter. She was back in Tufton Street before the end of 1804. Richard Thompson was to take the house off her hands, and she would thereafter visit

Mary occasionally, or at least that was how George understood the arrangement. He did not yet know, however, when the move would take place and where she would settle. He called on her in mid-December when he was over his injury, and for a few months an uneasy peace returned to their correspondence, perhaps because he was too busy to argue.[685]

His visits were infrequent, and he often wrote to alter the arrangements. Relations within the government were uneasy, and the Trotter-Melville affair was moving to a conclusion. Richard Thompson sent further unsolicited advice, prompting George to write irritably that everything he alleged was false, adding, 'I am in no way implicated. It is nothing to me or my character if Ld M and Mr T were both hanged.' In the event neither Melville nor Trotter was hanged, although the scandal meant the end of their careers.[i] In case Richard Thompson still hoped to profit from Trotter's dismissal, George told Mary Ann that a friend was returning from Jamaica[ii] in good time to succeed as paymaster.[686]

In June 1805, just before he was to take his family for a holiday in Hampshire, George arranged a further opportunity for Mary Ann to meet her grandchildren. He had no time, he said, to bring them to see her, but he invited her to call at Somerset House, accompanied by Mr Thompson and (since Mary was indisposed) Maria.[687] The visit again went smoothly. Afterwards it seemed to be accepted that she was to give up the Tufton Street house and stay with the Thompsons until she left town in the autumn to settle in the West Country for good.

Mary Ann dropped her resistance to the inevitable. Circumstances had changed since the previous summer. Mary seemed more content in her marriage, less in need of her mother's presence.[688] She was pregnant again, and Mary Ann, finding it tactful to keep out of the way, moved to the Thompsons' new

i The Commons voted in a memorable division, on the casting vote of the Speaker, to censure Melville, but the subsequent impeachment failed.

ii This was John Smith, a friend from Eton and one of the collaborators on the *Microcosm*. He had been sent to Jamaica five years earlier with a secret commission to gather accurate data on the slave trade (*HoP 1790–1820*).

house in Kennington. It was unsettling, living in an empty house in a new suburb. Letters reached her with no more precise address than *Mr Thompson's, Kennington*, but when George crossed the river to find her, he retreated, baffled by the maze of streets. And where was she to live when the Thompsons gave up the Millbank house and moved to Kennington? A final consideration was that the ointment business was not flourishing, and was leading to acrimony between Mary Ann and Richard Thompson. George, quoting the authority of Francis Newbery, pointed out that if it were to be revived and expanded it would need to be taken over by someone with the capital to finance an advertising campaign. But although it did not grow as Mary Ann had once hoped, it carried on. Over the next few years some of the work was done by Maria, who was welcome to stay at the Thompsons' house, so it no longer required Mary Ann's presence in London. But just a week before she left London, she referred to her *excursion* into the West, which alarmed George, since it seemed to imply an intention to return. He regularly complained that she examined the meaning of his words too minutely, but here he was doing exactly the same. She reassured him. They met to say goodbye, chaperoned by Mary to prevent renewal of painful arguments.[689]

Irritated though he was by Richard Thompson's interference over the Trotter affair, George could not afford a quarrel. For almost twenty years his own finances, and his mother's, had been handled by Walter Borrowes, but after a series of strokes Borrowes was becoming unreliable, and was told by his doctor to retire from business. Although he hung on, reluctant to admit defeat, he was often away from the office, leaving matters to his clerks, who George feared would gossip about his affairs. Borrowes had always managed to explain problems over the pension to Mary Ann, but the clerks only confused her. She contacted George's cousin, Harry Canning, a partner in the firm of Borrowes, French and Canning, which risked bringing her affairs to the notice of Mehitabel. To make things worse there was a legal dispute between the firm and the Navy over a contract to supply meat from Ireland; even if George had not influenced the award of the contract, he didn't want his connection with the firm to be brought to public notice. In the spring of 1806 the firm suspended payments, which began a protracted wrangle between the ailing Borrowes and his partners. George declared himself glad that his own account was in credit at the time of the firm's bankruptcy, preferring to lose money himself rather than contribute to the failure. The upshot was that someone else was needed to handle Mary Ann's affairs, and Thompson was both competent and discreet. Since the beginning of the year he had been negotiating a transfer of Mary Ann's business, and managed to save a remittance from Samuel. Mary Ann thanked providence for saving her money from the crash, which George criticised as 'the very reverse of piety'. It was her son-in-law's business acumen that had saved her.[690]

By this time Mary Ann was in Devonshire, having left London in October, travelling alone, leaving Maria with Mary. She stayed with Esther in Cullompton before moving on to her old friend Mrs Moore in Exeter, and then to Plymouth. George wrote to wish her well on her journey, promising to keep in touch with Mary and Maria, and provide them with franks. As soon as she reached Plymouth she found herself pestered by those who wanted her to pester George on their behalf. He responded with a long lecture on patronage, not the first he had delivered, nor the last. She must refuse absolutely; she must say 'I never do' if asked to pass on messages and requests. If people accused him of 'filial impiety' for ignoring her 'recommendations' she should reply that he had done enough – in fact, he said, some were accusing him of having already done too much for her family and friends.[691]

She stayed at various addresses in the West Country during most of 1806, and then spent a few months in Kennington before going to Bath, where she would remain for the rest of her life. It might have seemed, when George and Joan sent their servants away to the country and walked across the park with little Georgey in the stifling heat, that Mary Ann had won a sort of victory, that the Packet had gained its end, but of course it was not so. There was to be no familiar intercourse with George and his children; she was to be exiled from London. Apart from one short visit from Harriet almost twenty years later she saw no more of George's children, and was to see George himself only infrequently, when some business took him to Bath. He would visit her, as she had bitterly foretold in the opening of the Packet, 'as Benevolent Men give Alms to worthless Mendicants'. He had won, as he was bound to.

He tried, as always, to soften the blow. Despite all his warnings that she should not ask him to do favours, he took up the case of one of her friends, a London clockmaker, James Tregent.[i] A letter from Tregent to Mary Ann has survived. Describing her as 'the kind indulgent friend of my boyish days', he begged her to use her influence with her 'excellent son' to 'save me and mine from the cold hand of creditors.' His anxiety about his family may have been intensified by a realisation that he had not long to live. What his connection was with Mary Ann remains a mystery, buried in the unknown hinterland of her life. Mary Ann begged George to help James's son, Abraham, who was in the Marines. Mr Tregent's business, he said, was the last thing he did before leaving office following the death of Pitt in January 1806. It was, he thought, a case that was particularly close to her heart, and he was pleased to assure her that he had been thinking of her in his 'last official moments'. He secured a deputy barrack-master's place in Cheshire for Abraham Tregent.[692]

Maria stayed on in Kennington with the Thompsons, helping with the ointment business. While Richard Thompson conducted negotiations with agents and retailers (often difficult because sales were sluggish) she handled orders and sent out supplies. She remained in town until the summer of 1806, about the time of her eighteenth birthday, when she joined Mary Ann in Plymouth. Either in London or in Plymouth she met and fell in love with

i James Tregent, watch and clockmaker of Leicester Square, was active 1770–1805. He died soon after contacting Mary Ann in October 1805.

a young man called Powler. Before long they were engaged. Mary was anxious about Maria's health, thinking her too frail for childbearing. George thought it would be better to wait until Powler's circumstances were more settled, but did not interfere, beyond explaining that on marriage Maria would take the £100 that was her share of the pension, which hitherto had been part of the common purse on which Mary Ann depended. He was comparatively relaxed about his relationship with Maria, and if she married he could acknowledge her husband, in private at least, as his brother-in-law. The young people agreed to a year's delay, in the course of which the engagement was abandoned, without generating the unpleasantness of the Parker affair six years earlier.[693]

Meanwhile there was better news from India. Charles, it seems, had been in prison, but he was now free, and was married. He had written home in what George judged to be 'a much better tone than heretofore'.[694]

Samuel and his family were home on leave, and when Maria joined her Mary Ann was waiting for them to be released from quarantine. On Samuel's previous home leave, in 1803, Dorothy had stayed in Barbados, having just given birth, but this time she came with him, bringing the child, Mary, to be presented to George and Mary Ann who had been absent godparents. Nathan Ashby, Dorothy's brother, may have accompanied them. He had not found a post when he was in London in 1803 and had returned to Barbados, but the previous year, while still at the Navy Pay Office, George had 'pushed an old clerk into retirement' to create a vacancy, which Nathan could have if he was on the spot. In October they all went to London to stay with the Thompsons in Kennington, where George hoped to find time to see his goddaughter. Samuel tried to persuade him to intervene in his quarrel with a Jamaican judge, Henry Henchcliffe. George firmly declined to get involved.[695]

By December 1806 Mary Ann and Maria were in Bath. They stayed in lodgings over the new year while looking for a suitable house. The lodgings, in Orange Grove, belonged to a toyman[i] named Moore, possibly a connection of Mary Ann's Exeter friend.[696] While Samuel and Dorothy were with them George remembered that he had not fulfilled all the conventional duties of a godfather. To make good his omission he asked Mary Ann to buy a present on his behalf for little Mary's nurse. Samuel interfered, and George had to repeat his instructions: 'I did not mistake Sam's message,' he wrote. 'I understood what you say was intended. But it is customary to remember the nurse, so please carry out my commission.'[697] There's nothing to show what point Samuel had been making, perhaps simply that the christening had been three years ago, so it was late in the day to make this gesture. Another possibility is that he objected because the nurse was a slave and it was unnecessary to give presents to slaves. This would explain the acerbity evident in George's response. Although he took a gradualist approach to the abolition of slavery, and was prepared like most people to profit indirectly from slave labour, he voted consistently against the slave trade, and may well have been disgusted when confronted with slave-owning attitudes at close quarters. The issue was uppermost in the public mind at the time, with Wilberforce's bill abolishing the slave trade before parliament.

**

For Mary Ann the comings and goings of 1806 marked the end of what George had called her 'jigging about up and down'. From now on, although she made excursions to Devonshire and even once or twice to London, she was based in Bath. George's point had finally been made. In November she offered to help with looking after Georgey. The proposal, though well intentioned, may have looked to George like another attempt to gain a foothold in his family. If so, it was the last such attempt. He kindly but firmly turned her down. Joan refused to share the responsibility with anyone, he said.[698]

---

i Toyman: a seller of trinkets or fancy goods (*OED*).

For George 1806 marked other milestones. When Walter Borrowes ceased to act as his man of affairs it severed the last link with his Uncle Stratty. He realised how much he had depended on Borrowes when he lost his government residence and had to look for a house himself. Towards the end of the year his and Joan's home life was severely disrupted by their decision to entrust Georgey to the care of Dr Robert Chessher, a pioneer orthopaedist, who ran a hospital for disabled children at Hinckley in Leicestershire. Frightened by an accident that they blamed on a careless servant, they refused to leave the child to the unsupervised care of strangers, and so took a house close to the Chessher establishment, where Joan and the other children were to live for the next seven years. For Joan, George realised, this amounted to a 'sort of widowhood'.[699] For himself, devoted though he was to his wife and eldest child, the most significant break with the past was the death of Pitt on 23 January, which left him a sort of orphan.

Pitt had been more than a political leader, and his death meant more to George than just the loss of his job and the house and salary that went with it. From the outset he had made up his mind to be Pitt's man or nothing. For the first dozen years of his career he based everything on his loyalty to Pitt, and when they differed the intensity of their disagreements only emphasised their closeness. It was apparent to George's friends and enemies alike. John Frere recalled that they were more like father and son than political colleagues. The Whig Thomas Creevey described Canning as 'a true disciple… tho' in an inferior way, of the Arch villain Pitt.'[700]

George did not join the government of Pitt's successor, Lord Grenville, but when that government fell early in 1807 and the Duke of Portland became prime minister George gained the post he had long coveted, foreign secretary, only to lose it two years later as a result of his quarrel and duel with Castlereagh. George never acquired Pitt's knack for managing men. He could inspire genuine affection and loyalty, and his handling of George IV in the 1820s shows that he knew how to charm and flatter, but he made enemies too carelessly. Pitt had schooled himself to suffer fools gladly – too gladly, George thought, as he contemplated Pitt's 1804 cabinet from which he was excluded – a trick that George never learned. Determined to acquire a reputation for honesty and consistency, he would obstinately justify himself with pedantic and subtle arguments. Pitt foresaw that this arrogance and stubbornness would damage George's career. His anxiety is reflected in a letter that his niece and confidante, Lady Hester Stanhope,[i] wrote to Joan in 1804, warning her that George was making enemies by his cleverness and 'long face', and urging her to 'make Mr C as stupid as possible.'[701]

With the visit of 1805 and Mary Ann's subsequent removal from London, her story might be said to come to an end. George had made his tactical concession and emerged victorious. In agreeing to settle well away from London, Mary Ann gave up her dream of finding a place, however inconspicuous, in George's family life. The expectation that his fireside would be the haven for her 'shatter'd bark' had kept her afloat during her years of struggle and disappointment, and now it was gone. No more drama, no more conflict, she had given in. But both she and George had twenty-one more years to live.

For Mary Ann these were quieter years, largely free of the troubles of the preceding six decades. It's tempting to sum up this last quarter of her life in a few words, as Thackeray disposes of Becky Sharp: '... chiefly hangs about Bath... a very strong party of excellent people consider her to be a most injured woman... busies herself in works of piety... name in all the Charity Lists... always having stalls at Fancy Fairs...' Perhaps that is enough. Mary Ann belongs to the growing band of eighteenth and nineteenth century women who are emerging from the obscurity to which they were consigned first by the prejudices of their own time, and then by

i Lady Hester Stanhope (1776–1839) was the daughter of Pitt's sister. She was her uncle's companion and confidante between 1803 and 1806. After his death she embarked on the travels in the East for which she became famous.

the indifference of historians. From this point of view it's the years of struggle, injustice and resilience that count, not the years of retirement. Another reason for winding up her story soon after 1803 is that for the later years we don't have her own account. Her voice, heard loud and clear in the Packet, is largely silent from now on. Just a handful of her letters have survived, leaving us dependent on George's often witty and elegant replies, from which it's hard to see anything of her life beyond George himself and an endless succession of anxieties about health, money, lodgings and the obscure careers of her other sons. We risk being seduced into telling his story, not Mary Ann's. But by scrutinising his hurried scrawls with something of the intensity that Mary Ann herself bestowed upon them, we can sometimes guess at the thoughts and feelings expressed in her missing letters. We can build up a picture, patchy but vivid, of the fluctuating relationship between mother and son across the years.

26.
Settlement, 1807–1811

By the end of January 1807, Mary Ann was settled in 37 New King Street,[i] where she would remain for four years. Maria was with her, and Samuel and his family had not yet gone home. George, unable to keep up with the comings and goings, sent his kind remembrances to 'all about you'. The move seems not to have gone smoothly. George was alarmed when he did not receive his weekly letter from Mary Ann. The stress had made her ill. He then missed a week, explaining that he had been uncertain where to direct his letter: 'I have a horror of the miscarriage of a letter,' he said, fearing that information would leak out about his intimate affairs. Then Samuel went up to London, bearing messages, which George 'insensibly counted… as an interchange', so there is a further gap in the letters. In a depressed mood following her exertions, and perhaps also affected by not having heard from him, she urged him to retire from public life. He replied that he had obligations to his wife, who wanted him to continue in politics. Had he inherited a fortune he would have opted for the leisured life, he admitted, believing like many workaholics that he was 'naturally very idle'.[702]

i There were (and are) two King Streets in Bath, *New* and *Old*, and it seems that *New* was also known as Lower King Street. George directs at first to New King Street, but then to Queen Street, and Little King Street, before settling upon Lower King Street, occasionally reverting to New King Street.

The choice of Bath for Mary Ann's retirement was a compromise. George might well have preferred her to go further away, down into Devonshire. Bath was a satellite, almost a suburb, of London, journey times between the two cities being as low as twelve or thirteen hours, less than half that from Exeter to London. Fashionable gossip from Bath featured regularly in the metropolitan newspapers. George's first letter to Mary Ann in Bath contained a warning to avoid talking of his affairs as it could give rise to malicious talk. 'I have had proof of this – from Bath,' he wrote.[703]

Bath provided a wider range of social opportunities than the narrow and exclusive community of Totteridge, and Mary Ann seems to have found her own level. Although she had once threatened to bury herself in the country, she was a sociable person who enjoyed serious conversation and good company. She was wiser now, but just as open to excitement as she had been as a girl, when her Pump Room acquaintance Zephaniah Holwell captivated her with his talk of India. Proud of her medical knowledge, she prescribed for her friends' ailments.[704] Unashamed of her theatrical past, she cultivated the friendship of those in the profession, including, as we shall see, John Palmer, theatre manager and postal entrepreneur. George's appointment as foreign secretary under the Duke of Portland came soon after Mary Ann settled in New King Street, enabling her to borrow his reflected glory as she consolidated her position as a serious figure in Bath society – not in the first ranks of society, but quite at home among the resident tea-drinkers and whist-players.

One of her Bath acquaintances was Colonel Robert Hall, a Devon man who had led a regiment of Devon and Cornwall fencibles in Ireland during the brutal suppression of the 1798 rebellion. He claimed that he and his men behaved more humanely than other units of the army.[i] After the rebellion he devoted much

i Colonel Robert Hall (1753–1836) was the father of the journalist Samuel Carter Hall. His claim to have dealt humanely with the Irish rebels in 1798 is questionable, since he was stationed at the notorious Geneva Barracks, Co. Waterford, where prisoners were detained pending transportation.

of his fortune to mineral prospecting in Ireland, hoping, he said, to provide work for men thrown off the land. He had much in common with Mary Ann – Ireland and Devonshire, science and social improvement – and recalled her as an agreeable companion, despite her tendency to talk too much of her son in London.[705]

George's letters always to hand, Mary Ann gloried in his devotion to her and kindness to her children, which encouraged people to ask her to ask him to find jobs for their sons, brothers or nephews. In the absence of established procedures for securing government employment, aspirants had to exploit every opening. It could do no harm to ask, people thought. In Bath, which was full of elderly middle-class people with young relations eager to get onto the public payroll, it was probably considered bad form to refuse help. However often George repudiated the doctrine that it did no harm to ask and told her to ignore all such requests, she offended again and again. It was one of those endlessly recurring patterns of behaviour that grow up in families, an itch they couldn't help scratching. For Mary Ann there was more at stake than vanity or social pressure: she longed for George to prove his affection for her by doing her bidding, just because it was she who asked.

As soon as she was settled in her new home she passed on an application, to which he replied dismissively that he had no more influence in such a case than in the making of a bishop. She was hurt by the harshness of his tone, and upset because his letter gave no 'ostensible' explanation, but still, she said, she forgave him. He was horrified that she was prepared to treat his letters as 'ostensible', and her forgiveness both irritated and amused him. He reiterated that he could not have done anything to help her friend, and went on: 'I am not aware therefore that I have any "forgiveness" to ask or to receive from you my dearest Mother, though from a Mother I receive it even when not required, with thankfulness and submission.'[706] This sarcasm has the bantering tone of many of his letters, but it was a rebuke nonetheless. She had touched him in a sore place. In private, as in his public life, he was on the look out for slights.

George had no intention of providing Mary Ann with ostensible reasons when he failed to help. He didn't see the need for explanation. He told her not to pass on these requests and expected her to obey without question. But now and then he indicated which of the unwritten rules that governed the patronage system she was asking him to violate. The main problem was that she wanted him to seek favours on behalf of people with whom he had no genuine connection. The basis of the system was that a colleague could secure your support by doing a favour for someone whose prospects mattered to you, creating a network of mutual obligations which served to bind political allies together. But if the beneficiary meant nothing to you, was just a casual acquaintance, you would not be sufficiently obliged by the favour to make it worth your colleague's while. To make such a request was an impertinence, like asking for money out of a man's pocket. This had made it difficult for George to petition Henry Dundas for an Indian cadetship for Charles Reddish without revealing the closeness of his connection.[707]

In some respects George was now better equipped to take part in the game of jobs and favours. The patronage at the disposal of the foreign secretary gave him real influence, but the process of making appointments was more strictly circumscribed than outsiders imagined. Parliamentary scrutiny limited the scope of patronage. Wartime austerity and the Trotter-Melville scandal made the process more controversial than ever. When the Duke of Portland's government replaced Grenville's there was heightened awareness of corruption; the incoming administration uncovered the pensions and sinecures granted by their predecessors, and the outgoing party was keen to scrutinise the expense incurred by those who had replaced them. In a debate in which accusations were thrown back and forth, Canning summed up the atmosphere of recrimination with the 'vulgar proverb: Those who have many glass windows ought not to begin by throwing stones [*a laugh*]'. This jibe prompted one of the independent members to make an oblique reference to Mary Ann's pension. George replied that, yes, he had been awarded a pension during Mr Pitt's administration, half of which he retained for himself, and half he had given to 'two very near and dear relations who were dependent for their subsistence upon his labours'.[708] Technically the pension was paid to Mary and Maria, but the relations George probably had most in mind were Mary Ann and Esther, which was as close as he ever came to a public acknowledgement of his mother.

Within days of this exchange Mary Ann wrote to George offering to give up the pension. How she expected to live without it, when she could barely live with it, is unclear. She may still have placed hopes in the ointment business, or thought she could make do on casual handouts from George. Perhaps he would give her a regular allowance as he had proposed when she lived in Totteridge. Perhaps she would have to live with the Thompsons in London. Sensing that the pension was George's way of getting her off his hands, she may have hoped that the sacrifice would bring her closer to him. How far she thought through any of these implications is doubtful; whatever the deeper motives, it was a generous impulse. George sent a thousand thanks, declining her offer not for her sake but his own: 'It would look like having done wrong, which I have not. And for anything else I am not very solicitous'.[709]

In the following two months Mary Ann heard from George only three times, twice to say he was about to go into the country. The third letter, at the end of September, consisted of just two lines. A few days later he forwarded her a letter that had come addressed to him, adding a brusque note that as the sender had apologised for her intrusion Mary Ann did not need to find fault with her.[710] Perhaps feeling herself slighted by this grudging allowance, she sent him an 'injunction' whose nature we can only guess from his bemused response:

> I literally comply with your injunctions, by writing to you immediately, though… utterly at a loss to conceive what the

> object of your letter can have been – having complied with that injunction, I have nothing more to add than that I am, as ever, My Dear Mother's most dutiful and affectionate son, G.C.[711]

She had been ill and was about to go to stay with Esther. She may have feared she would die while away, and wanted this renewed assurance of his affection to take with her. Perhaps she wanted to prove to Esther that although George had driven her out of London his feelings for her were unchanged. During her month away she had three further letters in which he took care to demonstrate how burdened he was, telling her it was three months since he had seen Joan, and five since he'd seen his children. After repeated 'cruel' postponements he eventually snatched a brief visit to Hinckley at the end of October.[712]

When they were both back, he at the Foreign Office and she in Bath, a new embarrassment arose, when Abraham Tregent, the clockmaker's son whom George had helped the year before, presented him with a watch. George said it was an absolute rule that he would not accept gifts of this sort, even though he was sure there was no improper intention on Tregent's part. He returned 'poor Mr Tregent's' letter to Mary Ann, and arranged for Richard Thompson to return the watch and explain as best he could why it could not be accepted. He didn't want to give Tregent anything in writing.[713]

Despite such moments of irritation, Mary Ann's first year in Bath passed smoothly enough, but around the new year two things happened that caused George to erupt in anger. The first concerned Maria. We don't know how disappointed she was by the collapse of her marriage plans, but in Bath she threw herself into the life of the town. For Mary Ann the life of the town meant card-playing and conversation; for a nineteen-year-old girl it meant dances and assemblies. This illustrated the disadvantage of Bath. The London newspapers, which showed scant interest in the public entertainments of Plymouth or Exeter, regularly picked up stories from Bath, from which George learned that Maria had danced with not one, but both masters of ceremonies. The masters of ceremonies were public characters and Maria's association with them was uncomfortably like an appearance on a public stage. Brooding on the report, he delivered a furious warning to Mary Ann:

> For God's sake my dear Mother do not make a public Exhibition of your daughter. I cannot well express to you the feelings with which I first heard of her dancing with both Masters of Ceremonies!! a thing which nobody could have suffered their daughter to do – but which you had surely numberless additional reasons, arising (I should have thought from pleasing but I am sure) from many painful associations, to avoid. And the newspaper account of all this!! – I cannot but believe you must have felt it too strongly to require my impressing upon you what my feelings were ...[714]

There's more to this than his disdain for the tawdry Bath festivities. The awkwardness of his expression is a sign that he felt himself coming close to the painful topic of Mary Ann's own moral reputation. Much that could not be expressed openly was implied in the repeated underlining of you. You of all mothers must be careful. It would be hard enough to find a gentleman willing to marry the daughter of a woman with a sullied past; for Maria to flaunt herself in this way would make matters worse. But in the event Maria was to have no difficulty finding a husband.

No sooner had Mary Ann digested this onslaught than another arrived, even more hurtful, arising from an attempt to influence George's vote in Parliament. Her acquaintance John Palmer had other interests apart from the theatre, including postal reform. He had revolutionised the management of the mail, speeding up communications between Bath and London, and then extending the changes to other provincial centres. In the process he made enemies and was involved in a prolonged dispute with the government over the distribution of profits. As the date for a Parliamentary vote on Palmer's affairs drew near,

Mary Ann asked George to support her friend. George suspected that Mary Ann had put herself under an obligation by getting Palmer to lobby the Admiralty on behalf of Frederick, but she had another altogether different motive: twenty-one years earlier she had begged Stratty to approach Palmer on her behalf; if she could now be instrumental in furthering Palmer's case it might go some way to erasing the memory of her humiliation. Having rebuked her for her interference, George told her that he had not voted on the question because he had not read the papers, and that now he had read them he was not inclined in Palmer's favour. He gave no reason, but reminded her that she should adopt a policy, as his wife did, of knowing nothing of about his political views.[715]

For Joan the pretence of knowing nothing was just a pretence. Confident in Joan's discretion, her 'masculine' turn of mind, he felt free to fill his letters to her with his long-term ambitions and day-to-day manoeuvres. He had no such confidence in Mary Ann. She moved in circles of which he knew nothing, thoughtlessly incurring obligations to casual acquaintances. She discussed his letters with friends, and kept them as precious relics,[716] when it would be safer to destroy them, as he destroyed most of hers. His letter about Palmer, however, she marked 'Not to be opened'. She sent a detailed rejoinder, another packet, as George called it, to which he did not respond. Whether from annoyance or because of the pressure of work, over the next few months he let her go for long intervals without hearing from him.

Despite such occasional tempests the general tone of their correspondence was tranquil and good natured. Mary Ann's anger, always intense while it lasted, was short lived. Her way of smoothing things over was to make it clear that she understood him, appreciated the subtlety of his speeches and sympathised with his impatience at the petty cares of family and public life. As with her offer to give up the pension, she would assure him that she was on his side. For his part, whenever he felt obliged to scold her, he invariably followed it up with something emollient:

complimentary remarks about Samuel, assurances that he would do something for Frederick, concern over Mary's health, questions about Aunt Esther, or gifts of money.

Money was needed because every quarter Mary Ann ran up debts in anticipation of the next instalment of the pension. George, who never managed to live within his own income, cautioned her to avoid extravagance, but was always responsive to her needs. In March 1808, when the pension was late, he sent an advance of £75 plus £25 to cover various payments she had made on his behalf. These were either little things he wanted her to have for her house, or charitable payments that she made for him – but, as he always insisted, not in his name. He encouraged her to pass some of the money on to Esther.[717]

Mary Ann and Maria spent the summer of 1808 in Kennington. George promised to fix a day to dine with the Thompsons, but it was not until her two months in London were almost over that he found time. At first it was public business that detained him, but in mid-August he had to hurry down to Yarmouth where William Leigh was dying. Of all those who had helped and guided him in his youth, William Leigh had been the kindest and most patient. In return George was always willing, even eager, to use what influence he had on the Leighs' behalf, in contrast to his grudging response to requests from Mary Ann. Despite frequent claims that he had no influence over church appointments, he had procured a deanery for Leigh, who did not, however, live long to enjoy it. While George was engaged in comforting his aunt, Mary Ann irritated him by sending an unaddressed letter to be franked. Then she sent a letter about Samuel which he said testily 'was not well calculated for the moment at which it reached me'. After Yarmouth he spent a week or so with Joan in Hinckley, writing more calmly, asking after Maria's health, passing on a letter from Charles, and trying again to fix a day to dine in Kennington. 'Thursday sennight will do very well,' he wrote at last.[718]

During the visit conversation turned to a picture in Mary Ann's possession. When George told Joan about it she asked to see it, in order to correct one of her own of the same subject.[i] George passed on the request, saying that the canvas should be 'cottoned and papered' and entrusted to the post. This was too simple for Mary Ann for whom the picture had suddenly become a link with George's family. Shouldn't she speak to the postmaster in Bath to make sure it was well taken care of? Or one of her friends could easily deliver it by hand. There's a note of panic in his reply: no, there's no need to confide in the postmaster. 'Still worse,' he added, 'would be to introduce to me a new acquaintance in the bearer.' The picture duly arrived in London, and George took it to Hinckley at Christmas. He absentmindedly left it behind when he returned to London, and it wasn't until the following summer that Mary Ann eventually got it back.[719]

Maria came of age in 1809, bringing about a change in the arrangements for the pension. She was the titular beneficiary, along with Mary, and now she was managing her own affairs she needed to understand that it was intended primarily for Mary Ann's use. There's no reason to suppose that Maria wanted to make difficulties, but perhaps the legal niceties took time, so George sent £100 to keep them all afloat, including Aunt Esther, saying it was to mark the end of his second year in office. He wondered whether he would have another year. Maria also came into her legacy from her Hunn relations, and was contemplating sinking her money into a business enterprise. George's allusions to Maria's undertaking tell us nothing except that it was 'comfortable and creditable' but inevitably involved 'some risk'. For several years now she had been helping to distribute the ointment, so she may have planned to take it over on her own account, or perhaps she was proposing a business relationship with the Frome textile merchant Humphrey Noad, whom she eventually married. George was impressed by her energy, but warned her, through Mary Ann, not to jeopardise her whole fortune.[720]

---

i The subject of the picture is unknown. George refers to the painter as 'Wright'; it may have been Joseph Wright of Derby, who was a close friend of the portrait painter John Downman, the cousin of Mary Ann's Exeter friend Hugh Downman.

While Maria was in London making plans, Mary Ann was on her own in Bath. She was ill in May, and in July she suffered a fall. She was now just over sixty, but whether these mishaps were due to advancing age is hard to say. Nor do we know how serious things were – not too serious, to judge by the flippant way in which George referred to the fall. What is easier to imagine is that she was sometimes lonely. She scrutinised the newspapers for scraps of news about George. Why, for instance, were he and Joan not listed among those attending the King's birthday? George explained that the newspapers' information about the ladies in attendance was provided by the milliners, and Joan's milliner had left her off the list. As for him, he had gone in by the side door with the other ministers, and so escaped notice. He assured Mary Ann that Joan had been 'though not the finest, the best dressed woman there.'[721]

As Mary Ann pored over the newspapers, in the summer of 1809 she may have gathered something of the discord in the cabinet between George and the secretary of state for War, Robert Stewart, Viscount Castlereagh. George complained to colleagues, including the prime minister, the Duke of Portland, about Castlereagh's performance as secretary of state. The duke was a sick man and the dispute between George and Castlereagh was caught up in the larger problem of who should succeed as prime minister. Castlereagh accused George of plotting behind his back and challenged him to a duel. Although George had never handled a gun in his life, he felt he had no option but to accept the challenge. When the two men met on Putney Heath in the early morning of 21 September, Castlereagh's second shot hit George in the thigh.[i] George wrote to Mary Ann immediately after the event, hoping that his assurance that all was well would reach her before she heard anything from other sources. He warned her not to expect a daily bulletin, and fended off an attempt by Mary and Maria to call on him.[722] His suspicion that he would soon be out of

i George has generally been held responsible for the original dispute, although Castlereagh's response may be thought exaggerated. See Hinde, 218–28.

office had proved true, although he can hardly have foretold the dramatic circumstances.

George and Joan had recently acquired a substantial house, Gloucester Lodge, on the rural fringes of Kensington, where he spent the first few months of private life. His wounded thigh soon recovered, and he set about defending his wounded reputation against attacks from Castlereagh's supporters. He was well enough to travel to Hinckley for Christmas, and it was there that he received an alarming letter from Mary Ann, probably about her own health. It elicited an emotional response on the first day of 1810: 'But my dear Mother, what an alarm was the beginning of your last letter calculated to excite! God Almighty spare and protect you from such a calamity. No, I cannot dread it, as possible. God forbid! God forbid!' It may be that, in a gloomy mood, she had prophesied that she would not live to see the end of the year that was about to begin, but George's words seem to suggest some more specific calamity. He sent £50 from his last official salary for her to share with Aunt Esther.[723]

Over Christmas Joan was anxious about George's health. Fearing he would catch whooping cough from the children, she wanted to know from Mary Ann if he had ever had it as a child. The answer was yes. This exchange afforded a moment of intimacy that Mary Ann will have savoured. The children had barely recovered from whooping cough when they went down with measles. George could share with Mary Ann his anxiety over the children, the more so because she also was nursing a sick child, probably Samuel's daughter. In the event he didn't catch anything from the children, but back in London he caught a cold while attending upon the King. A little later he slipped and sprained his leg. Prepared for the worst after these mishaps, she noticed that he had been unexpectedly absent from the St Patrick's Day dinner at the City of London Tavern, organised by the Benevolent Society of St Patrick, a charity supported by many prominent London businessmen and politicians of Irish origin. Stratty had been a steward at its first dinner in the 1780s. Advertisements for the event listed George as one of the vice-presidents, but he was not named among those present on the night. He explained that his absence had been accidental and temporary, and for proof that he was well and active he referred her to newspaper reports of the prominent part he was playing in Commons debates. Why hadn't she thought of that for herself? he wondered. The society's mixture of patriotic speeches, sentimental songs and collections for charity was not the sort of thing George cared for. When he attended the 1804 dinner he described it sarcastically as being 'obliged to dine with a select company of 300 at the Crown and Anchor'. He attended the celebrations in subsequent years, and was chairman in 1820.[724]

While the children were ill, and George was himself suffering from his winter cold, letters arrived for him, Mary Ann and Samuel from Charles Reddish and his wife, pleading for help. The mail had taken ten months to arrive. Charles's pay had been reduced when he was invalided out due to a return of his fits, with further reductions going towards liquidating his debts. Now he aspired to a staff appointment, which he hoped would enable him to 'withdraw the ensigns of poverty from a beloved wife and children'. His wife Beatrice seconded his appeal, telling George that she had heard of all he had done in the past for 'Reddish'. George put his letters to one side, telling Mary Ann that he could do nothing. She does not seem to have pressed Charles's case.[725]

Samuel had been on leave in England during the winter of 1809/10 and at the end of February George forwarded his letter from Charles along with Mary Ann's. But by then he had left, forced to hurry back to Jamaica because his public dispute with Judge Henchcliffe was, after four years, about to come to a violent conclusion. According to the newspapers Samuel had sent a report to the commissioners of customs claiming that one of Henchcliffe's rulings was contrary to law and biased towards the commercial interests on the island. The accusation may have arisen from Samuel's research for his book on the laws of the customs, published in 1805.[726] Finally in March 1810 Henchcliffe issued a challenge, and the two men met outside Kingston and fired three shots at each other, without injury on either side. Reports of the duel reached the London newspapers, including the information that Samuel was 'brother-in-law to Mr Canning'. George felt that Samuel had displayed 'impudence and violence of temper', but Richard Thompson, who had regular dealings with the customs in Jamaica, established that Samuel, though not blameless, was substantially in the right. In particular George was relieved to learn that Henchcliffe, not Samuel, had issued the challenge.[727] Within six months, therefore, two of Mary Ann's sons had fought duels and survived.

In the summer of 1810 Frederick was stationed off Spain, where he attracted the attention of Admiral Francis Pickmore,[i] and the admiral's daughter, Emma. George refused to frank letters from Frederick to Emma until he had established that the admiral approved of the attachment. When he learned of Pickmore's reputation both as a sailor and as a pious and conscientious man, he admitted that it spoke well for Frederick to have won such a man's approval. George, as he had predicted when Frederick first entered the navy, was now drawn into the intricacies of Admiralty politics. Pickmore, having promoted Frederick to acting lieutenant, was pressing the Admiralty to confirm the promotion, but when George made enquiries he was told that nothing could be done. He explained the problems to Mary Ann in some detail, but she was encouraged by Frederick and the admiral to think he could have done more if he'd been willing to put himself under an obligation to the First Lord, Charles Yorke, who was not a political ally. The promotion was eventually confirmed the following April, but this did not put an end to the pressure on George, since Admiral

i Francis Pickmore (c.1746–1818): commissioned as lieutenant in 1777, he rose to be vice-admiral in 1812. Governor of Newfoundland from 1816, he was said to have worked himself to death during the severe winter of 1817/18. He was the first governor to spend the winter in Newfoundland, and was remembered for his humanity (*Dictionary of Canadian Biography*).

Pickmore would not allow the marriage until Frederick had been promoted further.[728]

At the end of September 1810 more letters arrived from Charles, written a year earlier. He wrote to Maria, grumbling at the conditions at Chunar, complaining with some justification about the inadequacy of the postal service.[729] His letter to Mary Ann is awkwardly written, straining for effect, and desperately sad. He reminded her of her promise that George would help him, and pointed out that he had heard nothing for eight years. He went on:

> Contentment is an inmate of my mind – reflection is an occasional intruder. But the incertainties of Life, without these proofs of its variegated walk – would be incomplete… I must leave this subject or may excite your displeasure for going beyond the rules I have laid down for my Guidance.…
>
> Oh that Fate woud so dispose of her favors, as to permit me the only blessing I ask of Heaven to bestow upon me this side of the Grave, I mean of being accompanied by my wife and beauteous Babes, to ask the embrace of my revered and truly beloved Parent.[730]

It is difficult to see past these stiff pomposities to the genuine sadness of Charles's situation. The style and content were not calculated to appeal to George. The letter's effect on Mary Ann is harder to guess. Charles was far away; there was nothing she could do for him, except through George. This time George was stirred to action. He replied at once, and also wrote to Lord Minto, the governor-general, describing Charles as 'a relation of mine'.[731]

But by this time Charles, his wife and their son were all dead. Only their daughter, another Mary Ann, survived. The news did not reach London until March 1811, almost nine months after the calamity. 'Poor Charles!' George wrote. 'Cruelly indeed has he expiated all his errors!' He and Joan put on mourning for a day in memory of this brother who was not a brother. Shocked to have lost the chance to make amends to Beatrice for ignoring her original appeal, he set about finding the best way of securing the orphan's future. He gave Mary Ann money to send to Beatrice's sisters. He then arranged for the little girl to be taken into an orphanage for the children of East India Company employees and, through Richard Thompson, established a trust fund. There was, he said, no point sending more money so long as the child was in the orphanage, but a trust fund would accumulate and provide maintenance for her in later life.[732]

What Mary Ann felt, as she contemplated the wrecked life of Charles Reddish, we cannot tell. In the Packet, when she described the circumstances of Charles's birth, she had wondered whether it might have been better if he had not been saved by the bounteous bosom of Mary's Irish nurse. During his early childhood Charles spent much of his time with his aunt and grandmother while Mary Ann was in Plymouth or touring in the North. Then he was at school with Mr Milner. Mary Ann neither defended him against George's criticisms, nor protested against his exile in India. But none of this means that she did not feel his death keenly. Charles had not lived to present his beauteous babes to her, but those words in his letter will have touched her heart. Once again the Embrace of Nature had been withheld. Her first instinct was to have her little namesake sent over to England so she could care for her; George's was to squash any such suggestion.[733] Mary Ann did not insist. George negotiated with Lord Minto on the orphan's behalf, but left detailed arrangements to Richard Thompson, and refused to open a direct correspondence with the aunts in India.

Samuel was sufficiently moved by his brother's death to insert a notice in the *Royal Gazette of Jamaica* recording the disaster that had befallen the family:

> Died – On 6th June 1810, at Chunar, in the Upper Indian Provinces, Capt. Charles Reddish, of the Honourable East-India Company's Native Cavalry – On the 23d of the same month, his infant son, and, on 28th August, on her journey to the Presidency of Calcutta, at the city of Patna, the afflicted wife and mother

> of the beforementioned, of a broken heart, leaving one solitary relict of a family two months before in health and happiness – an infant daughter, to regret the loss of parents, whose affection and protection she is too young to appreciate.[734]

Clearly touched by the fate of his orphaned niece, he hoped that when he eventually returned to settle in London he and Dorothy could give the orphan a home. George pointedly said that the little girl's aunts should not be told of this offer, since it would probably come to nothing. Mary Ann went along with the arrangements made by George, sympathising with him when he showed impatience with the two aunts.[735]

Charles's calamity, so far away and yet so intimate, was bound to affect Mary Ann's spirits, and the loss of yet another of her children made her think of her own death. George caught the note of melancholy in her letters, and wrote: 'Summon me when you want me', which suggests an understanding between them that he would come to her on her deathbed.[736] Grief and anxiety can coexist with all the more trivial concerns of life. Other things came to the surface to occupy her mind for a moment, but it didn't mean the sadness went away.

Some of George's letters at this period show a slight relaxation compared with earlier years. Though always attentive to parliamentary business, he had more time than when in office. He rummaged for pamphlets to send to Aunt Esther, probably for her husband to sell in his bookshop in Cullompton. Joseph Murch still had other interests, and Esther hoped George would support a canal linking Taunton to the River Avon. The bill to approve the proposed navigation was given a second reading on 18 March 1811. George said that he 'virtually' voted for it, because although he couldn't be present for the division himself, he took one of the canal's opponents away with him. Gone was the fury of a few years before when Mary Ann sought to influence his vote on the John Palmer controversy. Indeed, when she mentioned that Palmer's business was to be voted on again in May 1811, George, with none of the indignation he had shown before, gently assured her that though he could not support Palmer he would abstain from voting. Palmer's grievance against the government was not resolved, and when it came up yet again two years later George once more promised to be neutral.[737] He was less constrained as a private member than when he was a member of the government.

The ever active Richard Thompson did most of the work involved in setting up the fund for the Indian orphan, while at the same time preparing himself for a voyage to Jamaica on behalf of the customs service. It was a bad time to go to the Caribbean, with the threat from American privateers added to the usual risks of a sea crossing and a bad climate. During his absence Mary and her children, twin girls, a third daughter and two boys, spent some of the time with Mary Ann, starting with a long summer holiday in Weymouth. Preparations were also going ahead for Maria's marriage to Humphrey Noad, and just before he left the country Thompson undertook to act as trustee of her modest fortune. Noad's business was doing well and he owned a country house at Shawford, not far from Bath. The West Country textile trade was always uncertain, but when George looked into things he noted that Mr Noad was engaged in the more secure side of the business, by which he presumably meant that he was not a manufacturer with a large amount of capital at risk. The marriage took place in Weymouth on 5 October 1811. George wrote a brief message to Maria, and commissioned Mary Ann to buy a wedding present.[738]

27.
Seven Letters, 1812–1814

On her return from Weymouth at the end of 1811, Mary Ann did not go back to New King Street, but after a few weeks in lodgings moved into 13 St James's Parade, half a mile away. The reason for the move is unclear. It may be that with Maria's marriage she needed less space, or wanted more space to accommodate Mary and her children while Richard Thompson was on his West Indian journey. Perhaps St James's Parade was cheaper. Economy was needed. Although George would send an advance whenever the pension was delayed, and often provided small sums for extras such as medicines, so long as he was out of office he could not undertake regular payments. She depended on the pension, and as he admitted towards the end of 1811, rising prices made it difficult for those on fixed incomes. He noted that she had not yet allowed this to curtail her expenditure.[739]

From the years 1812 to 1814, seven of Mary Ann's letters have survived, four to George, two to a friend, and one to the post office in Bath. Most show her bursting with enthusiasm and pride in her son, but in the summer of 1813 we find her still brooding on her old 'disqualification', her exclusion from his family, the contamination that made her unfit to meet his wife and children. These seven letters, though they give some insight into the fluctuation of Mary Ann's thoughts and feelings, are a pitifully small sample. For most of the time we have to see her through the medium of George's weekly offerings.

She now expected George to write every Saturday, to reach her on Sunday, and for several years now he had been referring to 'my Saturday's debt to you' or to keeping 'my Saturday's custom inviolate'. He would apologise if he missed his day, and on his travels he tried to take account of the vagaries of cross posts to ensure that his letter would arrive on Sunday. In October 1813, when he 'missed [his] day', he thought it was the 'first time this century', which was not true, but shows how well established the habit had become.[740]

At the beginning of 1812, encouraged by newspaper speculation, Mary Ann dreamt of George returning to office, but when long awaited government changes were announced Castlereagh was brought in as foreign secretary, and George was left out. He confessed his disenchantment, expressing himself with unusual candour and telling Mary Ann it was for 'her ear only'. She responded by begging him to visit her, sensing perhaps that a withdrawal from public life might bring him closer to her. His reply was stiff and curt, as though regretting his earlier unguardedness. A meeting now was impossible, he said, but perhaps after the parliamentary session he might find time.[741]

In April came a reminder of past conflicts. Something she asked – it's not clear what – touched a raw spot. The answer to her letter, he said, was 'No'. Why must she turn their correspondence into controversy? he asked. Recalling the bitter arguments of the past, he told her not to read anything into this. It didn't mean he was changing towards her, or was refusing to communicate with her, just that the answer was No, and he would not discuss it further. To prove his continued goodwill he promised to send copies of his speeches, warning that they were on the 'dry' question of bullion. In May she was staying at Shawford, and wrote of hearing cuckoos from her window. George at Gloucester Lodge also heard a cuckoo, adding that he had been receiving delegations from

Birmingham and Liverpool which were 'less delightful than the cuckoo at my window and at yours.' He revealed nothing more about these delegations, whose significance would emerge later in the year.[742]

His next letter told of the assassination of the prime minister Spencer Perceval, which was followed by weeks of negotiations to form a new government. George wrote that he would be excluded so long as the 'H. influence' prevailed.[743] According to Mary Ann, in one of her surviving letters,[744] he managed to 'overset the H—d cabal',[i] but nonetheless the upshot of the negotiations was that he declined to enter Lord Liverpool's cabinet because of differences over Catholic emancipation. His refusal on a point of principle thrilled Mary Ann:

> … I must write – tho Heaven knows what! – for my brain absolutely turns round! – Tis not the increase of wealth – or even of Rank and Aggrandisement. – Tis the triumph of Honor – of Virtue – in my darling, that I contemplate with exultation – which only a Mother can feel. – had you ascended the highest pinnacle of power & wealth, by the sacrifice of one Atom of your Character – (which certainly was at Stake in your Decision) – I might have derived, a secondary kind of gratification from the hope that you thought it necessary for the public good – but – you were not born to be excused! – O my glorious Boy! – May this period of time, be ever dear in the annals of your Country! And Ages yet unborn, record your Name with Blessings! – Never was a moment of such magnitude in the History of this trembling Country. – With You and Virtue for her Supporters, She shall stand firm and triumph!

She didn't leave it at that. She went on to lay before George the plight of the poor, who were groaning for 'redress from

i It's not clear what is meant by the 'H. influence' and the 'H—d cabal'. It may be a reference to the enmity of Robert Hobart, Earl of Buckinghamshire, whose surname was pronounced *Hubberd*. Buckinghamshire became president of the Board of Control in Lord Liverpool's cabinet (Hinde, 266).

unnecessary hardships'. She recalled her travels at earlier periods of scarcity, when she had observed the suffering in the countryside. In 1795, 1800 and 1801 her 'intimacy with many different Classes of Society', had convinced her that the scarcity was artificially maintained by the 'inhuman owners' who held the 'monopoly of grain'. It was just the same now, she said. While staying at Shawford she learned that potatoes also were being hoarded, with 'Hundreds of Sacks rotting... whilst the laboring poor cannot purchase those produced for Sale – nor afford the bread for which they woud be a substitute'. Mr Noad was giving his workforce a field to grow their own potatoes. As for a solution, she had once believed that the French Revolutionary policy of imposing maximum prices could be 'modulated to assimilate with English Liberty', but she now understood that in France the *Loi du Maximum* had proved disastrous. Nonetheless she saw the necessity of some sort of control over the market, and suggested a limit on how much grain a farmer could keep in his barns. She recognised the difficulties involved, and believed that George was uniquely capable of resolving them:

> I am told that the freedom of the Subject forbids redress – tis for you – perhaps – Heaven has reserved for your mighty mind, the happy expedient of preserving due regard to freedom – & yet giving to the poor that bread which is withheld, even till it perishes in the granaries...

She addressed this suggestion to George, she said, because 'born for the general good – you cannot be insensible to anything that so materially Affects it.' Recognising that he might not be in a position to do anything about it immediately, she apologised for being 'obtrusive' and suggested that he should 'throw this letter by' for future reference. 'Methinks... that you can Effect anything – and my proud and exulting affection Thirsts for My Hero to claim a nation's thanks.' She ended by saying that she would 'restrain my full heart – from a further overflow', but then added a message to his wife: 'Tell Mrs Canning that I expect her to be as proud as any wife can be – but that she has long to wait, before she can estimate the feelings of a mother who has borne, & cherish'd with her heart's best blood – a son like mine.'

George's first response to this remarkable letter, with its kernel of sound sense embedded in what he must have regarded as exaggerated emotion, was a laconic comment that all was still at sea, and then a day or two later that he had nothing more to tell her.[745] But although he made no answer to her proposal, he did as she suggested: he kept her letter – why, we can only guess. Although such hero worship was not to his taste, he may not have outgrown (few of us do) the pleasure of pleasing his mother.

In July 1812 Mary Ann revisited old haunts in Plymouth and then stayed a month in Cullompton, keeping out of the way while Maria, attended by Mary, was awaiting her first confinement. While in Devonshire she heard from George of a projected visit to Lord Boringdon at Saltram, near Plymouth. He told her it was to redeem a promise made twenty years earlier, but did not add (perhaps he had forgotten) that back then the obstacle to visiting his friend had been her own presence in Plymouth. Since he was still free of the cares of office, he added, he could take his time over the journey, visit Aunt Esther in Cullompton, and stay a day or two in Bath on the way back to London. Mary Ann rushed home to make preparations. She hurriedly 'popped in' on Maria to share the good news with her and Mary, having first made sure that it was not the 'critical moment'. Her immediate response put him on his guard. He replied that the visit would not take place for two months, adding that she should abandon any thought of introducing him at the public Assembly Rooms. He counteracted his sternness by a qualified concession, agreeing to visit Maria at Shawford, and offering to stand godfather to her child, 'if needed'.[746]

The letter Mary Ann wrote in anticipation of this visit has survived, a delightful mixture of simple joy and stiff propriety. 'My Heart's own dear George,' she wrote, 'I never received a letter from your hand that gave me more complete gratification.' She went on to assure him that she had not been proposing to show him off in the Assembly Rooms. There were a handful of friends who would like to meet him, even if only to sit half an hour in his presence. She told him at some length how respectable these friends were, and how fervently they admired him. But pleased though she would be to gratify their wishes, her joy was centred on him. 'Three whole days happiness do you promise me? – oh tis worth living for,' she wrote, before going on to give advice on how he should travel, and which of the many Bath inns he should patronise.[747]

George set off from London towards the end of August, and for the next month Mary Ann could follow his westward progress in letters from Michelmersh in Hampshire, the Isle of Wight, Kingston Hall in Dorset, Mamhead near Exeter, and finally Saltram.[i] It was a long time since he had made such a tour of country houses. As he passed through Sidmouth he recalled that Mary Ann had stayed there the previous summer (it was, in fact, two years before that he had paid for her post-chaise from Cullompton to Sidmouth). He wrote of the prospects for the harvest, the romantic views, and the delight of 'moments of old intercourse'.[748] One might almost have believed that he was thinking of withdrawing from the political race. But George had no wish to become a gentleman of leisure. He wrapped up his account of the romantic delights of the Isle of Wight by saying he had 'seen quite enough'. His comments on the harvest did not signal a conversion to rustic interests, since the quality of the harvest was of prime political importance. He might tell Mary Ann that his visit to Saltram was just the fulfilment of a twenty-year-old promise to an old Christ Church friend, but Boringdon was also the leading spokesman of the Canningites in the House of Lords.

Saltram was the westernmost point of his tour and she could imagine him turning back towards Cullompton and then Bath. But

i George's hosts were an old Eton friend, now a clergyman, and various political allies, including Joan's uncle, Robert Dundas, Chief Baron of Scotland.

from Saltram he wrote warning that his visit might be cancelled. A dissolution of Parliament was likely, and far from abandoning politics he was planning a new departure. The next she heard was when the newspapers reported he was a candidate in Liverpool.

**

Hitherto his elections had been laughable affairs: he would turn up, eat a dinner with the shopkeepers and lawyers of some ancient borough, and in return for this condescension they would obligingly get drunk and vote him in. Liverpool on the other hand involved a real contest. There were some 3,000 electors, and in the course of his campaign George addressed audiences amounting to many times that number. He was accountable to an electorate which, because of the almost accidental way in which the franchise was acquired, included men from many different backgrounds, some with a substantial stake in the local and national economy, but also some small tradesmen and workmen. The voters of Liverpool represented a power in the land, and he would have to understand and defend their interests. It was far from a democratic election, and George was so far from being a democrat that he defended the system under which Manchester was still without parliamentary representation, claiming that as MP for Liverpool he also represented the mercantile and manufacturing interest in other towns, so that the unreformed Parliament could be said to represent 'not only the general interests of the kingdom, but the particular interests of every assignable portion of it'. He told Mary Ann that the position was equivalent to being in office, giving him status and influence beyond the confined world of Westminster, in the wider world of commerce and manufacture. He had to work to earn his votes, and he employed staff in the constituency to deal with things day to day.[749]

George's principal supporters in Liverpool were John Bolton and John Gladstone, a former slave trader and a slave owner. Bolton, for example, who was described in his obituary as an 'ornament of society, a gentleman in mind and manners', was vessel owner on sixty-nine slaving voyages between 1788 and 1807. Both George's fellow Liverpool MP, Isaac Gascoyne, and his predecessor, Banastre Tarleton, firmly opposed abolition. Liverpool MPs as a matter of course defended slavery – Tarleton once pointed to a group of slave owners in the gallery of the House of Commons, and said, 'There, there are my masters!' Henry Brougham, the Whig candidate in 1812, attributed his defeat to his prominence in the campaign for the abolition of the Atlantic slave trade.[i] Despite Canning's known abolitionist position, his supporters played on the fears of voters by distributing inflammatory extracts from Brougham's speeches. Liverpool electors were also traditionally on the Protestant side of the Catholic Question, but George retained the right to vote in accordance with his long-standing views. He soon grew weary of the ultra-Protestants, and refused to attend the annual Pitt dinners (which he had himself inaugurated) because he was disgusted by their anti-Catholic toasts.[750] He was less squeamish about enjoying the hospitality of slave owners.

George's October letters were all from the North, telling Mary Ann about his Liverpool campaign, his election, the triumphant procession round the town, and a succession of 'turtle dinners' with the great men of Liverpool. He returned to London by way of Manchester and Hinckley. There was no prospect of his coming to Bath that year, but he recognised that he remained in her debt for a visit in 1813, and offered himself as an absent godfather to Maria's child.[751] Mary Ann did not reveal the depth of her disappointment.

The last mention of Samuel was his offer to provide a home for Charles's daughter when he returned to England for good, which he hoped to do in 1816. As George had foretold, nothing would come of this gesture. Samuel died in August 1812, the news probably reaching England in the course of the excitement over the cancelled visit and the Liverpool election. By May

---

i Henry Brougham, first Baron Brougham and Vaux (1778–1868) was the leading Whig orator who clashed with George on numerous occasions. Brougham may have exaggerated the effect of his support for Wilberforce's Act (Dixon, 167).

1813 Dorothy Reddish was in London soliciting George's help in sorting out Samuel's disordered affairs. George approved of Dorothy; her letters were 'gentlewomanlike' and 'interesting', but probably what he most approved of was that she had a prosperous family in Barbados, and was going back to them. Samuel may have found some sort of contentment in the West Indies, but his life was unruly: in addition to his quarrel and duel with Judge Henchcliffe, in 1811 he faced two suits for defamation, with damages of £400 and £2,000 awarded against him. After the birth of his and Dorothy's daughter he fathered a number of bastards.[752] Neglected as a child, always coming second to his elder brother, he was forced into the army, exiled for years in Australia, and then sent off to an uncongenial job in an unhealthy climate. He was well enough educated at Milner's school for George to think him capable of writing about his experiences in Australia, and he did in fact produce his book on the laws of the customs service in the West Indies. He may well have felt that life had cheated him. We can hope, at least, that he achieved his schoolboy ambition of learning to dance.

George did not wear mourning, even for a day. Poor Samuel, did anyone really mourn him? His wife, perhaps, or was she only afraid his death might make the great Mr Canning withdraw his favour from her brother Nathan? His mistress back in Jamaica? His sister Mary? His mother? We don't know what Mary Ann felt at the loss of the oldest and most assertive of her player's brats. Perhaps her mind went back to the chaotic household in Bloomsbury, her mother quarrelling with Reddish, little Samuel's nurse protesting loudly, money short, Esther bringing stories of hostility in Clements Lane, trouble at the theatre. Perhaps she counted up the deaths. Six out of twelve had been lost in infancy or childhood. Now Charles and Samuel had died in what should have been their prime. Just four left: Mary, Maria, Frederick – and George. The loss of infants or young children was agonising; the loss of a grown-up son, seen only briefly at long intervals, who died far away, almost a stranger, is more likely to have evoked melancholy recollection. Had she expressed more violent grief George would probably have said something in his replies to comfort her. As it is, there is nothing.

The varied duties of the MP for Liverpool, and anxiety over his wife's expected confinement, meant George found no time to write to Mary Ann between 9 November 1812, when he gave his promise to visit her in 1813, and the start of the new year. In January he reported the birth of a fourth child, a healthy boy who 'sucks and thrives'. Two days later he heard that Richard Thompson's ship had reached England, and hurried to inform Mary Ann and Mary that the perils of the voyage were over.[753]By February Richard Thompson was out of quarantine and had joined Mary and the children in Bath. They were all ill, with Mary Ann looking after them. George wrote kindly, sending £50 to cover extra expenses. His daughter Harriet suffered a serious illness at about the same time, and as sometimes happened ill health provided common ground, prompting Joan to send Mary Ann her 'best good wishes'.[754]

Almost at once Richard was involved in George's efforts on behalf of Frederick, whose marriage to the admiral's daughter was still awaiting his promotion. Frederick expected Mary Ann to press George over it, and she had to put up with George's irritation at being pressed. From his experience of the workings of the Admiralty, Richard pointed out various obstacles, prompting George to exclaim that 'Mr T is so much more dextrous at raising than at smoothing difficulties'. Mary Ann sided with George in this disagreement. In the event George was glad of the delays because it was hard to find exactly the right moment to contact the Admiralty. In March, for instance, it seemed an opportune moment to approach the new First Lord, the second Viscount Melville, son of Henry Dundas and cousin of Joan's mother. Just two months later Melville's embarrassments over the failures of the American war meant George could not 'decently' ask for a personal favour.[755]

In May 1813, before going on to Exeter and Cullompton, Mary Ann spent a week or two at Shawford, where there was a delay in receiving her letters and newspapers. She complained at the post office, but the clerk did not take her complaint seriously. Stung by the man's insolence, she directed a fierce rebuke to the senior person in the post office in Bath. 'I consider,' she told him, 'attention to your office as a very important duty which you owe to the public and to me as an Individual.' She had a regular letter from Mr Canning, she said, every Sunday, and it should have been redirected to Shawford. A copy of her letter of complaint has survived, and it reads like the work of a regular complainer, a trimmer of shopkeepers and public servants, someone with a strong sense of her own worth.[756]

At Shawford a disagreement arose between Richard Thompson and Humphrey Noad. Noad, whose caution had impressed George, now planned to branch out into a riskier side of the textile trade. This may be the point at which he entered the dyeing business.[757] To finance his new mill he wanted to use Maria's fortune as security. Richard, as Maria's trustee, refused, and George strongly supported him. Humphrey commented that other members of the family used their wife's fortune for their own purposes, an obvious thrust at George. The situation was tense enough for Richard to ask to be relieved of the trusteeship. Mary Ann took Humphrey's side, perhaps because he was now the son-in-law she had most contact with, and perhaps because both the technical and commercial sides of the enterprise appealed to her imagination.[758] The daughter of Jordan Costello would not shy away from a gamble, and the business may have stirred memories of Henry Smith in Dublin, with his secret process for dyeing mohair.

At the beginning of 1813 George had been trying to secure promotion for Samuel's brother-in-law, Nathan Ashby, and when he failed it made him wonder whether he'd been right to refuse Lord Liverpool's offer of office. It was all very well enjoying the new experience of working for his constituents, but out of government he was of no use to his friends. He wondered, as others did, whether he had refused out of pride, but concluded that no, it was better to 'do what is right, and leave the rest to heaven'. His disenchantment with the uncertainties of public life was partly due to his money problems. He lived as a rich man amongst the rich, and people expected him to have enough to spare for subscriptions and charities, but, as he remarked ruefully in a letter to Mary Ann in Cullompton, 'a man may be very notorious, and yet very poor.' He was looking forward to the end of the session. The next Saturday would, he wrote in July, be the last parliamentary Saturday. The phrase must have stuck in his mind over the next few days. Knowing how minutely Mary Ann weighed every word, and how quick she was to jump to dramatic conclusions, he assured her a few days later that he meant it was the last Saturday of the session, not the last of his career.[759]

The end of the session brought no relief from parliamentary labours. Three weeks later he was still wading through his Liverpool correspondence. Things were not made easier by having his wife and family permanently in Hinckley. Little Georgey was not improving. Mary Ann advised taking him away from Dr Chessher's establishment, and reuniting the family at Gloucester Lodge. George could see the attraction of this, but said it was complicated. Even if he was getting no better, Georgey enjoyed the freedom at Hinckley to wander around without attracting attention.[760]

Mary Ann too was in melancholy mood. George planned another journey into the West, which he hoped would include a visit to Bath, but when Mary Ann received this news at Cullompton, she responded with none of the enthusiasm of the previous year, enthusiasm which had ended in disappointment. Her response[761] was full of thoughts of death, thanking him for his 'plan of operations', which enabled her to travel with him 'in Idea' – but her imagination conjured up not the joy of having him with her in Bath, but the joy of being united with him 'in a blissfull scene, purified from all disqualifications – and [travelling] on together thro Eternity'. As for his immediate plans, she pointedly wrote that she left 'their accomplishment to Heaven and you'. She longed to be at home, lonely and uncomfortable though that home was, she said. Esther wasn't well enough to accompany her, but intended to visit the following May. Mary Ann doubted whether the intention would be realised, but admitted that it was as likely as any plan which 'serves to amuse the Children of Sorrow and lighten the pressure of present calamity – and so far, the illusion is desirable.'

Mary Ann felt her proper place was with George, among the rich and powerful, not in the dreary provincial surroundings to which she was confined. Attached though she was to her sister, when she stayed in Cullompton she may well have reflected that the Murches were small town shopkeepers – the destiny that she herself rejected all those years ago. It might be tempting to conclude that her unhappiness came down to little more than thwarted pride. There is, moreover, a touch of the melodramatic in her style, and because most of her letters are known only through George's often ironical responses, it is easy not to take her moods seriously. But this letter shows the depth of her depression.

Then, calling on her old resilience, she turned from these thoughts to mention two interesting discoveries the sisters had made amongst Esther's belongings. First there was an etching of Melchior Guy-Dickens which she had believed lost, and then there was something that helped clear up the mystery of her date of birth. She doesn't say what this new evidence was, but it was enough to incline her to believe that she was twenty-one rather than eighteen at the time of her marriage. The discovery that she was three years older than she'd believed was, she said, of no consequence. 'I meet it without any of that regret which many old people woud do – who do not hail Death as a Deliverer.'

George had instructed her not to tell Maria of his proposed visit. She agreed, but warned him to remove his 'injunction' in time to prevent surprise, since Maria would be upset if she had no time to prepare her house for her distinguished visitor. 'I trust to both your Heart and your Head that you will not rob a kind act of its most gracious feature by doing it ungraciously… – My George was born – and formed by God and Nature – to scatter roses – without thorns.' But her devotion never blinded her to George's faults or prevented her from rebuking him; she proceeded to elaborate on what she regarded as his lack of social graces. She hoped that by throwing him into contact with his social inferiors, his Liverpool experience would 'have the effects of blunting – or rather of filing down the sharp angles – of – what shall I call it – my best beloved? – of conscious superiority, which form a Hedge of partition between him who feels – and those who see that he does feel it.' She would have agreed with the advice given by Hester Stanhope.

On reflection she decided that this letter was too pessimistic to send,[762] but what she wrote instead was still gloomy enough to make him anxious. There was a delay before he heard again from her, and not realising it was due to a brief stay in Taunton on her way home (perhaps to visit the grave of her daughter Ann), he begged her to write soon. He tried to cheer her up with upbeat accounts of his sea-bathing, and a discussion of inoculation, always a favourite topic. He also sent money for 'furnishing'. She had complained that her house in St James's Parade lacked comforts, and he paid for a mirror, and told her to buy a coffee pot, for which he would reimburse her.[763]

In August Mary Ann ran into Fanny Canning, George's unmarried aunt, who was visiting Bath. Fanny was, he agreed, bearing her years well. He was quite relaxed about this meeting, in contrast with his anxiety in the past to keep Mary Ann well away from the Cannings. Fanny, who knew George from the days when he used to visit the Leighs, was easy going, and like all the Canning women accustomed to softening the obduracy of the men. Mary Ann, warmed by George's willingness in this case to overlook her disqualification, hoped to elicit a further sign:

she wondered whether, in choosing the name Charles for his son, George had been thinking of her own poor Charles Reddish. She was unable to resist the temptation to probe discreetly. George replied disappointingly that the baby was named after Charles Ellis. 'There were none of our relations that we were particularly anxious to call in,' he wrote.[764]

After a holiday with Charles Ellis at Seaford, Joan and the children went back to Hinckley, while George spent a few days in London before setting off on his westward tour. While staying with a parliamentary supporter, John 'Dog' Dent,[i] in Christchurch he spent a day with his aunt Bess Leigh, who lived nearby. Since her husband's death and the divorce of her eldest daughter Tish, Bess had been living quietly. She was not well off, and had another daughter about to be married. Mary Ann had never felt as bitter towards Bess as towards Mehitabel, but she could hardly have forgotten that while she was struggling and suffering in Bury, Newcastle and Bristol, Bess had enjoyed George's company and confidence, and had watched over his first steps in the world. Mary Ann did not know it, but Mehitabel too resented Bess Leigh's intimacy with George.[765]

George wrote several times to make and re-make the arrangements for his visit to Bath. If Mary Ann wanted him to meet her friends it had to be on the last day of his stay (so he could not be pressed to accept any invitations) and she should provide the company with some occupation, such as cards, so there would be no awkward standing about. As though answering the accusation in the letter she had not sent, he admitted he had no 'common talk' and was afraid of being thought proud. Above all she should not tell the local newspapers. Three times he changed the projected date and time of his arrival. He didn't want to stay a night at Shawford, possibly because of the recent disagreement over Maria's settlement, but then changed his mind. The visit when it came failed to raise her spirits; more than ten days after

i John Dent (1761–1826): MP and director of Child & Co.'s bank. He was known as 'Dog' because he greatly disliked dogs and proposed a tax on them.

he left her he wrote anxiously saying that he had not yet heard from her.[766]

Events in the autumn and winter did little to cheer Mary Ann. Her hopes that George would return to office were disappointed. The hard-won victory of Britain's continental allies at Leipzig[i] vindicated the policies he had promoted as foreign secretary, he claimed, but would do nothing for his prospects, because Lord Liverpool would be too secure to need his support.[767] When Mary Ann's old friend Dr Gashing was travelling north he proposed calling on George, as though their having recently met at Mary Ann's house had established an acquaintance between them – the sort of consequence that George dreaded. He told Mary Ann to put a stop to the idea.[768] He came to London in November for the wedding of Bess Leigh's daughter Frances to Lord Berriedale, heir to the Earl of Caithness. He had warned Mary that on this visit he would not have time to call on her, but in the event he went to the Thompsons' new house in Hampstead, where they hoped the air would be more salubrious than in Kennington. There he met Samuel's widow, and was annoyed to learn that Mary Ann had told her that he had been unwell: he wanted to know how Mary Ann herself had found out.[769] He feared anything that encouraged familiarity and threatened to draw him into Mary Ann's family web.

George spent the Christmas of 1813 at Crewe Hall. It was twenty years since he had been there; the world had seen great revolutions in those years, he told Mary Ann, but the famous Crewe hospitality had not changed. He may have forgotten the circumstances under which he had turned down his first invitation to Crewe, but Mary Ann certainly remembered that the famous Crewe hospitality had not extended to sponsoring her benefit night. In the new year George went from Crewe to Liverpool, where he could not get over the enthusiasm of his supporters. Mary Ann had sent him a letter to be franked and forwarded to

i Napoleon's defeat in the so-called 'battle of the nations' (16–19 October 1813) led to his retreat from Germany.

Mr Tregent, who was stationed in Liverpool, and must have been surprised, and pleased, when George replied that he would deliver it by hand. In London George would not willingly have gone in search of a barrack-master to hand over a letter from his mother, but in Liverpool he felt less constrained.[770]

In the new year there was a renewed bout of politicking over Frederick's promotion. Frederick, aboard the *Royal George* in the Mediterranean, grumbled to Mary Ann and his sister Maria about the delays. His letters evidently contained complaints that George was not doing enough to help, and accusations, encouraged by Admiral Pickmore, against Lord Melville. George was embarrassed by Frederick's demands and the admiral's interference, which forced him to contact Melville, at a time when it was particularly awkward because, he told Mary Ann, the newspapers were suggesting that he might succeed Melville at the Admiralty. Mary Ann, taking George's side, replied angrily to Frederick, accusing him of having written while inebriated. Maria told him that his case was causing trouble for George, and making their mother unhappy. Frederick replied to Mary Ann, denying the charge of drunkenness, but unable to say anything about the many other 'distressing subjects' in her letter. He told her to stop pressing George to act, since it was making her uneasy.[771] George, however, pursued the matter for months more, not for Frederick's sake, but out of irritation with Lord Melville, and because Frederick's promotion and respectable marriage would be to Mary Ann's advantage.

Eventually, in July 1814, Melville gave a verbal assurance that the promotion would be accomplished, although Frederick was still complaining about delays at the end of August. When the promotion came through, Frederick wrote to thank George for his 'great and friendly exertions' on his behalf. George, who was on a visit to his Liverpool supporters, didn't want to write to Mary Ann in the middle of the week, but on the other hand he didn't want Frederick's letter lying around in his letter case. His first thought was to throw it on the fire, but instead he sent it on to Mary Ann. Later he congratulated Frederick, through Mary Ann, on his 'ultimate though tardy and difficult success'. With his promotion secure, even though he was without a ship, Frederick and Emma were at last married at St Martin's in the Fields on 15 October 1814.[772]

Meanwhile Mary Ann was having money problems. By the beginning of February 1814, less than halfway through the quarter, she needed an advance on the next instalment of the pension, and rather than have her dependent on an advance from Richard Thompson, George sent her £50. In addition she and her elderly servant Dennis were finding it hard to manage the house, so he promised to find £50 more to pay for an extra maid. He didn't have the money to hand, but would send it before the end of April; in the event he sent it at the end of March. Dennis was first mentioned by name in George's letters at the beginning of 1811, when he paid for medicine when she was ill, but from now on she will appear now and then. This may be a sign that as Mary Ann grew older her social life was beginning to contract, throwing her more into the company of her servant. She may already have started borrowing small sums from Dennis's savings. For some time past, and for months to come, Esther was ill, and staying in Bath to be close to medical advice. George, always through Mary Ann, never directly, sent money for her doctor's bills and in almost every letter he asked after his aunt and hoped for better news. 'I charge you, let me know when pecuniary assistance is wanting or will be welcome to her,' he wrote in May.[773]

In the first few months of 1814 there was a misunderstanding about a Christmas gift, probably something purchased at a Fancy Fair, that Mary Ann had sent to Gloucester Lodge. The servants failed to forward it to Hinckley. Since George had said nothing about it by mid-January she asked if it had arrived. He couldn't make out what it was she was asking about – a pair of guards, it looked like, or was it gloves? Several weeks passed and he didn't answer until he was on his way to London, when he said he would look for them at Gloucester Lodge. And there, on 23 April, he reported finding them, referring to them as 'comforters' and saying they would be useful next winter.[774]

In spite of everything, the trouble over Frederick, the uncomfortable and unmanageable house, her sister's illness and the money problems, Mary Ann's spirits seem to have risen slowly in the course of the spring. She was in touch with an old friend, Isaac Weld, brother of Stratty's friend and business associate Dick Weld. In his old age Isaac had married for a second time. His wife Lucy, who had recently given birth to a son, had evidently heard from her husband something of Mary Ann's past and expressed interest in learning more. Mary Ann asked George if he remembered the Welds. He didn't recall Isaac, he replied, but remembered Richard in Clements Lane and since. He remembered liking him. In all the two thousand or so letters that George wrote to his mother this is the only reference to his childhood in Clements Lane: that he liked Dick Weld. He was too young to remember the incident of the fish trowel, but no doubt there were later occasions when Dick was a good-natured presence at Mehitabel's dinner table. In the 1790s Dick was involved in the agitation for Reform (he died of apoplexy in the Tower of London while dining with a fellow activist who was imprisoned there) and George may have come across him then. They are unlikely to have discussed Mary Ann, although Dick could have told George the precise circumstances in which she took the decision to go on the stage, including the part played by Mehitabel. Memories of kind-hearted Dick Weld may account for the particular warmth of his letter – or it may have been due to its being Good Friday, or to the warmth of April after the bitterly cold winter. 'Heavenly weather,' he said, in an unusually expansive phrase. He hoped it would renovate her strength, but warned that sunshine was no substitute for her daily glass of Madeira.[775]

In June, after a placid few weeks in which George had hinted that he and Joan were planning, now that the war was over, to take Georgey and the rest of the family to the south of Europe, a complicated misunderstanding arose. George went to Oxford on 14 June, along with everyone else of importance, when the Prince Regent, the King of Prussia and the Emperor of Russia visited the university as part of the (premature) celebrations of victory over Napoleon. The royal and imperial parties returned to London the following morning, but George stayed on to receive the degree of Doctor of Laws. His Saturday letter to Mary Ann was dated from Oxford on 18 June. He planned to send it by direct post to Bath, and therefore did not include it with the bulk of his correspondence, which went to London. Unfortunately, he forgot to post it until two days later, Monday, by which time he was in Ryde on the Isle of Wight. He wrote again, the same day, from Ryde, enclosing £5 for Esther's medical expenses.[776] Both letters arrived at the same time. He did not write again on the Friday for her to receive her Sunday assurance that he was well.

When she had no letter on the 26th, knowing that he had had to make a sea-crossing from the Isle of Wight, and having also seen a newspaper report of Mr Canning in Calais, she didn't know what to think, particularly after the recent references to a voyage to the South. She complained not only that George had missed a letter, but that he had not told her in advance when he was to cross the sea. Irritated by her complaints, and perhaps thinking she might have shown more gratitude for the money, George, now back in London, replied at once. He had not missed a week, he said, because his letter of 20th enclosing the £5 note had fulfilled his weekly obligation to assure her he was well. There was, he said, no point in writing again to say he had 'continued well from Wednesday to Friday'. He had returned from the seaside by land, as most people do, he added sarcastically, although naturally he had been obliged to cross the sea from the Isle of Wight. 'How could you be so very – I will not add the epithet?' he asked. As for the Mr Canning at Calais, it was his cousin Stratford, on his way to take up his position as plenipotentiary to the Swiss Cantons.[777]

Since she had obliged him to write in the middle of the week, he made up his mind not to write again on the coming Saturday. But when Saturday came, he relented. The newspapers were reporting that he would be absent for a year or more, which forced him to tell Mary Ann something of his plans. He told her the journey was for Georgey's health, and assured her that he would inform her before he went. In his next letter (written two days later) he further conceded that in his hasty and sarcastic reply of 29 June he should have said 'from Monday to Friday' rather than Wednesday to Friday, although he didn't admit that this change weakened the force of his argument. He wrote again two days after this, asking her crossly, and unfairly, why she trusted the newspapers and imagined that they knew more about his family affairs than she did. To soften this acerbity he sent her some eulogistic comments from his supporters in Liverpool. This letter was sent on a Wednesday, and he told her firmly not to expect another that week, but once again he relented and wrote again, with positive news for Frederick.[778]

This exchange illustrates how closely they still scrutinised each other's letters, weighing every word just as during their fiercest battles, and how quick they were both to take offence, and to be reconciled. At the same time as she and George were irritating each other over this misunderstanding Mary Ann wrote the first of two surviving letters to a friend, probably Lucy Weld:

> … I often reflect with wonder on the variegated lots of human kind! Some pass their entire lives in a voyage on a smooth and temperate surface, whose tranquility neither joy nor sorrow, want nor abundance, the felicity of friendship nor the corrosion of enmity, disturb; whilst others, born in a tempest, go on through storms and hurricanes, tost by elements over which they have no control, until they are either shipwrecked finally on the rocks of unrelenting adversity, or landed, perhaps, when they least expect it, on a friendly shore. Of the latter class—and I trust there are

> many—it has pleased the Great Dispenser of Events to make the being you are pleased to think kindly of an eminent example.
>
> The first twenty years of my life was almost an uninterrupted scene of suffering. At twenty-three I was left a widow and my son an orphan… But my trust was in God, and nobly has His bounteous mercy justified my confidence in Him. For in that orphan boy He has given me every argument to soothe my sorrow, to justify my maternal pride, to rescue my age from adversity, and to crown my gray hairs with glory.

The unsent letter of 1813 shows that she still felt the weight of her 'disqualification', but such thoughts had no place in the enthusiastic declaration with which he ended her letter to her friend:

> … For forty years and more he has been my blessing—my pride—my guardian angel, and when I run up the account of a most eventful life I find the balance of good predominate, for George Canning is my son.[779]

By the end of July 1814 the newspapers were reporting that the journey to the South was not a private visit. After trying and failing to bring George back into the cabinet, Lord Liverpool appointed him ambassador to Lisbon, to meet the Prince Regent of Portugal on his expected return from exile in South America. George accepted the appointment, both because it might lead to a political comeback, and because he hoped it would benefit Georgey, while he and Joan could resume their interrupted family life. In view of their misunderstandings in June, when Mary Ann had accused him of deceiving her, it was unfortunate that now George was obliged to deceive her in order to control the release of information about the embassy. There was, however, one newspaper report he could truthfully deny. She had commented disapprovingly on reports that he was about to be awarded the 'red ribband' of a Knight of the Bath. He told her that she need be under no apprehension about this, since he felt exactly as she did about it. 'I get honours for others,' he wrote, thinking of new peerages procured for his friends Leveson-Gower and Boringdon, 'I want them not myself.'[780]

It was not until the end of August that Mary Ann received confirmation that George intended to visit her before leaving the country. He was about to go north to his constituency, he said, but afterwards he would spend three days in Bath, later reduced to two. By now Mary Ann was used to his stream of letters making and re-making his arrangements, and laying down what he would tolerate in the way of company. 'Pray, pray, no strangers,' he wrote, 'and pray pray pray no intimation to Mayor or Aldermen.'[781]

Mary Ann was in complete agreement. 'Fear not my best beloved,' she replied in the last of her surviving letters to George, 'Nor "Mayor nor Alderman" shall break in upon the sacred circle.' The Noads would come to Bath to meet him on the first day of his visit, but then go back home, taking Frederick with them. If Esther was well enough she would come up from Cullompton, but retire to Shawford after she had enjoyed her 'last look at the Being who from infancy to manhood has possessed her tenderest affection.' Whatever happened, Mary Ann said, she herself was determined on 'one days sacred Tete a' Tete – that done – my business with Life is over!' She said this not out of despondency; she didn't want George to suppose she was sinking back into the gloom of the previous year. She would not distress him with 'a weak mother's fondness,' she said. 'I will remember that I am your mother – and with his support in whom I have forever trusted – I hope – act accordingly.' Fourteen years earlier George's marriage had thrown her into a strange, depressed state of mind: 'I feel,' she wrote then, 'as I shoud if you had gone on a long Embassy – and I was – an Old Woman.' Now that he really was going on a long embassy her spirits were more buoyant. She begged him to visit the family in Hampstead. Mary was showing increasing symptoms of the disease that was to cripple her in later years, and Mary Ann said that next to God's blessing a visit from her brother George was the best support she could hope for. Anxiety over a chronically disabled child was a point of sympathy between Mary Ann and George. 'God prosper all your endeavours for the dear object of your constant and unparalleled Paternal care,' she wrote.[782]

After the usual last-minute rearrangements, George arrived in Bath on Tuesday 27 September, promising to stay until the Thursday. The first day, he dined with Joan's uncle, Robert Dundas and not only mentioned Mary Ann but actually encouraged him to visit her, probably in order to ensure some protection within the family for Mary Ann during his absence. Conscious that he might never see her again, George seems to have risen to the occasion. He stayed on until Friday, giving her after all a third day, prolonging his time with her, she felt, out of affection. This was all she wanted from him: unforced, spontaneous affection. Those extra hours they spent together, she told a friend (again, probably Lucy Weld), were 'the bonne bouche of life'.[783]

She went on to explain that the Lisbon journey was originally planned for the sake of Georgey's health, with the ambassadorship an afterthought – an honour, which she feared would lengthen the time George would spend in Lisbon.

> To say that I do not feel a kind of exaltation mingled with chastened pleasure would be to affect a degree of indifference foreign to my nature. I am proud of my son, proud of those distinctions which are due to his virtues and abilities united. In a private capacity he would not, in all probability, be more than a year absent; but as a public character of such high importance, who can calculate on the duration of his absence! It is more than mere philosophy can bear without wincing; but there is a power to whom I look for constancy, resignation and submission.

Foreseeing the melancholy that would threaten her when she had said goodbye, she had asked George for a large supply of franks. These would have to be used before he left the country, forcing her, she told her friend, to 'combat sorrow by doing duty'.

28.
The Lisbon Interlude, 1814–1816

Preparations for the voyage to Lisbon took another six weeks, during which the baby, Carlo, got over the effects of inoculation, and Georgey recuperated after the journey from Hinckley. 'Farewell, my dear Mother!' George wrote on 6 November from his cabin on the *Leviathan*, in Portsmouth. Finding that all his banknotes had gone he enclosed a bill for £50 that he said Mr Thompson would change for her. Held up by storms and contrary winds off Portland, *Leviathan* was visited by Princess Charlotte, who had been enjoying the benefits of sea bathing. Six days out of Portsmouth they had reached no further than Plymouth. When the ship took shelter inside the breakwater George thought of taking his family ashore and sitting out the storms at Saltram, but was advised that they would have to undergo all the qualms of their first days at sea a second time. It was not until 21 November that a north wind enabled *Leviathan* to get on its way.[784]

Finding a rumour going around that *Leviathan* had been blown up by a lightning strike, he hastened to reassure Mary Ann that they had arrived safely, in case the story had reached England. He didn't tell her about the princess's visit, probably because he wasn't sufficiently interested in it himself, and knew Mary Ann was no admirer of the royal family. Nor did he mention that his cousin Harry Canning had come to see them off from Portsmouth and had remained on board until Plymouth. But he told her about his attack of gout, because it was bound to get into the newspapers that he had been unable to present his credentials to the Portuguese government. He referred to it as a 'respectable complaint' and offered two explanations. First, he had not been seasick, and so had not 'thrown off the bile'; and secondly he had been tempted to leave off his flannel under-waistcoat. The weather in Lisbon, he said, was fine but treacherous. The newspapers reported heavy rain. When the family eventually came ashore their accommodation was cold, and there were no coal fires. Things were better when they moved into the former residence of the Duke of Wellington, which had been fitted up with stoves.[785]

During the eighteen months in Lisbon George spent more time with his family than at any other period, and his letters include little glimpses of home life, such as the children's excitement at the wild weather and rough sea, and their disappointment at sleeping through a minor earthquake. Mary Ann kept up her usual flow of questions and requests, and found it hard to adjust to the irregularity of their correspondence. She kept a log of letters sent and received[786] and they adopted the diplomatic practice of numbering their letters so that losses and delays would be apparent. George tried to forestall any anxiety that might arise from newspaper reports of his state of health or the state of politics. When she worried over apparent delays, he told her in irritation to check her newspaper to find out when the mail from Lisbon was due: 'Not to believe anything about me that you do not hear from me – and not to expect letters from me when there are no mails from Lisbon, are the two great secrets for keeping your mind quiet,' he wrote. Another annoyance was that when he said that the family were all in good health she would ask eagerly if that meant little Georgey's condition was improving, and it was disheartening to have to record that there was never any improvement, even though the boy's general health benefited from the climate of Lisbon.[787]

Now that he once more had an official salary, George undertook to supplement the pension with an annual allowance of £200, sending the first half-year's instalment in February. Because it was sent through his agent, Mr Heaton, Mary Ann would have to send a receipt, and he imagined her writing in her usual effusive manner, so he warned her to be dry and businesslike. Heaton, he said, 'is a mere man of business, and will file whatever you write to him in his office – and there is something ludicrous and painful in being filed with effusions of tenderness under one's hand.'[788]

George's horror of displays of feeling gave rise, a few weeks later, to an extraordinary outburst, exhibiting an extreme sensitivity, moral squeamishness and hypocrisy.[789] In addition to his official staff, he had brought with him a young man called John Young, then studying at Brasenose College, Oxford to act as private secretary and tutor to the children. Young was illegitimate. His father, 'Dog' Dent, was married and had cast off his mistress, but had taken their son into his family and brought him up along with his legitimate offspring. George employed him as an act of kindness both to Dent, who not only supported George in Parliament but had lent him a substantial sum of money,[790] and to the boy – he understood the difficulties faced by young men with a shadow on their birth.[i] Although he knew all about Young's birth, and Young knew that he knew, they never spoke of it. It happened that Young's mother, now married, was living with her husband in Bath, where she became friendly with Mary Ann. Naturally Mary Ann was intrigued to learn that her friend's son was employed by George. The friend, who is known only as Mrs G, had difficulty communicating with her son, difficulty that Mary Ann knew all about, since but for George's help she would have struggled to get letters through to Sam and Charles. She therefore suggested that when she next wrote to George in Lisbon she should enclose a letter from Mrs G to young John. Mrs G was pleased to take up this offer.

---

i Another of George's private secretaries, Augustus Stapleton, was believed to be the illegitimate son of George's friend Lord Boringdon, Earl of Morley (George to John Frere, Jan. 1825 (Festing, 265)).

Mary Ann was unprepared for the fury that this act of kindness provoked. George was angry both on his own account and on hers. For himself, he was embarrassed because it meant that Young would know that their mothers were friends, which would bring into the open the fact of his illegitimate birth. George felt he could hardly look Young in the eye with this knowledge between them. He said he feared it would be embarrassing for Young, but what really made the situation intolerable was that it introduced an unwelcome equality between his employee and himself: each of them had a mother whose character had been compromised. Mrs G, he said, was no doubt highly respectable now, a good wife to Mr G, but nonetheless she had borne this illegitimate child, and nothing could efface that fact. This made her an unsuitable friend for Mary Ann, whose own reputation in Bath was vulnerable. It was foolhardy to court attention by consorting with someone like Mrs G, who was, he said, as notorious as Mrs Robinson, the Prince Regent's 'Perdita', had been thirty years earlier, because Dent was incurably garrulous and quite open about his past connection with her.

George tried to base his objection on the impossibility of resisting the weight of public opinion against illegitimacy, but Mary Ann can hardly have missed the note of disdain that showed that he shared the public prejudice. The young man was, he wrote, 'as kind and dutiful to [his mother] as if she had come honestly by him'. It was a common enough phrase, which he probably used without considering what it revealed about his attitude to her and her Reddish children. Everything he wrote about Mrs G not being fit company cruelly underlined Mary Ann's disqualification. It's not known how she reacted. She could have pointed out that George found Dog Dent perfectly acceptable as a friend and colleague, but she may not have felt comfortable with what is, to us, the natural riposte. It was twenty years since her enthusiastic reading of Mary Wollstonecraft; she may well have believed still in a single moral code for both men and women, and still insisted that women's virtue did not begin and end with chastity, but if she pressed this point, George passed over it in silence; nothing more was said until, a month later, Mrs G left Bath, when George concluded 'all is well'. There is no further mention of her, which probably means that if Mary Ann continued to correspond in years to come she did not send the letters to George for franking. We must hope that Mary Ann was not cowed into ending the friendship. John Young remained with the Cannings for the best part of a year, taking Georgey and William to a spa in the mountains during the summer. George wrote warmly to Dent, praising the young man's conduct, particularly his kindness towards the two boys.[791]

In the summer of 1815 Mary Ann visited London. She stayed first with the Thompsons, who were back in Kennington. Richard Thompson's health had broken down following his trip to the West Indies, leaving him unable to work. He continued to receive his salary, but feared he would be pensioned off, and hoped George would find him a place on the Board of Customs. George repeatedly said he was sorry for him, and for Mary, but could do nothing beyond sending his love and presents for Mary Ann to distribute.[792]

Mary Ann then went on to Emma and Frederick in Eltham, where she may have coincided with Emma's father, the admiral.[793] Frederick was to remain without a command until he was appointed to the *Redwing* four years later, and may have had recourse to the coastal trade while waiting. His father-in-law encouraged him to believe that George could help, which led Frederick and Emma to lobby him without let-up. Frederick was never satisfied – when he eventually took command of the *Redwing* in August 1818 he complained that he was not given the rank of post-captain to go with it.[794]

After Waterloo, and the refusal of the Portuguese Prince Regent to come home, George's role in Lisbon came to an end. He became, he said, a private gentleman at the beginning of October 1815, but would remain until the following spring, to avoid an English winter. Meanwhile in London there were new rumours that he would be called back into the Cabinet. In the years before the embassy, Lord Liverpool's attempts to reshuffle his administration to make room for George had been frustrated by colleagues' reluctance to relinquish their positions. One of those who had refused to cooperate was Robert Hobart, Earl of Buckinghamshire, president of the Board of Control, and no friend to Canning. In February 1816, while the Cannings were preparing to leave Lisbon, the earl died following a riding accident, and Liverpool offered his place to George. It was the most junior post in the cabinet, below what he might have had if he had joined in 1812, but he accepted it gratefully. Perhaps because his name was so much in the public eye, several gentlemen in Bath presented themselves to Mary Ann as old school friends of Mr Canning, at least one of whom seems to have been an impostor. George warned her to beware of such people; there were, he said, 'a thousand little maliciousnesses in the world, more than you dream of'.[795]

It was the middle of April 1816 before the family left Lisbon. The frigate carrying them stopped at Bordeaux long enough for George to settle his family there, and to address the English merchants as they resumed normal commercial life after the war. He then continued his journey, landing at Plymouth and going at once to stay with Lord Boringdon, now Earl of Morley, at Saltram. He wrote to reassure Mary Ann that he was safe. He arrived at Saltram on Sunday, and intended to call on her in Bath on his way to Liverpool. He told her firmly not to write to him, and made sure she complied by not posting his letter until Monday, when it was accompanied by another informing her that he would be with her for a late dinner on Wednesday, so that any reply would not reach Saltram until after he had left. On Tuesday he wrote that he needed an extra day for his accumulation of correspondence and so would not be with her until Thursday. Probably he had intended all along to arrive on Thursday, and had said Wednesday merely to ensure she obeyed his underlined injunction not to write to Saltram. He removed any need to communicate further by telling her what to lay on for his late dinner: 'Beefsteak, fish and Madeira (if you have any left).'[796] Mary Ann, as she pored over his few brief lines, almost certainly detected this manoeuvre. However devoted she was to George, she understood the Cannings' compulsion to manage and manipulate those around them.

Unexpectedly, George brought someone with him to share the beefsteak, fish and Madeira, his cousin Stratford. The youngest of Mehitabel's children, Stratford, now thirty years old, was well launched on a long career that would make him a significant figure in British diplomatic history. He had come home from Switzerland to be married to the daughter of his father's friend Thomas Raikes. Mary Ann impressed him as a highly cultured woman, with 'an expressive countenance and commanding air', but Stratford's opinion is less interesting than his recollection that George prepared him to expect 'a person of high spirits and spirit also'.[797] This provides a rare glimpse of what George actually thought of his mother.

For Mary Ann this must have been a strange and moving occasion, meeting Stratty's son and namesake. Stratty had been dead almost thirty years, and it was more than forty since their tearful last encounter in the sponging-house. What can she have had to say to Stratford, who had been a baby when his father died? 'I remember your father visiting Mr Raikes in Gloucester', perhaps, or 'I knew your father well, he was a good man.' Anything more effusive would have embarrassed the two men. But her mind must have dwelt on 'sweet little Stratty', the sensitive and understanding man, whom she had idealised in the person of Marianne Clement's husband. She remembered the cruel decisions in 1783 and 1785 not to let her see George, but probably blamed them on Mehitabel. It was sweeter to dwell on the more distant time when Stratty had sustained her during her often gloomy marriage to George's father, and through the still darker days of her widowhood. Perhaps she reminisced about Stratty hiding banknotes for her to find, but she can hardly have told young Stratford that his father had wept when she was insulted by Mehitabel.

It's not clear why George brought Stratford with him.[i] We don't even know whether the two of them met by prearrangement or by accident – perhaps they crossed from France together. It was probably in George's mind that if he died before Mary Ann it would be useful if someone from the Canning family had met her, and seen where and how she lived. Otherwise all they would know was what Mehitabel told them, based on her memories of the fraught 1770s. For Mary Ann herself the visit was a sign of George's more relaxed attitude to her disqualification. Insisting that her connection was with him alone, he had resolutely insulated her from his family and circle of friends. Over the years he had seldom even mentioned Mehitabel to her, and when he referred to having assisted his aunt following the death of Charles Canning at Waterloo, he referred to her awkwardly as 'poor Charles Canning's mother'.[798] But with the visit of the Chief Baron in 1814, and now Stratford, the prohibition began to seem less absolute, although the concession had no sequel. Stratford's visit was also the final demonstration that George was no longer the Cannings' poor relation.

Having entered the government, George had to face his Liverpool electors in a sometimes violent contest. He was attacked as an 'itinerant orator' in allusion to his prolonged absence in Lisbon, while another insult, 'table-cloth orator', referred to his speeches to the merchants of Liverpool at their grand dinners. At the hustings the grateful Mr Tregent came forward to shake his hand. George, conscious of his vulnerability to accusations of being a government place-man, and fearing that a show of intimacy with one who had benefited from his patronage would only inflame the crowd still further, pretended not to know him. News of this snub reached Mary Ann, and when she upbraided him for his pride he had to explain the embarrassment that poor

i The two cousins had at one time been close. George had taken an interest in Stratford since his Eton days, and had encouraged him to attend parliamentary debates. Like George, Stratford had upset Mehitabel by transferring his political allegiance away from the Whigs. Stratford had accompanied George to Liverpool for his first election there in 1812 (*HoP 1820-32*; Hinde, 261).

Mr Tregent had unwittingly caused. When the poll closed George had secured 1,280 votes, his opponent 734.[799]

The embassy to Lisbon had seemed, at the outset, a difficult and worthwhile undertaking, which George approached with vigour and efficiency, but it was frustrated by the non-appearance of the Prince Regent. This failure tended to confirm the public perception of the whole thing as an expensive favour from Lord Liverpool to his old crony. George's role over the next five years would be to defend the government's controversial policies. One of his first parliamentary challenges was to justify his Lisbon adventure, in one of his most celebrated speeches. One of George's supporters, Sir Thomas Ackland, declared that it was a privilege to have been attacked since it gave occasion for such an eloquent defence. But like his mother's pension, the 'Lisbon Job' provided ammunition to George's enemies for the rest of his career.[800]

29.
Mother and Daughter, 1816–1823

On 1 June 1816, almost as soon as she had said goodbye to George, news reached Mary Ann of the death of Richard Thompson. Although part of Thompson's income had been threatened by his ill health, the family had lived comfortably enough, but he left his wife and five children with just £3,360 invested in the public funds, yielding barely £100 a year. On her marriage Mary had given up her £100 share of the pension to Mary Ann, but would now need it herself. George, in Liverpool for his election, told Mary Ann to make the amount over, as a voluntary gesture, and that he would reimburse her with an allowance out of his official salary. The arrangement could not be guaranteed to continue if he left office, he said, apologising for his curt manner. It wasn't until he got to London that he found time to write Mary a letter of condolence, with an offer to buy up Thompson's cellar of port. When he sent the first half-year's instalment of the promised allowance, he undertook to increase it to £200 and send more in October, but for now he found himself short of ready money because his investments in land in the Lincolnshire fens had not paid off.[801]

Mary went first to stay with Emma and Frederick in Eltham. George called on them once or twice during July, and met Emma's father. When he went to dine at the end of August, he disrupted

Emma's routine by asking to have his dinner at six o'clock, and declined the offer of a bed for the night. He told Mary Ann that Mary was well in health and spirits, and that Frederick and his wife seemed happy. The plan was for Mary to live with Mary Ann, which would involve finding a larger house. George approved of this both on economic grounds, and because it meant Mary Ann would have someone to keep an eye on her, as she had recently suffered another fall. To his relief, because he feared the changes might provide an excuse for Mary Ann to return to London, a suitable house was found in Bath, 35 Henrietta Street, in the newly developed suburb of Bathwick. Mary Ann and Mary moved at Michaelmas. Some of Mary's furniture and her stock of wine would be brought down from London.[802] By paying for Mary Ann's share of the wine George provided much needed support for the new household, without increasing his regular commitment.

Henrietta Street was to be Mary Ann's last home; she would be there longer than anywhere else in her life of jigging about. She may have looked forward to the comfort and convenience of having her daughter with her, but Mary was no longer a shy, docile girl; grief, anxiety and illness had made her nervous and irritable. Tensions would emerge as the years went by. Mary's eldest son was twelve, and George, who was the boy's godfather, promised to help him to a career once he had left school, but in the meantime he expected Richard's brother William to take responsibility for all the children.[803]

Mary Ann continued to annoy George by passing on requests for patronage from her friends; one he described as a 'discreditable scrawl such as no gentleman should write or receive'. He also objected to her habit of asking questions in the middle of the week, forcing him to interrupt his official labours to answer immediately for fear of losing her letter and forgetting the question. His way of handling his mail was to open everything and discard the covers (don't write anything important on the envelope, he warned) and then work steadily through the pile, leaving her letter until the end, and writing his reply just in time to catch the post to reach Bath on Sunday. Usually he destroyed her letters once they were dealt with, and returned or destroyed any enclosures, to keep his writing box clear.[804] Several times he described this routine, impressing on her that, barring emergencies, he could only spare time to think about her affairs once a week. Measuring out his time in such small spoonfuls smacked of the impersonal duty and charity that she had complained of in the Packet – 'as Benevolent Men give Alms to worthless Mendicants'. But as the years pass there are hints now and then that he did not put her out of mind quite as ruthlessly as his businesslike routine might suggest.

Joan, who was still in France with the children, reported another whooping cough scare. She thought Harriet and Carlo had caught it from a neighbour in Bordeaux, and told George to find out if he had had it as a child, evidently forgetting the answer Mary Ann had given six years earlier. At the beginning of October, just as Mary Ann was settling into Henrietta Street, George crossed the Channel to accompany the family home, via Paris. Because of the decades of revolution and war this was George's first time in Paris, and he said somewhat dismissively that he hoped to 'exhaust the wonders of this wonderful city'. After an absence of two months he reached London to find it in uproar following the second of three mass demonstrations in Spa Fields, when a group of demonstrators, including the government *agent provocateur* John Castle, broke away to attack the Tower of London. In what he originally intended as a brief note announcing his safe landing, George broke into a vehement denunciation of the agitators, probably once more countering something Mary Ann had written sympathising with the plight of the poor.[805]

It was a subject Mary Ann returned to repeatedly during these troubled years. George, she believed, didn't see or hear what was going on in the country at large; even in Liverpool he mixed with the wealthy families, and snubbed the small men. She was closer to the lives of ordinary people and, as his mother, had a duty to tell him what she saw. He was prepared to respect her intelligence, and so long as she confined herself to generalities he didn't protest at her interventions, but with very few exceptions his answers stuck to the government's public position. Through the summer of 1817 he was watching for a good harvest, which would, he said, 'put all to rights'. 'On the next three weeks,' he wrote at the end of August, 'depend the quality of the harvest and perhaps the peace of the country.' The following year Mary Ann suggested that the government was contributing to the unrest either by its repressive measures or by failing to relieve distress, which George conceded was partly true. He made the classic opportunist's appeal to pragmatism: he had to fall in 'with the current, to prevent it from being entirely guided by worse hands'.[806]

Bath offered an active social life, and George reckoned Mary Ann was spending more on entertainments than she had in the past. With political turmoil continuing into 1817, he criticised her for taking part in the Christmas and New Year celebrations: she used not to do so, he said (forgetting the incident of the two masters of ceremonies ten years earlier), 'and these are not the times to vary this prudent practice.' He may have been irritated to think that she, who lectured him so freely on the harshness of the times, could squander money on frivolities, while he was making himself ill with constant attendance in Parliament – till three in the morning four days a week. He suffered a return of his eye complaint (no talk now of Costello's Collyrium) and was so seldom at home that when for once he sat down to write a letter in his own study at Gloucester Lodge he found his pen had rusted in the inkwell.[807]

Mary Ann may have been pleased to hear during the summer of 1817 that Mrs Walker, the aunt of the Indian orphan, was planning to withdraw the child from the orphanage and bring or send her to England, but George was angry. A Captain Canning, who George thought was no relation, was advising the family, and suggested that since Mrs Walker's expenses would be growing as the orphan got older, it might be time to send her the income from the trust, currently between £15 and £18 per annum. George panicked; his contributions to the fund had fallen behind, and he hastened to make them good. He wondered whether Frederick had taken over the business of the fund from Richard Thompson, but it seems that Mary was handling it. In subsequent years there were further complaints from Mrs Walker, and also from the orphan's other aunt, Mrs Gardner. Mary Ann and George agreed that Mrs Gardner seemed a very silly lady.[808]

In August 1817 Mary Ann travelled down to Cullompton, no doubt taking observations of the state of the fields. She passed on a message from Esther thanking George for the £50 he had sent the year before. He recalled having sent ten guineas, and asked, in the teasing manner he often used with Aunt Esther, how it had fructified into £50 in one year. His plan for another French tour had been abandoned, and Mary Ann, hoping it meant she would have a visit, offered to cut short her stay in Devonshire. No, he said, there would be no time for Bath; his summer journey was to end at Welbeck, with Joan's sister Henrietta.[809]

Joan had been to Welbeck once or twice over the years, but George said it would be his first visit since 1802.[810] He was wrong about the year, having been there in the autumn of 1803, when his visit had been overshadowed by the heart-rending story of Mary Ann's sufferings which he had read on his journey from London. Henrietta's husband, the fourth Duke of Portland, was intent on restoring the family's fortune after the expenses of his father's political career. Welbeck may have been a less easy-going household than other country houses, such as Crewe Hall or Charles Ellis's house at Seaford.[i] Naturally, George does not complain to Mary Ann about it, beyond commenting on an inconvenient but economical custom of having all outgoing letters ready when the

i Henrietta, Duchess of Portland (1774–1844), acquired a reputation in later life for eccentricity and reclusiveness. From 1813 onwards she kept obsessively detailed records of housekeeping and estate management, contained in 23 notebooks filled with minute handwriting. (Private communication from Derek Adlam, Curator of the Portland Collection at Welbeck.)

postman delivered the incoming mail, which meant that he could not read Mary Ann's letters before fulfilling his 'weekly duty'.[811]

When Mary Ann returned to Bath in the last week of October 1817 the city was in a state of high excitement. The Queen was due to visit. Lavish preparations were made for her reception, and a subscription was got up to pay for illuminations. Mary Ann was sufficiently caught up in the general enthusiasm to contribute £3. George deplored the 'old lady's frisk', as he called the expedition, and thought two dozen tallow candles would have been more in keeping with the parsimonious tastes of the King and Queen. Mary Ann warned against such flippant allusions, lest like his poor father he might jeopardise his career by hostility towards the royal family. The visit coincided with a treason trial in Derby, where a small group of starving stockingers, quarrymen and iron workers who had staged a forlorn 'rebellion' during the summer were on trial for their lives. The *Morning Chronicle* placed its account of the planned illuminations underneath an epigram, signed 'Derbyensis', deploring inequalities of wealth and power.[812]

But by the time Mary Ann received George's fulminations another royal event had shocked the nation. After three days of civic celebration came the news that the Queen's granddaughter Princess Charlotte had died in childbirth. Since the Princess was the only popular member of the royal family, her death was received with intense public grief. George mentioned this 'overwhelming calamity' to Mary Ann, and also told her of the loss suffered by his friend Lord Morley, whose son had died of a freak accident. As though fearing he had displayed too much feeling he apologised for this 'unnecessary communication of sorrow', which he had only written, he said, because he had to provide a cover for a letter he was forwarding to her. He came to London to attend both funerals. Ever the politician, he hoped that the shared grief over the princess might do 'good to the publick mind of the country'.[813]

At the end of 1817 Mary was ill, which prompted George to think again of his godson. He asked the boy's age and mapped out the route he would need to take if he aimed at employment in India. Characteristically, Mary Ann had established close contact with 'the faculty' in Bath, including an apothecary called Turner, who lived in New King Street, and whose name will crop up now and then, as a friend and confidant as well as medical man. Mary Ann consulted him about Mary's case, and also wrote to William Thompson, who urged her to call in a second opinion. George endorsed this advice. Maria also fell ill at Christmas, and it was two months before Mary Ann could report a happy issue. 'Love to both your girls,' George wrote. He himself was suffering from a violent cough, and feared he had caught it from his children. Harriet in particular was poorly for several weeks, and Joan once more suspected whooping cough. George asked again whether he had acquired immunity as a child, and was relieved to learn once more that he had.[814]

Anxious all through the winter and spring about these invalids, Mary Ann also had money worries. The trustee of the pension was slow in making payments. In February 1818 George sent £50 to keep her going. She suggested changing the trustee; Humphrey Noad knew someone who might take it on. After checking the deed George agreed, and told her to get Mr Noad to arrange it. He was more alarmed to find that the trustee had failed to keep up payments on the life insurance for Mary and Maria, and told Mary Ann to make sure the policies were up to date. Changing the trustee proved more complicated than expected; eighteen months later the business was still not completed.[815]

At the general election of 1818, George's opponents had a new cry to add to his mother's pension and the Lisbon job. This was the case of William Ogden, a veteran campaigner for reform who had been imprisoned in 1817 along with other leaders of the 'Blanketeer' march on London by impoverished Lancashire weavers calling for political reform. While in prison the seventy year old Ogden had suffered a rupture, as a result of rough treatment, he claimed. After his release he and other leaders petitioned Parliament for redress.

Responding for the government, George alleged that Ogden had suffered from a hernia before his imprisonment and should have been grateful for having his truss fitted at public expense. Any credit the government might have gained from this argument was lost by George's heartless description of the sufferer as 'the revered and ruptured Ogden ... his bowels writhed around the surgeon's knife'. What the essayist William Hazlitt called this 'profligate alliteration' raised a laugh in the House of Commons, but gave campaigners in the streets and newspapers a cry to hurl at Canning for the rest of his career. Despite the publication of scatological verses on Ogden's 'writhing bowels', this was, George thought, the most peaceful of his Liverpool contests.[816]

After the election and the feasting, George travelled south in a leisurely way. He called at Welbeck, and then spent a day in Bath, dining in Henrietta Street on 10 July and setting off early the next morning for London. Over dinner Mary Ann told him of a disagreement with Mary, which had led to Mary moving out. Mary said the Bath air did not agree with her, but George suspected that in some domestic dispute Mary Ann had expressed herself too forcibly for Mary's sensitive nature. One likely ground for disagreement was the question of where Mary's daughters, now in their teens, should live. Mary felt obliged to comply with her husband's wish that their daughters should not reside with their grandmother, whereas Mary Ann is likely to have taken a more robust view that there could be no objection to the girls coming to Bath if their mother was with them. But Mary insisted, and went away with Maria, two invalids together, to Dawlish, and later to Weymouth.[817]

Money was another source of friction. Since her husband's death, Mary had needed her share of both the pension and the allowance provided by George, and she was afraid of not getting her entitlement. The pension payments were in some confusion because of the trustee's inefficiency and the irregularity of the sugar revenues, while the allowance from George was also irregular, depending on how much he had to hand. The issue was further muddled by the extra sums he sent for emergencies and his advances to cover delays in the pension. It's not surprising, therefore, that Mary Ann and Mary were uncertain whether the pension and allowance were paid in advance or arrears. George's view was that it didn't matter, provided the instalments came in every quarter, but he decided to remove the doubt, so far as the allowance was concerned, by paying a double instalment, £50 in arrears at the end of December, and a further £50 in January 1819, with the quarterly instalments from then onwards clearly paid in advance. Mary Ann feared he would think she had told him about the disagreement in order to extract this extra payment, but he assured her that no such suspicion had crossed his mind.[818]

The double instalment did not resolve the problems with the pension, nor did it get to the root of the matter, which was that Mary was in low spirits, was short of money and found her mother overbearing. The long-term solution was for young George Thompson to get on quickly so he could provide for his mother. George repeated that he would find a post for his godson when he was old enough. Mary Ann reminded him every now and then of his promise.[819]

As civil unrest persisted into 1819 Mary Ann tried to keep up with events. She now took the *Courier*, which George described as supporting the government, but not in the government's confidence. Like half the cabinet, it had been opposed to George's own pro-Catholic line, but was about to change its policy.[820] On other issues, he said, it was often wrong and alarmist, misleading her, for example, over the tea tax, which she thought was a new tax, and oppressive to the poor, whereas the government had merely increased an existing tax, and only on the more expensive kinds of tea.[821] This defence did not answer the fundamental objection to high taxes on commodities like beer and tea, which weighed disproportionately on the poor, but we don't know whether Mary Ann pressed the argument. In May she wondered why it was that, having told her that on the Catholic question he went his own way, he did not intervene when the matter was debated in Parliament. This was a sensitive topic because, as we shall see, some supporters of Catholic emancipation considered that he kept quiet for the sake of staying in office. Two months later she still looked in vain for his name in the debates. Recalling his complaint about the physical effort required to speak 'after sitting for six hours in an atmosphere of 77 or 80 in a room containing from five to seven hundred people', she feared he was ill. He said he had simply judged it better not to speak, adding that latterly, after the death of Joan's uncle the Chief Baron in mid-June, he had been confined to the house until he had a decent suit of mourning. He reminded her that much went on in Parliament that was not reported in the press.[822]

When she asked his sanction for a substantial donation to charity he replied sharply: 'There is a race of vanity (the word has slipped from my pen and I have not time to amend it into a more circumlocutionary phrase) in these times, for objects of piety and benevolence which [in other times] was confined to shew, equipage, and expensive amusements… I have not time for shading or softening.' He said £5 was ample 'for conscience and for shew'. The charity in question may have been for the new church in Bathwick; a fortnight later George was complaining that he had been forced to contribute £50 to a church-building fund. He believed that church-building was a 'work of national obligation' and should be paid for by the government.[823]

Such expressions of opinion are rare in George's letters. Another example was when Mary Ann, at the end of 1818, asked his opinion of *dandyism*. He replied primly that 'all nice and effeminate adornments of the person are in the highest degree discreditable both to the taste and the understanding.' Dandies had been an object of interest throughout the previous year, with several new plays incorporating the word in their title, and the newspapers, particularly outside London, regularly printing news stories, squibs and epigrams about 'the newly discovered species, termed Dandies'. Public reaction to the phenomenon ranged from ridicule to moral panic at what was regarded as a French import and affront to English manliness: 'Dandy's a gender of the doubtful kind'. There was a fracas between two dandies in a Bath coffee room. The Drury Lane Christmas pantomime that year, *Harlequin and the Dandy Club; or, 1818*, had to be withdrawn after three performances because of the great hubbub raised by, among others, the 'race of dandies'.[824] It may have been this theatrical incident that prompted Mary Ann's query.

Mary Ann hoped for a visit. Knowing that George was planning a three-month tour of the Continent, she suggested he might come to her before he left. He replied that it was impossible as the parliamentary session would last well into July. He held out the hope that he would visit after his tour. Before his departure, which was delayed by an attack of gout, he made sure she was not short of money. He sent the £50 allowance, reminding her that it was for the 'Quarter beginning July first', and then in the first week in August, since the third quarter of the pension had not arrived, he sent £125. Mary was in worsening health, depressed and unable to afford her house in Weymouth. Telling Mary Ann to send her money, which he would reimburse on his return, he hoped Mary could be persuaded to move back to Henrietta Street. With that, and with 'love to all around you', he set off for Rotterdam, Stuttgart and then Italy. His letters from the Continent were brief – from Milan he told her that she should look at a map if she wanted to trace his route. He was busy, and forgot to make arrangements for her next quarter's allowance, but made good the omission when he reached Genoa at the end of September.[825]

In August 1819 Mary came to Bath on a visit. Anxious about the future of her children, she needed to consult her mother, and, through her mother, George. She made her will.[826] She had little to bequeath, and the terms of her will follow those of her husband's, betraying the determination they both had to deal fairly with their children, in particular their 'scantily portioned' daughters. She expressed the hope that her elder son, aged fifteen at the time, would soon be able to provide for himself and his sisters. Her share of the pension, she said, should be divided among her daughters, unless one of the boys needed the money to complete his education. She proposed to draw up a schedule of the small stock of plate and books she had brought from her married home, to indicate who should inherit which items; an additional reason may have been to identify which items belonged to her and which to her mother. She repeated her husband's stipulation that their daughters were on no account to live with Mary Ann. This was a reminder for Mary Ann of her old disqualification, and the will's acknowledgement of her 'liberality and affection' in offering to take the girls is unlikely to have eased the pain. Having made her will, in which she described herself as residing in Henrietta Street, Mary returned to Weymouth.

Towards the end of October, George wrote from Rome that he was turning back and that his next letter would be from London. He recalled this when, almost a month later, he wrote from Dover to announce that he just landed: he'd be keeping his promise, he said, because although he was writing at Dover, the letter would be franked from London.[827] It often seems that he dashed off his weekly letters to Mary Ann and then forgot about her until the next Saturday. This throwaway remark is a rare sign that what passed between them, however trivial, lodged in his mind.

He had hurried home, leaving Joan and the children on a protracted European tour. Within days of landing he delivered a speech full of sophistry in defence of the government over the Peterloo Massacre (which had been perpetrated the day he left the country, 16 August). He hoped also to spend time with his son, whose hold on life was weakening. After so many years in the hands of doctors, Georgey had entrusted himself to one last practitioner whose treatment had at first seemed promising, only to disappoint like all the others. George had tried to keep his son's hopes alive, without feeling much confidence himself, and now after twenty months he denounced the surgeon as a quack. Georgey was at home at Gloucester Lodge, under the care of his great-aunt Fanny Canning. Parliamentary business continued right up until Christmas, to speed the passing of two laws to curb the press, but George managed to be at home for Christmas dinner with his son.[828]

Mary Ann was waiting for George to fulfil his promise to visit before the end of the year. When he told her that parliamentary business made it impossible she was free to go to Weymouth to spend Christmas with Mary. He sent £20 for travelling expenses there and back, and £5 to help with Mary's housekeeping. He promised to come to Bath at Easter, perhaps 11 April, his fiftieth birthday, although he disliked birthdays: 'The reflections which they bring are rather melancholy than exhilarating,' he wrote on 1 January 1820 – adding that the same applied to first days of the year.[829]

As a result of the Christmas visit, Mary agreed to return to Henrietta Street. So far as looking after her mother was concerned, there was little that Mary could do, since in addition to her lameness it appears from a rather unsympathetic remark made by George the following year that her eyesight was failing and she was becoming deaf. While Mary Ann must have had a sound constitution to have survived the rigours of her life, she was now seventy-three years old, and had suffered several falls over the last four or five years which, although George spoke of them lightly as 'tumbles', may have been a sign of failing strength.[830]

The times continued unsettled, with the death of George III at the beginning of 1820, and then in the week following the royal funeral the dramatic arrest of the Cato Street conspirators. The day after the arrests, Thursday 24 February, the London newspapers carried details of the plan to assassinate the whole cabinet while they were at dinner at Lord Harrowby's house, describing the gang's arsenal of pistols, knives, pikes and hand grenades and reporting that the leader, Arthur Thistlewood, was still at large.

Although the story did not reach the provincial press until Friday or Saturday, the London papers must have reached Bath by late on Thursday, and Mary Ann probably heard about it by early on Friday. Always quick to imagine the worst, she may have experienced an anxious few hours before the arrival of George's hurried note telling her that he and his colleagues were all safe. In his regular Saturday letter he told her, 'The constable visited our visitors just about the time that they meant to have visited us.' He did not add that since Thistlewood's second-in-command was a police spy, and the advertised gathering of the cabinet at Lord Harrowby's a hoax, he had not been in danger.[831]

The accession of a new king precipitated a general election. The result in Liverpool was never in doubt, but the contest was protracted, with daily speechifying and, when it was over, the unavoidable round of dinners and toasts and more speeches. George stopped at Welbeck on his way south, and wrote that he had not forgotten his promise to be in Bath on 11 April. He enjoyed the peace at Welbeck, evidently feeling more at ease now with his sister-in-law. As Aunt Fanny's bulletins on young Georgey's health were favourable he saw no need to hurry home. But when he reached Gloucester Lodge he found things had turned for the worse. The stoical young man was released from his sufferings in the early hours of 31 March. 'Never was human being of 19 so prepared for Heaven!' George told Mary Ann. The intellectual gifts of this favourite, suffering child had been a source of paternal pride, but also of anxiety. In his epitaph he wrote that Georgey had been kept secure from 'Pleasure's flowery snares', but years before he had shown a more natural reaction. Watching Georgey, and perhaps thinking of his own lonely, bookish boyhood, he had longed to throw the Latin grammar on the fire if only the little fellow could have joined the other children running and laughing in the sunlight.[832]

He assured Mary Ann that he would still keep his engagement with her, begging her to tell no one but Mary and Maria; the 'plague of notoriety' was particularly annoying at such a time. Joan urged him to put off the visit, but he replied that by spending his birthday there, 'a day which I hate spending anywhere', he would 'confer a much greater kindness' than by a longer visit at another time. He added that once it was over he would be 'free' for the rest of the year. When he reached Henrietta Street he was confronted with a large family gathering which included Maria, Mary and her children, and Samuel's daughter. He was shocked by Mary's condition, and left money for medicines, wine and a wheelchair, while once more concentrating his thoughts on the future of her eldest son. Mary Ann, aware of George's view that the Thompson family should take responsibility for young George Thompson, wrote pressing them to do more. She sent the letters to George to be franked, and he returned them with the comment that she had expressed herself too harshly. She was only echoing his own resentment, but he pointed out the risk of putting the family on the defensive – advice which, if he had followed it in his own political relationships, would have saved him many difficulties. When she sent a more emollient letter William Thompson's reply satisfied George, for the time being at least.[833]

The new reign caused an upheaval in the government apparatus which, among other things, delayed collection of the sugar revenue, interrupting the payment of the pension, so in April George again advanced the quarter's instalment. Irregularities in the administration of the revenues had caused delays the year before, and later on deep-seated problems with the sugar trade would cause the pension to dry up altogether. George was repeatedly having to pay the instalments, which, together with the regular allowance, meant finding £175 per quarter.[834] His ability to continue this subsidy was thrown in doubt by threats to his political position arising from the new King's unremitting hostility towards his wife, Princess, now Queen, Caroline.

George would not turn against his old friend and patroness, whatever his private opinion of the scandalous stories of her conduct abroad. It would be surprising if the subject did not come up during his birthday visit. The princess's story – forced marriage, a vicious husband, incarceration, followed by exile, and finally a protracted public humiliation – would not have been out of place among the tales of abused women in *The Offspring of Fancy*, and we can assume that Mary Ann applauded George's loyalty. The Queen was, one newspaper commented, 'of a character not likely to allow of her being overlooked or forgotten', something that might equally be said of Mary Ann. Two months later, when Mary Ann read reports of George's speech in Parliament on the Queen's arrival in London, she can hardly have missed the parallel with her own case. George declared that his advice to Caroline had always been that 'in the situation of incurable alienation and hopeless reconcilement' between her and her husband, she should live abroad, since her coming to England was 'a claim to be reinstated in all the rights and privileges of the station of Queen. And there was no longer any option, except between the immediate acknowledgement of all those rights and privileges, or a statement of the grounds on which any of them were withholden.' This echoes the painful argument he had used in 1804 to persuade Mary Ann to leave London – that her presence would force him to make known why he would never admit her to the rights and privileges of a mother and grandmother. George acknowledged the parallel when he said that he would have used the same argument 'were the party to whom it was given… one to whom he was bound by the dearest ties'.[835]

The Whitsun holiday afforded some respite from the political crisis. When newspapers reported that George was ill, he wrote to reassure Mary Ann that it was nothing more than his usual attack of gout, now no longer confined to the winter months. He was working day and night to clear his desk prior to leaving the country, to meet Joan in Italy, and to keep out of the King's way. He promised to take care of George Thompson's appointment before he left, and before the political situation forced him out of office. Mrs Walker in India plagued him, he said, with queries about the orphan's fund, which he was temporarily at a loss to answer.[836]

By mid-August he had finished his accumulated correspondence and dealt with all the plagues, and was ready to depart, impatient to see his family, and eager to visit Venice, 'a place of the most interesting character'. He thought of Thomas Otway's Pierre on the Rialto, of Shylock and Othello, of the city's past magnificence, and present decay, echoing Byron's recently published lines: 'Ours is a trophy which will not decay/ With the Rialto; Shylock and the Moor,/ And Pierre cannot be swept or worn away…' Mary Ann must have been struck by the theatrical allusions and unusually frank expression of enthusiasm. After Venice he escorted Joan and Harriet to Paris, and planned to leave them there for the winter, but in the event stayed on in order to avoid the autumn's proceedings against the Queen.[837]

By contrast with Venice, Mary Ann and her invalid daughter found Henrietta Street dull, their outlook narrowed by money worries and ill health. Yet always Mary Ann was reaching out in imagination to George, far removed though he was, both physically and socially – even his worries were on a grand scale, arising as they did from his intimacy with royalty. The passion that had animated her campaigns to secure a place in his life had not cooled, but her expectations were now reduced to a weekly letter. So long as it could be done easily, George cheerfully complied, but when it became difficult, as when he was travelling, he resisted her demands. He may well have seen her constant anxiety for his safety as an excuse to force him to write, force him to grant her a little more of his life than he was willing to spare. He wrote to confirm his safety after his Channel crossing, but she should not expect him to be constantly reassuring her during a land journey, where nothing could happen. But the fact was that she was now well into her seventies, and had been ill over the summer of 1820, while George was in his fifties and not robust; even without the perils of travel, the fear that death might come between them was not altogether unrealistic.[838]

He arrived back in Dover on 17 November, writing from there to prove he had survived the sea, but adding that there would be no need of a further letter from London because there were no perils between Dover and Westminster Bridge – once he came within sight of Parliament his perils would begin again. He resigned his position at the Board of Control and was determined to be out of the country again well before Parliament resumed on 23 January 1821, which he said ruled out a visit to Bath. Mary Ann must have complained at this disappointment, because his letter offers one excuse after another, as though his conscience troubled him. Looking for ways of consoling her, he sent her a copy of the eulogistic address from the directors of the East India Company, which he was sure she would find gratifying.[839]

He also reminded her what he had been doing for George Thompson. Now sixteen, young Thompson had declined the option of training for the Indian service, probably out of reluctance to leave his sick mother, and was to start at the Audit Office in Somerset House. Encouraged by his mother and other relations, he hoped for something better, and held out as long as he could before presenting himself at the office, almost missing the opening that George had worked hard to procure from the prime minister. The initial salary of £80 would not go far towards helping Mary, but promotion would come year by year. George wrote from Dover before embarking once more for the Continent, telling Mary Ann that he had seen the boy at Somerset House and hoped he would do well.[840]

Friction between Mary and Mary Ann grew worse. Mary may have felt she'd submitted to her mother for long enough. She was forty-three, in constant pain, with her sight and hearing impaired – if she complained, if for once she thought of herself, it was with good reason. The last straw may have been if Mary Ann passed on George's complaints about young Thompson's procrastination.

Mary made up her mind to leave Henrietta Street again and go into lodgings. Mary Ann's letters to George in Paris kept him informed of all the moves in the argument. He replied that it was selfish of Mary to want her own separate establishment, the only criticism he ever expressed of her. Their money problems were complicated and the details are unclear; George was prepared to help, if it would persuade Mary to stay put. He continued his allowance despite losing his official salary, and told Mary Ann to spend whatever was needed on medicines. But Mary moved out at the beginning of April.[841]

In March George left the family in Paris and returned to London to speak on the second reading of the Roman Catholic Disability Removal Bill on the sixteenth. He was therefore on hand to attend the 1821 dinner of the Benevolent Society of St Patrick. He had been chairman in 1820, and was succeeded this year by the Duke of Wellington. He and the Duke walked together to the City of London Tavern. As they were making their way along Cheapside, George recalled that it was Saturday and he had not written his usual letter to Mary Ann: 'it flashed upon my mind,' he told her.[842]

The dinner followed its fixed ritual: singing the national anthem, the orphans' parade and prize-giving, the collection and a long round of toasts and speeches, with the leading gentlemen withdrawing after the speeches, while the rest of the company enjoyed a concert of Irish songs and more eating and drinking late into the night. The Duke of Leinster toasted the Duke of Wellington, who returned the compliment; the Duke of Leinster then toasted Lord Castlereagh, who toasted Earl Darnley, who toasted his 'schoolfellow' Mr Canning, who toasted the Marquess of Lansdowne, who toasted Mr Vansittart the Chancellor of the Exchequer and so on, Tory complimenting Whig and Whig complimenting Tory. The previous year George, in his speech from the chair, had described himself as a usurper, being the first chairman of the society who was not a peer – a hint that one day he would usurp another position traditionally occupied by a nobleman.[843]

This year his display of humility was still more explicit. He spoke of his low birth and his lack of rank or property, confessing that his contribution to the collection was small compared with that of others. All he had to recommend himself to the gathering, he said, was his Irish 'derivation'.[844] This was conventional enough, an opportunity to praise the British constitution for enabling someone of humble origins to rise as far as his talents would take him. He might have been referring simply to his comparatively obscure upbringing in Clements Lane as the nephew of an unsuccessful banker, but with words like *birth* and *derivation* he seems to be going further, inviting his audience to think of his Irish mother. Even if knowledge of Mary Ann's past was no longer widespread amongst his colleagues, there was a risk that someone would recall the gossip. Like his Gregory Griffin 'memoir' in the *Microcosm* and his contribution to the debate on Queen Caroline, this speech was a relaxation of his habitual reticence. He may simply have been buoyed up and carried away by conviviality, but there may have been some more specific reason. Perhaps in the procession of Irish orphans he had seen his own six-year-old self on the road to the gallows; perhaps the recollection of Mary Ann that had flashed upon him on Cheapside was more troubling than he admitted.

George always denied that national sympathies lay at the root of his commitment to Catholic emancipation, and early in his career he had dismissed his Irish derivation, emphasising instead his English education and attachments. In 1825, however, he would turn this round, writing in a light-hearted letter to Sir Walter Scott: 'though I was accidentally born in London, I consider myself an Irishman.'[845] His 1821 speech to the St Patrick Society suggests that as he grew older he was becoming more emotionally committed to his Irish nationality. Another indication was given four years earlier when he went to hear the Scottish divine, mathematician and social reformer Thomas Chalmers.[i] Chalmers' sermon included a passage praising the Irish character for spontaneity, sociability and a capacity to break through the constraints of convention. George was seen to weep at this, much to the surprise of his fellow MP William Wilberforce, who thought him too hardened in debate to be so moved.[846] Perhaps it was the power of Chalmers' language that moved George to tears, but perhaps there was something more specific at work, something to do with the Irish person closest to him, his mother. Mary Ann was spontaneous and sociable, and during their bitter arguments had always urged him to follow Nature rather than the prejudices of Society.

After St Patrick's Day, George stayed to see the Catholic Bill through the Commons, and then watched its defeat in the Lords, before rejoining Joan, Harriet and Carlo in Paris. Harriet was now seventeen and on the family's return to London was presented at Court at the first 'Drawing Room' following the coronation. George characteristically forgot to inform the Court newsman, and Mary Ann noticed her granddaughter's absence from the published list. Out of office, George had too little to do, leaving him with no excuse to avoid watching Harriet dance until dawn at her first season's balls. After Princess Esterhazy's ball he declared it would be the last of the season's gaieties, adding that Harriet thought otherwise. He may have been pressed into service more than he liked because, he told Mary Ann, Joan was 'knocked up' by the season's festivities. Many of his letters are longer than usual – one included a circumstantial account of the procedure whereby blocks of type were passed from one newspaper to another. He at last got around to checking the accounts of the Indian orphan's trust fund.[847]

George promised to visit Bath during September. After putting the visit off for another week, and then changing back again he

i Thomas Chalmers (1780-1847): his *Astronomical Discourses*, attempting to reconcile the latest discoveries in astronomy with the truth of revealed Christianity, had made him a national celebrity, and his London sermons attracted large audiences. Later he would be a leading figure in the Disruption of 1843.

wrote to ask whether she wanted him to come to Shawford or Bath. Without waiting for a reply he announced his programme: he would call on her in Henrietta Street on the evening of Tuesday 2 October, spend Wednesday with her and then drive her to Shawford House on the Thursday. He added a postscript: 'I don't see why I should not eat my mutton chop or boiled fowl in H. St. on Tuesday at 7.' Since mutton chops and boiled fowl were typical bachelor fare such as he would have eaten regularly if he had never entered the great world of turtle dinners and country houses, this postscript offers a moment of intimacy, a glimpse of a different life in which he was content to work obscurely as a lawyer, without the need to separate himself from Mary Ann. But it was only a moment; two days later he was writing in his usual peremptory fashion. He had let slip that he did not propose to bring his own horses, prompting Mary Ann to offer to arrange a carriage for him; she could easily speak to the people at the White Hart, she suggested. He wrote back (his fourth communication within a week) telling her firmly that he was bringing his post-chaise, and 'post horses are to be had I suppose in all civilised countries'. On no account was she to give advance notice to the White Hart. He had no wish to be 'newspaper'd' or 'noticed' in any way.[848]

After their day together George drove Mary Ann in his post-chaise to Shawford. They found Mary in residence, and there was a long conversation about money and about her son. Mary Ann was caught in the middle, with Mary resentful and George defensive. George disapproved of a plan to make the entire £200 allowance over to Mary but did nothing to prevent it, only stipulating that the payment should not be in his name, and emphasising that it was not guaranteed to continue. The pension had failed for more than a year now, and he had already advanced £500 from his own pocket, so it was hard to find the additional £200. As for young George Thompson, he was dissatisfied with the Audit Office and Mary hoped for something better. George replied that he had been forced to ask Lord Liverpool for the clerkship, and it was the best he could get. While he was at the Board of Control he could have found a position in India, and it was a pity young George didn't grasp the opportunity at the time. He was angry at the continued failure of the Thompson family to take responsibility, in particular William Thompson's refusal to provide a home for his nephew.[849] There is no sign that Mary Ann tried to represent the Thompsons' side of the argument.

George might protest that he was a poor man and, having no prospect of returning to government (despite newspaper reports to the contrary), was also without influence, but when Mary Ann compared him with herself and her disabled daughter he seemed infinitely rich and powerful. Nonetheless, she could see things from his point of view. His letters at this time betray the strain he was under, and in their day together in Henrietta Street she could observe him carefully. Without knowing the details, she was aware that negotiations over a return to Lord Liverpool's administration were endless and wearisome. She may have picked up the rumour that he was to be the next governor-general of India, with all the anxious weighing of pros and cons that such a move entailed for him and his family. But however much she sympathised with him, however much it pained her to add to his plagues, she clung to him, and expected him to solve Mary's problems.

George left Shawford dissatisfied, fearing he had not made himself plain. After he had been back in London for a week he sent what he hoped was a clear summary of the conversation with Mary. This is one of the few occasions when, as in an epistolary novel, we are granted a glimpse of what had gone on when Mary Ann and George met face to face. How accurate it is, we don't know. George apologised for his abruptness, and sought as always to soften his words with much needed money. Three days later he sent a quarter's instalment of the allowance; she could pass it on to Mary if she wished, but he warned her not to take any binding decisions, and repeated his view that he had done as much as could be expected to help her and her family:

> My youth, my dear Mother, was devoted to you. In my manhood I have not been regardless of yours; but age brings other claims, and what remains of my life may be little enough for the claims of those who are mine, who are wholly mine, and to whom I have given being. I cannot take upon myself, nor allow silently to grow upon me, any new claim which would distract my attention from those first, natural interests.

Despite his usual horror of having his letters handed around, he hinted that she should pass a copy of this statement to the Thompsons, so they would understand that it was up to them to help young George from now on. It became starkly clear how short he was of ready money when he told her a few days later that the pension had once more failed, but he could not raise the latest instalment himself. He told her to let him know of any urgent needs.[850] There were always odd banknotes he could send.

Over the years George had admitted to being overwhelmed with work, too busy to write, plagued by endless demands on his time, on his pocket and on his stock of influence, but he had always been in control. Now his own affairs seemed to be getting out of hand. In response to further demands from Frederick, who in addition to his ceaseless search for promotion now wanted help in a dispute with the Admiralty,[i] George wrote: 'I am distracted with a thousand difficulties and solicitudes for those nearer to me, and for myself, and the time is ill chosen to set me a begging at all the departments of state. – I must not be burthened through life with the specifick and individual cases of each member of your family.' Then something remarkable happened. He changed 'your family' to 'the family'.[851] He seldom altered anything in his letters, occasionally apologising for a harsh word, but seldom offering to find a kinder one. Mary Ann was bound to notice this emendation, and understand the

---

i Frederick wanted the Admiralty to pay his legal costs in a court martial which had acquitted him of embezzling £4,000. Eventually he was granted £500, but complained that this left him £4,000 out of pocket, which suggests that although acquitted of embezzlement he had to pay the money back (Frederick to Mary Ann, 31 July 1823, filed with George's letter of 2 August 1823).

intention behind his acknowledgement that there was, after all, a connection between him and her other children.

As 1822 opened a note of panic was apparent. Having spent Christmas at Welbeck, George was detained there for six weeks by a severe attack of gout. His own money problems meant he could not immediately relieve Mary Ann's, so he suggested that she should '[make] glad poor Dennis's heart' by borrowing £25 from her savings.[852] How surprised the Duke and Duchess would have been had they known that their brother-in-law, now spoken of as the next governor-general of India, was reduced to soliciting small loans from an elderly servant. George's main concern, however, was his son William.

William was clearly intelligent but as early as 1809, when he was seven, George had described him as 'unamiable' and feared it was because he and Joan, always worried about Georgey and enchanted by Harriet, had neglected their middle child.[853] At the Naval College he had been in trouble over a watch, which he either stole or accused a comrade of stealing. Now it was gambling, at cards and billiards. What drove George to despair was that William was an inveterate liar. He had lied about the watch, even to his little sister, and was lying now about his accumulating debts. George pleaded, preached and threatened. If the lying continued he would do nothing more to help William in his career, and would cut him out of his will.[854] Untruthfulness was what had made George lose sympathy with Charles Reddish, but it had been easier to cast Charles adrift than his own son. William failed his navigation examinations and repeatedly went absent without leave.

From his sickbed, George mobilised friends and colleagues. He sent William to lodge with his private secretary John Backhouse, and begged him to take counsel from the Duke of Portland or Charles Ellis. He commissioned a parliamentary colleague, Lord Kensington, to seek information about William's activities in London from his son, who was a midshipman, and a few years older than William. A sympathetic Admiralty official called John

Barrow[i] and the experienced and understanding Captain Dawkins of the *Helicon* both offered advice. George even persuaded Lord Melville to order a special examination for William, and called on Frederick Hunn for help in tracing him when he risked being tried as a deserter. In November 1822 Dawkins declared William unfit to be an officer, but six months later he was made a lieutenant, and in less than three years would be promoted to his first command, the *Sappho*.[855]

Mary Ann knew none of this. When she continued to press Frederick's case George disingenuously pointed to the fact that he was not seeking promotion for William as proof that it was not a good time to solicit favours from Lord Melville.[856]

Although gambling at cards or billiards did not appeal to George – he had seen the danger early on when he associated with Sheridan and Fox – he had never been good with money. As a young man he had run up debts, had depended on the advice of Walter Borrowes, and had happily accepted the hospitality of wealthy friends. Since his marriage he had enjoyed constant access to ready money. He wasn't extravagant, but he lived like a rich man. Early in 1822, when he had been out of office for more than a year, he was faced, not with ruin, but with retrenchment. Scrabbling around for the money to send to Mary Ann when the pension failed was much like the old days, when as an undergraduate at Christ Church he had sent her odd £5 notes. The option of replacing the Marquess of Hastings as governor-general of India had been raised the year before, only to be withdrawn when it seemed that Hastings was not ready to retire, but now it became a real possibility. It would solve George's financial problems. Shortly after leaving Welbeck, he reluctantly decided to accept.[857]

His departure was set for August. The appointment offered a vast fortune, and a new and challenging life, but in his gloomier moments it looked like failure. 'I go into exile,' he told Mary Ann, 'because I do not feel myself where I ought to be at home.' He

i John Barrow (1764-1848), the son of a Lancashire tanner, had been on the staff of George Macartney in China and at the Cape before becoming second secretary at the Admiralty.

knew that all the world would catch the scent of Indian riches and want to come with him. His predecessor had grasped at the governor-generalship as a last chance of escaping bankruptcy, and had, George said, gone out 'with so many dependants that the whole of India will not satisfy them'. But as always George felt more constrained by the rules than his nobly born colleagues. The governor-general, he told Mary Ann, had no freedom except over the choice of his own personal staff, all other appointments being governed by the Company's procedures. Even before his appointment was confirmed he warned her that she would be overwhelmed by applications; now more than ever it was imperative that she should not forward anything to him.[858]

Among the applications that flooded in as soon as his appointment was made public, was one from young George Thompson, still keen to escape the Audit Office. He and his mother had not hitherto liked the idea of his going to India, but to go as the nephew and godson of the governor-general was too good an opportunity to miss. George was beside himself with fury. He wrote a letter of nine sheets – a whole morning's work, he told Mary Ann – explaining the Company's rules in detail. The only way young Thompson could go to India with him was as a member of his household, and he had no wish to inflict that sort of embarrassment and difficulty on his own children. He didn't specify why it would be an embarrassment for Harriet and Carlo to have their cousin living with them. It was partly, no doubt, because young Thompson was not a fine gentleman, but George was also conscious that it was only by pretending that Mary was his sister that he could explain the presence of her son in his household. To put an end to the matter he was driven to swear a solemn oath that he would not do it. Once again he summed up his position:

> I know my duties to you and I hope have fulfilled them. I admit <u>certain</u> duties to <u>yours</u>; and I hope have fulfilled these too, <u>for your sake</u>, without reluctance. But these duties do not swallow

> up others. They have their limits... I have children of my own... those children have a mother, whose connections have an equal claim upon me – not with my Mother – God forbid! – but with her connections...

Still talking the language of duty rather than affection, he was so exasperated that he reverted to his old line, that Mary Ann's family was not his family.[859]

We don't know what response this long letter elicited from Mary Ann. Did she sit down over it with Mary and Maria? Did they disagree about it? From one point of view George was right. It would not be in young Thompson's interest: he was not qualified to go to India as a Company employee, and if he went as a personal appointee he would have no security if George were to die or give up his post, and there would be no pension. Mary Ann may well have urged this consideration, but it is not to be wondered at that Mary was disappointed and resentful. The personal secretary George had chosen was his trusted Liverpool agent John Backhouse, a man in his forties with long administrative experience. None of this can have counted with Mary, who saw no further than that her son was not chosen. Accustomed all her life to look to George for help, she found that now, at the most sad and critical moment, he refused point blank to do what she asked. Having made his point, George, far from abandoning his godson, did what he could to smooth his path to either a civilian or military career with the East India Company.[860] It was as well that young Thompson was persuaded to take the official route, because sudden political changes meant that his uncle would not be governor-general after all.

By February 1823 it was clear that Mary was 'ripe for heaven', as George said, echoing the phrase he had used of his son. 'God's will be done,' he wrote, before turning to practical matters. The pension was for the lifetimes of Mary and Maria, so he asked pointedly after Maria's health. He also thought about the Thompson children, and to encourage the Noads to take responsibility for the girls, and perhaps sacrifice their share of the pension to them, he set about finding a post for Humphrey Noad's nephew, something he had earlier declared impossible. Mary lingered on until May. When George heard of her death he repeated, 'God's will be done.' It made his heart heavy; he was reluctant to set about his official labours, but, he said, to put off the business of the day 'would not be right or expedient'. He sent Mary Ann money, and a consignment of wine.[861]

30.
A Contingent Engagement, 1822–1826

Mary Ann's feelings about the governor-generalship are unrecorded, but she must have dreaded seeing George go to India. He would not be swallowed up as completely as poor Charles, but she would not see him again. More serious, because their face-to-face meetings were in any case rare, would be the loss of contact by post. The rhythm of her life was founded upon her opportunity to unburden herself to him each Friday, and the response which reached her two days later – brief, abrasive, sometimes sarcastic, but sometimes surprisingly affectionate; always dependable, and often accompanied by welcome banknotes. India would have disrupted the flow more drastically than during the Lisbon interlude. Given the scale of the impact on her, it is significant that, whatever she may have felt, she seems to have expressed not the slightest protest or disappointment. For a man, career and glory must come first.

But then other possibilities arose, allowing her to speculate on glories nearer home. In mid-August 1822 she was expecting a final visit once George had completed his farewell trip to Liverpool, when the newspapers reported the suicide of the Marquess of Londonderry (formerly Lord Castlereagh). Like everyone else who saw the news she must have speculated on how the tragedy would affect George's plans. She read the various contradictory predictions in the newspapers, but heard nothing from George until the end of the month, when all he said was that the public speculation made his grand speech to his constituents a matter of 'no small delicacy and difficulty'. Mary Ann added to his embarrassment by asking him to recommend one of her Bath friends for a job in Liverpool.[862]

Mary Ann visited Shawford in September, when the main topic of conversation was, no doubt, George's future, and how it would affect them all. She was back in Henrietta Street when George confirmed that he was to succeed Lord Londonderry. He couldn't visit her, but assured her that he would be remaining within reach, presumably alluding once more to her wish to have him with her at her death. The following week he expatiated on the sacrifice of giving up the £25,000 Indian salary in favour of the foreign secretary's £5,400, which, he said, would not even cover the expenses of the post. Thrilled by such disinterestedness she wanted to send his letter to the newspapers. He replied by return that on no account was she to do this. As always when George was in the news, Mary Ann's Bath acquaintances canvassed her in favour of sons and nephews in search of advancement. Unable to help herself, she passed on one of their letters, triggering the usual angry response.[863]

To celebrate his return to office, and in the hope of building up Mary Ann's strength, George planned to send a consignment of Madeira by canal. He asked in October whether there was a waterway all the way from London to Bath, but when she sent him a card containing details of the route he was too busy to act on it. Eventually he confessed that he remembered her sending the card, but had lost it. 'This is a sad account,' he wrote. She sent it again at the end of November, but it was not until Christmas that he found time to 'put out a case of Madeira' for her, prompted in the end by news that she had again been unwell. It was a cold winter in the south of England and the wine was still frost-bound at Paddington a fortnight later.[864] The saga illustrates both how much and how little George thought about his mother. For two months pressure of business repeatedly prevented him doing anything about the case of Madeira, and yet for those two months, and on into January as he waited for the thaw, he kept the project in mind.

In the meantime he arranged for her friend, Mr Turner, to keep him informed how she was getting on. In addition to Mr Turner the apothecary Mary Ann had another friend called Turner, Frewen Turner esq., a former MP who had been a business connection of Richard Thompson's and had known George in Leicestershire. The apothecary's information would be more useful, perhaps, but George might have been happier corresponding with a gentleman and former MP.[865]

Now he was back in office, George's hurried notes usually contained no more than that he was well, or exhausted, or suffering from gout. In March 1823 gout affected his 'writing knuckle' which prevented him writing for three weeks. He missed one Saturday, but on the other two his private secretary wrote for him, another sign that he was more relaxed about Mary Ann than in the past. He had come to resent attendance in the Commons, since it meant suspending his real work at four o'clock each afternoon, and spending up to eleven hours in a room as hot as a conservatory. When the session ended he escaped to a country house to carry on his official duties uninterrupted by personal interviews. His country house hosts would provide him with a table in the corner of the room and he would write letter after letter, shutting out the talk and laughter all around him. 'Think not that I enjoy the leisure very leisurely,' he told Mary Ann in the course of one of these visits. A letter from John Bolton's house near Kendal was more expansive than usual, describing the delights of the scenery and the benefits of exercise, but then ending abruptly when he decided that he'd given Mary Ann 'a fair share… of my day's work'.[866] Mary Ann may have felt this brusqueness was harsh, but equally may have seen it as a compliment to her intelligence, showing he trusted her to understand the needs of business.

In the autumn of 1823 George, accompanied by Joan and Harriet, went to stay some weeks with Lord Morley, formerly

Lord Boringdon, at Saltram, in the course of which he was to be made a Freeman of Plymouth. They travelled in leisurely stages, with the newspapers tracking their route.[867] They were to stay a night in Bath and George promised Mary Ann a quarter of an hour of his time, warning her to tell no one. From Cirencester he wrote ahead that if she could be sure to be alone he would bring 'other visitors'. So far as we can tell this was the first time since the clandestine visits of 1804 and 1805 that George had allowed any contact with his immediate family. For Mary Ann this tiny concession came too late to cancel the many painful years through which she had laboured under her disqualification. Neither she nor any of the other participants left any account of the meeting. We don't know, for example, what Harriet had been told in advance. Had she ever asked why she was not permitted to see her only surviving grandparent? Gossiping friends, perhaps, had pointed out taunts in the newspapers about the pension for 'Old Mother Hunn'. As for Joan, though always taking her lead from George, she may have wished, for his own sake, that he could take a more relaxed attitude. George almost certainly stood awkwardly in the background, looking at his watch and leaving the women to exchange polite conversation.

On their way across Devonshire the travellers stopped in Cullompton. True to her role throughout her life, Esther was providing a home for Mary's orphaned daughters, the twins Louisa and Mary Ann and their younger sister Caroline. George came to the bookshop alone, Joan and Harriet remaining at the inn, but Esther did not take offence. The sight of him was enough, as is evident from the account she wrote to Mary Ann in a letter which is moving both for the unaffected pleasure it expresses and because it is a rare moment when this patient and silent participant in the story breaks into speech.[868]

> We all still feel intoxicated from the effects of yesterday. We were all collected together in my best parlour. The girls with each a volume of The Life of Johnson—when we heard a voice

calling if Mrs Murch was home—we heard it once but paid no great attention to it—upon its being repeated I rose to see who the enquirer might be when I opened the door—you must judge of my feelings when I beheld the Delight of my—(of ours I must say)—[word missing] ready to enter. I cannot say that we received him very gracefully (at least I believe not) but to the feelings of the heart it must all be attributed. He staid with us twenty minutes perhaps half an hour. I ask'd him many questions one important one which was that He woud be in Bath to pay his long promis'd visit in December where he hoped he shoud see me—I told Him I hoped so too. The sweet attention He paid to the Girls I was delighted with He gave each of them a Soveraing —Said He must goe into the Shop to buy a Book. Mary Ann had the pleasure of choosing for him Crabbs poems. He turned round to Mr Murch shook hands with him and put in it ten pound. It gave me very great pleasure to find that you had a visit from Mrs C and Miss C—tell us is she as handsome as she [? ?] to be. You ask how I think he looks—I think him very much thiner but he was looking cheerful and happy and he told me he was very well. He asked us if we woud have some franks to which we said yes—then I produced the worst paper pens and Ink that coud be given to a Right Honble for to tell the truth I grudged the time I took to give him any. Then we were to think who to, the girls of course named one for Grandmama and Aunt—I named one for Wm—to be sure said he— and one for George— so they are filling up their franks… For to say truth they are not very expert with the pen… for they have been thinking how dearly their Dear Mama loved Dear Ancle Canning and it has been rather too much for them. He looked at the Books they were reading and was much pleased at their choice—he left us all gratifyed with the visit only wishing it longer—Bless him for the time it was. Do not expect us this coming week for I do not think it will be possible for me to do all I have to do early enough to move but as I hope the Dear Girls are content to stay—I feel

> satisfyed—we shall give you timely notice of our departure from here. Good night my dear Sister—Mr Murch (who is not very well) hopes his kindest regards—and believe me as ever my dearest sisters truly affect. E Murch

Having run out of red wax, Esther sealed her letter with black, but to avoid giving alarm by seeming to be in mourning she added four exclamation marks.

The ceremony in Plymouth was the occasion of one of George's most celebrated public (as opposed to parliamentary) speeches, in which he sought to justify his policy of non-intervention following the French invasion of Spain the previous May.[869] Inevitably, being in Plymouth, he spoke about the Navy.[i] Equally inevitable was his complete silence on the personal associations that the town had for him. Plymouth had been important to his mother: she had once cut a figure there. George, while still a schoolboy, had solemnly advised her to leave the town to find a more refined and appreciative audience. It was more than forty years since Mary Ann had gone there with Reddish, more than thirty since George had persuaded her not to go back to perform for John Bernard. Her patron Lord Courteney and her friend Dr Gashing were gone. Bernard was in America. There can have been few if any who still remembered her as the ruling favourite at Frankfort Gate, or as the heroine who braved the haunted carpenter's shop; few who remembered Richard Hunn, draper turned actor, and his father the master cooper and alderman. It was a new generation of dignitaries who were honouring George.

While at Saltram he went with his host to the theatre – not the old Frankfort Gate theatre, but the new Theatre Royal which had opened in 1813. When he arrived, the audience rose and

i He likened his apparent inaction in the Spanish crisis to the stillness of the great ships in the waters off Plymouth. 'You well know, Gentlemen,' he said, 'how soon one of those stupendous masses, now reposing on their shadows in perfect stillness – how soon, upon any call of patriotism or necessity, it would assume the likeness of an animated thing – instinct with life and motion – how soon it would ruffle, as it were, its swelling plumage – how quickly it would put forth all its beauty and its bravery – collect its scattered elements of strength and awaken its dormant thunder.'

cheered and the orchestra interrupted the overture to play 'God Save the King'. The newspapers described this as a spontaneous and heartfelt tribute, all the more remarkable because, they pointed out, it was in a place where he was 'without connections'. He left before the end, pleading a bad cold. The cold, which he blamed on the damp room in Bath, was genuine enough – its effects were to last for the rest of the year – but it was also a convenient excuse. The programme consisted of three recent one or two act musical comedies: *Simpson & Co.* by John Poole, *The Actress of all Work* by William Oxberry, and *Maid or Wife* by Barham Livius and Thomas Cooke. He was probably bored, and impatient to get back to Lord Morley's comfortable house to deal with his letters. Or perhaps there was something more to it, perhaps he was affected by that old unspoken connection, moved unexpectedly by the thought of his mother many years ago receiving the same 'universal applause' bestowed now upon the leading actress of the evening, Miss Brunton.[870]

If George was touched by the recollection of his mother's connection with Plymouth he didn't let her know it. He told her of his visit to the theatre and the civic ceremony and alluded briefly to the beauty of the countryside, but without a hint that she might have her own memories of the place. She seems to have sensed this, and displayed her disappointment by rebuking him for not having told her that he planned to stay several weeks at Saltram. If he could remain for so long away from London, surely he might have afforded her more than a quarter of an hour. It wasn't true that he had not told her his itinerary, and in any case a great deal had been made in the newspapers about his absence from London, but there was a deeper discontent underlying her complaint – a feeling, perhaps, that he had somehow missed an opportunity to show sympathy. Perhaps to make amends, he told her, briefly and unenthusiastically, a little more about his sightseeing in Plymouth – the Breakwater, Mount Edgecombe and 'other sights necessary to be seen'.[871]

In the weeks following his departure from Saltram, where he had enjoyed 'not holiday but relaxation', his letters to Mary Ann were more than usually brusque. Then, having a few days earlier told her firmly not to force him to write in the middle of the week, he broke his own rule in order to send her some reports with which, he said, he was greatly pleased. These probably referred to the progress of George Thompson, who with George's help had obtained a place at the East India Company College at Haileybury to train for service in India. Young Thompson had postponed his entry to Haileybury in order to spend time with his dying mother, a sacrifice of career to private feelings that George clearly found hard to sympathise with, although as it turned out he was glad of the delay, because it meant young Thompson was not involved in an outbreak of unrest among the cadets. He now seemed to be doing well. A week later, after Mary Ann had inveigled him into responding to a petition, he grumbled, 'If other people have no consideration for me, it is high time I had some for myself.' It must have been galling for Mary Ann to find herself lumped with 'other people'. At the end of December, sensing that his mother deserved an explanation for the fluctuations in mood reflected in his letters, he revealed that he had been ill since before his Bath and Plymouth journey, and that he had been laid up for almost three weeks, only getting out of bed while it was being made.[872]

Ill health thwarted his 'sincere' intention of visiting her at Christmas. Despite another bad cold, caught at the funeral of his nephew, Lord Titchfield, he managed a brief visit at Easter 1824 and promised another in the autumn, but when the time came the death of the King of France proved to be 'the annihilation of all my plans'. He consoled Mary Ann with the thought that kings of France do not die every year.[i] He would try again in December, he said. A return of the gout at Christmas 1824 threatened to

i Louis XVIII's death in September 1824 also prevented George from visiting Walter Scott, to whom he wrote on 17 September: 'it may perhaps sound unreasonable enough, to complain that the same stroke, which changes the condition of 30 million of men, stops also my visit to Scotland.' (BL Add Mss 89143/1/1/136).

annihilate this plan too, but he came despite his illness. Joan might well have stopped him, but she was in Paris with Harriet. The newspapers reported that he was in Bath for the sake of his health, in company with Lord Liverpool. The two old friends were jointly honoured with the freedom of the city of Bristol. After the ceremony there was a feast, more speeches and the ringing of bells and raising of flags. George returned to London with another desperate cold, which he blamed this time on the Bristol feast.[873]

In between the high points of George's visits, the correspondence between mother and son went on smoothly for more than a year, with George displaying nothing worse than occasional irritation. Mary Ann continued to anticipate the pension and run up debts. She tried to hide this by sending bills to the trustee of the pension, Mr Smith, asking him to pay them and recoup the money from her next instalment, the practice that had got her into trouble twenty years before when Walter Borrowes was the trustee. Mr Smith had not objected so long as he could repay himself, but now, because of the delays to the sugar revenue, George was paying the pension each quarter out of his own pocket, so Mr Smith had to send the instalments direct to him when they came in, which brought Mary Ann's bills to light. George suggested that he was annoyed for Mr Smith's sake, but went on to complain on his own account: 'I do not grudge the advance, my dear Mother, but I do object to being mixed up in the details of your expenditure… I really think this is hard upon me… I beg it may not happen again.'[874]

Similar irritation erupted as Frederick sought his help over the most serious of the many mishaps in his naval career. Now a post-captain in command of the 28-gun frigate *Tweed*, stationed off Brazil, Frederick quarrelled with his officers, and had one of them, Lieutenant Hannaford, the ship's master, incarcerated in a tiny cabin, which became an oven in the tropical heat. Although a court martial found Hannaford guilty of insubordination, on the *Tweed's* return to England he alleged that Frederick had exceeded his authority and launched a lawsuit against him. Frederick expected George to extricate him from his trouble, preferably by finding him a suitable civilian job. After two angry letters to Mary Ann on the subject, George felt he had gone too far: 'This, my dear Mother, you will know is not for yourself, but for those who importune you.' He added a note to say his wife and daughter had returned. Perhaps it was the thought of them that had made him soften his rebuke. The following week he said his wife and daughter sent kind remembrances to her.[875]

When at length the case came to court (with George's political opponent Henry Brougham representing Hannaford) the jury awarded damages of £250. Since Hannaford had claimed £10,000, Mary Ann felt that Frederick was vindicated. Saying as much to George, she asked him to lend her money towards the damages and costs, which amounted to £800. He grieved for her grief, he said, but was extremely careful not to 'impeach' the verdict of the court, nor to approve of it. As Emma Hunn wrote to a friend, he was 'too public a character to venture any open favour for a Brother', but he showed his sympathy by sending Mary Ann £200, as a gift not a loan, for her to use as she thought fit, obviously intending her to hand it over to Frederick. Frederick hoped that the Admiralty would contribute, but George found out that this would not be done; it showed, he said, that the Admiralty did not hold Frederick entirely blameless.[876]

Mary Ann and her family were not alone in incurring George's wrath by their ill-timed and inappropriate requests. Even his inoffensive Aunt Fanny sent him a 'strange and impudent' letter from an '<u>utter stranger</u>' seeking an introduction. 'I <u>will not</u> see Mr Sinclair,' George replied, 'I <u>will not.</u>' He apologised for writing such a disagreeable letter to his aunt, and ended 'Ever affectionately'. His cousin, Fanny Leigh, now Lady Caithness, received a still sharper rebuke when she wrote pressing her husband's claim to fill a vacancy in the representative peerage of Scotland. George protested that her letter was written 'in a tone to which I am not much accustomed, & by which I am not very likely to be swayed'. He tried to soften his rebuke by a touch of facetiousness that recalled that they had known each other since Fanny was a child, but he was angry at the attempt to involve him in 'Scotch arrangements', properly the business of Lord Melville.[877]

For closer members of his family George exerted all the influence at his command. When Harriet married Ulick John de Burgh, Earl of Clanricarde, in April 1825, George encouraged his son-in-law's political aspirations by making him a marquess and appointing him under-secretary of state at the Foreign Office. Clanricarde was a notorious womaniser, and a card-player every bit as reckless as poor William; gossip reported that George had to rescue him from a serious gambling scandal.[878]

As for William, it clearly was not 'transcendent merit' that advanced him from disgraced midshipman to commander in three years. His first command was not prosperous. He was charged with negligence when his ship the *Sappho* was damaged off Halifax. The gambling addiction was not cured, and at the end of 1825 George arranged to have the *Sappho* sent to the Cape, to separate William from his gambling 'ally'. Before leaving Halifax, however, the ship was declared unseaworthy, and the captain and crew were ordered back to England on board, as it happened, the *Tweed*, Frederick's ship. One wonders what uncle and nephew talked about on the voyage home, both of them beneficiaries of George's influence and victims of his dominant will. Meanwhile, the commander-in-chief intervened to have the charge of negligence dropped.[879]

Despite an attack of gout George was well enough in the weeks before Harriet's wedding to negotiate the settlement and attend the ceremony, but he then succumbed once more. His hands were affected. Twice he got his secretary to write to Mary Ann for him, and the first letter he wrote himself was to her. He was writing, he said, more than was prudent. A few weeks later he remembered he had not paid into the Indian orphan fund since coming to office three years before. He mentioned the fund several times in the next two months, each time saying he would look into it once

Parliament had risen, and asking Mary Ann to remind him.[880] Both of them were ill during the early summer, and the Indian orphan may have been overlooked again.

At the end of June, something Mary Ann wrote about her state of health was sufficiently alarming for George to ask George Thompson, who happened to be visiting Bath, to furnish a clearer and fuller account, and then to call at the Foreign Office. Thompson was now twenty-one, almost qualified for India, and his letters on his own affairs had made a good impression on his exacting godfather. George also asked for the address of Mary Ann's friend, Mr Turner, ostensibly so that he could direct her consignment of wine to him, but probably also in order to open a channel of communication about her health. And when Mary Ann annoyed him by forwarding a letter from a Mr Sigmond, who was seeking a post as private secretary, instead of sending Sigmond's letter back, he wrote to him, probably because he was related to Joseph Sigmond, one of the leading medical men in Bath, and therefore someone worth cultivating for Mary Ann's sake. It is possible that Mary Ann had been acquainted with Joseph since her Exeter days, but this passing reference is the only glimpse we have of the relationship. There are many such strands in Mary Ann's life story that are lost.[881]

George had hardly recovered from his gout when he went down with a stomach complaint. For most of July he stayed at Gloucester Lodge. He was bled in his right arm, losing 'by leeches and lancet' sixty ounces, which left him unable to write his weekly letter on 16 July. Fearing that the newspapers would publish his illness, George got Joan to write his Saturday letter, which she did in a stiff and formal note, starting 'My dear Madam…'. On the Monday she wrote again, this time a more friendly letter, commiserating on the uncomfortable heat, and including a piece of family news about Harriet. The letters were franked by one of the under-secretaries, Lord Howard de Walden, son of Charles Ellis. The next day George was able to write for himself. By the beginning of August he was 'essentially well', he said, promising to visit Bath before the end of the year, and adding that his wife sent her kind regards. The summer's exceptionally warm weather extended to the end of October. Enjoying the seclusion of Charles Ellis's house at Seaford, George wrote with an expansiveness as rare as the autumnal warmth, that 'I am always and everywhere my dear Mother's most dutiful and affectionate son.' The weather broke in mid-November, but George stayed away from London as long as he could.[882]

Mary Ann found the summer's heat oppressive. At the end of October she accidentally caused a small fire at home, and although not hurt was badly shaken, making it urgent to find her a companion. One suggestion was that she should move to a house she could share with someone else, but George immediately saw the difficulty: Mary Ann was not always tolerant, and in the event of friction it would be hard to extricate her from the arrangement without a 'squabble'. Mary Ann next considered taking a paid companion, and identified a possible candidate, whose letter of application she sent to George for approval, not waiting until her usual day for writing. He sent it back at once, refusing to advise on the person's suitability, and warning that he could not undertake to provide the lifetime pension that was customary in such cases; this had to be made plain at the outset, to check any implicit claim that might establish itself. He expressed himself in more emollient terms than often in the past, and did not complain at being forced to reply in the middle of the week, but still he feared that Mary Ann would feel he had been harsh. When Saturday came he wrote again, saying that he might have let his midweek letter count for his weekly tribute, but would not.[883]

A companion from the family would be best. He suggested having her granddaughters, Mary's twins, to live with her, although he admitted that they would not be able to remain alone with her if she became too feeble to 'superintend' them. Mary Ann replied that the twins could not live with her. He asked why, but she evaded the question, so he asked again. It can't have been easy for her to admit that it was because of the condition in Richard Thompson's will, which Mary had endorsed in hers. The Thompsons had accepted her in their family, and knew of her long years of blameless life, but had still deemed her unfit to superintend her unmarried granddaughters – the last cruel effect of her old disqualification. The immediate solution was, inevitably, that Esther came from Cullompton to be with her.[884]

For some time George had been saying he would visit Bath around Christmas time. As business built up he had to put off the trip: it would be just before New Year, and then it would be just after, then the middle of January, and then not before Easter. He could not make a promise, he said, but it was 'a contingent engagement' and 'sincere intention'. In making this distinction he was gently teasing Mary Ann, and there was self-mockery too, a recognition that they shared certain awkward characteristics, including a pedantic tendency to rake over small details. His regret sounds genuine, on his own account as well as hers. He begged her to keep Esther with her. With his letter on 31 December he sent £200, the quarter's instalments of the pension and the allowance, plus £25 to repair the ravages of the fire. He ended: 'I close the year 1825 with this letter to you and am for the next year as for all past years, my dear Mother's dutiful and affectionate son.'[885] Mary Ann, always so quick to detect a moment of coldness, could also appreciate the warmth of this expansion of his usual formula.

While Frederick was at sea in 1826 it was convenient for Emma to come to Bath to relieve Esther. She spent several spells on duty there. George, who had been irritated by her in the past, was pleased to receive her bulletins. He called her Mary Ann's kind nurse.[886] Her kindness was severely tested. Visitors like young Stratford might be impressed by Mary Ann's 'expressive countenance and commanding air'; such traits were more irksome to a daughter-in-law living in the house. It had never been an easy relationship. Emma, who could not forget that she was the daughter of an admiral and may have been frustrated by Frederick's comparatively unsuccessful career, hoped to change the family name to Pickmore,[i] but realised that it could not be done while Mary Ann was alive. She described her mother-in-law as 'a woman not to be offended with impunity; her disposition and feelings are of a violent character…'[887] It is unlikely that her growing infirmity made Mary Ann any milder or more tolerant.

When George eventually paid his flying visit, at the end of March 1826, he took note of the extra expense arising from having a companion, even if it was a member of the family, and undertook to send a contribution. He could tell Mary Ann about her great-grandchild, Harriet's baby girl, born the month before, although the demands of work meant he had seen little of her. He felt better for his visit, he said.[888]

As Mary Ann's health declined the flow of letters became thinner. The Hannaford case at the start of 1826 was the last time she troubled George over Frederick. In April she pressed him to intervene in the Admiralty on behalf of a friend, following it up with a lengthy memorial on the case, and provoking a complaint of the plagues he had to endure from those who did not understand the workings of government. After this there would no more inconvenient requests and applications, and no more teasing questions for him to answer. In the summer she again suffered from the heat, and at the end of August wrote something that George found seriously alarming; 'God grant your misgivings may be without foundation,' he replied.[889] He had to rely on Emma and Mr Turner for clearer information.

George's letters in 1826 told of his wife's illness, his own comparatively good health despite the strain of overwork, and his travels – back and forth to Brighton and Hastings for the sea air, to Eton College and Windsor to see Carlo and the King (with whom he was now, as a result of adroit manipulation, on better terms), and to Paris in the late summer. He warned her not to expect a

i Had Emma persevered with this scheme she would have had to decide which form of her family name to adopt, *Pickmore* or *Pickmere*.

letter on the first Sunday of his French trip, but in Calais found himself with a free moment to send her a line to reach her at the usual time. When Mary Ann, still keeping up her correspondence with friends, sent him a letter to forward without stating the addressee he returned it without the sarcasm he employed on similar occasions in the past. Perhaps he was too busy, or perhaps he realised that her mistake was a sign of failing faculties. When sending the October instalment of the allowance he included extra money for medicines, and also £100 to cover four missed contributions to the Indian orphan's fund.[890]

At this point his thoughts were already of the Christmas holidays. On his return from Paris at the end of October his thoughts were still of Christmas and his next visit to Bath. But before then there was an eventful session of Parliament to negotiate. All through November, as a crisis unfolded in Portugal and fears grew of a war with Spain, he counted the weeks. 'To Christmas I look forward for our meeting,' he wrote on the 11 November. 'God bless and sustain you my dear Mother till then.' In his next letter, a fortnight later, he wrote hurriedly in the midst of his work: 'A few weeks will bring me to the end of it, and then comes Christmas!'[891]

During Mary Ann's ten years in Henrietta Street, as she became an old woman, and George a prematurely aged man, mother and son may have softened towards each other, but the fundamentals of the relationship were unchanged; it was never anything but unequal. To all the inequalities arising from the structure of society and their material circumstances, there was added the inevitable asymmetry in the relationship between an elderly mother, confined to a narrow round of social activities, and a grown-up son, active in public affairs. The emotional investment cannot be the same on both sides. George's commitment, in everything except the absolute contract that bound him to provide for her comfort and well-being, remained in his phrase a 'contingent engagement'. His letters, except when he was very angry, were witty, light and bantering, which seems to be the only way he could bear to keep up this remarkable exchange, week after week. Mary Ann's letters were long and outspoken, as she poured her feelings into them, trying to engage George in the details of her life. It must have been galling to get back no more than his scribbled assurance of his duty and affection.

We should not, however, exaggerate the inequality between them by suggesting that her life was as narrow as it might appear through the lens of George's letters. As we have seen, she never stopped thinking about, caring for and interfering with her other children and her grandchildren. She had also to invest considerable time, effort and ingenuity in the practicalities of her life – arranging her journeys, juggling the demands of creditors, keeping up appearances. In Bath, unlike Totteridge, she found her social level, participated modestly in civic events, and had a circle of friends. Above all, she conducted a wide correspondence. George's frank meant that she was not restricted in her letter-writing by the high cost. She had always been thoughtful, read books and newspapers, and kept up with new ideas, and however much her range may have contracted with age, she enjoyed a broad hinterland of interest and activity.

31.
The Son of an Actress

Lord Liverpool and his cabinet have generally been regarded as a dull lot.[i] They distrusted George's brilliance, but felt the lack of it when he wasn't with them. In days when cabinet ministers drafted their own documents, his ability to make a detailed case was hard to replace – on the day he left the cabinet in 1820, he spent three hours carefully correcting and revising one of Castlereagh's dispatches – and he was acknowledged as the foremost orator in Parliament. Even now, when tastes in public speaking are so different, it's easy to be charmed by his wit, impressed by his imagery, seduced by the rhythms of his prose and the inventiveness of his expressions,[ii] but impossible not to be disgusted by the uses to which he put his gifts: defending the Peterloo Massacre, insulting the Blanketeers and extolling the virtues of the unreformed constitution. His speeches put him in the firing line as the member of the administration that the radicals most hated and most wanted to attack, but they also made him indispensable. He was, as a newspaper put it in 1819, 'the feather in the cap of the present dull-headed administration'.[892]

i Disraeli described Liverpool as an 'Arch-Mediocrity who presided, rather than ruled, over this cabinet of Mediocrities' (Coningsby ii. ch. 1), and the label stuck. More recent historians such as Asa Briggs and Norman Gash have shown greater appreciation of Liverpool's dull virtues, in particular his skilful management of difficult colleagues.

ii Not everyone has been seduced. Hazlitt brilliantly demolishes Canning's oratorical pretensions, dismissing him as a 'mere House-of-Commons man' having 'something vapid, something second-hand in the whole cast of his mind' (*Spirit of the Age*, 181).

George had resigned from the government over the prosecution of Queen Caroline, but as we saw he returned following the death of Castlereagh in 1822. With difficulty Liverpool persuaded George's enemies in the Cabinet to accept him, but the King, unable to forget his suspicion that George had been Caroline's lover, stubbornly refused until the Duke of Wellington, himself a reluctant convert, begged him to accept Canning as an act of 'mercy and grace', the prerogative of kings. Unfortunately the King wrote to Liverpool pluming himself on his exercise of royal clemency to one who had incurred royal displeasure.[893] When George saw the letter he was so angry that it was a further two days before he accepted the post. He had done nothing to require forgiveness; it was, he said, like receiving an invitation to join Almack's exclusive social club and finding 'Admit the rogue' written across the back.[i] There was truth as well as humour in this quip. For a quarter of a century or more he had been admitted to the best houses, to the innermost councils of the state, to the King's presence, but in many minds there had been a reservation: he was too clever, not altogether a gentleman, a conspirator, a penniless Irishman. He was a rogue, an outsider, a usurper, who had forced entry into a world that was not his by birth. Given all this, how important was it that he was also the son of an actress?

Among his enemies one of the most inveterate was Harriet Arbuthnot. Married to a Tory politician and fixer, Charles Arbuthnot, she was also the close friend and confidante of the Duke of Wellington. Having been attached to Castlereagh she felt Canning made a sorry replacement at the Foreign Office, and yet she was realistic enough to see that there was no alternative – the view eventually reached by the Duke. Shabby deals, she thought, unceasing intrigue, and support for Jacobinism abroad were all that could be expected from a government dominated

i The 'Almack's' quip is regularly quoted, but I've not traced it to its source; the wording given here is from *HoP 1820–1832*. Almack's Assembly Rooms was an exclusive social and gambling club in St James's, founded in 1765. Its membership was severely controlled by a committee of ladies.

by Canning. And yet she was fascinated by him, always wanted to know his doings and how he reacted to events; she filled her diary with speculation and gossip about him. As time went on her stories centred more and more upon his unpredictable moods, his volcanic temper and his bullying of colleagues and opponents alike, but after his death she complained that without him politics was less interesting.[894]

For all her prejudice and dislike, for all her feeling that he wasn't quite a gentleman, Mrs Arbuthnot was unaffected by learning about Mary Ann and the stage. Her husband's family was related to Henry Barnard, husband of Molly Canning, and one of Mr Arbuthnot's aunts remembered delivering the money collected by Molly to Mary Ann in her Holborn garret. Mrs Arbuthnot's interest in human nature was stronger than her malice and she was delighted by this tale of Canning's sordid origins. After half a century, the aunt's memory of the incident was not altogether accurate, but she recalled that Mary Ann had gone on to be the kept mistress of an actor. Mrs Arbuthnot's comment is nicely balanced: 'To those who, like me, think there is a good deal *in blood*, it may appear that Mr Canning's want of principle or high & honorable feeling may be derived from the stock he sprung from, while all must admire the institutions of a country where talent & genius can force their possessor into power & opulence in spite of the most adverse circumstances.'[895] What's clear is that nothing she found out about Mary Ann made her think any worse of George than she did already.

When urging Mary Ann to leave the stage, George made much of the world's prejudice against the theatre. His career, he said, and his ability to provide for her future comfort, would be damaged by a connection with the stage. When there was a question of either Charles or Mary going on the stage he reacted with horror, arguing again that the world, rightly or wrongly, was prejudiced against actors and actresses. This was clearly a genuine fear on his part. It was suggested earlier, when we were considering Mary Ann's choice of career, that the view of the stage as a scandalous trade, equivalent to prostitution, was not as prevalent as is sometimes alleged. Nonetheless there were clearly reservations about it, on moral and social grounds, and these may have been strengthened by changes in public attitude, such as the reaction to the French Revolution and spread of evangelical Christianity, between the 1770s and 1820s. To have a mother who had been an actress was never going to be an asset in a political career, but then neither was it an asset to be the nephew of a failed City banker. There were in George's family background many 'adverse circumstances', to use Mrs Arbuthnot's phrase, but the most adverse for a politician was that he was penniless and without powerful connections. Apart from the obvious disadvantages of not being able to buy his own seat in Parliament, and having no family or personal influence to use in bargaining for favours, his poverty meant that his motives were always suspect; he was always assumed to be out for what he could get. It was easy for opponents to represent him as that stock figure, an impoverished Irish adventurer. The *Examiner* for example likened him to Sir Lucius O'Trigger in *The Rivals*, with the additional vice of hypocrisy. When in 1813 he was trying to negotiate a return to Lord Liverpool's government, the saying was that he had made himself small like a weasel, to creep back into office.[896]

The radical journalist William Cobbett knew about Mary Ann, but although he might throw out the word 'play-actress' as an insult, what really mattered was the iniquity of the pension, and even that was insignificant compared with the still greater iniquity of the Lisbon Job. In an article attacking the government's bullion policy, Cobbett starts with an incidental reminder that 'we have already paid *ten thousand pounds* to this former play-actress and her daughter, who, it appears, has no higher honour than that of being a half-sister of the Portugal ambassador'. He then goes on to explain that the bullion policy will cause the price of grain to fall dramatically, so that the value of the play-actress's pension will increase from 666 to 2,000 bushels of wheat. 'Before it can come to this,' he added, 'Mrs Hunn must live upon the people's dead bodies, for nine tenths of them will be starved to death.' The whole passage is designed to be offensive, and 'play-actress' might make it slightly more so, but it doesn't affect the serious point that Cobbett is making.[897]

Like Cobbett and the satirist Peter Pindar, the radical Henry 'Orator' Hunt was aware of Mary Ann's history, and made good use of it in his attacks on George, which must have been hurtful for him, and for Mary Ann, but for the most part it could be dismissed as vulgar abuse, as part of the political rough-and-tumble, like dead cats. One of Hunt's attacks on Mary Ann included an accusation that she had torn down posters about his meetings in Bristol and Bath. It was a controversial matter at the time, because there was a public outcry over a case brought against a young boy called Dogood for tearing down pro-government posters in Birmingham. George didn't believe Hunt's accusation, but nonetheless warned Mary Ann to avoid drawing attention to herself: 'you cannot do, or say, anything that is observed or reported without my feeling the effects of it (though I may never know it) in aggravated difficulties.'[898]

Among George's parliamentary colleagues and opponents there were those who had come across Mary Ann in her youth. Sheridan, of course, knew all about her acting career, but he was too generous (and too aware of his own vulnerability) to attack George on her account. Others with less reason to be kind also knew. Lord Glenbervie, George's successor at the Pay Office in 1801, remembered having seen Mary Ann as Jane Shore, but there's no reason to think it increased his antagonism towards George. His reluctance to cooperate over the official residence can be accounted for by the bitterness of George's attacks on the new Addington administration. Fellow Pittite and one-time rival Lord Mulgrave had known Mary Ann even before her Drury Lane days. As a boy he had carried messages for his older brother Charles

Phipps, the lieutenant on leave from his ship who fell for Mary Ann in Dulwich in 1772. While we don't know what Mulgrave thought in private about George's origins, there's no indication that his behaviour towards him as a colleague was affected; any friction between them was explained by their jockeying for the position of foreign secretary, and by George's low opinion of Mulgrave's abilities, which he expressed freely in private and is unlikely to have disguised in public.[899] In general, Mary Ann's past may have confirmed the impressions of those who already had reason to feel that George wasn't quite a gentleman, but otherwise there's little sign that it affected his standing in Parliament.

There were two well documented occasions when Mary Ann's acting past became a matter of comment in elite circles. In 1822 a group of gentlemen were discussing the matter, and one of them expressed disbelief that Canning was the son of an actress. The question was decided a few days later when one of the disputants, Sir Robert Wilson, received a letter enclosing a playbill of 1788. It was from the theatre in Chester where Mrs Hunn was appearing in Nathaniel Lee's *Theodosius*. 'If any friends of yours keeps an album in after times it will be deemed a curiosity,' said Sir Robert's correspondent, suggesting that he at least didn't take it particularly seriously.[900]

It was during the last great crisis of Canning's career, the long negotiations leading to the formation of his short-lived ministry in 1827, that it was said, by the future Whig prime minister and hero of the Great Reform Act, Lord Grey, that the son of an actress was 'incapacitated *de facto* for the premiership of England'. Grey and Canning had a history of mutual animosity going back to when Grey had formed the Association of the Friends of the People, and Canning had gone over to Pitt. James Abercromby, a fellow Whig,[i] described Grey as 'violent, ill-tempered, and influenced purely by personal feelings'. For himself, Abercromby wrote, 'I am no defender of the life and character of Canning, but I should scorn

i James Abercromby (1776–1858) was an influential Whig MP, much involved in the parliamentary manoeuvring around the formation of the Canning administration of 1827.

to depreciate him or any other man by vilifying his parentage and reproaching him with the frailties of his mother.' The word *frailties* suggests that Abercromby either took it for granted that actresses were '*de facto*' immoral, or that he knew something of her liaison with Reddish, but he added that everyone on the opposition side of the House disowned Grey's 'vulgar abuse'.[901]

The need for a new government arose because, at the end of February 1827, Lord Liverpool suffered a stroke and was found unconscious on the floor of his study. George and other members of the Cabinet tried to carry on, but it was soon apparent that the case was hopeless and that Liverpool, even if he lived, would have to resign. As in 1822, the expectation was that Canning would fill the vacancy, but the obstacles were enormous. One was the personal animosity caused by his towering temper and imperious treatment of colleagues. He still had devoted friends, but anyone who crossed him inevitably suffered from his caustic tongue. There were also serious issues of policy. His support for Catholic emancipation, even though he had acquiesced in the postponement of decisive action, alienated most of his colleagues in Liverpool's cabinet, who refused to serve under him. Instead he had to cobble together a new Cabinet from his own friends and a few pro-Catholic Tories, along with as many of the Whigs as were not put off by his opposition to parliamentary reform and his perceived deviousness over the Catholic question. With so many real difficulties in his path, the actress taunt thrown at him by Grey can hardly have affected the issue. In the end it was only after six weeks of bruising negotiations that, just before Easter, he was able to kiss hands as prime minister.[902]

The actress story was still going around a few weeks later when a newspaper reproduced the playbill from Mary Ann's 1774 benefit, and incidentally reminded its readers that she had become 'in one way or other, Mrs Reddish'. But the sting in the tail had less to do with Mary Ann than with George's reputation for duplicity: 'Many of our readers are not probably aware that the

Prime Minister of ENGLAND is the son of an actress—but such is the fact … It ceases, therefore, to be a matter of surprise that her son should have turned out SUCH A CAPITAL ACTOR.'[903]

This son of an actress, however, had reached the place he had been working towards ever since he first glimpsed 'the mechanism and machinery by which the actions of the great Pantomime are guided'.

32.
Kind at Last

All through the autumn of 1826 George had been looking forward to Christmas, which he coupled with the prospect of visiting Bath. Never before had he expressed such sustained eagerness to see his mother. At the beginning of December he told her he was very busy but very well, and a week nearer the Christmas holidays. Then there was a blank, four weeks in which Mary Ann heard nothing from him. She could read in the newspapers that he was indisposed, suffering it was said from a cold and inflammation, for which he was bled, but two days later he was back at work. On 12 December he delivered a masterly defence of his Portuguese policy, and for many days the newspapers were full of the speech and its repercussions. Although he was preoccupied, and suffered something of a relapse after the strain of the Portuguese debate, it is hard to explain why he did not write for four weeks, not even to reassure her. Unless there were letters that have been lost (which so far as we can tell was almost unprecedented in their long correspondence) the likeliest explanation is that he knew, from Mr Turner perhaps, that Mary Ann was herself too ill to take notice. If so, she had recovered enough by the end of the month to ask after his health and remind him of the long anticipated Christmas visit. On New Year's Eve she had a letter at last, reporting that he was better, but about to go down to Brighton for the sea air. He promised a visit during January.[904]

At the start of 1827 Mary Ann was well enough to take note of her business affairs. George sent the January instalments of the pension and the allowance, along with £25 for Aunt Esther. To save Mary Ann the trouble of passing on a share of the pension to Maria, presumably for the benefit of Mary's daughters, he sent £50 direct to Shawford. Esther had come to Bath and George reminded Mary Ann to reimburse the costs of her journey. Her sister's presence may have signalled a sense that the end was drawing near. Over the years George had overseen the payment of well over a hundred quarterly instalments of the pension, and he may have guessed that this was to be the last. Mary Ann was, no doubt, relieved and thankful to receive the money, but will have been equally gratified by the thoughtfulness of the letter that accompanied it, and by the 'kindest remembrances' from George's wife.[905]

In the new year George had to travel to Windsor for the badly managed funeral of the Duke of York. The Bishop of Lincoln's death from pleurisy in February was attributed to the long wait in the freezing chapel. From Windsor George went straight down to Bath to repay Mary Ann for the cancelled Christmas visit and to discuss government affairs with Lord Liverpool, who had been too ill to attend the deadly funeral. The two old friends and rivals, sick and prematurely aged, were now indisputably hanging from the same lamp-post. George spent a whole day with Mary Ann, but dined with the prime minister, because, he said, she was not well enough to have company at dinner; possibly he was unwilling to sit eating his boiled fowl and mutton chop while Emma Hunn or Aunt Esther fed Mary Ann a diet of invalid slops.[906] This time there was no avoiding the aldermen of Bath, because he was to be presented with the Freedom of the City. In his speech accepting the honour (and the accompanying gold bar worth fifty guineas) he paid tribute to his friend Lord Liverpool, but made no allusion to his personal connection with the place which had been his mother's home for twenty years.[907] Perhaps he mentioned it in private conversation with Mayor Eleazer Pickwick – or was it something that each knew, and knew the other knew, but both kept quiet about? Whatever he said to the mayor, it's to be hoped that, when he left Lady Liverpool's dinner table to take tea with Mary Ann, he made no secret of where he was going. Surely the time was long gone when he had to make believe that his old friends knew nothing of Mary Ann.

Thirty years before, as a young MP enjoying his first taste of office, George had been bemused, condescending and somewhat scornful when his grandmother wished him to be present at her deathbed. Time had passed, teaching him to take such things more seriously. In the spring his aunt Bess Leigh had died of apoplexy, and he had hurried down to Brighton for the funeral. Shortly after Mary Ann's move to Bath, when he was stronger and less worn out by office, he had promised to come to her at once if she felt she was near to death; just four years ago, he had reminded her he was still within reach.[908] Now it was plain that his own feeble health and the overwhelming burden of work would make it impossible to drop everything and rush to his mother's bedside. So although Mary Ann was not yet on the point of death, he must have realised he was there to say goodbye. Mary Ann, who professed throughout her life that death would be a welcome release, also must have known.

George left Bath on the Wednesday, staying one night on the way with his colleague William Huskisson. As soon as he reached Brighton he collapsed and took to his bed. He managed a brief note to Mary Ann at the end of the week, apologising for being late, and speaking lightly of his illness as a 'cold I brought from Windsor'. He was ill all the next week, suffering as much from the remedies ('two cuppings and a proper bleeding in the arm') as from the rheumatic cold itself. He detected some improvement, he said, but not enough to 'facilitate the disobedience, of which I am at the moment guilty, to the positive Instructions of my Physician not to write. I must therefore shorten my sin, though I would not for the world have omitted it altogether.' The following week he wrote in the same straightforwardly affectionate tone. Having described the rheumatic pains that had attacked each part of his body in turn, he said he was currently enjoying a short pain-free interval; he must not abuse it, he wrote, 'nor would I have ventured to turn it to any other purpose than this of writing to you.'[909] It's always hard to say whether he gave her much thought in between his weekly letters, but in these last days, as he too lay sick in bed, it does appear that she was on his mind. And when he sends his wife's love and fond remembrance, perhaps it means that he and Joan had been speaking about her.

By then she may have been past noticing. Emma said that in her last days or weeks she was wandering in her wits.[910] The news of Lord Liverpool's stroke may have reached her. If so, perhaps the thought flitted through her mind that now her son's chance had come – a last flash of the electricity that had long ago propelled her on her picaresque journey. It is tempting to imagine that as she lay dying her thoughts, like so many of her letters and her conversations, centred on her glorious son, but it may not be so. She was not only the mother of George Canning. She had made a life of her own, and in her last secret moments other memories may have flooded back from her years of struggle and humiliation, achievement and disappointment, love and sorrow.

Two further letters from Frederick arrived, sent from Vera Cruz in December and January, and both franked by George on 6 March. If she was able to read them she will have been pleased by his expression of affection, but will have shaken her head over his mishandling of his affairs. He was an awkward man, always blaming his bad luck. He wrote of the 'dismal prospect' that awaited him as he contemplated his future, but said that her last letter, dated September, had removed a 'mountainous anxiety'. She had, it seems, finally convinced him that George's influence with the Admiralty was all used up, that nothing more could be done for him. 'Without hope,' he wrote, 'I shall be comparatively easy.' In December he complained that he'd been kept waiting for a good freight, and 'as usual I am disappointed'; in January he said he had got 'a something', enough at any rate to liquidate most of his debts. He asked after Maria's health, and said he was bringing a snug shawl for Aunt Esther and 'a box of cigars for Uncle Murch's whiffing'. 'God bless you, my Dear Mother,' he ended. 'Give my love to Maria and those around you desirous of hearing anything of Your Affect. Dutiful Son, Fred Hunn.'[911]

There is a melancholy about Frederick's surviving letters. He had long, lonely hours on his ship to devote to them, but he knew that nothing he could say would give his mother half the pleasure of George's hurried scrawls. He may have been afraid of his mother; he must always have known he was a disappointment to her. Who can tell what resentment, what sense of inadequacy, of not being loved, lay behind the obscene communication from school to his glamorous half-brother? He went through life doggedly pushing for advancement, expecting to fail, like his father, who had difficulty getting on with people and was, as Mary Ann said when she sought to make excuses for him, diffident and easily cowed. Emma was of a firmer disposition, and felt that Frederick had suffered from his mother's constant disparagement. 'Neither I nor my excellent husband stand high in her favour,' she told a cousin, 'Mr Canning is her favorite child, all others (as well they may) sink in the shade compared to him.'[912]

Emma herself left the house before the end, displaced, as she tartly remarked to another cousin, by an influx of relatives, as Maria and her family, and Mary's daughters, joined the faithful Esther. George was well enough to attend the House of Commons at the beginning of March, but then suffered a relapse.[913] His usual Saturday letter on 10 March was written on official notepaper still edged in black in honour of the Duke of York, and sealed with black wax. He warned Mary Ann not to believe exaggerated newspaper accounts of his indisposition. By the time the letter reached Bath, perhaps even by the time he wrote it at the end of his working day, she was dead. She was buried on 19 March in

Bath Abbey, which, since she was from a different parish, shows that someone was prepared to pay extra for this slight mark of distinction.[914] The precise place, however, is unmarked, possibly close to Letitia Canning's memorial stone, on which Mary Ann had reflected so bitterly in the Packet. The arrangements were presumably made by Maria or Esther, unless Mr Turner was commissioned to act on behalf of George, who was ill during the whole week between Mary Ann's death and her funeral.

On Sunday 11th George was visited by personal friends such as Lord Morley, who may have been alerted by first reports of his bereavement. At the Cabinet meeting next day George was reported to be unusually agitated, which was accounted for by a political crisis coming on top of his illness. By that night he was reported to be seriously indisposed. A week later, on the day of the funeral, he was sufficiently recovered to receive foreign ambassadors at his home. For most of the interim the newspapers reported that he was confined to his room and unable to conduct business. The illness was no doubt genuine enough, since he had mentioned it in his last Saturday letter, but one wonders whether the reports of his seclusion may have been cover for a very private visit to Bath. It is even possible that, perhaps with the help of Lord Morley, George left for Bath very early on Sunday, and was back in London in time for the Cabinet at two o'clock on Monday. This would certainly account for the turn for the worse on Monday night.[915]

Within six months George too was dead. The peerage he had never coveted was awarded to Joan, who became Viscountess Canning. William was drowned, in unexplained circumstances, while stationed in Madeira, about a year after the death of the father to whom he had been such a cruel disappointment.[i] The Canning name was kept before the public by Stratford, a

i William's body was discovered in a reservoir on the island and his death was attributed to cramp or an apoplectic fit while swimming. A comment in the *Times* (26 Oct. 1828) could be read as a discreet rebuttal of rumours of suicide ('the nature of Captain Canning's death need not therefore inflict an additional pang on those near connexions who now lament their loss…') . His body was brought to England and was buried in the cloisters of Westminster Abbey (*Times*, 4 Dec. 1828).

distinguished diplomat, in particular a notable ambassador to the Ottoman Empire in the 1840s and 1850s; and by Carlo, who inherited the viscountcy and became Viceroy of India, known as Clemency Canning for his comparatively conciliatory policy in the aftermath of the Sepoy Rebellion – pragmatism of which his father would have approved.

Mary Ann's story was forgotten, or worse than forgotten. She became a curiosity, a footnote to history, George Canning's scandalous actress mother. Biographers of Canning can't be blamed for dismissing her with a few words; Canning's life was politics, and until the Harewood archive became available his personal background, though well known in outline, was scantily documented. Mary Ann's contribution to his story is generally summed up in a series of stereotypes: the pretty young widow who hoped to exploit her charms by going on the stage; the middle-aged harridan, Mother Hunn, who badgered and embarrassed poor George; and finally the old woman of Bath chattering over the teacups about her glorious son.

About a century after Mary Ann's death the genealogist Frederick Gale, whose wife was descended from Frederick Hunn, saw through the stereotypes and guessed that behind them there was a 'remarkable woman'.[916] Over the course of twenty years Gale uncovered much about Mary Ann. His articles in *Notes & Queries* covering her parentage, husbands, descendants, and acting career have been invaluable. Without access to the Harewood papers he could not tell her story in her own words, but the Packet, her other writing, and George's weekly letters to her, confirm that Gale's intuition was right: she was indeed a remarkable woman, whose life deserves to be known.

Her story also contributes to the wider history of women in the man's world of Regency England. The early biographers of Canning asserted, against the Earl Grey view, that Mary Ann was a cultured, refined and well-born lady.[917] In the mid-twentieth century, Dorothy Marshall and Wendy Hinde caricatured her condescendingly as a pretty widow, and then highlighted her unpredictable and troublesome behaviour in later life, in order to show that George's treatment of her was reasonable and even generous. An exception to the patronising tendency among modern historians is P.J.V. Rolo, whose account of Mary Ann's life is brief and inaccurate, but captures something of her heroic and extraordinary character.[918] More recently still, there has been greater sensitivity, both among historians and in society at large, to the role and plight of women in history. When I have discussed my research with friends, the immediate response has usually been that Canning was a swine and Mary Ann his victim.

It's right to emphasise Mary Ann's helplessness in the face of overwhelming difficulties, frustrated and exploited as she was by one unsatisfactory man after another. Poverty, isolation, ignorance and the many vulnerabilities of women constrained her, limited her choices and directed the whole course of her life, from the time when she had to take in needlework to support her family in Dublin. Under a fairer dispensation for women, or if she had been surrounded by fairer-minded and less incompetent men, she would have found wider opportunities at every step of the way. But we should beware of consigning her to yet another stereotype. She was not a helpless victim. It's true that she was in all sorts of ways weak while George, and the other men in her life, were powerful, but she contrived to remain in control; she was never reduced to servitude. Her rackety life exemplifies many of the problems discussed in lofty generalities by authors like Mary Wollstonecraft and Priscilla Wakefield, who were arguing that women could and should take control of their destinies. Mary Ann's decisions, compromises and mistakes show how an intelligent and resourceful woman made sense of the world she lived in and navigated its dangers and difficulties.

The point is hard to grasp, because in her own account Mary Ann emphasises the image of herself as an injured woman, a helpless victim, forced by her father-in-law's irrational treatment to go on the stage, driven into Reddish's arms for protection, let down by Hunn, and all the time struggling under the legal disabilities and social restrictions imposed upon women. She presents this version of events because she has a case to make, but she undermines her case by showing how far she contrived to make her own judgements, take her own decisions, and even impose her will upon the world. There were times when everything collapsed: the death of her first husband; the revelation that Reddish could not marry her; the *Semiramis* disaster; Reddish's descent into madness; Hunn's refusal to let her leave the stage; her abandonment by the Whitlocks in Chester; George's outburst over the Newbery affair; the disastrous Totteridge experiment and its aftermath; the Parker affair. Every time, she extricated herself from the ruins, just as she pulled herself from the literal ruins of the theatre in Bury and was within days chatting with Elizabeth Whitlock in Wigan, boasting about George and his schoolboy achievements.

There are three character traits that Mary Ann highlights in the Packet: her elasticity, her predisposition to be happy, and her determination to live as a lady. We can see how the first two combined to carry her through the difficulties of her life, but what are we to make of the third? Was Mehitabel right? Could Mary Ann have saved herself and others a lot of trouble if only she had been less insistent on her social position? Living as a lady implies a level of refinement and respect from social inferiors, but above all what mattered to Mary Ann was her independence. Dragging herself around the country with a troupe of actors and subjecting herself to the hoots and hisses of provincial audiences, she clearly compromised on refinement and respect, but she kept her independence.

Mary Ann always avoided saying that she had any positive motive for choosing the stage. Any such admission would have confirmed Stratty's dreadful verdict, that she had all the time consulted her own pleasure. But her silence does not mean there were no positive reasons for choosing her career and staying in it. The glamour of the stage was one thing – the flattery of Garrick's attention and the attraction of working with him must have been almost irresistible – but it hardly accounts for the fifteen years during which she endured poverty, insecurity, illness and hostility for the sake of her work. We talk glibly of the lure of the greasepaint, and that is perhaps an adequate explanation for the foolish infatuation of Richard Hunn, but it hardly does justice to Mary Ann. Half a century later, a shrewd observer of women's lives would write this:

> Women, when they are young, sometimes think that an actress's life is a happy one – not for the sake of the admiration, not for the sake of the fame; but because in the morning she studies, in the evening she embodies those studies: she has the means of testing and correcting them by practice, and of resuming her studies in the morning, to improve the weak parts, remedy the failures, and in the evening try the corrections again. It is, indeed, true that, even in middle age, with such exercise of faculty, there is no end to the progress which may be made.[919]

Independence, taking responsibility for oneself, means more than earning one's own living – it includes learning, self-criticism, development, improvement. Florence Nightingale might not have chosen Mary Ann's chaotic life story to illustrate her point, but it's arguable, more than arguable, that what she wrote was true of Mary Ann and explains why she stayed in the theatre as long as she did. If that is what Stratty meant by consulting her own pleasure, then his accusation was partly true. Mary Ann could not admit it, and so presented herself as a helpless victim, but if we accept her plea we will distort and diminish her.

A further distortion arises from our tendency to cast the story in adversarial form. It's inevitable, because our sources consist of the letters of two people arguing with each other. Also, most of us have a propensity to take sides in what looks like yet another skirmish in the battle of the sexes. We adopt a figurehead: either

Mary Ann the downtrodden woman crying out for her natural rights as a mother; or George, the embattled outsider, plagued by her insatiable demands. We feel that in order to justify one protagonist we must denigrate the other, but it makes better sense to see two flawed but decent people trying to make the best of a situation which was appalling for both, and which they both rightly claimed was created by others. Their predicament originated in the dysfunctional family of Stratford Canning of Garvagh; it was the working out of the Abbey Street Logic, magnified by the tensions created by inequality.

The basic trajectory of their story is simple. In 1776 Mary Ann bowed to pressure and handed George over to Stratty and Mehitabel. Ten years later, following the meeting in Great Wild Street, George resolved in his heart that he would never live with his mother. When they took these fateful decisions, Mary Ann acted under duress, and George was little more than a child, so neither can be held entirely responsible, but from these two choices arose the separation between them. It was the great goal of Mary Ann's life to bring the separation to an end, while George was equally, obsessively, determined to maintain it.

That he would provide financial support was never in question; their differences were always about what more she was entitled to. As time went on Mary Ann conceded more and more, until she was content to live well out of George's way, expecting from him nothing more than a weekly letter and a few irregular visits. But she never lost her longing for spontaneous affection; she was never satisfied with mere duty. Their whole drama can be seen in their different interpretation of these two terms, affection and duty, which made up the formula that invariably closed George's letters: 'Ever my dear Mother's dutiful and affectionate son.' For Mary Ann, believer in Nature, and educated in love by a husband for whom all that mattered was the spontaneous sympathy between two hearts, affection transcended duty. For the sceptical and reserved George everything followed from and was measured by duty, including the affection which, as a son, he was bound to feel for his mother.

It's possible to exaggerate the extent to which George's behaviour was under firm rational control. His contemporaries sometimes described him as cold and calculating, and to us looking back he can appear the epitome of the dominant male in a patriarchal society, protected by layers of assertive self-confidence, elite culture and self-serving decorum. But alongside this we should remember his unhappy childhood, his social vulnerability and his ambivalence about his identity – a man without a father, an Irishman accidentally born in London. These weaknesses gave rise, no doubt, to his compulsion to control those around him, and in later years to his volcanic temper, but also, through these chinks in his armour, Mary Ann, with her predisposition to be happy, occasionally glimpsed signs of the spontaneous affection she hungered for, signs of Nature winning out over duty, over rationality and the constraints and prejudices of Society.

Even at the height of their conflict she was on the alert for these signs. In the final section of the Packet she recalled a recent meeting at which, she felt, he had looked on her more kindly than of late and had, without her asking, stayed with her for more than an hour. This flicker of warmth on his part, and her recent re-reading of old letters, made her think back to her reluctant decision to hand him over to Stratty's keeping – just after she had been forced to cut off his curls, when he was 'all my aching heart coud pray for'. Who could believe then that he would in time be 'taught to tread the <u>mere</u> cold path of duty'?[920] Later on she found what she was looking for in those moments in George's company which were the 'bonne bouche' of life, prompting her to declare that despite the troubles and struggles of her life the good predominated, 'for George Canning is my son'.[921]

There is no doubt that she was sincere, but we should not allow 'George Canning is my son' to be the last word. There are two objections to this way of summing up her eighty (or seventy-seven) years. First it smacks of monomania. Her obsession with her 'son in London' amused, bored and irritated her Bath friends, and by prompting their demands for patronage landed her in endless scrapes with George himself. It made her unkind to her other children, doing incalculable damage, leaving resentment in the family. Emma Hunn was clearly aware of its effect on Frederick's character. Even Mary Ann's well-loved daughter Mary suffered in comparison with George, and always bowed to his decrees. As for Samuel and Charles Reddish, they had many things against them, but it's hard not to see their mother's (and father's) preference for George as the first and most telling blight upon their lives. And in the end she was willing to see them shipped abroad, to Botany Bay, to Jamaica, to India, because it was inconvenient for George to have them in London.

The other objection to this view of herself is that, like that plea of victimhood, it diminishes her. One can see why, in old age, she found it appealing. Her acting career was a harsh struggle and more unsuccessful than successful; her professional writing stopped at one short novel; as a businesswoman marketing the Collyrium she prospered only briefly. Her glorious son, by contrast, was a public figure of great stature, a brilliant, fascinating and (in private at least) decent man, dutiful towards her, and, within limits, affectionate: nothing else she had achieved could match the glory of being the mother of such a son. But although old age has the privilege of passing judgement, we should not allow it to force a whole life into its narrow mould. We should not allow motherhood, even glorious motherhood, to blind us to Mary Ann's faults, nor to trump her other claims to our admiration. She was the girl for whom a 'wish pass'd like Electricity into my own Breast & never lost its force'; the woman whose mind possessed a large enough portion of 'elasticity' to recover from repeated humiliating failures; the woman 'not born for mediocrity', but with 'admiration for talent'. She was the bright eager girl who lapped up the Indian stories of the old sinner Holwell, and the trimmer catching the eye of young men in Islington, and the middle-aged woman just delivered of twins taking the nine-day sea voyage from Newcastle to London, or walking in the dark through the dirt of Gray's Inn Lane to her lodgings in Somers Town. Her two extended pieces of writing, her novel and the Packet, reveal a woman who had kept up with the advanced thinking of her day and had a genuine command of language. To sum her up, as she does herself, as the mother of George Canning, does no justice to her intelligence and courage, her resourcefulness, resilience and strength of mind.

Mary Ann and George may have been two decent people grappling with an impossible situation, but at times they fought each other fiercely and without scruple. He used his money (what money he had) and power, and the fact that she needed him more than he needed her, to dictate the terms of their relationship and keep her at a distance. For her part, during their bitterest years, from the Newbery incident of 1793 to her retreat from London in 1806, she pressed him sorely, exploiting his sense of duty and never letting up on her demands. We don't know what happened when they met face to face in those years; she could undoubtedly play the trimmer with him. But although her insistent demand for something more than cold duty may well have served, at the time of the Packet, as a cover for other demands – for recognition, money, patronage – in the end we can believe her when she said that what she wanted most from him was the natural love of a child for his mother. Still on the alert, she may have found signs of it in the expressions of affection he scrawled during their last winter. The fierceness had gone out of their exchanges. The disqualification, if not purified away, had become, as life drew to an end, increasingly irrelevant. He no longer felt the aftershocks of their meeting in 1786; she had lost her hunger for a share in his home life. He no longer had to keep her at bay; she no longer brooded over bitter words.

Appendix
When was Mary Ann Born?

Mary Ann knew that her birthday was 27 January, but she did not know the year. Her mother and aunt disagreed, her mother inclining to 1750, her aunt to 1747.[i] The issue became important at the time of Mary Ann's marriage in 1768, when on her aunt's reckoning she was 21 and so able to be married by licence without parental consent. The fact that the marriage was originally intended to take place on the day after Mary Ann's birthday suggests that her age was significant, presumably because she had not obtained her father's consent. Even if Mary Ann had been eighteen she and George could have got round the lack of parental consent by being married by banns, since Jordan Costello is unlikely to have come to hear of the marriage in time to forbid it, but George may have preferred to avoid the publicity of banns. As well as wanting to

i There is an additional complication due to the Calendar (New Style) Act of 1750, which moved the new year from 25 March to 1 January, starting in 1752. Prior to that year, official documents usually specify both the Old and New Style years for dates between 1 January and 24 March – for example *27 January 1746/47*, which would be 27 January 1747 N.S. We do not have an official document relating to Mary Ann's birth, but only her own statement that she was either 53 or 56 on 27 January 1803, placing her birthday in 1747 N.S or 1750 N.S. We don't know whether she took account of the O.S./N.S. factor, nor how she arrived at her beliefs about her age. If her calculations were based at any point on a written record of her birth, for instance in a family Bible or letter, it introduces the possibility that she mistook an Old Style for a New Style date, in which case the conclusions of this Appendix would have to be modified. I have proceeded on the assumption that Mary Ann understood the problem and that her statement in 1803 that she was either 53 or 56 was correct.

avoid asking Mary Ann's father's permission, he was unwilling to risk letting his own father hear of the marriage.[i] Also, the Guy-Dickens family, who wanted to see Mary Ann married but must have seen how unsuitable the marriage was, will have wanted to place responsibility upon Mary Ann – if she was of age, they could say there was nothing they could do to stop her.

Mary Ann remained undecided on the question until 1813 when she discovered documentary evidence that led her to accept the earlier date.[922] She doesn't say what this evidence was. She remained of the same opinion for the rest of her life, and when she died in 1827 her age was recorded as eighty. In the Packet Mary Ann recalls that in 1760, when Jordan Costello's business collapsed, she, Mary Ann, became the principal wage-earner for the family;[923] it is possible that she might have done this at the age of ten, but it becomes slightly more plausible if she was thirteen.

I have not found any record of Mary Ann's baptism, but there are four records for offspring of Jordan and Mary Costello (or variants of the name) baptised in St Catherine's RC Chapel, Meath Street, Dublin: Margaret (July 1744), Henry (November 1748), Edmund (August 1750) and Esther (October 1751).[924] There is no certainty that the Jordan and Mary in all or any of these records are in fact Mary Ann's parents, but if they are the most obvious consequence is that Mary Ann could not have been born in January 1750, just seven months before Edmund. Assuming therefore that Mary Ann was born in 1747 and that Margaret and Henry are her siblings, how do they all fit in with Mary Ann's statements in the Packet that she was the third of her mother's children, and that the second was a son called Melchior.[925] There would be time for these two births between Margaret in 1744 and Henry in 1748, with Melchior born in 1745–46 and Mary Ann on 27 January

i Under the Hardwicke Marriage Act of 1753, for marriage by licence a minor had to obtain written permission from his or her father or guardian, but a minor could be married following the calling of banns so long as there was no active intervention from the father or guardian. This at least is my reading of the act; according to Lawrence Stone (*Uncertain Unions and Broken Lives*, 33) the act required a minor to have the positive permission of a parent or guardian to be married, whether by licence or banns.

1747. These dates are, however, incompatible with Mary Ann's further statement that her father courted and married her mother after reading of Colonel Melchior Guy-Dickens's return from his embassy to Sweden, because Melchior was not recalled from Sweden until March 1748.

Even if we do not accept the evidence of the baptismal records for Margaret and Henry, the Packet's claim that Jordan first noticed Mary Guy-Dickens following her father's return from Sweden is at odds with what is said about Mary Ann's own birth. It makes it impossible for her to have been born in 1747, and also impossible for her to have been born in January 1750 if, as she believed, she was the third child, since that would require three children to be conceived and born in the 22 Months between March 1748 and January 1750.[i]

But if the events that triggered Jordan's interest in Mary Guy-Dickens were Melchior's recall from *Berlin* and *appointment* as minister to Stockholm in 1741 or 1742[926] we can construct a chronology that is otherwise compatible with the Packet and also fits with the baptismal records. There is time for their first child, Margaret, to be born by July 1744, after which, probably when Mary was pregnant with her second child, they met Captain de Brisay, Melchior's Dublin agent. This led to Jordan making contact with Melchior and obtaining £800 to help set up his business, plus a further £200 for Mary, to cover among other things the cost of their journey to London. Mary Ann says tentatively that this first contact was made in '47 or 48',[927] which would probably be while the Colonel was still in Sweden, or just after his recall, but it may have been a little earlier, since to encourage Melchior, or to show gratitude, they named their second child, born in 1745 or early 1746, after him. Then Mary Ann was born on 27 January 1747, being as she had always believed, the third child. Naming her after

---

i Three children could have been conceived and born in this period if two of them were twins. This is a possibility, but Mary Costello is likely to have remembered if she had borne twins, and is likely to have told Mary Ann, who would almost certainly have thought it interesting enough to mention.

her Huguenot grandmother would also have been in the hope of propitiating the Colonel. Mary Ann says that her mother had just recovered from childbirth when her parents went to meet Melchior in London; this birth was presumably Henry, who was baptised in November 1748, after which there was time for Jordan and Mary to visit the Colonel in London before his departure for Russia.

After Henry we have two further baptismal records, Edmund and Esther, born in 1750 and 1751. The Esther George knew as Aunt Hetty, and who later became Mrs Murch, is described in the Packet as about twelve years old when she came to London in 1770, meaning she was born in 1757 or 1758.[928] Her death notice says that she died on 10 March 1836, her 81st birthday, placing her birth in 1755. The 1755 date would make her 15 when she came to London, and it is quite plausible that Mary Ann might remember this as 'about twelve' (it's the same margin of error as in her recollection of her own age), but it is implausible that she would remember her sister as about twelve in 1770 if she had been born as early as 1751. Therefore it seems that the child born in 1751 died and her name was re-used for her younger sister. Mary Costello's former guardian, Mrs Esther Smith died in 1756, so using her name was either a way for the Costellos to ingratiate themselves with her, if the baby was born in 1755, or to commemorate her after her death. Mary Ann says her mother had eleven children,[929] so apart from Mary Ann, Melchior, Esther and the four for whom we apparently have baptismal records, there are four others unaccounted for.

Esther Murch's death notice in the *Exeter Flying Post* states that she died on her 81st birthday, and adds the following note: 'There is a singular coincidence herein with that of her late sister Mrs Hunn, Mr Canning's mother, who also died on the day in which she attained her 81st year.'[930] This is plainly false. Mary Ann was eighty on 27 January 1827, and died on 10 March, in her 81st year but not on her 81st birthday. What was true, and was a coincidence of sorts, was that both Mary Ann and Esther died on

10 March. A garbled memory of this may have led to the belief that they were the same age when they died. The mistake in the *Exeter Flying Post* has led some genealogists to believe that Mary Ann was born in 1746.

Why are Melchior and Mary Ann missing from the sequence of the children of Jordan and Mary Costello in the baptismal records at St Catherine's, Meath Street? It is possible that Melchior and Mary Ann were baptised in a Protestant church. If Melchior was named, as Mary Ann implies in the Packet, in order to please Colonel Guy-Dickens, then it may have been still more pleasing to the Colonel if the child was baptised as a protestant. Similarly it may be that when Mary Ann says her own birth affected a reconciliation with the Smiths this also was because she was baptised in a Protestant church and named after her Huguenot grandmother.[931] However, having searched the Dublin Church of Ireland records on the Irish Genealogy website, I have found no record for either Melchior or Mary Ann Costello, or any plausible variant, between 1744 and 1748. Another possibility is that for some of the time between the births of Margaret and Henry the Costellos were living outside Dublin. Mary Ann appears in numerous family trees on the Ancestry website, most of which say she was born in Mayo or Roscommon, where Jordan's family had an estate.[i] However, since most of these family trees also state that she was born in 1746, I am not sure how much reliance to place on them; the author of one of them reports that she has found no positive evidence that Mary Ann was born in Mayo or Roscommon.[932]

At the time of the Packet, as we have seen, Mary Ann inclined to the belief that she was herself born in 1750, and Esther in 1758. After 1813 she changed her mind and decided she was three years older; similarly, by the time Esther died it was accepted that she too was three years older. There are similar questions concerning

i After the failure of his business in 1760 Jordan acted as steward for his cousin in Mayo (Packet, 20). See Brian de Breffny, 'An Investigation into the Connacht Ancestry of Mary Ann Costello, Mother of George Canning', *The Irish Ancestor* (1980), 2–6 for information on Jordan Costello's Mayo connections.

the date of birth of Mary Ann's mother Mary Costello.

According to the Packet Mary was the only child of Melchior Guy-Dickens's brief marriage to the Huguenot widow Mariane Oiseau, who died in child-bed. Mary was fostered by Esther and Henry Smith in Dublin. The only date given in this account is 1736 when, it's said, she was about twelve or thirteen. This is unlikely since it would make her date of birth sometime around 1723, which is after Melchior's marriage to his second wife Hannah Handcock.[933] The significance of 1736, according to the Packet, was that it was in that year that Melchior went to Stockholm and sent for his daughter to accompany him. In fact Melchior's Stockholm mission did not begin until five or six years later. It could be that Melchior called for his daughter to accompany him on his first diplomatic mission, to Berlin, in 1731.

When Mary Costello died in January 1796, her age was given as 77,[934] which would place her date of birth in 1718 or early 1719 (and make her twelve or thirteen in 1731). I have found no baptism record for her under the name Guy-Dickens (or any plausible variant). However there is another possibility, if we assume that the Huguenot Oiseau family anglicised their name on coming to Dublin, with Mariane Oiseau becoming Mary Bird. A child, Mary Bird, daughter of Samuell and Mary Bird of [St] Francis Street, Dublin, was baptised at St Nicholas Without on 19 October 1718. Almost exactly a year earlier, Samuell Bird of Francis Street was buried at the same church.[935] Assuming this was the same Samuell mentioned in the baptism record, the child Mary Bird may have been his posthumous child. It's possible, however, that her father was Melchior Guy-Dickens, in which case, whether he and the recently widowed Mariane were married secretly, or not married at all, they may have felt it was preferable to pass the child off as Samuell's, although Melchior subsequently recognised her as his. Three years later, on 3 November 1721, another burial in the name of Bird is recorded at St Nicholas Without, this time the address is given as Plunk[et] Street,[936] which was a turning off Francis Street.

If this was Mariane her death would have left Melchior free to marry Hannah Handcock, which he did three months later. There was a family tradition, which Mary Ann adopted in the Packet, that Mariane died giving birth to Mary.[937]

This is highly speculative, depending on the assumption that the Birds in the St Nicholas Without records were originally called Oiseau, but if something along these lines is the case it offers a possible explanation for the uncertainty over when Mary Ann and Esther were born. Although we don't know what the evidence was, there was evidently some reason for believing that Mary was born in 1718, since this was the version adopted at the end of her life, making her 77 when she died. On the other hand, if Mary subscribed to the family story about her own birth, and knew that her mother Mariane died in 1721, she would assume that that was when she was herself born. There might therefore have been uncertainty about when she was born, 1718 or 1721. If Mary's calculation of her daughters' ages was based on her recollection of her own age at the time of their birth, the uncertainty about her own date of birth would generate equivalent uncertainty about theirs.

References

Unless stated otherwise all letters referred to are from the Canning Papers at the British Library, in the Personal and Family Matters series, BL Add. MSS 89143/3. In the endnotes the following frequently cited letters are referred to by date only:

89143/3/1/1-2:	letters from George Canning sen. to Mary Ann (the courtship letters)
89143/3/1/3:	correspondence between George Canning sen. and various friends and family members
89143/3/1/4:	correspondence between Mary Ann and Molly Barnard (née Canning), Stratty, Mehitabel, and John Beresford
89143/3/1/5-53:	letters from George to Mary Ann
89143/3/1/54:	letters from Mary Ann to George
89143/3/2/1-16:	letters from George to his aunt and uncle, Bess and William Leigh
89143/3/3/1-20:	letters from George to Joan Canning

The following abbreviations are used:

Bagot:	Josceline Bagot, *George Canning and his Friends.*
BDA:	Philip H. Highfill, Kalman A. Burnim, Edward A. Langhans, *A Biographical Dictionary of Actors, Actresses, Musicians, Dancers, Managers and Other Stage Personnel in London, 1660-1800.*
Bell:	Robert Bell, *The Life of the Right Honourable George Canning.*
Bernard:	John Bernard, *Retrospections of the Stage.*
Diary:	George's Diaries, BL Add. MSS 89143/3/7/1-30. See note on the sources.
Dundas Letter:	George to Lady Jane Dundas, 27 September 1799, BL Add. Mss 89143/3/3/21. See chapter 22.
Gale:	Frederick Gale, articles in *Notes and Queries* between 1920 and 1938, referenced by date and page number. For details see Bibliography.
Hinde:	Wendy Hinde, *George Canning.*
Hogan:	Charles Beecher Hogan, ed., *The London Stage 1776–1800* (part 5 of *The London Stage 1660-1800*).
Hooper:	Linley and Jim Hooper's Family History (online).
HoP:	History of Parliament Trust, *The History of Parliament: the House of Commons, 1754–1790*, ed. L. Namier and J. Brooke;

	1790–1820, ed. R. Thorne; 1820–1832, ed. D.R. Fisher (online).
Hunt:	Giles Hunt, *Mehitabel Canning, a Redoubtable Woman.*
Injured Woman:	Mary Ann's letters signed 'An Injured Woman' in the *Morning Chronicle*, Dec. 1776-Jan. 1777, referenced by date of publication. See chapter 6.
Letter Journal	*The Letter Journal of George Canning 1793-1795*, ed. P.E. Jupp.
Marshall:	Dorothy Marshall, *The Rise of Canning.*
Offspring:	*The Offspring of Fancy*, Mary Ann's epistolary novel published in 1778. See chapter 7.
Packet:	Mary Ann to George, January–June 1803.
Stone:	George Washington Stone, ed., *The London Stage 1747-1776* (part 4 of *The London Stage 1660–1800*).
Therry:	R. Therry, ed., *The Speeches of the Right Honourable George Canning, with a Memoir of his Life.*
Western Letters:	Canning Family papers formerly owned by Mrs M.D. Western, now held by West Yorkshire Archive Service, Leeds (WYL888).

Except where stated otherwise the authority for biographical details of minor figures is the relevant entry in the *Oxford Dictionary of National Biography* (online).

Bibliography

Place of publication is London except where stated.

'Account of Charges on Fund from Four and Half per cent Duties in Barbadoes and Leeward Islands', 19th Century House of Commons Sessional Papers, 6 (1801), 599.

ARBUTHNOT, HARRIET, *The Journal of Mrs Arbuthnot 1820–1832*, edited by Francis Bamford and the Duke of Wellington, 2 vols (1950).

ARMSTRONG, MURRAY, *The Liberty Tree* (Edinburgh, 2015).

ASPINALL, A., 'The Canningite Party', *Transactions of the Royal Historical Society*, Fourth Series, vol. 17 (1934).

— 'The Coalition Ministries of 1827' part one, *English Historical Review* (1927).

BAGOT, JOSCELINE, *George Canning and his Friends*, 2 vols (1909).

BARFOOT, PETER and WILKES, JOHN (compilers), *The Universal British Directory of Trade, Commerce and Manufacture*…, 5 vols (1791-98).

BARTON, BENJAMIN, *History of the Borough of Bury and Neighbourhood in the County of Lancaster* (Bury, 1874).

BELL, ROBERT, *The Life of the Right Honourable George Canning* (1846).

BENNETT, DOUGLAS, *Encyclopaedia of Dublin* (Dublin, 1994).

BERNARD, JOHN, *Retrospections of the Stage*, 2 vols (1830).
BICKFORD, J.A.R. and M.E., *The Private Lunatic Asylums of the East Riding* (East Riding Local History Society, 1976).
BOADEN, JAMES, *Memoirs of the Life of John Philip Kemble, Esq.* (1825).
— (ed.) *The Private Correspondence of David Garrick with the Most Celebrated Persons of his Time*, 2 vols (1832).
BURKE, JOHN, *Genealogical and Heraldic History of the Commoners of Great Britain and Ireland*, 4 vols (1838).
BURNIM, KALMAN A., *David Garrick, Director* (Carbondale, Ill., 1961, repr. 1973).
CANNING, GEORGE (SEN.), *A translation of* Anti-Lucretius *by Cardinal Melchior de Polignac* (1766).
— *Humanity, a Poem Inscribed to George Boden, Esq by G--- ---* (1766).
— *Poems* (1767).
— *A Letter to the Right Honourable Wills, Earl of Hillsborough, on the Connection between Great Britain and her American Colonies* (1768).
— *A Birthday Offering to a Young lady from her Lover* (1770).
CANNING, GEORGE (THE STATESMAN), *The Letter Journal of George Canning 1793–1795*, ed. P.E. Jupp, Camden 4th series, 41 (1991).
—, ELLIS, GEORGE and FRERE, JOHN HOOKHAM, *Parodies and other Burlesque Pieces, with the whole Poetry of the Anti-Jacobin*, ed. Henry Morley (1890).
CANNING, MARY ANN ('A LADY'), *The Offspring of Fancy*, 2 vols (1778).
CAWDELL, JAMES, *The Miscellaneous Poems of J. Cawdell, Comedian* (Sunderland, 1785).
CHALMERS, THOMAS, *The Doctrine of Christian Charity applied to the Case of Religious Differences, a sermon preached before the Auxiliary Society, Glasgow, to the Hibernian Society for Establishing Schools and Circulating the Holy Scriptures in Ireland* (Glasgow, 1822).
CHARKE, CHARLOTTE, *A Narrative of the Life of Mrs Charlotte Charke* (1755); repr. in *A Collection of the Most Instructive and Amusing Lives ever Published*, vol. 7 (1830).

CREEVEY, THOMAS, *A Selection from the Correspondence and Diaries of the Late Thomas Creevey MP (1768–1838)*, ed. Herbert Maxwell, 2 vols (1904).

DIXON, PETER, *Canning, Politician and Statesman* (1976).

ELMES, JAMES, *A Topographical Dictionary of London and its Environs* (1831).

FERGUSON, W., 'Dingwall Burgh Politics and the Parliamentary Franchise in the Eighteenth Century', *Scottish Historical Review*, 38 (Edinburgh, Oct. 1959), 89-108.

FESTING, GABRIELLE, *John Hookham Frere and his Friends* (1899).

FOSTER, R.F., *Modern Ireland, 1600–1972* (1988).

FRY, MICHAEL, *The Dundas Despotism* (Edinburgh, 1992).

GALE, FREDERICK, 'Colonel Melchior Guy Dickens', *Notes & Queries*, s12–7 (4 Sept. 1920), 194; 162 (30 Jan. 1932), 75–7.

— 'Marylebone Burial Ground Inscriptions', *Notes & Queries*, 151 (18 Sept. 1926), 208.

— 'Some Unpublished Letters of George Canning', *Notes & Queries*, 153 (20, 27 Aug. 1927), 129–33, 147–50.

— 'Canning's Mother and the Stage', *Notes & Queries*, 157 (14, 21 Sept. 1929), 183–5, 201–4; 158 (15 Mar. 1930) 190–1; 173 (4, 18 Sept. 1937), 164–6, 202–4.

— 'Richard Thompson, Canning's half-brother' *Notes & Queries*, 170 (7 Mar. 1936), 179.

— 'General Gustavus Guydickens', *Notes & Queries*, 171 (4 Nov. 1936), 352.

— 'Peter Pindar and Canning', *Notes & Queries*, 173 (9 Oct. 1937), 255–7.

— 'Canning's Mother and Reddish', *Notes & Queries*, 173 (23 Oct. 1937), 294–6.

— 'Popular Errors Regarding George Canning', *Notes & Queries*, 173 (6 Nov. 1937), 332-3.

— 'Where Canning Lived', *Notes & Queries*, 173 (20 Nov. 1937), 362–363.

— 'Richard Thompson, Canning's Brother-in-Law', *Notes &*

Queries, 173 (11 Dec. 1937), 420–4.
— 'Letters of a Naval Officer's Wife', *Notes & Queries*, 174 (8, 15 Jan. 1938), 22–7, 39–44.
— 'Maria Noad, Canning's Half-Sister', *Notes & Queries*, 174 (19 Feb. 1938), 131–2.
— 'Captain Hunn, Canning's Half-Brother', *Notes & Queries*, 174 (9 Apr. 1938), 256–60.
— 'The Last Years of Canning's Mother', *Notes & Queries*, 174 (30 April 1938), 311-3.
— 'The Living Descendants of Canning's Mother', *Notes & Queries*, 175 (6 August 1938), 92–6.
— 'Henry Keppel's first Skipper', *Blue Peter: the Magazine of Sea, Travel and Adventure*, 9 (July 1929).

GASH, NORMAN, *Lord Liverpool, the Life and Political Career of Robert Banks Jenkinson, 2nd Earl of Liverpool, 1770–1828* (1985).

GIFFORD, WILLIAM (ed.), *The Anti-Jacobin* Numbers 1–36 (20 Nov. 1797 – 9 July 1798; 4th edn, 1799).

GREVILLE, CHARLES, *A Journal of the Reigns of King George IV and King William IV*, ed. Henry Reeve, 3 vols (2nd edn, 1874).

'GREGORY GRIFFIN' (George Canning, John Frere, John Smith, Robert Smith) *The Microcosm* (Windsor, 1787; 2nd edn, 1788).

HAGUE, WILLIAM, *William Pitt the Younger* (2004).

HALL, SAMUEL CARTER, *Retrospect of a Long Life from 1815 to 1883*, 2 vols (1884).

HAZLITT, WILLIAM, *The Spirit of the Age* (1824–1825); ed. E.D. Mackerness (Plymouth, 1991).

HIGHFILL, PHILIP H., BURNIM, KALMAN A., LANGHANS, EDWARD A., *A Biographical Dictionary of Actors, Actresses, Musicians, Dancers, Managers and Other Stage Personnel in London, 1660–1800*, 16 vols (Carbondale, Ill., 1984).

HINDE, WENDY, *George Canning* (1973).

HOGAN, CHARLES BEECHER (ed.), *The London Stage 1776–1800* (part 5 of *The London Stage 1660–1800*), 3 vols (Carbondale, Ill., 1968).

HOLWELL, JOHN ZEPHANIAH, *A genuine narrative of the deplorable deaths of the English gentlemen and others, who were suffocated in the Black Hole* (1758).

HUNT, GILES, *Mehitabel Canning, a Redoubtable Woman* (Royston, 2001).

IRELAND, JOHN, *Letters and Poems by the late Mr John Henderson* (1786).

Journals of the House of Commons of the Kingdom of Ireland (Dublin, 1763).

KNIGHT, ROGER, *The Pursuit of Victory: the Life and Achievement of Horatio Nelson* (2005).

— *Britain Against Napoleon, The Organization of Victory 1793–1815* (2013).

KOHN, G.C. ed., *Encyclopedia of Plague and Pestilence: from Ancient Times to the Present* (3rd edn, New York, 2008).

LEVESON GOWER, GRANVILLE, *The Private Correspondence of Granville Leveson Gower, First Earl Granville, 1781–1821*, ed. Castalia, Countess Granville, 2 vols (1916).

'A MACARONI', *Theatrical Portraits Epigrammatically Delineated* (1774).

MACKINTOSH, ROBERT, *Memoirs of the Life of the Right Honourable Sir James Mackintosh*, 2 vols. (1835).

MARSHALL, DOROTHY, *The Rise of Canning* (1938).

MARSHALL, FRANCES, *A Travelling Actress in the North and Scotland, 1768–1851* [*The Memoirs of Mrs Charlotte Deans* (Wigton, 1837)] (Kendal, 1984).

'The Memoirs of Mr Reddish', *Covent Garden Magazine*, 2 (1773), 448–451.

NEWTON, J.F., *The Early Days of the Right Honorable George Canning, and some of his Contemporaries* (1828).

NICOLL, ALLARDYCE, *The Garrick Stage: Theatres and Audience in the eighteenth century*, ed. Sybil Rosenfeld (Athens, Ga., 1980).

NIGHTINGALE, FLORENCE, 'Cassandra' (1859, unpublished); Appendix 1 in Ray Strachey, *The Cause* (1928; Virago edn, 1978).

OBER, W.B., 'Boswell's Gonorrhea', *Bulletin of the New York Academy of Medicine* (June 1969), 587–636.

O'BYRNE, WILLIAM, *A Naval Biographical Dictionary: Comprising the Life and Services of Every Living Officer in Her Majesty's Navy* (1849).

OULTON, W.C., *History of the Theatres of London, 1771–1795* (1796).

PARTRIDGE, ERIC, *The Penguin Dictionary of Historical Slang*, abridged by Jacqueline Simpson (1972).

PIOZZI, HESTER, *Anecdotes of the Late Samuel Johnson*, 1786.

— *Autobiography, Letters and Literary Remains of Mrs Piozzi (Thrale)*, ed. A. Hayward (2nd edn, 1861).

POSTLE, MARTIN, '"Painted women": Reynolds and the Cult of the Courtesan' in Robyn Asleson (ed.) *Notorious Muse: The Actress in British Art and Culture 1776–1812* (New Haven, Conn., 2003).

PROBERT, REBECCA, 'Impact of the Marriage Act of 1753: Was it really "A Most Cruel Law for the Fair Sex"?' *Eighteenth Century Studies*, 38/2 (Winter 2005), 247–62.

PULLEN, KIRSTEN, *Actresses and Whores on Stage and in Society* (Cambridge, 2005).

RAVEN, J. 'Some letters of George Canning', *Anglo Saxon Review*, 3 (Dec. 1899), 45–54.

RHODES, R. CROMPTON, 'Early Editions of Sheridan: I – "The Duenna"', *Times Literary Supplement* (17 Sept. 1925).

ROBINSON, MARY, *Memoirs of the late Mrs Robinson (*1800), republished in *A Collection of the Most Instructive and Amusing Lives ever Published,* vol. 7 (1830).

ROLO, P.J.V., *George Canning, three Biographical Studies* (1963).

ROWE, NICHOLAS, *The Tragedy of Jane Shore* (2nd edn, 1714).

ROMILLY, S.H., *Letters to 'Ivy' from the first Earl of Dudley* (1905).

ROSENFELD, SYBIL, *The Georgian Theatre of Richmond Yorkshire* (London and York, 1984).

RUMP, ERIC, 'Sheridan, Congreve and *The School for Scandal*', in James Morwood and David Crane (eds) *Sheridan Studies* (Cambridge, 1995).

SCANLAN, PADRAIC XAVIER, 'The Rewards of their Exertions:

Prize Money and British Abolitionism in Sierra Leone, 1808–1823', *Past and Present*, 225 (Nov. 2014), 113–142.

SCOTT, WALTER, *Journal 1825–1832* (Edinburgh, 1890).

SMITH, HUGH, *Letters to Married Women* (2nd edn, 1768; 4th edn, 1785).

— *The Family Physician, being a Collection of Useful Family Remedies* (3rd edn, 1761).

STONE, GEORGE WASHINGTON (ED.), *The London Stage 1747-1776* (PART 4 OF *The London Stage 1660–1800*), 3 vols (CARBONDALE, ILL., 1968).

STONE, LAWRENCE, *Uncertain Unions and Broken Lives: Marriage and Divorce in England, 1660–1857* (Oxford, 1992, 1993; paperback edn, 1995).

TEMPERLEY, HAROLD, *Life of Canning* (1905).

THERRY, R. (ed.), *The Speeches of the Right Honourable George Canning, with a Memoir of his Life,* 6 vols (1836).

The Thespian Dictionary, or Dramatic Biography of the Present Age (2nd edn, 1805).

THOMPSON, E.P., *The Making of the English Working Class* (1963; Pelican edn, 1968).

WADE, JOHN, *The Black Book; or Corruption Unmasked!* (1820).

WAKEFIELD, PRISCILLA, *Reflections on the Present Condition of the Female Sex with Suggestions for its Improvement*, (1798; 2nd edn, 1817).

WATKINS, JOHN, *Memoirs of the Public and Private Life of the Rt Hon R B Sheridan*, 2 vols. (1817).

WOLCOT, JOHN, *The Works of Peter Pindar Esq*, 5 vols (1812).

WEATHERLEY, E.H. (ed.), *The Correspondence of John Wilkes and Charles Churchill* (New York, 1954).

WHEATLEY, HENRY B., *London Past and Present, Its History, Associations and Traditions,* 3 vols. (1891).

WILBERFORCE, A.M. (ed.), *Private Papers of William Wilberforce* (1897).

WILBERFORCE, ROBBERT AND SAMUEL, *The Life of William Wilberforce*, 5 vols (1839).

WILKINSON, TATE, *The Wandering Patentee*, 4 vols (York, 1795).
WILSON, FRANCES, *The Courtesan's Revenge* (2003; paperback edn, 2004).
WILSON, ROBERT, *Narrative of the Formation of Canning's Ministry* (1828).
WINSTON, JAMES, *The Theatric Tourist* (1805; Facsimile edn, 2008).
WOLLSTONECRAFT, MARY, *A Vindication of the Rights of Woman* (1792; Everyman edn, 1995).
WOOD, W, *The East Neuk of Fife* (Edinburgh, 1862)
WRIGHT, DANAYA C., 'The crisis of Child Custody: a History of the Birth of Family Law in England', *Columbia Journal of Gender and Law* 11/2 (2002), 175–270.
YONGE, C.D., *Life and Administration of Robert Banks Jenkinson, Second Earl of Liverpool*, 3 vols (1868).

Online resources

The following websites are referred to in the notes; they were all accessed on 20 January 2021.

ASHBEE, C.R. ET AL., *Survey of London*, 60 vols (1900–), at British History Online, http://www.british-history.ac.uk/search/series/survey-london
BENDALL, P.J., *Jewish Burial Ground, Combe Down, Bath, Supplementary Notes*, 2011, at Bath Archives website, https://www.batharchives.co.uk/sites/bath_record_office/files/JBG%20Supplementary%20Notes.pdf
BRITISH NEWSPAPER ARCHIVE, https://www.britishnewspaperarchive.co.uk (subscription required)
DEPARTMENT OF ARTS, HERITAGE, REGIONAL, RURAL AND GAELTACHT AFFAIRS, DUBLIN, *Irish Genealogy*, http://www.irishgenealogy.ie/

East Yorkshire Local History Society, http://www.eylhs.org.uk/

Emory University, *Voyages: The Transatlantic Slave Trade Database*, http://www.slavevoyages.org/

Gale Historical Newspapers, http://find.galegroup.com/dvnw/ (password required)

Gillray, James, *Online Exhibition Archive*, New York Public Library, http://web-static.nypl.org/exhibitions/gillray/index.html

Godwin, William, *The Diary of William Godwin*, Victoria Myers, David O'Shaughnessy, and Mark Philp (eds), (Oxford: Oxford Digital Library, 2010), http://godwindiary.bodleian.ox.ac.uk

History of Parliament Trust, *The History of Parliament: the House of Commons, 1754–1790*, ed. L. Namier and J. Brooke (1964); *1790-1820*, ed. R. Thorne (1986); *1820-1832* ed. D.R. Fisher (2009), http://www.historyofparliamentonline.org/

Hooper, Linley, *Linley & Jim Hooper's Family History*, http://www.linleyfh.com/main.htm

Horwood, Richard, *Plan of the Cities of London and Westminster, the Borough of Southwark, and Parts Adjoining, Shewing Every House*, (1792-9), http://www.romanticlondon.org

Kennedy, Maire, *William Flyn, Provincial Bookseller at the Sign of Shakespeare, Cork* (22 Feb., 24 Mar. 2016), https://mairekennedybooks.wordpress.com/tag/william-flyn/

King's College, London, *Clergy of the Church of England Database 1540–1835*, http://theclergydatabase.org.uk/

Mackenzie, Eneas, *Historical Account of Newcastle-upon-Tyne Including the Borough of Gateshead*, (Newcastle upon Tyne, 1827) at British History online: https://www.british-history.ac.uk/no-series/newcastle-historical-account

Mitchell, Don, *Mitchell's West Indian Bibliography* (11th edn, 2012), http://www.books.ai/ (http://216.92.185.108/)

PastPresented, transcription of *Cumberland Chronicle or Whitehaven Intelligencer*: http://pastpresented.info/cumbria/chronicle1776.htm

PROQUEST, *UK Parliamentary Papers*, http://parlipapers.proquest.com/parlipapers/search/basic/hcppbasicsearch (password required)

ROYAL ACADEMY, *Search the Collection*, https://www.royalacademy.org.uk/art-artists

ROYAL COLLEGE OF PHYSICIANS, *Inspiring Physicians*, formerly *Munk's Roll*, https://history.rcplondon.ac.uk/inspiring-physicians

THEATRES TRUST, *Theatre Database*, https://database.theatrestrust.org.uk/

UK PARLIAMENT, *Hansard 1803–2005*, http://hansard.millbanksystems.com/

UNIVERSITY COLLEGE LONDON, *Bloomsbury Project* (2012), http://www.ucl.ac.uk/bloomsbury-project

UNIVERSITY OF TORONTO/UNIVERSITÉ LAVAL, *Dictionary of Canadian Biography*, http://www.biographi.ca/en/index.php

WALFORD, EDWARD, *Old and New London*, 6 vols (1878), at British History Online, http://www.british-history.ac.uk/old-new-london

Endnotes

1 Dundas Letter.
2 Douglas Bennett, *Encyclopedia of Dublin*, 44, 104.
3 Packet, 12-3. For Mary Ann's antecedents and early life I have followed the Packet, supplemented by external sources cited in the Appendix 'When was Mary Ann born?'
4 Marriage of Henry Smith and Esther Bevins in St Luke's Church, Dublin, 11 Jan. 1718/19 (*Irish Genealogy*, DU-CI-MA-26967).
5 *Monthly Chronicle*, 3 (Aug. 1730), 156; *London Gazette*, 29 July–2 Aug. 1740, 26 Jan. 1741/42.
6 Packet, 12.
7 Packet, 5. Mary Ann says the Lord Lieutenant was the Duke of Dorset, but it was the Duke of Bolton who held the post in Melchior's time.
8 Packet, 6; Memorial to Hannah Guy-Dickens, cited by Hooper, s.n. Hannah Handcock.
9 Frederick Gale Collection at the West Yorkshire Archive (WYL682/15). Gale (14 Sept. 1929, 183) states that it is a portrait of Mary Ann, but does not give grounds for the statement; we must assume that it was the tradition in the family.
10 Packet, 16.
11 'A List of the Several Pensions now in being on the Civil Establishment of the Kingdom of Ireland, as presented to Parliament', *Gentleman's Magazine* 41 (1771), 531.
12 Hooper; *Clergy of the Church of England Database*; Sainty, *Office Holders in Modern Britain*, Queen Charlotte's Household; Packet, 17.
13 Packet, 22, 38.
14 George Canning, sen. to Mary Ann, 26 July 1767.
15 Packet, 42; George Canning, sen. to Mary Ann, 26 July 1767; Molly Barnard to Mary Ann, Nov. 1769.
16 Western Letters.
17 Molly Barnard to George Canning, sen., 8 Aug. 1769; George Canning, sen. to Stratty, 28 Sept. 1770; Letitia Canning to Stratty, 17 Nov. 1767 (Western Letters).
18 Molly Barnard to George Canning, sen., 8 Aug. 1769; George Canning, sen. to Stratty, 28 Sept. 1770; Letitia Canning to Stratty, 17 Nov. 1767 (Western Letters); Molly Barnard to Mary Ann, Oct. 1769 and 8 Nov. 1769.
19 Packet, 45.
20 E H Weatherley (ed.), *Correspondence of John Wilkes and Charles Churchill*.
21 George Canning, sen. to Stratty, 9 Oct., 5 Dec. 1766, 20 Feb., 22 Dec. 1767.

22 George Canning, sen. to Mary Ann, 26 July, 18 Oct. 1767.
23 George Canning, sen. to Mary Ann, 26 July 1767; Packet, 43.
24 George Canning, sen. to James Arbuckle, 14, 21 Apr. 1766.
25 Packet, 30.
26 George Canning, sen. to Stratty, 5 Dec. 1766.; Canning, *Poems* (1767), iii.
27 M. Canning to Stratty, 20 Oct. 1767; Letitia Canning, jun. to Stratty, 24 Feb. 1767 ; Stratty to Stratford Canning, sen., 3 Nov. 1767 (Western Letters).
28 Packet, 18. The Packet is the sole source for the events in Bath in 1765 and 1766.
29 *Offspring*, Letter 33.
30 Packet, 18.
31 Packet, 7, 26; *Gentleman's Magazine*, 18 (May 1748), 238; Thomas Carlyle, *Life of Frederick the Great* Book vii chapters 2-3.
32 Packet, 20-2.
33 Packet, 22.
34 Packet, 23.
35 Packet, 24.
36 John Lockman (1698-1771), 'The Humours of New Tunbridge Wells, at Islington' (excerpt in *Gentleman's Magazine*, 4 (Feb. 1734), 99, 112.
37 George Canning sen. to Mary Ann, 12 Aug. 1767; to Stratty, 9 Oct. 1766, 20 Feb. 1767.
38 'Introductory Address to Shem Thompson DD' in Canning, *Poems*.
39 Beresford to George Canning sen., Sept. 1768; Royal College of Physicians, *Munks Roll* s.n. Sir William Duncan; Carita Doggett, *Dr. Andrew Turnbull and the New Smyrna Colony of Florida* (1919), 18.
40 George Canning, sen. to Mary Ann, 1 Oct. 1767; Packet, 25.
41 Packet, 25-7.
42 George Canning, sen. to Mary Ann, 17 Aug., 13, 20 Sept., 16, 18, 20 Oct. 1767.
43 George Canning, sen. to Mary Ann, 21/22, 25 Sept. 1767.
44 George Canning, sen. to Mary Ann, 26 July 1767.
45 This is my understanding of paragraphs 3 and 11 of the Hardwicke Marriage Act of 1753 (26 George 2 c.33); see Rebecca Probert, 'Impact of the Marriage Act of 1753: Was it really "A Most Cruel Law for the Fair Sex"?', 254-5. Laurence Stone considers that under the Act consent of the father or guardian was required for any marriage of a minor in England (*Uncertain Unions and Broken Lives*, 33 and 194).
46 George Canning, sen. to Mary Ann, 29 Sept. 1767.
47 Packet, 12. The evidence, and lack of it, is discussed in the Appendix 'When was Mary Ann born?'
48 George Canning, sen. to Mary Ann, 28, 30 Dec. 1767.
49 George Canning, sen. to Mary Ann, 1 Oct. 1767
50 George Canning, sen. to Mary Ann, 27 Oct. 1767.
51 George Canning, sen. to Mary Ann, 6 Oct. 1767.
52 See W.B. Ober, 'Boswell's Gonorrhea', 607.
53 Packet, 28.
54 George Canning, sen. to Mary Ann, 11 Jan. 1768; *Anti-Lucretius* Book V (George Canning, *A Translation of the Anti-Lucretius* (1766), 394).
55 George Canning, sen. to Mary Ann, 16, 17/18 Jan. 1768.
56 George Canning, sen. to Mary Ann, 1, 6/7, 11 Jan. 1768.
57 Packet 44, 46; Beresford to George Canning, sen., Sept. 1768; *A Letter to the Right Honourable Wills, Earl of Hillsborough, on the Connection between Great Britain and her American Colonies* (1768).
58 *A Birthday Offering to a Young lady from her Lover.*
59 Packet, 31; Molly Barnard to George Canning, sen. and Mary Ann, undated. See below, chapter 31.

60 George Canning, sen. to Stratty, 6 May, 19 Aug. 1768, 3 Jan. 1769.
61 George Canning, sen. to Stratty, 9 Aug. 1768; to Mary Ann, 17/18 May 1768; Packet, 32.
62 Packet 31-2; LMA, *Church of England Parish Registers p89/mry1/164*; Stratford Canning, sen. to Mary Ann, 29 June 1771; Mary Ann to John Beresford, 29 Aug. 1771.
63 Packet 34; George Canning, sen. to Stratty, 9 June 1768.
64 Addressed to Mary Ann at Mrs Noble's, near the Church, Islington, bundled with George's courtship letters.
65 Stratty to Stratford Canning, sen., 25 May 1769 (Western Letters); George Canning, sen. to Stratty, 9 Aug. 1768.
66 Packet, 32.
67 Packet, 33; George Canning, sen. to Stratty, 9 Aug. 1768.
68 Molly Barnard to George Canning, sen., 28 May [1769].
69 Packet, 34; *The Independent Chronicle or Freeholder's Evening Post*, 11-13 Oct. 1769.
70 Wheatley and Cunningham, *London, Past and Present* 2:67; James Elmes, *Topographical Dictionary of London* 341. Mary Ann gives the address of their house as 'Queen Anne Street, Portland Chapel' (Packet, 33), and a letter whose cover has survived is directed to ' – Canning Esq, Queen Anne Street, Portland Road'.
71 Packet, 34.
72 Bell, 21; Molly Barnard to George Canning, sen., 8 Aug. [1769]; George Canning, sen. to Stratty, 20 Feb. 1770.; Dublin Directory (1764); *Journals of the House of Commons of the Kingdom of Ireland* vii. 145.
73 'The Progress of Lying' (1762), in Canning, *Poems*.
74 Packet, 35, 46; George Canning, sen. to Mary Ann, 26 July 1767; Beresford to George Canning, sen., 23 Sept. 1768.
75 Packet, 35-6. Smith, *Letters to Married Women* (2nd Edn, 1768), 91–92, 101, 125.
76 Stratty to Mary Ann, 22 Nov. 1769.
77 Molly Barnard to Mary Ann, 1 Sept. 1768.
78 Molly Barnard to Mary Ann, 24 Mar. 1770.
79 *Letters to Married Women*, 79.
80 Packet, 36–7; Molly Barnard to George Canning, sen., 19 Apr. 1770.
81 Packet, 37-8, 55. Mary Ann says Esther was about twelve at the time, but see 'When was Mary Ann born?'
82 George Canning, sen. to John Beresford, 9 Jan. 1770; Packet, 48–50.
83 Packet, 48, 50–1; Stratty to Stratford Canning, sen., 14 July 1769 (Western Letters); Molly Barnard to Mary Ann and George Canning, sen., 21 Feb., 17 Aug. 1770; George Canning, sen. to John Beresford, 28 Feb. 1770.
84 Packet, 38-9, 43.
85 Packet, 47, 54.
86 George Canning, sen. to Stratty, 28 Sept. 1770; Packet, 33.
87 *A Letter to the Right Honourable Wills, Earl of Hillsborough* 22–23, 45.
88 Packet, 168.
89 Packet, 52; Stratty to Stratford Canning, sen., 25 May, 14 July, 12 Aug. 1769 (Western Letters).
90 Packet, 51.
91 Packet, 44.
92 Packet, 53.
93 George Canning, sen. to Beresford, 1 Feb. 1771.
94 Packet, 54; George Canning, sen. to Beresford, 1 Feb. 1771; Robert Crowe to George Canning, jun., 22 June 1816 (BL Add Mss 89143/1/2/6); Catherine Jemmat to George Canning, sen. (BL Add MSS 89143/3/11/1). George Canning is listed amongst the subscribers of the 1771 edition of Jemmat's *Miscellanies*.
95 Mary Ann to Beresford, 3 Aug. 1771. The words are on a sheet of paper in BL Add. MSS

89143/3/1/3; I have not found any other trace of a sacred scroll.
96 Packet, 54–5.
97 Packet, 56.
98 Bell, 23.
99 Packet, 57, 62; Stratty to Beresford, 18 Apr., 28 May 1771; Mary Ann to Beresford, 25 May–20 June 1771.
100 Packet, 57.
101 Mary Ann to Stratford Canning, sen., 2 May, 21 June, 9 July 1771; Stratford Canning, sen. to Mary Ann, 29 June 1771; Mary Ann to Beresford, 25 May-20 June, 3, 29 Aug. 1771.
102 Stratty to Mary Ann, 5, 14 June, 28 Dec. 1771, undated letter marked August or September 1771.
103 Packet, 73; Marshall, ed., *A Travelling Actress in the North and Scotland*, 30. For Charlotte Johnston or Deans see below, chapters 5 and 13.
104 Packet, 73–4; Stratty to Mary Ann, 15 Sept. 1771.
105 Packet, 49; Mary Ann to Beresford, 25 May-20 June, 29 Aug. 1771.
106 Stratty to Mary Ann, 5, 14 June, 15 Sept. 1771.
107 See below, chapter 31.
108 Packet, 63; Stratty to Mary Ann, [Aug. 1771].
109 Mary Ann to Beresford, 25 May–20 June, 29 Aug. 1771, to Stratford Canning, sen., 9 July 1771; Beresford to George Canning, sen., 23 Sept. 1768.
110 Packet, 42.
111 Packet, 46, 71–2.
112 Packet, 64–5.
113 Remark attributed to Lord North, quoted in Vicary Gibbs (ed.), *The Complete Peerage* i (1910), 128.
114 Packet, 65, 71.
115 Packet, 58, 61. See Hesther Lynch Piozzi, *Anecdotes of the Late Samuel Johnson LLD during the last Twenty Years of his Life*: '... if we had put my Lady Tavistock into a small chandler's shop, and given her a nurse-child to tend, her life would have been saved' (154). In her *Autobiography* Mrs Piozzi quotes Johnson putting a similar point in different words: '... when condolence was demanded for a lady of rank in mourning for a baby, he contrasted her with a washerwoman with half-a-dozen children dependent on her daily labour for their daily bread' (1.17). Mary Ann had evidently come across both versions.
116 Packet, 61, 68.
117 Packet, 68–9, 85.
118 Packet, 69.
119 Packet, 86–8; Stratty to Mary Ann, 12 Sept. 1772; *HoP, 1754-1790*, s.n. Charles Phipps.
120 Packet, 70.
121 Stratty to Stratford Canning sen., 8, 31 July 1769 (Western Letters).
122 Packet, 70–1.
123 Packet, 67.
124 *London Evening Post*, 17-20 Apr. 1762.
125 Packet, 67.
126 Packet, 72-4.
127 Packet, 74-6. Mary Ann spells the sisters' name *Gower*.
128 Mehitabel Patrick to Mary Ann, 10 Jan. 1773.
129 Packet, 77-9; Mehitabel Patrick to Mary Ann, 31 Jan. 1773.
130 Packet, 77. *Prettrish* is not in the *OED*. I suppose Mary Ann meant *prettyish*.
131 Packet, 79; *London Gazette*, 25 May 1773.
132 Packet, 79; *Memoirs and Correspondence of George, Lord Lyttelton*, ii. 548.
133 *Injured Woman*, 26 Dec. 1776.
134 Mary Ann to Beresford, 6 July 1773.

135 For example Colley Cibber, James Boswell, Gentleman John Palmer, Hannah Pritchard and Jane Pope.
136 Packet, 80.
137 Mehitabel Canning to Mary Ann, 2 Sept. 1773; Packet, 80-1.
138 Packet, 181. See below, chapter 11.
139 Mehitabel Canning to Mary Ann, 23 Mar. [1774]; Packet, 81-2. Mehitabel seems to be using *trowel* in a comparatively novel sense. The earliest citation in the *OED* of its use in a culinary context is for this year, 1773.
140 Packet, 82–3.
141 Packet, 73, 80.
142 Stone, vol. i p. clxi.
143 Hogan, vol. i p. xx; Bernard, i. 2; Wilkinson, *Wandering Patentee*, i. 111.
144 *Town and Country Magazine* 4 (April 1772), 172; Robinson, *Memoirs of the late Mrs Robinson*, 91; Charke, *A Narrative of the Life of Mrs Charlotte Charke*, 113.
145 Priscilla Wakefield, *Reflections on the Present Condition of the Female Sex with Suggestions for its Improvement*, 104.
146 Postle, '"Painted women": Reynolds and the Cult of the Courtesan', 23; Pullen, *Actresses and Whores on Stage and in Society*, 58.
147 Packet, 83; 'A Macaroni', *Theatrical Portraits Epigrammatically Delineated*, 5; Bell, 28n.
148 Felicity Nussbaum, *Rival Queens*, 45.
149 *Morning Chronicle*, 24 Mar. 1773; 7 Nov. 1772.
150 Postle, 37.
151 Hunt, chapter 6.
152 Packet, 79–80.
153 Packet, 84; Stone vol. i pp. lxxxiv, clxxviii; Hogan vol. i p. cii. The capacity of the auditorium was estimated with surprising precision at 2,206 by H W Pedicord in *The Theatrical Public in the Time of Garrick* (Burnim, *David Garrick*, 65). Stone estimates it at about 1,800 (vol. i p. xxxi).
154 *Wandering Patentee*, iii. 16. Wilkinson tells how he once gave an opening to a promising amateur, who seemed to have all the necessary requirements of an actor, but the result was, he says, was 'Horrible! – Most horrible!'
155 Bernard, i. 26. The story as told by Bernard doesn't altogether hang together, because he says the other actor was Francis Aickin, who in fact seems to have come to Drury Lane two years before Reddish. Francis Aickin's brother James joined the Drury Lane company at about the same time as Reddish.
156 Burnim, *David Garrick*, 47–48.
157 *General Evening Post*, 6–9 Nov. 1773.
158 Burnim, *David Garrick*, 58–59, quoting from the memoirs of Edward Cape Everard; Wilkinson, *Wandering Patentee*, iii. 16
159 Packet, 83-4.
160 *Jane Shore*, II, i.
161 *Jane Shore*, I, ii.
162 *Jane Shore*, I, ii.
163 *Public Advertiser*, 21 Oct. 1773; A. H[ankey] to Mary Ann, 10 Oct. 1773, BL Add. MSS 89143/3/1/4; Stone, iii. 1759; Mary Ann (Packet, 83) gives the date as 3 November.
164 Mary Ann never describes the experience of appearing on stage. I have adapted Mary Robinson's account of her debut, with 'the keen, the penetrating eyes of Mr Garrick' upon her (*Memoirs*, 84). Garrick by then had retired and was in the audience watching his latest protégée.
165 In the second edition of the play this is described as the epilogue spoken by Mrs Oldfield, who played Jane in the original production. I have not established whether Mary Ann delivered the epilogue, or it was given to a better known actress. I assume it was the same epilogue.
166 Packet, 84.

167 *General Evening Post*, 9–11 Nov. 1773.
168 *Morning Chronicle and London Advertiser*, 8 Nov. 1773.
169 *London Chronicle or Universal Post*, 11-13 Nov. 1773.
170 *Morning Chronicle and London Advertiser*, 13 Nov. 1773.
171 *London Magazine or Gentleman's Intelligencer*, Nov. 1773; *Westminster Magazine* (Gale, 4 Sept. 1937, 166).
172 *General Evening Post*, 9–11 December 1773. This article contains the only references I've found in these reviews to Mary Ann's Irish origins.
173 *Injured Woman*, 2 Jan. 1777; Bernard, i. 22, 136–8, ii. 235; Stone, iii. 1759-71; Packet 84. Mary Ann remembered seven rather than six performances.
174 Packet, 85, 105–6.
175 Packet, 91; Stone, iii. 1809.
176 Correspondence and papers of George Simon Harcourt, Viscount Nuneham, later 2nd Earl Harcourt, and his wife Elizabeth, Bodleian Library MS. Eng. d. 2849, fols 109–110. A copy exists among the Canning papers held by the West Yorkshire Archive (WYL888/4). Nothing is known about the relationship between Mary Ann and Lady Nuneham, not even how they became acquainted; it may have been through the Duchess of Ancaster.
177 Mary Ann to John Beresford, 21 June 1772.
178 Bernard, i. 23; *BDA* xii. 282-7; Hannah More to Garrick, 28 July [1776] (Boaden, *Private Correspondence of David Garrick*, ii. 243); W.C. Oulton *History of the Theatres of London, 1771–1795*, i. 53. The hostile writer of 'The Memoirs of Mr Reddish' (*Covent Garden Magazine*, 2 (1773), 448–51) doesn't mention drunkenness, but concentrates on Reddish's supposed dishonesty and incompetence as an actor, and his liaison with Polly Hart.
179 Packet, 110–1; *Daily Advertiser*, 18 Nov. 1777; *BDA* xii. 284, quoting a clipping from the Burney collection that reports a two-horse race in which Reddish's lost.
180 Oulton, *History of the Theatres of London*, i. 28-31; *Courier*, 4 August 1797.
181 Packet, 91; *Private Correspondence of David Garrick*, ii. 243; Bernard, i. 23; Bell, 31; *BDA* xii. 287-288. Bernard attributes the pun to Samuel Foote, Bell to Garrick himself; Foote is the likelier author. Horace Walpole is cited as the authority for Polly's succession of keepers prior to Reddish. That Reddish married her for the money is an allegation made in the scurrilous 'Memoirs of Mr Reddish'.
182 Tate Wilkinson mentions Mrs Reddish at Hull in 1774 (*Wandering Patentee*, i. 202) and there are newspaper references to her being part of the Austin and Whitlock company at Chester, Newcastle and Whitehaven between 1775 and 1777. (*Chester Chronicle* 25 Apr. 1776; *Newcastle Courant*, 10 June 1775, 16 Mar. 1776, 19 Apr. 1777; *Cumbrian Chronicle or Whitehaven Intelligencer*, 7 Jan. 1777). Although it is theoretically possible that Mary Ann could have been in some of the places referred to at the relevant times, in other cases she was definitely elsewhere. At a later stage in her career (1786–8) she would herself go north and work for Whitlock, and her account implies that she had not previously been in contact with him.
183 *Injured Woman*, 26 Dec. 1776.
184 *Injured Woman*, 26 Dec. 1776; Packet, 90.
185 Mehitabel to Mary Ann, 23 Mar. [1774]; Packet, 91. The aborted elopement took place, according to Mary Ann, in Passion Week. The term was used to refer either to the fifth or sixth week in Lent; Mary Ann probably meant the sixth week, Holy Week, during which the theatre was closed. Easter being on 3 April that year, this was the week beginning 27 March. Reddish appeared in *The Earl of Warwick* on Saturday 26 March, and was back as Posthumus on the Tuesday after Easter (Stone, iii. 1796–8).
186 Packet, 91–2.
187 Packet, 84; Stone, iii. 1801-5.
188 *The Gamester*, III.
189 Packet, 90; Stone, iii. 1805-6.

190 Stone, iii. 1809; *Injured Woman*, 31 Dec. 1776.
191 Packet, 93; Allardyce Nicoll, *The Garrick Stage*, 41.
192 LMA, *Church of England Parish Registers*, p82/GIS/A/02 (St Giles in the Fields, Holborn).
193 Packet, 92–3.
194 Packet, 93–4.
195 Packet, 94–5; Wright, 'The Crisis of Child Custody: a History of the Birth of Family Law in England', 187, 190.
196 Packet, 92, 95–6.
197 Packet, 96–7.
198 *Public Advertiser*, 4 June 1774; *Private Correspondence of David Garrick*, ii. 98. See below, chapter 8.
199 Packet, 97; *Middlesex Journal & Evening Advertiser*, 16–19 July 1774.
200 *Felix Farley's Bristol Journal*, 4, 11 June, 9, 16, 30 July, 20 Aug., 3 Sept. 1774.
201 Aaron Hill and William Popple, *Prompter*, 11 Nov. 1735, quoted by Nussbaum, *Rival Queens*, 67.
202 Lee, *Rival Queens*, IV, i and V, i.
203 *Felix Farley's Bristol Journal*, 25 June 1774.
204 *Injured Woman*, 31 Dec. 1776.
205 *Felix Farley's Bristol Journal*, 10 Sept. 1774.
206 *Injured Woman*, 31 Dec. 1776; Packet, 100; *Felix Farley's Bristol Journal*, 10 Sept. 1774.
207 Packet, 98.
208 Packet, 100.
209 Packet, 100.
210 BL Add Mss 89143/3/11/6, dated 8 Sept. 1773.
211 Packet, 99.
212 *Injured Woman*, 31 Dec. 1776; Stone, iii. 1879–81.
213 Packet, 100; Stone, iii. 1882–97.
214 *Felix Farley's Bristol Journal*, 27 May, 3 June, 12, 26 Aug. 1775; *Private Correspondence of David Garrick*, ii. 61.
215 *Felix Farley's Bristol Journal*, 15 July 1775. Announcements of productions appeared each Saturday from June to September 1775.
216 *Felix Farley's Bristol Journal*, 26 Aug., 16 Sept. 1775
217 Reddish had written a similar penitential letter to Garrick the previous year (*Private Correspondence of David Garrick*, ii. 98, 352). In addition to the £50 that Reddish paid the theatre out of his Bristol earnings in 1775, the sum of £78 16s 6d was transferred over the summer from his Drury Lane benefit account towards satisfying his creditors (Stone, iii. 1898).
218 Stone, iii. 1983–5; Packet, 99; *Injured Woman*, 31 Dec. 1776.
219 *Morning Chronicle*, 25 Mar. 1776; Stone, iii. 1962–3.
220 Packet, 100, 106. *Public Advertiser*, 26 Feb. 1776.
221 Bell, 39; *Tom Jones*, bk. III, ch. ii; Packet, 106.
222 Packet, 105; Dundas Letter; BL Add. MSS 89142/3/11/6. George Canning's *ODNB* entry says he was adopted by Stratty in 1778.
223 Packet, 180, 107.
224 *Felix Farley's Bristol Journal*, 15 June, 24 Aug. 1776; *Private Correspondence of David Garrick*, ii. 243, where More's letter is assigned to 1777, an error which is followed by *BDA* and *ODNB* in their entries for Samuel Reddish. The events described in the letter are clearly those reported in the Bristol newspapers in 1776.
225 Tomalin, *Mrs Jordan's Profession*, 175; *Travelling Actress in the North and Scotland* 31, 77.
226 LMA, *Church of England Parish Registers*, P82/Geo1/002 (St George's Bloomsbury). The baptismal record gives the date of birth as 28 July.
227 *Private Correspondence of David Garrick*, ii. 251, 255; *Felix Farley's Bristol Journal*, 20, 27 July, 3, 24 Aug. 1776.

228 *Felix Farley's Bristol Journal*, 24 Aug. 1776; *Lloyd's Evening Post*, 26-28 Aug. 1776.
229 *Private Correspondence of David Garrick*, ii. 243.
230 *Private Correspondence of David Garrick*, ii. 251; *Felix Farley's Bristol Journal*, 3 Aug. 1776, 21 June, 9 Aug. 1777.
231 *Felix Farley's Bristol Journal*, 31 Aug., 14 Sept. 1776.
232 *Injured Woman*, 31 Dec. 1776; Packet, 101–2.
233 Packet, 107; Dundas Letter.
234 Hogan, i. 37–40; *Morning Chronicle*, 21, 22, 25 Nov. 1776.
235 Hogan, i. 32–3, 37; *General Evening Post*, 9–12 Nov. 1776; *Morning Chronicle*, 15, 18 Nov. 1776; *Morning Post*, 11 Nov. 1776; *New Morning Post*, 13 Nov. 1776.
236 *Injured Woman*, 2 Jan. 1777; Eric Rump, 'Sheridan, Congreve and *The School for Scandal*'.
237 Oulton, *History of the Theatres of London*, i. 51; *Middlesex Journal*, 25–27 June 1776; *Lloyd's Evening Post*, 11–13 Dec. 1776; *New Morning Post*, 14 Dec. 1776; *St James's Chronicle*, 14-17 Dec. 1776. The *St James's Chronicle* piece was presented as a first-night notice, but it makes no comment on the performance itself, so was probably written in advance.
238 Packet, 102.
239 Packet, 102; *Injured Woman*, 23 Dec. 1776.
240 Hogan, i. 43; *Memoirs of the late Mrs Robinson*, 29; *Gazetteer*, 13 Dec. 1776; *Morning Chronicle*, 25 Mar., 11, 12, 14, 17 Dec. 1776; *St James's Chronicle*, 10–12 Dec. 1776.
241 Packet 102-3; Hogan, i. 44; *St James's Chronicle*, 21–23 Dec. 1776; *Morning Post*, 18, 21 Dec. 1776; *Morning Chronicle*, 16 Dec. 1776.
242 Packet, 103; *Injured Woman*, 2 Jan. 1777; Hogan i. 45.
243 *St James's Chronicle*, 21–24 Dec. 1776; *Morning Chronicle*, 16, 18, 30 Dec. 1776; *Morning Post*, 16, 21 Dec. 1776.
244 *Injured Woman*, 26 Dec. 1776; *Morning Chronicle*, 26 Dec. 1776; Hogan, i. 37–8.
245 *Morning Chronicle*, 18, 26 Dec. 1776; 'Theatricus' in *St James's Chronicle*, 21–24 Dec. 1776. It's not clear when exactly Theatricus's letter was written; it is dated, obviously incorrectly, 10 December; *Injured Woman*, 23 Dec. 1776.
246 *Morning Chronicle*, 18 Dec. 1776.
247 *Injured Woman*, 23, 31 Dec. 1776; *Morning Chronicle*, 27 Dec. 1776; *St James's Chronicle*, 26–28 Dec.1776.
248 *Injured Woman*, 23 Dec. 1776; *Morning Chronicle*, 18, 26 Dec. 1776.
249 *Injured Woman*, 31 Dec. 1776. The two quotations in the passage come from *Jane Shore*.
250 Oulton, *History of the Theatres of London*, i. 51.
251 Packet, 104 and additional unnumbered sheet inserted between pages 104 and 105.
252 Packet, additional sheet. Mary Ann does not give the title of her novel, but says it was epistolary in form and amounted to two small volumes, published in 1777 or 1778 by Bew of Paternoster Row. Events to be described in the next chapter enable us to identify it conclusively as *The Offspring of Fancy*.
253 *Offspring*, Letter 46.
254 *Offspring*, Letters 20, 46 and 3.
255 Packet, 65; A. H[ankey] to Mary Ann, 10 Oct. 1773 (BL Add Mss 89143/3/1/4); Stratty to Mary Ann, undated probably 1773. *Offspring*, Letter 54. That Mrs Hankey lived in Arlington Street is a guess, based on allusions in her letter and Stratty's.
256 *Offspring*, Letters 3 and 57; Packet, 82.
257 *Offspring*, Letter 5.
258 *Offspring*, Letter 8.
259 A. H[ankey] to Mary Ann, 10 Oct. 1773.
260 *Offspring*, Letters 5 and 7.
261 *Offspring*, Letters 67 and 68.
262 *Offspring*, Letters 7, 70 and 77.
263 *Offspring*, Letter 75.

264 *Offspring*, Letters 76 and 77.
265 *Offspring*, Letter 79.
266 *Offspring*, Letters 10, 81 and 82.
267 *Offspring*, Letter 10, 11 and 81.
268 *Offspring*, Letter 11.
269 *The Runaway*, 72.
270 *Offspring*, Letter 70.
271 *Offspring*, Letter 64, referring back to Marianne's reception of Amelia in Letter 8.
272 *Offspring*, Letters 67 and 70.
273 *Critical Review*, 45 (June 1778), 474; *Monthly Review*, 58 (May 1778), 395; *London Review of English and Foreign Literature*, 8 (July 1778), 66.
274 Packet, 108–9.
275 Packet, 104–5; *Daily Advertiser*, 18 Nov. 1777.
276 George to Mary Ann, 29 Sept. 1782.
277 *Saunders' Newsletter*, 16, 21, 28 June 1777.
278 *Felix Farley's Bristol Journal*, 28 June 1777; *Saunders's News-Letter*, 21 June 1777.
279 Bell, 30; *Saunders' News-Letter*, 3 July 1777; Packet, 109.
280 *Hibernian Chronicle*, 7, 11 Aug. 1777.
281 *Hibernian Chronicle*, 8 Sept. 1777.
282 *Hibernian Chronicle*, 29 Sept., 6 Oct. 1777. *The Coopers* was presumably Thomas Arne's musical play *The Cooper*, which was produced at the summer theatre in the Haymarket in 1772 and 1773.
283 *Hibernian Chronicle*, 1 Sept., 2 Oct. 1777; Rhodes, 'Early Editions of Sheridan: I–"The Duenna"'; Oulton, *History of the Theatres of London*, ii. 96
284 *Hibernian Chronicle*, 25, 29 Sept., [7?] Oct. 1777.
285 Packet, unnumbered sheet.
286 *Hibernian Chronicle*, 1 Sept. 1777; *London Chronicle or Universal Evening Post*, 18 Mar. 1775.
287 Packet, 3, 12.
288 Maire Kennedy, https://mairekennedybooks.wordpress.com/Maire Kennedy (February and March 2016).
289 *Saunders's News-Letter*, 1, 4, 6, 8, 17, 27 Nov., 2, 9, 17, 22 Dec. 1777, 26 Jan., 9 Feb. 1778; Stone, iii. 1587.
290 Packet, 108–9, 117; Gale, 21 Sept. 1929, 203; *Saunders's News-Letter*, 28 Feb. 1778.
291 *Saunders's News-Letter*, 28, 30 Mar. 1778.
292 Packet, 110.
293 *Caledonian Mercury*, 29 June 1778; Packet, 110.
294 Packet, 110, 114; Hogan, i. 9.
295 Packet, 111; *Gazetteer*, 13 Oct. 1778.
296 *Gentleman's Magazine*, 46 (July 1776), 334.
297 Packet, 111.
298 Packet, 112.
299 Packet, 111–2; Hogan, i. 105, 123.
300 Packet, 112–3.
301 Packet, 113–4, 117.
302 Packet, 113–4, unnumbered sheet.
303 Packet, 114–6.
304 Packet, 116.
305 Ireland, *Letters and Poems by the late Mr John Henderson*, 57–60; Boaden, *Memoirs of the Life of John Philip Kemble*, xi–xii.
306 Packet, 114.
307 Packet, 188.
308 Packet, 117.

309 Canning et al., *Microcosm*, 434; George to Mary Ann, 19 Sept. 1800; Dundas Letter.
310 George to Mary Ann, 16 July [1782].
311 George to Mary Ann, 18 Apr. 1814.
312 An example of this trait was recalled many years later by his younger cousin, Stratford (*Nineteenth Century*, January 1880; Hunt, 48). Hunt points out that Cousin Stratford was sixteen years younger than George, so the incident must have been recounted to him, presumably by Mehitabel.
313 Packet, 52, 69, 81–2, 165–7.
314 Packet, 166; Hunt, 105-15.
315 Hinde, 23.
316 George to Mary Ann, 12 Feb., 16 July 1782.
317 Mary Ann to George, 10 Mar. 1782 (Raven, 'Some Letters of George Canning').
318 Dundas Letter.
319 Robert and Samuel Wilberforce, *Life of William Wilberforce* v. 139.
320 Gabrielle Festing, *John Hookham Frere and his Friends*, 52. Temperley, *Life of Canning* (1905), 22, quotes it as proof of the inadequacy of an Etonian education in the 1780s, which may be fair enough, but it's something that most boys would have picked up before they were old enough for Eton.
321 George to Mary Ann, 19 Nov. 1780.
322 Letter from 'Contemporaneus', *Times*, 17 Aug. 1827; *Standard*, 2 Oct. 1827.
323 Raven, 'Some Letters of George Canning'; Hunt, 190, 253; Henry Richman to George, 28 Aug. 1793, 17 Apr. 1799, 11 Nov. 1812, 20 Apr 1813 (BL Add. MS 89143/3/6/2); George to Henry Richman, 6 Sept. 1787 (Raven).
324 George to Mary Ann, 16 July, 11, 29 Sept., 19 Oct., 19 Nov. 1782.
325 *Life of William Wilberforce*, v. 139.
326 Francis Abell, *Prisoners of War in Briton, 1756-1815* (1914); *Gazetteer*, 23 Jan. 1779; *St James's Chronicle*, 28 Jan. 1779; *Morning Post*, 17 May 1779.
327 Allardyce Nicoll, *The Garrick Stage*, 68. For information on the location of the theatre and Burying Place Lane I'm grateful to the Plymouth local historian, the late Joan Stivey.
328 Bernard, i. 126, ii. 140.
329 *BDA*, xii. 282, quoting the unreliable 'Memoirs of of Mr Reddish'.
330 Packet, 117-8.
331 Packet, 118-9.
332 *Morning Chronicle*, 12 Jan. 1780 ; *London Courant and Westminster Chronicle*, 28 Mar. 1781; *Gentleman's Magazine*, 56 (Jan. 1786), 83; A R and M E Bickford, *The Private Lunatic Asylums of the East Riding*.
333 Packet, 118, 120.
334 George to Mary Ann, 19 Oct. 1782.
335 Packet, 119.
336 Packet, 120.
337 *Thespian Dictionary*, s.n. Richard Hughes.
338 Packet, 118, 119, 122; *Exeter Flying Post*, 7 Oct. 1784 (Gale, 14 Sept. 1929, 185); *HoP, 1754-90*; Bernard, ii. 127.
339 Packet, 117.
340 Wilkinson, *Wandering Patentee*, ii. 150; Packet, 124-5.
341 Bernard, i. 207, 219; *BDA*, ii. 52-8.
342 Bernard, i. 136-9, ii. 236-8.
343 *Exeter Flying Post* (Gale, 14, 21 Sept. 1929, 183-5, 201-4).
344 Bernard, i. 208-9; *Exeter Flying Post*, 6 Nov. 1778.
345 Gale, 14 Sept. 1929, 184; *St James's Chronicle*, 22-24 Jan. 1782.
346 *Editha*, I, iii.
347 *Editha*, II, ii.

348 Gale, 14 Sept. 1929, 184 ; *The World*, 4 Apr. 1788.
349 Bernard, ii. 264.
350 *London Chronicle*, 26 Oct. 1790; Gale, 14 Sept. 1929, 184.
351 Packet, 119.
352 England, Select Marriages, 1538-1973, FHL No. 547185; Gale, 4 Sept. 1929, 183-4.
353 George to Mary Ann, 28 May 1783; Packet, 120.
354 Gale, 14 Sept. 1929, 184.
355 Gale, 14 Sept. 1929, 184; Packet, 121, 126.
356 Gale, 14 Sept. 1929, 184.
357 Winston, *Theatric Tourist*, 67.
358 Bernard, ii. 263-4.
359 Gale, 14 Sept. 1929, 184.
360 Mary Ann to George, 10 Mar. 1782 (Raven, 'Some letters of George Canning', 46-7).
361 *Whitehall Evening Post* 2-4 Dec. 1783; George to Mary Ann, 15 Feb. 1784.
362 *Public Advertiser*, 9, 13 Dec. 1784; *Morning Herald*, 10 Dec. 1784; George to Mary Ann, 22 Dec. 1784.
363 England, Select Births and Christenings, 1538-1975, FHL No. 917101; George to Mary Ann, 22 Apr. 1785.
364 A. Wolff [or Wolfe] to Mary Ann, 16 Oct. 1785 (BL Add Mss 89143/3/1/4). The identity of the writer is not known. It could be Arthur Wolfe (later Viscount Kilwarden, one of the four friends whom Mary Ann chose as guardians for George) or his wife Anne. It is unlikely to have been the Wolfe involved in the theatre.
365 Gale, 14, 21 Sept. 1929, 185, 201-2.
366 Winston, *Theatric Tourist*, 67; Packet, 122. According to Winston, Hunn failed to pay for his share in the Plymouth theatre, so Wolfe had him arrested, and only released him on condition that he gave up his claim. Bernard had dealings with Wolfe, and suggests he was unscrupulous (ii. 267).
367 *Exeter Flying Post*, 19 Jan. 1786 (Gale, 21 Sept. 1929, 202); Packet, 122.
368 George to Mary Ann, 4 Dec. 1785.
369 George to Mary Ann, 22 Apr. 1785.
370 George to Mary Ann, 10 Aug. 1785; Dundas Letter.
371 George to Mary Ann, 23 May 1785.
372 George to Henry Richman, 27 Sept. 1786 (Raven, 'Some letters of George Canning'); Hunt, 56-7.
373 Hunt, 50.
374 George to Mary Ann, 10 Aug. 1785. Letitia Canning was in her 69th year when she died in October 1786 (memorial stone in Bath Abbey).
375 George to Mary Ann, 10 Aug. 1785.
376 George to Mary Ann, 5 Oct. 1785.
377 George to Mary Ann, 10 Aug. 5 Oct., 2 Nov. 1785.
378 George to Mary Ann, 17 Feb., 30 Mar. 1786.
379 George to Mary Ann, 4 Dec. 1785.
380 George to Mary Ann, 5 Jan., 27 Feb. 1786. To distinguish the three Palmers see *ODNB* entries for [Plausible] Jack Palmer (1744-1798), John Palmer [of Bath] (1742-1818), [Gentleman] John Palmer (1728-1768).
381 George to Mary Ann, 2, 17 Feb., 17 May, 16 Sept. 1786, 12 Nov. 1787.
382 George to Mary Ann, 5 Jan., 2, 17 Feb. 1786; *Times*, 20 Feb. 1786; Meteorological table in *Gentleman's Magazine*, 56 (Feb. 1786), 90.
383 Dundas Letter.
384 Packet, 122.
385 Mary Ann to George, 19 Aug. 1786.
386 George to Mary Ann, 16 Sept., 20 Oct. 1786.

387 *Times*, 27 July 1787.
388 Wilkinson, *Wandering Patentee*, ii. 154.
389 *Newcastle Courant*, 28 Apr. 1787.
390 *Newcastle Chronicle*, 25 Jan, 1766.
391 *Cumberland Pacquet*, 22 June 1775 (Marshall, ed., *A Travelling Actress in the North and Scotland*, p. x).
392 Rosenfeld, *The Georgian Theatre of Richmond Yorkshire*, 2-10.
393 Mary Ann's route can be followed from the direction on George's letters. On more than one occasion they had to be sent on after her, and one letter was returned to him at Eton. There is no letter addressed to Ripon or Kendal, but they formed part of Butler's circuit (*The Georgian Theatre of Richmond Yorkshire*, 6, 10).
394 *Newcastle Courant*, 25 Nov. 1786.
395 Packet, 123.
396 Mary Ann to George, 19 Aug. 1786.
397 Rosenfeld, *The Georgian Theatre of Richmond Yorkshire*, 15.
398 Wilkinson, *Wandering Patentee*, iii. 5.
399 *HoP 1820-1832*, s.n. Nathaniel Peach (1785-1835).
400 George to Mary Ann, 29 Aug. 1786.
401 Mary Ann to George, 24 Aug. 1788.
402 *Newcastle Courant*, 25 Nov. 1786.
403 Cawdell, *Miscellaneous Poems* (1785), 69-73.
404 Frances Marshall, ed., *A Travelling Actress in the North and Scotland*, 75-7.
405 *A Travelling Actress in the North and Scotland*, 57-8.
406 *A Travelling Actress in the North and Scotland*, 103-4.
407 *A Narrative of the Life of Mrs Charlotte Charke*, 113-4, 122, 77, 126-31. See above chapter 3.
408 George to Mary Ann, 2 June 1787.
409 Royal Academy website, www.royalacademy.org.uk/art-artists/work-of-art/strolling-actresses-dressing-in-a-barn-1
410 *Times*, 12 July 1787; *Whitehall Evening Post*, 10-12 July 1787; *Manchester Mercury*, 10 July 1787; Barton, *History of the Borough of Bury and Neighbourhood*, 18-23. Barton, who wrote some ninety years after the incident, does not cite any authority for his account. *Whitehall Evening Post* and *Manchester Mercury* identify the manager as Mr Bibby.
411 Packet, 125.
412 George to Mary Ann 16 Feb., 7 Aug. 1787; *Letter Journal*, 13 July 1795. *The Microcosm* was first published in 1787 by C Knight of Castle Street, Windsor. The second edition, again published by Knight, was distributed by London book-sellers, Robinson of Paternoster Row and Debrett of Piccadilly.
413 Canning et al., *Microcosm*, 434.
414 Marshall, 5.
415 George to Mary Ann, 2, 16 Feb. 1787.
416 Hunt, 62.
417 George to the Leighs, 31 May 1787; to Mary Ann, 7 Aug., 12 Nov. 1787.
418 Bell, 90n; *Life of William Wilberforce*, iv. 369-70; George to Mary Ann, 13 June 1791.
419 Dundas Letter; George to the Leighs, 24 May 1787 (Hunt, 64-5); to Henry Richman, 6 Sept., 11 Oct. 1787 (Raven, 'Some letters of George Canning').
420 Marshall, 14; George to Henry Richman, 11 Oct. 1787 (Raven, 'Some letters of George Canning').
421 Granville MSS, quoted in Marshall, 26.
422 Mary Ann to George, 24 Aug. 1788.
423 Packet, 125; *Cumberland Pacquet*, 1 Aug. 1787.
424 George to Mary Ann, 7 Aug., 12 Nov. 1787.
425 *Cumberland Pacquet*, 21 Nov. 1787.

426 Gale, 18 Sept. 1937, 202-4; *Chester Courant*, 6, 13, 20, 27 Nov., 4, 11 Dec. 1787; Packet, 126. Gale's playbills fill in some of the gaps in the newspaper record. There is a discrepancy: Gale says that on 28 November the mainpiece was *The Clandestine Wedding* [*sic*] whereas in the newspaper *The Gamester* was advertised for that night.
427 *Chester Courant*, 4 Dec. 1787; Hunt, 75.
428 *Chester Courant*, 25 Dec. 1787, 1 Jan. 1788.
429 *Newcastle Courant*, 19, 26 Jan. 1788; Mackenzie, *Historical Account of Newcastle-upon-Tyne*, 229-231; Winston, *Theatric Tourist*, 44 (where the date is given as 1789). After 26 January 1788 the Hunns do not appear in any of the announcements in the *Newcastle Courant*, although this is not conclusive as not all the plays were advertised there, and some of the advertisements are illegible.
430 Mary Ann to George, 11 Apr. 1788; Packet, 125.
431 Mary Ann to George, 24 Aug. 1788; *Chester Courant*, 6 May 1787; Kohn, *Encyclopedia of Plague and Pestilence*, 113; *Whitehall Evening Post*, 15-17 Apr. 1788; *London Chronicle*, 5-7 June 1788.
432 Packet, 126; George to Mary Ann, 26 Sept. 1788.
433 George to the Leighs, 26 Sept. 1788; to Mary Ann, 29 Sept. 1788; *HoP 1754-1790*.
434 *Chester Courant*, 16, 23 Sept,, 28 Oct., 4 Nov. 1788.
435 *Chester Courant*, 11, 18 November 1788; Gale, 18 Sept. 1937, 203.
436 Packet, 126.
437 Packet, 126-8.
438 George to the Leighs, 26 Sept. 1788.
439 George to Mary Ann, 26 Nov., 22 Dec. 1788; Hunt, 77; Packet, 129.
440 Packet, 126, 130.
441 Packet, 129; George to Mary Ann 28 June 1789.
442 *Universal British Directory* (1791), ii. 177; Packet, 129-30. Mary Ann doesn't say who her friends were in Newcastle; George's June letter is addressed to 'Mrs Reid's, New Gate Street'.
443 Packet, 129; George to the Leighs, 8 Aug. 1789; *Letter Journal*, 6 June 1794.
444 Packet, 129-30. Some of George's letters are addressed to Mary Ann at Stephens's shop on Wine Street, either because she lodged near the shop or because it was convenient to have her letters sent there. Wine Street is close to the river, so may have been damp and unhealthy.
445 George to Mary Ann, 9 Nov. 1789; *Chester Chronicle*, 18 Sept. 1789. The *Chronicle*'s correspondent judged the Eaton Hall company more kindly than George.
446 Packet, 130; George to Mary Ann, 4 Dec. 1789, 7 Feb. 1791.
447 *Times*, 9 Feb. 1791; George to Mary Ann, 13 Aug. 1794; 'Drury-Lane Theatrical Fund', *Standard*, 25 Mar. 1830. I am grateful to Linley Hooper for drawing my attention to this.
448 Packet, 131-2; George to Mary Ann, 7 Jan. 1790; George to Mehitabel, June 1792 (Western Letters).
449 George to Mary Ann, 9 Mar. 1790.
450 Packet, 130; George to Mary Ann, 26 March 1790.
451 Packet, 40.
452 George to Mary Ann, 7 Feb. 1791, 26 Feb. 1793.
453 Packet, 130.
454 Packet, 131. *Universal British Directory* (1791) lists 27 tea-dealers in Bristol
455 George to Bess Leigh, summer 1788 (Hunt, 76); to J F Newton, 1 Sept. 1788 (Newton, *The Early Days of the Right Honorable George Canning, and some of his Contemporaries*); Cyril Jackson to George, 1 Sept. 1788 and undated letter evidently written in 1791 (BL Add. Mss 89143/1/1/78).
456 George to the Leighs, 28 May 1791, 12 Dec. 1792; to Mary Ann, 24 Feb. 1791.
457 George to Mary Ann, 24 Feb., 13 June 1791; *Exeter Flying Post*, 2 June 1791.

458 George to Mary Ann, 9, 15 Nov. 1791.
459 George to Mary Ann, 8 June 1791.
460 George to Mary Ann, 13 June 1791; to Mehitabel, 16 Dec. 1791 (Hunt, 117-8).
461 George to Mary Ann, 26 June 1791.
462 Bernard, i. 22, ii. 235-7; Packet, 131-2.
463 The absence of evidence is not conclusive. I have not seen the Plymouth newspapers for that summer. *Exeter Flying Post* makes occasional mention of the Plymouth theatre, but does not provide the same detail as it does for Exeter.
464 Bernard, ii. 237-42.
465 Packet, 174, 185, 188.
466 Dundas Letter.
467 Wakefield, *Present Condition of the Female Sex*, 129; Wolcot, *Works of Peter Pindar*, v. 171; Hinde, 84; Marshall, 116.
468 Packet, 132; George to Mary Ann, 15 Nov. 1791, 11 Jan., 10 Feb. 1792.
469 Packet 132-3; Mary Ann to George, 21 Oct. 1792, 25 Mar. 1793.
470 Advertisements in *Exeter Flying Post*, January 1790.
471 Packet, 132, 182, 184; Diary, [?] Mar., 27 Aug., 6 Oct. 1792.
472 George to Bootle Wilbraham, 4 Dec. 1792 (Bagot, i. 29-35); to Lord Boringdon, 13 Dec. 1792 (Stapleton, *George Canning and his* Times, 4-9); Diary, 26 July 1792; Scott, *Journal*, 17 Apr. 1828; Godwin's Journal, 5 Jan., 22 Feb. 1792; Hinde, 22-9; Marshall, 30-46; Thompson, *Making of the English Working* Class, 115.
473 George to Sturges Bourne, Sept. 1792 (Marshall, 33-7); Festing, *John Hookham Frere and his Friends*, 29; Hague, *William Pitt the Younger*, 291-304, 387.
474 Diary, 21-27 May, 8 July, 3, 9, 15, 27 Aug. 1792 ; George to Mary Ann, 24 Jan., 14 May 1793.
475 *Times*, 9 Feb. 1791.
476 George to Mary Ann, 29 Aug. 1791, 26 Feb. 1793; Mary Ann to George, 21 Oct. 1792, 6 Jan. 1793.
477 Packet, 182-4.
478 Packet, 184-5.
479 George to Mary Ann, 10 Feb., 22 Sept., 21 Oct. 1792, 24 Jan. 1793.
480 George to Mary Ann, 17 Oct. 1792; Mary Ann to George 21 Oct. 1792; *Prerogative Court of Canterbury and Related Probate Jurisdictions: Will Registers, PROB 11/1225*, proved 10 Nov. 1792.
481 Packet, 133.
482 Mary Ann to George, 21 Oct. 1792; Wollstonecraft, *Vindication*, 5, 56-7, 81.
483 Mary Ann to George, 21 Oct. 1792.
484 *Letter Journal*, 30 June 1795.
485 George to Mary Ann, 4, 13 Jan., 26 Feb. 1793; to Mehitabel, 5 Oct. 1792 (Hunt, 122-3); Mary Ann to George, 6 Jan. 1793.
486 Packet, 134.
487 George to Mary Ann, 24 Jan. 1793; to the Leighs, 29 Jan. 1793; Packet, 134-5.
488 Mary Ann to George, 25 Mar. 1793. Mary Ann doesn't say who it is Maria went to live with, but the likeliest guess is her father's sister Mrs Featherstone.
489 Mary Ann to George, 25 Mar. 1793; George to Mary Ann. 14 May 1793.
490 George to Bootle Wilbraham, 12 Aug. 1793, quoted in Bagot, i. 44.
491 Packet 135; George to Mary Ann, 5, 9 July 1793; to the Leighs, 9 July 1793; *Lloyds Evening Post*, 1-3 July 1793.
492 Packet, 153.
493 Packet, 185.
494 George to Mary Ann, 18 Aug. 1793; Packet, 136.
495 Packet, 136.

496 Dundas Letter.
497 George to Mary Ann, 21, 26 Aug., 18 Sept., 14 Oct. 1793. There were other ointments marketed as collyrium, Sydenham's Collyrium, for example.
498 *Letter Journal*, 30 Nov. 1793; George to Mary Ann, 2 Dec. 1793.
499 George to Mary Ann, 2 Dec. 1793; Packet, 185.
500 *Letter Journal*, 31 Jan. 1794; George to Mary Ann, 3 Feb. 1794; Therry, i. 4–25.
501 George to Mary Ann, 10, 19 Mar. 1794; *Letter Journal*, 2 Mar, 17 Mar. - 1 Apr. 1794.
502 *Letter Journal*, 29 May 1794.
503 Therry, i. 30–42.
504 *Letter Journal*, 16 June 1795; Diary, 10, 23 Aug. 1795; George to the Leighs, 24 Dec. 1795, 5 Jan. 1796; to Mary Ann, 6 Jan. 1796.
505 George to Mary Ann, 22 Mar. 1794, 13, 20 Aug. 1795, 29 Mar., 29 Dec. 1796; to the Leighs, 15 Apr. 1795, 21 Jan. 1796; Diary, 6 Feb. 1796; Hinde, 44.
506 Dundas Letter; *Letter Journal*, 31 May 1794; George to the Leighs, 24 Jan. 1796; Diary, 16 July 1796.
507 Dundas Letter.
508 Diary, 17, 18 Aug. 1793; *Letter Journal*, 27 Jan. 1794.
509 *Courier*, 24 Feb. 1795; *Caledonian Mercury*, 5 Mar., 16 July 1795; *Hull Advertiser and Exchange Gazette*, 18 July 1795; Armstrong, *The Liberty Tree*, 320–6, 365–9.
510 George to Mary Ann, 6 July 1795; *Letter Journal*, 27 Jan. 1794, 8 July 1795.
511 George to Mary Ann, 27 Aug. 1794; Somerset Parish Records 1538-1914, ref D\P\tau.m/2/1/33 (burial record for Ann Hunn on 18 Aug. 1794, with no indication of age).
512 Packet, 137; George to Mary Ann, 25 Nov., 16 Dec. 1794.
513 Mary Ann to George, 6 Jan. 1793.
514 *Letter Journal*, 14, 24 May 1794; Hinde, 84; Marshall, 116.
515 George to Mary Ann, 4 May, 4 Sept. 1795.
516 *Letter Journal*, 27 Jan., 8 Feb., 3, 14 May 1794; George to Mary Ann, 27 July, 4 Aug. 1794, 26 Sept., 12, 28 Oct., 13 Nov. 1795, 16 July 1796.
517 George to Mary Ann, 13, 27 Aug., 18 Sept. 1794, 4 Mar. 1795; *Letter Journal*, 27 Nov. 1794.
518 *Letter Journal*, 10 June 1795; George to Mary Ann, 6, 13 June 1795, 16 Mar. 1796.
519 *Letter Journal*, 27 Jan. 1794; George to Mary Ann, 3 Dec. 1794, 23 Feb., 14 Mar., 13 Apr., 14 May 1796.
520 George to Mary Ann, 14, 16 July 1796.
521 *Letter Journal*, 28 Mar. 1795.
522 Mary Ann to George, 24 May 1812.
523 George to Mary Ann, 31 Jan., 4, 7 Feb., 4, 26 Mar., 6 June, 13 Nov., 1 Dec. 1795; *Letter Journal*, 30 June 1795.
524 Packet, 137; George to Mary Ann, 17 Dec. 1795; to the Leighs, 8, 22 June, 7 July, 9, 24, 26, 31 Dec. 1795, 20 Jan., 22 Feb., 14 May 1796.
525 George to Mary Ann, 3 Mar., 1 Oct., 13 Dec. 1796, 27 Feb., 28 Sept. 1797; to the Leighs, 25 Feb., 19 Sept. 1797.
526 LMA, England Marriages and Banns, St Pancras Parish Chapel, ref. P90/pan1/055.
527 George to Mary Ann, 29 Mar., 27 Dec. 1796; *Exeter Flying Post*, 19 May, 2 June 1791.
528 Diary, 25 Dec. 1795; George to Mary Ann, 13 Apr., 14, 26 May, 8, 14 July 1796.
529 George to Mary Ann, 26 Oct. 1796, 24 Jan. 1797, 11 Aug. 1798.
530 George to the Leighs, 5 Dec. 1798; Diary, 22 Mar. 1799.
531 Packet, 138; Diary, 13 Nov. 1796, 19 Jan. 1797.
532 Diary, 25 Sept. 1797; George to Mary Ann, 6 Oct. 1797; Marshall, 175; Wade, *Black Book*, 25. Marshall and Wade give different estimates of the salary, which presumably varied from year to year. The work of the office was carried out by deputy.
533 Packet, 139; George to Mary Ann, 23 Oct. 1797; to the Leighs, 19 Dec. 1798, 11 Sept. 1799.

534 George to Mary Ann, 29 Dec. 1797, 16 Jan. 1798; Packet, 140.
535 Packet, 139–43; Hunt, 83.
536 George to the Leighs, 17 Jan. 1798; Packet, 142.
537 Packet, 15; George to the Leighs, 11 Apr., 28 Nov. 1798; *Letter Journal*, 23 May 1795.
538 George to Mary Ann, 25 Aug. 1798; to the Leighs, 22 Jan. 1798; Gale, 9 Oct., 11 Dec. 1937, 256, 421.
539 George to Mary Ann, 24 Nov. 1798; to the Leighs, 28 Nov. 1798.
540 George to Mary Ann, 29 Aug., 26 Nov. 1798, 2 Jan. 1799; to the Leighs, 28 Nov. 1798; Charles to Mary Ann, 14 Sept. 1809 (see below, chapter 26); Dundas Letter.
541 George to Mary Ann, 23 Nov., 4 Dec. 1798.
542 Packet, 143; George to Mary Ann, 8, 9 Nov. 1798, 23 Jan. 1802; to the Leighs, 28 Nov. 1798.
543 *Times*, 31 Dec. 1798, 7 Jan. 1799; George to Mary Ann, 28 Nov., 25 Dec. 1798, 10, 18 Jan., 17 Feb. 1799.
544 George to Mary Ann, 11, 17 Feb., 6 Mar. 1799; to the Leighs, 28 Nov. 1798.
545 George to Mary Ann, 3 Nov. 1794, 29 Mar., 13 Apr. 1796, 10 Apr., 4 Dec. 1798; to the Leighs, 21 May 1799; *Letter Journal*, 28 Mar. 1795.
546 George to Mary Ann, 4 Dec. 1798, 3, 10 Jan. 1799; *Lloyd's Evening Post*, 31 July–2 Aug. 1799.
547 George to Mary Ann, 7, 19 Apr., 21 May 1799.
548 Packet, 144; George to Mary Ann, 21, 27 May 1799.
549 George to the Leighs, 6 June 1799; to Mary Ann, 23 Jan. 1802.
550 George to Mary Ann, 21 May, 3, 26 June 1799.
551 George to the Leighs, 24 Dec. 1795, 5 Jan. 1796; George to John Sneyd, 17 Dec. 1795, 10 Jan. 1796 (Bagot, 54, 59); Diary, 21 Aug. 1795.
552 Diary, 15, 17 Mar. 1799; George to Mary Ann, 8 Aug. 1799; 'Account of Charges on Fund from Four and Half per cent Duties in Barbadoes and Leeward Islands', 1801.
553 Packet, 143–4.
554 George to Mary Ann, 26 July, 17 Sept. 1799; Sam Reddish to Mary Ann, 17 Sept. 1799 (enclosed in George's letter of same date).
555 George to Mary Ann, 17 Sept. 1799.
556 George to Mary Ann, 15, 24 July, 16 Oct., 25 Nov. 1799, 15, 24 Feb., 22 Mar. 1800.
557 George to the Leighs, 8 Apr. 1800.
558 Packet, 166; Hunt, 86–7.
559 George to the Leighs, 5 Dec. 1798; Diary, [February] 1798.
560 Bess Canning, writing to her mother from Bath in December 1798, named Miss Newenham and described her as 'an angel of a creature', adding: 'Do you know that our cousin G.C. lost a piece of his heart to her last year?' (Hunt, 154.) Hunt assumes that 'GC' is Irish George but it's clear from what he wrote to the Leighs and in his diary that it was English George.
561 *Lloyd's Evening Post*, 20 Aug. 1792, 28 Jan., 27 Feb. 1793; *World* 19 Oct. 1792; *London Packet*, 3 Apr. 1793; *Sun* 24 June 1793; LMA, C of E Parish Registers, ref P69/BRI/A/013/MS06543/001; Packet 31–2.
562 *Letter Journal*, 31 Jan., 26 May–3 June, 16 Nov. 1794,
563 *Letter Journal*, 24 Apr. 1794, 23 May 1795.
564 *Letter Journal*, 4 Feb. 1794.
565 *Private Correspondence of Granville Leveson Gower* i. 217.
566 George to Leveson-Gower, 22 Aug. 1799 (*Private Correspondence of Granville Leveson Gower*, i. 250–2); Marshall, 195–6; Hinde, 87–8. There's no direct evidence that the woman who almost led George into ruinous indiscretion was the Princess of Wales, but the circumstantial details in the letter to Leveson-Gower make it very likely.
567 *Exeter Flying Post*, 17 Apr. 1800.

568 George to Mary Ann, 22, 26 June, 15, 17, 24, 26 July, 23 Aug., 5 Sept., 4, 16 October 1799.
569 George to Mary Ann, 1, 6 June 1802.
570 Hinde, 73n; *Sun*, 22 Aug. 1799; *Letter Journal*, 9 Apr. 1794; *Times*, 7 June 1794.
571 George to Lady Susan Ryder, 15, 24 Aug. 1799 (BL Add MSS 89143/3/3/21).
572 George to John Sneyd, 17 Sept. 1799 (Bagot, i. 154–5); to the Leighs, 21 Mar., 8, 9, 10 May 1800.
573 George to the Leighs, 12 Apr. 1800; George to Lady Susan Ryder, undated draft.
574 Bell, 175 and Walter Wood, *The East Neuk of Fife*, 391. Joan's marriage settlement lists various amounts invested in the funds, totalling £52,685, plus 'divers sums' from the estates of her father, mother and uncle, and ready money and other effects 'to a considerable amount'. (West Yorkshire Archive WYL412)
575 *HoP 1754–1790*, s.n. John Scott. I'm grateful to the late Brenda Webster for information about General Scott.
576 Ferguson, 'Dingwall Burgh Politics and the Parliamentary Franchise in the Eighteenth Century'; Leneman, *Alienated Affections*, 128–31.
577 Hinde, 79.
578 Portland London Collection, F6/1, University of Nottingham ; West Yorkshire Archive Service, WYL412. Final administration of Scott's will was not granted to Henrietta until 1802.
579 George to Mary Ann, 16 Dec. 1799, 15 Feb. 1800; to the Leighs, 14 Feb. 1800.
580 George to Mary Ann, 6, 15, 30 Jan., 15 Feb., 22 Mar. 1800, 20 Dec. 1801.
581 George to Mary Ann, 29 July 1800, 17 June 1801.
582 Packet, 144; George to the Leighs, 26 May, 7 , 11 June 1800; to Mary Ann, 3 June 1800; Mary Ann to George, 24 May 1812.
583 George to the Leighs, 1 Jan., 1 Mar., 23 Apr., 4, 28 June 1800; Hunt, 179.
584 Dundas Letter; George to the Leighs, 1 Mar., 13, 15 May 1800.
585 George to the Leighs, 13 May, 7, 14, 18 June 1800; Festing, 31; Hague, *William Pitt the Younger,* 458.
586 Packet 144–5; Joan to Mary Ann, 15 July 1800 (included with George's letters); Mary Ann to George, 19 July 1800.
587 Packet, 151–2.
588 It is not certain that Mary's Captain was Edward Parker, but see endnotes 594 and 609 below.
589 *Lloyd's Evening Post*, 21–23 Oct. 1799; *London Gazette Extraordinary*, 22 Oct 1799; *Commissioned Sea Officers of the Royal Navy 1660–1815*, s.n. Edward Thornb[o]rough Parker (Ancestry website); Knight, *The Pursuit of Victory* (2005), 330–45; Burke, *Genealogical and Heraldic History of the Commoners of Great Britain and Ireland*, vol. 4, s.n. Thornbrough of Bishopsteignton.
590 He was London agent for John Frewen-Turner of Cold Overton, Leicestershire and Brickwall, Sussex (Frewen family papers, East Sussex Record Office).
591 Packet, 147; George to Mary Ann, 30 July, 30 Nov. 1798; Diary, 15 Aug. 1798.
592 Packet, 145; George to Mary Ann, 17, 27 Sept., 3, 12, 20, 26 Nov. 1800; to Joan, 4 Dec. 1800.
593 George to Joan, 1 Dec. 1800 ; to Mary Ann, 23 Jan. 1802.
594 George to Mary Ann, 13 Dec. 1800; to Joan 1, 3, 5, Dec. 1800. If Mary's Captain was Nelson's aide-de-camp it would explain George's anxiety on this point.
595 George to Mary Ann, 20 Nov. 1800.
596 George to Mary Ann, 26, 29 Nov., 6 Dec. 1800; to Joan, 26 Nov., 1 Dec. 1800.
597 Packet, 147.
598 Joan to Mary Ann, 27 Jan. 1801; George to Mary Ann, 20, 30 Jan. 1801.
599 George to Mary Ann, 4 Feb. 1801; Packet, 151.
600 George to Mary Ann, 1, 3 Apr. 1801; *Morning Chronicle*, 27 Feb. 1801; *Exeter Flying Post*, 30 Apr. 1801.

601 Joan to Mary Ann, 11 Oct. 1800.
602 George to Mary Ann, 25, 27, 29 Apr., 5 June 1801; LMA, ref. DL/T/093/001.
603 George to the Leighs 4 Mar., 22 Oct. 1802; to Joan, 10 June 1803. It could be *gee* rather than *gcc*. The handwriting is unclear, but in the documents I've examined it looks more like *gcc*, which is the sort of humorous conceit that George might well have indulged in.
604 Packet, 160.
605 Packet, 147–8.
606 George to Mary Ann, 22 Nov. 1801; Richard Thompson to John Frewen, 19 Nov. 1804 (Frewen Papers, FRE/1597); Maria to Mary Ann, 19? Nov. 1805, BL Add Mss 89143/3/11/2.
607 George to Mary, 1 Dec. 1801 (Gale, 20 Aug. 1927, 130).
608 George to Mary, 1 Dec. 1801 (Gale, 20Aug. 1927, 130); to Mary Ann, 24 Mar. 1802.
609 Knight, *Pursuit of* Victory, 662; *Times*, 16 Oct. 1801; Packet, 146–7. The assumption that Mary's Captain was Edward Parker makes sense of the comment which would otherwise remain unexplained.
610 Hinde, 92–5.
611 George to the Leighs, 27 Feb., 20 Mar., 1, 3 July 1801; to Mary Ann, 16 June, 17, 27 July 1801; to John Sneyd, 14 Feb. 1801 (Bagot, i, 180).
612 Packet, 146; George to Mary Ann, 23 Jan. 1802.
613 George to Mary Ann, 19 Mar., 17, 25 June 1801, 7 Apr., 21 June, 24 Aug. 1802.
614 George to Mary Ann, 20 Dec. 1801, 1 Jan. 1802.
615 George to Mary Ann, 23 Jan. 1802.
616 George to the Leighs, 4 Feb. 1802.
617 Packet, 165–6; George to Mary Ann, 26 Feb. 1802.
618 George to Mary Ann, 4 Feb., 24 Mar., 7, 15 Apr., 3 May, 6, 14, 21, 27 June, 12 July 1802; to the Leighs 31 Jan., 2 May 1802; Hinde, 108–9.
619 Packet, 157–61.
620 Packet, 159, 163.
621 Packet, 163.
622 George to Mary Ann, 25 Sept. 1802; to the Leighs, 2 Aug. 1802; Packet, 136.
623 George to the Leighs, 18 July, 13 Sept., 22 Oct. 1802; to Mary Ann, 4, 8 Oct. 1802.
624 George to Mary Ann, 16, 20, 21, 28 Dec. 1802, 4 Jan. 1803.
625 Packet, 161, 164, 176; George to Mary Ann, 11 Nov. 1804.
626 Packet, 161–3; George to Mary Ann, 22 Jan. 1803.
627 Packet, 162.
628 Packet, 1, 175.
629 Packet, 45.
630 Marshall, ed., *A Travelling Actress in the North and Scotland*, 3; *Memoirs of the late Mrs Robinson*, 8; *Narrative of the Life of Mrs Charlotte Charke*, 16; Pullen, *Actresses and Whores*, 58.
631 Packet, 15.
632 Packet, 24–5.
633 Packet, 117, 172, 174; George to Mary Ann, 6 Mar. 1803.
634 Packet, 38, 44.
635 Packet, 45.
636 Packet, 86.
637 Packet, 89.
638 Packet, 166.
639 Packet, 167–168.
640 Packet, 168.
641 *Jane Shore* I ii; *Vindication of the Rights of Woman* (chapter 4), 81.
642 Packet, 14, 33, 40, 174, 185.
643 Packet, 154, 170.

644 Packet, 169.
645 Packet, 127 (dated 27 Feb.); George to Mary Ann, 28 Feb. 1803.
646 Packet 175; Diary, 27 May, 14 Nov. 1804; George to Mary Ann, 6 Mar. 1803.
647 *ODNB* s.n. John Heriot (1760-1833), editor of *The True Briton*; 'Change of Ministry', *Political Register*, 30 Apr. 1803.
648 George to Mary Ann, 15 Mar. 1803; Packet, 173-4.
649 Packet, 176.
650 George to Mary Ann, 23 Mar., 7 Apr. 1803; Packet, 177.
651 Packet, 179-80.
652 Packet, 180-1.
653 Packet, 182-184.
654 Packet, 185.
655 Packet, 187.
656 Packet, 187-8.
657 Packet, 186; George to Joan, 10 June 1803; to Mary Ann, 27 July 1803.
658 George to Mary Ann, 14 Aug., 14 Sept. 1803.
659 George to Mary Ann, 16 Apr., 14 Sept. 1803; Hooper.
660 George to Mary Ann, 5, 14, 27 July 1803.
661 George to Mary Ann, 1 Aug., 29 Sept. 1803.
662 George to Mary Ann, 30 Aug., 21 Sept., 8 Nov. 1803.
663 George to Mary Ann, 21, 30 Aug., 21 Sept., 14, 28 Oct., 4, 16, 21 Nov., 4 Dec. 1803.
664 O'Byrne, *Naval Biographical Dictionary*, 554; George to Mary Ann, 7, 14 Sept. 1803, 20 Jan. 1804.
665 George to Mary Ann, 10 Feb., 15, 30 Apr. 1804.
666 George to Mary Ann, 10, 18/19 May 1804; Hinde, 124-5.
667 George to Mary Ann, 18/19 May 1804.
668 George to Mary Ann, 6, 7, 9, 11 Sept. 1804; to Joan, 10 Sept. 1804; to the Leighs, 17 Sept. 1804.
669 George to Mary Ann, 1 July 1804.
670 *Great Cry and Little Wool* Epistle IV (*Works of Peter Pindar Esq*, v. 172-3). I have not identified Uncle Tommy. 'Uncle' and 'Somerstown' both suggest a connection with Esther or her husband Joseph Murch.
671 George to Mary Ann, 27 Sept. 1804.
672 George to Mary Ann, 27 Sept. 1804; Fry, *Dundas Despotism*, 262-74; Hinde, 131-3.
673 *The Times*, 17 Sept. 1804, where the weather story comes immediately after a report of the fitting out of two new 74-gun warships, the *Bellona* and the *Alexander*.
674 George to Mary Ann, 17 Sept. 1804.
675 George to Mary Ann, 17, 27 Sept., 1 Oct. 1804; to the Leighs, 13 Sept. 1804.
676 George to the Leighs, 17 Sept. 1804.
677 George to Mary Ann, 23 Oct. 1804.
678 George to Mary Ann, 24 Sept. 1804.
679 George to Mary Ann, 1, 14 Oct., 4 Nov., 2 Dec. 1804; Diary, 7 Oct., 8 Dec 1804.
680 George to Mary Ann, 1, 14, 23 Oct., 11 Nov. 1804.
681 George to Mary Ann, 8 Nov. 1804.
682 *Prerogative Court of Canterbury and Related Probate Jurisdictions: Will Registers PROB 11/1582, 11/1679*; Gale, 12 Dec. 1937, 422.
683 Diary, 17 Feb. 1805.
684 Diary, 14 Nov. 1804; George to Mary Ann, 11 Nov. 1804.
685 George to Mary Ann, 11 Nov., 14 Dec. 1804, 17 Feb. 1805.
686 George to Mary Ann, 2, 9 Apr. 1805.
687 George to Mary Ann, 26 June 1805.
688 Maria to Mary Ann, 19 Nov. 1805 (BL Add MSS 89143/3/11/2).

689 George to Mary Ann, 7 July, 10, 15 Oct., 4 Nov. 1805; Richard Thompson to Mary Ann, 21 Nov. 1805; Mary to Mary Ann, 15 June 1806 (BL Add MSS 89143/3/11/2).
690 George to Mary Ann, 25, 29 Aug., 25 Oct. 1805, 1 Jan., 13 May, 26 June 1806; Hunt, 251, 277.
691 George to Mary Ann, 15, 17, 25 Oct., 27 Dec. 1805.
692 George to Mary Ann, 29 Jan. and 1 Feb. 1806. Tregent senior to Mary Ann, 16 Oct. 1805 (BL Add. Mss 89143/3/11/2); Science Museum website: collection.sciencemuseumgroup.org.uk/ people/cp105482/james-tregent; *London Gazette*, 1 Feb. 1806, 28 May 1808.
693 Richard Thompson to Mary Ann, 21 Nov. 1805; Mary to Mary Ann, 15 June 1806; George to Mary Ann, 26 June, 18 July 1806.
694 George to Mary Ann, 3 Dec. 1805.
695 George to Mary Ann, 1 Sept. 1805, 18 July, 10, 26 Aug. 1806, 3 Jan., 16 Feb. 1807; Mary to Mary Ann, 15 June 1806.
696 George to Mary Ann, 5 Dec. 1806, 8 Jan. 1807; Barfoot and Wilkes, *Universal British Directory*, ii. 104, 112. The information relates to the 1790s, so it is not certain that Mr Moore was still there in 1806. Even if he was, it isn't certain that he had any connection with Mrs Moore of Exeter.
697 George to Mary Ann, 3, 8 Jan. 1807.
698 George to Mary Ann, 11 Nov. 1806.
699 George to Mary Ann, 24 Apr., 7, 11 Nov. 1806 ; to Joan, 20 Sept. 1809.
700 Festing, *John Hookham Frere and his Friends*, 31; Dixon, *Canning, Politician and Statesman*, 162.
701 [Lady Hester Stanhope] to Joan, n.d., filed among George's letters to Joan, 1804, BL Add Mss 89143/3/3/4. The signature is illegible, but the likeliest author is Lady Hester. The letter contains a reference to the writer's sister Lucy, which would tend to support this.
702 George to Mary Ann, 30 Jan., 16 Feb., 6 Mar. 1807.
703 George to Mary Ann, 5 Dec. 1806.
704 Inside the cover of one of George's letters (17 Oct. 1812) is a note: 'My Mother's blessing. She sends you the enclos'd cure for your headache.' It's not clear who this was addressed to, nor why, if it was actually sent to someone on Mary Ann's behalf, the paper came back to remain among George's letters.
705 Hall, *Retrospect of a Long Life*, 93, 585-7 (Gale, 30 Apr. 1938, 312). Hall's information about Mary Ann's earlier life is inaccurate, but that doesn't invalidate the colonel's recollection of the general impression made by Mary Ann in Bath.
706 George to Mary Ann, 10, 12 June 1807.
707 George to Mary Ann, 27 Dec. 1805 , 28 Jan. 1814, 27 Jan. 1816, 27 Aug. 1818, 16 Jan. 1819, 17 Jan., 10 Apr., 29 Aug. 1822, 25 Jan., 13 Dec. 1823, 19 Mar. 1825; to Mary Thompson, 9 Nov. 1812, (Gale, 27 Aug. 1927, 148); Dundas Letter.
708 *Times*, 1 July 1807; *Hansard 1803-2005*, Debate on the Finance Committee, 30 June 1807, column 703. When George says he kept half of the award for himself he was probably thinking of the stipend from the Alienation Office. The controversy continued, with newspapers over the next weeks publishing lists of 'Places, Pensions and Reversions' paid to members of the government. Compared with some of his colleagues' emoluments, George's were quite modest. See for example *Jackson's Oxford Journal*, 18 July 1807.
709 George to Mary Ann, 10 July 1807. His letter does not mention the nature of Mary Ann's generous offer, but his reason for refusing it, and the context, suggests strongly that it was to do with the pension.
710 George to Mary Ann, 3 Oct. 1807.
711 George to Mary Ann, 6 Oct. 1807.
712 George to Mary Ann, 17 Oct., 5 Nov. 1807.
713 George to Mary Ann, 18 Nov. 1807.
714 George to Mary Ann, 30 Dec. 1807.

715 George to Mary Ann, 8 Jan. 1808; *HoP 1790-1820*, s.n. John Palmer.
716 Bernard, ii. 242.
717 George to Mary Ann, 25 Mar. 1808.
718 George to Mary Ann, 10, 17, 24, 31 Aug., 9, 12 Sept. 1808; Hunt, 221. Leigh was made Dean Hereford in March 1808 (Clergy of the Church of England).
719 George to Mary Ann, 11, 13 Nov. 1808, 15 Feb., 20 June 1809.
720 George to Mary Ann, 2 Apr., 19 Nov. 1809, 27 Feb., 10 Apr. 1810.
721 George to Mary Ann 30 May, 22 June, 22 July 1809.
722 George to Mary Ann, 21, 26, 29 Sept. 1809.
723 George to Mary Ann, 4 Aug. 1809, 1 Jan. 1810.
724 George to Mary Ann, 20 Mar 1804, 27 Dec. 1809, 21 Jan., 27 Feb., 16, 22, 31 Mar. 1810; *Morning Chronicle*, 6, 19 Mar. 1810.
725 George to Mary Ann, 27 Feb. 1810; Charles to George, 5 Apr. 1809; Beatrice Reddish to George, 10 Apr. 1809 (BL Add Mss 89143/3/11/2).
726 Samuel Reddish, *A Digest of the Laws of the Customs, as they relate to the plantations, carefully compiled from the statutes at large* ([?Bridgetown] [?1805]). It is listed in Don Mitchell, West Indian Bibliography with the note 'Exceptionally rare, no copy known'. Don Mitchell, in private correspondence, confirms that this is all that is known of the book.
727 George to Mary Ann, 27 Feb., 10, 29 Apr. 1810; *Morning Chronicle*, 19 Mar. 1810.
728 George to Mary Ann, 1, 7 Aug., 1, 11, 19 Sept., 9, 13, 17 Nov. 1810; 4 May, 29 Aug. 1811. Frederick's naval record shows him as Acting Lieutenant from 25 May 1810, and Lieutenant from 21 Apr. 1811 (National Archives, ADM/196/4/623).
729 Charles to Maria, 14 Sept. 1809.
730 Charles to Mary Ann, 14 Sept. 1809.
731 George to Mary Ann, 11 Oct. 1810. George wrote to Lord Minto in May 1811 (enclosed in George to Mary Ann, 1 May 1811), referring back to an earlier letter of October 1810.
732 *Alphabetical list of the Bengal Army* (1838) 222-3; *India Deaths and Burials 1719-1948*, FHL 498609; George to Mary Ann, 23 Mar., 22 Apr., 1, 4 May 1811; George to Richard Thompson, 4 May 1811 (Gale, 23 Oct. 1937 , 295).
733 Packet, 113; George to Mary Ann, 19 Apr. 1811.
734 *Royal Gazetteer of Jamaica*, 22 June 1811. I am grateful to Linley Hooper for drawing this to my attention.
735 George to Mary Ann, 25 May, 6 Sept. 1811, 12 Sept. 1818.
736 George to Mary Ann, 25 May 1811.
737 George to Mary Ann, 1, 19 Mar., 18 May 1811, 17 May 1813; *Journals of the House of Commons* vol 66 (Session 1810-1811), 178, 181.
738 George to Mary Ann, 3 Apr., 4 May., 23, 29 Aug., 19 Sept. and 5 Oct. 1811, 2 Jan., 5 June 1813; *Exeter Flying Post*, 10 Oct. 1811.
739 George to Mary Ann, 29 Nov., 13 Dec. 1811.
740 George to Mary Ann, 17 Feb., 22 Aug. 1812, 23 Jan., 1, 13 Mar., 30 Oct. 1813, 25 Aug. 1814
741 George to Mary Ann, 31 Jan., 22 Feb. and 7 Mar. 1812.
742 George to Mary Ann, 18/19, 27, 30 Apr., 9 May 1812.
743 George to Mary Ann, 12 May 1812.
744 Mary Ann to George, 24 May 1812.
745 George to Mary Ann, 28, 30 May 1812.
746 Mary Ann to George, 24 May, 16 Aug. 1812; George to Mary Ann, 3, 8, 15 August 1812; *Letter Journal*, 28 Mar. 1795.
747 Mary Ann to George, 16 Aug. 1812.
748 George to Mary Ann, 28 Aug., 3, 11, 18, 25 Sept. 1812; 1 Sept. 1810.
749 George to the Leighs, 26 March 1799; to Mary Ann, 9 Nov. 1812, 16 Jan., 29 May 1813; Dixon, *Canning*, 158; Hinde, 261; Therry, iv. 185-94; vi. 398-409.

750 George to Mary Ann, 29 May 1813; *Gentleman's Magazine* (Apr. 1837), 431; *Transatlantic Slave Trade Database*; *Life of William Wilberforce*, ii. 147; Hinde, 260; Dixon, 165, 167.
751 George to Mary Ann, 12, 17, 23, 29, 31 Oct., 9 Nov. 1812.
752 *Royal Gazette of Jamaica*, 27 July 1811, 29 Aug. 1812; George to Mary Ann, 6 Sept. 1811, 1, 22 May 1813; Hooper.
753 George to Mary Ann, 2, 4 Jan. 1813.
754 George to Mary Ann, 2, 4 Jan., 1, 6 Feb., 13, 20 Mar. 1813.
755 George to Mary Ann, 4 Mar., 10 Apr., 1 May, 3 July 1813.
756 Mary Ann to an unnamed recipient, dated Shawford, 24 May 1813 (BL Add Mss 89143/3/1/54).
757 Humphrey Noad is listed in 1830 as a woollen dyer in Frome (*Pigot and Co.'s National and Commercial Directory* (1830), 707).
758 George to Mary Ann, 5, 12, 19 June 1813; Richard Thompson to Mary Ann, 7, 12 May 1813 (filed with George's letters).
759 George to Mary Ann, 2 Jan., 10, 14, 24 July 1813.
760 George to Mary Ann, 3 July 1809, 30 July, 7 Aug. 1813.
761 George to Mary Ann, 7 Aug. 1813; Mary Ann to George, 10 Aug. 1813.
762 George's letter of 7 Aug. 1813 is endorsed: 'Memo. Inclosed is an answer intended for this letter – but not sent – it may be seen at a better time! MAH!' I am assuming that the letter of 10 August included in the bundle with Mary Ann's other letters is the one she never sent.
763 George to Mary Ann, 21, 27 Aug., 17, 24 Sept. 1813; Diary, 17 Sept. 1813. The letter of 21 Aug. was redirected to Taunton.
764 George to Mary Ann, 27 Aug., 3 Sept. 1813. Fanny was at least seventy in 1813.
765 George to Mary Ann, 29 Sept., 4 Oct. 1813; Diary, Oct. 1813; Mehitabel to her son Stratford, 17 Mar. 1809 (Hunt, 221).
766 George to Mary Ann, 29 Sept., 4, 22 Oct. 1813; Diary, 9, 11 Oct. 1813.
767 George to Mary Ann, 5 Nov. 1813.
768 George to Mary Ann, 30 Oct. 1813.
769 George to Mary Ann, 30 Oct., 5, 12, 27 Nov. 1813; *Morning Post*, 23 Nov. 1813.
770 George to Mary Ann, 24, 31 Dec. 1813, 14 Jan. 1814.
771 Frederick to Mary Ann, 11 Mar. 1814 (filed among George's letters to Mary Ann); George to Mary Ann, 28 Jan., 23 Apr. 1814.
772 George to Mary Ann, 15 Apr., 14 May, 8 July, 31 Aug., 4, 8 Sept. 1814; LMA, ref *DL/T/093/010*
773 George to Mary Ann, 4, 11 Feb., 28 Mar., 7, 27 May 1814, 31 Dec. 1821 (by which time Mary Ann owed Dennis £25).
774 George to Mary Ann, 11 Feb., 18 Mar., 1, 23 Apr. 1814.
775 Non-Conformist and Non-Parochial Registers 1567–1970, RG4/3665, Swansea High Street Chapel, 26 Aug. 1813; *General Evening Post*, 12 Dec. 1799; George to Mary Ann, 18 Apr. 1814.
776 George to Mary Ann, 27 May, 11, 18, 20 June 1814; Diary, 16 June 1814; *Morning Post*, 15 June 1814.
777 George to Mary Ann, 29 June 1814.
778 George to Mary Ann, 2, 4, 6, 8 July 1814.
779 Mary Ann to unnamed, 28 June 1814 (*Bath Chronicle*, 21 Feb. 1867). That the recipient was Lucy Weld is a guess based on the fact that the letter was sent to the newspaper by C R Weld, Lucy's son, who states that they were addressed to a 'deceased member of my family'. From the opening paragraph it appears that the addressee was a woman who was younger than 65. I have not seen the original letter, so cannot say whether the published text accurately reflects Mary Ann's spelling and punctuation.
780 *Morning Chronicle*, 27 July, 1 Aug. 1814; *Times*, 4 Aug. 1814; George to Mary Ann, 29 July, 1, 6 Aug. 1814; Hinde, 269.

781 George to Mary Ann, 30 Aug., 20 Sept. 1814.
782 Mary Ann to George, 19 July 1800, 21 Sept 1814.
783 George to Mary Ann, 22 Sept., 8 Oct. 1814; Mary Ann to unnamed, 30 Sept. 1814 (*Bath Chronicle*, 21 Feb. 1867).
784 Shipping News, *Morning Post*, 7 to 23 Nov. 1814.
785 George to Mary Ann, 29 Nov., 9, 30 Dec. 1814, 14, 23 Jan. 1815; to Bess Leigh, 14 Nov. 1814.
786 BL Add. Mss 89143/3/11/2.
787 George to Mary Ann, 28 Apr., 12, May, 22 Dec. 1815, 10 Feb., 13 Apr. 1816.
788 George to Mary Ann, 10 Feb. 1815.
789 George to Mary Ann, 17 Mar. 1815.
790 George refers to Young's father as Mr D., but his identity is clear from a letter from George to Dent, 21 Aug 1815 (BL Add. Mss 89143/3/6/2). The loan of £4,500 (on the security of South Hill) is mentioned in a receipt signed by George's agent John Heaton on 14 Nov. 1806, and again in Heaton's accounts for 24 Aug 1808 (BL Add. Mss 89143/3/4/1 and 89143/3/4/3).
791 George to Mary Ann, 15 Apr. 1815; to Dent, 21 Aug 1815.
792 George to Mary Ann, 15 Apr., 27 May, 18 June, 25 Aug. 1815, 10 Feb. 1816.
793 Mary Ann's movements can be deduced from the direction on George's letters from July to October 1815. A letter from Admiral Pickmore to George, dated from Frederick and Emma's home, was enclosed in George to Mary Ann, 26 Jan. 1816.
794 George to Mary Ann, 26 Jan. 1816, 19 Dec. 1818; National Archives, ADM 196/4/623; *Liverpool Mercury*, 13 Jan. 1815; *Bury & Norwich Post*, 5 Nov. 1817. .
795 George to Mary Ann, 22 July, 4, 29 Sept., 12 Oct., 2 Nov., 22 Dec. 1815, 17 Feb. 1816; *Times*, 25 Sept. 1815; Hinde, 266, 277.
796 George to Mary Ann, 8 Mar., 13 Apr., 26, 27, 28 May 1816; *Morning Post*, 21 May 1816; *Times*, 29 May 1816.
797 Lane-Poole, *Life of Lord Stratford de Redcliffe*, i. 272 (Bagot, i. 17).
798 George to Mary Ann 18 Aug. 1815.
799 George to Mary Ann, 6, 10 June, 7 Dec. 1816; *Morning Chronicle*, 10 June 1816.
800 George to Mary Ann, 10 May 1817; Therry, iii. 543; Hinde, 266-76.
801 The sum left by Richard Thompson is given in Mary's will; see endnote 826 below. George to Mary Ann, 6, 21, 29 June 1816; John Heaton to George, July 1815 (BL Add. MSS 89143/3/4/1).
802 George to Mary Ann, 29 June, 6 July, 17, 24, 31 Aug., 29 Sept., 1 Oct. 1816; Mary to George, enclosed in George's letter to Mary Ann of 24 Aug.
803 George to Mary Ann, 27 July 1816.
804 George to Mary Ann, 4 Sept. 1814, 29 June, 27 July, 31 Aug., 7 Sept. 1816, 9 Aug. 1817, 2 Dec. 1823, 1 Dec. 1825.
805 George to Mary Ann, 17, 24 Aug., 21, 29 Sept., 1, 17 Oct., 3 Dec. 1816; Hinde, 280; Thompson, *Making of the English Working Class*, 693-5.
806 George to Mary Ann, 12 Apr., 28 June, 30 Aug. 1817, 31 Jan. 1818.
807 George to Mary Ann, 11 Jan., 22 Feb., 15 Mar. 1817.
808 George to Mary Ann, 14 Sept. 1816, 4 Jan., 19 Apr., 2, 9 Aug. 1817, 5, 12 Sept. 1818, 30 July, 7 Aug. 1820.
809 George to Mary Ann, 23 Aug. 1817.
810 George to Mary Ann, 30 Aug. 1817.
811 George to Mary Ann, 30 Oct. 1817.
812 George to Mary Ann, 6, 15 Nov. 1817; *Morning Chronicle*, 10, 11, 25, 28 Oct. 1817; Thompson, *Making of the English Working Class*, 723-34.
813 George to Mary Ann, 8, 15, 22 Nov. 1817; *Morning Chronicle*, 8 Nov. 1817.
814 George to Mary Ann, 2, 12, 25 Dec. 1817, 24 Jan., 7, 14, 28 Feb., 14, 21 Mar. 1818.

815 George to Mary Ann, 23 Feb., 7, 8, 14 Mar. 1818, 12, 13, 15, 17 Apr., 19, 24 July 1819.
816 Therry, iv. 32-7; Hazlitt, *Spirit of the Age*, 190 ; George to Mary Ann, 18, 25 June 1818; *Liverpool Mercury*, 19 June 1818.
817 George to Mary Ann, 25 June, 5, 12, 25 July 1818, 25 Dec. 1819.
818 George to Mary Ann, 11 Jan., 5 July 1817, 24, 31 Oct. 1818.
819 George to Mary Ann, 27 July 1816, 24 Oct. 1818, 20 Feb. 1819, 15 Jan. 1820.
820 George to Mary Ann, 1, 29 May 1819.
821 George to Mary Ann, 19 June, 10 July 1819; Debate on Excise Bill, 18 June 1819 (Parliamentary Debates, Series 1 vol. 40 1207-21).
822 George to Mary Ann, 20 Feb., 1, 8, 29 May, 12, 19 June, 3, 10 July 1819.
823 George to Mary Ann, 23, 28 Feb., 7 March 1818. The new church of St Mary, Bathwick was consecrated in 1820.
824 George to Mary Ann, 9 Jan. 1819; *Exeter Flying Post*, 27 Aug., 5 Nov. 1818; *Lancaster Gazette*, 10 Oct. 1818; *Liverpool Mercury*, 6 Nov. 1818; *Morning Chronicle*, 26 Dec. 1818; *Examiner*, 3 Jan. 1819.
825 George to Mary Ann 15 May, 3 July, 7, 15 Aug., 30 Sept., 13 Oct. 1819.
826 *Prerogative Court of Canterbury and Related Probate Jurisdictions: Will Registers; PROB 11/1679.*
827 George to Mary Ann, 25 Oct., 20 Nov. 1819.
828 George to Mary Ann, 4, 11 Apr. 1818, 25 Dec. 1819, 8 Jan., 31 Mar. 1820; Hinde, 294-5.
829 George to Mary Ann, 11, 18 Dec. 1819, 1 Jan. 1820.
830 George to Mary Ann, 10 Jan. 1816, 21 Nov. 1818, 19 Feb. 1821.
831 George to Mary Ann, 24, 26 Feb. 1820; Thompson, *Making of the English Working Class*, 772-3.
832 George to Mary Ann, 29 Sept. 1806, 9, 23, 31 Mar. 1820, 4 Feb. 1821.
833 George to Mary Ann, 8, 15 Apr., 17 , 27 May 1820; to Joan, 6 Apr. 1820; Diary 10 Apr. 1820.
834 George to Mary Ann, 24 Jan. 1819, 29 Apr. 1820, 29 Jan., 26 Oct., 1 Nov., 31 Dec. 1821.
835 *Examiner*, 26 Mar. 1820; *Morning Post*, 8 June 1820; Therry, iv. 245-53; Hinde 297.
836 George to Mary Ann, 1, 8, 18 June, 15, 29, 30 July 1820.
837 George to Mary Ann, 28 Aug., 12, 26 Oct. 1820; Byron, *Childe Harold* IV, iv., published 1818. Pierre is a character in Thomas Otway's *Venice Preserv'd.*
838 George to Mary Ann, 15 July, 11 Aug. 1820. An endorsement shows that the August letter, from Antwerp, was prepaid by George, but it is stamped 'more to pay'.
839 George to Mary Ann 17 Nov., 23 Dec. 1820, 13, 16 Jan. 1821.
840 George to Mary Ann, 25 Nov., 9, 11, 16, 20, 23 Dec. 1820, 16 Jan. 1821.
841 George to Mary Ann, 19, 26 Feb., 7 Apr. 1821.
842 *Morning Post*, 17 Mar. 1821; George to Mary Ann, 19/20 Mar. 1821.
843 *Morning Post*, 8 May 1820. The event was postponed from 17 March because of the election and then because of George's bereavement.
844 *Morning Chronicle*, 19 Mar. 1821; *Times*, 19 Mar. 1821.
845 George to Charles Arbuthnot (draft), 24 Mar. 1793 (BL Add Mss 89143/3/11/5); to Walter Scott, 24 July 1825 (BL Add Mss 89143/1/1/136).
846 Chalmers, 'The Doctrine of Christian Charity applied to the case of Religious differences'; *Morning Chronicle*, 26 May 1817; *Life of William Wilberforce*, iv. 324-5; Hanna, *Memoirs of the Life and Writings of Thomas Chalmers*, ii. 98-104. The published text of the sermon is as preached in Glasgow; the London sermon may have differed in detail. Hanna quotes an eye-witness, Lady Elgin, who noticed that it was the passage on the Irish character which moved Canning to tears.
847 *Times*, 18 Apr. 1821; *Morning Post*, 23 June, 13, 27, 28, 30 July 1821; George to Mary Ann, 26 Apr., 14, 21, 28 July, 10, 24 Aug. 1821.
848 George to Mary Ann, 31 Aug., 14, 22, 25, 26, 27 , 29 Sept. 1821.

849 George to Mary Ann, 14 Sept., 13 Oct. 1821.
850 George to Mary Ann, 13, 16, 26 Oct., 1 Nov. 1821.
851 George to Mary Ann, 20 Dec. 1821, 17 , 25 Jan., 5 , 11 Feb. 1822; Frederick to Mary Ann, 2 Feb. 1822, filed with George's letter of 5 Feb.
852 George to Mary Ann, 31 Dec. 1821.
853 George to Joan, 20 Sept. 1809.
854 George to William, 17 May 1817, 5, 7 Feb 1822; to Captain Giffard (Royal Naval College) 17 May 1817; Giffard to George, 18 May 1817 (BL Add Mss 89143/3/5/ 'Correspondence with and regarding William Pitt Canning').
855 George to Barrow, 21 Jan. 1822; to Backhouse, 12, 16 Feb. 1822; to Dawkins, 25 July 1822; to William, 5 Feb. 1822; to Frederick, 23, 25 July 1822; Barrow to George, 23 Jan., 22, 25 July 1822; Dawkins to George, 7 Nov. 1822; *Morning Post*, 2 Apr. 1823, 4 July 1825.
856 George to Mary Ann, 5 Feb. 1822.
857 Hinde, 311-6; George to Mary Ann, 16, 22, 27 Mar. 1822.
858 George to Mary Ann, 6 June 1814, 6 Jan. 1815, 11 Mar., 1, 10 Apr. 1822.
859 George to Mary Ann, 10 Apr. 1822.
860 George to Mary Ann, 10, 17 , 19 Apr., 29 June, 1 July 1822.
861 George to Mary Ann, 25 Jan., 22 Feb., 22 Mar., 12, 24 May 1823.
862 George to Mary Ann, 28, 29 Aug. 1822; *Morning Chronicle*, 13 Aug. 1822; *Morning Post*, 14 Aug. 1822.
863 George to Mary Ann, 14, 21, 24 Sept., 1 Oct. 1822.
864 George to Mary Ann, 19 Oct., 26, 30 Nov., 21 Dec. 1822, 10 Jan. 1823.
865 George to Mary Ann, 14, 21 Dec. 1822. *Hunt's Bath Directory* (1824) includes Mr S Turner, apothecary, at 12 New King Street, and Frewen Turner esq at 28 Crescent.
866 George to Mary Ann, 8, 22 Mar., 29 Aug., 8 Nov. 1823; Romilly, *Letters to Ivy*, 327.
867 George to Mary Ann, 11, 24 Oct 1823; *Morning Chronicle*, 16, 20, 21 Oct. 1823; *Exeter Flying Post*, 22 Oct. 1823.
868 Esther to Mary Ann, 19 Oct. 1823, filed with George to Mary Ann, 24 Oct 1823.
869 *Exeter Flying Post*, 6 Nov. 1823; Therry, vi. 420-5.
870 *Morning Post*, 27 Oct. 1823.
871 George to Mary Ann, 24, 31 Oct., 3 Nov. 1823.
872 George to Mary Ann, 17, 20 July, 19 Oct., 16, 22, 29 Nov., 8, 13, 16, 27 Dec. 1823.
873 George to Mary Ann, 27 Dec. 1823, 20 Mar., 17 Apr., 15 May, 1, 29 Oct., 25 Dec. 1824, 15 Jan. 1825; *Morning Post*, 10, 15 Jan. 1825.
874 George to Mary Ann, 14 Aug. 1824.
875 George to Mary Ann, 16, 19, 26 Mar. 1825.
876 George to Mary Ann, 17, 20 Jan. 1826; Emma Hunn to Miss Pickmere, 29 Mar. 1826 (Gale, 15 Jan. 1938, 40).
877 George to Frances Canning, 24 Feb. 1827; to Lady Caithness, 31 Aug. 1823 (BL Add. Mss 89143/3/11/4).
878 Harriet Arbuthnot, *Journal*, ii. 55; *Times*, 10 Sept. 1825; *Morning Post*, 10 Oct. 1825.
879 George to William, 9 Nov. 1825; to Lord Melville, 20 Aug. 1825; Lord Melville to George, 22 Aug., 4 Sept. 1825; Barrow to George, 3 Dec. 1825; Captain Houston-Stewart to George, 5 Nov. 1825; *Morning Post*, 5, 16, 19 Dec. 1825; *Morning Chronicle*, 19 Dec. 1825.
880 George to Mary Ann, 23 Apr., 7, 28 May, 11, 25 June 1825; unsigned letters to Mary Ann, 27, 30 May 1825.
881 George to Mary Ann, 27 June, 2, 9 July, 25 Aug. 1825.
882 Joan to Mary Ann, 16, 18 July 1825; George to Mary Ann, 19, 30 July, 4 Aug. 1 Sept., 14, 22 Oct., 12, 18 Nov. 1825.
883 Joan to Mary Ann, 18 July 1825; George to Mary Ann, 18 Aug., 28 Oct., 12, 23, 25 Nov., 31 Dec. 1825.

884 George to Mary Ann, 18 Aug., 23 Nov., 1, 9, 17, 30, 31 Dec. 1825.
885 George to Mary Ann, 17, 24, 30 Dec. 1825, 14 Jan. 1826.
886 George to Mary Ann, 11 Nov. 1826.
887 George to Mary Ann, 11 Nov. 1826; Emma to John Pickmere, 3 Apr. 1825 (Gale, 8 Jan. 1938, 25).
888 George to Mary Ann, 25 Feb., 4, 11, 27 Mar., 1, 8 Apr. 1826.
889 George to Mary Ann, 12, 29 Apr., 23 June, 25 Aug. 1826.
890 George to Mary Ann, 6, 24 May, 10, 17, 23 June, 7, 14 July, 11, 25 Aug., 12, 14, 25 Sept., 6 Oct. 1826.
891 George to Mary Ann, 13 Oct., 4, 11, 25 Nov., 2 Dec. 1826.
892 Hinde, 305; *Examiner*, 20 June 1819.
893 George to Mary Ann, 14 Sept. 1822; to Joan, 2, 3 Sept. 1822; Arbuthnot, *Journal*, i. 25, 186-90; C D Yonge, *Life and Administration of Robert Banks Jenkinson, Second Earl of Liverpool*, iii. 199–201; Hinde, 300, 318-9.
894 Arbuthnot, *Journal* i. 55, 90–1, 187, 192, 208, 250, ii. 88–9, 121, 130, 404.
895 Arbuthnot, *Journal*, i. 354. See above, chapter 3.
896 Examiner, 22 July 1821; Romilly, *Letters to Ivy*, 215, where the jibe is attributed to Canning's enemies, without naming the originator.
897 Cobbett, *Political Register*, 35 (13 Nov. 1819), 369-70.
898 George to Mary Ann, 15 Feb. 1817; *Times*, 4 Feb. 1817.
899 Hinde, 129–30; George to George Bagot, 10 Aug. 1808 (Bagot, i. 260).
900 British Library Add MS 30147A f19 (Gale, 18 Sept. 1937, 203–4).
901 Wilson, *Narrative of the Formation of Canning's Ministry* (Hinde, 448); Aspinall 'The Coalition Ministries of 1827', 214.
902 Hinde, 435–51.
903 *The Age*, 13 May 1827.
904 George to Mary Ann, 2, 30 Dec. 1826; *Morning Post,* 8, 9 Dec. 1826; *The Times*, 11 Dec. 1826; *Bristol Mercury*, 11 Dec. 1826; Hinde, 423.
905 George to Mary Ann, 4 Jan. 1827.
906 George to Mary Ann, 18 Jan. 1827.
907 *Times*, 26 January 1827.
908 George to Mary Ann, 25 May 1811, 14 Sept. 1822, 6, 20 May 1826.
909 George to Mary Ann, 27 Jan., 2, 9 Feb. 1827; *Morning Post*, 26 Jan. 1827.
910 Emma to Miss Pickmere, 10 Mar. 1827 (Gale, 15 Jan. 1938, 40).
911 Frederick to Mary Ann, 17 Dec. 1826, 15 Jan. 1827, franked by George, 6 Mar. 1827.
912 Emma to John Pickmere, 3 Apr. 1825 (Gale, 8 Jan. 1938, 25).
913 Emma to Miss Pickmere, 10 Mar. 1827 (Gale, 15 Jan. 1938, 40); George to Mary Ann, 3, 10 Mar. 1827; *Morning Chronicle*, 7, 9 March 1827
914 Somerset Heritage Service, Taunton, Somerset Parish Records, Bath Abbey 1813-1853 (Ref. D\P\ba.ab/2/1/9).
915 *Morning Chronicle, Morning Post* and *Times*, 12-20 March 1827.
916 Gale, Introduction to unpublished manuscript, *Canning's Mother*, WYL682/10.
917 Bell, 20; Therry, i. 6.
918 *George Canning, Three Biographical Studies*, 19-21.
919 Florence Nightingale, 'Cassandra', p 407.
920 Packet, 180.
921 Mary Ann to [?Lucy Weld], 28 June, 30 Sept. 1814.
922 Mary Ann to George, 10 Aug. 1813.
923 Packet, 14.
924 Irish genealogy, DU-RC-BA-301980/304336/305627/ 306316.
925 Packet, 11.
926 *London Evening Post*, 26–28 Jan., 24 Apr. 1742.

927 Packet, 11.
928 Packet, 38.
929 Packet, 12.
930 *Exeter Flying Post*, 24 Mar. 1836.
931 Packet, 10.
932 Private communication from Ros Muspratt.
933 Packet, 8; Irish genealogy, DU-CI-MA-26418 (Marriage of Melchier Guy Dickings and Hannah Handcock, Parish of St John, Dublin, 6 February 1721/22).
934 LMA, St Marylebone Parish, Ref. P89/MRY/1/314.
935 Irish genealogy, DU-CI-BA-159959 , DU-CI-BU-197942.
936 Irish genealogy, DU-CI-BU-199304.
937 Packet, 5.

Acknowledgements

Since I have been preoccupied by Mary Ann and George for a quarter of a century I must first of all thank my wife, Anna, and my children, Jessica, Swithun and Christopher, for their forbearance and love, and for the many helpful insights they have given me. My children have contributed with breathtaking generosity to the fundraising effort. Two dramatised versions have helped to bring her story to life. The first was devised and performed by my sister Rosalind, and the second by my son Christopher, his wife Daphne and their friends in the Footnotes Theatre Company.

Without Cedric Collyer this book would never have happened, since it was among his collection of notes from the Harewood archive that I found the transcript of the Packet and so learnt Mary Ann's story. My visits to Cedric's widow, Mary, both while sorting through the papers and for years afterwards, provided some of the happiest hours of my life. I can't measure the debt I owe to Mary and Cedric.

I should also like to acknowledge the work of Cedric's research assistant. I regret to say that I have forgotten her name, but Cedric and Mary spoke highly of her, and quite apart from her scholarly contribution she was a much better typist than Cedric.

Like my family, my friends have had to follow the twists and turns of my research and have often fretted over my inability to bring it to a close. Thanks in particular to Bernard Barker, Simon

Taylor, and Elspeth Wills, all of them proper historians, who have helped and prodded me over the years. Bernard persuaded his friend Roger Knight to read an early draft of my book and Roger's encouragement and advice were most valuable. While I was working in the University of St Andrews many members of staff listened patiently to my tales of the Cannings when I was supposed to be attending to their computer problems. I remember with particular pleasure the enthusiasm of the late Nora Bartlett.

The University of St Andrews has been an important part of my life, giving me my wife, my education, my job of twenty-two years and my pension. Without all these benefits, and without access to the resources of the university library, this book could hardly have been written.

Most of my archival research was carried out at the West Yorkshire Archive Service, Leeds, first in Sheepscar and then in Morley. The staff over the years have been invariably kind and helpful. After the Canning papers were removed to Harewood House access was restricted, but Tara Hamilton Stubber helped me get the most out of the single afternoon I was granted. I also received assistance from the Devon Archive Service in Exeter, the British Library in Colindale and the Euston Road, and the National Library of Ireland in Dublin. In recent years, much has been possible via the internet, and I am particularly grateful to the Chawton House Library for preserving and putting online one of the two known copies of *The Offspring of Fancy*.

I am grateful to Trevor Griffiths, editor of *Theatre Notebook*, and the Society for Theatre Research for publishing three articles on Mary Ann's theatrical career; the comments of the anonymous reviewers of my articles were extremely useful. Among the scholars who have answered my questions over the years are Derek Adlam, Dr Camilla Campbell Orr, Nina Hamric, Linley Hooper, Bruce Lenman, Don Mitchell, Hamish Scott, Richard Sharpe and the late Joan Stivey. In particular I am grateful to the late Tony Upton for his advice on dealing with Cedric's papers.

I should also record my debt to Frederick Gale, who unearthed so much about Mary Ann's life and background. He appreciated that she was a 'remarkable woman', and if he had been given access to the Canning papers at Harewood House he could have presented her story to the public ninety years ago.

In 1995 the late Earl of Harewood responded generously to my request to use the Canning archive and encouraged me in my work. I am grateful to the present Earl and to the Harewood family for permission to quote from the letters and other documents.

Finding a publisher is a dismal occupation and I was relieved when Unbound agreed to take on this project. I'm grateful to the subscribers whose confidence, interest and generosity has made this publication possible, and to Andrew Chapman for his editorial advice and guidance, and his hard work on a book which is longer than he bargained for.

Finally, I dedicate my telling of Mary Ann's story to my two actor sisters, Rosalind Crowe and the late Imogen Claire.

Index